In Gods We Trust

EVOLUTION AND COGNITION General Editor, Stephen Stich, Rutgers University

Published in the series

Gerd Gigerenzer, Peter Todd, and the ABC Research Group, *Simple Heuristics to Make Us Smart*

Gerd Gigerenzer, *Adaptive Thinking: Rationality in the Real World*

Scott Atran, *In Gods We Trust: The Evolutionary Landscape of Religion*

SCOTT ATRAN

In Gods We Trust

The Evolutionary Landscape of Religion

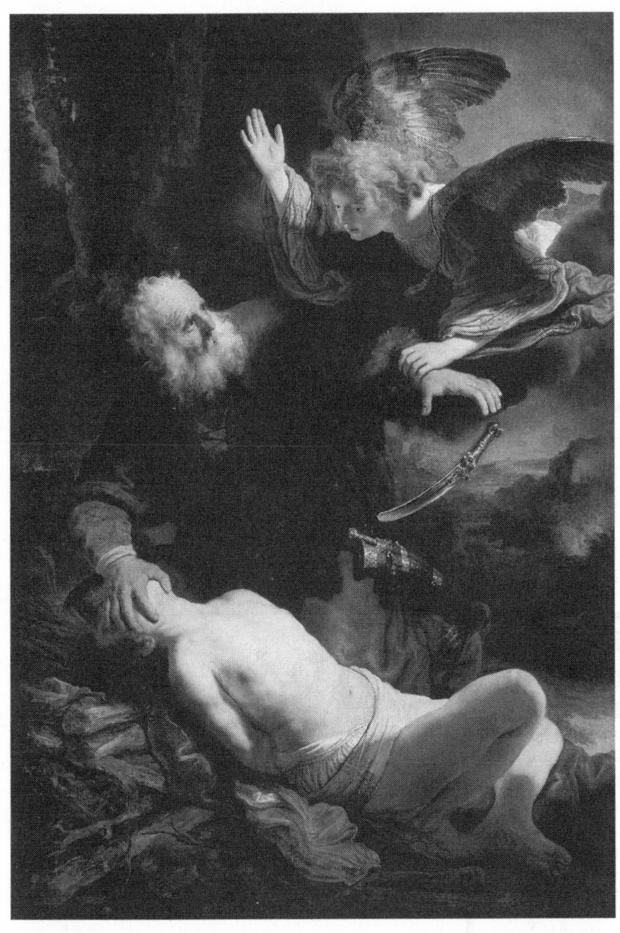

OXFORD
UNIVERSITY PRESS
2002

OXFORD
UNIVERSITY PRESS

Oxford New York
Auckland Bangkok Buenos Aires Cape Town Chennai
Dar es Salaam Delhi Hong Kong Istanbul Karachi Kolkata
Kuala Lumpur Madrid Melbourne Mexico City Mumbai Nairobi
São Paulo Shanghai Singapore Taipei Tokyo Toronto

Published by Oxford University Press, Inc.
198 Madison Avenue, New York, New York 10016

www.oup.com

Library of Congress Cataloging-in-Publication Data
Atran, Scott, 1952–
In gods we trust : the evolutionary landscape of religion / Scott Atran.
p. cm.—(Evolution and cognition)
Includes bibliographical references and index.
ISBN 0-19-514930-0
1. Psychology, Religious. 2. Genetic psychology. I. Title. II. Series.
BL53 .A88 2002
200'.1'9—dc21 2002074884

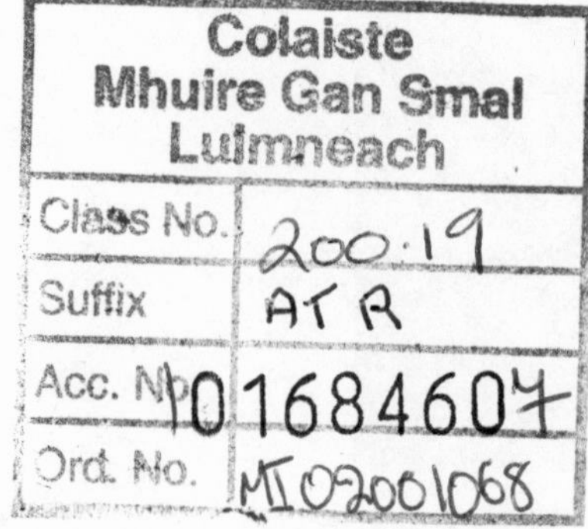

9 8 7 6 5 4 3 2 1

Printed in the United States of America
on acid-free paper

For Leonard, Harris Keith, Hazel Dawn, and Velvel,
and Tatiana, Laura, Emiliano Dean, and Ximena Fatima

Preface

Stone Age Minds for a Space Age World?

Faith presupposes natural knowledge.
—Saint Thomas Aquinas, *Summa Theologiae* (1265)

Reason is, and ought only to be, the slave of the passions.
—David Hume, *Treatise of Human Nature* (1739)

Evolutionary and psychological inquiries into the origins of religion are hardly new. What is new is the recent convergence of evolutionary biology and cognitive psychology, with its alluring promise of novel solutions to age-old problems of human, and perhaps cosmic, nature. The general idea is that the brains and minds of the human species were naturally selected over millions of years of biological and cognitive evolution to deal with important and recurrent problems in the ancestral past, such as finding mates, protecting offspring, fleeing predators, and pursuing prey. Circumstances have surely changed since the Pleistocene, and many of today's problems are far different from those faced by our hominid forebears. But the biological and cognitive structures that make human life possible on Earth seem to have changed little, or not at all—at least since our descent from some "Mitochondrial Eve," who punctuated the African savanna over a hundred thousand years ago.

Evolutionary psychology is still in its infancy and is not yet the new scientific paradigm some love and others hate. Some find the idea of Stone Age minds for a Space Age world bold and irreverent; others find it false and demeaning; many find it ridiculous. As the field stands now, all may garner uncertain support for their position. This new field surely will not solve all of the problems its fervent supporters say it will. But neither will it face the massive road blocks to understanding that its unrelenting detractors see at every turn. At present, the field is a promissory note, much as Darwin's theory was at its beginning.

Little by little, biologists were able to deliver on Darwin's promises. This process has speeded up considerably—almost irreversibly—thanks to access at the molecular level. There is still a long way to go. Through recent advances in cognitive science, evolutionary psychology has gained entrance to mental structure and so potentially to the brain's evolved neural architecture. It has an even longer way ahead: much less is currently known about how the mind/brain works than how body cells function. Perhaps, in the end, evolutionary psychology's interpretations of complex mental designs as telltale signs of ancient environments will prove no truer than phrenology's readings of bumps and other conformations of the skull as indications of mental faculties and character (phrenology was a very serious and hotly debated discipline a century ago). Then again, perhaps not, which makes the effort worthwhile.

Religion is a hard test for this gambit. Sincere expressions of belief in supernatural agents, sacred rites, and other aspects of devout faith and practice seem to vary as much as anything possibly can in human imagination. And it isn't easy to see what biological advantages or ecological functions bodiless spirits or costly sacrifices may have afforded simian ancestors in Pleistocene scrub. What follows is an attempt to show that in all cultures supernatural agents behave and sacred rites are performed in ways predictable under evolved cognitive (inferential) and emotional constraints. This implies some humbling truths about our kind, in the limits of our reason, the chaos behind moral choice, and the fatality of our anxieties and passions.

Other evolutionary approaches to human thought and culture, which pay little mind to cognitive structure, my own experiments and fieldwork do not abide. These include some versions of sociobiology (direct attempts at explantion of behavior in terms of genetics or behavioral ecology), group selection (individuals in a population share norms that compel them to sacrifice their own fitness so that the group as a whole benefits in competition with other groups), and memetics (wherein ideas invade and avail themselves of individual minds for their own propagation, much as genes and viruses make use of individual bodies to replicate themselves and spread). To be fair, I might have given these views the benefit of the doubt. I haven't, for reasons I expose.

On another plane, this work is agnostic and so prone to charges of insincerity from either side of the religious divide. The cognitive perspective I have chosen for this book is a biological and scientific perspective that focuses on the causal role of the mind/brain in generating behavior. From this vantage, religion is not doctrine, or institutions, or even faith. Religion ensues from the ordinary workings of the human mind as it deals with emotionally compelling problems of human existence, such as birth, aging, death, unforeseen calamities, and love. In religion, these "facts of life"are always inherent problems of society, caused by the very same intentional agents that are thought to constitute society. They are never *just* random or mechanical incidents of a physical or biological nature, as science might suggest. For religion, there is always an intentional, socially relevant reason for this particular person to have been born a man rather than a woman, or for a wave to have knocked over and drowned a person at that specific place and time.

Religious beliefs and practices involve the very same cognitive and affective structures as nonreligious beliefs and practices—and no others—but in (more or less) systematically distinctive ways. From an evolutionary standpoint, these structures are, at least proximately, no different in origin and kind from the genetic instincts and mechanical processes that govern the life of other animals. Religious explanations of religion may or may not accept this account of proximate causes, but no faith-based account considers it to be the *whole* story. I do not intend to refute such nonscientific explanations of religion, nor do I pretend that they are morally worthless or intellectually unjustified. The chosen scientific perspective of this book is simply blind to them and can elucidate nothing about them—so far as I can see.

From this vantage, human cognition (re)creates the gods who sustain hope beyond sufficient reason and commitment beyond self interest. Humans ideally represent themselves to one another in gods they trust. Through their gods, people see what is good in others and what is evil.

The reasons for this book are both far and near in time. As a graduate student almost three decades ago, I spent some years with the Druze people of the Middle East. I wanted to learn about their religious beliefs, which appeared to weave together ideas from all the great monotheistic faiths in intriguing ways. Learning about Druze religion is a gradual process in the Socratic tradition, involving interpretation of parables in question-and-answer format. Although, as a non-Druze, I could never be formally initiated into the religion, the elders seemed to delight in my trying to understand the world as they conceived it. But every time I reached some level of awareness about a problem, Druze elders reminded me that anything said or learned beyond that point could not be discussed with uninitiated persons, including other Druze. I never did write on Druze religion and wound up with a thesis on the cognitive bases of science.

Perhaps because the Druze asked me never to discuss the content of their beliefs, my background thoughts about religion began to telescope on some sort of scientifically describable structure. As I went on to study and live with other peoples, the structural outline of Druze religious beliefs and practices appeared to crop up everywhere I sojourned: among forest Maya, desert Bedouin, steppe-roaming Pashtuns, Indian farmers, Tibetan mountaineers. At times, some of these general reflections on religion insinuated themselves into my thoughts and writings about other things. But these ideas were always a bit too austere, even under the cold light of science, because they ignored the passion with which religious beliefs are often held—a passion some willingly die (or kill) for.

Then, a colleague and friend of mine, who is also a world-class cognitive scientist, told me why he just couldn't buy cognitive theories that ignored emotion or social commitment theories that neglected individual minds. His grandmother had loved his grandfather as much as anyone apparently could love another person. But when grandfather committed suicide, grandmother was unforgiving in her judgment that her husband merited going straight to hell to suffer eternal damnation, even though he had been a good and decent man. She didn't cherish her husband's memory any less and wasn't particularly angry about his killing himself. Yet she was resigned to her husband's real suffering in afterlife, and to her own unending anguish about it, because of her religious beliefs. That's when the notion of a book about religion, addressed chiefly to a scientifically minded audience, became serious. (I apologize to the general reader for the dense argument this choice sometimes entails.)

The actual writing of this book developed in response to three events held at the University of Michigan in spring 1999. The first was a conference organized by the Culture and Cognition Program on "Cognitive Theories of Religion" under the direction of Richard Nisbett and Lawrence Hirschfeld. Presenters included Justin Barrett, Pascal Boyer, Thomas Lawson, and Brian Malley. They offered new data and interpretations for a convincing view of religion, namely, as a family of cognitive phenomena that involves the extraordinary use of everyday cognitive processes to produce minimally counterintuitive worlds that are attention-arresting, hence readily memorable and liable to cultural transmission, selection, and survival. But to the question I posed—"How, in principle, does this view distinguish Mickey Mouse from God, or fantasy from beliefs one is willing to die for?"—there was acknowledgment that nothing in the cognitive literature at the time offered an answer.

The second event was Dan Sperber's Culture and Cognition Workshop on "Cultural Epidemiology": same question, same response. This question first emerged in print the year before (Atran 1998:602). It soon after came to be known in e-mail circles as "the Mickey Mouse problem."

The third event was a conference organized by Randy Nesse for the Evolution and Human Adaptation Program on "The Biology of Belief and Trust." The discussants included an impressive array of evolutionary thinkers from biology and philosophy (Richard Alexander, David Sloan Wilson, Bobbi Low), political science and economics (Robert Axelrod, Robert Frank, Thomas Schelling, Elinor Ostrom), and anthropology (Robert Boyd, Peter Richerson, William Irons). Most discussions dealt at some point with evolutionary arguments favoring religion as a naturally selected design for social commitment (see Nesse 2002). But apart from a few rather silly, throwaway lines about a "God module" or "faith module" and numerous but largely irrelevant references to a "cheater-detection module," virtually nothing was said about the cognitive structure of the human mind/brain, its evolution, and its formative contribution to religious commitment or any other culturally recurrent behavior.

For those of us listening who do experimental work on modular cognitive processes, it was hard to know what some of this discussion was about. To the last question that the conference's moderator posed—"What more needs to be done?"—the final commentator replied: "We might consider the role of the mind." Let's.

Acknowledgments: For comments and suggestions on various parts of this work, I thank Michael Baran, Justin Barrett, Susan Carey, Francisco Gil-White, Joe Henrich, Lawrence Hirschfeld, David Hull, Nicola Knight, Philip Kukulski, Thomas Lawson, Elizabeth Lynch, Luther Martin, Dan Moerman, Randy Nesse, Richard

Nisbett, Stephen Nugent, Marshall Shearer, Paulo Sousa, Dan Sperber, Peter Todd, Edilberto Ucan Ek', and Harvey Whitehouse. I am also grateful to those who generously shared their unpublished materials with me: Susan Johnson, Robert McCauley, Patrick Macnamara, Brian Malley, and Steven Pinker. There is much I owe to Ximena Lois and Douglas Medin for the keen and patient attention that they gave this work when we were supposed to be doing other things. And, thanks to Laura Reynolds and Jessica Ryan for all their help during the editing process.

Note: Bits and pieces of this book have appeared in other places, most notably much of chapter 9 in *Human Nature* and *Evolution and Cognition,* and some of chapter 8 in *Proceedings of the National Academy of Sciences* and *Current Anthropology.*

Contents

In Gods We Trust

1 Introduction

An Evolutionary Riddle

God ain't no white-bearded old man up in the sky somewhere. . . . He's a spirit. He ain't got no body. . . . The only body he's got is us. *Amen. Thank God.*

—Brother Carl Porter, Evangelical Holiness Minister from Georgia, preaching in Scottsboro, Alabama, March 1992, cited in Annie Hillard, *For the Time Being* (2000)

A girl was asked by the gunman if she believed in God, knowing full well the safe answer. "There is a God," she said quietly, "and you need to follow along God's path." The shooter looked down at her. "There is no God," he said, and shot her in the head.

—Nancy Gibbs, "The Littleton Massacre: In Sorrow and Disbelief," *Time* (3 May 1999)

Just in terms of allocation of time resources, religion is not very efficient. There's a lot more I could be doing on a Sunday morning.

—William (Bill) Gates III, President of Microsoft Corporation, cited in Garrison Keillor, "Faith at the Speed of Light," *Time* (14 June 1999)

Most of us think we're more important than we really are, Charlie. Their universe isn't watching. It mostly, for the most part, doesn't care.

—Harlan Ellison, "Incognita, Inc.," *Hemispheres Magazine* (January 2001)

1.1. Why Is Religion an Evolutionary Dilemma?

Explaining religion is a serious problem for any evolutionary account of human thought and society. Roughly, *religion is (1) a community's costly and hard-to-fake commitment (2) to a counterfactual and counterintuitive world of supernatural agents (3) who master people's existential anxieties, such as death and deception*. All known human societies, past and present, bear the very substantial costs of religion's material, emotional, and cognitive commitments to factually impossible worlds.

From an evolutionary standpoint, the reasons religion shouldn't exist are patent: religion is materially expensive and unrelentingly counterfactual and even counterintuitive. Religious practice is costly in terms of material sacrifice (at least one's prayer time), emotional expenditure (inciting fears and hopes), and cognitive effort (maintaining both factual and counterintuitive networks of beliefs). Summing up the anthropological literature, Raymond Firth concludes:

> "Sacrifice" implies . . . that the resources are limited, that there are alternative uses for them, and that . . . sacrifice is giving something up at a cost. . . . [N]o direct counter-gift of a material kind is normally expected, although ensuing material benefits—in the form of fertility of crops or health of persons maintained or restored—are frequently regarded as its outcome. But even where no material benefit is thought to arise, religious offering and sacrifice have other compensatory functions . . . benefits arising from belief in the establishment of appropriate relations between the offerer or sacrificer and some spirit entity or extra-human power. . . . [S]acrifice expresses more than almost any other concept the heart of a religious system. (1963:13)

Religious beliefs are counterfactual insofar as they are anomalous (e.g., God is gendered but sexless; Saturn devours his own children; lambs lie with lions), implausible (e.g., Athena bursts forth from Zeus's head; the Zaïrean Nkundo hero Lianja springs fully armed from the leg of his mother; Lao-Tse either emerges with his white beard from the left side of his mother, who bore him for eighty years, or is born immaculately of a shooting star), and, most significantly, counterintuitive (e.g., the Judeo-Christian God is a sentient and emotional being with no body; Greek, Hindu, Maya, and Egyptian deities are half-human half-beast; the Chinese monkey god can travel thousands of kilometers at one somersault). In religious thought, a person may ride a horse into the sky (Mohammed), ascend to heaven in a chariot of fire (Elijah), rise to the stars in a carriage drawn by six dragons (Huang Ti, the founder of the Chinese empire), or gain knowledge and afterlife in passing through the digestive tract of a feathered serpent (Maya kings).

In all religions, argued the empirical philosopher and religious believer Thomas Hobbes, there are bodiless but sentient souls and spirits that act intentionally, though not in ways that can be verified empirically or understood logically. As for "one infinite, omnipotent, and eternal God," even the enlightened "choose rather to confess He is incomprehensible and above their understanding than to define His nature by 'spirit incorporeal,' and then confess their definition to be unintelligible" (1901[1651]: I, xii:69).

Everybody, whether they are religious or not, implicitly knows that religion is costly, counterfactual, and even counterintuitive. The more one accepts what is materially false to be really true, and the more one spends material resources in displays of such acceptance, the more others consider one's faith deep and one's commitment sincere. For the moral philosopher and Christian votary Søren Kierkegaard, true faith could be motivated only by "a gigantic passion" to commit to the "absurd." Abraham's willingness to sacrifice more than his own life—that of his only and beloved son—is exemplary in this regard: "For love of God is . . . incommensurable with the whole of reality . . . there could be no question of human calculation" (1955 [1843]: 35–46).

Much the same sentiment is represented on a panel of the Chola temple at Dārāsuram in Tamil Nadu, South India (ca. A.D. 1000): "A great Śaiva devotee offered his son's flesh to his guest who was no other than Śiva in disguise and demanded this ghastly food. When, however, it was cooked, the guest refused to take food in the house of the childless couple but finally appeared before them and restored life to the child, whom the mother received with joy" (Archaeological Survey of India 1992:42). For the Judaic-Christian-Islamic and Hindu faithful, Abraham and the Śaiva devotee aren't would-be murderers or child abusers. On the contrary, their willingness to commit what they and everyone else know to be a horribly self-sacrificing act *for nothing* save faith makes them religious heroes.

To take what is materially false to be true (e.g., people think and laugh and cry and hurt and have sex after they die and their bodies disintegrate) and to take what is materially true to be false (e.g., people just die and disintegrate and that's that) does not appear to be a reasonable evolutionary strategy (cf. Pinker 1998). Imagine another animal that took injury for health, or big for small, or fast for slow, or dead for alive. It's unlikely that such a species could survive competition with many other species or that individuals that acted this way could proliferate among conspecifics that did not act this way.

If people literally applied counterfactual religious principles and prescriptions to factual navigation of everyday environments they would likely be either dead or in the afterlife in very short order—probably in too short an order for individuals to reproduce and the species to survive. Imagine that you could suspend the known physical and biological laws of the universe with a prayer (or, for those who are less institutionalized, by crossing your fingers). The trick is in knowing how and when to suspend factual belief without countermanding the facts and compromising survival. But why take the risk of neglecting the facts at all, even in exceptional circumstances?

As for costly material commitment to the supernatural, it is all well and good to argue for analogy with some evolutionary principle of "sacrifice the part to save the whole" (Burkert 1996). But given that the probability of certifiably obtaining the desired outcome, such as a rewarding afterlife or freedom from catastrophe, ranges between zero and chance, there is no more likelihood of this being a functional analogy than an adaptive homology. For a bear to sacrifice its paw in a bear trap by gnawing it off, or a lizard to leave behind its tail for a predator to chew on, or a bee to die by stinging an intruder to save the hive seem reasonable trade-offs for survival. Yet, what could be the calculated gain from:

- a lifetime of celibacy (Catholic priests and nuns, Lamist monks, Aztec sun priests, Hindu sadhus)
- years of toil to build gigantic structures no person could use (Egyptian, Mesoamerican, and Cambodian pyramids)
- giving up one's sheep (Hebrews) or camels (Bedouin) or cows (Nuer of Sudan) or chickens (Highland Maya) or pigs (Melanesian tribes, Ancient Greeks), or buffaloe (South Indian tribes)
- dispatching wives when husbands die (Hindus, Inca, Solomon Islanders)
- slaying one's own healthy and desired offspring (the firstborn of Phoenicia and Carthage, Pawnee and Iroquois maidens, Inca and Postclassic Maya boys and girls, children of South India's tribal Lambadi, adolescents caught up in contemporary Western satanic cults or Afro-Brazilian Vodoo)
- chopping off a finger to give to dead warriors or relatives (Dani of New Guinea, Crow and other American Plains Indians)
- burning your house and all other possessions for a family member drowned, crushed by a tree, or killed by a tiger (Nāga tribes of Assam)
- knocking out one's own teeth (Australian aboriginals)
- making elaborate but evanescent sand designs (Navajo, northern tribes of central Australia)
- giving up one's life to keep Fridays (Muslims) or Saturdays (Jews) or Sundays (Christians) holy
- forgoing eating pigs but not cows (Jews and Muslims) or cows but not pigs (Hindus)
- just stopping whatever one is doing to murmur often incomprehensible words while gesticulating several times a day?

There can't be individual fitness advantages of the sort that part-for-whole sacrifice among animals may convey. Religion costs resources that rarely are fully repaid. This is also the case for entire societies. For example, the Crusades brought unforeseeable, long-term benefits to Western Europe, such as recovery of ancient knowledge and importation of new technologies from the Middle East. Still, knowledge seeking did not drive the Crusades, either explicitly or implicitly. Rather, for nearly three centuries European societies carried on at incalculable expense in money and human lives in a distant land to regain possession of an empty grave. Gains that followed were largely serendipitous, and advantageous only to later generations who did not take part and sacrifice (much as some future generations might serendipitously find a vast new supply of energy in our polluted waste).

Evolutionary arguments in favor of religion usually attempt to offset these apparent functional disadvantages with even greater functional advantages. Ever since recorded history began, there have been numerous different attempts to explain why religion exists in terms of what function it serves. For example:

Intellectual functions: It tries to answer the question Why? It prevents answers to the question Why? It creates meaning for an arbitrary world. It postulates an imaginary world that hides reality's reason. It discovers the origin of nature's regular recurrences, such as the sun and the stars, day and night, plants and animals, men and women. It disguises the origin of nature's regular recurrences. It clarifies mental phenomena, such as thoughts and dreams. It occludes mental phenomena. It stimulates intellectual and artistic creativity. It stifles creativity. It's the explanation of first resort. It's the explanation of last resort. It reduces complexity. It befuddles. It's the repository and residue of ignorance after knowledge is factored out. It's the utter understanding that all the tribe of logic-mongers can't describe.

Affective functions: It compensates for separation from father. It offsets weaning away from mother. It generalizes family feelings to the group. It internalizes group affections in the individual. It's a projection of ego to the world. It's the reduction of the world into ego. It extends sexual drive. It displaces sexual drive. It's deeply sensual. It's profoundly asensual. It relieves anxiety. It terrorizes. It enables one to cope with chaotic and episodic events, such as earthquakes and eclipses, hail and heartache, injury and illness. It fosters denial and escape from chaotic and episodic events. It aims to overcome evil, suffering, misfortune, and injustice among believers. It aims to cause evil, suffering, misfortune, and injustice among nonbelievers. It enables people to bear death. It enables people to enjoy life. It incites optimism and belief in the rightness of one's course. It instills pessimism and doubt to compel change in one's course. It supports stupidity and stubbornness. It commends caution and care. It's childhood fantasy. It's all that's serious.

Socio-economic functions: It benefits elites. It benefits the downtrodden. It intensifies surplus production. It wastes surplus production. It fosters cooperation. It drives competition. It binds society. It cements the self. It's the opiate of the masses. It's the motor of the masses. It's the workhorse of war. It's a player for peace. It's the mouthpiece of monarchy. It's the oracle of oligarchy. It's a friend of fascism. It's a foe of communism. It's the spirit of capitalism. It's whatever money can't buy.

Most of these proposals may have been true at one time or another, depending on the cultural context. All could also be said, and most could have been true, of cultural phenomena besides religion. None predicts the cognitive peculiarities of religion. For example, none provides a glimmer of an answer to these questions:

Why do *agent* concepts predominate in religion?
Why are *supernatural*-agent concepts culturally universal?
Why are *some* supernatural-agent concepts *inherently better* candidates for cultural selection than others?
Why is it necessary, and how is it possible, to *validate* belief in supernatural agents that are logically and factually inscrutable?
How is it possible to prevent people from deciding that the existing moral order is simply wrong or *arbitrary* and from *defecting* from the social consensus through denial, dismissal, or *deception*?

This book tries to answer these and related questions.

1.2. Why Are Religions and Cultures Not Entities or Things?

In *Leviathan*, Hobbes outlined the tale of a progressive development of mind, religion, science, and society that continues to agitate modern thinking. In the beginning, goes the story, mankind lived in a magical world where dreams could not be distinguished from reality (giving rise to waking visions of fairies and ghosts), where signs and objects were causally interchangeable (e.g., actual lions, drawings of lions, and utterances of the word "lion" would be equally feared), and where rash inductions were made routinely on the basis of propinquity in space or time (e.g., stop the clock from striking 6 and day may never come) or perceptual similarity (e.g., in Ancient and Medieval Europe, caressing walnuts sympathetically calmed troubled brains; among contemporary Itza' Maya, eating howler monkeys' heads cures whooping cough). From this dreamworld that confounded the sign with what is signified and correlation with cause "did arise the greatest part of the religion of the Gentiles in times past" (Hobbes 1901[1651]:I,ii:7).

This magical world, which supposedly defines the "savage" or "primitive" mind, overlaps with a simultaneous or later developing mythical universe that transcends the bounds of sense perception and observation in unverifiable and unwarranted ways. Thus, according to Edward Werner, an encyclopedic student of Chinese history and folklore:

> Chinese thoughts have not been, and are not now, as our thoughts. . . . Minds which conceive of persons drowned in a river as still alive, of corpses capable of resuscitation, of human souls passing into inanimate objects, plants, animals and other human beings, of stones becoming human beings and talking, are not likely to draw from the same data the conclusions we should draw from them. . . . [They] would almost seem subject to different psychological laws. (1961[1932]:xv)

Where some see magic as a precursor of myth, others see magic as the practical and behavioral expression of the mythical imagination. In any event, both magic and myth are thought to stem from ignorance as to relations between cause and effect and from hasty and incorrect attempts to explain perceptual phenomena. They are part and parcel of unscientific man's explanation of things (B. Russell 1948; Piaget 1967; Hallpike 1976).

Some, like Hobbes, see "religion" in its more modern guises as a concomitant of science, or at least as not incompatible with science. With progress in methodical understanding of material causality based on controlled observation, religion could purge myth of its fanciful visions and take over its foundational function of establishing a shared, moral understanding of the nature of human society. Others hope instead that religion is but the last vestige of humankind's uneducated folly, to end up on the garbage heap of history as science triumphs in all spheres of knowledge and understanding.

Such sentiments are common to the positive philosophies of scientific empiricism initiated in England by John Locke and on the European continent by Auguste Comte (cf. Lévy-Bruhl 1966[1923]; Tyler 1930(1881). They are also ethnocentric and wrongheaded. Judeo-Christian belief is no more or less imbued with magical or mythical thought than are the supernatural beliefs of Chinese, Hindus, Maya, African animists, or Australian aboriginals. And the psychology that leads to such beliefs is common to us all.

In this book, I make no principled distinctions between magic and myth, between primitive and modern thought, or among animistic, pantheistic, and monotheistic forms of religion. Magic and myth are complementary aspects of the imperfect causal community of ideas and behaviors that we dub "religion," that is, costly communal commitments to hard-to-fake beliefs in the supernatural. Although I look at some fundamental differences between science and religion, I don't see religion as a psychologically primitive attempt at causal explanation of physical facts, or science as a pyschologically more complex development or substitute for religion.

Granted, social and economic complexity, as manifest in hierarchical divisions of labor and government, are associated with less animistic and zoomorphic beliefs (Swanson 1967; Lemert 1974; Sheils 1980; Simpson 1984; Diamond 1997). Monotheistic religions are on the whole historically more recent than pantheistic religions, emphasizing broad concepts of social obligation (justice for all, care for the anonymous needy). Their principal mode of transmission is literate and therefore impersonal. This allows the Abrahamic faiths (Judaism, Christianity, Islam, and their offshoots) to espouse relatively disembodied and abstract forms of doctrine that override (or annihilate) specific cultural and environmental attachments—a development that arguably expands what counts as humanity but also continues to have serious consequences for the world's cultural and ecological diversity.

Similarly, Buddhism's nearly exclusive focus on mental causation and on the teachings of a single mind (Buddha's) as a model of enlightenment extends Hinduism's literate but pantheistic notions of spirit, karma, and reincarnation to a transcultural audience, as a doctrine of rebirth in a world without spatial or temporal dimensions. It makes little sense to have a Hindu elephant god and a sacred mango tree, or to be reborn into the loom-weaving caste, if most people have never seen an elephant or eaten a mango or if their communities have no looms. But Buddhism is no more simply a later stage of Hinduism than Christianity is of Judaism or Islam of Christianity.

For my purposes, the differences among animistic, pantheistic, and monotheistic religions can be ascribed to differences in the content of beliefs in the supernatural, not to differences in the cognitive structure of those beliefs. These content differences concern the relative psychological "distance" between representations of society and representations of nature. In animistic beliefs, representations of nature and society tend to merge (e.g., social groups descended from animal totems); in pantheistic societies they are often mixed (e.g., some deities are part animal and part human, others have only human form, still others have no present human form); and in monotheistic societies they are mostly separate. Still, even the most animistic of tribal cultures have disembodied notions of intentional spirits and even the most rigidly monotheistic cultures have animistic representations (e.g., the snake in Eden, God speaking to Moses through the burning bush).

All religions, I claim, involve counterintuitive beliefs in supernatural beings. Moreover, such beliefs are systematically counterintuitive in the same basic ways. As we shall see, these basic ways of entertaining supernatural beliefs are more or less predictable from a fairly limited set of species-specific cognitive structures.

These claims stem from a cognitive perspective. This is a perspective that I used earlier to study the psychological foundations of scientific developments in *Cognitive Foundations of Natural History* (Atran 1990a). It focuses its subject not from the more traditional philosophical, historical, or sociological standpoints, but from a vantage that I think is more basic and necessary to all of these: that of cognitive culture theory. By cognition, I mean simply the internal structure of ideas that represent the world and that directs behaviors appropriate to the world represented. By culture, I intend only the distributed structure of cognition, that is, the causal networking of ideas and behaviors within and between minds. Religion, science, and any or all regularities of culture are just more or less reliable (statistically identifiable) causal distributions of mental representations, and public displays of those representations, among a given population of minds in a specified ecological context.

Cultures and religions do not exist apart from the individual minds that constitute them and the environments that constrain them, any more than biological species and varieties exist independently of the individual organisms that compose them and the environments that conform them. They are not well-bounded systems or definite clusters of beliefs, practices, and artifacts, but more or less regular distributions of causally connected thoughts, behaviors, material products, and environmental objects. To naturalistically understand what "cultures" are is to describe and explain the material causes responsible for reliable differences in these distributions.

The anthropologist's task, then, is not to account for ideas and practices in terms of culture or religion, as layfolk and social scientists alike often commonsensically do. Rather, it is to scientifically explain cultures and religions in terms of their material causes. Cultures and religions exist, and are explained, to the extent that they reliably express stucturally enduring relationships among mental states and behaviors and where these material relationships enable a given population of individuals to maintain itself in repeated social interaction within a range of ecological contexts. Cultures and religions are not ontologically distinct "superorganisms" or "independent variables" with precise contents or boundaries. They are no more things in and of themselves, or "natural kinds" with their own special laws, than are cloud or sand patterns.

Although many of the specific points made herein must ultimately be revised or rejected, this book is in a sense a plea for a naturalistic approach to anthropology that would harness for science the insights gained from studying and living with other peoples. Naturalism in cognitive anthropology describes the attempt to causally locate the commonsense objects of study—cultures—inside the larger network of scientific knowledge. This approach posits no special phenomena, ontologies, causes, or laws beyond those of ordinary material objects and their interrelationships. It studies the structure and content of representations, both private and public, and their variously patterned distributions within and between human populations.

1.3. What Is an Evolutionary Landscape? A Conduit Metaphor

Think metaphorically of humankind's evolutionary history as a landscape formed by different mountain ridges. Human experience that lies anywhere along this evolutionary landscape converges on more or less the same life paths, just as rain that falls anywhere in a mountain landscape converges toward a limited set of lakes or river valleys. This notion of landscape is a conduit metaphor in the sense that it serves as a guide for a multisided approach to the evolutionary riddle of religion.

The random interactions of people as they walk through and experience life bottoms out in some well-trodden, cross-culturally recurrent paths in the basin of this evolutionary landscape (Waddington 1959; Kauffman 1993; Sperber 1996). The class of humanly plausible religions is one such set of paths in the landscape's drainage basin. From this viewpoint, humankind's evolutionary landscape greatly reduces the many possible sources of religious expression into structures that seem always to reappear across history and societies. This landscape functions everywhere to canalize, but not determine, development.

The existence of a physical path depends jointly on:

the nature of the path's ecological setting, which constrains where it can be made to go
the animate bodies that actually groove the path into the landscape
the behavioral itineraries that determine where in fact the path leads
the cognitive models that give purpose and direction to the path

Likewise, the existence of religion—indeed, of any cultural path—results from a confluence of cognitive, behavioral, bodily, and ecological constraints that neither reside wholly within minds nor are recognizable in a world without minds. Theories of religion that concentrate on only one of these factors, however correct or insightful in part, can never be thorough or comprehensive.[1]

Each mountain ridge in this landscape has a distinct contour, with various peaks whose heights reflect evolutionary time. That is, within humankind's evolutionary landscape there are several naturally selected systems that contribute to channeling human experience toward religious paths. In the processing of human experience, these systems, and their components, interact and develop interrelated functions—as do geological, hydrological, and organic systems in the drainage process.

One such evolutionary system, or ridge, encompasses panhuman emotional faculties, or affective "programs." These include the basic, or primary, emotions that Darwin first identified: surprise, fear, anger, joy, sadness, disgust, and perhaps contempt. Certain reactions characteristic of the neurophysiology of surprise and fear are already evident in reptiles, and the other primary emotions are at least apparent in monkeys and apes. Then there are the secondary, mostly "social" emotions, such as anxiety, grief, guilt, pride, vengeance, and love. These may be unique to humans—hence, at the lower level in our evolutionary mountain landscape—and somewhat more liable to cultural manipulation and variation than the primary, "Darwinian" emotions. Thus, only humans seek revenge or redemption across lifetimes and generations, whatever the cost, although the nature of the deeds that trigger insult or remorse may vary considerably across societies, and the means to counter them may range even wider.

Another ridge includes social interaction schema. Some of these schema may have aspects that go far back in evolutionary time, such as those involved in detecting predators and seeking protectors, or that govern direct "tit-for-tat" reciprocity (you scratch my back, and I'll scratch yours; if you bite me, then I'll bite you). Other social interaction schema may have elements common to some species of social mammals (e.g., bats, wolves, monkeys, and apes). Examples include certain systematically recurrent forms of delayed reciprocity (you help me now and I'll help you later), indirect reciprocity (I'll help those who help those who help me; the enemies of my enemies are my friends), and greeting displays of submission-domination. Still other social interaction schema appear to be unique to humans, such as making decisions to cooperate on the basis of social signs of reputation rather than on the basis of individual observation and experience, or in offering and obtaining future commitments of an indeterminate nature (when the chips are down, I'll help you, whatever the situation). Only humans, it appears, willingly commit their lives to groups of nonkin.

Yet another ridge encompasses panhuman mental faculties, or cognitive "modules," such as folkmechanics (the mostly unreflective understanding of how whole objects physically move and interact), folkbiology (the often automatic taxonomic assignment of any perceived organism to one and only one essential, species-like group), and, especially for our purposes, folkpsychology (the largely spontaneous attribution of intentional beliefs and desires to other minds). In this evolutionary system, folkmechanics is clearly the oldest component, with aspects perhaps stretching back to amphibian or reptilian brains. Folkpsychology is the newest, with glimmerings in the great apes but apparently not before. Only humans seem able to formulate a nonobservable, causal notion of "controlling force" that empowers agents, including all supernatural agents. Only humans generate multiple models of other minds and worlds, including those of the supernatural.

In the course of life, all such systems (i.e., the different evolutionary ridges) are somewhat functionally interdependent, as are components within each system (i.e., the different programs, schema, modules). Nevertheless, each system and system component has a somewhat distinct evolutionary history and time line. There is no single origin of religion, nor any necessary and sufficient set of functions that religion serves. Rather, there is a family of evolutionary-compatible functions that all societies more or less realize but that no one society need realize in full.

Religions are not adaptations and they have no evolutionary functions as such. Religion did not originate exclusively or primarily to:

- cope with death (Feuerbach 1972[1843]; Freud 1957a [1915]; H. Bloom 1992) or existential anxieties generally (Malinowski 1961[1922]; Lowie 1924; Geertz 1966)
- keep social and moral order (Durkheim 1955[1912]; Evans-Pritchard 1965; Douglas 1973; Irons 1996a)
- recover the lost childhood security of father (Kant 1951[1790]; Freud 1955 [1913]; Foster and Keating 1992), mother (Erikson 1963; Obeyesekere 1984; Kirkpatrick 1997), or family (Spiro and D'Andrade 1958; Fortes 1959)
- substitute for, or displace, sexual gratification (Wallin 1957; Taylor 1959; Mol 1970)
- provide causal explanations where none were readily apparent (Tyler 1930; Horton 1967; Dawkins 1998)

- provoke intellectual surprise and awe so as to retain incomplete, counterfactual, or counterintuitive information (Sperber 1975; Atran 1990a; Boyer 1994)

It is not that these explanations of religion are all wrong. On the contrary, they are often deeply informative and insightful. It is only that, taken alone, each such account is not unique to, or necessary or sufficient for, explaining religion. Rather, there are multiple elements in the naturally selected landscape that channel socially interacting cognitions and emotions into the production of religions. These include evolved constraints on modularized conceptual and mnemonic processing, cooperative commitments, eruptive anxieties, communicative displays, and attentiveness to information about protective, predatory, and awe-inspiring agents.

1.4. Why Are Mickey Mouse and Marx Different from God? Limitations of Cognitive and Commitment Theories of Religion

In every society known, there is:

1. widespread counterfactual belief in supernatural agents (gods, ghosts, goblins, etc.)
2. hard-to-fake public expressions of costly material commitments to supernatural agents, that is, sacrifice (offerings of goods, time, other lives, one's own life, etc.)
3. a central focus of supernatural agents on dealing with people's existential anxieties (death, disease, catastrophe, pain, loneliness, injustice, want, loss, etc.)
4. ritualized and often rhythmic coordination of 1, 2, and 3, that is, communion (congregation, intimate fellowship, etc.)

In all societies there is an evolutionary canalization and convergence of 1, 2, 3, and 4 that tends toward "religion," that is, passionate communal displays of costly commitments to counterintuitive worlds governed by supernatural agents. Despite important contributions to each, there has been no concerted attempt to unify 1, 2, 3, and 4 in ways that preserve what is specific and insightful in these recent contributions. This book is an attempt to fill the void. Consider the following.

Cognitive theories of religion primarily concern 1. These concentrate almost entirely on the micropsychological processes of cultural transmission. They are the processes that causally generate, transform, and connect chains of mental and public representations into "cultures" and parts of culture like religion. Empirical studies in this area have almost wholly concerned memory and cognitive constraints on the structuration and transmission of religious beliefs, ignoring motivation (Sperber 1975, 1985a; Atran 1990a, 1996; Lawson and McCauley 1990; Whitehouse 1992, 2000; Boyer 1994, Boyer and Ramble 2001; Malley 1995; J. Barrett and Keil 1996; J. Barrett and Nyhof 2001; for an exception, see Guthrie 1993).

Commitment theories of religion primarily concern 2. These focus almost exclusively on the macroinstitutional dynamics of socially distributed traits, rules, norms, and other cultural prototypes. Empirical studies have almost wholly concentrated on material measures of individual and group costs and benefits and have paid little attention to the mind's cognitive architecture and processing constraints (Alexander 1987, 1989; R. Frank 1988; Irons 1996a, b; Sober and Wilson 1998; D. S. Wilson 2002; Nesse 1999; Boyd and Richerson 1985, 2001a, b).

Experiential theories primarily concern 3. These mainly target states of altered consciousness and personal sensations. Empirical studies focus on tracking participants' neurophysiological responses during episodes of religious experience and recording individual reports of trance, meditation, vision, revelation, and the like. Cognitive structures of the human mind/brain in general, and cognitions of agency in particular, are described either cognitively in simple-minded terms (e.g., binary oppositions, holistic vs. analytical tensions, hierarchical organization) or in psychoanalytic terms that have little input from, or pertinence to, recent findings of cognitive and developmental psychology (Persinger 1987, 1997; Beit-Hallahmi and Argyle 1997; d'Aquili and Newberg 1999; Newberg et al. 2001).

Performance theories primarily concern 4. These attend to the psychosocial dynamics of liturgy and ritual practice, that is, to the affective character and sociological implications of what Durkheim (1995[1912]) called "collective effervescence." Empirical studies have almost wholly focused on normative and ceremonial expressions of religion. They neglect the more mundane cognitive processes of categorization, reasoning, and decision making that underlie all religious beliefs and commitments and that make such beliefs and commitments comprehensible (Turner 1969, 1983; Tambiah 1981; Rappaport 1999).

Cognitive theories of religion are motiveless. They cannot, in principle, distinguish Mickey Mouse and the Magic Mountain from Jesus and the burning bush, fantasy from religious belief. They cannot explain why people are able to willingly sacrifice even their lives to uphold religious belief, or how thoughts about death and anxiety affect feelings of religiosity. If religious belief and fantasy are pretty much the same, then why, for example, do individuals who are placed inside a sensory deprivation tank have an easier time evoking religious images than cartoon images, but not when those individuals are outside the tank (Hood and Morris 1981)? Why do people in all societies spontaneously chant and dance or pray and sway to religious representations, but do not rythmically follow other factual or fictive representations so routinely?

Commitment theories are mindblind. For the most part, they ignore or misrepresent the cognitive structure of the mind and its causal role. They cannot in principle distinguish Marxism from monotheism, ideology from religious belief. They cannot explain why people can be more steadfast in their commitment to admittedly counterfactual and counterintuitive beliefs—that Mary is both a mother and a virgin, and God is sentient but bodiless—than to the most politically, economically, or scientifically persuasive account of the ways things are or should be. For commitment theorists, political and economic ideologies that obey transcendent behavioral laws do for people pretty much what religious belief in the supernatural is supposed to do. One frequently cited example of religious-like ideology is Lenin's (1972) doctrine of dialectical materialism. An equally plausible candidate is what financier George Soros (2000) calls "market fundamentalism."[2] Like more familiar religious doctrines, these promissory ideologies seem to maintain the faith no matter how many contrary facts or reasons they face. But if such secular ideologies perform the same functions as religious ideologies, then why did at least 50 percent of Marx-fearing Russians feel the need to preserve their belief in the supernatural (survey by Subbotsky 2000)? And why is the overwhelming majority of market believers *also* God-fearing (Novak 1999; Podhoretz 1999). What is it about belief in the supernatural that thwarts social defection and deception, underpinning moral orders as no secular ideology seems able to do for long?

1.5. Overview

In the chapters that follow, I seek to reconcile cognitive and commitment theories of religious belief on the basis of evolutionary arguments that mobilize data from numerous psychological studies and anthropological observations, including some of my own studies with colleagues. This reconciliation motivates, and bootstraps in, a new examination of experiential and performance theories of ritual practice and mystical experience and the evidence they harness. The results are then assessed against competing evolutionary theories of religion.

Part I, "Evolutionary Sources," sets the stage. Because there is no such entity as "religion," it makes no sense to ask how "it" evolved. Rather, religious belief and practice involves a variety of brain and body systems, some with separate evolutionary histories and some with no evolutionary history to speak of.

Supernatural agents are critical components of all religions but not of all ideologies. They are, in part, by-products of a naturally selected cognitive mechanism for detecting agents—such as predators, protectors, and prey—and for dealing rapidly and economically with stimulus situations involving people and animals. This innate releasing mechanism is trip-wired to attribute agency to virtually any action that mimics the stimulus conditions of natural agents: faces on clouds, voices in the wind, shadow figures, the intentions of cars or computers, and so on. Among natural agents, predators such as snakes are as likely to be candidates for deification as are protectors, such as parent-figures.

Part II, "Absurd Commitments," looks into the cognitive structures and social commitments that make up belief in the supernatural and that also ensure stability within and across cultures. People everywhere understand the world in terms of "modular" conceptual systems, such as folkmechanics (tracking objects and movements), folkbiology (categorizing and reasoning about living kinds), and, especially, folkpsychology (attributing to others intentions, beliefs, desires, and "minds"). All religions have core beliefs that confound these innate expectations about the world, such as faith in physically powerful but essentially bodiless deities. These beliefs grab attention, activate intuition, and mobilize inference in ways that facilitate their social transmission, cultural selection, and historical persistence. New experiments suggest that such beliefs, in small doses, are optimal for memory. This greatly favors their cultural survival.

Mature cognitions of folkpsychology and agency include metarepresentation. This involves the ability to track and build a notion of self over time, to model other minds and worlds, and to represent beliefs about the actual world as being true or false. It also makes lying and deception possible. This threatens any social order. But this same metarepresentational capacity provides the hope and promise of open-ended solutions to problems of moral relativity. It does so by enabling people to conjure up counterintuitive supernatural worlds that cannot be verified or falsified, either logically or empirically. Religious beliefs minimally violate ordinary intuitions about the world, with its inescapable problems, such as death. This frees people to imagine minimally impossible worlds that seem to solve existential dilemmas, including death and deception.

Religious ritual invariably offers a sacrificial display of commitment to supernatural agents that is materially costly and emotionally convincing. Such ritual conveys willingness to cooperate with a community of believers by signaling an open-ended promise to help others whenever there is true need. These expensive and sincere displays underscore belief that the gods are always vigilant and will never allow society to suffer those who cheat on their promises. Such a deep devotion to the in-group habitually generates intolerance toward out-groups. This, in turn, leads to constant rivalry and unending development of new and syncretic religious forms.

Part III, "Ritual Passions," explores ritual practice and religious experience and the existential anxieties that motivate religious thought and action, such as those associated with stress, trauma, and death. Because religious beliefs and experiences cannot be reliably validated through logical deduction or observational induction, validation occurs only by satisfying the emotions that motivate religion in the first place.

Religious ritual survives cultural transmission by embedding episodes of intense, life-defining personal experiences in public performances. These performances involve sequential, socially interactive movement and gesture (chant, dance, murmur, sway) and formulaic utterances that rhythmically synchronize affective states among group members in displays of cooperative commitment. This is often accompanied by sensory pageantry, which further helps to emotionally validate and sustain the moral consensus.

As with emotionally drawn-out religious initiations, neurobiological studies of stress disorders indicate that subjects become intensely absorbed by sensory displays. The mystical experiences of schizophrenics and temporal lobe epileptics, which may be at the extreme end of the "normal" distribution of religious experience, also exhibit intense sensory activity. These may help to inspire new religions. There is no evidence, however, that more "routine" religious experiences that commit the bulk of humanity to the supernatural have any characteristic pattern of brain activity.

Part IV, "Mindblind Theories," compares this book's take on religion with other current evolutionary theories of religion and culture formation. These other theories make scant effort to describe how hypothesized units of cultural selection and evolution are formed and represented in the minds that produce and process them. Such theories also fail to causally spell out how norms actually work to produce behaviors.

Sociobiology and group selection theory both assume that cultures are systems of widely shared rules or norms that maintain heritable variation. Evidence for norms as units of cultural selection comes mainly from colonial anthropologists and lone fieldworkers trying to make sense of alien cultures as "social machines" to reduce a lot of information to readily manageable proportions. In fact, widely accepted, sacred, or morally absolute norms are only signposts of behavioral tendencies. They are not shared rules. Like the Ten Commandments, they have little if any context-free content or directive. Lacking reliable content or boundaries, they cannot replicate with any degree of fidelity adequate for Darwinian selection. An experiment in the Maya Lowlands offers an empirical demonstration of cultural modeling without norms and throws new light on the role of supernatural spirits in resolving a particular kind of moral and environmental dilemma known as "the Tragedy of the Commons."

Meme theory, or memetics, resembles evolutionary theories of norm selection but with an original slant. A meme is supposed to be an element of culture, an idea or practice, passed on by imitation much like a norm. But whereas norms are presumably selected to benefit the group that has them, memes serve only themselves. Just as genes or viruses use individual bodies to replicate and propagate, so memes allegedly use the minds that host them as (potentially disposable) transport vehicles. Cultures and religions are coalitions of memes seeking to maximize their own fitness, regardless of fitness costs for their human hosts. Unlike genetic transmission, however, cultural transmission involves rapid and constant "mutation" of information. Without fidelity in transmission, there is no meme to naturally select. Stability in cultural transmission occurs not via imitation and replication, but through modularized constraints and inferences. These crucial parts of our evolutionary endowment canalize human interactions into cultural paths that always include recognizable religious paths.

The final chapter offers a summary of preceding arguments that is meant to address the question Why does religion seem here to stay? It ends with a comparison of science and religion. Religion survives science and secular ideology not because it is prior to or more primitive than science or secular reasoning, but because of what it affectively and collectively secures for people.

From the cognitive perspective of this book, the most stable and recurrent cultural patterns, and those that provide the material bases for cultural patterns less steadfast, are generated by specialized core adaptations of the human mind/brain. These include the various naturally selected peaks of emotion (e.g., fear, guilt, love), social interaction (e.g., avoiding predators, attaching to protectors, tracking prey), and cognition (e.g., folkmechanics, folkbiology, folkpsychology) in the evolutionary landscape of human existence. Even the apparently incommensurable aspects of different cultural groups are conceivable only against a rich background of universally commensurable cognitions and emotions. If this weren't true, anthropology would be impossible and psychology would never amount to more than ethnocentric fiction.

Ignorance or disregard of our evolutionary heritage, and of the fundamental biological, emotional, cognitive, and social similarities on which much in everyday human life and thought depend, can lead to speculative philosophies and empirical programs that misconstrue the natural scope and limits of our species-specific abilities and competencies. The intellectual and moral consequences of this misconstrual have varying significance, both for ourselves and for others, for example, in the ways relativism informs currently popular notions of "separate but equal" cultural worlds whose peoples are in some sense incommensurably different from ourselves and from one another. Relativism aspires directly to mutual tolerance of irreducible differences. Naturalism—the evolutionary-based biological and cognitive understanding of our common nature and humanity—aims first to render cultural diversity comprehensible. If anything, evolution teaches us that from one or a few forms wondrously many kinds will arise.

PART 1

Evolutionary Sources

In the beginning of things, the *kaos* was created.

—Hesiod (ca. 700 B.C.)

We are placed in this world, as in a great theatre, where the true springs and causes of every event are entirely concealed from us; nor have we sufficient wisdom to foresee, or power to prevent those ills, with which we are continually threatened. We hang in perpetual suspence between life and death, health and sickness, plenty and want; which are distributed amongst the human species by secret and unknown causes, whose operation is oft unexpected, and always unaccountable. These *unknown causes,* then, become the constant object of our hope and fear; and while the passions are kept in perpetual alarm by an anxious expectation of events, the imagination is equally employed in forming ideas of those powers, on which we have so entire a dependence. . . . Where is the difficulty in conceiving, that the same powers or principles, whatever they were, which formed this visible world, men and animals, produced also a series of intelligent creatures, of more refined substance and greater authority than the rest? That these creatures may be capricious, revengeful, passionate, voluptuous, is easily conceived; nor is any circumstance more apt, among ourselves, to engender such vices, than the licence of absolute authority. And in short, the whole mythological system is so natural, that, in the vast variety of planets and worlds, contained in this universe, it seems more than probable, that, somewhere or other, it is really carried into execution.

—David Hume, *The Natural History of Religion* (1757)

Imagination and intelligence enter into our existence in the part of servants of the primary instincts.

—Albert Einstein, *Out of My Later Years* (1950)

2 The Mindless Agent

Evolutionary Adaptations and By-products

Evolutionary adaptations are functional biological designs naturally selected to solve important and recurrent problems in ancestral environments, such as hands for grasping objects. Evolutionary by-products are necessary concomitants of adaptations that were not selected to have any direct utility. Nevertheless, by-products can acquire or co-opt functions for which they were not originally designed, such as knuckles for fighting and fingerprints for tracking personal identities. There are several sources of evidence for adaptation: analogy, homology, functional trade-offs among traits in phyletic lines, ontogeny, and complexity of design. Owing to lack of phylogenetic parallels and a poor hominid fossil record, much of this evidence is unavailable to evolutionary accounts of human cognition. Claims for cognitive structures as adaptations are often simply "just-so" tales. Alternative views of language, religion, and myriad other forms of human cognition and sapient behavior as by-products, or "spandrels," of big brains—akin to the indefinitely many novel software configurations and uses for a computer—are mostly opaque "it-just-happened" stories.

Evolutionary psychology's emphasis on reverse engineering of complex design is a promising but problematic method for distinguishing human mental adaptations and by-products. Unlike the case for language, for religion there is no likely direct evolutionary resolution of its cognitive components. Rather, religious belief and practice involves cognitive systems, some with separate evolutionary histories and some with no evolutionary history to speak of. Of those with an evolutionary history, some parts plausibly have an adaptive story and others are more likely by-products.

2.1. Introduction: The Nature of Biological Adaptation

> Thus, from the war of nature, from famine and death, the most exalted object which we are capable of conceiving, namely, the production of higher animals, directly follows. There is grandeur in this view of life, with its several powers, having been originally breathed by the Creator into a few forms or into one; and that, whilst this planet has gone cycling on according to the fixed law of gravity, from so simple a beginning endless forms most beautiful and most wonderful have been, and are being, evolved.
>
> —Darwin, *On the Origin of Species by Means of Natural Selection* (1859)

The idea of adaptation most congenial to evolutionary psychology is that of George Williams (1966). An adaptation is any trait that enhances fitness and was modified by selection to perform that role (cf. Gould and Vrba 1982). Invoking adaptation is appropriate when there is evidence of a functional design that solves some recurrent problem in an ancestral environment and when there is evidence of fitness-promoting modification of design by natural selection.

The delayed effects of William Hamilton's (1964) theory of inclusive fitness have shifted attention somewhat from adaptation as a characteristic of organisms to adaptation from "a gene's-eye view" (Dawkins 1976). Hamilton puzzled over the apparently altruistic self-sacrifice of worker bees in forsaking the opportunity to breed in favor of caring for the queen's young. He realized that the hive's peculiar genetic structure resulted in workers being so closely related to one another that, in slaving for the queen, they were promoting their own gene pool. It follows that the genetic disposition of a human parent to forgo personal advantage for the sake of his or her child is just a special case of genes selfishly looking out for their own best interests, as is their disposing of the individual who carries them to self-sacrifice (*ceteris paribus*) for the sake of two siblings, four cousins, or eight second-cousins.

There is suggestive evidence that at least some primate species have evolved abstract computational mechanisms for constructing kin categories, which allow context-dependent flexibility in monitoring and mobilizing genetic relationships and obligations. For example, female vervet monkeys respond to the screams of their own juvenile offspring, but when another's offspring screams they look to its mother. Even more intriguing is the report that when two vervets fight, the close kin of one may attack the kin of another (Cheney, Seyfarth, and Smuts 1986).

Genes are DNA-encoded units of information for body building and behavior programming that dependably survive reproductive division (meiosis). By contrast, the whole genotype, which is a temporary and unique sampling from a population's gene pool of all the DNA-encoded information that makes an individual organism, cannot survive reproductive division—except perhaps under some divinely inspired forms of personal reincarnation. From the gene's-eye view, adaptations promote the fitness of genes of which those adaptations are the naturally selected phenotypic expressions. Adaptations promote fitness by increasing the representation of those genes in the population's gene pool. Put a bit differently, an adaptation is a set of phenotypic effects, in an organism, of genes that were modified under selection to reliably produce such effects as led to the genes' propagation in ancestral environments. The basic idea is a functional design selected for solving past environmental problems.

Environmental contexts may be geographic (adaptation to land, sea, air, climate, etc.), ecological (e.g., predator avoidance), sexual (competition for mates), social (e.g., hierarchical access to resources), or internal (accommodation to prior mechanisms). Different contexts may impinge on selection by imposing somewhat antagonistic task demands. Adaptations often have to balance conflicting, context-dependent selection factors. For example, peacocks apparently evolved long and colorful tail feathers to better compete with one another for the attention of peahens. Long and weighty tail feathers, however, arguably render peacocks slower than if they had short tail feathers; moreover, colorful tail feathers are more likely to attract predators than dull tail feathers.

Similar considerations likely applied to the extinct mammoth. Like elephant tusks, mammoth tusks almost surely served for defense. The problem with mammoths is that the tusks of larger, older, and presumably dominant bulls were so long, twisted, and heavy that they dragged on the ground and so lowered defense capabilities. Compared to the evolutionary emergence of ecologically adapted designs, the appearance of sexually selected traits seems rather arbitrary and chaotic (G. Miller 2000). One might suppose that ecological factors would eventually lead to peahens having a genetically driven preference for shorter, duller tail feathers and for mammoth cows to privilege shorter, less twisted tusks.

The mathematical biologist R. A. Fisher (1958:151–153; cf. Cronin 1992) explained such ecologically odd, "aesthetic" behaviors as follows: if the majority in a population prefers some arbitrary trait, then it is best to go with the majority preference. Suppose that a bit earlier in mammoth evolution tusks that were moderately long and curved properly signaled adequate defense capabilities and virility. Cows would then be under selection pressures to evolve a mating preference for those bulls having longer and more curved tusks than other bulls. Once the majority in the population was inclined to prefer long tusks, there would be selective pressures on bulls to evolve even longer tusks to attract cows. This would still be true even if longer tusks actually reduced adaptive advantage in regard to the defense function for which tusks were originally designed under selection. Thus, a cow that mated with a long-tusked bull would have sons who inherited long tusks and daughters with preferences for long tusks (not phenotypically expressed but transmissible). A cow that preferred short-tusked bulls would have short-tusked sons who might be less burdened and swifter than their long-tusked competitors, but they would fail to attract the majority of cows (who still prefer the long-tusked variety) and so would be less likely to reproduce than their slower rivals.

The evolutionary concept of adaptation differs from more general notions of adaptation or "adaptiveness" current in anthropology and ecology. For example, the ecological anthropologist Roy Rappaport defines adaptation as "the processes through which living systems of all sorts—organisms, populations, societies, possibly ecosystems or even the biosphere as a whole—maintain themselves in the face of perturbations continuously threatening them with disruption, death or extinction" (1999:6). The evolutionary concept of adaptation differs from this more general notion in two respects.

First, the processes that currently maintain a system may be quite different from those that created the system in the first place. For example, historical processes produced modern railroads that function nowadays to transport freight and people; however, the span of railroad tracks may be largely a historical vestige of an earlier design, perhaps owing to the carriage width of the earlier battle chariot. Similarly, the selective social pressures for white-skinned persons in South African suburbs or black-skinned persons in Chicago ghettos are very different from selective climatic pressures related to intensity of sunlight that were originally responsible for the emergence of white or black skin. Similarly, some of the social processes that affect the ways and reasons people today use language (e.g., storage of thoughts and formal arguments in written words) may have little to do with the selective forces that led to the creation of these abilities, presumably in the Pleistocene.

Second, current fitness or lack of fitness with respect to present environments is not evidence of adaptation or lack of adaptation. For example, fear of snakes conveys little, if any, fitness benefit on people who live in urban areas, especially in temperate climates (where there are few noxious snake species). Nevertheless, a universal and easily triggered fear response to snakes in humans and other primate species makes adaptive sense in terms of the threat of snakes in ancestral environments (R. Morris and Morris 1965; Mineka et al. 1984; Marks 1987). By contrast, fear of automobiles or atom bombs, which are far more dangerous in today's world than snakes, is not so nearly as universal or as easily triggered, in part because natural selection has not had the time to alter genes to better face these modern threats (E. O. Wilson 1978).

Similarly, religious fundamentalism may be adaptive in some contexts without being an adaptation in an evolutionary sense. In theocratic societies, adherence to fundamentalism may enhance the fitness of fundamentalists, as opposed to nonfundamentalists, because fundamentalists are more likely to obtain productive resources and have successful offspring, whereas nonfundamentalists are less likely to have access to productive resources and more likely to be punished or killed. It is not likely, however, that natural selection has had the time to cause the difference.

Conversely, the accumulation of resources by high-status individuals in technologically advanced societies does not appear to translate into the production of more offspring than in lower-status individuals or to greater representation in the population's gene pool. Nevertheless, comparative studies of other primate groups, as well as comparative and historical analysis of human societies, suggest that high-status individuals generally have had more surviving and successful offspring than lower-status individuals. The implication is that resource- and status-seeking behavior is an adaptation widespread among primates, including humans, regardless of present consequences.

2.2. Evidence for Adaptation: Analogy, Homology, Functional Trade-off, Ontogeny

There are several types of comparative analysis for garnering evidence for an evolutionary adaptation: structural or behavioral resemblance in different phyletic lines owing to ecologically driven functional convergence (analogy), functional transformations from the same ancestral character (homology), functional trade-offs between traits in the same phyletic line, intrageneric or intrafamilial species comparisons, and ontogenetic development. Analogy (homoplasy) reveals adaptation in similar traits that solve similar environmental problems in phylogenetically unrelated species, for example, the wings of bats and birds and flying insects, the eyes of humans and the octopus, and bipedality in therapods (carnivorous dinosaurs such as Tyrannosaurus) and humans.

Homologies are traits derived from the same ancestral character, such as the relatively long human thumbs that evolved from shorter simian thumbs and bipedality in therapods and birds. Traits whose homologies are functional may themselves be nonfunctional, for example, the structural vestiges of tetrapod limbs in snakes and whales, or the coccyx in humans and other tailless apes. Some homologies share little form and nothing by way of function, for example, the structure of the mammalian inner ear and the jaw bones of ancestral fish. Other homologies share only broad resemblances in form and function, such as bird wings, seal flippers, and simian arms.

Homology is critical to understanding adaptation in three ways. First, considerations of homology allow understanding of adaptations that make perfect functional sense but that initially appear to violate the incremental requirements of natural selection. For example, the panda's opposable "thumb" has no functional counterpart among other nonprimates. Moreover, the panda also has five fingers, which suggests that the panda's thumb could not have evolved through a process parallel to the evolution of primate thumbs from one of five digits. As it turns out, the panda's thumb is not a true digit; it is the adaptation of a wrist bone to grasping and stripping bamboo, the panda's essential food (Gould 1980). In other words, the panda's thumb is analogous to, rather than homologous with, simian thumbs.

Second, homologous structures or behaviors that share much in the way of form but function very differently may still be related to the same ancestral problem context. For example, the baring of teeth in humans and other social primates is used to communicate anger or aggression, whereas the baring of fangs in other mammals is a motor priming for actual biting. Nevertheless, this particular form of signaling behavior, snarling, makes sense only as a derivative adaptation from the original adaptation of such behavior for attack (Lorenz 1965a).

Third, homologies allow one to understand why otherwise highly functional designs can include features that are apparently nonfunctional or functionally suboptimal. For example, the blind spot of the vertebrate eye owes to an inverted retina. The inverted retina is an evolutionary transformation of the planar light-sensitive surface of some primitive ancestor, which was adapted to the cylindrical form of the evolving vertebrate nervous system (Goldsmith 1990).

Functional trade-offs occur when one trait decreases in a phyletic line as another increases in the same or a related line, or when modification of a trait in one direction is offset by modification in another direction, in accord with changes in environment or mode of life. One example is the reduction in the length of the primate snout relative to other mammals, which favored vision at the expense of olfactory sensibility. Another example is the decrease in the length of the fingers relative to that of the thumb from apes to hominids, which increased precision grip of objects on the ground but handicapped tree climbing and branch swinging (brachiation).

Another indication of adaptation involves comparisons between closely related taxa, that is, when variants of a trait arise in closely related species and conform to differences in environments or modes of life, for example, species-specific fur patterning among large felines (e.g., Siberian tigers, rainforest jaguars, savanna lions), and ecologically fitted nesting behaviors of different falcon species living in the same area.

Finally, ontogenesis provides evidence of adaptation when variants in the different life stages of a trait or set of traits conform to different environments or modes of life, for example, the transformation from internal to external gills in the aquatic life of a tadpole and metamorphosis to frog lungs as an adaptation to life on land and the change in starfish and other echinoderms from bilateral symmetry in the larval stage to radial pentamerous symmetry in adults.

2.3. Sui Generis Human Cognition

Unfortunately for our understanding of higher-order human cognition, including language and reasoning, these sorts of clues hold only limited promise. General solutions to problems of animal thought and communication, for example, provide only glimmers of insight into human strategies of representation and reference. There appear to be no meaningful analogies elsewhere in the animal kingdom to the peculiar designs of, say, syntactic structures or to the mechanisms by which inferences carry truth or lead to falsehood.

Let's dwell a bit on human language. Language, particularly syntax, interests us here for three reasons: (1) the theory of generative grammar (the explanatory system of principles and parameters underlying all manifestations of human syntax, in whatever language) is arguably the best theory of any human cognitive capacity; (2) syntax is perhaps the most unmistakably specieswide and species-specific (higher-order) cognitive faculty that we know of; and (3) there have been more evolutionary stories offered for language than for all other aspects of cognition (although no evolutionary story has yet produced a single new theoretical structure, principle, or rule of language; see section 2.7).

Briefly, linguist Noam Chomsky (2000), who originated the theory of generative grammar, outlines a language system, LS, of the human brain. LS reflexively discriminates and categorizes parts of the flux of human experience as "language" and develops complex abilities to infer and interpret this highly structured, and structurally peculiar, type of human production. There is nothing intrinsically different about LS—concerning innateness, evolution, or universality—from the visual system (VS), immune system (IS), respiratory system (RS), or any other complex biological system. Much polemic is driven by distaste for "innateness," "genes," and "evolution." Historical and ideological reasons explain this aversion, some well-justified. None bear on universal grammar.

LS is no more (or less) "autonomous" from the ambient social environment, or other mental systems, than VS is detachable from ambient light and object patterning or other physical systems (including, in humans, linguistic and other cognitive systems of meaning; Marr 1982). LS and VS neither exist nor develop in isolation, but only as subsystems of even more intricate structures (Hubel 1988). Claims of biological "autonomy" for LS or VS refer only to a specifiable level of systemic functioning within a system hierarchy.

One might be able to show some prelinguistic or prehuman analogies to concepts of agent (action initiator), instrument (action bearer), and patient (action receiver) in the way certain primate and bird species use twigs to obtain food. However, there is no apparent order in the ways these conceptual roles and their relationships are represented in other species. Or, if there is an order, it bears no apparent resemblance to anything in human syntax (Atran 1980). No pertinent information on extinct hominid species is available that directly bears on these issues. Speculations based on the extant material record of hominid tool making in this regard are spurious (Atran 1982).

The only example that hints at the possibility of rudimentary representational order in apes comes from work with Kanzi, a bonobo (bonobos and chimps are congeners but distinct species). Kanzi has learned to respond to over 500 sentences, such as "Give the doggie a bone." Chimps, such as Washoe (B. Gardner and Gardner 1971) and Nim Chimpsky (Terrace 1979), have also learned to make several dozen hand signs as labels for specific objects and actions. Only Kanzi, however, shows possible evidence for a primitive rule-based system of two- and three-item signal strings. Kanzi appeared to have suddenly developed "spontaneous" comprehension and production abilities without formal training at 30 months of age, after leaving his foster mother. For example, when signaling a place he wanted to go to or an object he wanted to have: "Kanzi placed his goal (object or location) first and his action (go, chase, carry, etc.) last. His word order differed from that of spoken English, and many of these action words, such as "go" and "chase," were conveyed by gestures. Thus, we found that whenever Kanzi combined a symbol with a gesture, he tended to place the gesture after the symbol. This was a rule of Kanzi's own making and one that only Kanzi followed" (Savage-Rumbaugh, Shanker, and Taylor 1998:64–65).

Although certainly intriguing and suggestive of a prelinguistic capacity to invent and sustain a conventional representational order when stimulated by a rich social learning context, Kanzi shows no consistent subject-predicate structure. Many of his strings are action-action combinations, such as "Chase bite." These strings employ two "predicates" and no subject (Rumbaugh, Savage-Rumbaugh, and Sevcik 1994:330). No human language allows sentences that have no arguments and thus cannot express a proposition. By contrast, the imperative sentence "Chase and bite!" in English has an *underlying* syntactic structure that obligatorily includes a subject and an object. Even more significant, there is no indication that Kanzi or any other nonhuman creature can recursively embed structured strings within strings, which allows practically limitless expression and production of information (Atran and Lois 2001).

Perhaps the most informative use of the evolutionary concept of homology in understanding adaptations in human thought and behavior is in the field of emotion. A number of researchers follow Darwin in identifying a few basic emotions common to all human societies: surprise, fear, anger, disgust, sadness, happiness (Darwin 1965[1872]; Tomkins 1962; Izard 1977; Plutchik 1980; Ekman 1992; Damasio 1994). Ecological eliciting conditions and bodily responses that are typically associated with basic emotions appear to be much the same in many primate species (e.g., fear of snakes), and the neural bases of certain emotional stimulus-response patterns may be common to all vertebrates (e.g., fear in general; LeDoux 1994). These primary emotions appear to be like reflexes in that they may be "automatically" triggered by stimuli and need not be mediated by higher-order cognitive processes.

The evolutionary bases of "higher-order feelings" or "secondary emotions" are more problematic. Arguably, at least some secondary human emotions are naturally selected solutions to recurrent conflicts between the short-term and long-term interests of individuals living in hominid (and perhaps other, nonhominid) social groups (R. Frank 1988; Tooby and Cosmides 1990a; Griffiths 1997). For example, anxiety over competing obligations generates commitment even when it is incommodious for the individual. Grief and despondency motivate shifts away from previous commitments that are no longer available or have become dysfunctional (Nesse 1989).

All animals behave selfishly in some contexts, as they must to survive any immediate competition for resources. Reliance on others is also often necessary for survival, for example, food sharing when there is substantial individual variation in access to food supply and common defense when predators or opportunities for predation abound. The individuals in a cooperative social group cannot afford to tolerate repeated defections by selfish "free riders," such as those who hoard food or shirk responsibility for the common defense. Any group too tolerant of defectors would be subsidizing them at its own expense, which would amount eventually to collective suicide. Organisms that temporarily forsake immediate personal advantage in the expectation of equivalent near-term reciprocation from nonkin ("reciprocal altruism"; Trivers 1971) or deferred and roundabout forms of long-term reciprocation through third parties ("indirect reciprocity"; Alexander 1987) must therefore evolve ways of reliably discriminating between a cooperator and a defector.

Thus, romantic love possibly signals an individual's enduring commitment to another, even in situations where forsaking the loved one would accrue more benefits (e.g., a younger, richer, or more fertile partner). Guilt signals that an individual who has reneged on a relationship desires to recover it and is committed not to defect again even if an opportunity should arise when defection would go undetected. Vengefulness signals that a breach in contract will not be tolerated at any cost, even at the price of the avenging individual's own life or fortune. In each case, the emotion was presumably selected in response to a statistical range of specific ancestral problems that required abeyance of short-term calculations of self-interest. Such emotions would have to be "eruptive" to be believed and to convince others, that is, sincerely out of control, hard to fake, and unsuited to apparent self-interest.

This sort of evolutionary narrative for certain secondary emotions is plausible. Nevertheless, the comparative study of animal behavior (ethology) provides little sign of homologies for such higher-order emotions. For such emotions to have the desired functional effect on the signaler's audience, the audience would need the ability to represent the communicator's emotion. Only by representing the emotion could the audience form a belief *about* it, namely, the communicator's intention in expressing the emotion. This implies that such communicative emotions could have evolved only within a context of *beliefs* about these emotions. There is no more evidence that other animals form beliefs about emotions or any other mental states (e.g., other beliefs) than there is evidence that other animals have syntactic structures.

Phylogenetic comparisons of humans with other primates show some evidence for rudimentary forms of basic higher-order cognitive functions, such as conceptualization of species differences and number relations. Vervet monkeys even have distinct alarm calls for different predator species or groups of species: snake, leopard and cheetah, hawk eagle, and so forth (Hauser 2000a). Only humans, however, appear to have a concept of (folk) species as such, as well as taxonomic rankings of relations between species. The human taxonomic system for organizing species appears to be found in all cultures (Atran 1990a; Berlin 1992; Berlin, Breedlove, and Raven 1973). It entails the conceptual realization that, say, apple trees and turkeys belong to the same fundamental level of (folk)biological reality, and that this level of reality differs from the subordinate level that includes winesap apple trees and wild turkeys as well as from the superordinate level that includes trees and birds. This taxonomic framework also supports indefinitely many systematic and graded inferences with respect to the distribution of known or unknown properties among species (Atran 1998). No species concept and no taxonomic system is evident for other animals, even in rudimentary form.

Rhesus monkeys and other primates can count up to four and apparently understand that the difference between one unit and three units is not the same as the difference between one unit and four units or between one unit and two units. But they show no understanding that the difference between three units and four units is the same as that between 15 units and 16 units, or that there even is a difference between 15 and 16 units (Hauser 2000b). Nonhumans apparently lack the combinatorial skills that permit infinite (or indefinitely many) combinations of finite means or any combinatorial operations that range freely over quantities. The computational gap between even great apes and humans appears too wide to be able to assess possible selection factors responsible for the massive processing differences between humans and other species in any of these higher-order cognitive domains.

Similar considerations apply to human folkpsychology, or "theory of mind," that is, the attribution of intentions, beliefs, and desires to other minds in addition to one's own. From recent studies in child development (cognitive ontogeny) comes evidence that some basic structures of this aspect of higher-order human cognition pass through different functional stages (Wimmer and Perner 1983;

Wellman 1990; Leslie 1994; Spelke, Phillips, and Woodward 1995; Baron-Cohen 1995, Johnson, Slaughter, and Carey 1998; Johnson, Booth, and O'Hearn 2001; J. Barrett, Richert, and Driesenga 2001). During the first year of life, a child acquires the concept of *teleomechanical agency*: the child is able to perceive an object's physical movement as goal-directed. In the second year, the child develops comprehension of *mentalistic agency*: the child attributes internal, mental states, such as perception and desire, to actors in predicting or explaining their actions. Around the start of the fourth year, the child begins to elaborate an understanding of *metarepresentational agency*: the child attributes intentional attitudes, such as belief and pretense, to people's representations of the world. Only then can children examine whether their and other people's thoughts about the world are true or fictive, likely or incredible, exaggerated or imprecise, worth changing one's mind for or forgetting.

Many animals, including most common pets and primates, have cross-modal abilities for sensory integration that result in a comprehensive representation, or *perception*, of events in the outside world that occur over a short duration (Ettlinger and Wilson 1990). Such perceptions allow for anticipatory, goal-directed actions that are obviously adaptive and indicate some conception of teleomechanical agency. For example, a cat watching a mouse go from point A to point B, and then hearing or smelling the mouse continue on a straight path behind a barrier at point C, can expect to intercept the mouse when it emerges from behind the barrier at point D. Some of the great apes (chimps, bonobos, gorillas, orangutans), but not monkeys or other animals, are apparently able to construct alternative representations, or *mental models*, of the world to plan, create, and implement novel solutions to recurrent problems.

Captive chimps, for example, can spontaneously hit on the solution of stacking boxes to reach bananas that initially hang beyond their grasp (Köhler 1927[1917], although this may be simply trial and error learning). In the wild, chimps (Goodall 1986; Boesch 1991) and organgutans (Fox, Sitompul, and Van Schaik 1999) produce different tools for different tasks (e.g., wood hammers and stone anvils for cracking nuts, reworked twigs for digging out termites) and take their tools with them to different locations. Captive gorillas also modify tools for specific tasks (Boysen et al. 1999), although there is as yet no evidence of this for wild gorillas.

There is some anecdotal evidence that apes raised with humans engage in play that involves rudimentary forms of pretense, as when the gorilla Koko uses her plastic alligator to "scare" her human caretakers (Patterson and Linden 1981; cf. B. Gardner and Gardner 1971). Chimps, but not macaques, appear to be able to understand the different perspectives of their conspecifics, as when a subordinate male chimp aroused by the presence of a female covers his erection when a dominant male approaches (de Waal 1982; cf. Kummer et al. 1996). Chimps, but not rhesus monkeys, also seem capable of role reversals in cooperative tasks that involve empathetic recognition of another's perspective (Povinelli, Nelson, and Boysen 1992; Povinelli, Parks, and Novak 1992). In sum, the great apes arguably manifest at least some aspects of teleomechanical agency and mentalistic agency (Suddendorf and Whiten 2001); however, there is no convincing evidence that any animals other than humans possess metarepresentational agency (Heyes 1998; C. Wynne 2001).

Because we interact with, say, dogs and can predict some of their behavior as a function of our own, we may be inclined to attribute some conceptual belief structure to a dog's "pretending" (e.g., to let you take the ball off the ground before snatching it up at the last possible moment). Such behavior, however, can plausibly be explained on the basis of associative learning (Heyes 1993). Moreover, we also readily intuit profound differences between a dog's or even a chimp's pretending and a child's, if "only" in the number of embedded levels of propositional attitude. Recent experiments in child development show that even 3-year-olds understand that other animals can't recognize false beliefs in the sense that people can (J. Barrett and Newman 1999).

For example, a child pretending to peel the telephone believes *that* (level 1) the mother knows *that* (level 2) the child knows *that* (level 3) the telephone is not a banana *because* (level 4): the child believes *that* (level 1) the mother believes *that* (level 2) the child believes *that* (level 3) the mother remembers *that* (level 4) yesterday the child pretended to talk to a banana. Recent experiments by behavioral ecologist Robin Dunbar and colleagues indicate that, at best, chimps and orangutans may be able to represent level 1 aspects of intention but cannot embed levels further (Hare et al. 2000; Hare, Call, and Tomasello 2001; Dunbar 2001).[1] Most people can readily follow up to four levels of embeddings of intention, although with effort they can train themselves to follow five (e.g., novelists; L. Barrett, Dunbar, and Lycett 2001). As with embeddings of relative clauses in language, this limit may owe to memory constraints that are extrinsic to the mental module or faculty in question (theory of mind, universal grammar). Just as language, if left to its own devices, allows production of indefinitely many and complex novel sentences, so may folkpsychology, if unconstrained by a person's practical needs, allow production of indefinitely many and complex representations of (other people's) possible worlds.

The developmental stages of folkpsychology are functionally specialized in the sense of being domain-specific (Atran 1989a; Hirschfeld and Gelman 1994). They are stages in the maturation of a particular mental faculty, or processing module, that takes only certain kinds of data as input (e.g., perceptually likely candidates for animacy, such as self-propelled objects) and produces highly organized outputs whose structure is not apparent in other domains (e.g., psychological motives, such as beliefs and desires, as opposed to purely mechanical causes, such as push and pull). Domain-specific developments and structures indicate that the human mind consists of at least some functionally differentiated "mental organs" that cannot be attributed to any sort of (selection for) general intelligence. Ape and other animal minds, too, likely consist of differentiated mental organs: some different from those of humans (e.g., echolocation), some also common to humans (e.g., visual perceptions of object permanence), and some—like the chimp's rudimentary counting, classification, and perspective-taking abilities—homologous lower stages or inchoate forms of human capacities.[2]

Unlike the case of the tadpole's gills and the frog's lungs, these domain-specific conceptual stages are overlaid rather than mutually exclusive. More like the starfish, where radial symmetry appears to be overlaid on earlier bilateral symmetry, the child's primitive conceptual schema survive even as more advanced forms appear. Progression through these stages appears to be fairly uniform, regardless of culture or learning experience (Avis and Harris 1991; N. Knight et al. 2001). Nevertheless, as I argue later, such stages may reflect increasing complexity with respect to certain ancestral problem contexts, such as ability to negotiate predator-protector-prey relationships. Within such a context, hominids ultimately evolved conceptual abilities particularly suited to dealing with the most dangerous predator of all: other hominids.

2.4. Adaptations as Solutions to Ancestral Tasks

Although comparative perspectives from ethology, phylogenetic analysis, and ontogeny can occasionally provide clues to whether an adaptation is likely, such clues are few and meager. Fortunately, there is a somewhat more accessible criterion for assessing the likelihood of an adaptation: "A good but not infallible rule is to recognize adaptation in organic systems that show a clear analogy with human implements" (G. Williams 1966:8–12). There are numerous examples: the wings of birds and planes, the fins and flippers of aquatic animals and the rudders and airfoils of boats and planes, skeletal structures and building structures, blood circulation and an urban traffic system, hearts and pumps, eyes and cameras, and so forth. For G. Williams, such "demonstration of conformity to design specification is superior to phylogenetic comparison as a way of demonstrating adaptation" (1992:104). This is because it is usually possible to show that the relationship between a recurrent adaptive problem and the structural features of the adaptation that solve the problem is not random.

In evolution, the causal processes that produce the evolutionary novelties on which selection operates (e.g., genetic base-pair substitution) are largely random with respect to any function that those novelties might assume. Selection is the only known process that leads to nonrandom changes in organic design with respect to function. When the logical probability is vanishingly low that the fit of form to function owes to random combinations of DNA, then it is highly probable that the design is selected. Coincidences are logically possible, but any such closed thermodynamic system tends to disorder (entropy) in the absence of a countervailing cause, such as selection. Miracles may be imagined as possibilities, but these require arbitrary suspension of the known physical laws of the universe.

The preferred analogy that Williams and those who follow him use is that of an adaptation as the solution to an "engineering" problem. The founders of evolutionary theory, too, viewed adaptations as designs functionally "perfected for any given habitat" (Darwin 1883[1872]:140), having "very much the appearance of design by an intelligent designer . . . on which the wellbeing and very existence of the organism depends" (Wallace 1901[1889]:138). Nevertheless, G. Williams (1992) emphasizes that natural selection often behaves as a flawed or downright stupid engineer. This is because there never can be a natural selection of tools and materials from scratch. Natural selection is always bound by historically antecedent compromises between organic structures and environments.

For example, the alimentary system evolved in aquatic animals before the respiratory system of land animals was first jerry-rigged to share the digestive tract's anterior structure, including the mouth and pharynx (throat). In terrestrial vertebrates, the pharynx has become a short passage linking the mouth to the esophagus and the windpipe (trachea). Any mistiming of the swallowing mechanism, which blocks off the air passage in routing food to the esophagus, causes choking. Choking episodes usually occur over the course of a lifetime and some are fatal.

For humans, the problem is even worse. The digestive and respiratory systems cross at the top of the larynx. The human larynx evolved into a complex organ to serve a dual function: as a canal that controls the access of air to the lungs and as the organ of phonation in speech (cf. Laitman 1983). The jerry-rigged functioning of the larynx in humans thus involves the coordination of three evolved mechanisms: digestion, respiration, and speech. Both in swallowing food and in articulating speech sounds, respiration is temporarily inhibited as the larynx rises to close (in swallowing) or constrict (in speaking) the opening to the air passage (glottis). Humans are even more liable to choke than other animals, as they attempt to simultaneously coordinate eating, breathing, and speaking. Moreover, the swallowing capacity of humans has become much weaker than that of other animals. These apparent "design flaws" were likely outweighed as selection factors by the cascading effects of speech on the ability of humans to proliferate across environments. Still, when parents tell their children "Don't talk with your mouth full," they may be promoting more than just social etiquette; they may also be promoting survival.

Another apparent example of flawed design is the procrustean fit of the reproductive, urinary, and excretory tracts to the same anatomical region. In men, the urethra serves both as a urinary canal and a genital duct. This results in dysfunctions and diseases that affect one function often affecting the other. In women, these two functional passages are anatomically separated but are sufficiently close to one another, and to the anus, to facilitate the spread of infection from each of the three systems to the others. During pregnancy, urinary and excretory afflictions are common as the uterus expands and presses the organs of the other two systems. The most nefarious consequences for the childbearer's health and life, however, owe to evolution's parsimonious resolution of the outlets of all of these major expulsive functions into the same narrow basin. In particular, the expulsion of the large-headed human fetus through this narrow region at childbirth occurs at considerable cost.

The "design flaw" of human childbirth has had cascading effects: humans profit from the benefit to fitness of big-brained offspring, but only at substantial cost to fitness of relatively high fatality rates for child and mother, long periods of postnatal care, reduction in fertility rates, decrease in resource procurement, and so forth. Many aspects of social life, in turn, may have emerged under natural selection, and subsequent cultural selection, as compromises to such design problems. Modern societies are still trying to work out these compromises for "the working mother."

Creationists often point to the apparent perfection of human adaptations as evidence of God's design and good disposition toward His creatures; palpable imperfections are evidence of God's anger at His creatures' hubris or selfishness. A closer look reveals that God may never have been wholly pleased with His most preferred creations in granting them the parts they have. Why did He invert the retina and give humans (but not the octopus) a blind spot? Why, in making us upright, did He render us so liable to back problems? Why did He give us just one head, heart, and liver instead of two? After all, having two lungs and kidneys is surely better than having one of each: if you have only one and it fails, you die; if you have two and only one fails, you live. As G. Williams (1992:80) notes, however, such mutations seem to be catastrophically disruptive for other adapted functions so that the individuals that bear such mutations cannot survive on their own. These examples suggest that adaptations can develop only under mutual constraint with other preexisting structures.

Some fish species can have different numbers of cephalid vertebrae (Boetius and Harding 1985), but mammals have just seven cervical vertebrae (apart from eight in sloths and six in Sirenia). From an engineering standpoint, that is odd.

Consider: ancestral species of the camel family originated in the American Southwest millions of years ago, where they evolved a number of adaptations to wind-blown deserts and other unfavorable environments, including a long neck and long legs. Numerous other special designs emerged in the course of time: double rows of protective eyelashes, hairy ear openings, the ability to close the nostrils, a keen sense of sight and smell, humps for storing fat, a protective coat of long and coarse hair (different from the soft undercoat known as "camel hair"), and remarkable abilities to take in water (up to 100 liters at a time) and do without it (up to 17 days). Moles, which are an order of magnitude smaller than camels in size, evolved for burrowing in the earth in search of earthworms and other food sources inaccessible to most animals. A number of specialized adaptations evolved, but often in directions opposite to those of the camel: round bodies, short legs, a flat pointed head, broad claws on the forefeet for digging, and velvety fur that brushes in any direction without resistance. In addition, most moles are blind and hard of hearing, which makes burrowing less onerous than if they had functional eyes and external ears. Given such a stunning variety of specialized differences between the camel and the mole, it is curious that the structure of their necks remains basically the same.

Surely the camel could do with more vertebrae and flex in foraging through the coarse and thorny plants that compose its standard fare, whereas moles could just as surely do with fewer vertebrae and less flex. What is almost as sure, however, is that there is substantial cost in restructuring the neck's nerve network to conform to a greater or fewer number of vertebrae. To connect to the sympathetic trunk and the rest of the nervous system, each of the first seven cervical spinal nerves in the spinal cord exits the vertebral canal through an opening at the top of its corresponding cervical vertebra (the last cervical nerve exits at the bottom of the last cervical vertebra). Different spinal nerves innervate different aspects of the body. The effects of adding or subtracting spinal nerves to conform to any addition or subtraction of cervical vertebrae would likely ramify through the upper body (arms, chest, etc.) in unforeseen, and therefore likely dysfunctional, ways.

A limitation on adaptation that is related to mutual constraint concerns the idea of a "fitness landscape." A functional design in such a landscape represents a "local optimum," a mountain summit that selection has incrementally reached from a given base. For example, the evolution of a comparatively long human neck relative to that of other primates also began and ended with seven vertebrae. Although neighboring mountains may represent better designs, selection is unable to backtrack down the fitness slope into the deep valleys between the mountains and recommence climbing toward a more advantageous peak. A precipitous descent would reduce fitness dramatically. Gradual descent would amount to successfully reversing the process of natural selection, the probability of which is astronomically low.

The local optimum of two arms and two legs suits human purposes better than the vertebrate base camp of four legs. But why not four arms and two legs, two arms and four legs, or a pair each of wings, arms, and legs? Mythologies the world over intimate the likely functionality of such designs for human purposes. In fact, the insect world provides examples of various designs with three pairs of limbs and one or two pairs of wings. But despite cinematic morphing programs and makeup artistry that can produce the illusion of a human fly or Spiderman, even a small step in that direction would be likely to fatally compromise an individual's chances of survival. Although genetic engineering has begun to bridge across fitness valleys, some valleys may be just too wide for any bridge. Other designs may be optimal but nearly impossible because there is simply no genetic basis, and hence no genetic variation, to start the selection process. That's why there almost certainly can be no Superman with earthly DNA that can hear a whisper miles away, see through solid walls, bore through steel, fly faster than a speeding bullet, jump tall buildings in a single bound, and still uphold Truth, Justice, and the American Way.

2.5. Reverse Engineering and Its Limits

The adaptive relationship of structure to function is often manifest, as with the giraffe's neck for foraging in trees and the rhinoceros's horns for defense. But often it is not. This is especially the case with long-extinct species, like the dinosaurs, or for relatively isolated species whose extinct antecedents have left little trace of the adaptation, as with humans and human cognition. In such cases, evolutionary theorists adopt a strategy of "reverse engineering." Reverse engineering is what military analysts do when a weapon from a potential enemy or competitor in the arms market falls into their hands and they try to figure out how it was put together and what it can do.

Reverse engineering is easiest, of course, if the structure contains some signature of its function, like trying to figure out what a toaster does given the telltale sign of toasted bread crumbs left inside. But in many cases, recognizing the appropriate signs already requires some prior notion of what function the structure may have served. For example, a Martian scientist trying to figure out what corkscrews were originally made for would have a big problem if universal Prohibition had been in place for thousands of years, grape vines and cork oaks had become extinct, and corks themselves had long ago rotted into oblivion.

Any number of highly plausible functions could be imagined for the advent of corkscrews in the late eighteenth century, some of which might still be in existence: a primitive drill, a paper porter, a torture device, a co-opted symbol of the Society for Spirochete Research. One can imagine debates among rival schools of corkscrew theorists, including participation by a revisionist group that denied corkscrews constituted a unitary design or "kind" at all. Meanwhile, perhaps a Martian archaeologist had begun independent work on the ruins of a series of ancient wineshops and wine cellars and published her findings. By chance, one of the Martian biologists or anthropologists engaged in the great debate noticed the intriguingly high concentration of corkscrews in the reports. After much detective work, the Martian scientist discovered a high correlation between corkscrews and bottles with certain residues and . . . Eureka! Corkscrews functioned to suspend small grapes in bottles of alcohol so as to flavor the liquor that ancient humans called "wine." Close but no cigar.

After a century and a half of debate, it is only now that scientists clearly favor the hypothesis that bipedality was primarily selected to enhance field of view. Comparative studies of humans with bipedal birds and dinosaurs, as well as experiments comparing energy expenditure and running speed in two-footed versus four-footed running and walking, appear to exclude the competing hypotheses that bipedality evolved for running or energy conservation. The moral is that reverse engineering can be helpful, and occasionally successful, but success is by no means guaranteed even in the richest of evidentiary contexts.

Consider the long, ponderous tails of the sauropods (e.g., Brachiosaurus and the "brontausaurs") and the huge bony neck frills of Triceratops. The best argument for the functionality of these designs is that if they didn't have some highly advantageous function, they would almost certainly have been maladaptive. The fact that these creatures carried the burden of all that extra weight and cumbersomeness for tens of millions of years clearly suggests that whatever functions these designs served, they must have been highly adapted to the environment in which these creatures lived. But what functions might these have been?

One hypothesis is that they were defensive traits: the sauropod's tail acted as a whip, whereas Triceratops's frill shielded its head and neck from attack. Another hypothesis is that these traits were selected for thermal regulation: the sauropod's tail improved heat loss over a large surface, whereas the vast network of blood vessels in Triceratops's frill pulsed with overheated blood or helped to absorb solar heat. Still another hypothesis is architectural: the sauropod's great tail anchored the huge leg muscles that supported the creature's enormous weight; similarly, the wide bony neck frill of Triceratops functioned as an attachment site for the strong neck muscles that were required to wield head horns. Perhaps the brontausaur's tail helped balance its unwieldy body. Perhaps Triceratops evolved the neck frill as an ornament for recognizing conspecifics. Perhaps we will never know for sure.

Notice that the problem is not simply one of antiquity, or the general quandary in science that the proposed solution to a problem will always have a residue of uncertainty. Other functional designs of sauropods and Triceratops do not pose difficulties. The foraging function of Brachiosaurus's long neck is no more a mystery than is the similar function of a long neck in camels or giraffes. Triceratops's horns are as surely defensive as the horns of a rhinoceros or a bull. In sum, reverse engineering is not a general solution to design problems, but it is often useful to try.

Because any functional mental structure bears the signature of the ecological problem that selected for that function, there are two ways to approach an evolutionary description and explanation of mental structures. First, it should be possible to infer that a given cognitive structure is an adaptation by considering how it could have functioned to solve some ancestral problem-set vital to hominid survival. For example, if hominids had to consistently distinguish a large number of species in order to range over a wide area in search of food and to avoid being eaten or poisoned, then selection for a cognitive device dedicated to systematically and automatically comparing and contrasting species would likely have been advantageous (Atran 1998).

Second, it may be possible to infer the ancestral problem-set by considering what ecological survival functions the current structure would have been able to perform in the Pleistocene. This is the process of reverse engineering. For example, a computational ability to keep track of social obligations and monitor contractual violations is required for any flexible regimen of social exchange, collaboration, and reciprocation among nonkin (i.e., among whom there is no genetic calculus of cooperation; Cosmides and Tooby 1992). One possibility, consistent with speculations about environments where hominids roamed, is that this ability emerged to allow social composition to vary as a function of wide fluctuations in supply of food and other resources—a scenario much like the case of modern nomads and hunter-gatherers. This is certainly plausible, but the case must be made in terms of the structural details. Efforts thus far are laudable but not convincing (cf. Sperber, Cara and Girotto 1995).

2.6. The "Just-So" Story of the Self

Consider, first, the broader evolutionary arguments for the emergence of the concept of self, for human language, or for our big brains. Such arguments are numerous and as varied and contradictory as the theories they are intended to support. Evolutionary considerations in these areas are also all backward-looking rather than forward-looking, in the sense that they have produced no significant or surprising scientific predictions or discoveries. Neither have they contributed to unraveling componential structures associated with the time-traveling self, the principles and parameters of human syntax, or the representation of creative abilities that subserve many of the brain's uniquely human mental functions (i.e., the ability to meaningfully add a number, quality, idea, or inference to any prior string of quantities, qualities, concepts, or inferences). Are evolutionary arguments for the self, language, and big brain all "just-so" stories?

According to Sedikides and Skowronski, for example, the symbolic self is a "flexible and multifaceted cognitive representation of an organism's own attributes" that "serves adaptive functions" (1997:80). The authors claim that the concept of self plausibly evolved in *Homo erectus* in response to Pleistocene environmental pressures, especially ecological and social conditions. The supporting arguments are speculative, uninformative as to any specific computational structures, and generally too vague to assess their truth or falsity.

Consider: the initial ecological and social pressures associated with collective hunting that the authors cite in favor of selection for a concept of the self could apply equally to coordinated group life among wolves: keen visual perception and rapid coordination of information among hunters, efficient memory and recognition devices for tracking the habits and spatial distributions of different prey, and so forth. Apparently, such conditions set the stage for the emergence of the self in *Homo erectus* rather than some lupine ancestor because *Homo habilis* already had "good memory," "cognitive maps," and "primitive tool use." Given this evolved baseline, environmental pressures "may have also contributed to evolution of both automatic and controlled processing capabilities (ibid.)," such as rapid emotional assessments of potentially immediate life-threatening situations (e.g., fear response toward intruders) as well as more reasoned assessments of long-term costs and benefits (e.g., assessing the likelihood of a newcomer's becoming an ally).

The self, which tracks past achievements and projects future likelihood of achievements, would presumably further the ability of hominids to form group alliances that would allow ranging far from home base to track diverse prey. The self would also further the ability to resolve social dilemmas inherent in such alliances, to efficiently distinguish friend from foe, and to match personal objectives to collective goals. Now, factor in considerations of social hierarchy and status, the descent of the larynx in *Homo* relative to *Australopithecus* (suggesting "verbal communication skills"), big brains, runaway social competition and deception, bonding of nonkin through systematic mate exchange, and so forth. And from this evolutionary stew emerges the self, along with introspection, counterfactual thinking, fantasy, humor, planning, awareness of mortality, morality, and the United Nations (Sedikides and Skowronski 1997:95).

Of course, we know next to nothing about the mental faculties and computational structures of *Australopithecus* or *Homo*, and cannot rule out any of indefinitely many alternative causal sequences that might involve or exclude these putative selection factors. Even if some chapters of this fulsome story may be locally falsifiable, the overall tale is virtually immune to refutation. For example, Sedikides and Skowronski claim that "biased perceptions of the symbolic self serve to maintain positive evaluations" in the face of apparent adversity or defeat (1997:85). Although experiments in social psychology tend to support this generalization to North American and Western European populations, similar experiments show negative rather than positive self-evaluation for East Asians under similar circumstances (Markus and Kitayama 1991). Whatever the case, these arguments on the self and affect bias could be deleted without changing the rest of the story. This is so for any number of other arguments, such as the self's relation to spatial mapping, species recognition, resource sharing, cheater detection, mating, and language.

An alternative approach to understanding the evolutionary origins of the self is to concentrate on specific design features of self-awareness, such as the ability to retrieve episodic memories and to mentally travel in time. These features are intimately related to theory of mind and the metarepresentational ability to embed levels of intention (representations of representations). In being able to purposefully retrieve episodic memories, people are able to (1) access and assess the sources of present knowledge for accuracy and reliability, (2) creatively combine and recombine familiar events to explain the present or anticipate the future, and (3) dissociate or maintain different mental states and scenarios simultaneously. The metarepresentational, time-traveling self can thus imagine itself in indefinitely many alternative worlds so as to best choose among them. In this way, the human organism is able to perspicaciously navigate the present and actual world and to plan for and transform future worlds to its advantage (Suddendorf and Corballis 1997).

Neuroimaging associates the development and functioning of episodic memory and the time-traveling self with the prefrontal cortices, the most recently evolved part of the hominid brain (Wheeler, Stuss, and Tulving 1997). Neanderthal burial sites indicate that by roughly 50,000 to 100,000 years ago the time-traveling self was conscientiously imagining and reshaping its own mind and body, as well as that of the surrounding terrestrial environment, to suit its own imagined ends, for example, creating a religious world where death is only the passage of another stage in life, like the stages of birth or achieving full adult membership in a group. Extrapolating from what is known of the later Upper Paleolithic and Neolithic burial sites of *Homo sapiens sapiens*, the collective evidence from Neanderthal burial sites (accompaniment of artifacts, remains of game animals, vegetable pigments, flowers and medicinal plants, group hearths, and the remains of family members) "betrays a keen self-awareness and a concern for the human spirit" (Leakey and Lewin 1977:125). According to paleoanthropologist F. Clark Howell: "Evidence . . . clearly indicates that Neanderthal man believed in life after death and that it was probably not unlike the life he lived on earth, since he seemed to be trying to help his corpses along on their journeys with tools and food. Death itself appears to have been regarded as a kind of sleep, since corpses were carefully arranged in sleeplike positions" (1965:130).[3] No other extinct or extant animal appears to have traveled so freely in time with a reliably intact sense of self. As we shall see in later chapters, metarepresentation, mental time travel, and self-awareness in the face of death are all critical aspects of religious development.

2.7. The Mystery Tale of Language

Evolutionary scenarios for the emergence of language tend to range even further over evolutionary time and space, including bee dances, fish courtship, bird songs, dog barking, simian aggression displays, ape tool use, ape signing, hominid fire making, object recognition, gesturing, sensorimotor intelligence, self-awareness, food sharing, hunting, spatial mapping, cheater detection, and social hierarchy. A favorite among anthropologists is hominid tool making as a source of insight into the various structures of language (Leroi-Gourhan 1964; Holloway 1969; Marschack 1976; Leakey and Lewin 1977; T. Wynn 1979). Lithic artifacts provide the only sustained evidence of emerging hominid behavior over time; however, the analogies between tool making as "action grammar" (Matasuzawa 1996) and linguistic grammar are extremely tenuous. Both forms of behavior may involve agents, instruments, and patients, but language assigns them specific syntactic structures that have no formal counterparts in nonlinguistic cognition. Both forms of behavior may involve hierarchical processing, but only language allows infinite (or at least indefinitely many) structural recursions and movements, and so forth.

There is little way of scientifically pursuing such analogies, or for verifying speculative evolutionary scenarios that language did not evolve alongside material tool making but rather "began as a kind of tool for implementing intentionality in social interaction" (Goodenough 1990:608). Given structural descriptions of one form of behavior it is simply not possible to deduce specific structures associated with the other form of behavior. This is the case for any of the presumed relationships between human language and other forms of human or nonhuman behavior.

A particularly ingenious claim is that language allowed gossip to substitute for grooming and so enabled larger and larger social groups to be maintained (Dunbar 1996; cf. Paine 1967). The account, though, provides little by way of insight into specific linguistic structures, such as principles of structure dependence and theta-role assignment. Without specific structures to analyze it is difficult, if not impossible, to verify or falsify speculations.

Another intriguing argument by a leading theoretical linguist based on consideration of the specific structures of human syntax concludes that the intervention of God may have been an evolutionary necessity to account for the parameterization of language that underlies linguistic diversity (M. Baker 1996:509). Some languages (e.g., Spanish and Maya but not English) can drop pronouns from sentences because their verbs incorporate information about subjects; other languages (e.g., Maya but not Spanish or English) can incorporate objects into verbs. The structural consequences of these different "parameter settings" may be far-ranging in the syntax of the language. The fact that languages have different parameter settings impedes mutual comprehension and the free flow of information across languages. Arguably, this would be maladaptive compared to a universal grammar that allowed no parametric variation—unless God wanted this to happen, say, for the reasons given in the Tower of Babel tale (Genesis 11,1:5–9). Alternatively, selective comprehension and miscomprehension may have adaptively favored in-group cooperation for between-group competition. In any event, present evolutionary considerations furnish no definite solution to the problem "What is X that UG developed out of," where X is the set of mental structures that Universal Grammar evolved out of, and where X has the property P that was the ancestral seed of UG's parameters.

By far the best story to date of language as an evolutionary adaptation centers on the claim that language shows signs of design "tailored to the transmission of propositional structures through a serial interface" (Pinker and Bloom 1990:585). Pinker and Bloom describe how specific syntactic structures conform to this language-specific design in ways that provide functional advantage, for example, through certain structure-dependent rules (phrase structure) and principles of embedding (recursion) that allow the formulation and expression of infinitely many discrete ideas by finite and few means. This enables the multiple thoughts of multiple individuals to be combined, tested in imagination, and consequently included in or excluded from having a role in some future action. A population whose individuals could contemplate alternative scenarios in any sequence and at any rate, benefit from the cognitive travails of others, and let conjectures die instead of themselves would surely have had an evolutionary advantage over a population that couldn't.

Their agument is not simply another just-so story. There is a well-reasoned analysis of the evolutionary trade-offs involved in opting for linear communication through an auditory medium: visual displays are much better at communicating highly complex topological relationships ("A picture is worth a thousand words"), gestures are much better at conveying emotion, and language is terribly inefficient at transmitting information associated with taste or smell. For all its insight and plausibility, however, the Pinker and Bloom account remains wholly backward-looking: no structural discovery, novel prediction, or theoretical reformulation ensues within the Chomskyean framework of generative grammar that the authors adopt. The problem of linguistic diversity and the origins of parameterization is left hanging. Although any number of evolutionary scenarios can be imagined for diversity, none carries even backward-looking retrodictions as to the origins or functions of specific parameters.

For Chomsky himself, although no evolutionary account of the origins of language seems remotely persuasive, his own guess is this:

> It may be that at some remote period a mutation took place that gave rise to the property of discrete infinity, perhaps for reasons that have to do with the biology of cells, to be explained in terms of the properties of physical mechanisms, now unknown . . . evolutionary pressures may have shaped the further development of this capacity, at least in part. Quite possibly other aspects of its evolutionary development again reflect the operation of physical laws applying to a brain of a certain degree of complexity. We simply do not know. (1988:170)

Chomsky's speculation deserves attention. Ever since Darwin, the focus in evolutionary theory has properly been on the ways that a general, three-part process (variation → inheritance of variation → selection of inherited variation) has unfolded in specific causal contexts (to perform particular environmental tasks), so leading to the adaptive radiation of life on earth. By contrast, the consequences for evolution of broader physical laws and complexity theory are only beginning to be explored.

For example, it remains a mystery why most warm-blooded animals (i.e., birds and mammals) have nearly the same body temperature (G. Williams 1992: 136–138). Surely, a tropical toucan could save energy if it didn't have to maintain the same body temperature as a polar bear. Nevertheless, only a certain relatively narrow range of body temperatures permits a stable balance among general processes of cell hydration, heat retention, and heat dissipation (cf. McArthur and Clark 1988). Consider just two general processes, hydrobiological and thermal, as jointly determining a viably stable interval for body temperature. Imagine their joint canalizing function as operating like fitted parts of a funnel. No matter how wide the funnel at the top (the range of possible ambient temperatures), whatever enters the funnel (whichever species evolves) must converge into a narrow passage at the bottom (the range of allowable body temperatures).

Complex and heterogeneous structures can spontaneously emerge from simpler and more homogeneous structures, for example, in reaction to the influx of energy from some outside source. If water is heated gently from below, water warmed at the bottom of the pan is less dense than water higher up and tends to move upward gently. But if the water heats up rapidly so that the temperature difference from bottom to top becomes large, then rising columns of hot water become surrounded by descending columns of cooler water to form striking rolls or hexagonal patterns. The appearance of structure thus depends on an arbitrarily small critical difference in temperature, just as the formation of a whirlpool in running water depends on an arbitrarily small difference in water speed. Certain aspects of pattern formation in embryos may result from similar processes (Kauffman 1993:180), possibly even the beginnings of life itself. Highly specific and constrained structures can also arise from initially more general and independent structures when unforeseeable internal thresholds or critical values are attained, such as in the sudden emergence of unplanned Internet or neural pathways and blockages.

Imagine the gross anatomy of the brain as a croissant roll (cf. LeDoux 1996). The brown, flaky crust is the cerebral cortex. When the croissant is pried apart as if for a sandwich, each half corresponds to one of the cerebral hemispheres. The cerebral crust is about three millimeters thick and consists of multiple, parallel layers of nerve cells (neurons). The softer crumb inside contains unlayered neurons (subcortical nuclei). On average, every neuron forms between 1,000 and 10,000 connections (synapses) to other neurons. The brain functions as a supergovernment of systems that govern behavior. Each system consists of multiple interconnections (local circuits) between small cortical areas in the crust and subcortical nuclei in the crumb.

Human brains have between two and three orders of magnitude more connections per cell, or "fanout," than do the most powerful computers existing today. This allows the human brain a nonlinear increase in the number and complexity of possible local circuits, assemblies of local circuits, and interconnected assemblies (Holland 1995). This may be one factor in why people are easily able to perceive that some activity is a game or a party without knowing rule or reason. It also may help to account for humans finding art fun, religion compelling, and the pigeon on a statue's head amusing, whereas computers show no signs of being able to comprehend what all the fuss is about.

According to Jerry Fodor (1998), whose reasoning is close to Chomsky's, it is not likely that natural selection gradually produced an adaptive mutation for a language instinct. Rather, selection pressures unrelated to language simply made human brains a little larger and more complex. Unlike gradual and incremental adaptations, a little added complexity can go a long way fast to produce multiple novel structures: "Make the giraffe's neck just a little bit longer and you correspondingly increase, just by a little, the animal's capacity to reach the fruit at the top of the tree. . . . But make an ape's brain just a little bigger (or denser, or more folded, or, who knows, grayer) and it's anybody's guess what happens to the creature's behavioural repertoire. Maybe the ape turns into us" (8).

Much ink has spilled and nearly as much acrimony has been vented in the debate between evolutionary psychologists and the scientists who criticize them. In the case of language, however, no empirical issue has yet to turn on the debate. Despite very different evolutionary stories, Chomsky and Fodor as well as Pinker and Bloom fundamentally agree on the specific computational structures that characterize language, on its innateness, on its highly specialized mode of operation (modularity), and on the fact that all of this is uniquely the product of evolution, whether adaptation or by-product.

2.8. Evolutionary "By-products"

On the use of a spandrel:

> From the tip of his index, András traces her profile, starting with the forehead, at the hairline, then delicately descending between the eyebrows, following the fine ridge of the nose and sliding into the hollow between the root of the nose and the lips.
>
> "It is here," he said, "that the angel presses a finger to the baby's lips, just before birth. Shshtt!—and the child forgets everything. All he learned there, before, in paradise. Like that, he comes innocent to the world."
>
> "And when does it end, innocence?" asked Saffie in a dreamy voice, barely moving the lips against which the finger of András was still pressed. "You, are you innocent?" (Huston 1998, my translation)

Leading evolutionary biologists, such as Stephen Gould and Richard Lewontin (1979) also do not consider it likely that language and most other peculiarly human cognitive faculties are adaptations selected for functional design. Gould and Lewontin describe the products of higher-order human cognition as evolutionary "by-products" or "spandrels." A spandrel is an architectural term that describes the structural form or space that arises as a necessary concomitant to another decision in design and is not meant to have any direct utility in itself. For example, the space beneath a flight of stairs is a by-product of constructing an inclined stairway rather than a vertical ladder. The fact that people might subsequently use this "leftover" space for storage does not entail that the space was designed to be a storage space.

A recurrent spandrel in different cultures around the world is the sometimes ornamented space between the right or left exterior curve of an arch and an enclosing right angle. This results from the simple fact that any arched passageway that pierces a rectangular wall will produce two "leftover" triangles, one in the left upper corner and one in the right. In some cases, as at the entrance to a railway tunnel, these spandrels do not merit attention and are not ornamented. In other cases, as at the arched entrance to a mosque or a church, the spandrels are richly ornamented with ornate designs or saintly figures and are often more the focus of attention and devotion than the archway itself. Although a pair of such religiously ornamented spandrels may be structurally identical to a pair of spandrels at the entrance to a railway tunnel, their cultural functions and values could not be more different.

It would be meaningless to investigate the different spandrels at the entrances to railway tunnels as differences in cultural "phenotypes" of the same architectural "genotype." In the natural selection of an adapted biological genotype (or the cultural selection of a functionally designed architectural form), the phenotype itself functions in a given environment to cause the further propagation or perpetuation of the genotypic design. Railway tunnel spandrels contribute no reason to having railway tunnels; rather, it is the contextually proven functionality of the arched tunnels that causes the continued or renewed use of the arched tunnel design. By contrast, in some mosques and churches, archway spandrels have been subsequently culturally selected and designed to enhance ornamentation.

In biology, spandrels, or sequelae, arise nonadaptively as incidental effects. Darwin (1859) describes them as "correlations to growth," which may serve as "preadaptations" that become available for later co-optation to useful function in the evolutionary lineage. For example, evidence suggests that the thoracic horns of male beetles are presently adaptations for fighting and are only incidentally or secondarily used during mating and digging (West-Eberhard 1980). But future reproductive success might come to depend on the ability of horns to hold down females for mating or the ability to dig faster or deeper.

To some degree all adaptations were originally functionless or secondary consequences of prior adaptations, then co-opted and subsequently modified under selection to perform new functions (Dennett 1995:281). Thus, insect wings and bird feathers appear to have been initially selected for thermal regulation and only later co-opted for flight in the subsequent evolutionary history of insects and birds. Similarly, the human chin seems to have originated as a secondary consequence of the adaptation of human mandibles, a prominence left behind when the dental arcades shrank from prehominid to modern size. Sexual selection may then have acted on the chins of later hominids as signaling health and potential mate value (Thornhill 1997). Human language, too, might be a co-opted secondary adaptation that was subsequently modified under selection—what Gould and Vrba (1982) refer to as an "exaptation."

For biologists such as Gould, Lewontin, and G. Williams, however, most higher-order human cognitive abilities are not biologically co-opted exaptations. Instead, they originated as functionless spandrels that have been subsequently modified under cultural selection rather than natural selection. Biologically functionless, or nearly functionless, spandrels supposedly include religion, writing, art, science, commerce, war, and play. These evolutionary by-products are cultural "mountains" to the biologically "adaptive molehill" (Gould 1991:58–59; G. Williams 1992:77–79). On this account, evolutionary psychology would have little to reveal about the emergence and structure of such culturally elaborated spandrels: "The number and complexity of these spandrels should increase with the intricacy of the organism under consideration. In some region within a spectrum of rising complexity, the number and importance of useable and significant spandrels will probably exceed the evolutionary import of the primary adaptation" (Gould 1997:10754–10755; cf. Fodor 1998).

Admittedly, exaptations and spandrels always involve structural exploitation of preexisting biological mechanisms. Nevertheless, it may not always be the case that detailed knowledge of those preexisting mechanisms is necessary, or even informative, for understanding cultural functions. Consider the cultural exploitation of three spandrels of human anatomy: the lines in a palm, belly buttons, and the hollow between the upper lip and the nose. Understanding the evolutionary history of the hand, the umbilical cord, or human facial structure would shed little light on cultural practices of palmistry (fortune telling) and omphalopsychitism (mystical contemplation of the navel) or on wondrous musings like *The Mark of the Angel* cited at the beginning of this section (Huston 1998).

Evolutionary psychologists counter that even in cases where a culturally elaborated spandrel, like folklore or religion, is hypothesized to have no evolved biological function, scientific evidence must be garnered in support of the hypothesis. At a mimimum, this requires specification of the original biological adaptations or exaptations that were co-opted in cultural life to produce religion (Tooby and Cosmides 1992; Buss et al. 1998; cf. Pinker 1997; Plotkin 1997). More generally, one can't claim that a feature is a biologically co-opted exaptation (e.g., as with language) or a culturally elaborated spandrel (e.g., as with religion) without prior identification of the adaptation(s) that the feature is a secondary adaptation or by-product of. Furthermore, although some aspects of a putative spandrel, such as war or religion, may appear to have little evolutionary history (cf. Sahlins 1976), such as prisoner exchanges or churches, other aspects may. For example, socially organized raids, fights, and killing occur throughout all human history and, if similar behavior by chimpanzees is any indication, throughout hominid prehistory as well (cf. Otterbein 1999).

2.9. Is the Big Brain Just a Spandrel Maker?

For Gould and other critics, evolutionary psychology is prone to the same foolishness as those who would fall for Rudyard Kipling's "just-so" stories for the origins of odd behaviors, or the explanations of Dr. Pangloss in Voltaire's *Candide*, where noses were made to support eyeglasses and legs were intended for pants. Of course, humans couldn't wear pants if their legs were not designed for walking, but figuring out how walking biologically originated would tell little, if anything, about the cultural emergence of pants. Just as a computer that was originally built or bought for word processing can be used for any number of other tasks for which it was not originally designed, so the human brain may have grown larger under selection for cooperative hunting and gathering, "but the implicit spandrels in an organ of such complexity must exceed the overt functional reasons for its origins" (Gould 1997:10755). Built for some tasks, it can do many others—"and in this flexibility lies both the messiness and the hope of our lives" (Gould 1980:58; cf. Dawkins 1976:215).

Gould's alternative account of the emergence of distinctly human cognitive abilities as spandrels of a big brain is hardly convincing. First, the very notion of a big or large or complex brain is too vague to empirically constrain the evolutionary story about how it might have evolved. The big brain is taken as an adaptation from which all cognitive spandrels arise. But an adaptation to what? A design for what? What are its evolutionary-relevant computational structures? Big brain stories tend to be even broader in scope and hand waving than language-evolution stories. Human brains supposedly broke away from ape brains under selection pressures that run the gamut from runaway social competition (Alexander 1989), to gut reduction (Aielo and Wheeler 1995), to hunting large game (Hill 1999), to niche construction (Laland, Olding-Smee, and Feldman 2000), to runaway sexual selection (G. Miller 2000). Alternatively, the big brain primarily evolved as a conduit for culture (M. Harris 1975), as a vehicle for language (Jerison 1976), or as a host for the independently evolving ideas, or memes, that compete to colonize it (Dennett 1995; Blackmore 1999). Finally, the big brain may have evolved under any number of "positive feedback" pathways involving some or all of the factors mentioned.

But even if true, and even if we knew the reasons (the selection pressures responsible), we are unlikely to learn anything of particular interest about how the mind works. The notion of a big brain is as uninformative about cognitive structures and functions as the notion of a big body is about bodily structures and functions. Never mind exaptations such as chins or spandrels such as palm lines. From the fact of a bigger body, what could one possibly deduce about hearts, livers, kidneys, hands, faces, placentas, and so on? And never mind exaptations such as language or spandrels such as religion. From the fact of a bigger (or denser, or more folded, or grayer) brain, what could one possibly deduce about perception, emotion, categorization, inference, or any of the other capabilities humans share with apes but in more vastly elaborated form? Probably nothing at all.

Preoccupation with the evolution of the big brain, rather than with the evolution of its cognitive structures and functions, likely stems from three sources of relative ignorance (shared by all of us who work in the cognitive sciences).

First, there is still precious little detailed description of the abstract conditions of cognitive structures that could guide neurophysiologists to look for something interesting in the brain. To be sure, brain imaging, including positron emission tomography (PET) and magnetic resonance imaging (MRI), is currently a very hot and well-funded area. Applications in clinical studies of cerebral disorders are becoming ever more critical to the development of new drugs and other treatments. In cognitive psychology, however, its use appears to be driven largely by the technological innovations and the industry it supports rather than by insight. Important exceptions occur when neuroimaging studies are designed to test or refine details of well-thought-out cognitive theories. There can no more be a theory derived directly from observations of neuroimaging than there can be a theory derived directly from observations of meter readings. It is only in the service of some prior abstract theory that such observations can make sense.

Second, nobody has any reliably tested idea of how any specific higher-order cognitive function maps onto brain structure. There has been some progress in ability to localize certain cognitive functions, such as certain types of word comprehension, episodic memory, and image formation; however, these mappings are far from complete and, in the best of cases, are barely inchoate. This is complicated by the likelihood that localization of mental functions is distributive.

Imagine that the brain runs itself like an airport (cf. Damasio 1994). At any moment in the airport (a given mental state), airplanes are coming in (input, stimuli) and going out (output, behavior), as numerous interconnected systems operate: controllers direct air traffic, ticket agents direct passengers, police monitor passenger flow, passengers congregate to chat or eat or wait, catering and janitorial services perform their duties, administrative personnel coordinate services and schedules, and so forth. Imagine some cognitive faculty, such as language, as the luggage that flows into, through, and out of the airport. There is no single area in the airport (brain) where the luggage (language) is localized. Nevertheless, there are several areas where luggage is concentrated to varying degrees, such as the baggage claim area (Broca area of word comprehension) and the preloading area (Wernicke area of word production). Problems (cerebral damage) to one of these concentration areas are likely to affect the overall luggage distribution system more than damage to other areas where luggage is present but not concentrated (passenger waiting areas, ticket purchase lines, etc.). Even if one of the concentration areas is seriously disturbed, however, it still may be possible to eventually reroute the luggage (rewire language's brain circuits) to its proper destination. In this scenario, it is quite appropriate to consider there to be a functionally distinct and physically localized luggage system in the airport (a distinct and localized language system in the brain) even though function and localization are topologically distributed throughout the brain in varying ways. Still, plotting these localized paths can be an analytic nightmare.

Third, there is scant evidence of historical changes in the brain's internal structure from protohominid to human. The fossil record is spotty and poor. Even when skull remains are fairly whole, their endocasts lack the resolution (of sulci and gyri) needed to indicate anything more than gross changes in cortical morphology, much less cognitive function. Nevertheless, strong opinions based on coarse and fragmentary evidence abound. According to Holloway, by about two million years ago:

> There is clear evidence for a *homo* lineage showing brain endocast patterns suggestive of a more modern and enlarged third inferior frontal convolutional complex, expanded brain size (e.g. 750+ ml), and cerebral asymmetries . . . (i.e. left-occipital-right-frontal). In so far as these patterns correlate with . . . a left-right asymmetry of cognitive functioning regarding symbolic language behavior (left) and visual spatial integration (right), it is possible to speculate that early [*Homo habilis*] cognitive patterns were similar [to those of *Homo sapiens*], albeit less advanced. (1983:113)

Barber and Peters (1992) indicate that the defining moment in the evolution of language may have occurred about half a million years ago, as indicated by the apparent enlargement of the prefrontal region of the *Homo rhodesiensis* cranium and presumably in other archaic *Homo sapiens*. Leiberman, Crelib, and Klatt (1972) take the fossil evidence to show plainly that only *Homo sapiens sapiens* could have produced speech and therefore language, although other work indicates that monkeys and apes can at least discriminate and imitate some of the same speech sounds that human infants can (Hayes and Hayes 1951; Kuhl and Miller 1975). In brief, almost nothing about human cognition is clear from the fossil record.

2.10. Evolutionary Psychology: A Tentative Research Paradigm

It may well be true that little insight is to be gained into higher-order human cognitive structures by considering possible evolutionary origins and functions. Adopting Gould's hypothesis, which assumes this truth, is practically guaranteed to block insight, whether or not it is true. By contrast, in adopting evolutionary psychology's requirement that candidates for exaptations and spandrels be described, as far as possible, with reference to evolved adaptations, it might be possible to find out if Gould's hypothesis is true or not. If it is true, then evolutionary psychology would have provided the empirical evidence that shows it to be a significant and surprising scientific insight and not one that depends entirely on intuition, analogy, eloquence, and wishful thinking. If it is not true, then evolutionary psychology will have helped to discover something new about human nature.

Granted that many evolutionary psychology accounts are "just-so" stories, and that there may be no higher-order computational structures yet discovered by applying the concerns and techniques of evolutionary psychology, still, there is often enough specificity in particular claims about the evolutionary functions and origins of certain computational structures to suggest new lines of inquiry and empirical testing. For example, one might compare the problem-solving capabilities of some hypothesized adaptation, such as a computational device that favored investment in detecting cheaters over investment in detecting altruists, with various logically possible devices that made no such distinction. One could compare the statistical consequences of operating these devices in hypothetical ancestral environments over different time periods and under different demographic conditions. In addition, one could see whether people currently perform faster, more economically, or more reliably with algorithms that describe one device rather than others under a variety of culturally natural and ecologically real conditions.[4]

Empirical research programs are being developed to test evolution-inspired hypotheses about the long-term benefits of mild depression on reorienting individual career decisions to yield better payoffs, on the benefits of guilt in fostering social reintegration, on the merits of rage in forestalling aggression, and so forth. Perhaps we will discover that, after all, depression is more a "social disease" that historically descended from the nearly defunct "nervous breakdown" of decades past (which, in turn, may have "mutated" from the syndrome of "hysteria" current among women in the West for the half century before the First World War).[5] But even so, historical descent may well follow along biological tracks (e.g., Why have women been statistically more prone than men to suffer depression, nervous breakdown, and hysteria? Why are certain physiological symptoms and emotions more relevant and recurrent than others?). Formulation and testing of alternative computational strategies that might drive whatever results emerge is likely further down the line. For example, computational theories of optimal foraging have already proven reliably predictive, although there may be much room for critical improvement and reformulation (much as the case with classical economics and theories of marginal utility; cf. Ingold 1996).

Surprising predictions from evolutionary theory appear borne out, such as the presence of more male offspring among groups of high socioeconomic status and the corresponding presence of more female offspring among groups of lower status. The responsible computational mechanisms (if there are any) are wholly unknown, but there is at least a plausible argument that there is now something to look for. In the cognitive domains of language, number, folkmechanics, folkpsychology, folkbiology, and folksociology, evolutionary speculation is leading researchers to reevaluate or better confirm specific assumptions about corresponding computational structures: Can children computationally distinguish the movement of shadows from the motion of solid objects? Can there be counting or calculations of frequency without a concept of discrete infinity? Can there be metarepresentation without theory of mind, or understanding of agency without self-propulsion? Can there be limited syntactic structure with added communicative value but without full recursion, or a specified subject condition with absolutely no communicative value? Can apes and monkeys have partial taxonomic orderings of species or causal presumptions that imply a concept of underlying essence? Can people avoid social stereotyping? Can there be moral truths without concepts of God(s)?

2.11. Summary: The Mindless Agent

For Richard Dawkins, the chosen metaphors for evolution are given in the titles of his books: *The Selfish Gene* (1976), *The Blind Watchmaker* (1986), *Climbing Mount Improbable* (1996). Better than allusions to the perfect designer or the clumsy engineer, Dawkins's metaphors convey the lack of foresight, the tentativeness, and the luck (or providence) of natural selection. Perhaps an even more telling metaphor is provided by the French term *bricoleur*. As the French anthropologist Claude Lévi-Strauss describes him in another context, the bricoleur is a combination of handyman, odd-job man, and jack-of-all-trades:

> The "bricoleur" is adept at performing a large number of diverse tasks; but, unlike the engineer, he does not subordinate each one of them to the availability of raw materials and tools conceived for the purpose of the project. His universe of instruments is closed and the rules of his game are always to "make do with whatever is at hand," that is to say with a set of tools and materials which is always . . . heterogeneous because what it contains bears no relation to the current project . . . but is the contingent result of all the occasions there have been to renew or enrich the stock or to maintain it with what remains of previous constructions. (1966:16)

Common to all of these metaphors, of course, is the idea of some agent-like initiator as the cause of complex developments and behaviors. The introduction of agent metaphors in science is ironic and not fortuitous. It is ironic because scientific explanation differs from both religious and commonsense interpretations of complex events of uncertain origin by excluding rather than conjuring up agent-based accounts. Agent-based interpretations of complex events, as I later try to show in the next chapter, appear to represent a default strategy of the human mind, that is, an evolved strategy that is universal, innate, easily triggered by the appropriate input, and difficult to inhibit.

That is why the use of agent-based metaphors in scientific explanations—and especially in scientific expositions for popular audiences—is not fortuitous. Human minds appear to be programmed to look for, and readily countenance, agents as the causes of complex and uncertain happenings. Scientists intellectually wean people away from reliance on this psychological bias by encouraging withdrawal from it by degrees. In this sense, the "lazy God" (*le Dieu fainéant*) of Enlightenment physics is kith and kin to the blind bricoleur of evolutionary biology.

For evolutionary psychologists generally, any functional biological design that is too complex to result from pure chance must be either an adaptation or a by-product of an adaptation—the product or waste of the Mindless Agent of Evolution (Pinker 1997; Plotkin 1997; Buss et al. 1998). Thus, "Given any sensible analysis of the probabilities involved, a system with so many complexly interdependent subcomponents that together interact to produce complex functional output cannot be explained as anything other than an adaptation, constructed by the process of natural selection" (Tooby and Cosmides 1990b:761). Moreover, "each Darwinian adaptation contains in its functional design the data of the cause—the selective force—that created it. These data are both necessary and sufficient to demonstrate scientifically the historical environmental problem that was causal in creating the adaptation" (Thornhill 1997:5).

Complexity alone, however, is not sufficient to show adaptation. This is especially obvious in the case of humans because almost any culturally selected cognitive output has complex, nonrandom structure and functionality (e.g., writing, religion, rhyme, rowing, reverse engineering). One can easily imagine scenarios in which these abilities could have provided functional advantage in historical contexts. It is almost as easy to imagine plausible adaptive scenarios in the Pleistocene for such abilities. Only in the case of writing does our knowledge of the facts appear to definitely rule out a Pleistocene adaptation. The problem is that there are often no facts to rule out any of an indefinite number of plausible narratives that make evolutionary sense.

In the following chapters, I describe the various cognitive systems involved in religious belief and practice. Even those systems with an evolutionary history, whether as adaptation or by-product, have often been culturally "exapted" to new functions absent from ancestral environments. And these may have little, if any, systematic relationship to genetic fitness: encouraging xenophobia or opposing injustice, supporting ruling cliques or their overthrow, facilitating social communion or con games, relieving or inciting anxiety, enhancing or suppressing sexual pleasure, promoting or impeding artistic creativity, fostering or hindering insight into ourselves and the world around us, seeking or inventing truth, and the like.

3 God's Creation

Evolutionary Origins of the Supernatural

Religion involves extraordinary use of ordinary cognitive processes to passionately display costly devotion to counterintuitive worlds governed by supernatural agents. The conceptual foundations of religion, like those of culture itself, are intuitively given by highly specialized, universal cognitive domains that are the evolutionary endowments of every human being, such as folkpsychology, folkbiology, and folkmechanics. These domains provide the cognitive means that people use, often unawares, to sort out the supernatural from the natural. A critical feature of the supernatural agent concepts common to all religions is that they trigger an "innate releasing mechanism," whose proper (naturally selected) domain encompasses animate objects but that actually extends to moving dots on computer screens, voices in the wind, faces on clouds. This mechanism consists of evolved predator-protector-prey detection schema that renders dangerous snakes and other beasts just as likely natural candidates for deification as caregiving parents.

3.1. Souls and Spirits in Dreams and Shadows

> That we come to this earth to live is untrue. We come but to sleep, to dream.
>
> —Aztec poem, anonymous, cited in Joseph Campbell, *The Mythic Image* (1975)

> In the beginning when there was darkness everywhere, the creator, Karora, lay sleeping in Ilbalintja, covered by rich soil and a myriad of

> flowers and plants. . . . [I]n his head were thoughts that became real. Huge bandicoots slithered out from his navel and his armpits—male wombs—and broke through the soil above, and the sun began to rise over Ilbalintja.
>
> —Arandan creation myth, northern Australia, cited in D. Leeming and M. Leeming, *A Dictionary of Creation Myths* (1994)

In all religions, and thus in all societies, people believe that agents unseen have intentionally generated the world we see. God created the world for us on purpose and knows what is true. Given that people believe in truthful and purposive supernatural agents, they are able to sanctify the moral order and hold the group to commitment. But this is not the only value of such agents. In all cultures and religions, people believe that conscious souls live on after bodies die, like actors in a dream; they survive in the unseen realm of spirit, where the purposes and truths pertaining to all existence are known. In every society, people believe that ritual can provoke spirits to alter the world for the better and make clearer its meaning, like stage directors called on to change and improve a play.

Just as the intentional thoughts housed in brains and minds would direct human bodies to act, so bodiless but intentional spirits would direct the world. This, according to British social anthropologist E. B. Tylor (1958[1871]), is a basic characteristic of "savage," "primitive," and "barbarian" religions. The most widespread, and apparently convincing, argument for the independent reality of the spirit is by analogy to the play of thought in dreams. The deceptive and deathlike aspects of sleeping and dreaming are readily conceived as sympathetic elements of a supernatural solution to real-world problems of death and deception. Thus, among the Pokoman Maya of Highland Guatemala:

> Dreams are held to be real actions carried on by the soul of the person when it leaves him in sleep at night. The soul, like the air, can travel at great distances in a matter of seconds. It finds itself with other spirits, who are the persons about whom one has dreamed. When the body is left without the soul, it will appear to be dead; and if the soul decides not to return to the body, the person dies forever. . . . Dreams are interpreted in reverse. . . . When a person dies in a dream, it actually means a long and healthy life. But to dream of a child in a healthy state . . . , on the other hand, is cause for concern. (Reina 1966:186)

Unlike most conscious—or at least conscientiously thought out—beliefs about events, dream happenings appear to be unbounded by considerations of consistency and noncontradiction or factual and intuitive plausibility. To the waking mind, dreams produce worlds that are obviously absurd and materially impossible yet still seem to contain most of the elements of the everyday world.

In many cultures, dreams provide both inductive evidence and elements of interpretation for religious beliefs. Sometimes there are also culturally fixed rules of interpretation. Among Maya groups, for example, dream happenings are often interpreted as foretelling future events in reverse. Among the Lacandon Maya, the most important form of reversal between the dream and the future event is the alternation between people and the animal of their totemic Onen (from *ojel*, "that by which one is known"):

> For example, if one dreams that a certain person of the K'ek'en (wild boar) Onen attacks him with a knife or machete, the most logical interpretation of the dream is that the dreamer is seeing the person's Onen, and will be attacked by a boar clearly showing its tusks. There does exist the option, however, that the dream represents hach u pixan, "his real soul" (the person himself) and that the attribute which could be defined as "aggressiveness" is seen in reverse. In that case, the dream would foretell an encounter with the person in question, who would be uncommonly friendly and solicitous. (Bruce 1975:25)[1]

Like the Lacandon, the Itza' Maya refer to such prophecy, or "enlightenment" (*uk'in* = "its sun/day"), as a "kind of lie" (*b'aik utus*) that carries a deeper truth (*jach jaj utzikb'al* = "really true story"). Joseph's biblical dreams are much the same.[2] In these prophetic interpretations, the "rules of correspondence" for relating dream to waking events often provide analogical bases for linking the otherwise merely conventional social order to the true and apparent order of the natural world.

A common theme in religious creation myths across the the world's cultures is the supernatural establishment of order from the midst of primordial chaos. The order that is establishment derives from the thoughts and intentions of divine beings. These thoughts and intentions, which can never be observationally transparent or fully comprehensible to people, are often represented as divine visions very much like human dreams. For example, in the creation myth of the Uitoto of Colombia:

> First there was only a vision, an illusion that affected Nainema, who was himself the illusion. Nothing else existed, Nainema took the illusion to himself and fell in thought. He held the vision by the thread of a dream and searched, but he found nothing. Then he searched it again and tied the emptiness with magical glue. Then he took the bottom of the phantasm and stamped on it until he could sit down upon this earth of which he had dreamed. As he held onto the illusion, he spat out saliva and the forest grew. He lay down the earth and made a sky above it. Gazing at himself, the One who was the story created his story for us to hear. (Leeming and Leeming 1994:281)

In Hindu religious iconography, Vishnu is often represented dreaming the world, as he hovers over the Milky Way while lying on the serpent Ananta ("Unending"). He dreams his wife, Draupadi, and the five Pandava brothers of the heroic epic *Mahabharata*. These dreamed beings are the manifestations of Vishnu's mind and senses: "Eyes open and ready to fight, the youths address themselves to this world of light in which we stand regarding them, where objects appear to be distinct from each other, an Aristotelian logic prevails, and *A* is not *not-A*. Behind them a dream-door has opened, however, to an inward, backward dimension where a vision emerges against darkness" (J. Campbell 1975:7).

Among the Kayans, a head-hunting tribe of Borneo, as among the Menominee, Ojibwa, and many other Native American groups, professional soul catchers go out in search of the souls of sick and slumbering persons who are too weak to bring their own souls back. After having been instructed to take up this calling by some spirit met in dreams—often a dream experienced during sickness—the soul catcher decides that the soul of the patient has left that person's body and has gone some part of the journey toward the abode of departed souls. The soul catcher's task is to fall into a trance and to send his or her own soul to overtake that of the patient and to persuade it to return (House and McDougall 1912: II:28–32).

Although Tylor, like Hobbes before him, saw an unbridgeable gap between the dreamlike souls of animists and pantheists on the one hand, and the monotheistic spirit on the other, they occupy much the same cognitive and emotional space.[3] Consider, for example, what Eleazar, the Jewish commander of the Masada garrison in the revolt against Rome, told his followers to convince them that killing their bodies to preserve the spirit of their faith would be ultimately more rewarding than enslaving their bodies to Rome:

> Ever since primitive man began to think, the words of our ancestors and of the gods, supported by the actions and spirit of our forefathers, have constantly impressed on us that *life* is the calamity for man, not death. Death gives freedom to our souls and lets them depart to their own pure home where they will know nothing of any calamity; but while they are confined within a mortal body and share its miseries, in strict truth they are dead. . . . But when, freed from the weight that drags it down to earth and is hung about it, the soul returns to its own place, then in truth it partakes of a blessed power and an utterly unfettered strength, remaining as invisible to human eyes as to God himself. . . . Sleep will provide you with the clearest proof of what I say. In sleep souls left to themselves and free from bodily distractions enjoy the most blissful repose, and consorting with God whose kin they are, they go wherever they will and foretell of many things to come. Why, pray, should we fear death if we love to repose in sleep? And isn't it absurd to run after the freedom of this life and grudge ourselves the freedom of eternity? . . . After all, we were born to die, we and those we brought into this world: this even the luckiest must face. (Josephus 1981[66–73]:403–405)

The separation of the spiritual soul from the body is evident in Christian theology and Enlightenment philosophy as well. For Saint Thomas Aquinas, the soul gives life to the body but does not require the body to act: "I am not my soul" (*Anima mea non sum ego*). For Descartes, the soul and mind are one, and they enable material existence: "I think, therefore I am" (*Cogito ergo sum*). The soul has both intellect and passions, but for Aquinas and Descartes, the passions once released from the body become "pure" passions of love and light. The rational intellect is the immortal side of the soul, whose only true raison d'être is to manifest the spirit and love of God.

On this account, the mind and body occupy different ontological planes. They are different and independent modes of being. The "proof" is that nonhuman animals have no soul, or mind, to speak of (they are "automatons"). In humans, the soul drives much of the body's active behavior but separates from the body at death. Like thoughts that wander from the sleeping body in a dream and regain coherence as the body wakes, so the soul wanders the world until it is reunited with the body on Judgment Day.

Perhaps the one significant distinction between the souls and spirits of philosophical monotheism and those of animism and pantheism is the illusion of the rational intellect as the one unmistakable vision of God Almighty. For Ibn Sīnā (Avicenna) and Baruch Spinoza, as for Aquinas and Descartes, whatever is clear and distinct in the mind and pure of soul owes directly to God. If we rightly believe, and know to be true, Aristotle's dictum that *A* cannot also be *not-A*, it is only because God made this aspect of His spirit the very heart and essence of our human souls.

In other words, believing in the inviolable truth of the law of noncontradiction can *only* be a pure act of faith. In this view, only clear and distinct ideas can be known for sure. The full character and essence of God Himself remains confessedly incomprehensible. Most practicing (as opposed to philosophical) monotheists, however, neither religiously adhere to the law of noncontradiction nor confess to God's being incomprehensible. As with other believers, they hold that the world is the creation of a divine and somewhat disembodied imagination. There is something of a paradox in this *need* to believe, which, as we shall see in Parts II and III, owes very much to the affective and indissociable nature of the human mind and body.

The Western conception of separation of body from soul is similar to such conceptions in other cultures. For example, among the Eskimo (Inuit):

> Man himself is thought to consist of two parts, the body and the soul, which are entirely distinct from one another. The soul [*innua*] can be seen by the medicine man only, to whom it appears in the same shape as the body, but of a more airy composition. . . . The soul of man is quite independent and can leave the body at any time to wander at will; this it does every night when, in dreams, it goes hunting or enjoys merrymaking. This soul can be lost or stolen by means of witchcraft. (Nansen 1893:228)

Finally, the dissociated thoughts of dreams are often religiously allied with the disembodied movements of shadows. For example, among numerous tribes of West Africa:

> The *kra* escapes through the mouth of a sleeper, and if the mouth is left open a strange *kra* may enter and take up its abode there, thus causing much trouble. If a man is awakened suddenly, his *kra* may be taken away, so that the man becomes ill. The witch doctor is called in and he gets a new one for the man. In daytime the *kra* will follow a man around in the form of a shadow, and so people will avoid losing their shadows and hence their *kras*. Alligators may pull a man into the river by seizing his shadow, and murders are sometimes committed by secretly driving a nail or a knife into a man's shadow, but if the murderer be caught redhanded at it, he or she would be forthwith killed. (Kingsley 1899:208)

Movements of shadows fall under agency's natural domain (proper and actual, see section 3.2); however, the motions of shadows violate many of the constraints that humans universally apply to the movements of solid objects.

Different objects maintain their boundaries and edges as they move and cannot occupy the same spatiotemporal position. Shadows can lose their boundaries and coincide in space and time. When an object moves off the edge of a surface, it maintains its connectedness and traces a continuous path. The same shadow can simultaneously occupy multiple surfaces, change size and shape, disappear, move in spatially discontinuous fashion, and so forth. Objects move with the surfaces on which they are located. A shadow moves with the object(s) that cast it and may remain fixed in space as the surface on which it is cast moves. When an object in motion contacts an object at rest, the object in motion changes motion and the object at rest goes into motion. When a moving shadow touches a stationary shadow, they merge and then the moving shadow may go on just the same.

Human infants 5 to 8 months old react to these shadow movements with surprise, but not so to object movements (Spelke et al. 1995). The children seem to overgeneralize innate principles of folkmechanics to shadows, which renders the movement of shadows inherently surprising and attention arresting. Being able to track agents, however imperfectly, by following the distorted and faint reflections of their shadow images has obvious survival value (e.g., tracking furtive predators) in addition to intrinsic surprise and cognitive interest.

Like dreams, shadows are also often thematically associated with darkness and night, when people generally feel least secure and in control. Thus, Itza' sorcerers, *ajwaay*, are said to kill their quarry by conjuring a night shadow spirit (*ak'ä' pixan*) to represent a dead relative of the victim, which frightens the victim into illness and death. Sometimes the *ajwaay* change themselves into animals, including small gekkos (*chib'il b'o'oy* = "shadow biter") that cart off the souls' (*'ool*) victims by biting their shadows. These and other common thematic associations (e.g., with the moon, night predators, dark caves, death, disease; or sun, songbirds, light, open spaces, reason, health, life) are readily available candidates for cultural manipulation. A culturally ubiquitous example is the ghost:

> DUNCAN: Wicked dreams, abuse the curtained sleep; witchcraft celebrates Pale Hecate's offerings; and wither'd murder, Alarum'd by his sentinel, the wolf, towards his design Moves like a ghost. . . .

> MACBETH: The times have been, That when the brains were out, the world would die And there an end; but now they rise again . . . And push us from our stools. . . . Thy bones are marrowless, thy blood is cold; Thou hast no speculation in those eyes Which thou dost glare with. . . . Approach though like the rugged Russian bear, The arm'd rhinocerus, or the Hyrcan tiger; Take any shape . . . horrible shadow! Unreal mockery, hence! [Ghost vanishes.] (Shakespeare, *Macbeth*, Act II, scene 1; Act III, scene 4)

These near-universal thematic co-occurrences account for much convergence in thematic content of religious beliefs across cultures. As we shall see in the following sections, however, this cross-cultural convergence is possible only because of the universal structural framework on which these thematic associations are pegged. This universal structural framework involves innate and modularized expectations about object movements (folkmechanics), essential kinds (folkbiology), and the intentional nature of agents (folkpsychology). It is this cognitive architecture that makes it natural to render a supernatural interpretation of events under conditions of uncertainty.

3.2. Modularity and Domain Specificity

Supernatural agency is the most culturally recurrent, cognitively relevant, and evolutionarily compelling concept in religion. The concept of the supernatural agent is culturally derived from innate cognitive schema, "mental modules," for the recognition and interpretation of agents, such as people and animals. By "culturally derived," I mean that numbers of people acting together causally manipulate innate, specieswide processing schema in historically contingent ways, much as makeup and masks involve culturally collective, contingent, causal manipulation of innate, modular sensibilities to secondary sexual characteristics and human facial cues.

A naturally selected, mental module is functionally specialized to process, as input, a specific domain of recurrent stimuli in the world that was particularly relevant to hominid survival. The module spontaneously produces, as output, groupings of stimuli into categories as well as inferences about the conceptual relationships between these categories. The innately constrained cognitive structure of this output presumably was designed under natural selection. It allowed humans to adaptively navigate ancestral environments by responding rapidly and economically to important, statistically repetitive task demands, such as distinguishing predator from prey and friend from foe.

Within the current approach of domain specificity, then, human knowledge of the world can be characterized in terms of autonomous mental faculties. There are roughly four classes of evolved mental modules: perceptual modules, primary emotion modules, secondary affect modules, and conceptual modules.

A *perceptual module* is "informationally encapsulated" insofar as it has automatic and proprietary access to a specific range of sensory inputs. It has its own exclusive database for accessing and processing input (perceptual stimuli) and does not draw on information produced by other cognitive systems. A perceptual module is usually associated with fairly fixed neural architecture and fast processing that is not accessible to conscious awareness. Examples are modules for facial recognition, color perception, identification of object boundaries, and morphosyntax (Fodor 1983).

Like perceptual modules, *primary emotion modules* operate more or less autonomously and automatically, much like instincts and reflexes, in response to particular stimulus situations (either external and "real" or internal and "imagined"). A first-order emotion module has automatic and proprietary access to specific physiological arrays of body states. Although there is some disagreement as to the exact character and scope of so-called basic or primary emotions, the list generally includes the six affective states for which Darwin detailed homologies in other species: surprise, fear, anger, disgust, sadness, happiness (Darwin 1965[1872]; Tomkins 1962; Izard 1977; Plutchik 1980; Ekman 1992; Damasio 1994). An apparent characteristic of basic emotions is that they need not be mediated by higher-order cognitive processes (cf. Zajonc 1984; LeDoux 1994), although in humans they can be.

Much more controversy surrounds the possible evolutionary underpinnings of *secondary affect modules* and second-order conceptual modules. One position is that secondary affect programs, or "higher-order feelings," may be variants or specific cognitively mediated elaborations of primary emotions: anxiety is fear provoked by an internal rather than external stimulus, grief is sadness prolonged by inference to the finality of the eliciting condition, contempt is disgust in a social context, outrage is anger in the social context of insult, and so forth. Another position is that secondary emotions are all acquired by learning or are "socially constructed." For example, guilt, vengefulness, love, and pride all seem to involve fairly abstract social cognitions (breach of contract, meeting expectations) whose eliciting conditions and forms of expression can vary considerably across cultural settings. A third position, which I adopt, is that at least some secondary human emotions are naturally selected solutions to recurrent conflicts between the short-term and long-term interests of individuals living in hominid (and perhaps other, nonhominid) social groups (R. Frank 1988; Nesse 1989; Tooby and Cosmides 1990a; Griffiths 1997).

A *conceptual module* has privileged, rather than proprietary, access to inputs (external or internal stimuli) that are provided by other parts of the nervous system (e.g., sensory receptors or other modules; Atran 1990:285). Like perceptual modules, each conceptual module has its own innately constrained database for processing inputs. There is somewhat more leeway in the way that conceptual modules interact with one another and somewhat less exclusive access to inputs (including access to the outputs of perceptual modules). But these distinctions between conceptual and perceptual modules may turn out to be more of degree than of kind.[4]

A central issue in recent cognitive and developmental psychology concerns the scope and limits of conceptual modules, such as folkmechanics, folkpsychology, folkbiology, and folksociology. One problem is demarcation of the ontological boundaries of a given domain, that is, the nature of the selection processes involved in the identification of the entities that fall under a given domain. Presently, there is considerable debate about how people decide, for example, when it is appropriate to invoke psychological versus mechanical principles (Leslie 1994; Csibra et al. 1999), or psychological versus biological principles (Carey 1995; Atran et al. 2001), or mechanical versus biological principles (Au and Romo 1999), or sociological versus biological principles for categorizing and reasoning about groups of individuals (Hirschfeld 1996; Atran 1998) to explain or predict regularities in the world.

In what follows, I take the position that there are separate modules that govern interpretation of agency (folkpsychology) and essential kindhood (folkbiology), but no separate modules for human versus nonhuman agency or for biological versus social essentialism (Atran 2001c). Nevertheless, there are differences between the ways humans and nonhumans are processed as agents and between the ways biological kinds and social groups are processed for essences. People cannot fail to comprehend humans as always being intentional agents or living organisms as essentially belonging to one and only one (folk) species, just as they cannot fail to perceive rocks as solid or the sky as blue on a cloudless day. The input conditions that activate comprehension of human agents or species essences drive modular processing to a completed end state that has a fixed, if inchoate, factual core (with additional factual knowledge and revision subsequently possible; Atran 1987a; Medin and Ortony 1989; see Ahn et al. 2001 on essence as a causal "placeholder"). By contrast, the input conditions that activate comprehension of nonhuman agents or social essences allow more degrees of freedom in processing, which yields much greater variability in output and permits much wider flexibility in interpretation across individuals and cultures. Successful performance of computations over information specific to a domain does not depend on a complete specification of perceptible properties of the entities that may fall under the domain (Keil 1994).

To clarify the point, I will elaborate liberally on insights by Tinbergen (1951) and Sperber (1996) concerning modular processing structure and stimulus conditions. This is important for understanding the approach I adopt to cultural cognition in general and to religious cognition in particular.

3.3. Agency

Agency is triggered by evidence of complex design. Indeed, this is one of the classic arguments for the existence of God (Paley 1836). Whether in nature or society, directly observable, short-term productions of complex design are caused by animal or human agents. Unobservable or longer-term productions, such as the complex spatiotemporal patterns of stars, geography, seasons, plants, animals, societies, and people themselves, have no intuitively natural causal interpretation. Human cognitive architecture does not appear to have been selected to spontaneously appreciate such long-term causal histories, in the sense that such an appreciation would represent a solution to a problem of some functional relevance to hominid existence. Agency detection is deployed as the default program for processing and interpreting such information, but in an "extended mode," much as layfolk, philosophers, psychologists, and even many biologists readily (over)extend the concept of a class or lawful "natural kind" to species and other groupings of similar but genetically distinct individuals.

Agents are entities that instigate and control their own actions as well as those of other objects and agents. Developmental and cognitive psychology have experimented with several related theories of how humans come to make sense of one another. An overarching theoretical framework has emerged, known as folkpsychology, naïve psychology, or theory of mind. The central idea is that people, and perhaps other animated objects, are *intentional agents* who act, and cause others to act, on the basis of *internal motivations*.

Unlike inert objects and substances, such as rocks and water, intentional agents do not just react mechanically to physical contact and environmental change, such as air pressure, temperature, or light. Intentional agents can simply decide to get up and move "at will" without anything apparent causing them to do so; that is, they seem to be self-propelled by some inner force. More often than not, they appear to act "on purpose" to achieve some preexisting goal; that is, they appear to act *teleologically*. Finally, intentional agents are generally thought to have more than just purposes. They are also ascribed beliefs and desires: attitudes toward propositions, or to the sorts of would-be propositions that religious utterances often express, such as "God is merciful" or "The Devil wants to own you" (I'll say more in the next chapter about what I mean by the would-be "quasi propositions" of religion). Intentional causal mental states, such as beliefs and desires, cannot be directly perceived. They are nonobvious and unobservable constructs, much like universal attributions of underlying causal essences to animal and plant species (Atran 1998).

If people didn't understand and interact with one another as intentional agents with minds that function something like our own, there would be no point in using words or gestures to motivate or manipulate behavior, except perhaps as one might utter sounds to physically induce a robot to action. In the structure of human language, agents are initiators and possessors of actions. Praying to the gods to get them to turn their attention toward acts favorable to human concerns implies that the gods understand human intentions and that humans, in turn, can divine at least enough of the gods' true beliefs to motivate action on the suppliants' behalf. Intentional agency is a critical part of human beings' cognitive ability to engage and navigate the social world: to figure out whom it would be wisest to cooperate with and whom it would be best to do without. Figuring out how to interact with God may not be much different (Brams 1980).

Mental states are inferred from poor and fragmentary triggering experiences that indicate only a physical event, such as interruptible movement toward a goal (Csibra et al. 1999), self-propulsion (Premack 1990), coordinated motion between subjects (Premack and Premack 1995), pointing (Leslie 1991), eye gaze (Baron-Cohen 1995), facial expression (Tomasello, Strosberg, and Akhtar 1996), and interactive gesture or signaling (S. Johnson, Slaughter, and Carey 1998). Attributing internal motivation allows people to understand how they and others can react to and act on objects and events at a distance, without physical contact. For example, your smile or frown as the cat meows may cause someone else in the room to infer your desire or reluctance to feed the cat and so feed the cat. Unlike essences, which concern inherent properties *of* the things that possess them (e.g., the capacity of a cat to meow), mental states are *about* other things in the world (wanting it to be a true state of affairs in the world that the cat has food).

Agency is a complex sort of "innate releasing mechanism" (Tinbergen 1951) whose proper evolutionary domain encompasses animate objects but that actually extends (as an inadvertently but spontaneously activated evolutionary by-product) to moving dots on computer screens, voices in the wind, faces in the clouds, and virtually any complex design or uncertain circumstance of unknown origin. For each *natural domain*, there is a proper domain and (possibly empty) actual domain (Sperber 1994). A *proper domain* is information that it is the module's naturally selected function to process. The module's function is a set of outcomes that causally contribute to making the module a stable species feature. Thus, stimuli that track behaviors of animals, including people, fall under the proper domain of an AGENCY module. Identifying animate beings as agents, with goals and internal motivations, would allow our ancestors to anticipate goal-directed actions of predators, prey, friends, and foe and to profit from this in ways that enhanced hominid survival and reproductive success.

The *actual domain* of a module is any information in the organism's environment that satisfies the module's input conditions whether or not the information is functionally relevant to ancestral task demands—that is, whether or not it also belongs to its proper domain. For example, cloud formations and unexpected noises from inanimate sources (e.g., a sudden, howling gush of wind) readily trigger inferences to agency among people everywhere (Hume 1956[1757]; Guthrie 1993). Although clouds and wind occurred in ancestral environments, they had no functional role in recurrent task problems with animate beings. Similarly, a number of experiments show that children and adults spontaneously interpret the contingent movements of dots and geometrical forms on a screen as interacting agents who have distinct goals and internal motivations for reaching those goals (Heider and Simmel 1944; Premack and Premack 1995; P. Bloom and Veres 1999). Moving dots on a screen do not belong to AGENCY's proper domain because they could not have been involved with ancestral task demands. Like clouds and wind, moving dots on computer screens can belong to AGENCY's actual domain.

A parallel example is food-catching behavior in frogs. When a flying insect moves across the frog's field of vision, bug-detector cells are activated in the frog's brain. Once activated, these cells in turn massively fire others in a chain reaction that usually results in the frog's shooting out its tongue to catch the insect. The bug detector is primed to respond to any small dark object that suddenly enters the visual field: "Every time it moves, with even the faintest jerk, there is a burst of impulses that dies down to a mutter that continues as long as the object is visible. If the object is kept moving, the burst signal discontinues in the movement, such as the turning of corners, reversals, and so forth, and these bursts occur against a continuous background mutter that tells us the object is visible to the cell" (Lettvin et al. 1961). If flying insects belong to the proper domain of a frog's food-catching module, then small wads of black paper dangling on a string belong to the actual domain.

In sum, cognitive schema for recognizing and interpreting animate agents may be a crucial part of our evolutionary heritage, which primes us to anticipate intention in the unseen causes of uncertain situations that carry the risk of danger or the promise of opportunity, such as predators, protectors, and prey. If we, or our ancestors, were to find that the scratching at the door or the howling in the air was not the stalker that seems "automatically" to first come to mind but only the play of branches and leaves in the wind, we would suffer nothing. But if there were a stalker, we would be prepared and likely to suffer less than if we weren't. Natural selection may have prepared us to induce agency in potentially important but causally opaque situations, like the way it seems to have mentally prepared our ancestors to avoid snakes (Marks 1987). Apes raging against thunderstorms may be incipiently homologous to Masai herders blustering at storms or to other peoples conjuring up supernatural agents as bowmen shooting or deflecting arrows of outrageous fortune (Van Lawick-Goodall 1971)—but incipient only insofar as apes seem to lack the critical notion of an abstract CONTROLLING FORCE that supernatural agency requires (see section 3.5).

3.4. The Natural Domain of Agency: Evidence from Infant Development

Developmental studies are crucial to our understanding of the evolved, innate character of the mind because they reveal how cognition is biologically primed to infer rich conclusions and consequences from poor and fragmentary data. As Hume (1955[1758]) showed, it isn't logically possible for people to consistently generalize from one or a few scattered instances to a complex set of intricately related cases in the absence of prior structures that guide projection. For the infant to go so far beyond the information given requires innate, domain-specific mental faculties, like that responsible for detecting and inferring agents.

Beginning at 4 to 8 months of age, infants are able to track eye gaze and pointing. This indicates that the infant can represent how agents act, and a bit later how they interact, to achieve goals. By the second half of the first year, infants reliably "request" and "refuse" to be picked up; that is, the children enlist others in achieving a goal or deliberately blocking others from achieving a goal (Bates et al. 1979). Using computer animations, Premack and Premack (1995) surmised that 1-year-olds spontaneously attribute emotions to objects that move in specific ways. The children were habituated to one of two positive (caress, help) or negative (hit, hinder) situations, each involving a black and a gray circle. For example, when "caressing," neither circle deformed the other on contact; when "hitting," the gray circle deformed the black. If habituated to a positive situation, the children would become attentive to a negative situation that followed and vice versa. These results suggest the possibility of a modular device that interprets visual displays of apparently self-initiated movement as belonging to distinct kinds of goal-directedness, such as helping or hindering and harming (Premack 1990).

By 18 months, children clearly relate an adult's emotional expression to goal-directed behavior (Tomasello, Strosberg, and Akhtar 1996). In one experiment, an adult used a nonce word to announce her intention to find an object (e.g., "Let's find the gazzer"). She picked up an object and, frowning, rejected it. She then found an object and, smiling, gave it to the child but used no language. Children learned the new word for the object smiled upon as well as in a condition in which the adult found the object immediately. Children at this age are also able to meet adult food requests as a function of the adult's prior emotional reactions to food choices (Repacholi and Gopnik 1997). For children 1 year old and younger, a parent's emotional expression affects the degree of the child's interaction with a stranger (Feinman and Lewis 1983) and the probability of touching an unfamiliar toy (Hornick, Risenhoover, and Gunnar 1987; Walden and Baxter 1989). A plausible evolutionary advantage would be to allow for a quick visual evaluation of potentially noxious versus beneficial relationships with interactants, including vital assessments of likely predators or parasites and prey or symbionts.

S. Johnson, Slaughter, and Carey (1998) tested the reactions of 1-year-old children to an object somewhat resembling a stuffed animal without limbs. When the infant babbled, the object beeped; when the infant moved, the internal light flashed. After the child's habituation to the novel object, the object made an attention-grabbing beep and turned to orient itself to one of two targets. Infants followed the orientation of the object to the relevant target in three of four familiarization conditions: (1) if the object had a face; (2) if, when the infant babbled or moved, the object beeped and flashed lights; or (3) both conditions together. Although the object in the (4) noncontingent, faceless condition had the same shape and orientation movements as in the other three conditions, the infants did not reliably follow its orientation to a target. The authors suggest that at 12 months children are able to attribute mental states such as perception and attention to people, as well as to novel entities that are not people. Moreover, they identify "contingent interactivity" at a distance as yet another possible "intention marker," that is, as a perceptual basis for categorizing an object as belonging to the domain of folkpsychology.

Additional experiments further support the argument. S. Johnson, Booth, and O'Hearn (2001) found that 15-month-olds infer goal-directed behaviors of an orangutan puppet (e.g., children place beads in a cup when the puppet "tries" but nonetheless "fails" to place beans in the cup), direct social communicative gestures toward it (children wave hello to it, offer it toys, etc.), and follow its "gaze" (children look at the target to which the puppet is oriented). The children do not respond in any of these ways to objects, such as mechanical pincers, that lack a face or that fail to interact contingently with the child (cf. Meltzoff 1995a). This indicates that communicative gesturing, inferencing to unachieved and unseen goals, and social referencing (alternating gaze between object and agent) spontaneously co-occur as a behavioral "package" that is driven by domain-specific principles of mentalistic attribution. Such attributions spontaneously apply to humans and animals, as well as to entities whose associated stimuli resemble or mimic corresponding features or behaviors of humans and animals, such as faces or contingent interaction.

Supernatural agents often have both abstract and group qualities, with a minimum of associated substance (e.g., ghosts) and specieslike characteristics (e.g., the Furies). Again, experiments encourage the view that the attribution of intentional agency to abstract objects is spontaneous and natural. For example, Heider and Simmel (1944) found that adults attribute intentionality to objects interacting on a screen (e.g., a first shape "chases" a second shape to the screen's upper corner, "capturing" the first shape by blocking its movement and "keeping it prisoner"). P. Bloom and Veres (1999) used essentially the same experimental set-up, but with each "agent" separated into five small shapes on a computer screen. Subjects interpreted each agent as a group of identical actors, suggesting that agency can be attributed to individuals as well as to groups of individuals. Lawrence Hirschfeld, Susan Gelman, and Michael Baran have preliminary evidence that 4- to 5-year-olds reason in much the same way (Baran 2000).

From an evolutionary standpoint, the proper domain of the human infant's agency detector is the range of animate objects that could initiate action in ancestral hominid environments; however, the module need not know anything about biological animateness: "Automobiles might appear to be Agents to the extent that they keep changing motion" (Leslie 1994:145 n. 7). In other words, the actual domain of the infant's agency detector can extend to inanimates, including geometrical shapes on a computer screen and machines.

3.5. Telic Structures and the Tragedy of Cognition

> I simply can't build up my hopes on a foundation consisting of confusion, misery and death. . . . I hear the ever approaching thunder, which will destroy us too; I can feel the sufferings of millions; and yet, if I look up into the heavens, I think that it will all come right, that this cruelty will end, and that peace and tranquility will return again. . . . I want to be useful or give pleasure to people around me who yet don't really know me. I want to go on living after my death!
>
> —Anne Frank, *Het Achterhuis*, 1944, from *The Diary of a Young Girl* (1993 [1947])

Recent studies by Csibra et al. (1999) challenge the idea that infants can interpret an object's movement as goal-directed only in the presence of perceptual cues indicating agency, such as self-propulsion. In particular, the Csibra et al. study implies that humans spontaneously attribute agentive, goal-directed behavior to certain types of *event structures*, regardless of the agent's physical character and even in the absence of any direct perception of an agent.

Using computer-animated visual events, the experimenters first habituated 9- and 12-month-old children to the appearance of a stationary rectangular column on the right side of the screen and a large, stationary circle on the left side. In one experiment, the large circle then moved further left and stopped; in another experiment, it was simply positioned to the far left of the screen and never moved. A small circle then entered the screen from the right side at a level somewhat lower than the top of the column. It traced a parabolic trajectory over the column and landed, immediately stopping at a position adjacent to the large circle. The screen was then cleared for two test events in which the column was no longer present. In the familiar test event, the behavior of the small circle was identical to that of the habituation event: it entered from the right side and "flew" to the position adjacent to the large circle along a parabolic trajectory. In the unfamiliar test event, the small circle approached the same end-point in a novel way, taking the shortest straight path at ground level.

In both experiments, children at both ages paid more attention to the familiar test event, presumably because they understood it to be a less efficient (or "rational") approach to a given goal (landing next to the large circle) than either the habituation event or the unfamiliar test event. By occluding the origins of the small circle's movement (it entered the screen like a tennis ball in midflight), the movement of the small circle could just as easily be attributed to an external cause as to an internal cause, or to no causal source at all. This indicates that children do not need to perceptually disambiguate the causal source of behavior in order to interpret it as goal-directed action. In particular, the results call into question the claim that perceptions of self-propulsion are necessary to attribute intentionality (Premack 1990; Leslie 1994; Baron-Cohen 1995). These results also indicate that neither humanlike facial or bodily features nor biomechanical movements are necessary for the attribution of psychological principles, such as goal-directed behavior, motivation (e.g., emotion), intention to communicate, or social referencing (via physical orientation or "gaze"). One implication is that *spontaneous attribution of agency to physically unidentified sources isn't counterintuitive.*

Let's consider that agents may be identified as operators in *telic event structures* without regard to initiation of movement. In other words, the agent identification process might be based on the analysis of event structures rather than object cues as such. This implies that the natural domain of AGENCY is not an ontological category of objects as such, like ANIMATE BEING, ANIMAL, or PERSON, but a domain of event structures, such as those crucial to understanding interactive goals of PREDATOR-PREY and FRIEND-FOE. Indeed, many mammals, such as social carnivores and primates, evince behaviors consistent with an integrated appreciation of predator-protector-prey event structures. For example, in "chase play" the young typically "dare" a protector (e.g., parent, sibling) to chase them as a predator would, only to "surrender" to the pettings, lickings, and other comforting behaviors of the chaser.

I borrow the idea of a telic event structure from linguistics (Greek *télos* = end): "In expressions referring to telic situations it is important that there should be both a process leading up to a terminal point as well as the terminal point" (Conrie 1976:44). Thus, "John is singing" or "Cats drown in deep water" do not express telic events because there is no terminal point, whereas "John is singing a song" and "The cat is drowning" are telic. In the unfolding of a telic situation, earlier stages of the process are not so intimately bound up with the final outcome that once the process is underway it cannot be prevented from occurring (Vendler 1967:103). For example, "John is dying" is not telic because the process cannot be interrupted (if it could, John would not be dying, only seeming to be dying or almost dying).

The critical feature of a telic situation is not the initiation of an action, but contingent control of its outcome, such that the outcome could have been different if control had been lost. The concept of CONTROLLING FORCE is a key to proper analysis of the situation (cf. Leslie 1994). If there were no control involved in determining the smaller object's path, then there would be no purpose to its stopping short of the large object and the results could be interpreted without any reference to teleology. If there were no inference about a CONTROLLING FORCE, then one could expect the same response from a child looking at the movement of a stream of water around a rock: if the rock were removed from the stream's path, then, all other things being equal, the most efficient movement of the water would be straight and not curved.

This suggests that teleological reasoning about objects needn't specify the source of the CONTROLLING FORCE (e.g., internal self-control vs. external control at a distance). Objects are thought to behave teleologically even when their causal origins are unseen and unknown: the moving object may be just an *experiencer of agency* rather than the instigator of agency. All that is required is that presence of contingent variation between the behavior of objects and changing aspects of the environment elicits attribution of CONTROLLING FORCE. Before age 2 years, children learn to seek out a causal source for the CONTROLLING FORCE in such contingent variation. Objects that evince facial or vocal emotion, contingent reactivity at a distance, biomechanical movement, self-propulsion, and so on will be good candidate sources. Once a source is identified as an agent it is bundled with all sorts of attributes, which usually identify an animate agent instigator.

Agent instigators in a telic event can be external (a player who throws a ball toward a goal) or internal (a fly that moves toward a goal). The perceptual structure of a telic event may be compatible with either external or internal agent instigators. Telic event structures that recurrently trigger concepts of supernatural agency, such as shooting stars or the birth of an individual, readily lend themselves to interpretation as either external instigators (e.g., God the Unmoved Mover) or internal instigators (e.g., animating spirits; cf. Evans 2001). Apes seem unable to abstractly represent the perceptually neutral causal relation of CONTROLLING FORCE that assimilates the two (Tomasello and Call 1997; Povinelli 2000).[5]

Humans are cognitively susceptible to invoke supernatural agents whenever emotionally eruptive events arise that have superficial characteristics of telic event structures with no apparent CONTROLLING FORCE. These include chaotic or chance events (earthquakes, thunderstorms, floods, drought), uncertain events (disease, war, famine, loneliness), and future events that are normally beyond a person's control but that people cannot avoid trying to manage, such as critical periods in the human life cycle (birth, puberty, old age, death). Awareness of death is one universal cognition that is especially anxiety-provoking.[6]

For example, in a British television survey, 64 percent of respondents associated thinking about "death" with God, compared with 2 percent who related God to "lovemaking" and other emotionally charged notions (cited in Beit-Hallahmi and Argyle 1997:195). Consistent with these findings, Norenzayan and Atran (2002) recently found that inducing mortality salience directly affects religious feelings. Compared to control group participants who were asked to reflect on their favorite foods, experimental group participants who were asked to reflect on their own death scored higher on self-reports of religiosity and belief in God.[7] We also found that death-related scenes that were emotionally stressful (i.e., with increased adrenalin activation) were stronger motivators for religiosity, including belief in God and supernatural intervention, than mere exposure to unstressful religious scenes, such as praying (see section 7.2). Consistent with these observations, numerous polls show a significant spike in Americans' feeling of religiosity immediately following September 11.

Evolutionarily, at least some basic emotions preceded conceptual reasoning: surprise, fear, anger, disgust, joy, sadness (Darwin 1965[1872]; Ekman 1992). These likely further evolved to prime reason to make inferences about situations relevant to the course of life and its continued existence. Arguably, this was a foremost selection factor for the emergence of reason itself. Existential anxieties are by-products of evolved emotions, such as fear and the will to stay alive (LeDoux 1996), and of evolved cognitive capacities, such as episodic memory and the ability to track the self and others over time (Wheeler, Stuss, and Tulving 1997; Suddendorf and Corballis 1997). For example, once you can track even the seasons—and anticipate that leaves will fall off the tree in autumn and that squirrels will bury nuts—you cannot avoid overwhelming inductive evidence favoring your own death and that of those you are emotionally bonded to. Emotions compel such inductions and make them salient, and terrifying. This is "the Tragedy of Cognition."

Dying is by nature not a telic event because once the process of dying starts (from birth on) it cannot be stopped to avoid the inevitable end state. By introducing a supernatural agent, religion resolves the Tragedy of Cognition. Dying is converted into a telic event whose goal state is an extended afterlife. The result is, in part, an allaying of an otherwise recurring and interminable existential anxiety: people are compelled by ordinary workings of cognition (unavoidably tracking the self over time) to become aware of impending death, and by emotion to do something about it so as to continue to survive (anxiety, which is usually distinguished from fear by lack of an immediate external eliciting stimulus, nevertheless includes primitively powerful neurophysiological fear reactions; LeDoux 1996: 228–230). In sum, existential anxieties (evolutionary by-products of inevitably converging biological tracks of cognitive inference and emotion) are further channeled through adaptations for agency (modular telic-event structure) into the evolutionarily constrained paths of "religion."

3.6. The Supernatural: Agency's Cultural Domain

> Lo the poor Indian! Whose untutored mind
> Sees God in clouds, or hears him in the wind.
>
> —Alexander Pope, cited in E. T. C. Werner, *A Dictionary of Chinese Mythology* (1961 [1932])

> I saw in the night visions, and behold,
> one like the Son of man came with the clouds of heavens.
>
> —Book of Daniel 7:13

Humans everywhere interpret animals as agents, both natural and supernatural. For humans, animals are typically predators, prey, or (at least since domestication at the end of the last Ice Age) companions. Anyone who has ever visited the Ice Age cave paintings of Lascaux and Chauvet in southern France or Altamira in northern Spain cannot fail to be impressed by the highly accurate—but formulaic, repetitive, and ritualized—scenes of animal movements in acts of hunting and being hunted.

In many, and arguably most, human cultures throughout history, supernatural agents have been associated with animals and apparently self-propelled inanimate objects like the sun, moon, and stars. This is the case for all known state-level priestly civilizations of the ancient Old World and New World before the rise of monotheism (enduring, however, even in the popular lore of monotheistic cultures). The attribution of intentions to animals and moving objects also seems to be a spontaneous product of agency cognitions that children acquire early on (Coley 1995; S. Johnson, Booth, and O'Hearn 2001). These attributions apparently do not involve violations of ordinary processing routines. Neither do they require formal instruction or ritualized cultural learning.

For humans, agents are the primary purveyors of goals and emotions and also the primary elicitors of goals and emotions in others. Fear in humans, as in animals, is often paralyzing (ceasing all movement offers predators fewer cues to guide attack). But along with paralysis in action fear often motivates, is a hopeful search for an even more knowing intelligence who could help save the day by stepping into the situation, as in a scene in a play, to conjure up a design for some way out.

Although seemingly contradictory, the emotions of hope and fear are closely allied, cognitively and religiously. As social psychologist Gordon Allport and colleagues (Allport, Gillespie, and Young 1948) found in a study of returning frontline soldiers, fear was remembered along with heightened faith in God's deliverance, or hope in some other kind of providential outcome: "Allport interviewed us returning [WWII] vets at Harvard. He found that most of the frontline soldiers who had been under fire had either prayed or hoped to God for deliverance—or they had just hoped, which Allport believed [in that context] to be the same as religion" (Donald R. Brown, Professor of Psychology, University of Michigan, personal communication, 7 June 1999). More recently, Sethi and Seligman (1993) found strength of religious belief to be strongly correlated with hope.

From the standpoint of appraisal theory, fear and hope may differ only in valence, being cognitively—although not physiologically—composed of otherwise identical elements (Ellsworth 1991). Such an evolutionary landscape could well favor the cultural selection of gods and devils, demons and good fairies: "Here therefore is a kind of contradiction between the different principles of human nature, which enter into religion. Our natural terror presents the notion of a devilish and malicious deity: our propensity to adulation leads us to acknowledge an excellent and divine" (Hume 1956[1757]:65).

But even more than present and perceptible events, the emotionally eruptive and cognitively inescapable dreads of a perilously unknown future of relentless enemies and seemingly inevitable death would favor the cultural survival of humanlike supernatural agents. These entities with extraordinary, promissory powers and attributes that go beyond observed realities and human capabilities are nevertheless naturally accessible to human understanding. As Hume noted:

> There is an universal tendency among mankind to conceive all beings like themselves, and to transfer to every object, those qualities, with which they are familiarly acquainted, and of which they are intimately conscious. We find faces in the moon, armies in the clouds; and, by a natural propensity, if not corrected by experience and reflection, ascribe malice or good-will to every thing, that hurts or pleases us . . . trees, mountains and streams are personified, and the inanimate parts of nature acquire sentiment and passion. (1956[1757]:29)

For example, the Renaissance artist Michelangelo and Hollywood director Cecil B. DeMille both found God and goodness in the clouds, as did Old Testament Daniel (7:13) and New Testament Luke (21:27). By contrast, Julius Caesar's wife, Calpurnia, saw that "Fierce warriors fought upon the clouds" (Shakespeare, *Julius Caesar*, Act II, scene 2). Chinese villagers, too, regularly see certain malicious dragons with partly human features in particular types of cloud formations (Werner 1961 [1932]:xii).

Recently, numbers of devout American Catholics eyed the image of Mother Theresa in a cinnamon bun sold at a shop in Tennessee. Latinos in Houston prayed before a vision of the Virgin of Guadalupe, whereas Anglos saw only the dried remnants of melted ice cream on a pavement. Cuban exiles in Miami spotted the Virgin in windows, curtains, and television afterimages as long as there was hope of keeping young Elian Gonzalez from returning to godless Cuba. And on the day of the World Trade Center bombing, newspapers showed photos of smoke billowing from one of the towers that "seems to bring into focus the face of the Evil One, complete with beard and horns and malignant expression, symbolizing to many the hideous nature of the deed that wreaked horror and terror upon an unsuspecting city" ("Bedeviling: Did Satan Rear His Ugly Face?" *Philadelphia Daily News*, 14 September 2001).

In all these cases, there is culturally conditioned emotional priming in anticipation of agency. This priming, in turn, amplifies the information value (by reducing the signal: noise ratio) of otherwise doubtful, poor, and fragmentary agency-relevant stimuli. This enables the stimuli (e.g., cloud formations, pastry, ice cream conformations) to achieve the mimimal threshold for triggering the hyperactive facial recognition and body movement recognition devices that all human beings possess (save those with specific brain damage). This hair-trigger agency detector is evident, for example, in people's "automatic" reconstruction of three-dimensional full-face memories from very incomplete two-dimensional profiles (e.g., incomplete drawings, partial photographs), or in the illusion produced by a rotating mask: as the face of a mask rotates away (e.g., clockwise) from an onlooker, who now gazes on the mask's hollow back, the onlooker perceives a three-dimensional face emerging in the other direction (e.g., counterclockwise) from inside the back of the mask.

Our brains, it seems, are wired to spot lurkers (and to seek protectors) almost anywhere. People interactvely manipulate this hypersensible cognitive aptitude—or rather, the groupwide distribution of peoples' thoughts and actions causally sequence a series of firings—so as to create the agents who creatively order and unite the culture and cosmos. This gives the same order of meaning to all manner of existence, including one's own.

Such a prepared, or modularized, processing program would provide a rapid and economical reaction to a wide, but not unlimited, range of stimuli that would have been statistically associated with the presence of agents in ancestral hominid (and perhaps all higher primate) environments. Mistakes, or "false positives," would usually carry little cost, whereas a true response could provide the margin of survival (Seligman 1971). Thus, for the Carajá Indians of central Brazil, intimidating or unsure regions of the local ecology are religiously avoided: "The earth and underworld are inhabited by supernaturals. . . . There are two kinds. Many are amiable and beautiful beings who have friendly relations with humans. . . . The others are ugly and dangerous monsters who cannot be placated. Their woods are avoided and nobody fishes in their pools" (Lipkind 1940:249). Nearly identical descriptions of supernaturals can be found in ethnographic reports throughout the Americas, Africa, Eurasia, and Oceania.[8]

Arguably the most dangerous and deceptive predator for the genus Homo over a substantial portion of the past few million years has been Homo itself, which may have engaged in a spiraling behavioral and cognitive arms race of individual and group conflicts. According to evolutionary biologist Richard Alexander (1989), this "runaway social competition" led to larger groups of a nonkin sort that is absent from the rest of the animal world. Larger groups would greatly allay the threat from nonhominid predators, such as prides of wild felines and canids, and greatly enhance success in capturing nonhominid prey, such as large game. But as genetic ties weakened, large groups would also generate more and greater threats from defecting nonkin within and prod competitors to form even larger groups that would threaten from without. Given the ever-present menace of enemies within and without, concealment, deception, and the ability to both generate and recognize false beliefs in others would favor survival.

In potentially dangerous or uncertain circumstances, it would be best to anticipate and fear the worst of all likely possibilities: the presence of a deviously intelligent predator. How else, for example, could humans have managed to both constitute and survive such similar yet deadly competitive groups as the Nāga mountain tribes of Assam (northern India)?

> All the Nāga tribes are, on occasion, head-hunters, and shrink from no treachery in securing these ghastly trophies. Any head counts, be it that of a man, woman, or child, and entitles the man who takes it to wear certain ornaments according to the custom of the tribe or village. Most heads are taken . . . not in a fair fight, but by methods most treacherous. As common a method as any was for a man to lurk about the water Ghāt of a hostile village, and kill the first woman or child who came to draw water. Sometimes expeditions on large scales were made, several villages combining. . . . Every tribe, almost every village is at war with its neighbour, and no Nāga of these parts dare leave the territory of his tribe without the probability that his life will be the penalty. (Crooke 1907:41–43)

Recognizing the minor differences in dialect and tatoo marks among Nāga groups would alone hardly guarantee safety, especially against night infiltrators in disguise.

Throughout the world, societies cast their enemies as physically or mentally warped supernatural beings, or at least in league with the supernatural. Originally, *nāga* "applied to dreaded mountain tribes, and [was] subsequently used to designate monsters generally" (Werner 1961 [1932]:284). The dragons of ancient India (*nāga*) and their Chinese derivatives (*lung*) are often depicted as creatures half-human and half-animal who emerge from the clouds to wreak havoc on humankind.

In sum, humans *conceptually create* actual-domain entities and information to mimic and manipulate the natural input conditions of evolutionarily proper-domain entities and information (Sperber 1996). That is, they create *cultural domains* that ride piggyback on mental modules. Masks, makeup, Mickey Mouse, geometry, governments, gods, and so on are made by and for human beings. Because the phenomena created readily activate modular processes, they are more likely to survive transmission from mind to mind under a wide range of different environments and learning conditions than entities and information that are harder to process (Atran 1998, 2001b). As a result, they are more likely to become enduring aspects of human cultures, such as belief in the supernatural.

Another example from ethology offers a parallel. Many bird species have nests parasitized by members of other species. Thus, the cuckoo deposits its eggs in passerine nests, tricking the foster parents into incubating and feeding the cuckoo's young. Nestling European cuckoos often dwarf their host parents: "Consider the ludicrous site of a Garden Warbler . . . standing atop a cuckoo to reach the mouth of the gaping parasite. . . . The most rudimentary eyesight should suffice to show that something has gone seriously wrong with the normal parental process" (Hamilton and Orians 1965). How does the cuckoo manage to fool its otherwise visually acute host? According to Lack, "The young cuckoo, with its huge gape and loud begging call, has evidently evolved in exaggerated form the stimuli which elicit the feeding response of parent passerine birds. . . . This, like lipstick in the courtship of mankind, demonstrates successful exploitation by means of a 'super-stimulus'" (1968). Late nestling cuckoos have evolved perceptible signals to *manipulate* the passerine nervous system by initiating and then arresting or interrupting normal processing. In this way, cuckoos are able to subvert and co-opt the passerine's modularized survival mechanisms.

Humans, too, can have their innate releasing programs "fooled," as when people become sexually aroused by lines drawn on wood pulp or dots arranged on a computer screen, that is, pornographic pictures. Indeed, much of human culture, for better or worse, can be attributed to focused stimulations and manipulations of our species' innate proclivities. The soft drink and fast food industries manipulate our evolved but evolutionarily unconstrained likings for sweets and fats. Sweet and fatty foods (fruits and animals) are not easy to find in nature (which is why humans domesticated fruit-giving plants and edible animals). Natural selection gave us only the motivation to take what we could get. Now that we can get almost anything of this kind that we want, we have to learn to control our intake to prevent harm to ourselves, like having our teeth rot or arteries clogged. Art and medicine likewise involve stimulations and manipulations of our innate dispositions and susceptibilities for attention-arresting forms and feelings of pleasure and pain, but arguably to better ends.

In all cultures, supernatural agents are readily conjured up because natural selection has trip-wired cognitive schema for agency detection in the face of uncertainty. Uncertainty is, and likely will always be, ubiquitous. And so, too, the sort of hair-triggering of an agency-detection mechanism that readily lends itself to supernatural interpretation.

3.7. Attachment Theory: Are Deities but Parental Surrogates? The Devil They Are

> The crocodile be against him in the water, the snake be against him on land—(against) him who may do a thing to this (tomb). I never did a thing to him. It is the god [the image of a menacing snake] who will judge him.
>
> —Tomb-chapel inscription, 6th Dynasty mastaba of Meni, Giza, Egypt (ca. 2300 B.C.), cited in Patrick Houlihan, *The Animal World of the Pharaohs* (1996)

> The North Indian peasant considers that he is environed by a world of spirits which control all the conditions of his life. These spirits, as a rule, affect him more for evil than for good, and, as might be expected, those that are malignant in their nature require special

> propitiation, while those that are benevolent are accepted as normal, and receive only slight and infrequent worship.
>
> —W. Crooke, *Natives of North India* (1907)

Attachment theory is a competing theory about religion and the supernatural that weds psychoanalysis and Darwinism. It postulates an evolved motivational system designed by natural selection to maintain physical and psychological closeness between infants and parents (Bowlby 1969). The parent (or primary caregiver) is an attachment figure that functions as a refuge when the helpless infant senses danger, and as a safe and secure base for exploration of the environment in the absence of threat.

Recent studies by Lee Kirkpatrick (1997, 1998) are designed to support the claims of attachment theory. In one study, Kirkpatrick (1998) measured religious belief among students at the College of William and Mary during two academic years. Students rated adjectives, on a scale from 1 to 9, in terms of how well the adjective described God. Scores were averaged to create three scales: a Loving God scale (forgiving, caring, loving), a Controlling God scale (wrathful restricting, controlling), and a Distant God scale (distant, unavailable, impersonal). Students were also asked whether or not "you feel that you have a *personal relationship* with God?" Finally, students were asked to indicate whether "God is a living, personal being who is interested and involved in human affairs" or an abstract, impersonal, or nonexistent force in the universe.

In this study, students with positive self-models (secure and dismissing) were more religious than students with negative self-models (preoccupied and fearful). Students with negative self-models showed greater positive religious change than those with positive self-models. Students with positive models of others showed greater positive religious change than did those with negative self-models. The Loving God scale correlated strongly with mental models of the self: students with positive self-models tended to view God as loving and caring; students with positive models of others were more likely to believe in close personal relations with God and to believe that God is a living being interested in human affairs.

Kirkpatrick interprets these and other findings as confirmation of attachment theory. Thus, people who have negative self-models and who recall being in avoidant relationships with others as children are more prone to seek out God as an attachment figure (and undergo religious conversion). People with positive models of others see and seek God as an attachment figure with whom one can have a close personal relationship. In short, "the worshipper-God relationship more closely parallels the infant-mother relationship than does an adult romantic relationship" (Kirkpatrick 1997:972). This scenario is also consistent with psychoanalyst Erik Erikson's (1963) notion that God is the result of a search for mother love.

Although Kirkpatrick never identifies the cognitive processes that enable the evolved infant-mother paradigm to be extended to God concepts, a possible scenario is the following. The infant-mother paradigm may be considered a complex "innate releasing mechanism" of the sort discussed earlier (Tinbergen 1951). For example, a greylag gosling will follow the first adult goose it sees if the goose calls in response to the gosling's calls. This "imprinting" evolved to allow the gosling to attach itself to its genetic parent. However, the gosling will also initialize its innate "maternal recognition template" if a nongenetic relative or even a human is the first it sees that calls in response to the gosling's calls (Lorenz 1965b). Thus, any number of animals can fall within the actual domain of the gosling's maternal attachment module, although only its genetic parents fall under its proper domain.

Similarly, cultural manipulation of the actual domain of human maternal attachment would enable people to acquire God concepts that satisfy (trigger) minimal evolutionary requirements for bonding securely with a primary caregiver as well as social requirements for group bonding. In other words, notions of God would also engage manipulations of our innate faculties. The God concept would arise through culturally contrived stimulations of the evolved motivation faculty that directs emotions and behaviors toward infant-mother bonding. Presumably, this faculty emerged as naturally selected means of protecting the mother's offspring from predators and other natural threats, thus assuring reproduction and survival of the parents' (and species') genes.

There are a number of difficulties with attachment theory, and the evidence for it, some more critical than others. First, if religion is an extension of mother love, why do many societies mark religious initiation by violently rupturing childhood relations with the mother? Anthropologists Whiting, Kluckholn, and Anthony (1958) found that in societies were boys were closest to their mother (late weaning, sleeping with mother until puberty), male initiations were most severe. One might argue that such initiations serve to replace mother love with group devotion. In that case, argues Mary Douglas, "religion is not compensation," but replacement "by a fair representation of social reality": "Psychoanalysis takes account of a very restricted social field. It makes of parents and siblings the social framework into which all subsequent relationships are slotted. . . . But it is difficult to extend its categories in a controlled way to the wider experience of society" (1973:110–111; cf. Durkheim 1995[1912]; Evans-Pritchard 1965). Moreover, *all* psychoanalytic explanations of religion in terms of deprivation projection (mother, father, sibling, family, superego, love partner, group, etc.) fail to account for the specificity of religion. These same "mechanisms" of compensation also figure in psychoanalytic accounts of many types of "normal" (e.g., Oedipal) and "abnormal" (e.g., hysterical) behaviors that have nothing especially to do with religion.

Second, Kirkpatrick (1998) reports that female subjects are reliably more prone than male subjects to consider God to be loving and to see themselves as having a close personal relationship with God. Other attachment-like theories, such as Freud's, have "God . . . in every case modelled after the father," a more distant and authoritarian figure (1955[1913]). These differences in attachment style may simply reflect differences in the social times or milieux. In Freud's Vienna, the father occupied the dominant parental role, as he still may in much of the Western world (Foster and Keating 1992). For William and Mary College students, especially the females, Mom has the role. In both cases, God is identified with the primary caregiver, which is still consistent with attachment theory. Thus, according to anthropologist Meyer Fortes (1959:78), African Tallensi religion is an "extrapolation" of parent-offspring relations.[9] In this vein, Vergote (1969), who studied Catholics in Belgium, argued that children before ages 5 to 7 cannot distinguish between God and parents of whatever gender.

More recent experiments indicate that the idea of deities as surrogate parents is overgeneralized and, at least from the standpoint of folkpsychology, wrong. For example, in false-belief tasks, J. Barrett, Richert, and Driesenga (2001) found that 3- to 4-year-old children attributed true beliefs to God, mother, bear, ant, elephant, snake, and tree, whereas the majority of 5- to 6-year-olds attributed true beliefs only to God. In a perspective-taking task (where the contents of a box are partially occluded on initial observation and subsequently revealed on later inspection), most 3- to 4-year-olds responded that God, a girl named Maggie, a monkey, and a special kitty with night vision could see the occluded contents of the box. For the majority of children 4 to 5 and 6 to 8, only God and the special kitty would be able to see the hidden contents. The older children do not consider infallible beliefs and special night vision to be properties of ordinary human agents; hence, it is difficult to argue that understanding infallible nonhuman agents, like God, and special nonhuman agents, like the kitty, are based entirely on projections from parents in particular or personification or anthropomorphism in general (contra Piaget 1969). Other experiments also indicate that young children distinguish God from people in thinking that God primarily creates natural objects (sky, rocks, animals, people), wheareas people make artifacts (Petrovich 1988, cited in Beit-Hallahmi and Argyle 1997:147; Evans 2001).

In a recent study of Yukatek Mayan speakers in Quintana Roo, Mexico, N. Knight et al. (2001) found that children's attributions of false beliefs reliably increase from God to lesser supernatural beings to people. Children ages 4 to 7 were shown a familiar container for tortillas and told: "Usually tortillas are inside this box, but I ate them and put these shorts inside." After the box was closed, the children were pretested in their home for their knowledge of its present contents. The experimenter then asked every child a set of randomly ordered questions about what each of the following beings who entered the child's house would think was in the box: a person (*winik*, represented by a doll), God (the Christian *dyoos*), the sun (*k'in*), the principal forest spirits (*yumil k'ax'ob'*, "Masters of the Forest"), and other minor spirits (*chiichi'*). In line with the American children in the J. Barrett (2001) study, the youngest Yukatek children (4-year-olds) overwhelmingly attribute true beliefs to both God and people in equal measure (including mothers); after age 5, the children attribute mostly false beliefs to people but continue to attribute mostly true beliefs to God (Figure 3.1). Note that figure 3.1 indicates that beliefs about people cannot be the basis for beliefs about God because the developmental trajectories of these two sets of beliefs diverge significantly from the outset. Beliefs about God are statistically flat across age groups, whereas beliefs about people change (ANOVA, $F(1,44)=6.51, p=.01$).

This study is one of very few cross-cultural replications of "theory of mind" claims about false belief. A novel finding was that Yukatek children from age 5 on attribute true beliefs according to a supernatural hierarchy, with God at the top, followed by the sun and principal forest spirits, then minor spirits, and finally people (Figure 3.2). For pre-Columbian Maya, the sun was the most venerated cosmic body, and the Sun Priest (Aj K'in) was the chief religious official. Our other studies show that Yukatek children believe that God, the sun, spirits, and people "are alive" (*kukuxtal*), but that only people "die" (*kukimil*; see Atran et al. 2001). As with Itza' Maya, the Yukatek villagers still consider the Forest Masters to be pow-

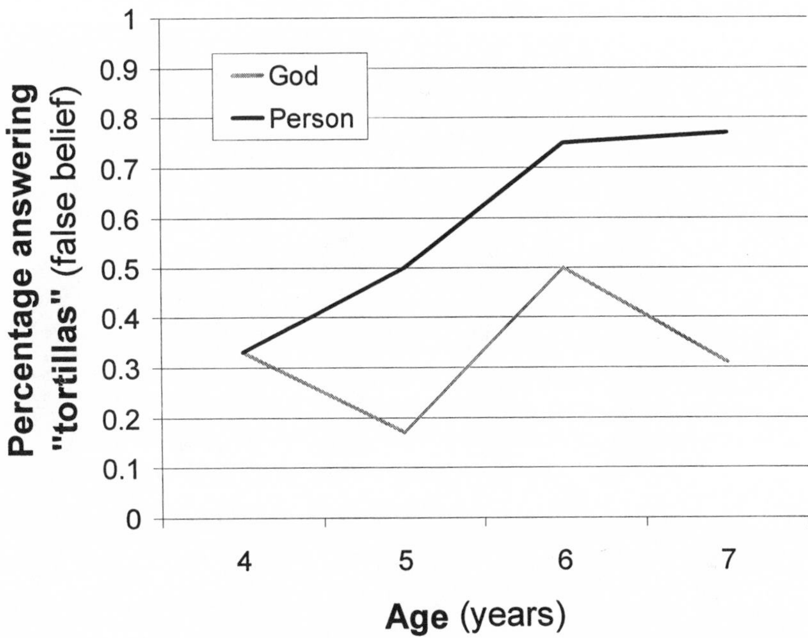

Figure 3.1. Percentage of Yukatek Maya children's attributions of false beliefs to God and persons by age.

erful and knowledgeable spirits who are able to monitor and punish people who try to "deceive" and exploit forest species. These beliefs have reliably measurable behavioral consequences for biodiversity, forest sustainability, and so forth (Atran et al. 2002, see section 8.10).

A third, and equally serious, objection to attachment theory is that social interactions with parents are customarily very different from social interactions with deities. With parents, children usually practice a form of "communal sharing" that does not involve "equality-matching" negotiations over terms for reciprocity or tit-for-tat exchanges (Fiske and Tetlock 1997): a child usually doesn't give thanks or sacrifices to his or her mother for a meal, and neither does a mother petition or give offerings to a child for a kiss. In most societies and times, most deities require materially measured sacrifices and offerings. Worship often involves an "authoritarian ranking" relationship (e.g., when a superior gives you a present, you render deference or respect, not reciprocity or payment in kind) or even a "market-pricing" relationship (e.g., as when you pay money for a service or good). Such relationships typically characterize people's social interactions with nonparents: "gifts, petitions, thanks, submission of body," payments, and so on (Hobbes 1901[1651]: 69–70).

A fourth critical difficulty for attachment theory is that supernatural deities can be just as menacing as they can be protective. Among the pre-Columbian Maya and Mexicans, for example, there appears to have been no entirely benevolent deity, and all were feared (to greater or lesser degrees) for their ability to bring death on almost anyone, almost anywhere. The primary Lowland Maya deity was the fearsome male thunder god Chaak, whose emissaries were the jaguar and the

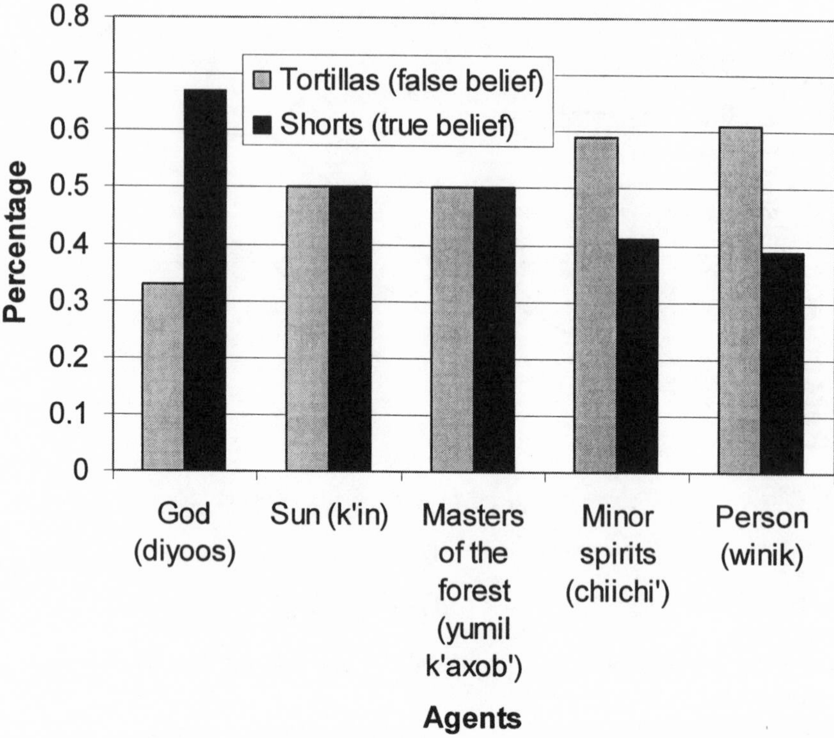

Figure 3.2. Percentage of responses by all age groups of Yukatek Maya children's attribution of false beliefs or true beliefs to persons and various supernatural agents.

tropical rattlesnake. The dominant Toltec god was Quetzalcoatl ("feathered serpent"). Both deities required frequent and bloody human sacrifice, which involved opening the victim's chest cavity with an obsidian knife and ripping out the beating heart. Moreover, even protector deities may altogether lack endearing or affectionate qualities. For example, the Egyptian scorpion goddess, Selket, the "protector" who guarded tombs, is always represented menacingly with her dangerous tail upraised.

For the rural peoples of south India, the primary village deities are goddesses of variable character: "The villagers do not regard them as evil spirits, but neither do they regard them as unmixed benefactors. They are rather looked upon as beings of uncertain temper" (Whitehead 1988[1921]:30–32). Chief among the goddesses in many villages is "Mahakāli, i.e., great Kāli . . . a deity of furious temper, and . . . the cause of the prevalence of cholera. . . . The people worship her to avoid falling victims to her unquenchable anger, since her main object is said to be to devour and consume everthing that comes in her way. She is said especially to have a great relish for bones! Kāli is often regarded as especially the protectress against evil spirits that haunt forests and desolate places, and against wild beasts" (30–32). As with the primary Maya deity, Chaak, India's Kāli is both a bloodthirsty destroyer and defender against destruction, a beastly predator and protector against beasts and monsters, a disease carrier and safeguard against diseases, a keeper of one's own group and despoiler of other groups. She is often depicted with a black face and hideous expression, her lips dripping blood and her neck encircled with snakes, skulls, and heads of human victims. As a village deity, she demands the sacrifice and slaughter of many animals, despite mainstream Hinduism's doctrine of nonviolence toward all living things, or *ahimsa*.[10]

The dominant deities of the pre-Columbian Maya and Mexicans, like those of pre-Aryan India and contemporary south India's Tamil villagers and tribal peoples (*adivāsis*) and the avenging God of radical Islamists and certain Christian and Jewish fundamentalists, may symbolize many things, but not your typical (Mesoamerican or Subcontinental) Mom or Pop.[11] A Mom-like figure may be a particularly good God candidate in modern North America, where women have acquired sustained economic and political authority for the first time in human history and where expressions of "I love you" and "self-esteem" prevail even in commercial advertising. But it is doubtful that like conditions applied in the Pleistocene, when natural selection for a parental paradigm presumably took place.

Snake worship is at least as culturally widespread and historically deep in human religion as is the worship of personalized family or group deities. Even in the great monotheistic religions—Judaism, Christianity, Islam—the snake appears as Satan, the primary Other God, and often becomes a cult object in more radical monotheistic sects (Gerrard 1968). In part, this may be because humans and other primates have specially evolved predator detectors that are dedicated to snake avoidance (Mineka et al. 1984; Marks 1987). Once targeted, snake behavior, such as molting, becomes a privileged focus of attention for thinking about death and rebirth, resurrection, or reincarnation (Henderson and Oakes 1990). Ancient China, India, the Middle East, and Mesoamerica similarly worshipped deadly serpents and serpent-men who especially lurked in forbidding mountains, deserts, and forests; so, too, did chiefdoms in subsaharan Africa and aboriginal Australia (Munkur 1983). They are often equal with, or superior to, a society's more beneficent deities, for example, Apophis, the embodiment of evil and the implacable enemy of Ra, the Egyptian sun god.

The evolutionary imperative to look out for predators, such as poisonous snakes, ferocious beasts, and, especially, dangerously deceptive humans, breeds ubiquitous cognitions of supernatural demons, demiurges, devils, ghouls, goblins, vampires, and other more or less overtly rapacious agents. Chinese, Japanese, Hindus, Assyrians, and Babylonians worshipped dragons, whereas Medieval Europeans looked to God, saints, and angels to ward them off. Judaism, Christianity, and Islam again needed God to fend off this primal danger.

In many, if not all, societies religious expressions of supernatural beings include monsters, that is, physically incongruous beings that counterfactually exaggerate or recompose human physiognomy, such as the pointed-ear Devil or the many-limbed Kāli. More often than not, supernatural monsters have characteristic features of animal predators, such as fangs, large canines, hooked beaks, claws, and other means of tearing and consuming flesh, like the reptilian World God of the Maya, Itzam Na'. Caves, caverns, cliffs, pits, sinkholes, deep bodies of water, and so forth are often represented in the world's religions as the gaping mouths of monstrous gods to whom sacrifice must be made. This characterizes the Great Cenote at Chichen Itza in Yucatan (Tozzer 1957) where Chaak gave rain for blood, just as it does in the ancient Fertile Crescent where Moloch and other terrible deities also extorted their human due: "The yawning gap is a memorable projection of anxiety, linked to the image of devouring jaws. One person must be swallowed to save the rest. . . . Anxiety is removed and normalcy secured by way of a specific payment" (Burkert 1996:52). Medieval Europe abounds with religious representations of cannabalistic monsters devouring sinners on Judgment Day (e.g., the writings of Dante and the paintings of Heironymous Bosch).

Although these predator monsters attempt to lure and deceive, believers generally think it difficult to deceive them in return. In many, if not most or all religions, one and the same deity can be both protector and destroyer of oneself as well as others. The Jewish God Almighty doesn't refrain from killing Jews, neither did the ancient Middle Eastern deities Baal and Moloch shrink from devouring the people they protected. The Hindi deity Shiva destroys those he brings to life, as did the ancient Maya deity Itzam Na'.

In sum, it is not an infant-mother, infant-father, or infant-family template per se from which God concepts extend, but a more encompassing *evolutionary program for avoiding and tracking predators and prey*. It is *an innate module for detecting agency and intention, whether good or bad*. Moreover, unlike the actual world of nature, in religion's counterfactual and counterintuitive worlds one and the same deity can have the dual role of predator and protector, or prey and protector. These may well be humankind's most popular deities.

3.8. Summary: Supernatural Agency Is an Evolutionary By-product, Trip-Wired by Predator-Protector-Prey Detection Schema

Supernatural agent concepts critically involve minimal triggering of evolved agency-detection schema, a part of folkpsychology. Agency is a complex sort of "innate releasing mechanism." Natural selection designed the agency-detector system to deal rapidly and economically with stimulus situations involving people and animals as predators, protectors, and prey. This resulted in the system's being trip-wired to respond to fragmentary information under conditions of uncertainty, inciting perception of figures in the clouds, voices in the wind, lurking movements in the leaves, and emotions among interacting dots on a computer screen. This hair-triggering of the agency-detection mechanism readily lends itself to supernatural interpretation of uncertain or anxiety-provoking events.

People interactively manipulate this universal cognitive susceptibility so as to scare or soothe themselves and others for varied ends. They do so consciously or unconsciously and in causally complex and distributed ways, in pursuit of war or love, to thwart calamity or renew serendipity, or to otherwise control or incite imagination. The result provides a united and ordered sense for cosmic, cultural, and personal existence.

Souls and spirits, which derive much of their inductive force from analogy to the dissociated thoughts of dreams and the disembodied movements of shadows, are near universal candidates for cultural manipulation and elaboration. There is much cross-cultural convergence in the religious realization of souls, spirits, dreams, and shadows for two reasons. First, they readily lend themselves to common thematic associations (e.g., with the moon, night predators, dark caves, death, disease; or inversely, with the sun, songbirds, light, open spaces, reason, health, life). These psychologically ubiquitous thematic co-occurrences account for much convergence in thematic content of religious beliefs across cultures. Second, dreamlike souls and shadow spirits systematically violate innate and modularized expectations about object movements (folkmechanics), essential kinds (folkbiology), and the intentional nature of agents (folkpsychology). This provides the structural framework to which all contents may be attached, whether those contents are general and thematic or particular and episodic. Within this framework of systematically violated innate expectations, *any* beliefs so structured will be inherently attention-arresting, memorable, and everywhere culturally transmissible. (There will be much more to say about this in Part II.)

Attachment theory also proposes an evolved motivational system designed by natural selection to produce supernatural beings. Such beings allegedly come to mind to recover something of the physical and psychological intimacy between the infant and parents who provide care. But recent experiments indicate that young children's beliefs about God differ appreciably from beliefs about parents and other persons. People's interactions with deities also manifest asymmetrical forms of reciprocity, unlike the kind of sharing that typically takes place among family members. Finally, the evolutionary imperative to detect rapacious agents favors emergence of malevolent deities in every culture. Worship of serpent deities and would-be destroyers is at least as prevalent as God the Father and mother goddesses.

PART 2

Absurd Commitments

Holy scripture cannot err and the decrees therein contained are absolutely true and inviolable. I should have only added that, though Scripture cannot err, its expounders and interpreters are liable to err in many ways . . . when they would base themselves always on the literal meaning of the words. For in this wise not only many contradictions would be apparent, but even grave heresies and blasphemies, since then it would be necessary to give God hands and feet and eyes, and human bodily emotions such as anger, regret, hatred, and sometimes forgetfulness of things past, and ignorance of the future.

—Galileo Galilei, letter to Benedetto Castelli, 21 December 1613, in Dava Sobel, *Galileo's Daughter* (2000)

And, for the matter or substance of invisible agents so fancied, they could not by natural cogitation fall upon any other conceit, but that . . . the soul of man was of the same substance with that which appeareth in a dream to one who sleepeth . . . which, men . . . think them to be real and external substances, and therefore call them ghosts; as the Latins called them *imagines* and *umbrae*, and thought them spirits, that is thin aerial bodies, and those invisible agents which they feared to be like them, save that they appear and vanish when they please. But the opinion that such spirits were incorporeal, or material, could never enter into the mind of any man by nature, because, though men may put together words of contradictory significance, as "spirit" and "incorporeal," yet they can never have the imagination of anything answering to them; and therefore men that by their own meditation arrive to the acknowledgement of . . . God chose rather to confess that He is incomprehensible and beyond their understanding. . . . [F]or the worship which naturally men exhibit to powers invisible, it can be no other but such expressions of their reverence, as they would use towards men; gifts, petitions, thanks, submission of body, considerate addresses, sober behaviour, premeditated words, swearing, that is assuring one another of their promises by invoking them. Beyond that, reason suggesteth nothing.

—Thomas Hobbes, *Leviathan* (1901[1651])

Ivan Fyodorich . . . solemnly declared . . . that there was nothing in the whole world to make men love their neighbours . . . and that, if there had been any love on earth hitherto, it was not owing to natural law, but simply because men believed in immortality. . . . [T]he whole natural law lies in faith. . . . He ended by asserting that for every individual . . . who does not believe in God or immortality, the moral law of nature must immediately be changed into the contrary of the former religious law, and that egoism, even to crime, must become, not only lawful but even recognised as the inevitable, the most rational, even honourable outcome.

—Fyodor Dostoyevsky, *The Brothers Karamazov* (1880)

4 Counterintuitive Worlds

The Mostly Mundane Nature of Religious Belief

Religious traditions do not consist of cultural "worldviews," "theories," "systems," "codes," "grammars," or any such determinate structures. The beliefs current in religious doctrine and liturgy consist of logically unintegrated counterintuitions and anecdotal episodes that evoke a much richer substrate of everyday, commonsense beliefs. These commonsense beliefs, which are usually readily available to everyone, remain implicit and are rarely articulated. Transmission and survival of religious creed and ritual depends, for the most part, on the facility with which explicit religious beliefs and practices are able to elicit, and render relevant, underlying commonsense beliefs.

Fully developed cognitions of folkpsychology and agency involve metarepresentation, which makes deception possible. This threatens social order. But these same metacognitive capacities provide the hope and promise of open-ended solutions through representations of counterintuitive supernatural worlds that cannot be logically or empirically verified or falsified.

Core religious beliefs minimally violate ordinary intuitions about how the world is, with all of its inescapable problems, thus enabling people to imagine minimally impossible worlds that appear to solve existential problems, including death and deception. The dual aspect of supernatural beliefs—commonsensical and counterfactual—renders them intuitively compelling yet fantastic, eminently recognizable but surprising. Such beliefs grab attention, activate intuition, and mobilize inference in ways that greatly facilitate their mnemonic retention, social transmission, cultural selection, and historical survival.

4.1. Natural and Supernatural Causality

The angels stopp'd their ears and died their pinions;
The devils ran howling, deafn'd down to hell;

> The ghosts fled, gibbering, for their own dominions—
> (For 'tis not yet decided where they dwell,
> And I leave every man to his opinions).
>
> —Lord Byron, "The Vision of Judgement" (1998[1812])

There is a long-standing claim on the "relativist" side of anthropology, psychology, and the philosophy and history of science to the effect that people who live in "traditional" cultures—where magic, myth, and religion are interdependent and socially prominent—live in conceptual worlds that are profoundly and incommensurably different from our own world (and each other's worlds). I believe this claim is mistaken in light of the following facts:

1. There is considerable recurrence of symbolic content across historically isolated cultures (e.g., incorporeal spirits, immortal beings, monstrous species hybrids, metamorphosis and reincarnation, animated substances, etc.).
2. This recurrence owes chiefly to universal cognitive mechanisms that process cultural input (information) in ways that are variously triggered but subsequently unaffected by the nature of that input (e.g., spirits and immortals are not mindless, and so have memories, beliefs, desires, sufferings, etc.).
3. These universal mechanisms are the very same core set of cognitive modules that are responsible for the sorts of factual, commonsense beliefs about the everyday world that are intuitively obvious to everyone (folkmechanics, folkbiology, folkpsychology, etc.).

As for supernatural beliefs:

4. They are just as counterintuitive for the people who think them true as for those who think them false (e.g., wine as the blood of Christ, a wafer as His body).
5. People who believe such counterintuitive beliefs to be true do so by ritually proscribing situations of conflict with intuitively mundane beliefs (e.g., devout Catholics aren't routinely cannibals); such people routinely invoke nonconflictual aspects of intuitive belief systems to give mundane content to "impossible worlds" (e.g., God is everywhere but likely not in the trash, and He ought to behave like a good family man, except in bed).

The most striking support for cultural relativism is thought to come from those "primitive," "exotic," or "traditional" societies where, from a Western standpoint, natural and supernatural phenomena are so seemingly intermeshed that the people in those societies just live in "another world." Consider, for example, the sorts of "symbolic propositions" typically stated by Itza' Maya speakers and recorded in my field notes:

I. The sorcerer (*ajwaay*) transformed himself (*tusutk'esaj ub'aj*) into a dog (*ti pek'*). The *waay* makes bad sickness (***kumentik k'ak'as ko-***

ja'anil) and steals (*uyoklik*) one's soul (*uyool*). You need a *waay* to catch and kill a *waay*. I remember a *waay* who turned into a pig (*k'eke'n*) and another into a small gekko (*chib'il'b'o'oy* = "shadow biter"), but all the other sorcerers I heard about turned into village animals (*b'a'alche'il kaj*) to be near the [victim's] house.

II. A person (*kristyaanoj*) ensouls (*kutz'ik uyool*) a house (*ti naj*) and the house has a soul (*yan uyool*). A person can ensoul (*patal utz'ik uyool*) what he makes (*ta' b'a'ax kumentikej* = artifacts). A bad wind (*k'ak'as ik'*) brings sickness and takes its soul. Then you need a curer (*aj pul yaj*) to make a sacrifice (*sakrifiisioj*) with incense (*pom* = copal resin).

III. Some persons (*kristyaanojoo'*), the Kanté family (*ajk'änte'*), they say their name is howler monkey (*ajb'aatz'*) because they were howler monkeys before; the spider monkey (*ajtuuchaj*) is Tesukun (another family).

IV. One animate wood fairy (*juntuul arux*), it follows you into the forest (*ti k'aax*). Sometimes you can feel it because it comes as the possessor of the wind (*uyumil ik'*). Sometimes you can tell it's there because it turns itself into a small child (*mo'nok paal*). But once it stole my moccasins just before I caught a glimpse of it. You have to catch it before it turns to wind. . . . Now when an *arux* comes all you have to do is turn on a radio. They hate listening to radios. You don't see them much in the forest anymore. They don't like [newcomers] who are felling the forest.

V. One round *sastun* (*junkuul sastun*), you can hear it whirl as it flies by. I saw one on the table in [a curer's house]: a clear stone, you can see things in it like in your thing [pointing to my computer]. It flies when it's looking for a curer who will treat it well, bathe it in "strong water" [*yek' ja'* = drinking alcohol]. Once the *sastun* came to a curer but left the next day. The curer looks into the *sastun* to see if a sick person will live or die, seeing the way lines lie [that form in the clear center]. It can tell who stole your pig. Nobody, not even a curer, can ever find the *sastun*; it finds you.

VI. The fer-de-lance and its companions (*uyet'ok k'ok'o*, i.e., vipers, coral snakes, and other snakes considered poisonous), only deaf people can see their feet. When a *k'ok'o* gets old (*chämach kujok'ol*), it opens up the earth (*kujenkesik a' lu'um*), sprouts horns (*kuch'iil ukaachoj*) and has wings also (*yan uxik' xan*), two more heads (*maas kap'el upol*), and flies to East (*tak ti chik'in*) to the sea (*ti k'ak naab'*) with its [human] prey.

Itza' clearly believe what they say here is true. We, just as clearly, cannot believe what they say here is true. Although we may try to translate what they say in terms that make some factual sense to us, it is unlikely that any factual sense we make out of what they say would make relevant sense to them. For if such statements do represent commonsense facts for the Itza', then obviously their ways of deciding what the facts are differ significantly from ours. And if such statements don't represent commonsense facts for the Itza', then our giving them some factual sense misses the point. From the foregoing we might conclude that we and the Itza' just live in conceptually different everyday worlds. That people abide such apparently different worlds may, in turn, be taken as support for the flexibility of the human mind, that is, a mind unconstrained by cognitive structures that are evolved and task-specific or innately determined and content-constraining. But this conclusion is wrong.

If it were true that we and the Itza' live in profoundly different conceptual worlds, then how could the anthropologist ever become aware of this? We can observe, say, goldfish and infer from their behavior that it is not likely motivated by the same conceptual structures that motivate our own behavior. But we cannot as easily infer how *different* goldfish conceptual structures are from our own, or even what conceptual structures, if any, they might have.

By contrast, anthropologists seeking to demonstrate deep cultural differences invariably do so by attempting to show how curious native life is in terms of, for example:

> joking, punning, metaphor, irony, gossip, lying, insult, skepticism, storytelling, betting, marriage, cooking recipes, folkbiology, ways of counting, solar and lunar time reckoning, litigation, gift exchange, etiquette, hospitality, feasting, mourning, interpretation of dreams, sex and food taboos, negotiation, morality, crime, punishment, navigation plans, landscape mapping, medicine, nosology, disaster-relief routines, common-defense policy, food-sharing obligations, kin reckoning, property rights, residency rights, politics, song, dance, architecture, deceit, conceit, pride, and so on.

These analytic categories and many more that are used to show difference may themselves be universal or near universal (cf. D. Brown 1991). Hedges to the effect that the natives do not "mean" what we "mean" about something requires at least some overlap in what we both mean (i.e., local commensurability).

If not for this common "something" it would be inconceivable that an anthropologist would be able to penetrate the "worldview" of a native group in the year or two it usually takes to do so (about the same time it takes an infant to "learn" a language). This is not to say that the anthropologist learns all there is to know about the native culture (indeed, neither the anthropologist nor the native may ever learn all there is to know about their own respective cultures). But even the dullest anthropologist quickly intuits that, in most respects, the native thinks pretty much like the anthropologist. Because this fact is intuited so rapidly and effortlessly, the anthropologist is then able to leisurely search for the profound "differences" that will earn a dissertation, tenure, or renown as "the Sorcerer's Apprentice."

The notion that people in different cultures live in different conceptual worlds is rooted in a false premise, namely, that people process symbolic beliefs in the same way that they process commonsense beliefs and therefore don't recognize a principled distinction between intuitive and counterintuitive beliefs. There are two objections to this premise. First, if symbolic beliefs were processed in the same way as commonsense beliefs, then the former would invariably contradict the latter. Second, magical, mythical, and religious beliefs are as counterintuitive for the people who hold and transmit them as they seem to us.

If symbolic beliefs were processed just like beliefs of brute fact, then any conclusion would logically follow from any belief because people would assent to blatantly contradictory facts. Consequently, any systematic intentional behavior, much less any systematic knowledge, would be unimaginable. Suppose, for example, that Itza' held stories I–VI above to be true states of affairs in the same way that they hold the following to be true states of affairs:

i. Humans and animals belong to mutually exclusive commonsense ontological domains, whose respective members behave in accordance with distinctive causal schema. For example, only humans usually behave in accordance with embedded beliefs and desires, so that animals cannot intentionally *plan* a person's sickness or death. Moreover, members of one animal species, such as pigs, can't just transform themselves into members of another species.
ii. Humans and artifacts belong to different ontological domains. For example, houses do not live and therefore cannot get sick.
iii. Same as i.
iv. Animate beings and inert, nonsolid physical phenomena belong to different ontological domains. For example, stones are not sensate and therefore cannot fear the sound of a radio or just get up and run away.
v. Inert solid objects, animate beings that can fly by themselves, and entities with minds belong to different ontological domains. For example, inert solid objects can't defy gravity, remember things, or have beliefs, desires, and knowledge.
vi. Winged creatures that fly (*ch'iich'* = bats and birds save chickens) and snakes (*kan*) belong to mutually exclusive folkbiological taxonomies, whose respective members behave in accordance with uniquely distinct underlying causal essences. For example, snakes can displace themselves over long distances only when the full length of their body is in contact with a hard surface. Birds run on two legs or fly.

Anyone processing beliefs I–VI and i–vi in the same register should suspect that someone eating a pork chop might be a cannibal, expect healthy houses to give birth to little houses, believe that animal species can interbreed as indiscriminately as people can mate, turn on the radio to stop the wind from spreading fire, avoid provoking rocks that could fly up and strike you dead, look for flocks of snakes flying in from the East but not the West.

Not only is there no evidence that Itza' behave in accordance with a defective or alternative rationality in going about their daily affairs, but there seems to be a cross-cultural method to the apparent madness of their symbolic beliefs. Thus, Itza' *waay* have many of the characteristics of sorcerers, witches, and shamans the world over, including a capacity and desire to do evil in animal guise. Itza' "ensoul" some of their more important artifacts much as other "traditional" peoples do, like the native folk of West Futuna-Aniwa in Polynesia (Keller and Lehman 1993). Itza' association of families to animal species is likely a vestige of totemism, which was common among the historical Maya and widespread over all the Earth's habitable continents. Itza' *arux* have many of the same characteristics of Irish elves and Russian wood fairies. The Itza' *sastun*, which is rooted in pre-Columbian tradition, has many of the same features as the Arabic *tilasm* (talisman, or crystal ball). The Itza' story of flying serpents, which is related to the pre-Columbian "feathered serpent" cults of *quetzalcoatl* (Toltec) and *kukulkan* (Maya), has many similar or inverted aspects of the Ancient Egyptian myth of the phoenix. If we reject the unlikely possibility that these thematic recurrences stem from historical contact and diffusion or are spontaneous instantiations of a Platonistic set of innate religious forms (e.g., Jungian archetypes), then how else could such apparent recurrences independently take place across cultures without specific and strong universal cognitive constraints?

4.2. Mythical Episodes

Public expressions of supernatural beliefs rarely, if ever, take the form of generalized or universally quantified statements, such as "God reasons," "All spirits fly," and "Every frog turns into a prince." Instead, supernatural phenomena are usually embedded in explicitly contextualized episodes; for example, "The *arux* [an Itza' Maya forest spirit] came as a child to steal my moccasins but disappeared as a gust of wind before I could catch it." Such personalized instances suffice to generate an anticipation in anyone hearing the story that *all* such imaginary entities are ethereal, elflike tricksters. This expectation, in turn, activates the interlocutor's specific intuitive schemas about wind behavior, child behavior, and cheating behavior, as well as more general causal schema associated with basic conceptual domains: solid and nonsolid physical substances, nonhuman living kinds and persons, and social life (contractual obligations for cooperative behavior).

These singular events personalize the phenomena so as to enhance their memorability (Tulving 1983). In so doing, they also provide specific contextual scripts that other people can alter or embellish, thus enhancing transmissibility (Abelson 1981). Such episodes balance and optimize the personal and social relevance of the information by flexibly accommodating idiosyncratic requirements of individual understanding to the more general requirements of fable and folklore (Bartlett 1932). A good myth, then, must be open to variant readings, which allows speakers and hearers to best fit their personal experiences into the story's episodes (cf. Bruner 1990: chap. 2).

In preliterate societies, which do not have the option of storing their accumulated knowledge and history in an indefinitely expandable public repository of information, this cognitive negotiation between the requirements of personal and social relevance is crucial to the cultural survival of "collective memory" in myth. As Claude Lévi-Strauss (1969[1964], 1971) illustrates in his multivolume *Mythologiques*, the aboriginal myths of the Americas are structured so as to interrelate cosmic happenings, local environments, social requirements, and so on to personal memories in ways that optimize their mutual saliency and redundancy for a given population. Because conditions of optimal cognitive salience change from population to population and environment to environment, the myths of any one native group undergo more or less profound structural transformations in the way information is organized and content selected as the myths are diffused to other groups.

Nevertheless, Lévi-Strauss is able to show that the myths of Alaskan and Amazonian tribes share not only certain recurrent themes but also predictable patterns of transformation. These predictable patterns follow the lines of differences between indigenous populations and their environments as observed by anthropologists or gleaned from the historical record (following European contact), for example, differences in kin reckoning, residency arrangements, architecture, hunting strategies, species distributions of local fauna and flora, and the patterns of seasons and the night sky at various latitudes. Although Lévi-Strauss pays little attention to the actual operation of psychological processes, his magnum opus is tantamount to a cognitive history of the prehistorical Americas.

Like most other anthropologists, Lévi-Strauss's own approach is "interpretive" rather than cognitive, in that it describes generalized "meanings," or "themes," in terms of synthetically broad, culture-wide categories, such as "kinship," "religion," "myth," and "politics." For the cognitive anthropologist, such synthetic categories reflect important regularities in the distribution of representations, but they tell us little about the material processes whereby minds in their physical environment actually produce these distributions. Interpretive categories help cognitive anthropologists to focus their research by targeting the end-products of a complex causal story of information processing, communication, and transformation that is yet to be told.

Unlike Europe's written folktales or fables—which may be the "frozen" vestiges of myths outworn—the public content of a myth changes at each telling through a dynamic process of cognitive negotiation between teller(s) and audience. Such "collective memories" or "cultural representations" are never fixed once and for all even within a population, but constitute a more or less loosely connected (fuzzy) set of public representations that share and evoke informational content only in a "family resemblance" sort of way. In this sense, myths are more typical of cultural representations generally than the fixed representations that popular conceptions of culture focus on.

4.3. Cultural Representations

Consider the rather mundane cultural representation of health care in the United States today. Many people have very many thoughts about health care, whereas others have few or none. The overwhelming majority of the mental representations produced by the many minds that think about health care never become public. Only a small fraction of what people are actually thinking about health care is ever communicated from one person to another. The overwhelming majority of the public representations, in turn, never become culturally widespread. For example, frequent discussion of the issue among family members rarely gets beyond the dinner table. By contrast, when the President of the United States or candidates for the presidency utter something about health care, a small portion of his public representation (i.e., a portion that can fit into an average eight-second "sound bite") is communicated to millions of people on the evening television news.

Television commentators and other media "experts" (doctors, politicians, insurance executives, etc.) give their own rendition of the President's public representation, which almost invariably changes the content of the original representation. These variously altered versions then elicit "comment" and inevitable alteration. Parts of these versions are then mentally represented by television listeners who, in turn, "automatically" alter the information content to make it personally relevant.

These personally relevant versions are, in their turn, uttered, discussed, and transformed as public representations (cf. Sperber 1996). Some of these do get beyond the dinner table and eventually find their way after innumerable other transformations to the media commentators, experts, and even the president. The president may then internally revise, and publicly express, yet a different version of health care, and so on. Notice that the flow of information is conditioned by certain "ecological" aspects of the culture that constrain interactions between public representations, for example, the dinner table and the sound bite, themselves the complex causal products of social history.

Meanwhile, the communication media intone with the oxymoron that nobody seems to know exactly what health care is "all about," although almost everybody seems to think it is "about something" that is socially relevant. This, of course, is how most cultural representations actually manifest themselves. But the media's message is that the time has come for politicians, experts, and "the public" to sum up their cognitive negotiations on the issue of health care and decide on a policy written into law.

Policies and laws are established as parts of cultural *institutions*. Institutions are physically constituted public mechanisms, which are variously composed of selected "ecological" features of the cultural environment, such as police batons, jails, parliamentary buildings, archives, and other cultural representations. Institutions—whether political, religious, or scientific—serve the cognitive function of providing conduits for sequencing the flow and interpretation of information through what may be indefinitely many versions of "a" (or "a set" of) cultural representation(s).

Religious institutions usually embrace *ritual* displays of information. Religious ritual displays serve both to ensure activation of intuitive beliefs and to restrict them to more or less definite contextual frames for imagining the supernatural: the public display of supernatural episodes in ritualized ceremonies. Anthropologists have interpreted the "social function" of such ceremonies as creating a "liminal space" between the natural and supernatural realms (Leach 1976). Here, select persons (priests, shamans, sorcerers, etc.) are jointly "annointed" by supernatural beings and appointed by the public to mediate the flow of information between the two realms. From a cognitive standpoint, the mediator's task is to focus attention on precisely those counterintuitive assumptions whose liminal, public expression serves as a "conduit metaphor" for activating and constraining the far more wide-ranging subliminal assumptions and inferences that the audience intuitively shares.

In sum, the episodic expressions and ritual performances associated with symbolic beliefs are instrumental in activating and focusing the intuitive assumptions and inferences that underlie religion and cosmology. But they do no more than that. The overwhelming bulk of information that is stored and evoked with symbolic beliefs is rarely, if ever, rendered public, explicitly communicated, and culturally transmitted. Nobody, even the most faithful believer or religious functionary, ever articulates more than a fraction of the intuitive beliefs that underpin devotion. Indeed, people are largely oblivious to them unless expressly prodded to become mindful (e.g., in theology class, by a persistent anthropologist). Even the relatively sporadic and loosely articulated public expressions of symbolic belief are parasitically rooted in the deep range of ordinary assumptions and inferences that make counterintuitive beliefs both remarkable and memorable.

4.4. Relevance and Truth: Why God's Word Cannot Be Disconfirmed

> The vedas are authorless and eternal, divinely inspired by Lord B'rhma, revealed through vedic sages who were greatly intellectual and intensely spiritual persons who in their mystic experience came face to face with Reality.
>
> —Chitralekha Singh Prem Nath, *Hinduism* (1996)

One clear and important distinction between fantasy and religion is the knowledge of its source. People generally attribute their personal fantasies and dreams to themselves and to events they've experienced. They also know or assume that public fictions (novels, movies, cartoons, etc.) were created by specific people who had particular intentions for doing so.

A religious text is another story. Followers believe it to be the work and word of deities themselves. Believers assume that sacred doctrine was first heard or transcribed in some long-forgotten time by chosen prophets or sages who were faithfully repeating or imaging what the deities had directly said or shown to them.

Accepting a text on authority and faith implies that the listener or reader suspend the universal constraints on ordinary communication, that is, pragmatic considerations of *relevance* (Sperber and Wilson 1986).[1] In ordinary communication, the listener or reader "automatically" attempts to fill the gap in understanding between what is merely said or written and what the communicator *intends* the listener or reader to think or do as a result.

In ordinary communication, there is almost always such a gap. For example, if someone says to you "That's just fine," you will immediately try to figure out what in the previous conversation or immediate environment "that" could possibly refer to, what is "fine" about it, and why it is "just" fine. This search, in turn, takes cues from the phonetic and syntactic structure of the utterance itself (e.g., phrasing, stress, intonation), surrounding environment (the presence of a broken wine bottle on the dining room floor), recent memory (you had just asked to taste your dinner host's special reserve), and background knowledge (your host tends to be ironic when angry).

Moreover, you, the hearer, automatically assume that the speaker also shares many of these same background assumptions with you and, furthermore, that the speaker made the utterance knowing that the two of you shared enough of these background assumptions for you to readily understand what the speaker intended. Both of you also automatically assume that you, the hearer, will make the appropriate *inference* to the speaker's intentions on the basis of considerations of relevance: you will attempt, with the least cognitive effort, to infer sufficient information to understand the speaker's intentions. You *stop* cognitively processing information the moment the communication makes sense. (If there were no such stopping rule, inference and interpretation would go on forever.)

Depending on the circumstances and what you know or don't know about the speaker's past intentions, you may suspect that the speaker is attempting to lie or deceive. Alternatively, you may doubt that the speaker really knows what he or she is talking about, or is adequately aware of the kind or extent of knowledge that you share, or properly assesses your readiness or willingness to make the appropriate inferences. Finally, you may have reason to interpret the speaker's utterance figuratively, say, as a metaphor or parable, or perhaps simply as a bit of fanciful fun.

In everyday communication, humans effortlessly, but necessarily and unmistakably, make these many assumptions and inferences. Often, they do so very many times in a single minute of ordinary conversation. In interpreting a religious utterance or text, however, people need do very little of the sort. Ordinarily, believers assume that the utterances or texts connected with religious doctrines are *authorless, timeless, and true*. As a result, people do not apply ordinary relevance criteria to religious communications.

Because divine statements are authorless, it makes little sense to try to infer intent from their mode of presentation. For example, the bodily gesticulations, phrasings, and intonations in the utterance of a biblical, Quranic, or Later Vedic passage cannot be God's, Allah's, or Vishnu's. It can be only the speaker's (unless there is cause to believe that God is directly communicating through the deity, as in a public revelation). Interpreting what the speaker intends by uttering the passage is one thing; interpreting what the deity intends can be indefinitely many things (expressed, in part, by indefinitely many speakers and interpreters).

Timelessness implies that cues from the surrounding environment, background knowledge, and memory are all irrelevant—or equipotentially relevant, which amounts to irrelevance. God's message, therefore, can apply to any and all contexts and to each context in indefinitely many and different ways. To be sure, people interpret God's message in particular ways for specific contexts, but they have no reason to ever *stop* interpreting.

Finally, the fact that God's word is accepted as true on faith—come what may—entails that it can never be false or deceptive or merely figurative. Ordinary preoccupation with lying and false belief in communication therefore plays no role in interpretation (or at least no consistent role). Neither can failed attempts at verification or confirmation of this or that aspect of the information represented in a religious statement, or inferred from it, undermine the audience's belief in the statement's truth.

On the contrary, apparently disconfirming evidence only seems to make believers try harder to understand the deeper truth and to strengthen religious beliefs. For example, after reading a bogus article on a new finding from the Dead Sea Scrolls that seemed to contradict Christian doctrine, religious believers who also believed the story reported their religious beliefs reinforced (Batson 1975). For believers, then, confidence in religious doctrine and belief can increase through *both* confirmation and disconfirmation of any factual assumptions that may accompany interpretation of those beleifs.

Faith in religious belief is not simply another manifestation of a general psychological propensity to reduce "cognitive dissonance" by ignoring or reappraising information that is contrary to one's views (cf. Festinger, Riecken, and Schachter 1956). It is the direct cognitive result of suspending the relevance criteria that universally apply to ordinary communication. *If faith is, in part, willingness to suspend ordinary pragmatic constraints of relevance, then beliefs held in faith become not only immune to falsification and contradiction but become even more strongly held in the face of apparent falsification or contradiction.* Apparently disconfirmed religious beliefs show only the superficiality of one's current interpretation and point to an even deeper but more mysterious truth.

4.5. Quasi Propositions

At first glance, it may seem that agents, especially supernatural agents, vary as much as anything possibly can in human imagination. Supernatural agents around the world include magic mountains, flying carpets, talking trees, philosophizing animals, and bodiless thinkers and at least as many possible variants of these sorts of things as there are different types of mountains, carpets, animals, and thinkers. Nevertheless, the scope of supernatural agency is actually quite restricted on two counts. First, the ways that supernatural agents can surprise us is cognitively systematic. Second, what's left over after we're surprised is remarkably predictable, ordinary, and mundane.

If it's somewhat surprising that our God is an eternally disembodied being that can still (without a body, heart, or brain) feel and conceptualize grief, jealousy, and anger on some occasions, it's remarkably unsurprising that our God can then also feel and conceptualize joy, love, and compassion on other occasions, just as most of us do. If it's surprising that our God can move mountains, then it's not surprising that our God can also move rocks, trees, people, and boats and generally pick out the same kinds of objects in space that we do. Gods and other supernatural beings are systematically unlike us in a few general ways—more powerful, longer lived, more knowledgeable, more intelligent, more vehement, more forgiving, able to act at a distance, able to act in two places at once, able to travel in time, able to take nonhuman bodily forms—and predictably like us in an enormously broader range of usual ways (Boyer 1994; Atran 1996).

Supernatural agents are always *humanlike* but never quite human. For example, recent experiments indicate that children in the United States from about 5-years-old on up more readily attribute epistemic mental states (see, think, know) to beings in the afterlife than psychobiological mental states (hunger, thirst, sleepiness) (Bering and Bjorklund 2002). Ordinary distinctions between mind and body (e.g., dreaming) provide at least some intuitive support for extraordinary beings with disembodied minds.

What does the *nonhuman* aspect of supernatural agency cognitively consist of? To set the stage for an answer, consider further what supernatural agents aren't.

First, they're not collectively verifiable in the way common sense and scientific facts are. Most cultural anthropologists have witnessed individual informants sincerely claiming to have seen and talked with spirits of one sort or another. As far as I am aware, though, no anthropologist has reported multiple individuals seeing the same spirit, or interacting with it in precisely the same way. Each person has his or her own vision and account, unlike usual perceptions of rocks, pots, pigeons, and persons. Supernatural agents have no fixed reference and descriptions of them have no determinate or determinable propositional content. Each person's conceptual representation of a supernatural agent is different from every other person's conceptual representation, even when the public description or expression used by all individuals in a community is the same.

Consider the expression "God is omnipotent, omniscient, and omnipresent." I suspect no one before me has thought this to mean that God can simultaneously catch dust particles with a boxing glove, instantly compute the full decimal value of a circle's circumference, and jump out of the garbage can. Experiments with adults in the United States (J. Barrett and Keil 1996) and India (J. Barrett 1998) further illustrate the point. When asked to describe their deities, subjects in both cultures produced abstract and consensual theological descriptions of gods as being able to do anything, anticipate and react to everything at once, always know the right thing to do, and be able to dispense entirely with perceptual information and calculation. When asked to respond to narratives about these same gods, the same subjects described the deities as being in only one place at a time, puzzling over alternative courses of action, and looking for evidence to decide what to do (e.g., to first save Johnny, who's praying for help because his foot is stuck in a river in the United States and the water is rapidly rising; or to first save little Mary, whom He has seen fall on railroad tracks in Australia, where a train is fast approaching). Indeed, the Bible itself is written as if God were sometimes less than omnipotent or omniscient. Thus, after eating the forbidden apple, Adam and Eve hid in the trees (out of God's sight). God had to ask, "Where art thou?" Adam answered that he hid because he was afraid and naked. And God inquired (wanting to know), "Who told thee thou wast naked?" (*Genesis* 3: 8–11).

The culturally consensual, or "theological," description of gods includes many of the same extrahuman features, but actual attempts to interpret gods in real-world or narrative contexts and to *complete* reference produce understandings of beings that are remarkably like everyone's everyday conceptions of mundane human agents. There are no significant differences in this respect between theologians and ordinary believers. In brief, implicit, underlying conceptions of human agency in supernatural beliefs involve commonsense propositions that invoke other commonsense propositions by means of straightforward inductive and deductive inferences. By contrast, explicit and superficial theological form is nonpropositional and the inferences it evokes are idiosyncratic.[2]

Earlier rational and empirical philosophers, such as Descartes (1681) and Hume (1955[1758]), argued that religious beliefs could not be judged by the same criteria of (logical) coherence and (empirical) correspondence as factual commonsense or scientific beliefs. Kant (1951[1790]: sec. 59) considered "symbolic cognitions," including religious beliefs, to be possibly valid but only partially intelligible, "quasi-schematized" thoughts for which "no intuition commensurate with them can be given." What happens, roughly, is that one seeks some empirically intuited situation that can serve as a model by reference to which the idea can be made more or less comprehensible (e.g., God putting nature in order on the model of a father disciplining his family). But the fact that the model is undetermined with respect to its structure leaves many features in the dark. Because there is, in principle, no complete isomorphism between the real model and the imagined situation, questions of literal truth, falsity, or fact cannot arise.

For Sperber (1975, 1985b), the superficial form of a religious "semiproposition" is "p," and is superficially interpreted as the belief that "p" is true. But the underlying form is really "'p' is true," where the content p is bracketed off from analysis (see also Ayer 1950:117 on religious "pseudo-propositions"). The general idea is: "OK, we accept *that* p is true; now, what does *that* mean?" In other words, the truth of a religious quasi proposition is assumed, not verified, and this assumed truth serves to evoke further thought and inference like a metaphor in poetry, without implying or referring to anything directly. This further thought and inference is evocation in pursuit of emotional validation. The significance of a religious quasi proposition, and the inferences it evokes, resides in the ways it participates in a process of cognitive coordination between social actors so as to enhance their emotional commitment to one another.

Truth validation of factual propositions can be direct and observational (e.g., "The snow is white" is true if and only if I observe that the snow is in fact white) or indirect and theory-embedded (e.g., "Birds descended from dinosaurs" is true if and only if the theory of evolution is factually true). Emotional validation of religious quasi propositions is always indirect. It is achieved only by implicating a larger network of other propositions and quasi propositions (e.g., "My husband committed suicide and will therefore go to Hell" is not a quasi proposition many would find emotionally persuasive or satisfying in itself; only in the larger context of belief in the cosmology of Heaven and Hell is it emotionally validated). In sum, religious quasi propositions may have *truth value* (e.g., Baptists believe that "after you die you either go to Heaven or Hell" has truth value), but they are *not truth-valuable* in the sense of being liable to verification, falsification, or logical evaluation of the information. Truth is taken on faith and emotionally validated with little reasoning required for support.

4.6. Counterintuitions

All the world's cultures have religious myths that are attention-arresting because they are fundamentally counterfactual and counterintuitive. Nevertheless, people in all cultures also recognize that such beliefs are fundamentally counterfactual and counterintuitive, whether or not they are religious believers. In our society, for example, Catholics and non-Catholics alike are unquestionably aware of the difference between Christ's body and ordinary wafers and between Christ's blood and ordinary wine. Likewise, the Native American Cowlitz are as aware of the difference between the deity Coyote and everyday coyotes and between Old Man Wild Cherry Bark and ordinary wild cherry bark: "Coyote fell down, his limbs entirely wrapped and tied with the cherry bark. . . . He got his knife, and cut at the cherry bark. . . . Coyote got to his feet, no more tied up by the cherry bark, he had cut it all to pieces. Old Man Wild Cherry Bark fell down and died. Coyote went on directly. He burst into laughter as he went. 'Ha! Ha! Ha! Wild cherry bark could never kill me, its only *mere* cherry bark'" (Jacobs 1934:126–133).

Religious beliefs are counterintuitive, hence also necessarily counterfactual, because they violate innate, modular expectations about basic ontological categories, such as those of LIVING KIND (ANIMATE [PERSON, ANIMAL], PLANT) and STUFF (ARTIFACT, SUBSTANCE) (Sperber 1985a; Atran 1990a; Boyer 1994). As Atran and Sperber note, though, religious beliefs nonetheless remain integrally bound to factual, commonsense beliefs and inferences:

> They are generally inconsistent with commonsense knowledge, but not at random: rather they dramatically contradict basic commonsense assumptions. For instance, they include beliefs about invisible creatures who can transform themselves at will or who can perceive events that are distant in time or space. This flatly contradicts factual commonsense assumptions about physical, biological and psychological phenomena. . . . As a result, these beliefs are more likely to be retained and transmitted in a human group than random departures from common sense, and thus to become part of the group's culture. . . . To the extent such violations of category distinctions shake basic notions of ontology they are attention-arresting, hence memorable. But only to the degree that the resultant impossible worlds remain bridged to the everyday world can information be stored and evoked in plausible grades. (1991: 52)

As a result, *religious concepts need little in the way of overt cultural representation or instruction to be learned and transmitted.* A few fragmentary narrative descriptions or episodes suffice to mobilize an enormously rich network of implicit background beliefs.

Public expressions of religion are the tip of the iceberg of underlying religious evocations. For example, it suffices for any person to hear once that an angel flew into a cold prison at night to comfort someone for that person to infer indefinitely many other physical, emotional, and intellectual properties of angels. Many of these inferences will tend to converge regardless of the person's culture or individual learning experience: if angels can fly through walls they can probably fly through any solid barrier and even go underground; they can sympathize and reason and therefore likely understand injustice, acknowledge mitigating circumstances, feel sorrow, make inductions, probably count, and so on; they can see in the dark and very well may have something like X-ray vision and hindsight; they don't get cold and therefore you could bet that they don't get hot or feel physical pain. Other inferences will be channeled by background information that is specific to the culture or a person's experiences: modern angels are as likely to fly like airplanes or rockets as like birds; angels in a war zone are probably busier than angels on a tranquil prairie. Indefinitely many other possible inferences may never be articulated: Do angels like the smell of flowers? Can they eat pizza? Still others may be articulated but irresolvable and evocative by turns: How many angels can fit on the head of a pin? Can angels pass through one another?

Within a given religious tradition, one might "predict that the likelihood of a transformation from one thing into another should decrease as the distance . . . between [universally intuited ontological] categories of these two things increases" (M. Kelly and Keil 1985). For instance, the metamorphosis of humans into animals and animals into plants may be more common than that of humans or animals into artifacts or substances. Analyzing Ovid's *Metamorphoses* and other similar folktales, Kelly and Keil showed that metamorphoses were far more frequent between adjacent categories of universal ontology, for example (PERSON ↔ ANIMAL ↔ PLANT) > PERSON ↔ SUBSTANCE. There are thus systematic, experimentally testable ways in which *some* supernatural agent concepts are *inherently better* candidates for cultural selection than others.

Consider the following candidates for selection as deities in some unknown culture (an asterisk marks the cognitively less likely candidate):

(A) *a talkative infant / a talkative bush
(B) *a one-eyed mouse / a one-eyed mountain
(C) a pensive pig / *a pensive pot
(D) *a bellowing rabbit / a bloodthirsty rabbit
(E) omniscient or omnipotent spirit that burns people from the sky / *omniscient or omnipotent spirit that eavesdrops from the sky

All things being equal, some supernatural beliefs are better candidates than others for cultural transmission and retention in any given population of human minds because (1) they are more attention-arresting; (2) they have greater inferential potential; (3) they cannot be processed completely; (4) they are more emotionally provocative.

Each of these selection criteria depends on the evolutionarily poised and prepared architecture of the mind/brain. For example, (A) a talkative bush is more cognitively compelling than a garrulous infant because a talkative PLANT implies attributes that are unique to the PERSON category, such as social use of language. A talkative infant is "merely" counterfactual. Still, in being counterfactual, the infant with adultlike properties is a better candidate for deification than, say, a talkative man. Similarly, (B) a one-eyed mountain is more intuitively dramatic, hence more attention-arresting and memorable, than a one-eyed ANIMAL as it violates innately based intuitive expectations about inanimate SUBSTANCE. Insofar as a one-eyed animal is abnormal and also attention-arresting, it is a better candidate than a normal animal. Anomalous but factually plausible conditions are also reasonably good religious candidates. As Hume noted: "The more regular and uniform . . . the more he is familiarized to it, and the less inclined to scrutinize and examine it. A monstrous birth . . . alarms him from its novelty; and immediately sets him a trembling, and sacrificing, and praying" (1956[1757]:25).

By contrast, (C) a pensive pot is *less* evocative than a pensive pig. Although both are intuitively absurd, a pensive object is *too far removed* from the natural category of entities with thought and mood to be richly evocative. As Kant might have said, little or no "intuition commensurate with them can be given." Such cognitions are less likely to be retained in memory, transmitted, and culturally selected for survival. In other words, some ontological violations have what Boyer (1994) refers to as greater "inferential potential" than others.

Incomplete processing of supernatural agents implicates two cognitive aspects of religious belief: (1) activation of innate conceptual modules and (2) failed assignment to universal ontological categories. The processes responsible for activating conceptual modules and those responsible for fixing ontological categories are intimately related but not identical. Conceptual modules are activated by stimuli that fall into a few intuitive knowledge domains, including folkmechanics (object boundaries and movements), folkbiology (species configurations and relationships), and folkpsychology (goal-directed and interactive behavior).

Ontological categories are generated by further and more specific activation of conceptual modules. Among the conceptually primary ontological categories are PERSON, ANIMAL, PLANT, ARTIFACT, SUBSTANCE (Atran 1989a). All ontological categories involve more specific processing over the folkmechanics domain (nonliving objects and events).

- Only SUBSTANCE involves further processing that is exclusive to folkmechanics.
- PERSON involves more specific processing over the folkpsychological domain (human behavior is scrutinized as indicating friend or foe and possibly predator or prey) and the folkbiological domain (essentialized group assignments, e.g., race and ethnicity).
- ANIMAL involves supplemental processing over the domains of folkbiology (every animal is assigned uniquely to a folk species) and (some aspects of) folkpsychology (animal behavior is scrutinized as indicating predator or prey and possibly friend or foe).
- PLANT involves additional processing over the folkbiological domain (every plant is assigned to one and only one folk species).
- ARTIFACT involves further processing over the folkmechanics and (some aspects of the) folkpsychology domains (intentionally produced nonliving object).

The combination of (3) conceptual modules and (5) ontological categories results in a 3 X 5 matrix with 15 cells. Changing the intuitive relationship expressed in any one cell generates a minimal counterintuition (cf. J. Barrett 2000). For example, switching the cell (– folkpsychology, SUBSTANCE) to (+ folkpsychology, SUBSTANCE) yields a thinking talisman, whereas switching (+ folkpsychology, PERSON) to (– folkpsychology, PERSON) yields an unthinking zombie.

Whenever stimuli activate a conceptual module they are processed until assigned to an ontological domain. Within their assigned domain, the stimuli are further assigned to some basic-level category (e.g., woman, turkey, oak, hammer, rock; cf. Rosch et al. 1976). For example, all naturally occurring clusters of plant and animal stimuli are uniquely assigned to a particular plant or animal (folk) species (Atran 1998). Once assigned a basic-level category in some ontological domain they can be further classified into superordinate (e.g., bird) and subordinate concepts (e.g., wild turkey) and integrated into the general mental encyclopedia of factual knowledge and background belief.

All religious traditions include, as key elements responsible for learning and transmission, public expressions of beliefs in which assignment to one of the primary ontological domains fails because further processing in accordance with intuitively innate expectations about folkmechanics, folkbiology, or folkpsychology is blocked. For example, the Arab talisman, European black magic crystal ball, and Maya *sastun* are naturally inert substances or artifacts with supernatural animate and sentient powers. As such, they violate intuitive expectations about folkbiology and folkpsychology, and cannot be assigned to PERSON or ANIMAL, nor can they remain simply SUBSTANCE or ARTIFACT. Talkative, vengeful, or pensive animals cannot be assigned to either PERSON or ANIMAL; one-eyed, lame, or helpful mountains cannot be assigned to either PERSON or ANIMAL; omniscient but bodiless gods cannot be assigned to PERSON, and so forth.

At initial stages of processing, supernatural agents do not represent ontological violations of the universally innate cognitive categories of PERSON or ANIMATE BEING because the minimal conditions for activating cognition of agency require only a *telic event structure*, that is, indications, however schematic, of interruptible movement toward a goal. The sudden movement of an object stirred by the wind may trigger the agent-detection system that operates over the domain of folkpsychology and a ghost invoked to interpret this possibly purposeful event. In normal circumstances, a sudden movement of wind might activate cognitve processing for agents but would soon deactivate on further analysis ("It's only the wind"). But the object-boundary detectors that operate over the domain of folkmechanics, and that are required to identify the agent, cannot be activated. As a result, assignment to the PERSON or ANIMAL category cannot be completed. Ontological violations kick in at later stages of processing supernatural agent concepts. By violating innate ontological commitments—for example, endowing spirits with movement and feelings but no body—processing can never be brought to factual closure, and indeterminately many interpretations can be generated to deal with indefinitely many newly arising situations. Notice that bringing processing to factual closure does not require actual verification, but only the reasonable possibility of such verification. Someone who is heard but not seen is visible in principle, whereas an invisible being is not.

Supernatural agent concepts tend to be emotionally powerful because they trigger evolutionary survival templates. This also makes them attention-arresting and memorable. Thus, (D) a bloodthirsty rabbit and a bellowing rabbit are both counterfactual rather than counterintuitive, in the sense that they violate encyclopedic knowledge about known animal behavior rather than intuitive ontological expectations. Both are, therefore, better candidates for deification than normally behaving rabbits. But carnivorous rabbits also activate universal sensitivities to predator and prey and so are even better candidates. In (E) the entity described violates intuitive ontological expectations (nothing can be knowledgeable without a body that stores information or physically powerful without bodily cause). But something that knows to physically harm people is more alarming than a do-nothing that knows and just listens in.

All things being equal, then, supernatural concepts that join ontologically distant categories (e.g., PERSON-SUBSTANCE, ANIMAL-SUBSTANCE) should be less prevalent than supernatural concepts that join ontologically nearer categories (e.g., PERSON-ANIMAL). Intervening perceptual, contextual, or psychothematic factors, however, can change the odds. For example, a stone viewed by a South Indian villager that looks vaguely like an ox (oxen being objects of worship and sacrifice) may be a good candidate for an ox god that can turn itself into a stone (Whitehead 1988[1921]:124–125). A pastry whose form vaguely resembles Mother Theresa's face and habit, a photograph of which is posted on the Internet shortly after her death, may be taken by some devout Catholics to be a material manifestation of her spirit.

Women are often thematically identified more with watery and weak things than hard and strong things. So they are as or more likely to be transformed into streams and lakes than into bulls and jaguars, as in ancient Greece and Mayaland. According to a Hindu legend, a demon imprisoned many gods by turning itself into a mountain enclosure. When Murga, son of Shiva, attacked the demon, it became half-peacock half-cock. The first transformation into a mountain is perhaps attributable partly to context (a natural stronghold for a prison), partly to a near universal thematic association of mountains with sacred places. Certain natural substances—mountains, seas, clouds, sun, moon, planets—are associated with perceptions of great size or distance and with conceptions of grandeur and continuous or recurring duration. They are, as Freud surmised, psychologically privileged objects for focusing the thoughts and emotions evoked by existential anxieties, such as those concerned with death and eternity.

4.7. Memorability for Minimally Counterintuitive Beliefs and Belief Sets

Many factors are important in determining the extent to which ideas achieve a cultural level of distribution. Some are ecological, including the rate of prior exposure to an idea in a population, physical as well as social facilitators and barriers to communication and imitation, and institutional structures that reinforce or suppress an idea. Others are psychological, including the ease with which an idea can be represented and remembered, the intrinsic interest that it evokes in people so that it is processed and rehearsed, and motivation and facility to communicate the idea to others. Of all the psychological factors, the mnemonic power of an idea is one of the most important. In fact, Sperber (1996) puts forth memorability as a "law" of the epidemiology of representations, as a necessary (but of course not sufficient) condition for cultural success. The *memorability test* has two components:

1. Memorability places severe constraints on the cultural transmission of ideas. In oral traditions that characterize most human cultures throughout history, an idea that is not memorable cannot be transmitted and cannot achieve cultural success.
2. Moreover, even if two ideas pass a minimal test of memorability, a more memorable idea has a transmission advantage over a less memorable one (all else being equal). This advantage, even if small at the start, accumulates from generation to generation of transmission, leading to massive differences in cultural success at the end.

One of the earliest accounts of the effects of memorability on the transmission of natural and nonnatural concepts was Bartlett's classic study of "the war of the ghosts." Bartlett examined the ways British university students remembered and then transmitted a culturally unfamiliar story (a Native American folktale). Over several successive retellings of the story, some culturally unfamiliar items or events were dropped from the retelling. Other unfamiliar items were distorted, being replaced by more familiar items; for example, a canoe (an unfamiliar item) was replaced by a rowboat (a familiar one). Bartlett reasoned that items inconsistent with the cultural expectations of British students were harder to represent, harder to recall, and so less likely to be transmitted than items consistent with expectations (see also Kintsch and Greene 1978). Another striking finding was that the very notion of the ghosts—so central to the story—was gradually eliminated from the retellings. However, this finding may be explained by the idea that the effect of memory on cultural transmission also operates at the level of belief sets, such that the elimination of the ghost from the retellings contributed to the overall cultural survival of the story as a whole.

Recent studies that have followed up on Bartlett's seminal work suggest that, under some conditions, counterintuitive beliefs are actually *better* recalled relative to intuitive beliefs. For example, J. Barrett and Nyhof asked people to remember and retell stories containing natural as well as nonnatural events or objects. Participants read three of six different Native American folktales and then remembered as much of each as they could. A content analysis of what they remembered was revealing: participants remembered 92 percent of minimally counterintuitive items but only 71 percent of intuitive items.

Although suggestive and insightful, these and other studies (e.g., Boyer and Ramble 2001) leave unresolved a number of issues. One issue is the problem of incompatibility of this finding with existing cultural materials. Why don't we see minimally counterintuitive concepts take over most of the narrative structure of religions, folktales, and myths? Even a casual perusal of culturally successful materials, such as the Bible, Veda, or Popul Vuh, or even popular folktales, such as the Grimm Brothers' collection, suggests that counterintuitive concepts and occurrences are in the minority. The Bible, for example, is a succession of mundane events—walking, fishing, eating, sleeping, copulating, dying, marrying, fighting, suffering rainstorms and drought—interspersed with a few counterintuitive occurrences, such as miracles and the appearance of supernatural agents such as God, angels, and ghosts.[3]

An answer to this puzzle may lie in examining the memorability of an entire set of beliefs as a single unit of transmission rather than individual beliefs. The unit of cultural transmission is often, but not always, an individual idea. Under many conditions, a series of events or concepts are transmitted together as a single unit. So cognitive optimality might be at work not only at the level of individual beliefs but at the level of belief structures as well.

Ara Norenzayan and I (Norenzayan and Atran 2002) conducted a study to examine the memorability of intuitive (INT) and minimally counterintuitive (MCI) beliefs and belief sets over a period of a week (see examples in Table 4.1). Participants were 107 undergraduate students at a large U.S. university in the Midwest. MCI beliefs were generated by transferring a property from its intuitive domain to a novel domain (e.g., thirsty door, closing cat). For each MCI belief, there was a corresponding INT belief (thirsty cat, closing door). Thus, each word—"cat," "door," "closing," and "thirsty"—was equally likely to appear in an INT item as in an MCI

Table 4.1. Examples of intuitive statements (INT) and bizarre (BIZ), minimally counterintuitive (MCI), maximally counterintuitive (MXCI) counterparts in counterbalanced design

Version 1	Version 2
INT	
1. Crumbling Ice	Crystallizing Ice
2. Crystallizing Glass	Crumbling Glass
3. Gossiping Child	Chanting Child
4. Chanting Man	Gossiping Man
5. Grazing Cow	Wandering Cow
6. Wandering Deer	Grazing Deer
BIZ	
7. Nauseating Cat	Dangling Cat
8. Dangling Squirrel	Nauseating Squirrel
9. Blinking Newspaper	Floating Newspaper
10. Floating Pencil	Blinking Pencil
MCI	
11. Giggling Seaweed	Sobbing Seaweed
12. Sobbing Oak	Giggling Oak
13. Cursing Horse	Admiring Horse
14. Admiring Frog	Cursing Frog
15. Solidifying Lady	Melting Lady
16. Melting Grandfather	Solidifying Grandfather
MXCI-Control	
17. Cheering Limping Turtle	Chattering Climbing Turtle
18. Chattering Climbing Pig	Cheering Limping Pig
MXCI	
19. Squinting Wilting Brick	Squealing Flowering Brick
20. Squealing Flowering Marble	Squinting Wilting Marble

item. This resulted in a set of four statements that achieved a counterbalanced design, each word in each statement serving as its own control. Recall was measured in two ways: planned free recall after a three-minute delay, and a surprise free recall after a one-week delay. This latter measure was the more important one, as it better reflects the role of recall in oral traditions.

Participants were told that they were in an experiment about memory and were given a list of items to remember without a story context. This list-learning format provided a neutral context to measure recall, rather than participants' notions of what is interesting to report. Although stories are an important part of culturally successful materials, elements of these stories often begin life as a set of discrete images, events, and beliefs, not unlike lists of items, with little or no story structure (consider the sketchy nature of early Christian beliefs about the life events of Jesus, which cohered into a chronological narrative centuries later). This format simulated the degraded informational context of nascent cultural materials. Finally, unlike previous studies, basic-level concepts were used, such as door, cat, infant. The basic level is where (1) many common features are listed for categories, (2) consistent motor programs are used for the interaction with or manipulation of category exemplars, (3) category members have similar enough shapes so that it is possible to recognize an average shape for objects of the category, and (4) the category name is the first name to come to mind in the presence of an object, for example, "table" versus "furniture" and "kitchen table," or "dog" versus "mammal" and "collie" (Rosch et al. 1976).

A complex pattern of recall emerged for intuitive and minimally counterintuitive beliefs (for details, see Norenzayan and Atran 2002). Unlike other recent studies, intuitive beliefs showed better recall rates than minimally counterintuitive beliefs. This was the case immediately (Figure 4.1)[4] as well as after a one-week delay (Figure 4.2).[5] The only exception to this pattern was when counterintuitives made up the majority of beliefs, in which case there were no differences in recall rates. Because the two kinds of beliefs were matched (i.e., each term in each belief was equally likely to occur in an intuitive and counterintuitive belief), we can conclude with relative confidence that it was the intuitiveness factor, not other unknown factors left to vary, that contributed to the recall advantage of the intuitives.

We have subsequently replicated this finding with a different set of ideas, where a sharper distinction was made between counterintuitive ideas and ideas that are intuitive but bizarre and between degrees of counterintuitiveness. Recall was measured in two ways: planned free recall after a three-minute delay and incidental free recall after a one-week delay. The latter measure was the more important, reflecting the role of recall in cultural transmission.

Participants were 32 undergraduates at a different U.S. university. Participants received ideas that were (1) intuitive and ordinary, (2) intuitive but bizarre, (3) minimally counterintuitive, and (4) maximally counterintuitive. Two-word or three-word statements that represented INT, BIZ, MCI, MXCI-Control, and MXCI beliefs were generated (Table 4.1). Each statement consisted of a concept and one or two properties that modified it. INT statements were created by using a property that was appropriate to the ontological category (e.g., closing door). BIZ statements were created by modifying the concept with an intuitive but bizarre property (e.g., blinking newspaper). MCI statements were created by modifying with a property transferred from *another* ontological category (e.g., thirsty door). Finally, MXCI statements were created by modifying a concept with two properties taken from another ontological category (e.g., squinting wilting brick). For each MXCI statement, a matching MCI statement was generated, where just one of the properties was counterintuitive (e.g., chattering climbing pig). Each participant received only one of two different versions.

Results revealed a linear effect of intuitiveness on recall, immediately as well as a week later.[6] Intuitive ideas enjoyed the highest rate of recall, and maximally counterintuitive ideas received the lowest rate of recall (Figure 4.3). There were a total of 71 distortions. A recalled item was classified as "distorted" if it did not appear in the original study materials. Most distortions occurred within the same ontological category (39 items, or 55 percent). Of those, the majority were distortions within the minimally counterintuitive (MCI) category (23 items, or 59 percent of all same-category distortions). For example, "cursing horse" was remembered as "laughing horse" (both MCI). There were 7 distortions in the INT category, or 18

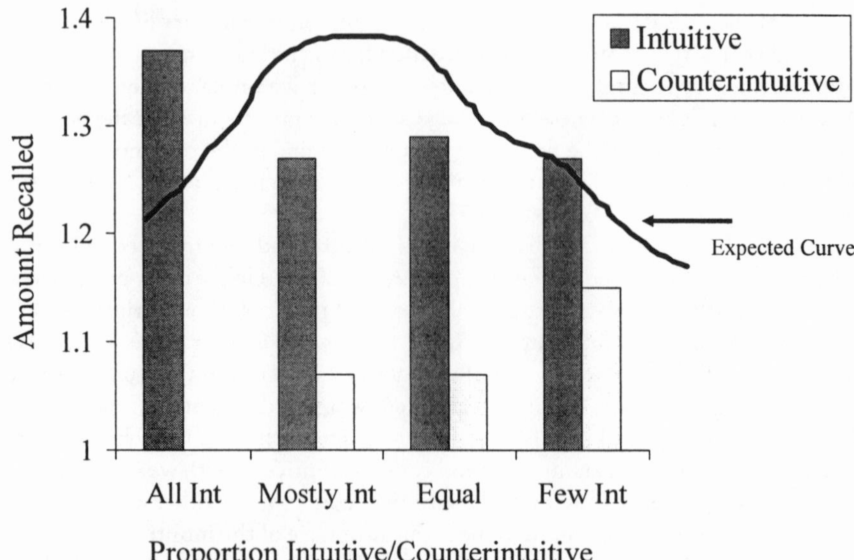

Figure 4.1. Immediate recall by proportion of intuitive and minimally counterintuitive beliefs.

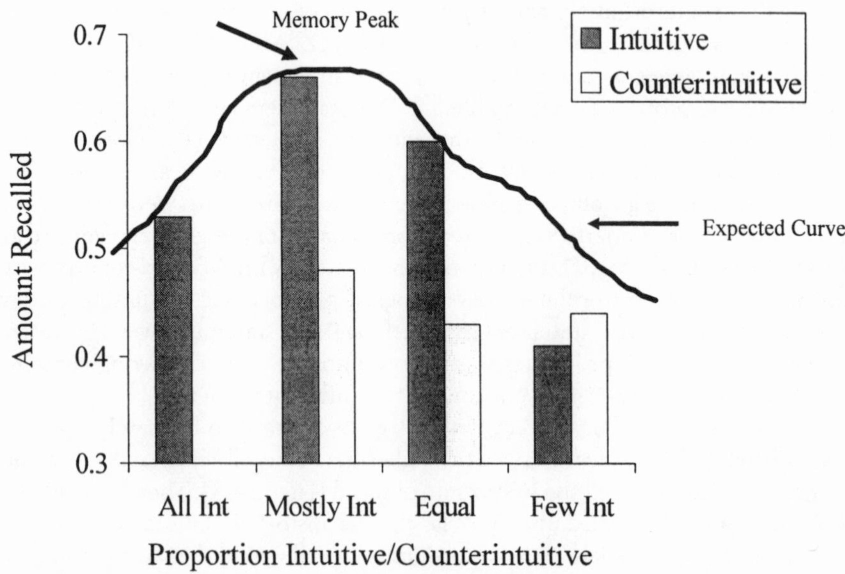

Figure 4.2. Delayed 1-week recall by proportion of intuitive and minimally counterintuitive beliefs.

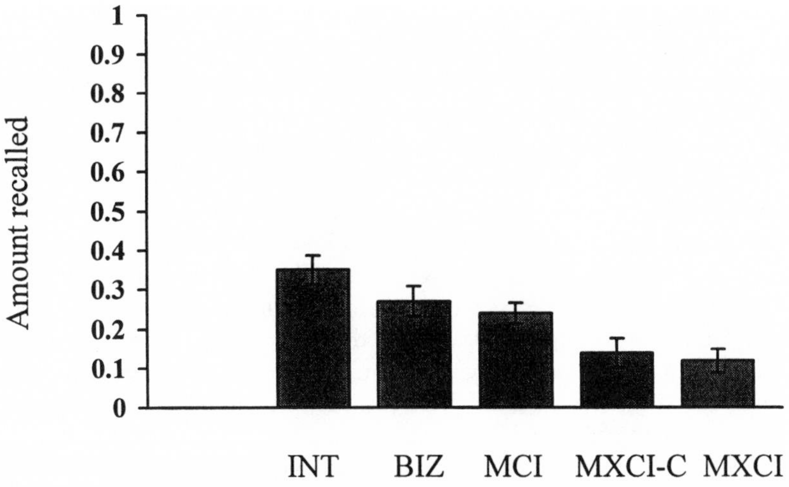

Figure 4.3. Delayed 1-week recall by proportion of intuitive, bizarre, minimally counterintuitive, and maximally counterintuitive beliefs (vertical bars represent margin of error at $p = .05$)

percent of all same-category distortions. For distortions that crossed ontological boundaries, the most common type was from counterintuitive to intuitive. There were a total of 14 such distortions (20 percent). The least common distortion was from intuitive to counterintuitive: only 1 such distortion was found (1.4 percent).[7] The pattern of results for distorted items, with a preference for rendering counterintuitive beliefs intuitive, follows the main lines of Bartlett's (1932) study.

How can we account for this pattern of results in light of previous findings? One important difference between our experiments and those of J. Barrett and Nyhof (2001) and Boyer and Ramble (2001) is that in our studies, participants were not led to expect nonnatural events (as in listening to a science fiction tale) and were not motivated to tell an interesting story. In a context in which people expect that information will conform to a natural course of events, they are likely to attend to and remember beliefs that are consistent with ontological assumptions. This process would break down when the majority of the to-be-remembered beliefs are minimally counterintuitive. In such a situation, it is possible that people develop the expectation that the task is about recalling nonnatural events or about reporting the "interesting stuff." As a result, intuitive beliefs would lose their privileged status and recall would be no different for intuitive and minimally counterintuitive beliefs. Under such conditions, it may even be possible to reverse the phenomenon, such that minimally counterintuitive beliefs are better recalled, as we saw earlier.

An intriguing finding that converges with previous studies was that minimally counterintuitive beliefs were more cognitively resilient than intuitive ones, in that they degraded at a lower rate after immediate recall; this, despite the fact that the former had an overall lower recall rate than the latter. Minimally counterintuitive beliefs may have a potent survival advantage over intuitive beliefs: once processed and recalled, they degrade less than intuitive ones. It's easy to see how this difference in cognitive resilience may be a significant factor in cultural survival. The disadvantage in recall may be offset by resilience, so that over numerous generations of transmission, an idea that is less remembered, but also less degradable, can, in some situations, prevail over an idea that is initially remembered well but then eventually dies out because of a higher rate of degradation.

The picture that emerged at the level of belief sets confirmed that cognitive optimality at this level is at least as important as at the individual belief level. The effect of belief proportions on delayed recall followed an inverted U-shaped curve. The belief set that was mostly intuitive combined with a few minimally counterintuitive ones had the highest rate of delayed recall and the lowest rate of memory degradation over time (Figure 4.4).[8] This is the recipe for a successful transmission of cultural beliefs, and it is the cognitive template that characterizes most popular folktales and religious narratives. The "equal proportions" belief set had moderate memorability. Critically, the belief set with a majority of minimally counterintuitive beliefs had the lowest rate of delayed recall and the highest level of memory degradation. In fact, this is a cognitive template rarely encountered in existing culturally successful materials. Possibly, narratives with such a template may have been introduced by cultural innovators but failed to pass the test of memorability. As a result, they faded from cultural life. Thus, the way natural and nonnatural beliefs are combined is crucial to survival of a cultural ensemble of beliefs, such as those that form the core of any religious tradition.

Minimally counterintuitive beliefs, because of minimal incongruity with ontological assumptions, are surprising and interesting. Although they themselves are not as memorable as intuitive beliefs, they may draw attention to the entire belief set in which they are embedded. They encourage paying more attention to the belief set as a whole and thinking about it more often over time. The majority of intuitive beliefs, supported by ontological assumptions and theories, then do the actual conceptual work by enhancing overall recall. Thus, a cognitive bootstrapping may be in operation between a minority of counterintuitives and a majority of intuitives. The former draw interest, the latter ensure recall over time.

This process depends on the particular mix of beliefs. It works as long as minimally counterintuitive beliefs exist in small proportions. Once their proportion increases to high levels, the belief set becomes too incongruent. It loses its capacity to arouse surprise and interest. In addition, because of massive inconsistency with ontology, it also becomes harder to recall and transmit. If this reasoning is correct, the following prediction ensues: assuming that immediate recall is a rough measure of initial "noteworthiness," immediate recall of the counterintuitives should predict delayed recall of intuitives, but not when counterintuitives are in the majority. This was indeed the case. Immediate recall of minimally counterintuitive beliefs predicted delayed recall of the intuitive beliefs in the "majority intuitive" condition and "equal proportions" condition but not in the "majority counterintuitives" condition. Another follow up study with Yukatek Mayan speakers revealed the same recall pattern as in the United States follow up, including greater resiliency for MCI than for INT beliefs. In addition, we found *the same pattern* for the Yukatek after three months as after one week, which indicates cultural stabilization of that pattern.

In sum, minimally counterintuitive beliefs, as long as they come in small proportions, help people remember and presumably transmit the intuitive statements.

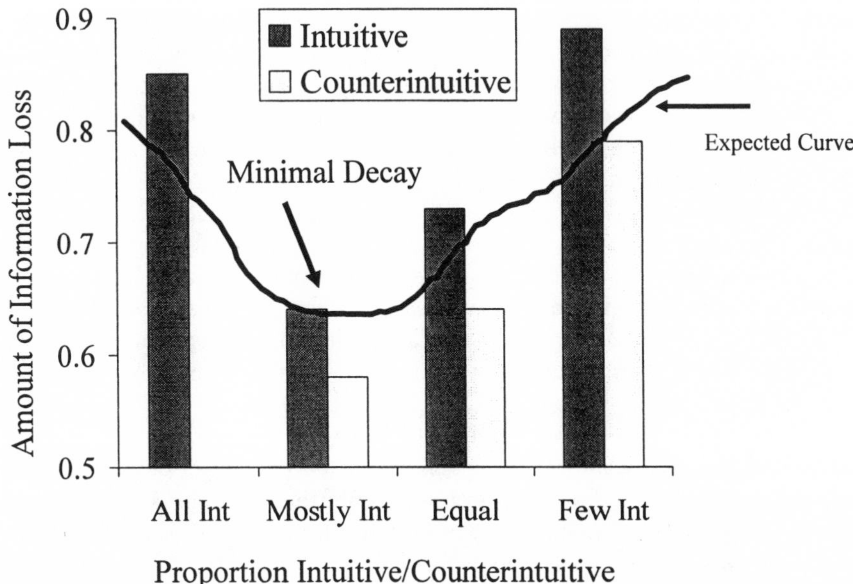

Figure 4.4. Memory degradation (immediate minus delayed recall) by proportion of intuitive and minimally counterintuitive beliefs.

A small proportion of minimally counterintuitive beliefs give the story a mnemonic advantage over stories with no counterintuitive beliefs or with far too many counterintuitive beliefs, just as moderately spiced-up dishes have a cultural advantage over bland or far too spicy dishes. This dual aspect of supernatural beliefs and belief sets—commonsensical and counterintuitive—renders them intuitively compelling yet fantastic, eminently recognizable but surprising. Such beliefs grab attention, activate intuition, and mobilize inference in ways that greatly facilitate their mnemonic retention, social transmission, cultural selection, and historical survival.

4.8. Displaying Truth: Metarepresenting Supernatural Worlds

> *Sienim fallor, sum* (If I doubt, I am)
>
> *Decivitate Dei* (*The City of God*)
> —Saint Augustine 2000 [413–426]

> God ain't in the killing business; God is in the giving business. *Hallelujah*. It's the Devil that's out to get you. . . . Peter [I, 5:8] says "The Devil wants to consume you"—"consume" is the Greek—he wants to eat you . . . So when the Devil comes you need armor. Your helmet of salvation, your shield of faith . . . The Devil wants to eat your job, eat your marriage, to take the honey out of your moon. . . . The Devil is mad, the Devil is a liar and The Truth is not in him.
>
> —Bishop Wayne Jackson, preaching "Miracles Do Happen," Ann Arbor television (18 February 2000)

Thus far I have claimed that the presence of minimally counterintuitive beliefs in religious belief sets favors the production, transmission, and cultural survival of those belief sets over time. We have also provided initial experimental support for the claim, although clearly much more needs to be done. (We are currently testing several cultural groups involving children and adults over a wider range of contents, conditions, and time periods. Initial results conform to our predictions.) But this claim leaves open the issue of how counterintuitive beliefs can be formed at all. If counterintuitive beliefs arise by violating innately given expectations about how the world is built, how can we possibly bypass our own hardwiring to form counterintuitive religious (or even scientific) beliefs? The answer is that we don't entirely bypass commonsense understanding but conceptually parasitize it to transcend it. This occurs through the species-specific cognitive process of metarepresentation.

Humans have a metarepresentational ability to form representations of representations. This ability allows people to understand a drawing or picture of someone or something *as a drawing or picture* and not the real thing. It lets us enjoy novels and movies *as fiction* that can emotionally arouse us without actually threatening us. It lets us think about being in different situations and deciding which are best for the purposes at hand *without our having to actually live through (or die in) the situations we imagine*. It affords us the capacity to *model the world in different ways, and to conscientiously change the world by entertaining new models* that we invent, evaluate, and implement. It enables us to become aware of our experienced past and imagined future *as past or future events that are distinct from the present that we represent to ourselves* and so permits us to reflect on our own existence. It allows people to comprehend and interact with one another's minds.

Equally important for our purposes, metarepresentation allows humans to retain half-understood ideas (Sperber 1975, 1985b; Atran and Sperber 1991). By embedding half-baked (quasi-propositional) ideas in other factual and commonsense beliefs, these ideas can simmer through personal and cultural belief systems and change them. Children come to terms with the world in similar ways when they hear a new word. A half-understood word is initially retained metarepresentationally, as standing in for other ideas the child already has in mind. Initially, the new word is assigned an ontological category; for example, if "An andro chases balls,"then an andro must be an ANIMAL or PERSON, Fido or Fred.

This metarepresentational capacity, and the learning functions it serves, is common to everyday cognition and communication and not particular to religion. Without it, though, representations of what gods are or do, and the entertaining of other religious quasi propositions, would not be possible. Supernatural causes and beings are always metarepresented as more or less vague ideas about other ideas, like a metaphor that metarepresents the earth as a mother but not quite.

After Dennett (1978), most researchers in "theory of mind" maintain that the attribution of mental states, such as belief and desire, to other persons requires metarepresentational reasoning about false beliefs. Not before the child can understand that other people's beliefs are *only* representations—and not just recordings of the way things are—can the child entertain and assess other people's representations as veridical or fictional, truly informative or deceptive, exact or exaggerated, or worth changing one's own mind for or ignoring. Only then can the child appreciate that *God thinks differently than most people, in that only God's beliefs are always true*. This capacity seeems to emerge in humans sometime between the ages of 3 and 5 years (Barrett 2001; Knight et al. 2001).

Suppose a 2- or 3-year-old thinks there is candy in a box but finds out the box has pencils inside. If you ask her what she thought when she first saw it, or what someone else seeing the closed box for the first time thinks, she'll say "pencils" and not "candy" (Wimmer and Perner 1983; Flavell 1986; Avis and Harris 1991). She fails to understand how someone can believe something different from what she knows is really the case. She has no *metarepresentational* understanding of beliefs about other beliefs, such as Sally believes *that* (Mommy's belief *that* the proposition ["there are pencils in the box"] is true) is false. Metarepresentation allows both an embedding of beliefs and a decoupling of semantic inferences connected with those beliefs; that is, an embedded belief in brackets need not have any implications for one's belief about reality (e.g., Sally need not believe that Mother's belief really describes the world).

Work on "infantile amnesia" also indicates that only around age 3 can a child use metarepresentations to remember *that* (semantic encoding) she remembers *that* something occurred in her life (episodic memory). For example, at 13 to 14 months children could recall aspects of novel events at delays of up to one year (Fivush, Gray, and Fromhoff 1987) and defer imitation for novel acts at delays of four months (Meltzoff 1995b); however, before age 3 children generally cannot remember themselves remembering: "A two-year-old can be aware, for example, that 'a dog is in the yard' and may be able to recognize the dog later as one that was in the yard. The same child could not, however, encode an entire episode, such as 'I am now watching (experiencing) a dog in the yard'" (Wheeler, Stuss, and Tulving 1997:346). The metarepresentational ability to recall past representations of events, often at will, appears to be intimately related to self-awareness and mental time travel (Suddendorf and Corballis 1997). It is functionally associated with the recently evolved prefrontal cortices of the hominid brain (Wheeler, Stuss, and Tulving 1997).

One evolutionary story is that metarepresentational agency, and understanding of false belief and deceit, emerged as a later development of intentional communicative displays that signaled possibilities for hominids to cooperate (or deceive) in a wide variety of situations: "Thus, I gesture towards a vase of flowers with an upturned palm. There is little or no interest in the primary description of this stimulus as an end in itself: a hand oriented with such and such a geometry for such and such a time. What *is* interesting is what someone *means* by making it" (Leslie 1991:75). Intentional communicative display is what autistic children often lack. Although they can often imitate the gesture, and so represent it, they can't go beyond this primary representation to infer that the gesture stands for something else. For example, unlike nonautistic 1-year-olds (Masur 1983), older autistic children cannot signal communicative intent by pointing. They cannot metarepresent a relation, INTENTIONALLY COMMUNICATE, among a person as an agent (e.g., mother), a stimulus situation (e.g., an upturned palm oriented toward a vase of flowers), and an inferred situation (e.g., the child giving the flowers to the mother).

Religious acts of faith incorporate universal, metarepresentational features of pragmatic communication, including PRETEND (that *p*), EMPATHIZE (about *p*), and

PROMISE (to do *p*). These are *social* acts common to all normally interacting human agents. A principal difference between religious and nonreligious employments of these behaviors is that the situation that is represented (*p*) in a religious act is not a state of affairs by which the truth, adequacy, or accurateness of the representation is evaluated. Rather, a religious representation (statement or other display) is *always right* and the situation to which it is properly applied *is made* to fit what is conventionally stipulated to be the case.

This is possible because a quasi-religious proposition *p* has no fully specifiable or fixed content, even in principle. In pretense, person A believes that (person B believes that ["*p* is true"] is false) because not-*p* *is* demonstrably or verifiably the case. In faith, person A believes that (person B believes that ["*p* is true"] is meaningful) because "*p* is true" is the Word of God and because God always speaks the truth. Faith, like pretense, necessarily involves metarepresentation (the embedded brackets). In pretense, however, the content of *p* is transparent and the state of affairs it represents can be fully assessed by observation and inference for truth or falsity. In faith, the quasi proposition to be assessed is not *p*, but the conceptually fused and opaque quasi proposition "*p* is true," which can be evaluated only for its indeterminately many possible implications (all necessarily true by fiat; Sperber 1975). Such religious quasi propositions are held metarepresentationally (Atran and Sperber 1991): one believes that_1 ("*p* is true" means that_2 [. . . .]). Although co-believers may all share belief that_1 "p is true," they may all differ in their representations of what that_2 means (see section 9.7).

As with pretense, religious acts of faith involve exaggerated gestures that are intended to connote a situation that differs from or goes beyond the one that is perceptually manifest. These ostentatious displays, which are always part of religious ritual, are intended to grab the perceiver's attention while also shifting that attention from mechanical aspects of the action itself to what the actor intends by it. For example, the act of receiving the host during Mass is an extraordinary eating display, where people are atypically fed on their knees with no chewing of the wafer allowed. It is obvious to everyone that the intended goal of the display is not eating, but communion. Communion is not a fixed relation of the attitude of faith to specifiable imaginary or counterfactual propositional content, although it may variously contain such partial contents. The meaning of an act of faith is not an inference to a specific proposition or set of propositions, but to an emotionally charged network of partial and changeable descriptions of counterfactual and counterintuitive worlds.

Religious displays of faith involve expressions of empathy that signal commitment (on development of empathy, see Eisenberg and Strayer 1987). To empathize is to cognitively match emotions. For example, suppose B feels grief and guilt because of her father's death, and that A feels sadness and regret in empathy. The cause of B's feeling of grief or guilt (her father's death) and A's feeling of sadness or regret (that B feels grief or guilt because of her father's death) are different. The physiological reactions are different (grief and guilt often are associated with increased heart rate; sadness for and regret for someone else are often associated with decreased heart rate). At a limit, A can arrive at B's state, although this is not usually the case. A's sadness and B's grief are causally related through cognitive appraisal.

Experimental studies of emotion indicate that people cognitively appraise situations in terms of elements such as pleasantness, certainty, anticipated effort, control, legitimacy, and perceived obstacle (Ellsworth 1991). Different emotions tend to be associated with different combinations of appraisals. A perceived obstacle (barrier to a goal) thought to be caused by an external agent is associated with anger; a perceived obstacle that is a person's own responsibility is associated with guilt; a perceived obstacle that has no readily apparent source is associated with sadness; and a perceived obstacle characterized by uncertainty is associated with fear and anxiety (Keltner, Ellsworth, and Edwards 1993). Using appraisal theory, let us define empathy as follows: A empathizes with B's experience of emotion E(b) if, and only if, A has emotion E(a) and A believes *that* there exists a situation, S, such that S causes B to have emotion E(b) and E(a) matches the appraisal of E(b) in important respects. Thus, A's sadness may match B's guilt in nearly all respects except that of "perceived obstacle."

Often in empathy, A and B both represent situation S with same propositional content (e.g., B's father died). But this needn't be so. At a limit, the situation may not be specified for any content or context (e.g., "I started to cry and started the whole world crying"). A common belief suffices that there is *some* situation at cause, whatever it is. As a form of empathy, religious compassion often involves cases where S is underspecified for propositional content or not specified at all (e.g., S = God's will). Even when a common cause is fully specified (e.g., B's father died), it is conceived of only as a *proximate* causal event that arises from an *ultimate and ultimately inscrutable* causal situation (e.g., God has called B's father to Him).

Ritualized religious displays are examples of what is known in pragmatics as performative (Austin 1962) or illocutionary (Searle 1969) acts. The relationship of a performative display to the situation it is concerned with is very different from that of an utterance or statement to some propositionally represented state of affairs (cf. Tambiah 1981). For example, when a woman is invested as a Catholic nun and faithfully married to Christ, those who do the investing are not describing acts of investiture or marriage to the woman; they are making her a nun. Moreover, if the nun has a child with a man, it is not the investiture that is wrong, it is the nun's behavior that fails to live up to what the investiture prescribes (cf. Rappaport 1999:132). Utterances and acts of religious ritual do not report or interpret antecedently existing states of affairs; they function to create and conjure into being conventional and communal commitments to counterfactual and counterintuitive worlds.

Many ritual performances convey the "illocutionary force" of the act of promising. Promising is among the strongest linguistic devices for conveying *commitment* to perform some future deed, D: *"It is not obvious to both [person A] and [person B] that [A] will do [D] in the normal course of events"* (Searle 1969:58–59). In religion, however, the future deeds to be performed need not be specified in detail, or even at all. All that is required is the convincingly expressed commitment to perform appropriately when some as yet unarticulated need arises. For example, if someone promises to do "God's bidding," then that person, or others, may interpret any number of as yet undetermined actions as satisfying the promise.

Embedded within religious liturgies are also promises that refer to more or less determinate situations that can be observed or discovered to conform to the promise made in rather straightforward and ordinary ways (e.g., I promise to obey the Commandment "Thou shalt not steal"). More often, religious prescriptions and commandments do not constitute social norms in the sense of shared rules or injunctions that determine behavior (contra Alexander 1987; R. Frank 1988; Sober and Wilson 1998; Boyd and Richerson 2001b). Instead, they stipulate only a bare, skeletal frame for collectively channeling thought and action: "Here O Israel, the Lord Thy God, The Lord Is One. . . . Thou shalt not bow down to other gods nor serve them" (for a fuller discussion and supporting experiments, see chapter 9). Their expression performatively signals and establishes a cognitive and emotional commitment to seek convergence but doesn't specify (the propositional content of) *what* people should converge to. Supernatural agents are guarantors and placeholders for appropriate actions in future circumstances. The truth about them is accepted on faith and communicated through ritual display, not discovered or described as a set of factual or logical propositions.

In sum, human metarepresentational abilities, which are intimately bound to fully developed cognitions of agency and intention, also allow people to entertain, recognize, and evaluate the differences between true and false beliefs. Given the ever-present menace of enemies within and without, concealment, deception, and the ability to both generate and recognize false beliefs in others would favor survival. But because human representations of agency and intention include representations of false belief and deception, human society is forever under the threat of moral defection.

Simple consent between individuals seldom, if ever, successfully sustains cooperation among large numbers of people over long periods of time. Displays of commitment to supernatural agents signal sincere willingness to cooperate with the community of believers. Supernatural agents thus *also* function as moral Big Brothers who keep constant vigil to dissuade would-be cheaters and free riders (R. Frank 1988; Dennett 1997; Pinker 1997). To ensure moral authority survives without the need for brute force and the constant threat of rebellion, all concerned—whether master or slave—must truly believe that the gods are always watching even when no other person could possibly be looking. Once these sacred relations become a society's moral constitution, as in our "One Nation Under God," they cannot be undone without risking collapse of the public order that secures personal welfare. This is one way that the conceptual ridge of our evolutionary landscape connects with the ridge of social interaction (in particular, with the imperative to cooperate so as to compete).

4.9. Summary: Making Possible Logically Impossible Worlds

Across cultures throughout the world people can readily identify beliefs that they consider religious, mythical, or magical. In most cultural settings where such beliefs arise, they arise together. Anthropologists, philosophers, and psychologists have customarily regarded such networks of beliefs as symbolic systems or cosmological theories that pervade or determine a culture's worldview. The apparent diversity of worldviews is the main support for cultural relativism: the doctrine that peoples in different societies think differently about how the world is constituted and conceive different ranges of empirical knowledge and ways of attaching meaning to things.

But there are no such bounded domains of culture, any more than culture itself constitutes a bounded domain of thought, meaning, or practice. Beliefs and practices become more or less "cultural" only to the extent that they become causally distributed among a population of minds with some (statistical, not categorical) reliability. To attain a culturally reliable level of distribution requires that most such beliefs and practices be compatible with, and constrained by, universal cognitive dispositions. Even the apparently incommensurable aspects of different cultural groups are only *conceivable* against a rich background of universally commensurable beliefs. If this weren't true, anthropology would be impossible.

Religious doctrines, rites, and liturgies are only diversely connected sets of examples that serve as public entry points into the vast network of mostly unarticulated commonsense beliefs that nearly all human beings share or have ready inferential access to. In fact, the so-called norms and values of religious traditions are not rules, principles, axioms, or injunctions with fixed factual or propositional content. They are public representations of *quasi-propositional beliefs*. Quasi-propositional beliefs may have the superficial subject-predicate structure of ordinary logical or factual propositions, but they can never have any fixed meaning because they are counterintuitive. Their cognitive role is to mobilize a more or less fluid and open-textured network of ordinary commonsense beliefs in order to build logically and factually impossible worlds that are readily conceivable, memorable, and transmissible.

By minimally, yet unmistakably, violating ordinary factual intuitions about how the world is, the religious counterintuitions that depict supernatural agents draw attention to those aspects of the world that people wish were otherwise. Such counterintuitions evoke other, logically and factually impossible worlds that are nonetheless readily conceivable because they leave intact most of the everyday world—minus a few worrisome facts and inferences. In this way, most of what religion conveys need never be made explicit or even transmitted.

Human metarepresentational abilities, which arise in fully developed cognitions of agency and intention, enable people to entertain, recognize, and evaluate the differences between true and false beliefs. These cognitive abilities allow lying and deception, which perpetually endangers any moral order. At the same time, they provide the hope and promise of eternal and open-ended solutions through representations of counterintuitive supernatural worlds. This enables people to imagine minimally impossible worlds that appear to solve existential problems, including death and deception. Attempts to replace intentional worlds governed by supernatural agents with secular ideologies are at serious disadvantage in the moral struggle for cultural selection and survival.

5 The Sense of Sacrifice

Culture, Communication, and Commitment

Religious offerings always involve nonrecuperable costs, no matter how economically flexible they appear. Why? Because human representations of agency and intention include representations of false belief and deception, human society is forever under threat of moral defection. Simple consent among individuals seldom, if ever, successfully sustains cooperation among large numbers of people over long periods of time. Emotionally hard-to-fake and materially costly displays of devotion to supernatural agents signal sincere willingness to cooperate with the community of believers. Supernatural agents reign over the emotions as imagined moral supervisors—fictive Wise Fathers, Attentive Mothers, Big Brothers, Watchful Wardens—who keep constant vigil to dissuade would-be cheaters and free riders.

Commitment is useless unless it is successfully communicated. It follows that displays of credible commitment are as significant as the behavioral commitments they are meant to signify. Displays also are more frequent than actual commitments, because they are usually less costly. Nevertheless, for cooperation to work, displays of commitment must be thoroughly convincing, and to be convincing people must be willing to make the ultimate sacrifice, however rare.

Just as a marriage commitment to one person usually precludes similar commitment to another, so a religious commitment to one society or moral order usually precludes commitment to another. This leads to constant conflict and competition between groups. The result of this process is an unending development of new religious forms.

5.1. Sacrifice: A Nonrecuperable Cost

> As a mother, even at the risk of her own life, protects her son, her only son: so let the *Arahat* [person set free by insight] cultivate

> goodwill without measure among all beings . . . unmixed with any feeling of differing or opposing interests.
>
> —"The Path of the *Arahat*," attributed to Siddharta Guatama (Buddha) (6th or 7th century B.C.)

> Cruelty and intolerance to those who do not belong to it are natural to every religion.
>
> —Sigmund Freud, *Group Psychology and the Analysis of the Ego* (1955[1921])

Religious sacrifices are not only designed to be materially costly, they also aim to be emotionally arousing. Blood, especially human blood, is optimal for sacrifice on both accounts. Among the ancient peoples of the Middle East, Europe, India, Africa, Mesoamerica, North America, South America, and Oceania, sacrificial use of human blood expressed many important ritual ideas. Such costly offering of a significant part of a particular human life was made to the gods to obtain an even fuller and more enduring life for the congregation as a whole. Blood offered at the altar was usually conceived to be drunk by the deity.

The blood offered was sometimes drawn from the sacrificers (Maya, aboriginal Australians, ancient Semites, West Africans), the sacrificers' children (in India, Phoenicia, Carthage, the Iroquois confederation of Native North America) or, more generally, the sacrificers' slaves and captives (in Mexico, Assyria, Rome, Scythia, Melanesia; cf. Pliny 1829[ca. A.D. 70]; de la Vega Inca 1986[1609]; Diaz del Castillo 1989[1632]; Villagutierre 1701; J. Wilson 1855; Lowie 1924; Havemeyer 1929; Freidel, Schele, and Parker 1993; A. Baker 2001). Apart from circumcisions and letting of one's own blood, blood sacrifice usually meant the sacrificial victim's death. The flesh of the victim was often shared among the congregation (Mesoamerica, Inca), burned to etherealize the food for consumption by the gods (Middle East), or buried to fertilize the earth and renew its creative powers (Incas and others).

In many of the world's religions, blood sacrifice has persisted in one form or another. Usually it survives as animal sacrifice, with animal blood replacing human blood. Among the Old Testament Hebrews, for example, the sacrificial bull was called "food of the gods" (*lehem elohim*). The Homeric deities, too, were said to "feast on hecatombs" (*Iliad* ix, 531). Particular Greek gods were designated by special epithets, such as "the goat-eater," "the ram-eater," "the bull-eater," and even "the cannibal," with the allusion to persistent human sacrifices (Robertson Smith 1972[1891]:224).

Often the animal is consumed by the congregation, at least in part. This serves to redistribute meat and affection among members of the community. For example, among Moslems in the vicinity of Mecca in 1890:

> a sheep or goat, is thrown down upon its left side, and its throat is cut, as has been customary, doubtless from time immemorial. . . . [T]he one killing the animal, says: "In the name of God, God is great" [Bismillah! Allahu Akbar], and the minister of the shrine, known as the religious sheik, sometimes reads the first sura of the Koran. After the minister has re-

> ceived his quarter, the rest of the animal is boiled, and may be served as in any other feast, with boiled rice, or wheat, or with loaves of Arab bread. . . . When there are many guests, and the one who offers the sacrifice fears there is not enough flesh to provide for all, he may ask the minister to give up his share. (Curtiss 1902[1892]:172–173)[1]

According to British social anthropologist Edward Tylor, the advantage of animal sacrifice over human sacrifice is that "cost may be economised without impairing efficiency. The result is seen in ingenious devices to lighten the burden on the worshipper by substituting something less valuable than what he ought to offer, or pretends to" (1958[1871]: ii,485).

In the Arabian case described above:

> A cock may be offered if the one paying his vow is too poor to bring a more expensive offering. A bullock or camel is considered a sufficient offering for seven persons. (Curtiss 1902[1892]:174)

Similarly, among the Nuer of Sudan:

> Oxen were never killed for food, only for ritual purposes; yet the meat provided (along with natural death) apparently satisfied meat requirements; barren cows were sacrificed rather than fertile ones, sheep or goats substituted when ox sacrifice might deplete the herd, and even cucumbers substituted. (Evans-Pritchard 1940:26)

Also for the Inca, sacrifice included something of a scale of economic substitutability:

> The sacrifices that the Inca offered to the sun were of many and diverse things, such as domesticated animals big and small. The principal and most esteemed sacrifice was that of lambs [of the llama], next to which came that of sheep [llama], then that of barren ewes. They also sacrificed rabbits, and all birds used for food, all cereals, even the coca herb, and the finest cloths. All this they burned in the place of incense as a thank-offering to the sun, for having created them for the support of man. (de la Vega Inca 1986[1609]: bk. 2, ch. 8, 76–77; my translation)

Although economic calculations often influence the choice and practice of sacrifice, the conclusion that sacrifice is a purely economic strategy is mistaken. In religious offerings, there is *always a nonrecuperable cost* involved both in the selection of the item offered and in the ceremony itself. Thus, in the Arabian case: "The offerings must be without a blemish [a perfect male of the flock, at least a year old]" (Curtiss 1902[1892]:174). For the Nuer, substitution is allowable only to a point, after which "a religious accounting might reveal that the spirits and ghosts were expecting a long overdue proper sacrifice, because accounts were out of balance so to speak" (Evans-Pritchard 1940:26).

Religious sacrifice invariably costs something for the persons on whose behalf the offering is made. That is why "sacrifice of wild animals which can be regarded as the free gift of nature is rarely allowable or efficient" (Robertson Smith 1894:466). In many cases, the first or best products of one's livelihood must be given to the gods, as with the first fruits of the Hebrews or the most perfect maize kernels of the Maya.

Most, if not all, religions specify obligatory circumstances under which a sacrifice *must* be performed, *regardless* of economic considerations. For example:

> The Pawnee "Morning Star" sacrifice; the "year-minding" of the Beduin for their deceased male kin and ancestors; the Ketsá and other rituals of the Kede to secure the welfare of the people on the Niger River; or the sacrifices of the Tallensi at sowing and harvest . . . sacrifice at the installation of a chief among the Ashanti; to rectify a homicide, as among the Tallensi and Nuer; to cure illness or avert accident as among the Swazi and Nuer; or after it as with the Lugabara; to expiate incest as among the Ashanti and Dinka; or to expiate fighting at some very sacred rites, as among the Owele Ibo. There are also the sacrifices to avert disasters of nature, as when the Lovedu try to secure rain. In all such cases the regular religious need, to establish communication with god or with the spirit world . . . would seem to be pressing and primary. "Afford it or not," the attitude might seem to be. (Firth 1963:16)

To these examples of animal or plant offerings may be added numerous other types of costly abnegation, such as sacrificing one's own procreative capacity, fingers, teeth, labor, artifacts, and so forth. The issue, then, is not whether religious sacrifice is costly, but why?

5.2. Altruism: Cooperating to Compete

In any human society, there is always a risk of cheating in joint endeavors and lying in communication. The same metarepresentational cognitive capacities that allow humans to conceive of nonexisting states of affairs and to conceptually modify present ones also allow for deception (see Chapter 4). Social competition virtually guarantees the exercise of deception. Supernatural agents contribute to maintaining the cooperative trust of actors and the trustworthiness of communication by sanctifying the actual order of mutual understandings and social relations as the only morally and cosmically possible one (cf. Rappaport 1999). Thus, invocation of supernatural agents constitutes an ecologically rational (and self-rationalizing) response to enhanced possibilities of deception inherent in the evolution of human interaction. For if people cannot believe that the moral basis of community life is directed by the fundamental nature of the world in an intelligent, purposeful, and meaningfully designed way, there is nothing except brute force to prevent defection and nothing except individual goodwill to prevent deception (which is hardly a sure thing).

From this perspective, the evolutionary problem of religion in particular, and commitment in general, is one of explaining how and why biologically unrelated individuals altruistically sacrifice their own immediate material interests to form genetically incoherent relationships under an imagined permanent and immaterial authority. Altruism occurs when an organism's behavior diminishes its own fitness and enhances the fitness of some other organism or organisms. Fitness is a measure of an organism's reproductive success. The sacrifice of an organism for its relatives—a mother for her children, a brother for his siblings, an ant for its colony, a bee for its hive—lowers an organism's individual fitness (also called "classical" or "Darwinian" fitness) because it compromises the individual's ability to bear and raise offspring. Nevertheless, such kin altruism may also enhance the individual's "inclusive fitness" by allowing surviving relatives to pass on many of the individual's genes to future generations (Hamilton 1964).[2]

Other situations of apparent altruism involve requiting strategies between nonrelatives. In direct cases of what biologist Robert Trivers (1971) calls "reciprocal altruism," an individual donates its own short-term benefit to another when it is likely that the beneficiary will return the favor in the future. Such direct reciprocity can occur within or between species. Among many primate species, for example, nonrelatives often groom one another to remove small parasites from hard-to-get-at body parts. In symbiosis, direct reciprocity between different species may involve repayment in entirely different "currencies"; for example, certain plant species of the genus *Acacia* give ants shelter and the ants, in turn, protect the plants by stinging any animal that brushes by.

The practice of reciprocal altruism, however, poses an evolutionary problem. A group of individuals that always cooperated would not likely survive an invasion of cheaters, unless the cooperators could identify and exclude the cheaters. Otherwise, the cooperators would be in effect subsidizing cheaters at significant cost to themselves and thus driving themselves to extinction. Detecting cheaters usually carries some cost in terms of time or energy allotted to marking, monitoring, and punishing them. As a population tended to full cooperation, the (selection) pressures to pay the cost of detecting cheaters would lessen, but the opportunities for cheaters to invade undetected would thereby increase. As cheaters began succeeding, cooperators would again have to evolve cheater detectors or die out.

These antagonistic selection pressures work against populations of interacting nonkin consisting wholly of cooperators or cheaters. One evolutionarily recurrent, simple, and stable strategy for maintaining reciprocal altruism is what political scientist Robert Axelrod (1984) calls "tit-for-tat." If individual X cooperates with individual Y during their first interaction, then Y cooperates with X in succeeding interactions; if X cheats on Y during any interaction, then Y no longer cooperates with X.

As human groups get larger, the occasions for interaction with strangers become more frequent, as does vulnerability to deception. Successful strategies for maintaining direct reciprocity usually require repeated encounters between individuals. This allows for the return of an altruistic act by the beneficiary to the benefactor. But what if two individuals who are unlikely to ever meet again must decide how to treat one another? Suppose individual X decides to take a chance in cooperating with individual Y. Why shouldn't Y just take the benefit and run off, leaving X in the lurch? This vexed question is famously known as "the Prisoner's Dilemma" (as any police officer, prosecutor, or judge knows, there's little to keep one crook from ratting on another to get the better side of a plea bargain).

One solution hinges on what biologist Richard Alexander (1987) calls "indirect reciprocity." Indirect reciprocity provides more opportunity for mutual benefit, and for swindling, than direct reciprocity. Direct reciprocity helps to bond individuals together in exchange, as when a person pours a glass of wine for another or exchanges gifts at Christmas. It is a mainstay of small-scale societies (Mauss 1990[1925]). Direct reciprocity provides advantages that the reciprocating parties would otherwise lack, as when a person barters one item she needs less for another she needs more or exchanges money for goods. With indirect reciprocity, instead of receiving benefits only when a person can afford to give up some, a person can receive aid when most in need. In food sharing, for example, if a person gives up a surplus to others his loss may be minimal; but if he has nothing, the same quantity could mean the difference between life and death. People not only save for a rainy day by storing food surplus in another's stomach, as vampire bats do (Wilkinson 1984). In sharing food, people also intentionally *invest* that surplus to reap dim or unforeseen future benefits (friendship and cooperation, social security and energy savings, etc.). Moreover, depending on reputation, a person can receive aid not just from acquaintances but also from practical strangers. Indirect reciprocity is a necessary condition for the emergence of large-scale societies.

Indirect reciprocity occurs when individual X knows that individual Y cooperates with others, and this knowledge favors X's cooperating with Y. Consider a population whose individuals have the option to cooperate or not. Suppose individual X randomly meets individual Y. If Y has a reputation for cooperation and if X cooperates with Y, then X's reputation likely increases. If X does not cooperate with Y, then X's reputation likely decreases (see Novak and Sigmund 1998 for various simulations). The basic idea is to help those who are known to help others.

Humans, perhaps unlike other animals, invest heavily in acquiring and adhering to social reputations. Reputation is a public "image" allowing members of the society to see who the nice guys are. Reputations are continually evaluated and reevaluated by different subgroups of "onlookers" in the population, with different subgroups often assigning different weights to similar interactions. For example, leaders and landlords may be more inclined to downgrade subjects and tenants for failing to pay taxes or rent, whereas subjects and tenants may tend more to diminish leaders and landlords for withholding benefits and amenities.

A plausible hypothesis is that the mechanisms for successful promotion of indirect reciprocity were naturally selected in response to the environmental problem-context of "runaway social competition" (Alexander 1989). Unlike other primate groups, hominid groups early on grew to sizes (Dunbar 1996) that could not function exclusively on the basis of kin selection (commitment falls off precipitously as genetic distance increases between individuals) or direct reciprocity (ability to directly monitor trustworthiness in reciprocation decreases rapidly as the number of transactions multiply). Larger groups of individuals outcompete smaller groups in love and war (Axelrod 1984).

As "fictive kin" (Nesse 1999), which cognitively retains natural kinship's emotional valence, members of large groups also perform and profit from many tasks that they could not do alone, one by one, or only with family.[3] Thus, "Among the Hebrews and Phoenicians . . . the worshipper is called brother (that is, kinsman or sister of the god)" (Robertson Smith 1972[1891]:44 n. 2). "Brotherhood" is also the common term applied today among the Christian faithful and to the fraternity (*ikhwan*) of Islam.

5.3. Fundamentalist Intolerance of Other "Species"

> The U.S. knows that I have attacked it, by the grace of God, for more than 10 years now. . . . God knows that we have been pleased at the killing of American soldiers. This was achieved by the grace of God and the efforts of the *mujahedin*. . . . We expect to be rewarded by God. . . . Fighting is a part of our religion and our Shari'a [an Islamic legal code]. Those who love God and his Prophet and this religion cannot deny that whoever denies even a minor tenet of our religion commits the gravest sin. . . . Hostility toward America is a religious duty, and we hope to be rewarded for it by God.
>
> —Osama bin Laden, interview from Afghanistan, 22 December 1998, *Time* (11 January 1999)

> God continues to lift the curtain and allow the enemies of America to give us probably what we deserve [referring to the terrorist attack by Islamic extremists on Washington and New York]. . . . We make God mad. I really believe that the abortionists, and the feminists, and the gays and the lesbians who are actively trying to make an alternative life style, the ACLU [American Civil Liberties Union], People for the American Way—all of them who have tried to secularize America—I point the finger in their face and say, "You helped this happen."
>
> —The Reverend Jerry Falwell, on the Christian Broadcasting Network's *700 Club* (13 September 2001)

> Islam is not a peaceful religion that wants to coexist. They want to coexist until they control, dominate and then if need be destroy.
>
> —Pat Robertson on CBN Television, February 21, 2002, *The Washington Post* (February 22, 2002)

The evolutionary and cognitive flip side of in-group commitment is out-group intolerance. In tribal cultures, religion is inseparable from polity, and all tribal cultures engage in intertribal warfare.[4] In modern societies, orthodox and fundamentalist congregations tend to be associated with higher in-group cohesion and commitment than traditional or mainstream religious groups (Alston and Aguirre 1979; Welch 1981; Kaldor 1994) but also with less tolerance for out-groups.

Numerous studies indicate that the stronger one's religious commitment to fundamentalist beliefs, the less tolerant one's politics and sense of justice (Smidt and Penning 1982; Powell, Steelman, and Peek 1982; Eckberg and Blocker 1989; Young 1992; Greeley 1991,1993). During the Vietnam War, for example, Americans who associated themselves with orthodox or fundamentalist religious beliefs were more inclined to support the war and its resolution through military action alone (Tygart 1971; E. Russell 1971; Granberg and Campbell 1973; McClelland 1975). Among Catholics and Protestant Baptists, fundamentalists tend to be more authoritarian, ethnocentric, dogmatic, and prejudiced toward other groups (Rokeach 1960; Putney and Middleton 1961; L. Brown 1962). This also appears to be the case for fundamentalist Moslems, Hindus, and Jews (al-Thakeb and Scott 1982; Hunsberger 1996). In Guatemala and El Salvador, the Pentacostalist movement has been associated with the most conservative right-wing elements of society, including those who manned and supported the infamous "death squads" (Arias 1990; Martin-Baro 1990; Stoll 1994).

Fundamentalist sects, as well as more transient religious cults, often emerge initially from the economic fringe or politically disenfranchised margins of society (Beit-Hallahmi and Argyle 1997). They are most dynamic as millennial movements that tend to arise in times of crises that involve social oppression (Baer and Singer 1993), political dislocation (Crapanzano 1985), economic dislocation (Cochrane 1970), war (Thrupp 1962; Beit-Hallahmi 1992), or epidemic (Barkun 1974). Recent historical examples include the Native American Ghost Dances of the late nineteenth century (Thornton 1986), post–World War II Melanesian Cargo Cults (Worsely 1968; Whitehouse 2000), and any number of revitalization and salvation movements in sub-Saharan Africa (Blakely et al. 1994) and elsewhere in developing countries (B. Wilson 1973). In the United States and throughout the industrialized world, fundamentalist sects and religious cults may be, in part, reactions to institutionalized social mobility and economic "flexibility." This has permanently removed traditional (i.e., transgenerational) family and community moorings, making the self's disorientation a chronic condition for large population segments of our "culture."

Fundamentalist sects distinguish themselves from more ephemeral and unstable (socially fluid) religious cults by creating more intense and integrated forms of practical cooperation and religious commitment (Kanter 1972; Stark and Bainbridge 1980).[5] Sometimes they manage to affiliate with more orthodox groups and to claim for themselves the role of proactive vanguard and reformist protector of mainstream religion (e.g., the Protestant Christian right in mostly Catholic Latin America, the Shi'ite Moslem Hezbollah in the mostly Sunni Moslem Middle East).

Fundamentalism often exacerbates social and national conflict, if only by associating other causal factors (economic or social inequalities, territorial or resource-control disputes, etc.) with absolute, categorical discriminations that thwart negotiation and compromise (Atran 1990b). Social and conceptual differences become essentialized as ahistorical and acontextual differences of race, caste, class, or "civilization."

For example, Uri Tsvi Greenberg, the ultranationalist Jewish poet and ideologue, explained the Palestine conflict as a millennial struggle between Jews and Arabs in these terms: "Double blood for blood. Double fire for fire . . . for thus races repay their enemies; across generations and throughout time. . . . A country is conquered in blood . . . from the River of Egypt to the Euphrates" (1937). To the zealot, religious group differences seem no less insurmountable than the biological barriers that appear to separate animal species. Thus, during the first intifada, Rabbi Meir Kahane, a leader of the extreme religious right in Israel and among Jews in the United States, declared: "The Arabs are cancer, cancer, cancer. . . . Let me become Defense Minister for two months and you will not have a single cockroach around" (cited in *Ha'aretz Magazine*, Israeli weekly, 31 May 1985; my translation).

Similar thoughts are current during the second intifada. For example, Rabbi Ovadia Yosse, chief spiritual leader of the ultraorthodox Shas Party in Israel, declaims: "The Arabs must be annihilated, these evil ones, these accursed ones, they should be bombarded with supermissiles" (cited in *Le Point*, French weekly, 13 April 2001; my translation).

Such anti-other sentiments, of course, feed off one another and are often mutually generating (Atran 1990b). Thus, beginning in the 1920s, the Moslem religious leader (*mufti*) of Jerusalem, Hajj Amin al-Husseini, and numbers of other Moslem fundamentalists ever since, have routinely denounced the Jews as a "filthy race" intent on subjugating humankind. For example, as outlined in the *Protocols of the Elders of Zion*, a preposterous forgery of the Russian Czarist police that outlines a Jewish plot to dominate the world: "You [the English colonial power in Palestine] bring with you dangerous Thieves, Impostors and all sorts of Filth from Europe [i.e., Jews], while you profess that you are bringing civilization" (for sources, see Atran 1990b:511 n. 30). Such notions are still current: "Oh, Allah, destroy America for it is controlled by Zionist Jews . . . Allah will avenge, in the name of his Prophet, the colonialist settlers who are the descendants of monkeys and pigs . . . forgive us, oh Muhammad, for the acts of these monkeys and pigs who wished to profane your holiness" (Ikrima Sabri, Mufti of Jerusalem, weekly Friday prayer, radio broadcast on the Voice of Palestine, 11 July 1997).

In May 2001, the Moslem Taliban ("religious students"), who then ruled most of Afghanistan, ordered Hindus in the country to wear yellow identification badges to distinguish themselves from Moslems—a practice mimicking the preextermination stage in the Nazi persecution of European Jews in the late 1930s and early 1940s. In August 2001, the Taliban Ministry for the Promotion of Virtue and Prevention of Vice (religious police) declared that persons convicted of teaching the Bible "will be imprisoned for life, or hanged" ("Les employés afghans d'ONG chrétiennes risquent la peine de mort," *Le Monde*, 3 September 2001). Ever since the late 1940s, extreme Hindu pietists have been violently advocating expulsion or liquidation of Moslems from India. Today on the Internet, militant Hindus and Jews have teamed up on joint Web sites to explain that fighting Moslems everywhere in Southwest Asia is really a struggle against the anti-God—an idea that resonates with Christian militants who support U.S. domination in the area ("Hindu Holocaust," www.ghen.net/forum/; www.hinduunity.org).

As fundamentalist groups become more dominant, other groups that were formerly part of the mainstream may attempt to counter fundamentalist encroachments. One reaction to fundamentalism is religious humanism, which seeks to break down the social and ideological barriers that keep certain groups subordinated to, or outside of, the mainstream (e.g., the "liberation theology" espoused by popular elements of the Catholic Church in Latin America). Another reaction is the splintering off of new, antagonistic fundamentalist groups from the mainstream or the margins. From an initial position of weakness, some fundamentalist groups may eventually adopt a more humanist strategy for group survival (early Christianity, twentieth-century European Moslem Brothers), whereas from a position of strength they may adopt an even more uncompromising stance (late Medieval Christian monastic orders, early Islam). Whatever the balance of forces, however, religious competition and conflict endure and social change ensues in the constant production of new sects, cults, and ever-evolving syncretic forms of religion.

5.4. Syncretism, Social Competition, and Symbolic Inversion

> There was then no sickness, they had then no aching bones; they had then no high fever; they had then no smallpox . . . they had then no headache. At that time the course of humanity was orderly. The foreigners made it otherwise when they arrived here. . . . It was only that these priests of ours were to come to an end when misery was introduced by the real Christians. Then with the true God, the true *Dios*, came the beginning of our misery.
>
> —*Chilam Balam of Chumayel*, "The Jaguar's Spokesman," Yukatek Maya text (16th–17th century), in Inga Clendinnen, *Ambivalent Conquests* (1987)

> In advance, and spread my word, I, Spokesman of the Jaguar. For I recount the word of the True God, Whose day will come to help or punish the born and engendered children of the Itza.
>
> —Final passage of the *Chilam Balam of Tizimin* (19th century), in Munro Edmonson, *The Ancient Future of the Itza* (1987)

In one sense, all religions are syncretic, or at least all currently existing religions are syncretic. This is because every existing society communicates with, and exchanges beliefs and practices with, other societies.[6] In some societies, different social groups have competing religions that involve many of the same elements, but in different relationships that symbolize their differing social relations.

For example, in the Candombolé Nagô sects of Afro-Brazilian Bahia, "values and behaviors characteristic of . . . Brazilian society at large are *inverted*" (Omar 1994:140). Upward mobility in the Candombolé religious hierarchy depends on adherence to African and not European customs and values: "Thence comes the prestige of Africa . . . where everything has religious value. . . . The highest qualifications are to be . . . the son or grandson of Africans, with no mixture at all of white blood" (Carneiro 1940:278). Impressive investments of time (active membership), energy (in communion through trance), and bodily sacrifice (months of seclusion and deep incisions of the occiput during initiation) help to secure a moral and social order somewhat resistant to enslaving pressures of the dominant society.

Another example concerns the Itza' Maya of northern Guatemala. The Itza' are the last surviving Maya native to the Petén tropical forest, a former epicenter of Classical Lowland Maya civilization (Atran 1993). The Spanish waged a particularly brutal campaign of conquest against this last independent Maya confederacy, which was finally conquered at the end of the seventeenth century (Atran and Ucan Ek' 1999; Jones 1998). Within a decade or so of conquest, the priesthood and ruling elite were eliminated and the native population fell by between one and two orders of magnitude through warfare, disease, the hardships of corvée labor, and flight. The Itza' language is presently moribund owing to the delayed effects of a violent anti-Maya language policy inaugurated by the Guatemalan dictator General Jorge Ubico in the 1930s. Their physical environment also faces imminent destruction owing to sudden and massive immigration of landless farmers from southern Guatemala. Nevertheless, aspects of pre-Columbian Itza' religion and society survive in subtle ways (Atran, Lois, and Ucan Ek' in press).

Most Itza' are devoutly Catholic, although a small but increasing minority recently has been joining the local Pentacostal church. A few Itza' Catholics are sorcerers-shamans-healers (*ajmen yaj*) who practice "white magic" (*säk maajiyaj*), as opposed to the *ajwaay*, who practice black magic. One Itza' shaman described his beliefs and practices to me as follows: Diyoos, the Christian God (i.e., the Spanish Dios), came after the Great Men (*Nojoch Winikoo'*), the Itza' ancestors who built the cities with pyramids and whose spirits (*upixanoo'*) still dwell there. The coming of Diyoos engendered the coming of the devil, *Kisin* ("the Killer"), who works in league with the spirits of the Nojoch Winikoo' at the behest of Diyoos.

Itza' sorcerers-shamans-healers contract themselves to Kisin. Every year they must arrange for some unworthy Christian soul (*uyool kristiyaanoj*) to go to Kisin, often by conjuring a night shadow spirit (*ak'ä' pixan*) or "wind" (*ik'*) to represent a dead relative of the victim. This may frighten the victim to death in either of two ways. In one case, the victim merely sights the spirit, which triggers a "hot" (*chokoj*) reaction of the blood (*k'ik'*): the "thin blood" (*bekech k'ik'*) races through the body, causing the heart (*pusik'al*) to explode. In the other case, the spirit touches the victim as a "cold wind," which freezes the "nerves" (*nerb'ios*). Once dead, the victim, in turn, becomes an *ak'ä' pixan*.

In exchange, the Itza' sorcerer-shaman-healer obtains the power to heal the souls of Christians with the help of Kisin and the *ak'ä' pixan*. Most often, physically and mentally troubled individuals come to the Itza' sorcerer-shaman-healer when neither the Catholic church nor medical personnel from nearby towns seem able to provide relief. Through the sorcerers-shamans-healers vast amounts of Itza' Maya ethnomedicinal knowledge and practice endure, as does a somewhat distinct sense of Itza' religious identity that is linked to the pre-Columbian past. Without this knowledge and cultural sense, the last Itza' may simply disappear among the mass of poor Spanish-speaking Ladinos (mestizos).

Of course, behind present syncretic forms of religion may lie a tortuous course of historical development. For example, in the mid-sixteenth century, when the Spanish conquered the Maya of Yucatán (who are closely related to the Itza'), the Yukatek seem to have first assimilated the crucifixion to their own notions of blood sacrifice: instead of spread-eagling the victim over a rock to cut the heart out, the victim was first nailed or tied to a cross (Clendinnen 1990). During the Yukatek rebellion known as the Caste War, which lasted from the mid-nineteenth to the early twentieth century, the "Talking Cross" at the rebel capital of Chan Santa Cruz (present-day Carillo Puerto in Quintana Roo, Mexico) commanded the execution of white and mestizo Mexicans as "false Christians" and "devil worshippers," whose horns were hidden from view, like those of Jews (conversations with the son of a Maya soldier of the Cross, Noh ha, Quintana Roo, October 1993; cf. Reed 1964). In the Maya Highlands of Mexico and Guatemala, loss and revival of cultural sovereignty is celebrated in the passion of the Indian Christ as the last Maya king (Bricker 1981).

A final example of syncretism and symbolic inversion concerns the Tamil (Dravidian) and tribal peoples (*adivasis*) of south India. Hinduism was introduced into Dravidian and tribal south India by Indo-European Aryans who invaded from the north. By the time the Aryans reached south India, Hinduism had taken the form of post-Vedic Brahminism (700 B.C.–A.D. 1100). This included the caste system (*Dharmasastras*). That system essentially lifted all Aryans into the "twice reborn" high castes of priest (*Brāhman*), warrior (*Kshatriya*), and farmer or tradesman (Vaiśya). They were granted the lands and labor of the conquered Dravidians and aboriginals. Most Dravidians became low-caste servants (*Śūdra*). They could enter, but not officiate, in the temples. Aryan women convicted of immorality would be branded prostitutes, whereas low-caste women of ill repute were sold as slaves (Manickan 1993).

Some Dravidians, and most aboriginals, became "fifth-class" outcasts (*Pañchama*). Eventually, outcasts were deemed too "unclean" to be admitted into the temples or even to be seen or touched by a Brāhman.[7] They were not allowed to live independently within the confines of the settled villages (Gough 1981). They were known as Pariahs (*Parayar*), and many became bonded laborers inseparably attached to the soil (Manickan 1993). They were allowed no hope of improving their lot in this life or the next, and so became de facto hereditary slaves (*adimai*). The outcasts were clearly the ancestors of today's "untouchables," or Harijan (Gough 1973).

In Brahminism, the cosmos is ruled by a sacred triumvirate: Brahma the Creator, Vishnu the Protector, and Shiva the Destroyer. All three are male deities. In north India today, Vishnu is often the dominant focus of worship; in south India, Shiva predominates, as the creative force of life through death. Until recently, many of the tribal peoples were animist or only nominally Hindu, some practicing various forms of totemism (Devasahayam 1990).

Perhaps more important than Brahminism for the everyday life of south India's Tamil and tribal villagers is worship of the village deity (*grāma-devata*). Village deities protect the community from public catastrophes, such as epidemics, droughts, floods, and bandits. If they are not properly honored, these deities introduce the very calamities they are supposed to protect against. Unlike the principal deities of the Hindu Pantheon, the primary village deities are almost always female (Whitehead 1988[1921]). The only important Hindu deity who is also a primary village goddess is Kāli, the "black" wife of Shiva (as opposed to his "white" wife, the goddess Devi). She is the goddess of death and time (*kaal*). Unlike the Brahministic deities who discourage the taking of animal life (*ahimsa*), the village goddesses demand frequent and sometimes massive animal sacrifices. The village holy man (*pūjārī*), who presides over such sacrifices, is customarily low-caste. Harijan, too, participate and officiate in these ceremonies.

In north India as well, village religion often deviates appreciably from Brahminism. This seems especially so among the lower castes and tribal peoples of largely Dravidian or aboriginal descent, even though Dravidian languages are no longer spoken: "The rural classes do indeed know the names and attributes of some of the greater [Hindu] gods, like Vishnu and Siva. . . . But worship here is confined to the higher classes, and the cultivator and labourer are content to propitiate the village deities" (Crooke 1907:235). Like many south Indian villages, the poorer north Indian villages also venerate Kāli as a principal village deity, or *grāma-devata*. Here, too, she demands blood and animal sacrifice to ward off epidemics and enemies; she also brings such catastrophes to the village if she is not adequately propitiated.

As among the Itza' and in other parts of the world, in India a clear distinction is drawn between white magic and black magic:

> White [Magic] . . . is a recognised method of promoting the interests of the community, as, for instance, in rain-making and by other devices for the general benefit of all members of the tribe. It is different when any one who has gained this power employs it for his own interest—to bring others under his power, or to punish an enemy or a rival. This is Black Magic, or Witchcraft, which is naturally regarded as an offence against the community. . . . The Shaman, medicine-man, wizard, or warlock, is recognised as the agent [of White and occasionally Black Magic] who controls the unseen spiritual powers and compels them to cure disease, foretell the future, rule the weather, avenge a man upon his enemy, and generally intervene for good or evil in human affairs. (Crooke 1907:248)

In sum, Afro-Brazilian Candombolé Nagô, Itza' Maya sorcery-shamanism-healing, and the village religion of India all contain inverted elements of dominant or mainstream religion. These elements sustain the links between the minority, small-scale societies and the mainstream religions of larger-scale society. These elements also carry vestiges of earlier religions and social orders that were once dominant but later subject to near annihilation by the now dominant religion and society. As a result, these minorities endure with some semblance of their own history and moral autonomy. Finally, this discussion of syncretism suggests that when different subgroups in the society have unequal status but competing religious priorities, there is no clear sense to the claim that religion is a form of social domination.

5.5. Social and Supernatural Hierarchy

> [I]t makes sense why an otherwise highly competitive and testy male baboon should ever allow another male literally to hold his future reproductive parts in the palm of his hand. It is hard to imagine a more tangible expression of trust than to invite excruciating punishment for a real or perceived betrayal. . . . Among the Walbiri of central Australia, men from different communities express their willingness to support each other through a public presentation and grasping of the supplicant's subincised penis [Meggitt 1965]. Similarly, in Genesis (24:9), Abraham's servant swears an oath while placing his hand under his master's "thigh," a probable euphemism for the genitals. . . . Of course, Australian aboriginals are no more ba-

> boons than they are Old Testament prophets . . . but their very incongruity suggests an enduring nexus in ritual between . . . willful individuals and social promises, fragile trust and elusive truths.
>
> —John Watanabe and Barbara Smuts, "Explaining Ritual without Explaining It Away" (1999)

> I have sinned. . . . It is important that everybody know the sorrow I feel. . . . And if my repentance is genuine . . . and if I can maintain both a broken spirit and a strong heart, then good can come of this for our country as well as for me and my family.
>
> —U.S. President Bill Clinton on the Monica Lewinsky affair, *Yahoo! News* (11 September 1998)

In primate societies, including human societies, high-status individuals have a discretionary range of behavioral choices unavailable to low-status individuals. Exercise of these choices often coercively imposes costly behavior on the subordinate individuals that benefits the dominant individuals. For example, subordinate male baboons must avoid estrous females when dominant males are around, thus decreasing chances for propagation, or suffer attack and decrease chances for survival. Either way, subordinate individuals suffer loss of fitness. Nevertheless, the social harmony and maintenance of the troop requires that, in the absence of a contested resource, dominant males engage in a greeting display that allows them to approach subordinates without evoking an avoidance response and subordinates to approach dominants without provoking attack (Zahavi 1977).

Religions in large-scale societies all show evidence of social dominance (Irons 1996a). Kneeling, bowing, prostration, hand spreading, and throat baring display primate submission and occur in *all* religions. They are everywhere understood in human society as conveying a message of humility, supplication, or subordination in social exchange.

Nevertheless, human society differs from other primate societies in this respect. Human worship requires even dominant individuals to willingly submit to a higher moral authority in displays of costly, hard-to-fake commitment or risk losing the allegiance of their subordinates: "Submission and sovereignty inhabit the same hierarchical structure. . . . God is to ruler as ruler is to subjects. . . . The ruler . . . ceases to be alone at the top of the pyramid as a target of potential aggression" (Burkert 1996:95; cf. Aristotle 1958a). The more a ruler sacrifices and suffers, the more the ruler earns respect and devotion. For example, Maya priests once required peasants to offer hard-won food and even to sacrifice their children to gods whose interests the priests represented. Such practices held for a time even after the Spanish conquest (Tozzer 1957; Clendinnen 1990). Human sacrifice kept the world going by cycling back the bounty and blood of life that the gods provided and distributed to the people via their representatives. Many an ancient Maya priest and peasant alike willingly partook of human sacrifice, which they called "no pain death" (*ma' yaj kimlal*; Edmonson 1982:101).

The Maya priests and kings, in turn, also made costly and hard-to-fake commitments to gods for whom the peasantry stood in as witness. At important events, the priests and kings bored into their penises or tongues to draw sacrificial blood, and they understood that they would be first to have their heart sacrificially ripped from their body when their policies and predictions failed, as always threatened to happen in war. In 1952, the Mexican archaeologist Alberto Ruz uncovered the tomb of Pacal the Great, ruler of Palenque, which contained a record of his funerary rites and the ascension of his successor Chalum-Bahlum II on January 10, 634. Epigraphers Linda Schele and David Freidel narrate the events described in the glyphs:

> Chan-Bahlum grabbed the young ahau's [lord's] hair. . . . [H]e plunged [the knife] into the captive's chest and struck up into the heart. . . . With the sacrifice completed, Chan-Bahlum . . . reached down and grabbed his [own] penis . . . he pierced it three times with the point . . . he pulled long strands of bark through the wounds and watched them turn red. . . . It was his first sacrificial act as patriarch of the royal clan, an act of symbolic birth in the midst of death. . . . The people of the kingdom in their thousands had come to witness the great king's [Pacal's] journey . . . toward Xibalba [the Underworld]. Hundreds began their song of grief and cut their own flesh in pious prayers for the king. Drums beat a mind-numbing rhythm accompanied by the piercing notes of clay whistles by people exhausted by days of dancing and fasting. (1990:233–234)

Some would argue that religion is primarily a coercive means of social domination. It involves a mixture of overt force and covert persuasion of the Godfather type, "an offer one can't refuse." The coercion argument holds that religion was created by and for rulers to materially exploit the ruled, with derivative or secondary benefits to the oppressed masses of a low but constant level of material security and productivity (Marx 1972[1842]). By brute force and punishment, rulers block physical opportunities for heretical social forms to emerge and competitively spread over a population. In this situation, only bloody upheaval would likely effect a change, but at great cost and with dubious results. In subtler and less violent ways, rulers tie personal security and public order to religion, which actually may render the local world a less uncertain and violent place to live. And so, for Protestant leader John Calvin, God commands support of injustice and tyranny against sedition and chaos: "Those who rule in an unjust and tyrannical world are raised by Him to punish the iniquity of the people. . . . If we have this . . . impressed on our hearts, that the most iniquitous kings are placed on their thrones by the same decree by which the authority of all kings is established, those seditious thoughts will never enter our minds that a king is to be treated according to his merits" (1956[1559]:74–77).

According to Jared Diamond, who relates a form of the "religion is oppression" argument: "Bands and tribes already had supernatural beliefs, just as do modern established religions. But the supernatural beliefs of bands and tribes did not serve to justify central authority, justify transfer of wealth, or maintain peace between unrelated individuals" (1997:277–278). True "religion" arose only when a central authority, or what Diamond calls a "kleptocrat," co-opted preexisting supernatural beliefs to set up a pyramid scam. In this game of social deception, wealth flows up the social hierarchy from plebes to patricians on its way to the gods. Of course, the plebes never see wealth get past the patricians, but they *believe* it does. The kleptocrat's trick is not entirely a con. He gets people to cooperate with one another under the belief that Big Brother is always lurking about in search of defectors. The plebes hope to emulate Big Brother by spying on and policing one another, which helps maintain personal security through public order. It also gives people a motive to sacrifice themselves for nonkin: "At the cost of a few society members who die in battle as soldiers, the whole society becomes much more effective at conquering other societies or resisting attacks" (p. 278). Self-sacrifice needn't even result in loss of an individual's inclusive genetic fitness: the martyr's relatives are usually rewarded with extra goods and elevated status.

Diamond's view of religion acknowledges the ubiquity of supernatural beliefs but is not obliged to account for them. For whatever reason, they happened to be around. What needs to be explained is how the kleptocrat gets the populace to go for the co-optation of such beliefs in a pyramid scam. Banging people over the head won't get ideas committed to it. Rewarding a person's kinfolk if a person dies for a cause is an inefficient way to spread the cause; to compensate for the lost martyr requires dispensing benefits to the martyr's family, which is costly for the kleptocrat. Maintaining personal security through public order and belief in Big Brother still leaves open issues of the origin and validation of such belief.

Diamond's restriction of religion to chiefdoms and state-level societies is arbitrary. Supernatural agents can serve in all small-scale societies to mitigate selfishness. Religious beliefs discourage abandoning the elderly and infirm who are about to become ancestors, as with Australian aboriginals, or exploiting children who are ancestors reincarnated, as in Bali. Among hunter-gatherers, religious beliefs underscore commensal relations such as food sharing.[8]

For Ibn Khaldûn, and contrary to Calvin, religious law is designed especially to thwart injustice. Ibn Khaldûn surveys the long-term cycles of civilizations and finds that even rulers must be accountable. If authorities become greedy and unjust, the populace follows suit. This undermines governance and social cohesion. It renders society liable to sedition from within and attack from without. Even in the absence of dramatic events "injustice must bring . . . the ruin of civilization" (1958[1318]: II, iii:41).

In fact, religion can be, and historically has been, as liberating as it has been domineering. As Adam Smith suggested, religions are co-opted and created by the disaffected to mobilize the populace *against* the kleptocrats: "Almost all religious sects have begun among the common people, from whom they have generally drawn their earliest as well as their most numerous proselytes. The austere system of morality . . . was the system by which they could best recommend themselves to . . . their plan of reformation" (1993[1776]:439). Indeed, Benjamin Franklin proposed that the revolutionary American Republic adopt the motto "Rebellion to tyrants is obedience to God" (cited in Novak 2000). American Presidents and other politicians must constantly, and more or less convincingly, display faith in God and adherence to beliefs like Franklin's to be elected by the people they serve and govern. They must also religiously display contrition when the people show moral discontent.

5.6. The Evolutionary Rationality of Unreasonable Self-Sacrifice

> My loyal followers, long ago we resolved to serve neither the Romans nor anyone else but only God . . . now the time has come that bids us prove our determination by our deeds. . . . The fire that was being carried into the enemy lines did not turn back of its own accord towards the wall we had built: these things are God's vengeance for the many wrongs that in our madness we dared to do to our own countrymen. For those wrongs let us pay the penalty not to our bitterest enemies, the Romans, but to God—by our own hands. . . . One thing only let us spare our store of food: it will bear witness when we are dead to the fact that we perished, not through want but because . . . we chose death rather than slavery. . . . Eleazar had many more arguments to urge, but all his listeners cut him short and full of uncontrollable enthusiasm made haste to do the deed. . . . These [dead] numbered nine hundred and sixty, women and children included. . . . Masada had fallen thus, the [Roman] general left a garrison in the fortress and returned with the rest of his army to Caesarea. For nowhere was there any enemy left.
>
> —Josephus Ben Matthias, *The Jewish War (67–73 A.D.)* (1981)

> Volunteers for "martyrdom" are subject to a veritable liturgical preparation. Before the attack, the body is oiled and perfumed. Often the clothes they have have never been worn before. It is truly a marriage with death in which the sexual dimension plays a determinant role . . . once in the "Garden of Delights" each young *shohada* can have the benefit of 70 virgins. So, awakening in an Israeli hospital, one of the "martyrs," gravely wounded by the explosives he carried, asked the nurses who were bent over his dressing table whether he was in Paradise. Another, who also survived . . . had even carefully wrapped his penis in bandages in the hopes of it being ready for use.
>
> —J.-P. Perrrin, "Oints et parfumés avant le 'martyre'," my translation

The commitment problem involves two seemingly antagonistic evolutionary imperatives. On the one hand, it is of obvious biological value to be able to react immediately to the most pressing events. This requires discounting events that are farther away in space and time as well as discounting the interests of others. To escape a fire you may need to leap from a building onto a crowded street below, whatever consequences might follow other than your own salvation, such as breaking the back of the person who breaks your fall. On the other hand, there may be distant risks and rewards that require consideration of information beyond present concerns. Helping the elderly or infirm may bring you no immediate advantage, but it may increase the chances of being helped by others as you in turn age or fall ill.

For economist Robert Frank (1988), uncontrolled passions are keys to the problem of commitment and the origins of social and moral sentiment. Passionate commitment cuts through the Gordian knot of various and opposing assessments of reputation by welding public perception to self-image in materially costly and emotionally hard-to-fake displays. Indirect reciprocity also requires more than just giving and receiving benefits; it requires *promises*, that is, displays of commitment to give future aid. Because promises can be broken, they have to be *convincing* for indirect reciprocity to be successful. To be convincing they have to be passionately expressed. Emotionally driven moral sentiments, then, could be regarded "as a crude attempt to fine-tune the reward mechanism" (90). They do so by mitigating the necessary tyranny of short-term interest when structural conditions in a present situation resemble those of a recurrent problem situation from our hominid past.

Some critical situations require immediate reactions to once-in-a-lifetime events. Although we may have scant preparation for action based on actual experience or learning, we do come biologically poised to react categorically to certain phylogenetically encountered classes of situations, such as finding a mate, fleeing from a predator, and fighting against long odds to defend what is dear. These built-in parts of cognitive and physiological architecture are "automatically" triggered by stimuli that fall within the natural domain of an ancestral problem task (Tooby and Cosmides 1990a; Nesse 1989; Griffiths 1997).[9] The exaggerated, telltale signs accompanying the eruption of ancestral emotions in particular contexts override everyday reasoning and occupy a special legal staus in our society, commonly known as "temporary insanity": "I once helped prosecute a prostitute who had stabbed a victim 81 times; I remember thinking that the jury would surely convict once they were made to count out the time it takes to stab someone 81 times. But what I learned afterward was that the sheer number of stab wounds seemed to the jury like evidence that the woman was telling the truth when she said she was responding more out of fear of attack than any deliberate plan to murder" ("A Story the Jury Never Heard," *New York Times*, 26 February 2000, A31).

Emotions provide rapid and economical responses when rational analysis is impractical, either because reason fails us for lack of available information to analyze or because systematic exploration of cause-effect relationships would take too long. They are cognitively thrifty, efficiently energizing, and lifesaving in a pinch. These are fitness gains, but there are costs. Emotions can be uncontrollable, unbalanced, and blind to differences between cave life and civil life. They function as if the present were the distant past, as if their likely implications in today's societies of laws and traditions mirrored their statistical implications for overall hominid fitness in Pleistocene environments. Arguably, murderous revenge and jealous rage are less likely aids to securing resources, allies, and mates in our time than in the Stone Age.[10]

As an example of passionate commitment among extended kin, take the case of blood "honor" (*ard*) or blood "revenge" (*tha'r*) among many nomadic and sedentary Arab (and likely ancient Hebrew and other Semitic) groups. In these societies, the rule of descent is patrilineal; that is, inheritance of wealth and responsibility goes primarily through the father's line (Atran 1985a). If a person from patriline A insults or injures a person from patriline B, then any patrilineal kinsman of B can take revenge on any patrilineal kinsman of A. Several aspects of blood honor are represented in the Old Testament Pentateuch and the Quran, including taking vengeance on the enemies of God "unto the fourth generation" and stoning to death any woman who casts "a stain upon [her] father's house."

The initial unit of revenge is usually the "blood group," or *khams* ("five"), which extends unto five generations from each of the persons in question (i.e., ego plus four generations, including all male collaterals). Person C can be in B's *khams* as well as D's, whereas person D can be in C's *khams* but not B's. Thus, if a person in A's *khams* kills person C in B's *khams*, then the obligation for counterrevenge now extends to person D in C's *khams*. In this way, a vendetta may come to encompass the whole society, including generations yet unborn.

Such a result obviously can be to no one's benefit. At the very least, A's realization that acting against B commits all of B's close kin to retaliate against A or A's close kin, no matter what effort is required or how long it takes, should diminish the likelihood of A's acting against B. The solidarity of the blood group is underscored with other elaborate and costly social displays, such as wedding feasts and sharing gain in time of need.

Notice that although genealogical reckoning is ego-based and different individuals are obligated to different groups of kin, moral obligations to members of one's kin group are absolute, not relative: all *khams* members must be defended equally. Moreover, the biological constitution of one's kin group is asymmetrical: obligations to maternal relatives, who carry just as many of one's genes as paternal relatives, are not prescribed. From the standpoint of a strictly genetic theory of inclusive fitness, absoluteness and asymmetry are arbitrary.

In fact, allies are sometimes adopted into a patrilineal group and given genealogical status, which makes the whole notion of patrilineage somewhat fictive. Rather than a patrilineage as such, the basic component of Arab "kinship" systems is often the patronymic group, or *hamula*. This is a quasi patrilineage that functions as a corporate and moral unit where legal rights and obligations follow *putative* patrilineal descent, that is, descent from a commonly accepted or supposed male ancestor. Nevertheless, genealogical reckoning and social duties remain exclusively couched in a patrilineal idiom. As a result, any doubts about a woman's fidelity anywhere in the patronymic group threaten to undermine the whole group's legitimacy and thus to sunder its social, economic, and political unity. For example, a person without a patrilineal pedigree cannot count on kin to avenge him if he is injured or killed. This makes him more susceptible to being injured or killed. Thus, upholding the lineage's pedigree is the paramount social commitment.

This is true as well for other patrilineal groups whose political economy is religiously tied to the male line, as it is throughout the Middle East among Christian Maronite Arabs (Cresswell 1976) and Moslem Kurds (Barth 1953), Baluchis (Pehrson 1966), and Pathans and Pashtuns:

> The Afghan [Pashtun] noblemen maintain the strictest *parda*, or seclusion of their women, who pass their days monotonously behind the curtains and lattices of their palace prison-houses. . . . The poorer classes cannot afford to seclude their women, so they try to safeguard their virtue by the most barbarous punishments, not only for actual immorality, but for

> any breach of decorum. . . . The recognized punishment in such a case of undue familiarity [e.g., talking to an adult male nonrelative] would have been to cut off the nose of the woman . . . as a rule a woman has no redress. (Pennell 1909:192)

The last century has witnessed little change in this regard, at least in fundamentalist regimes such as Saudi Arabia and Afghanistan, where the mere suspicion of adultery warrants almost any punitive measure short of mutilation or death, and where even circumstantial evidence usually brings death to the woman by stone, knife, axe, or gun (as in present-day Nigeria and Pakistan).

The passionate and religious defense of a woman's honor among male kin in patrilineal societies, where personal cost appears to be no object, illustrates two poles of commitment. For male kin, commitment is *volitional* in the sense that individuals have ample latitude in choosing how to act: courageous and honorable men face their responsibilities head on and even ostentatiously court danger when it is possible and permissible to avoid it. For women, commitment is *imposed* in the sense that they have little choice in how they may act and the limited range of choice they do have is determined by others (i.e., men): a woman might try to avoid shaking the hand or embracing the glance of any man she meets or avoid going out of the house altogether.

Of course, male commitment is not entirely voluntary and female commitment is not entirely coerced. Men who fail to respond in appropriate ways to social expectations suffer various degrees of ostracism (*herem*), ranging from contempt to exile. Females who show sincere and voluntary acceptance of imposed, stereotypical behavior receive honors that range from greater trust to increased material opportunities for their children. Commitment can never appear to be wholly coerced. If it were, then it would also show itself to be insincere and potentially deceptive. To be effective and convincing to others, commitment must be emotionally heartfelt and hard to fake. Neither can commitment be wholly voluntary. If it were, it would also show itself to be calculating and potentially untrustworthy when the chips were down. To be trusted, commitment must be unaffectedly submissive to some emotionally eruptive moral impulse and authority outside the individual's control.

Displays of vengeance in Arab societies are interdependently public and private. The public and often religious expression of norms of "honor" are manifest through all spheres of social life, from rigid modesty in women's dress to revenge as a legitimate motive for "holy war" (*jihad*). But they are also often deeply heartfelt, so much so that a father or brother kills a beloved sister for family honor and so spends years in jail, or carries out a suicide bombing as an avenging martyr. Still, fratricide and martyrdom are exceptional consequences of such displays. They are exceptions because the displays are intended to ensure that drastic consequences will be rare.[11]

It is enough that people believe that devoted individuals would carry out commitments if necessary and that there is occasional evidence that individuals do, in fact, live up to group commitments when they must.[12] Although without such group commitments, the consequences to individual fitness, well-being, and survival could be much worse on average, there is always some trade-off. This involves small but real risk that the cost may be exorbitant, even unto death.

Why suicide martyrs are not suicidal. Although relatively rare, there are nevertheless recurrent and striking examples of group commitment to fight to the death or commit collectively supported suicide rather than suffer another's rule or religion. These include the Jewish zealots at Masada (73 A.D.), the Christian martyrs at Rome (80–330 A.D.), members of the People's Temple at Joneston in Guyana (1977), and radical Islam's *shohada* ("martyrs") throughout the world today. Most often, these people willingly die not as psychotics or sociopaths or even under the immediate impulse of stress or anxiety.

Willing martyrs believe sincerely in the goodness of a religious fraternity that is menaced by outside evil. They often cement their personal identity through religious alliances established during childhood, adolescence, or early adulthood, that is, when sense of self and position in society is least sure. For example, documents found in Kabul used by *Harkat al-Ansar* (now *Harkat al-Mujahedin*), a Pakistani-based ally of Al-Qaida and the Taliban, contains biographical sketches of 39 recruits, all of whom were unmarried. Although few had gone beyond secondary school, most had studied the Quran (Rohde and Chivers 2002). Sacrificing themselves, they help to secure their "family" in this world by directly joining it in the next: "Each [martyr] has a special place—among them are brothers, just as there are sons and those even more dear" (ibid.). *"Jihad"* is often the first word children learn to spell in Taliban schools (*madrasa*). Taught as "God's Path to Paradise," the idea matures if need be into war unto death, as in the following Harakat "oath of allegiance to Jihad": "I, Amir Maawia Siddiqi, son of Abdul Rahman Siddiqi, state in the presence of God that I will slaughter infidels my entire life" (ibid.).

Studies by Ariel Merari (2002) indicate that suicide terrorists span a population's normal distribution in terms of education, socioeconomic status and personality type (e.g., introvert vs. extrovert). His research team interviewed 32 of 34 families of suicide bombers in Palestine and Israel (before 1998) and collected data on dozens of Lebanese and Tamil Tiger families of suicide attackers. The team also interviewed trainers and recruiters for Hamas and Islamic Jihad, as well as would-be suicide bombers who survived attacks. Mean age for suicide bombers was in the early twenties. Almost all were unmarried (and not engaged). Merari attributes primary responsibility for attacks to recruiting organizations, which seek out prospective candidates from this youthful and relatively unattached population. Charismatic trainers then carefully and intensely cultivate mutual commitment to die within small cells of 3–5 members. The final step for these human bombs is usually a formal social contract in the form of a videotape, with a set speech and symbols, such as a rifle in one hand and the Quran in the other.

Except for generally being young unattached males, suicide bombers differ in almost every respect from members of violent racist organizations to whom they are often compared (cf. Ezekiel 1995). Overall, suicide terrorists exhibit no socially dysfunctional attributes (fatherless, friendless, jobless) or suicidal symptoms (e.g., affective disorders, substance abuse, repeated suicide attempts) (Ariel 2002). They clearly aren't the cowards often portrayed in the U.S. media, nor do they vent fear of their enemies (as racists are wont to). They don't express "hopelessness" or a sense of "nothing to lose" for lack of life alternatives that would be consistent with "economic rationality" (i.e., if there is only one option, and no reasonable alternatives, you take it)—although despair is often the interpretation given by and to Western media in statements targeted for United States and European audiences. On the contrary, supporters in the Arab media emphasize expressions of hopefulness and "everything to lose" by those who sacrifice personal future for that of their people, and the strategic use of this hope by recruiting organizations as a political weapon (cf. Bennett 2002).

Psychologist Brian Barber (2002) surveyed 900 Moslems who were adolescents during the first Palestinian Intifada ("Uprising," 1987–1993) in Gaza. Results show high levels of participation in and victimization from violence. For males, 81% reported throwing stones, 72% burned tires, and 29% tossed Molotov cocktails (vs. 51%, 9%, and 5%, for females, respectively); 73% of males reported being verbally abused, 66% were hit or kicked, 63% shot at, and 23% imprisoned (vs. 38%, 19%, 20%, 3% for females). Involvement in violence was not strongly correlated with depression or antisocial behavior. In fact, adolescents most caught up in the Intifada displayed a strong sense of individual pride and social cohesion. This was reflected in their activities: for males, 87% reported delivering supplies to activists, 83% visited families of martyrs, and 71% cared for the wounded (vs. 57%, 46%, and 37% for females). A less formal follow up with subjects involved in the second Intifada (2000–2002) indicate that those still unmarried now play roles that are considered personally more dangerous but socially more meaningful. Increasingly many view the martyr's role as most meaningful of all. By spring 2002, nearly two thirds of Palestinians supported martyr actions (Brinkely 2002).

In contrast, surveys with a control group of Bosnian Moslem adolescents from the same time period reveal markedly weaker expressions of self-esteem, hope for the future, and pro-social behavior (Barber 2002). One key difference between the two groups is that the Palestinians routinely invoke religion to invest their personal trauma with proactive social meaning that takes injury as a badge of honor. Many of the Bosnian Moslems say that they did not think of religious affiliation as a significant part of their identity until seemingly arbitrary violence forced awareness upon them through senseless pain and humiliation ("we were just sitting ducks"). Most continue to feel hopelessness born of senselessness, but some are no doubt turning to radical Islam for a sense of hope.

These studies indicate that both psychosocial (unattached males in supportive religious and peer groups) and socioecological factors (small cells organized under charismatic leadership) shape the causal network of interconnected representations, emotions, and behaviors that are broadly characteristic of contemporary suicide bombing. Individual psychopathology seems not to be an important factor here, whereas ecological context may be decisive: institutionalized creation of intimate social cells works to canalize inference (as might a classroom) and affect (as might a commune) into sufficient causes of violent martyrdom actions. This further suggests that attempts to account for individual variations in religious behavior solely in terms of personal selection factors are misguided. One's performance in the network of religious and cultural behaviors often has a complex causal determination that involves any number of variously interrelated selection factors. These pertain to the internal environment of personal ideas and emotions as well as to external conditions of social and physical context.

5.7. Sincere Self-Deception: Vengeance and Love

> Revenge may form the most important duty in life for a [Solomon Islander]. If a man is injured he picks up a stick or stone where he cannot help but see it, to keep him constantly in mind of the duty of revenge. If a man abstains from food or keeps away from the dance, it is a bad sign for his enemies. The man who goes about with his head half shaved or . . . allows a long twisted bunch of hair to hang down his back is thinking of revenge. Sometimes there hangs from the gable of a house a bundle of tobacco which is only to be smoked over the corpse of an enemy; or the bloody clothes of a slain relation to preserve the memory of an unatoned deed. Nor is there any lack of friends to keep a man reminded of his duty, with songs either lamenting or censuring. . . . A dead man often takes a whole generation with him.
>
> —Loomis Havemeyer, *Ethnography* (1929)

> These degrees [of unreciprocated love] are ten in number, and are distinguished by the following marks: 1. Love of the eye. 2. Attachment of the mind. 3. Constant reflection. 4. Destruction of sleep. 5. Emaciation of the body. 6. Turning away from objects of enjoyment. 7. Removal of shame. 8. Madness. 9. Fainting. 10. Death.
>
> —Vatsyanyana, *The Kama Sutra* (1984 [ca. A.D. 100–500])

Religious commitment always involves public expression and exercise of moral sentiment. Consider, for example, a recent display in front of television cameras by Fayez ul-Rahman, leader of the Jamiat Ulema e-Islami, an association of militant Quranic teachers and "students" (*taliban*) centered in Peshawar, Pakistan: "'We will never allow infidel soldiers to soil our Moslem land!' he burst out to the hurrahs of his supporters in skull-caps. 'America must know that we will defend our Afghan brothers by whatever means and at whatever cost!'" (*Le Monde*, 22 September 2001; my translation). Convincing displays of vengeance are often dissuasive against aggression by stronger or more numerous adversaries. In such cases, the more powerful party must reckon with the added cost that an emotional commitment by the weaker party is likely to carry. This, for example, is a key consideration and justification for acts of suicidal terror as legitimate means of struggle for the weak and downtrodden. (Of course, the potential attacker is a lot less likely to be swayed from an assault if the feeling is one of vengeance for aggression previously initiated by the "weaker" party.)

As Darwin (1965[1872]) noted, emotions such as fear and anger are able to significantly augment the energy available for action by closing down or minimizing bodily functions that are not immediately required for fleeing or fighting. Many animal species have also evolved means for both displaying and detecting these energy commitments. All things being equal, a potential aggressor is less likely to attack another animal that earnestly bares its fangs or thumps its chest. In such cases, the more powerful party must reckon with the added cost that an emotional commitment by the weaker party is likely to carry for the aggressor.

Passionate commitments are useless unless successfully communicated. Derivative displays of commitment are therefore as significant to human societies as fundamental commitments. In general, a promissory display to commit is generally less costly to the individual than the act of carrying out the commitment; that is, the actual costs of sacrificing self-interest are generally well below anticipated costs and often also below the punitive costs of failing to display sincere commitment. Displays of willingness to act vengefully or altruistically are themselves taken as acts of vengeance or altruism, albeit less costly than direct acts of vengeance or altruism.

In addition to the basic Darwinian emotions that erupt on and motivate human cognition, including religious cognition, moral passions have evolved, such as feelings of empathy and fairness, guilt and remorse, vengeance and love. These "social emotions" allow people to thrive in cooperative groups of nonkin under a wide range of environmental conditions and structurally recurrent social situations. Someone who can communicate understanding of other people's anxieties is a potentially safer ally in perilous situations than someone who does not appear to understand what people's problems are. Those who make a costly show of regret over breach of a social contract need not be forever left alone and lost to the community. Those who, when the stakes are low, refuse a no-cost gain because it seems a slight are less likely to allow themselves to be taken advantage of when stakes are high.

The more costly and heartfelt a person's commitment, the more persuasive is the public image of that commitment, as in the above account of commitment to vengeance among native Solomon Islanders. Displays of vengefulness are simultaneously public and private. They serve both to signal inflexible adherence to a social more and to continually trigger and reinforce the urges of an avenging self-image. Vengefulness can pay off in the long term by convincing others that the avenging party will never allow itself to be victimized. But the payoff, again, requires an incalculable personal risk to pursue vengeance even when the personal cost far outweighs any potential personal benefit, for example, in committing one's family to an endlessly cycling vendetta, or dying for the cause, or slitting one's own throat in the hope of righting an insult:

> In the Warangal taluq of the Hyderabad State [India] there are numerous slabs of stone with figures of a man in the act of cutting his throat carved on them in bas-relief. The story goes that in ancient days a king of Warangal promised some wudders (navvies) a sum of gold for digging a large tank. When they appeared before him for payment, he offered them silver instead . . . all cut their throats in the presence of the king, so that their spirits might haunt and torment him for the rest of his life. They have been worshipped from that day to this, and are among the most popular gods of the district. . . . I have often heard of similar acts of retaliation even in modern times. (Whitehead 1988[1921]:124)

In a set of experiments, Nisbett and Cohen (1996) explored differences in reactions to insult between people raised in the southern versus northern United

States. Subjects were told they would be participating in an experiment on some other topic. A confederate of the experimenter—a big man—then bumped into the unsuspecting subject as he walked down the hallway and called him an "asshole." Northern subjects tended to shrug off the apparent insult and do nothing. Southerners generally responded with behavior accompanied by physiological changes of a sort that mediate real violent aggression, such as shouting abuse and fervently trying to bang down the door that the "assailant" had disappeared behind.

Nisbett and Cohen attribute the Southerners' reaction to a vestigial "culture of honor" similar to that of herding peoples in other parts of the world, such as Bedouin and Mongols. They note that the original settlers of the Old South were primarily herders (e.g., Highland Scots), whereas settlers in the southwest continued herding cattle and sheep. In herding societies, there is easy opportunity for theft and other forms of cheating, such as overgrazing or abuse of water rights. To exclude cheaters, members of these societies display signals of uncompromising commitment to defend their property and also monitor displays that might signal inattention to such commitment. For Southerners, reaction to any perceived insult displays sincere commitment to defend what is theirs at all costs. Indeed, perhaps the worst insult of all, and the one that incites the most violent reaction, is an insult to one's honor, that is, a display that communicates an intention not to take seriously one's display of commitment. Whether or not Nisbett and Cohen's account of historical differences between Southerners and Northerners is correct (e.g., pre–Civil War behavior differences are not clear-cut), the data show robust effects for the present and recent past. More important, the results underscore the claim that displays of commitment are as significant as actual commitments.

To be perceived as genuinely vengeful or honest, it does not suffice to issue a declaration espousing vengeance or utter honest words. Vengefulness and honesty, like love and guilt, must be internalized to be convincing. To be persuasive, people need to perceive vengefulness or honesty in a person's affect: in a gaze, in a spontaneous movement of the mouth, in an unmistakable tone of voice, or in any number of minute movements of posture or other behaviors that appear to be beyond the person's conscious control (Darwin 1965[1872]; Ekman 1992; Baron-Cohen 1995). That is why juries want to see and hear the accused for themselves before deciding guilt or innocence.[13]

Actors learn to mimic or camouflage emotions, and we like them for being able to touch our hearts and minds just as we like fantasy for exercising our cognitive modules. Lovers may learn to deceive with their bodies and lawyers may teach guilty defendants to "look the jury in the eye." This kind of foolery we detest because we feel cheated. But even untrained observers are fairly good at detecting emotional fakery and bluff, especially if they are on the lookout (e.g., by monitoring manifestations of blood flow around the eyes). Moreover, even the best fakers do tend to get caught eventually simply because fakers tend to reveal their true nature when they think the coast is clear. Because the coast is sometimes not as clear as might be thought—someone could be watching by accident or a recording of the occasion could be made inadvertently—there is always *some* chance of being caught on such occasions.

Where vengeance provokes negative emotion, love incites positive affection. Romantic expressions of love are seductive because they are costly, irrational, and emotionally compelling. Arduous pursuit costs time, energy, and material outlay. Vows of abiding love are irrational because one or both parties claim that no other person could ever hope to compete with the present object of one's affections and also because such claims for true love's insatiate and immortal thirst are believed regardless of ample inductive support for doubt that comes from the world around.

Falling in love is emotionally compelling because, although one may be aware of just how costly and irrational it is, it feels and looks to others as irresistible as the need for food, water, or air. This is as true today as in Ancient India, China, Greece, Egypt, Mesopotamia, Mesoamerica, or the Gold Coast of Africa in times past: "The African . . . seeks its [love's] gratification, regardless of the greatest sacrifices," such as reckless charge in battle to impress or suicide when obstacles to union prove insurmountable (Cruickshank 1966[1853]: 2:207). As with other emotions, such as fear (LeDoux 1996), love involves involuntary arousal, signaled internally by butterflies in the stomach and high levels of neurotransmitters in the brain stem, such as dopamine (H. Fisher 1995). (Perhaps, in part, this is why people often fall in love with those who share a dangerous experience.)

Vatsyayana's *Aphorisms of Love*, or *The Kama Sutra*, written in India sometime between the first and sixth centuries, is an abridgment of several ancient works that makes romantic love the cornerstone of a religious philosophy (1984:102–110). It analyzes the art of amorous display and lists the telltale signs of costly commitment and hard-to-fake signaling. Thus, women and men alike should be on the lookout for unplanned gestures that indicate readiness to give oneself over to one's beloved and for indirect reciprocity. But whereas women should monitor signs of wealth, status, and generosity, men should watch for signs of kindness and emotional attachment to the prospect of maternity and for the physical strength and beauty to make maternity successful. There is some empirical evidence for similar mating and monitoring priorities in other societies, including our own (Buss 1995). Finally, a costly and hard-to-fake commitment to genuine love increases in intensity from one degree to another when that love is not reciprocated.

This notion of love as an uncontrollably passionate solution to a rational problem (stable and secure mating) involves a compromise between searching for the perfect or ideal solution and making do with what's readily available. But manifestation of compromise indicates willful self-interest, whereas irrational manifestations of lack of compromise signal abandonment of self-interest to blind commitment. This is akin to Alexander's (1987) notion of evolutionary self-deception. Self-deception makes sense only in a social setting: one deceives oneself to better deceive and convince others (of course, one may deceive oneself for other reasons as well). For example, concealment of female ovulation from consciousness and the more or less unchanging male interest in the copulatory cycle may have been naturally selected to simultaneously increase likelihood of conception (at the beginning and end of ovulation) and secure enduring protection and parenting from a mate (Alexander and Noonan 1979; Daniels 1983). Similarly, "If people learn that all apparent altruism is mere exchange . . . then their capacity to believe in love is corroded. And if they cannot believe, then for them, love is impossible" (Nesse 1999:3).[14]

The reality that commitments of loyalty endure, argues R. Frank (1988), does not primarily owe to costs imposed on disloyalty by others (society), but to the emotionally self-imposed costs of guilt that accompany binding commitments of love or loyalty. Guilt and sympathy reignite, if not passion, at least compassion: "when love implies sympathy and affection arising from mental qualities, there is a tie . . . which lasts long after youth and beauty are gone" (Westermarck 1922: 3:104). From this perspective, marriage vows function like the signposts of revenge that the Solomon Islander and those around him keep in view. Such cultural displays rekindle an emotional commitment whose fire may wane with time, preventing it from ever dying out.

The communicative intent of a religious ritual display is somewhat different from many of the "mundane" displays of vengeance or love described above. Often, it is not to signal readiness to act in a particular way on a given occasion (although in some circumstances a religious display does target a specific event or context). Rather, routine religious rituals mostly serve to display pledges of mutual assistance and conviction in resolving recalcitrant and even rationally irremediable problems. In these cases, there is no principled distinction between the performative display and the behavior intended. The display is not a derivative of the behavior or a representation of the behavior. Instead, such ritual displays are themselves *episodes* of social commitment; they create the messages that they instantiate. The ritual message has no fixed reference or content, but depends for its interpretation on the network of quasi-propositional beliefs in which it is embedded. Each occasion of ritual use can, and usually does, mobilize different parts of the network that the circumstances encourage. Moreover, different commonsense propositions are also activated for each actor at the same occasion, as each personal situation warrants. Thus, the authorless, eternal and divinely inspired Bible, Quran, Hindu Vedas, or Mayan Popul Vuh have a true and personal message for anyone, anywhere, anytime.

5.8. Ceremonial Mediation, Magic and Divination

> [A]t the shrine of Kulanthalamman . . . when a creditor cannot recover a debt, he writes out a statement of his claim against his debtor on dried palmyra leaves, presents it to the goddess, and hangs it up on a spear before her image. If the claim is just and the debtor does not pay, it is believed that he will be afflicted with sickness and terrifying dreams, and that in his dreams the goddess will warn him to pay his debt at once. . . . When the claim is acknowledged, the debtor brings the money to the pujari [village holy man], who places it before the goddess, and then sends for the creditor and informs him that the debt is paid. All the money thus paid into the temple coffers is handed over to the various creditors during the festival in April or May, after deducting the amount due to the temple treasury. This is certainly a simple method of doing justice in the manner of debts, and probably just as effective as the more elaborate and more expensive processes of our courts of law.
>
> —Henry Whitehead, *The Village Gods of South India* (1988[1921])

There is a common view among many scientists and modern empirical philosophers that the mythicoreligious beliefs of children, uneducated people, and tribal peoples crucially misinform thinking about the everyday factual world, so that there is no clear distinction in their unfortunate lives between natural and supernatural phenomena (B. Russell 1948; Quine 1960; Popper 1963). In "traditional" societies, such ceremonial displays are generally required for the practice of magic: the art of controlling events by incantations or ritualized gestures that conjure a combined intervention of natural causes and supernatural spirits. Many psychologists and anthropologists still see magic as a special mode of causal thinking that supposedly pervades the whole of the society in which it is practiced and that obeys its own set of "laws" or "rules." This, despite the obvious fact that *the very same* magical or divinatory practices can very often be interpreted in seemingly contradictory ways by the very same person.

More "positivist" views hold that such magical causation is "prerational," "preoperational," or "prescientific" (Horton 1967; Piaget 1970; Hallpike 1976). More "romantic" views treat magical thinking as reflecting "alternative" modes of rationality and causation (Douglas 1966), or "counterculture." For example, to understand ancient and modern Maya, one must learn "a different rationality just as one learns a new language," that is, an "alternative reality" different from "our worldview—that thing we call science" (Freidel, Schele, and Parker 1993:11,36,172).

Whether positivist or romantic, all-encompassing views of magic as pervading everyday thought are somewhat surprising given the oft-reported fact that magic in traditional societies is generally associated with explicitly choreographed and quite extraordinary public displays (even if only a dyadic display, such as between a voodoo "doctor" or priestess and her client). Years ago, Margaret Mead (1932) performed psychological experiments indicating that magical thinking and "animism" were decidedly *less* common among children than adults in traditional societies, such as Manus (New Guinea). Children in Manus, she argued, understood events in straightforward terms of material causality: canoes go adrift because ropes are unfastened and water cuurents move them. By contrast, Manus adults *who had gone through special rites of initiation* might "explain" events in terms of ghosts, "the evil eye," or animistic forces.

Granted, some of Mead's experiments left much to be desired in terms of precision and replicability (e.g., Rorschach ink blot tests). Nevertheless, her conclusions were much better empirically informed than contrary speculations current at the time, such as those of Freud and Piaget. These latter views were largely extrapolated from Lucien Lévy-Bruhl's thesis of a thoroughly "mystic" notion of causation that dominates "primitive reality"—a thesis based largely on tendentious interpretations of nineteenth-century ethnographic reports. For Lévy-Bruhl, the "African races," the Eskimo, and other "uncivilized peoples, in South America, Australia, and so on" exhibit a "primitive mentality" that "shows such indifference to, one might almost say dislike of, the discursive operations of thought, of reasoning, and reflection" (1966[1923]:27–29).

More recent controlled experiments by Sheila Walker indicate that "the absence of supernatural explanations even in older Yoruba [Nigeria] children suggests the inclusion of principled supernatural knowledge in the representations of living kinds occurs much later than the shift to more refined biological concepts"

(1992:656; cf. Jeyifous 1985). The most "traditional" adult Yoruba assent to transference of "essences" between natural kinds only when "supported by supernatural explanations in the ritual contexts." For Lévi-Strauss (1962, 1963b), the myths and rites of totemism—that is, the institutionalized relationship between human groups and natural species—explicitly mark the fact that human totemic groups, unlike their natural species namesakes, generally may not interbreed. In other words, people organize their cultures not by blindly mimicking nature, but by commonsensically carving nature at its joints and then symbolically restructuring it.

In reporting magic, researchers often *assume* but do not show that the practice aims at causal efficacy in curing or producing illness, bringing or stopping rain, and so on. Descriptions are often accompanied by references to "mystical forces," "occult powers," or "invisible hands." Rarely, if ever, are such terms used by the practitioners themselves (so far as can be ascertained from the few literal transcriptions available). Rather, as Tambiah (1973) notes, these terms were invoked in the historical development of Western science to underscore the obscure parts of rival theories or to discredit hermeneutical approaches, such as astrology and alchemy. "Explanations" of magic that employ such notions without further justification thus unwittingly assume what they seek to demonstrate.

Religious magic, suggests Tambiah, endures as a social phenomenon *not* because of some presumed causal efficacy, but because it creates a social context that allows participants to conceptually integrate an important situation for which they believe no causal explanation exists: "a sacrifice which creates the cosmos persists because it 'creates' the world in a sense that is different from what is known in the laboratory" (1973: 210). Magic is usually practiced precisely in situations where no mundane causal sequence of actions and events is known to affect an outcome that is both personally relevant and socially desired. As Evans-Pritchard (1937) observed in regard to Zande (African) magic, curing rites are most "mysterious" when the diseases they deal with are most acute and chronic.

This attempt to give cultural representation to causally inscrutable situations does not altogether ignore the mundane causal factors in the situation. Such factors are as neccessary (but insufficient) for understanding what in the situation constitutes the causally opaque, that is, "mysterious" or counterintuitive, part of the magic. Moreover, by preserving what causally efficacious information there is in a magical representation, the representation may, in fact, optimize mundane causal efficacy.

Consider, in this respect, magical practice associated with the Itza' divining stone, called *sastun*. The purported causal powers of the *sastun* are allegedly intrinsic to it, in much the same way that causally efficacious intentions are intrinsic to people. One cannot make a stone into a *sastun* any more than one can give a person a mind. But what, exactly, are the *sastun*'s causal powers beyond those of a restricted set of human intentions (i.e., *sastun* never lie, engage in irony)? The *sastun* can "recognize" unknown events of the past (e.g., who stole the pig) and unknown events of the future (e.g., who will die or get well). The *sastun*'s knowledge, however, is only intermittently apparent to the curer/diviner whom the *sastun* has chosen as its medium.

The curer/diviner usually consults the *sastun* at the request of a "client" who wishes to know, for example, who stole the family pig or whether a sick child will die or get well. The curer/diviner typically asks for all of the information that the client deems relevant to the event, much as a detective or a doctor would. Only then does she consult the *sastun*. For someone possessed by a supposedly "prerational" or "alternatively rational" mentality, this sequence of behavior is odd indeed. Why not just consult the *sastun* directly, without bothering with this mundanely "rational" routine?

A partial answer may be that the curer/diviner uses the client's information to build up a "best hypothesis" causal scenario involving only mundane causes. Because not enough information is known (and is unlikely ever to be known) to complete the scenario, it can never be deterministic. The scenario must remain somewhat uncertain, that is, probabilistic. This uncertainty makes it difficult to act. Suppose the wrong person is accused of stealing the pig, or the child who was predicted to live actually dies? Such uncertainty can block action aimed at rationally maximizing benefit, even if the likelihood of a positive outcome is greater than the likelihood of failure (Kahneman and Tversky 1979).

Arguably, consultation of the *sastun* allows the curer/diviner to take decisive action in somewhat risky cases where it would be most rational to do so, that is, where the benefit of the action taken, less the cost of a failed action, is greater than the benefit of inaction: B (action) – C (failed action) > B (inaction).

For example, suppose a child is ill, and the curer/diviner knows from experience that about four out of every five persons with this type of illness dies if not treated: B (inaction) = 20 percent. From experience, she also knows that every other person who is given an herbal potion (whose recipe she jealously guards) survives: B (action) = 50 percent. However, she also knows that the potion can sometimes kill people who might otherwise get well without treatment. Suppose, as a worst-case scenario, she imagines that the treatment could kill half the people it is given to. Given that the expectation of the untreated child's survival is only 20 percent, then the worst case would halve this expectation: C (failure) = 50% × 20% = 10%. Thus, even in a worst-case scenario, the decision to give rather than not give the potion is more likely to produce the happy outcome of seeing the person well: [B (action) = 50% – C (failure) = 50% × 20% = 10%] = 40% > B (inaction) = 20%.

This is not to say that all, or even most, magical acts are designed to encourage and maximize rational decision making. It is only to suggest that there is nothing in magic per se that opposes, blocks, or substitutes for mundane conceptions of "rationality" and "causation"—conceptions that are likely the same for humans everywhere. In some cases, magic and divination may even enhance rational decision making and causal analysis. But this usually occurs within the broader context of optimizing the relevance of such practices by symbolically binding personal problems of mind and body to the larger cultural ecology: "The question [the *sastun* divinator] asks his clients can be as subtly penetrating as those of a trained and experienced psychiatrist. But most of all, the divination gives clients a chance to focus on their problems, to share them with other people, and to receive advice that often links them back to their community and the greater cosmos. In our world, medicine addresses the body, while divination and healing in the Maya world work with the mind and spirit" (Freidel, Schele, and Parker 1993:231). Far from indicating an "alternative reality" that has "no rational explanation" (230), such experiences partake of panhuman cognitive principles applied to a different ecological context. This different context is one where sustaining a millennial communal tradition is as much a part of the epidemiological environment as combating the pathogens of disease.

In sum, belief in the supernatural does not involve causal thinking that is inappropriately applied or distinctive. Rather, by variously mobilizing the thoughts and actions of people, as well artifacts and elements of the environment, priestly actors aim to change relevant aspects of the society's cultural ecology. This includes changes in the distribution of intentional psychological states of the people who make up the society and of the behaviors that those intentions cause. In the south Indian case above—as in Maya divination, Afro-American voodoo, and various forms of institutionalized magic—the ceremony makes a person keenly aware that he or she is the focus of the attention, and of the intentions, of others. Being in the social spotlight and believing that the spotlight is ultimately controlled by an all-seeing, all-knowing deity may well cause a person to change behavior in accordance with those intentions.

5.9. Summary: Religion's Enduring Embrace

> Organized religion is a sham and a crutch for weak-minded people who need strength in numbers. It tells people to go out and stick their noses in other people's business.
>
> —Minnesota Governor Jesse Ventura, *Playboy* (November 1999)

> Tonight I ask for your prayers for all those who grieve, for the children whose worlds have been shattered, for all whose sense of safety and security has been threatened. And I pray they will be comforted by a power greater than any of us spoken through the ages in Psalm 23: "Even though I walk through the valley of the shadow of death, I fear no evil for you are with me." . . . None of us will ever forget this day, yet we go forward to defend freedom and all that is good and just in our world. Thank you. Good night and God bless America.
>
> —U.S. President George W. Bush, televised address to the nation (11 September 2001)

Invocation of supernatural agents constitutes an ecologically rational response to the enhanced possibilities of deception inherent in the evolution of human representational skills and social interaction. Religion, or any moral order, could not long endure if it were unable to forestall defection and escape from the Prisoner's Dilemma (i.e., if you don't cheat others before they have a chance to cheat you, you will be left in the lurch; but if all reason this way, then everyone will lose). Clerics, rulers, and elders who are about to become ancestors can only intermittently monitor peasants, workers, and youth to verify that commitments to God, country, and authority are kept. To keep the morally corrosive temptations to deceive or defect under control, *all concerned*—whether beggar *or* king—must truly believe that the gods are always watching. They must believe this even when they know that no other person could possibly be looking (R. Frank 1988; Pinker 1997; Dennett 1997). Once the relationships are constituted in a union, as in our "One Nation Under God," they can be sundered only by seeming to risk collapse of the public order that secures personal welfare.

All religions require their members to sacrifice immediate self-interest in displays of moral commitment to a particular way of community life whose rightness and truth is God-given. For these displays to work their magic, however, they must be convincing. In the statistical long run, and on the average, displays of commitment are convincing only if people *are* sincerely committed to live up to their promises no matter the cost. To be convincing, then, displays of commitment must be uncontrollable and unreasonable enough to be hard to fake. They must be emotionally expressed and passionately held. (Of course, some control is often necessary as well; you probably wouldn't want to be in a fox hole with someone just because they have an uncontrollable desire to stick by you.)

The successful communication of commitment through display implies that the displays themselves are critical to commitment. Displays of credible commitment are also far more common than the behavioral commitments themselves. For God, and for the monotheistic societies that pledge allegiance to Him, it is Abraham's sincere display of willingness to sacrifice his son that is important, not whether his son was actually sacrificed or not (Kierkegaard (1955[1843]). In general, a promissory display to commit is less costly to the individual than the act of carrying out the commitment. That is, the actual costs of sacrificing self-interest are generally well below the potential costs, and often also below the punitive costs, of failing to display sincere commitment (cf. Sober and Wilson 1998). Displays of willingness to act with commitment are themselves ultimately taken as acts of commitment.

In religion, as in love and war, sanctified displays of passionate commitment to others are given in the face of existential anxieties for which no predictable outcome or rational solution is possible, as at weddings, send-offs, and funerals. These sacred vows are promises to help one another in *future* situations where there is need and no hope of reward. This enables people to trust and do uncalculating good for one another. Thus, in tight-knit religious communities where displays of commitment are routine (e.g., Jews, Mormons, Christian fundamentalists), there appears to be a negative correlation between religious commitment on the one hand and cheating, crime, and delinquency on the other (reviewed in Beit-Hallahmi and Argyle 1997:211–213).

But religious commitment also allows harm and evil. As Allport (1956:413–426) found in his classic study of prejudice, the higher the degree of religious identification with a particular group, the greater the tendency to discriminate against other groups. This leads to constant conflict between groups and shifting of cooperative alliances within groups. In fostering cooperating groups that compete with one another, religion generates unending social evolution and experiments in syncretism.

Attempts to replace intentional supernatural agents with intentionless supernatural agents (Thomas Jefferson's Unitarian God, the Deity of the French Enlightenment), historical axioms (Marxism), or physical laws (natural science) that do not intervene directly in personal affairs and whose actions humans cannot directly influence are at a serious disadvantage in the struggle for cultural selection and survival as moral dogma. This is because no matter how passionate one's commitment to an ideology, the ideology remains, to some extent, *transparently arbitrary*. As such, it can be no more than a necessarily imperfect attempt to figure out what is right. This leaves open the possibility—indeed the eventual likelihood—that *another* ideology is truer. And if that is the case, then the current ideology must be false in some sense.

Purely ideological commitments to moral principles also lack interactive aspects of personal agency—and the emotional intimacy that goes with it—as well as the promise to allay the eruptive and uncontrollable existential anxieties for which there appears to be no rational expectation of resolution, such as vulnerability (to injustice, pain, dominance), loneliness (abandonment, unrequited love), catastrophe, or death. As we shall see in chapter 8, this intentional (goal-directed) and affective sense of agency can extend to nonhuman elements of the surrounding environment, creating intimacy with and care for Nature.

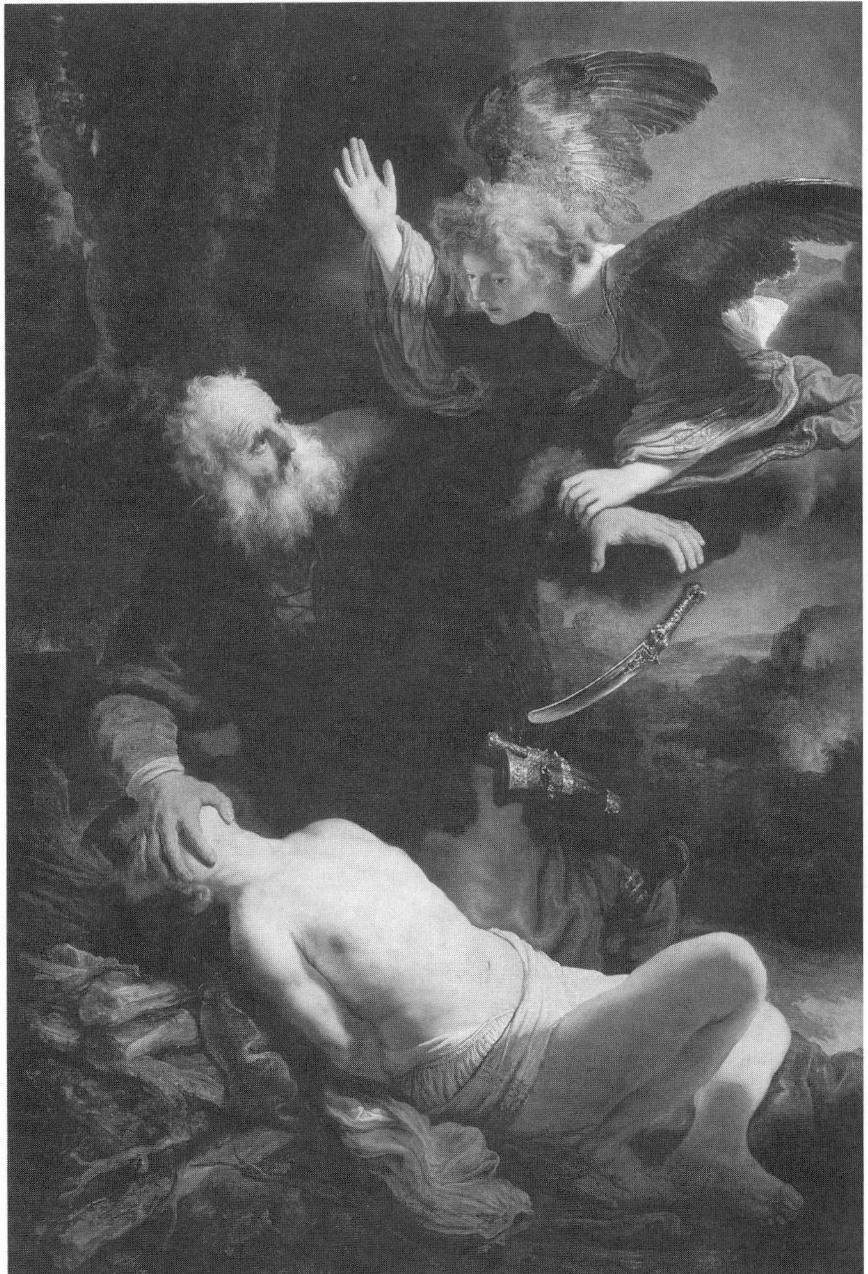

Figure 1. "Sacrifice of Isaac," oil painting by Rembrandt van Rijn, 17th century, Hermitage Museum, St. Petersburg, Russia. Courtesy of Art Resource, New York

Figure 2. Moses with horns, marble sculpture by Michelangelo, 16th century, Rome (author's photo)

Figure 3. "Fall and Expulsion," oil painting by Michelangelo featuring a snake with woman's torso in Eden, Sistine Chapel, Vatican, 16th century

Figure 4. Heaven's Gate on a spandrel, column capital, Cloister of Monreale, Sicily. Engraving of drawing by G. Vuiller, 1894 (author's possession)

Figure 5. Vishnu dreaming the world while slumbering atop the world serpent "Endless," Dasavatara Temple, 1st millennium A.D., Deogarh, central India (author's photo)

Figure 6. "L'Orgie Satanique à Travers les Siècles" (Satanic Orgy Across the Centuries) engraving, by Roland Brèvannes, France, 19th century. Courtesy of the Division of Rare Book and Manuscript Collections, Cornell University

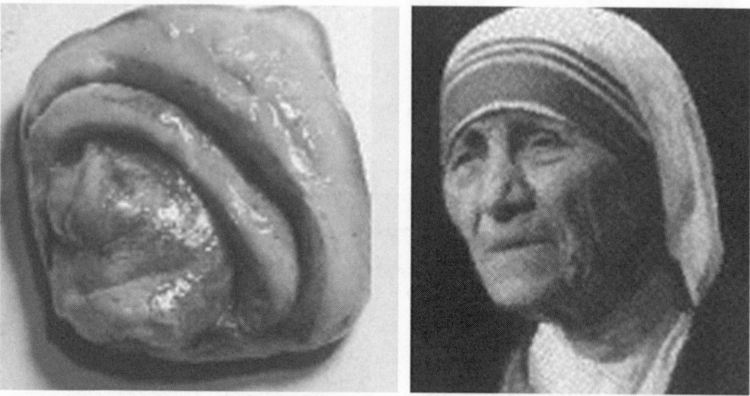

Figure 7. "The Nunbun," a cinnamon bun from a Nashville, Tennessee, pastry shop that became an Internet icon after the death of Mother Theresa

Figure 8. "Bedeviling: Did Satan Rear His Ugly Face? Title of article in the *Philadelphia Daily News* (14 September 2001) featuring photograph by Mark Phillips of smoke from World Trade Center bombing, 11 September 2001 (Note: The cutout is an enlargment of the area of the building and smoke just below.) Copyright SLPStock Agency, New York

Figure 9. Adouma fetishes, West Africa, 1887, engraving by Riou (author's possession)

Figure 10. Aleut death mask, Unalaska Island, 19th century. Courtesy of the Smithsonian Institution, Museum of Natural History, Washington, D.C.

Figure 11. "Der Teufel und die Geschichte" (The Devil and the Angel of History), Germany, 19th century. Courtesy of the Division of Rare Book and Manuscript Collections, Cornell University

Figure 12. Chaak, the Maya Thunder-God, stone relief from Main Acropolis, Tikal, Guatemala, 1st millennium A.D. (author's photo)

Figure 13. Kali, the Hindu Death Goddess, seated in intercourse with a corpse, Punjab, India, 18th century. From Phillip Rawson, *Tantra: The Cult of Indian Ecstasy* (New York: Avon Books, 1973) Estate of Ajit Mookerjee

Figure 14. Natesa (Dancing Shiva) Subduing a Demon, Gangakondacholapuram, south India, ca. 1000 A.D. (author's photo)

Figure 15. Minoan Snake Goddess, earthenware statue, Knossos, Crete, 2nd millennium B.C. Courtesy of Heracleion Museum, Greece Ministry of Culture

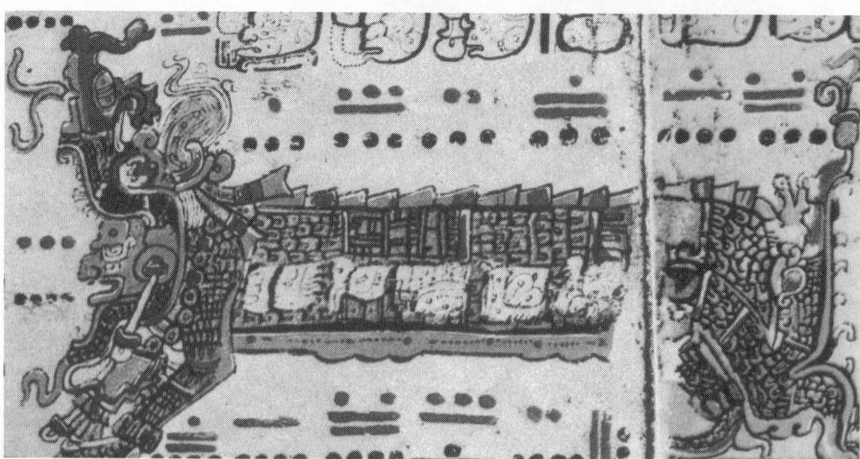

Figure 16. Maya birth and learning as passage through the Dragon-Snake, Drawing from *Dresden Codex*, pre-Columbian, 1st millennium A.D.

Figure 17. Street shrine of sacred Hindu family: Shiva (center), wife Parvati (Shiva's right), and Elephant-Headed son, Ganesh (Shiva's left), Chidambaram, south India, 21st century (author's photo)

Figure 18. "Le Temple de Satan" (The Temple of Satan), woodcut by Stanlislas de Guaita, France, 19th century. Courtesy of the Division of Rare Book and Manuscript Collections, Cornell University

Figure 19. "Construction d'une Cathédrale" (Construction of a Cathedral) oil painting by Jean Fouquet, 15th century. Courtesy of the Bibliotèque National de France, Paris

Figure 20. Ghost House, Polynesia, early 20th century. Courtesy of the American Museum of Natural History, New York

Figure 21. Maya Temple of the Jaguar, Tikal, Guatemala, 1st millennium A.D. (author's photo)

Figure 22. Kailasthanatha Temple, Kanchipuram, south India, 1st millennium A.D. (author's photo)

Figure 23. Toda Tribal Funeral and Buffalo Sacrifice, south India, engraving by P. Fritel, 1882 (author's possession)

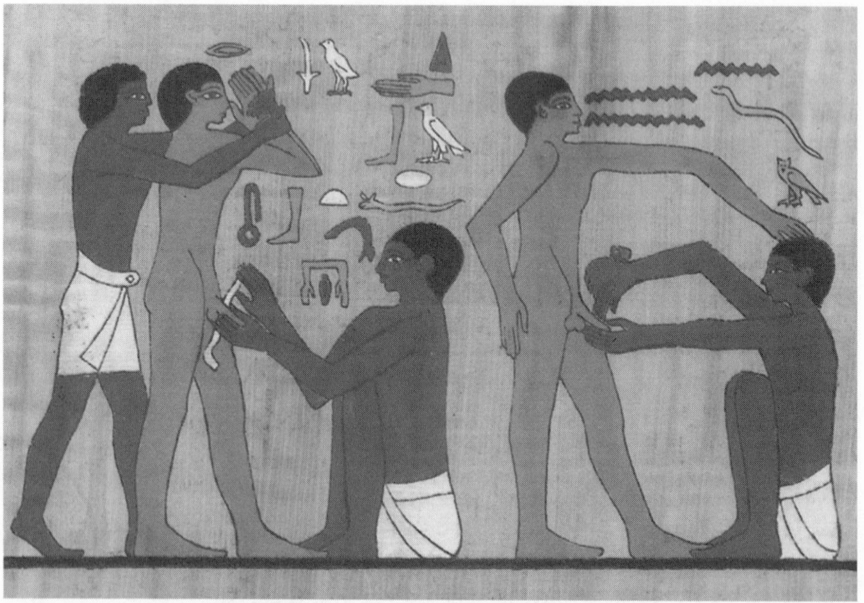

Figure 24. Egyptian circumcision, tomb of Ankh-Mator, 3rd millennium B.C. (Old postcard, drawing by Lambert & Landrock, Art Publishers, Cairo)

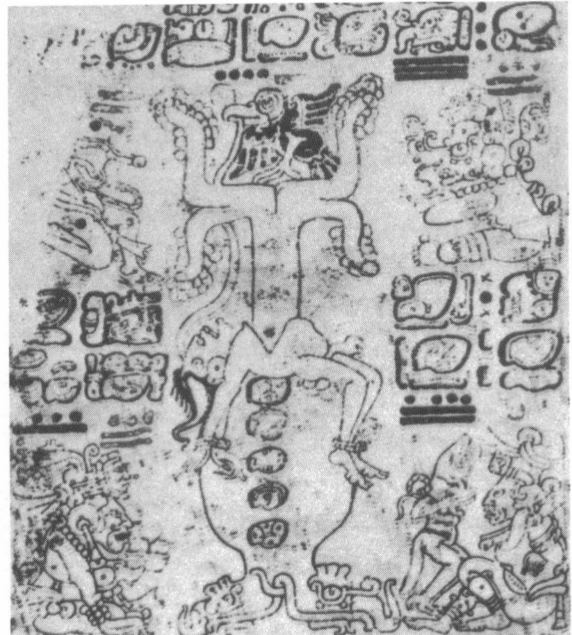

Figure 25. Maya human sacrifice, drawing from *Dresden Codex*, pre-Columbian, 1st millennium A.D.

Figure 26. Forms of Christian Martyrdom, detail from *Frontal de Sant Quirze i Santa Julita de Durro*, painted wood altarpiece from village chapel, Catalonia, Spain, 12th century. Courtesy of the Museu Nacional d'Art de Catalunya, Barcelona, Spain

Figure 27. Divine Toffa King and subjects, Dahomey, African Slave Coast, 1894, engraving by Devos (author's possession)

Figure 28. Buddha's Temple, Kandy, Ceylan (Sri Lanka), engraving of drawing by Marius Perret, 1894 (author's possession)

Figure 29. Moslems bowing and praying on the Esplanade of the Dome of the Rock, Jerusalem. (Old postcard, photo by I. Amad, Jerusalem)

Figure 30. Pope kneeling and praying before a painting of Jesus. (Old postcard dated 1879)

Figure 31. Once-in-a-lifetime Australian Aboriginal initiation, with candidates led blindfolded, over totemic sand designs and under chanting spearbearers, to learn their history and how to kill an enemy, early 20th century, after photos printed in Loomis Havemeyer, *Ethnography*, New York: Ginn and Company, 1929

Figure 32. Periodic pageantry, Semana Santa, Antigua, Guatemala, 1986. (Old postcard, photo by Diego Molina)

Figure 33. Yumbo Wedding, Ecuadorian Amazon, drawing by Charles Wiener, 1883 (author's possession)

Figure 34. Highland Maya wedding, Lake Atitlan, Guatemala. (Old postcard, anonymous)

Figure 35. Maya magic in music and dance, Bonampak, Chiapas, Mexico, 1st millenium A.D., computer-reconstructed fresco by Doug Stern for *National Geographic Magazine*, February 1995. Courtesy of National Geographic Image Collection

Figure 36. Hindu Dancer and Musicians, stone relief from Purāna Mahādeo Temple, 1st millennium A.D., Sikar Museum Rājasthān, after reproduction in S. Karmisch, *The Art of India Through the Ages* (London: Phaidon Press, 1954)

Figure 37. Egyptian musician girls, Tomb of Nakht, Egypt, 2nd millennium B.C. (Old postcard, drawing by Lambert & Landrock, Art Publishers, Cairo)

Figure 38. Dakota Indian Dog Dance, 19th century print. Courtesy of the American Museum of Natural History, New York

Figure 39. Samoan Dance, early 20th century, after photo by H.C. Walters, printed in Loomis Havemeyer, *Ethnography* (New York: Ginn and Company, 1929)

Figure 40 (*left*). Tibetan with prayer wheel and trumpet, early 20th century print. Courtesy of the Peabody Museum, Harvard University, Cambridge, MA

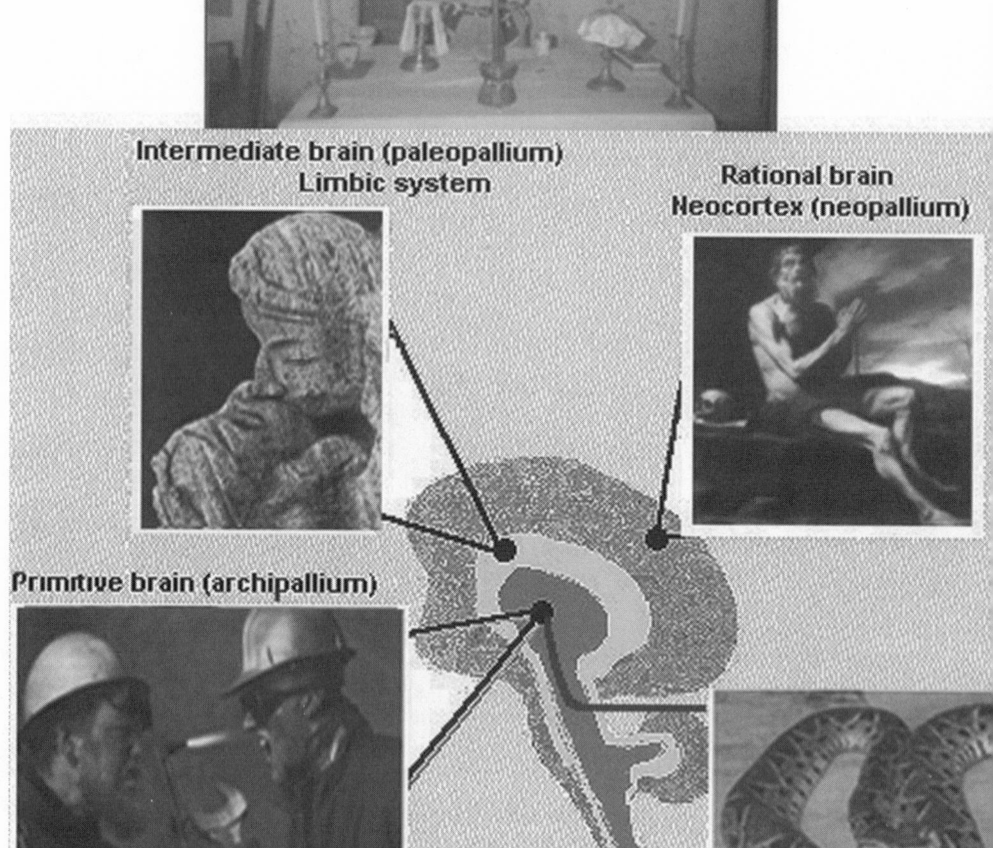

Figure 41 (*clockwise*). Itza' Maya elder giving his blessing, San José, Petén, Guatemala, 1995 (photo by Valentina Vapnarsky for author); "Saint Paul the Hermit," oil painting by Jusepe de Ribera, 17th century, Louvre, Paris; "Fear," fer-de-lance, Petén, Guatemala (author's photo); "Rage," 2000 (anonymous, Internet); "The Kiss," Srya Temple, Konarka, India, 13th century, after reproduction in S. Karmisch, *The Art of India Through the Ages* (London: Phaidon Press, 1954)

PART 3

Ritual Passions

Most people live dejectedly in worldly sorrow and joy; they are the ones who sit along the wall and do not join the dance. The knights of infinity are dancers. . . . To this end passion is necessary. Every movement of infinity comes about by passion, and no reflection can bring movement about.

—Søren Kierkegaard, *Fear and Trembling: A Dialectical Lyric* (1955[1843])

I recorded an inconspicuous electrical seizure from the temporal lobe of a meditator and heard reports of cosmic bliss. . . . Here sat a person waiting with anticipation for a few short seconds of seizure. There were no convulsions . . . just a slight smile and the facial expressions of cosmic serenity. . . . For a few brief seconds, the person had mingled with the Great Mentality whose rudiments are found in every culture.

—Michael Persinger, *Neuropsychological Bases of God Beliefs* (1987)

The most common type of recruitment [to the cult of Olokun, son of the creator god] is through suffering. As I talked to priestesses, I heard story after story about periods of dissociative states, disturbed pregnancies, failed marriages, marketing disasters, and terrible diseases, all experienced because someone did not realize that the sufferer was really a child of Olokun. . . . As the years went by with no resolution or relief, these women experienced great misery. From the descriptions an interesting pattern emerged: those very illnesses that Olokun inflicted on his recalcitrant children were the symbolic opposites of the benefits and glories of his kingdom: lameness from a god who loves dancing, blindness from a god who demands beauty, barrenness from a god who blesses humans with children.

—Paula Girschik Ben-Amos, "The Promise of Greatness: Women and Power in an Edo [Benin, Africa] Spirit Possession Cult" (1994)

6 Ritual and Revelation

The Emotional Mind

People cannot cognitively avoid awareness of emotionally inescapable threats and opportunities that have no positive logical, plausible, probable, or reasonable outcome. Existential anxiety appears to be a significant factor in inducing religious experience. Religious beliefs and experiences cannot be validated by social consensus either through deductive inference or consistently reliable induction from observation and experience. Validation occurs only by satisfying the very emotions that motivate religious beliefs and experiences. This is what religious rituals help to accomplish.

Religious rituals tend to be rigidly formulaic, sequentially typed public performances that conceptually forge personal identity and memory according to cultural parameters. These publicly held parameters are set by signs and displays that somewhat arbitrarily exploit and exaggerate elements of the surrounding natural environment: in movement (e.g., dance), sound (e.g., chant), smell (e.g., incense), touch (e.g., immersion), and sight (e.g., masks). Ritual signs and displays affectively manipulate individual sensations and bodily states in ways that causally coordinate the minds and bodies of the various individuals involved into convergent expressions of public sentiment—a sort of N-person bonding that communicates moral consensus.

6.1. Remembering Rituals: Doctrines and Images

> Purpose is but the slave of memory, of violent birth, but poor validity. . . . The passion ending, doth the purpose lose.
>
> —William Shakespeare, *Hamlet*, Act III, scene 2

> It is difficult to be religious, impossible to be merry, at every moment of life, and festivals are as sunlit peaks, testifying above dark valleys, to the eternal radiance.
>
> —Clement A. Miles, cited in Oscar Hijuelos, *Mr. Ives' Christmas* (1995)

Like oral tribal myths and enduring folktales (Lévi-Strauss 1971), religious doctrine and liturgy lack any thoroughgoing logical or empirical constancy. Nevertheless, their quasi-propositional elements are well-tuned for human memory. As I noted some time ago, myths optimize storage and retrieval of information that is culturally general and personally idiosyncratic. The myth-teller adapts a theme inherited from his or her audience in such a way that the specific time and space of the telling and participation become instantiations of universal themes:

> The distinction involving the storage and retrieval of these two types of information may well correspond to a more general distinction between "semantic" and "episodic" memory (Tulving 1976). Here is an illustration. For the common person, the folkstory of "Jack-the-Giant-Killer and the Beanstalk" may evoke ruses that can be used against social oppressors (Darnton 1984:15). And the guarantee that one's personal genealogy somehow links that person to the King of France may instill a certain pride and feeling of security that can be used to structure one's relationship to the social past and present (Fox 1967:13). But combining both types of tale, say, in the biblical history of David-Killer-of-Goliath and King of Israel, is liable to mutually reinforce their narrative effect in the memory of [David's would-be descendants and followers, including Jews and worshippers of Jesus]. True myths, which vary over each telling in oral societies, are likely to be even more conditioned in this way by the audience's memory propensities. (Atran 1991:638–639)

This is because without writing, logic, or empirical observation to fix content, there is no other readily apparent way to stabilize a tale's transmission.

In his recent book, *Arguments and Icons*, anthropologist Harvey Whitehouse (2000) proposes that religions can exhibit two modes of ritual development: imagistic and doctrinal. Each mode selectively favors certain kinds of cognitive, emotional, social, and political organizations, although the two modes often interact in complex ways. The overriding distinction between the two owes to different memory requirements: the doctrinal mode is predominantly "semantic," and the imagistic mode is "episodic." In this account, "semantic memory" is confounded with propositional representation, and "episodic memory" with iconic representation. Psychologists familiar with Tulving's (1972) original semantic-episodic distinction may find this confusing because both types of memory were supposed to be verbal and propositional. I'll clarify the distinction in section 6.3, but for now I just want to present Whitehouse's account.

In the doctrinal mode, religious practices tend to be frequently repeated and routine, such as daily prayer, weekly services, and annual celebrations. Frequent repetition supposedly builds an accurate memory routine for the ritual's abstract, schematic organization, or "script," like the formulaic order of events in a Moslem prayer, Catholic Mass, or Jewish Passover. Participants customarily perform these scripted actions almost automatically but retain little long-term memory of the changing details and content of the rites in question, such as who was actually present or what exactly was preached on a given occasion. Particular details and content of scripted actions can vary substantially from one ritual performance to another. Yet the schematic sequence of events repeats with fairly high fidelity over time.

By tuning out the scripted routine and forgetting changing details, participants are able to turn their attention to the "logical" structure and implications of religious doctrine presented in exegesis, argumentation, and sermonizing. As the "inexorable implicational logic" of religious doctrine becomes transparent to participants, the "codification and transmission" of religious belief takes on a "high degree of ideological integration, coherence, uniformity, stability" (Whitehouse 2000:93). Indeed, "the systematic, logically integrated character of . . . [doctrinal] institutions is an adaptation to conditions of frequent reproduction" (106).

The repetitive routine is usually directed by a rigid social hierarchy. Routinization minimizes the risks of unintended innovations; hierarchization enhances monitoring, policing, and sanctioning of nonconformity. This normalizing design not only encourages indoctrination and preservation of orthodoxy but also favors identification with masses of anonymous worshippers, which often promotes universalist and humanist notions of common fellowship: "The political implications of this cannot be underestimated. . . . One's identity, as part of this community, was conferred on the basis of presumed commonalities in the schematic and behavioural patterns of people one had never met, and did not even need to meet in order to be united with them" (Whitehouse 2000:40). The doctrinal mode depends chiefly on "verbal codification" for transmission and semantic memory of a general cultural and encyclopedic sort. There is usually little accompanying sensory pageantry or deep emotional communion. Verbal doctrine, which can be greatly amplified by writing and literacy, facilitates rapid cultural (and cross-cultural) spread and proselytization.

A good example of dominance of the doctrinal mode is the Protestant Reformation. In his pamphlet to the German nobility, Martin Luther proclaimed that any man's soul could have direct access to God, without intermediary. The first to interpret Luther's *writings* as the key to a direct line to God and a signal for revolution were those who could *read* both Luther's pamphlet and God's Bible and who were also strongly motivated to change their lives. These were not the peasants (who could not read), nor the clergy and princes (who were favored by the existing social order), but the imperial knights (Koenigsberger 1966). From the beginning of the sixteenth century, the nobles increasingly encroached on knights' rights of jurisdiction in the seigneurial courts, taxing their peasants and so reducing their ability to extract income from rents without risking social unrest. Squeezed between knights and nobles, the peasants, too, had cause for change. But for them it was first necessary to *hear* the word of God from preachers who could *explain* how to call directly to Him for help.

The invention of the printing press and the breakup of the feudal regime were thus catalysts for the sweeping changes engulfing Europe. But "At no stage of this process could literate transmission be regarded as indispensable in principle, although it was clearly relevant in practice" (Whitehouse 2000:153). For the Protestant message to spread among Europe's illiterate minds, the new faith required a doctrine that privileged an oral alliance between the ministers and the masses. For John Calvin and his Church of God, in principle anyone could become a minister. But, before being recognized:

> [H]e had to be tested, ruthlessly and reverently, by the existing ministers as to his beliefs, his conduct, his knowledge, his capacity for preaching, his determination to continue on his chosen course, his ability to inspire faith and devotion in others. Then, after a severe oral examination, the candidate was presented to the Council, given leave to preach, and hands were laid on him as a sign that his authority came from heaven. From then on he must preach to his congregation frequently, advise, pray, administer the two sacraments of baptism and holy communion, visit the sick, relieve the poor, call sinners to repentance, rebuke vice and indifference. In conjunction with his fellow ministers, he must study, discuss doctrine and share in their corporate guardianship of the conduct of the faithful. (Potter 1966:42–43)

Herein lie all the basic elements of the doctrinal mode: repetition and routinization of fairly abstract and austere theological doctrine in conjunction with rigid practices and principles of behavior. For Calvin, conformity and submission to orthodoxy guaranteed the social stability necessary for reformist thought and practice to spread, steadily and uniformly, to an expanding mass. Humanism, though, was generally extended only to those who unsuspiciously rendered their submission.

The early Christian Church likewise grew exponentially out of disaffected elements of the Roman Empire's scattered Jewish communities (Stark 1997). It preached, and practiced, a fairly abstract and inclusive doctrine of personal grace and salvation through self-sacrificing works of social compassion and fidelity (caring for the sick, sexual control). By co-opting the Empire's dominant languages (Latin and Greek) and deploying along its vast communication infrastructure (trade and road system), the early Christians were able to reach out from their originally circumscribed Jewish social networks to the Empire's alienated gentiles (slaves, oppressed minorities, unsettled Greek thinkers, estranged Roman women). By 350 the Roman emperor Constantine himself had joined.

Following the collapse of the Western Roman Empire in the fifth century, the Eastern Empire that continued to rule in parts of Europe, Asia Minor, and North Africa gradually dissipated over the next millennium, disappearing altogether with the fall of Constantinople to the Moslem Ottoman Turks in 1453. Already in the seventh century, however, its outlying parts were ripe for another messianic doctrinal reformation. Mohammed's conception of Allah rapidly diffused over and beyond the Eastern Roman Empire through promissory words of salvation and self-sacrificing works of charity. But this rapid conquest of mind and heart was mightily assisted by a doctrine that sanctifed the use of the sword and the quest for spoils of war as means to incorporate or eliminate the infidel. This strategy was subsequently adopted with even more uncompromising ferocity by the Crusaders and Counter Reformation against Moslems and Jews, by the conquistadores against the indigenous peoples of the Americas and parts of Asia, and, ultimately, by the colonial powers against the rest of the world.[1]

Strict doctrinal regimes do not well tolerate exaggerated or artificial forms of earthly sensory arousal, such as alcohol and drugs, nudity and sexual promiscuity, and unofficial art. Whatever other reasons the ruling Moslem Taliban of Afghanistan may have had for the recent destruction of two ancient statues of the Great Buddha of Bamiyan (winter 2001) and innumerably many other antique icons, their justification for destruction was clearly doctrinal. Some of the more zealous Christian missionaries also industriously practice what they preach concerning intolerance of "graven images," especially the images of those tribal cultures they covet.

In contrast to the "logocentric iconophobia" of the doctrinal mode (Whitehouse 2000:156), the imagistic mode relies mainly on unverbalized, emotionally arousing experiences and episodic memory of a spatiotemporally localized and autobiographical sort. The most sacred and revelatory rites in the imagistic mode are highly arousing, once-in-a-lifetime events. These are often physically excruciating and sensorially invasive: hideous masks and grotesquely painted dancers, horrifying cries and hoots, piercing whistles and pounding drums, overexposure to direct sunlight and heat or darkness and cold, extended sleep and food deprivation, anonymous pummeling and deep body laceration, and more. Possible examples of what Whitehouse (1996) calls "rites of terror" include initiations among Native American Cheyenne and Arapaho (Lowie 1924) and Navajo (Kluckholn and Leighton 1974), Walbiri (Meggitt 1965) and other aboriginals of the central Australian desert (B. Spencer and Gillen 1904), and Mountain Ok Baktaman (Barth 1975) and Ilahita Arapesh of Highland Papua New Guinea (Tuzin 1982). Consider, for instance, the initiation of Ituri Forest Pygmies in the African Congo:

> Sansiwake . . . cried not only for himself, but because his mother was crying bitterly at being parted from a son. . . . Sansiwake was brought to the village, and his head was shaved as the first of a series of ritual acts symbolizing the casting off of an old life. Then Sabani appeared, dressed and painted in a terrifying manner, to smell out his next victim. His face was covered with a mask, his body was daubed with white clay, and his arms and legs were bound with great bundles of raffia so that as he danced he looked half animal and half bird. With him were a number of nkumbi drummers, beating a wild and ear-shattering tattoo, driving all women and uninitiated children into their houses, where they locked and barred the doors. . . . The trials of the nkumbi candidate only begin with the actual circumcision. During the succeeding months . . . the torture is sometimes mental rather than physical. For instance, one boy . . . was made to ridicule his father almost every daylight hour. . . . A crouching dance that might be fun for a few minutes becomes agony after half an hour. A mild switching on the underside of the arm with light sticks is of no concern until, after several days, the skin becomes raw. And then the villagers notch the sticks so that they . . . pinch the skin sharply, often drawing blood. When the boys have become used to being beaten with leafy branches, thorny bushes are substituted. (Turnbull 1962:225)

According to Whitehouse (1995, 2000), such highly infrequent episodes seem to be engraved in detail in participants' minds, confidently and forever, as especially vivid "flashbulb memories," akin to the memories of Americans who experienced such personally momentous social events as Pearl Harbor, the Kennedy assassinations, the explosion of the *Challenger* space shuttle, or the recent terrorist attack on Manhattan and Washington. Such flashbulb effects presumably endure even if the episodes last for days, months, or years, such as the experience of warfare or the Holocaust. These haunting episodes seldom need to be repeated or discussed to ensure the intense and intimate social solidarity of coparticipants. Although limited forms of communication among initiates may be tolerated, there are often severe penalties for those who dare talk about their experiences to others, including social ostracism, physical punishment, and the menace of supernaturally driven psychological harassment unto death. The imagistic mode thus fosters unspoken, emotionally powerful, and long-lasting ties among relatively small groups of specific individuals but hinders wider inferential elaboration and public dissemination of religious theology and cultural ideology.

Whitehouse avoids identifying the doctrinal, or "digital," mode with large-scale Western religions or literacy, and the imagistic, or "analogic," mode with small-scale tribal religions and cults. Nevertheless, he argues that imagistic rituals are historically primary, dating at least to the "religious" cave art of the Upper Paleolithic (and perhaps as far back as Neanderthal; see section 2.3). The dark and labyrinthine subterranean environment, which distorted sound and sight, arguably favored the production of exaggerated and stylized animal and human forms in conditions of heightened emotional and sensory arousal (cf. Pfeiffer 1982). Burial sites from the time clearly indicate religious funerary rites that intimate communal awareness, anxiety, and hopes for avoiding the finality of death. Doctrinal religions first emerged in lower Mesopotamia some 6,000 years ago with complex chiefdoms and state-level literate societies.[2]

To demonstrate how the two modes operate, Whitehouse examines four Melanesian cases. Two are predominately imagistic and highly localized (Baktaman and the Taro cult of northern Papua) and two are predominantly doctrinal and more widespread (the Paliau movement of Manus and the Pomio Kivung of East New Britain in Papua New Guinea). In each case, though, the imagistic and doctrinal modes interact in complex ways.

For example, shortly after World War II, Paliau preached a revision of Christian doctrine known as "the New Way." The central doctrine was contained in "the Long Story of God," and focused on the dual nature of Jesus and the rest of humankind, in which the body housed the spirit or *tingting* (Pidgin "thinkthink") that derives from God (T. Schwartz 1962). The Long Story illuminated differences with missionary doctrine, thereby clarifying the ways in which the colonial ideology allegedly sought to confound and conquer the native spirit. Like missionary Christianity, however, the Paliau movement relied on highly repetitive observances and routine orations and discussions. According to Margaret Mead, who knew Paliau and followed developments in his movement over the years, Paliau even commanded a form of roll call, "the line": "[W]hen church was over 'the line' was formed. Like the rising gong, 'the line' was reminiscent of plantation discipline when all the labourers formed into a line to be given assignments for the day, although in the minds of young European critics of The New Way, who had never seen an old-style plantation, 'the line' was regarded as part of the militaristic 'totalitarian regimentation' introduced by Paliau" (1956:249). Moreover, the Paliau movement, like late Medieval or modern Evangelical Christianity, wound up incorporating numerous imagistic forms into the main doctrinal mode: celebrations of miracles, spirit possessions, ecstatic visions and trances, and so on.

More generally, repetition and routinization eventually produce a "tedium effect" that undermines religious motivation, ultimately causing decay of ritual script and religious doctrine. In fact, Stark and Glock (1968) report that few Christians in the United States are presently familiar with routine Church doctrine. For example, 86 percent of Catholics and 79 percent of Protestants in a survey could not name even one Old Testament prophet. Whitehouse suggests that ignorance about doctrine ensues because increasing the frequency of emotional outlay raises energy costs associated with information processing and storage while yielding diminishing returns.

Periodic imagistic revivals, driven by iconoclastic heresies and cults, then become necessary to rejuvenate mainstream ideology and ensure long-term doctrinal survival. This might be one part of the explanation for the current rise of the "theological passion" seizing fundamentalist sects across traditionally Christian, Jewish, and Moslem societies (cf. Talbot 2000). Conversely, some ritual scripting and narrative consolidation may be required to forestall excessive localization and splintering of imagistic sects and to allow dissemination of beliefs and assimilation of individuals across increasingly permeable and mobile community boundaries. Finally, some relatively large-scale religious movements appear to fall somewhere in between the doctrinal and imagistic modes. Sufism and Zen Buddhism, for example, pointedly discourage any doctrinal formulation in the quest for mystical experience, and Quakers make little or no attempt to enforce doctrinal conformity or to achieve a mystical experience (W. Alston 1967:144).[3]

6.2. Some Problems: Liturgy Isn't Logical, Frequent Arousal Isn't Rare

There is much to commend Whitehouse's (2000) analysis. It parsimoniously assumes no special cognitive features for religion over and above those (logical, inferential, mnemonic, sensory, and emotive) modalities of everyday, nonreligious life. It predicts interesting links between different modes of religious practices and distinctive aspects of small- versus large-group social cohesion and political integration. It connects differences in how rituals are structured and remembered (semantically vs. episodically) with differences in religious motivation (ideological coherence vs. emotional arousal). And it describes subtle structural interactions among modes of religiosity as they historically unfold, avoiding a static and overly simplistic typology.

Nevertheless, there are some serious problems. First, there is no evidence for the claim that the doctrinal mode of religion tends toward some "logically integrated and coherent ideology" that is inferentially connected by "complex strings of implicational logic" (Whitehouse 2000:18–19, 58–60). Preliminary studies indicate that even the content of the most hardcore elements of liturgical doctrines, such as the Ten Commandments, lacks any semblance of conformity and propositional agreement across (secular or religious) informants who actually know one another (from the same classroom or church; see chapter 9). Consequently, the inferences generated from such content are not logically bound to converge. At best, one might claim that the doctrinal mode is more concerned with discursively connecting and elaborating certain judgments and behavioral commitments. This may involve local development of implications from some propositions, as well as more global and evocative connections between various local bits of doctrine.

Many students of religion argue that theology is a thoroughly logical discipline of the sort that Whitehouse describes: "Theology proper represents intellectual deductions from a foundational myth . . . as well as "reasonable" extrapolations on such a myth. The beginning point of theology proper . . . in the West . . . in primitive societies . . . in Hinduism . . . is . . . a marked admixture of deduction from ancient foundational myths" (d'Aquili and Newberg 1999:7). As we saw earlier, though, religious doctrine *cannot* aspire to logical integration because it is fundamentally counterintuitive and quasi-propositional at its core (see chapter 4).

Logic itself is merely a tool for shifting one's intuitive feelings of confidence about premises to the conclusions that the rules of logic generate. Nevertheless, if logic is to do its work, then any premise to which the rules of logic are applied must be a proposition. A proposition is an expression in language, signs, or mental representations expressing a definite relation between a subject and a predicate that can be doubted or denied to be true or false. Religious "foundational myths" (d'Aquli and Newberg 1999), "ultimate postulates," or "cosmological axioms" (Rappaport 1979) aren't propositions, at least if any notion of the supernatural is involved. The violations of intuitive categories that any supernatural phenomenon manifests preclude any possibility of inferential consistency and completeness; that is, there is no clear, replicable, or context-free standard for testing the truth or falsity of any utterance about the supernatural.[4]

If liturgical doctrines were truly integrated through logical inference, then frequent repetition would seem superfluous. Once a logical procedure is known, inferences can be "automatically" generated and applied to indefinitely many new or old cases and situations. That's chiefly why people use logic in the first place, whether in mathematics, science, law, or everyday argument. One can imagine a group of mathematicians, scientists, or lawyers congregating to repeat some formula as a mantra for the purpose of some social convention; however, no amount of repetition would make mathematics, science, or law more "logically integrated," consistent, or coherent.

So far, the discussion has concerned mainly deductive inference; however, religious belief also invariably violates canons of inductive inference, such as relying on the cumulative weight of evidence after multiple comparisons and repeated observations. Thus, religious belief is often justified by reference to a singular happening, such as a supposed miracle or revelation. Induction from miracles and revelations does not involve cumulative weighing of evidence, multiple comparisons, or repeated observations.

In fact, Whitehouse's important observation about frequent repetition of liturgy arguably leads to a conclusion diametrically opposed to his own: people may need to repeat such rituals precisely because the ritual elements are not, and cannot be, logically integrated or independently induced from multiple experiences. Rather, the elements are woven into a script that must be acted out and *performed* to be reliably connected, remembered, and retransmitted. Although any performance necessarily involves bodily excitation and arousal, performances that consist mainly in low-arousal, verbal rites and repetitions may well favor the ready application of these doctrinal rites to indefinitely many persons and situations, much as the sense-neutral description of a plant in terms of the general configuration of its parts can be readily copied and used to categorize and communicate about indefinitely many plants of the same "type," regardless of the particular colors, smells, or environments with which actual exemplars are associated.

The second major problem with Whitehouse's case studies is that there are glaring counterexamples. The inverse relation between emotional arousal and performance frequency is far from constant. For example, the shrine of Reza in the Iranian city of Mashad has been a pilgrimage center of the world's Shi'ite Moslems for centuries. Nowadays, each month, more than one million devotees visit the large shrine complex dominating the center of the city. Many are repeat visitors. On special mourning days, men in black shirts rhythmically beat their chest and act out the death of Reza, who legend claims was killed in A.D. 817 with poison grapes offered by a rival caliph. Outside the shrine, visitors sob and cry as holy men recount Reza's life and death. Inside the shrine, under a great golden cupola, crowds strain to kiss or touch the silver cage housing Reza's tomb, and babies are passed by thousands of hands over hundreds of heads to absorb its blessed power:

> The sick and the lame—men, women and children—attach themselves by lengths of a thread to a latticed window looking on to the shrine, camping and praying there for days and weeks in the hope of being healed. From time to time, someone leaps up with a cry of salvation and is pursued across the courtyard by those hoping to be touched by the miracle. . . . There is no doubting the religious intensity surrounding Iran's holiest place, with its constant stream of visitors, day and night. (*Financial Times*, 9–10 June 2001, p. 1)

Another example of a relatively frequent, highly arousing ritual is the annual festival of La Tirana de Tarapaca in Chile. Thousands of frenetic dancers with elaborate, diabolical masks whirl until exhausted. Thousands more chant and wail in procession as they agonize their way on their knees through the streets and up to the Virgin's blessed altar (Echevarría 1963). Many, if not most, performers and participants are repeaters. Similarly, during the annual pilgrimage at Lourdes in southern France, more than a century after Bernadette Soubirous had visions there, up to 50,000 people daily participate in an emotionally charged service directed at healing physical and mental handicaps (Cranston 1988). During Holy Week (Semana Santa), millions of worshippers throughout Latin America participate in emotional re-enactments of Christ's Passion.

In the Roman Catholic world, ever since the Middle Ages, pilgrimages have been proofs of penitence: the greater the pain and suffering, the greater the likelihood of forgiveness. In many of the world's large and small religions, periodic pilgrimages and seasonal ceremonies routinely and profoundly rouse votaries to costly and intense commitments. One also gets the impression from reports of repeated human sacrifice, as among the Aztecs, that few witnesses or participants ever got bored. Vivid visions of death and the sight and stench of human blood everywhere, especially on the Aztec priests, who were caked in it from head to toe, would likely offset any tedium effect (Díaz del Castillo 1989 [1632]).

The same is probably true of animal sacrifices in south Indian villages. Whenever an epidemic breaks out, a relatively frequent occurrence in the region, there is a public festival lasting for days or weeks. Sensory pageantry and emotional impact are evident:

> First the buffalo is washed with water, smeared with yellow turmeric and red kukuma, and then garlanded with flowers and the leaves of the sacred margarosa tree. It is brought before the image; and a Mādigā cuts off its head . . . over a heap of boiled rice, which becomes soaked with blood. The right foreleg is then cut off and placed crosswise in its mouth . . . the fat of the entrails is smeared over the eyes and forehead. A lighted lamp is placed [either on the head itself or on the heap of rice soaked in blood]. . . . The people shout out as they go [in some villages with music or tom-toms] "Poli! Poli!" ["Food! Food!"] and clap their hands and wave sticks above their heads to keep off the evil spirits. . . . Sometimes an extraordinary number of animals is sacrificed on occasions of this kind, as many as a thousand . . . on a single day. . . . The function lasts from about ten a.m. to five p.m. (Whitehead 1988[1921]:56–58)

Even much more frequent performance of rites, such as weekly Pentacostal church services, can involve extraordinary displays and levels of sensory arousal.

There are also infrequently repeated events that are accompanied by no affective pageantry. For example, whereas a Lebanese Druze wedding is a delightful sensory feast, the occasional once-in-a-lifetime divorce is an emotional wash. The man simply utters "I divorce you" three times and swears he means it before the religious judge (qādi). Closer to home, the Church of Scotland is occasionally called on to bless Scottish motorways. This is usually a rare occurrence for a clergyman and his congregation, as it was when the Reverend Samuel J. Knox performed his once-in-a-lifetime motorway blessing for the A68 out of Edinburgh. For the participants, emotions did not run especially high (Garth Knox, personal communication). Still, it is a credit to Whitehouse's insight that counterexamples to low-frequency, high-arousal rites are not very easy to come by.

Finally, the interpretations offered are so abstract that the natives themselves would hardly be able to recognize, much less confirm, the analysis offered. This, too, would be acceptable if the abstractions were precise enough for other scientists to independently test them. Despite the laudable (and, for anthropology, increasingly rare) attempt to connect ethnographic description and interpretation with the methods and findings of the larger scientific community (in particular, cognitive psychology), the interpretive framework needs considerably more refinement and definition to be tested. It is in the spirit of refinement and correction, and not rejection, that I want to probe deeper into the relationship among memory, emotion, and ritual.[5]

6.3. Schemas and Encoding Specificity: Episodic versus Semantic Memory

Cognitive psychology, argues Whitehouse (2000), provides solid experimental grounding for distinguishing modes of religiosity: the doctrinal mode is based on verbal semantic memory and embedded in noncontextualized schema, whereas the imagistic mode is based on nonverbal and highly contextualized episodic and flashbulb memories. The key insight into schema comes from Bransford and Johnson (1973); the distinction between semantic and episodic memory is Tulving's (1972); the original account of flashbulb memory owes to R. Brown and Kulick (1982). Whitehouse's (and McCauley and Lawson's 2002) use of these somewhat technical terms from experimental psychology is more in the realm of interpretive evocation than empirical description or generalization.

Tulving's distinction involved different modes of encoding verbal information. Both sorts of memory were based on the classical semantic-feature accounts of concepts in memory (Bower 1967), rather than currently more popular and powerful theory-based approaches to concept formation and memory organization (Medin, Ross, and Markman 2001): "our conceptualization of memory traces as aggregates of elements is in keeping with . . . notions of concepts and words being represented in memory as bundles of attributes and features" (Tulving and Watkins 1975:261). For Tulving, the key dimensions that distinguish between semantic and episodic encoding are temporal specificity and novelty, not verbal versus iconic information.

For example, a person may learn on one occasion that bears like honey, on another occasion that bears eat fish, and on yet another occasion that bears hibernate in winter. Encoding all three facts under the semantic concept BEARS then allows the person to infer that bears are omnivorous and thus are also likely to eat beef and fruit, although they probably don't each much of either in the winter. Alternatively, each of these facts might have been encoded episodically, for example, as part of what a mother told her daughter in the course of three separate visits to the local zoo. The facts would then be stored within a perceptually and temporally contextualized event, such as (information pertaining to) VISITING THE ZOO WITH MOTHER and not under an abstract and decontextualized category of (information about) BEARS.

Episodic encoding "does not include the capabilities of inferential reasoning" (Tulving 1972:390). According to Tulving, the episodic system is fairly unstable and more susceptible to transformation and loss of information than is the semantic system. Nevertheless, the two systems can, and often do, interact. Semantic cues "can be effectively and quickly used to locate information stored in episodic memory" to build up richer semantic structures (e.g., knowledge about ZOO BEARS) as well as more abstract episodic schema (e.g., VISITING bears in ZOOS; Tulving 1976).

One way that semantic and episodic memory appear to be integrated is through the use of general knowledge structures called schema or scripts (Schank and Abelson 1977). A schema or script does not encode information about any one particular situation but about a certain type of situation. Consider, for example, the following scenario. The bear roared as little Mary continued to throw things at it from her bag; her little brother cried; her mother hurried over; and her father asked if bears like salty things more than sweets. If presented as an isolated episode, the scene might just as well seem frightening or bizarre. But as part of the zoo-visiting schema, it's pretty routine.

A schema or script may be viewed as a structured "frame" that includes certain "slots" for information. A zoo-visiting frame would have slots for which individuals came along on the visit (parents, friends, teachers), what the visitors were doing (eating popcorn or ice cream, watching animals), what kind of animals were seen, what the animals were doing (roaring, playing, eating), what animals appear to "go together" (reptiles, felines, monkey and apes), and so forth. A frame may contain other frames embedded within it. For example, the zoo-visiting frame may contain a popcorn-buying frame (with slots for who buys, who sells, how it's bagged, etc.).[6]

Unschematized episodic memory is unstable and liable to degenerate because the lack of coordinating context makes otherwise related episodes incoherent or incomprehensible (Moser 1976); for example, "the notes were sour" and "the seam was split" contain two events that seem to be unrelated until the context information "bagpipes" is added (Bransford and Johnson 1973). Similarly, the seemingly bizarre events of a Pygmy or Baktaman initiation rite would simply remain bizarre for the initiate if not incorporated into a socially relevant initiation schema.

Two factors clearly operate to channel initiates' personal experiences into a socially convergent schema. First, religious initiates are often inducted in cohorts, so that fellow participants all more or less experience the same manipulations by elders (and spirits) within the same spatiotemporal frame. Second, accompanying sensory displays are customarily targeted on central elements of the rites, so that all participants tend to focus attention, and affectively project personal sufferances, onto the most culturally relevant themes. Personal identities are thus fired and forged under a public brand.

Moreover, although community members may *undergo* initiation into such thematic experiences only once in a lifetime, they generally *witness* a few, several, or many ceremonial repetitions of the same ritual themes. This includes generally unpleasant ceremonies, such as a Cheyenne Sun Dance or Navajo hazing, as well as generally pleasant ceremonies, such as baptisms, confirmations, bar mitzvahs, and weddings. Through repeated witnessing, people review, recollect and renew the general, social effects of these rites on multiple but distinct individuals like themselves. They also *report* these effects to one another during repassage.

For rites to become socially scripted and schematized, at least some verbalization and "narrative consolidation" seems indispensable, whether in the repeated mode or the once-in-a-lifetime mode. Granted, initiates are often afraid to talk about the manifestations and meanings of any occult forces encountered (Barth 1975:258–260). Nevertheless, novices usually come to understand how initiation events evocatively cohere—emotionally and poetically rather than logically or as factually interdependent—within a partially verbalized frame. The initiates are *told* what to do and what not to do by elders who were previously *told* much the same thing; elders explain what the social and supernatural consequences of the initiates' actions are likely to be; and cohorts of initiates *speak* about and *discuss* some aspects of their shared experiences.

6.4. Affecting Memories

Whitehouse (1995, 2000), though, suggests that important religious episodes, such as initiation, require little or no narrative consolidation because they are encoded as emotionally vivid "flashbulb memories." Psychologists Roger Brown and James Kulik (1977) pioneered the study of such flashbulb memories. They asked 40 white and 40 black adults to recall the circumstances when they first heard of an important event, such as the assassinations of John Kennedy and Martin Luther King Jr. All but one of the participants could remember the circumstances surrounding Kennedy's assassination 13 years before. Three-fourths of blacks but only one-third of whites had vivid memories of King's more recent assassination. Brown and Kulik speculated that such memories are triggered by a biologically evolved "Now Print" mechanism, specially adapted for remembering surprising, highly consequential events. These are emotionally imprinted in memory as alarm (re)calls that selectively focus energy and attention for appropriately reacting to low-probability, high-risk situations. Without emotional priming, the cognitive system is liable to undervalue the risk of low-probability events and forget them, like a natural calamity (e.g., an earthquake), a man-made catastrophe (e.g., Chernobyl), seeing a deadly snake, or terrorist attack.[7]

Additional experiments on flashbulb memory, though, suggest much narrative consolidation, dubious accuracy, and little emotion. Christianson (1989) studied memories of the assassination of the popular Swedish prime minister, Olaf Palme. Young adult Swedes remembered Palme's assassination far better than an uneventful happening from the same time. Subjects' initial feelings of surprise reliably predicted recall of central details about the assassination a year later; however, recall consisted of fairly standard and stable social narrative (perhaps gleaned informally from discussions and news accounts) that excluded contextual details and peripheral information.

Neisser and Harsch (1992) asked undergraduates at Emory University how each had heard of the *Challenger* shuttle explosion that occurred the day before. A questionnaire elicited detailed reports about students' emotions. Two and a half years later the same students were asked for their memory of how they heard about the 1986 *Challenger* explosion. Each student's reported recall received a score between 0 and 7; a score of 7 indicated almost perfect recall. The mean score was 2.95, and half of the participants scored 2 or less. Moreover, for students who said that they accurately remembered the circumstances, there was no reliable correlation between accuracy of recall and their confidence in recall. Some students reported highly imagistic memories, but these proved no more accurate. Different codings schemes for emotion also failed to reliably predict accuracy of recall. Six months later (three years after the explosion) the stories told were highly consistent with those told at two and a half years, suggesting that flashbulb memories endure more through narrative consolidation based on "TV priority" than through relived emotion. In brief, many so-called flashbulb memories stabilize with systematic distortions that are in line with social reports and expectations.[8]

One problem in the literature on flashbulb memories is the confound between memories for striking experiences and memories for stressful experiences. For Emory University students, memories of the *Challenger* explosion may have been striking as a shared public event, but not as an intensely felt, frightening personal experience. For children, however, events such as the Kennedy assassination, the *Challenger* explosion, and the terrorist attacks on New York and Washington may be much more emotionally unsettling. In line with this possibility, Warren and Swartwood (1992) found that children who reported higher emotional responses to the *Challenger* explosion had more consistent recall over a two-year period than children reporting lower initial arousal.

There seems to be no clear and simple relation between severity of stress and memory. A number of clinical studies indicate that children's memories for single traumatic experiences tend to be fairly accurate and long-lasting. Too much stress, however, appears to hinder memory.[9]

Longitudinal studies show that acute stress suffered during a single traumatic event, as among children who have witnessed a murder (Pynoos and Nader 1989), leads to detailed and long-lasting recall of core elements of the event, although there is also evidence for significant decay and distortion of peripheral elements. For example, child psychologist Leonore Terr (1983) studied children who had been kidnapped at gunpoint from a school bus in Chowchilla, California, in 1976. Most of the children, age 5 to 14, furnished "a fully detailed account of the experience" four to five years later. But about half the children showed marked distortion in recall, including those whose initial memory of the event had been quite accurate. One possible interpretation is that the more severe the stress, the greater the attention paid to core, autobiographical elements of the situation (the most personally relevant agents, patients, and instruments involved) and the less paid to specific setting of the event (actual location and time of occurrence, as well as preceding, surrounding, and following incidents).[10]

A number of laboratory and real-life case studies of memory loss through trauma also indicate that people forget many peripheral details of information preceding, surrounding, and following a traumatic event. Nevertheless, there is frequently accurate and persistent "tunnel vision" of the event's critical and core details. For example, victims of a rape or hold-up tend to focus on particular physical aspects of the aggressor and details of the means used in the aggression (e.g., the gun), but initially fail to recall aspects of the event's location or of what preceded or followed it. Experiments indicate that the effects of tunnel memory decrease over time (Safer et al. 1998).

There is also extensive documentation that victims of combat, torture, and abuse often show initial amnesia and inability to retrieve consciously information relating to the precipitating event. Still, retention of isolated memory fragments of critical details—present in intrusive flashbacks and nightmares—resembles tunnel memories for traumatic events, although spontaneous recall is apparently nonconscious. This suggests that central aspects of repressed memories may be somehow indirectly available, even if not willfully accessible (Davis 1990). Such memories often can be successfully retrieved later, depending on the type of retrieval cues present (Christianson 1992; Heuer and Reisberg 1992). For example, memory retrieval for an event can be facilitated if the person experiences an emotional state similar to that associated with the original event (Bower and Mayer 1989; Eich 1995), especially if the eliciting emotional state is one of marked pleasantness or unpleasantness (Macauley et al. 1993). Specific sights, sounds, and particularly smells seem to be more effective than words or stories in retrieving emotional memories, perhaps because stressful or traumatic experiences—including severe religious initiations—are indeed first imprinted as affective and bodily sensations in the limbic system (cf. Cain 1974). This is a topic explored in the next chapter.

6.5. Ceremonially Manipulating Memory's Evolutionary Imperatives

In sum, a review of the psychological literature on memory for stressful events suggests that memory for trauma is conditioned by competing evolutionary imperatives. On the one hand, severe stress seems to facilitate long-term remembering of traumatic events as threatening situations that critically merit attention for survival. Without social support and narrative consolidation, however, ready recall of such events tends to be fragmentary and spare, limited mainly to high-priority, core aspects of the situation. There is an attentional focusing, or tunneling effect, that results in blocked access to background and peripheral information associated with the event. As with euptive emotions themselves, such as terror and rage, this attentional narrowing to the most critical aspects of the situation may help to optimize information processing and energy expenditure for the purpose of acting in ways most directly relevant to survival (Darwin 1965[1872]).

On the other hand, recall of traumatic events often lacks a coherent verbal account. This can render such memories more subject to distortion and forgetfulness. From an evolutionary vantage this, too, may be crucial to long-term individual survival under conditions of uncertainty. By marginalizing or provisionally forgetting aspects of events that a person is forced to suffer but has little or no control of (combat, terrorism, sexual or physical abuse, rape, sudden infirmity, natural disaster, etc.) personal identity and self-esteem may better endure, especially under the threat that such dispossessing, potentially ego-shattering situations might again arise (Freud 1957b[1915]; Horowitz 1979).

Novices who undergo terrifying initiations, like many people experiencing abuse, are often prevented from discussing their experiences. Yet accurate recall of details still appears to be a possibility under two broad sets of conditions: if mood-dependent or emotionally arousing aspects of the original situation reoccur, so that a person feels compelled to better recall in order to cope with it; or if a socially secure environment (family, friends, support group, doctors, psychoanalyst, social worker, community structure, etc.) is convincingly provided so that the person feels better able to integrate adversity and overcome it. For religious initiates, the ceremonial repetition of situations that bring to mind their own initiations—witnessed as part of a congregation rather than suffered as individuals—seems to fulfill both conditions.

Finally, there is some clinical evidence that the stressful aspects of group initiation result in greater social cohesion. For example, in a classic test of Leon Festinger's theory of cognitive dissonance, Aronson and Mills (1959) looked at the effect of severity of initiation on liking for a group. They found that persons who undergo an unpleasant initiation to become a member, by having to read "embarassing material" before the group, find the group more attractive than do persons who become members without undergoing a severe initiation (for a replication, see Gerard and Mathewson 1966). Moreover, Mills and Mintz (1972) found that by increasing physiological arousal through an unknown source—a frequent aspect of severe group initiations—subjects would increase their desire to affiliate with other persons in the same situation and show stronger affiliative tendencies than when the increase came from a known source. The desire to affiliate was greater when subjects were given a stimulant and told that it was an analgesic than when they were given a placebo and told it was an analgesic or when given a stimulant and truly told it was a stimulant.[11]

In the social context of religious initiation, the startling and acute production of stress is often scaled to the prior forbiddenness and significance of the new knowledge shared and higher status attained. Thus, for the Navajo:

> Boys and girls are made recognized members of The People and are introduced to full participation in ceremonial life. . . . The first boy is led out beside the fire. The figure in the white mask makes a mark on each shoulder with sacred cornmeal. . . . Then, using a different falsetto cry, the black-masked figure lightly strikes the cornmeal marks with some reeds. . . . This is repeated for other places on the body, and the one who uses the reeds varies the time interval between touching the boy and uttering his cry, so its unexpectedness causes the boy to start convulsively. . . . Then the one who wore the black mask places it over the face of each child in turn. . . . All the children are told to look up and always remember the Holy People. The reversal of the masks is a very intelligent psychological act, for it allows the child to see that the dread figure is actually someone he knows, or at least a human being, and thus the ritual is robbed of some of its terror. . . . The ceremony closes with the admonition to each child not to betray to uninitiates what he has seen. (Kluckholn and Leighton 1974[1946]:207–208)

Through the stress they induce, such rites of passage (akin to "chase play") emotionally enduring, costly, and hard-to-fake commitments to group membership.

The exaggerated, sensual displays associated with such ceremonies thereby also accomplish a conceptual task. They "miraculously" create a coherent frame for a person's group identity from almost arbitrary manipulations of the surrounding natural environment. Forever affecting, these originally traumatic manipulations become the cultural coordinates for personal memory and social security.

6.6. Spirit Possession, Sudden Conversion, Mystical Experience: Ritual Resolution without Rehearsal

Extreme religious rituals of initiation arouse existential anxieties by culturally mimicking and manipulating the seemingly capricious and uncontrollable situations that naturally provoke them: terror and risk of death from unidentifiable sources, the menace of infirmity and starvation through physical ordeal and deprivation, the injustice of whimsical oppression, sudden isolation and loneliness. Through such contrivance, participants rehearse life's travails, surviving them all just fine. The novices behold how the beliefs and artifacts circulating in their society appear to *recreate*, and thereby regularize and control, what would otherwise be nature's despairing arbitrariness. By the initiation's end, the novices realize that they and their people ultimately dispose the supernatural means to manage anything that might arise.

These life rehearsals incite the very emotions and existential anxieties that motivate religious beliefs and quests for deliverance. Then, by assuaging and resolving the ensuing distress, successful completion of the ritual perfomance authenticates the religious thoughts and actions that stage-manage both the rehearsal and the real thing. In fact, the rehearsal avows itself to be reality's wellspring. For the religious initiate, therein culture becomes the causal core of the cosmos.

Ritual displays of religious conviction and commitment can also offer direct resolution without rehearsal, as in cases of spirit possession, sudden conversion, or spontaneous mystical experience. Take demon possession. It is generally associated with "a relatively long term pyschological state in which an individual believes he is unwillingly possessed by one or more intruding spirits and exhibits contingent (usually maladaptive) behavioural responses which he attributes to the spirits' influence" (C. Ward and Beaubrun 1980:202). Recurring cases are reported from Africa and Afro-America (Leiris 1958; Douyon 1966; Lewis, 1971; Kilson 1972; S. Walker 1972; Pressel 1974; Ben-Amos 1994), European America (Freed and Freed 1964), Native America (Lowie 1924; Reina 1966), China (Yap 1960), India (Crooke 1907; Whitehead 1988[1921]), North Africa, and the Middle East (Jaussen 1948[1907]). Cases in the United States often involve possession by devils, witches (Galvin and Ludwig 1961; Warner 1977), and, more recently, aliens (Spanos et al. 1993; Mack 1994). Variants of demon possession include "soul kidnapping" (Lowie 1924:177–178) or "soul loss" (Warner 1977) through the agency of malevolent spirits. Black magic and bewitchment, in which spirits cast charms or spells on victims, can also exhibit aspects of possession. This is especially so in regard to the onset of symptoms and debilitating pathology, as with depression and disease (Redfield and Villa Rojas 1934:177–180). If not exorcised, death may be expected.

In places where demon possession occurs, society usually recognizes a fine line between supernaturally caused possession and organically caused madness:

> Between madness and possession, the difference is small in the eyes of the Arab. There is nevertheless a different term . . . the madman is designated by the word *mağnoun*; the possessed person is called *madroub* or "struck"

> by a spirit. To chase away the intruding spirit from the possessed body, one turns to a faqir [an indigent wanderer or street person who practices healing and sorcery by virtue of being "gifted with supernatural power, because of his friendship with Allah"]. . . . A *faqireh* [sorceress] seizes the possessed person, places him in the middle of the room and begins turning around him as she plays the tambourine. At the sound of this primitive music, the spirit stirs restlessly; the afflicted person has convulsions. "Where do you want to leave from?" asks the *faqireh* of the malevolent spirit; "From the head?"—"No."—"From the eyes?"—"No."—"From the mouth?"—"No." She continues the enumeration of the parts of the body in this way, until finally, she obliges it to leave by the little toe of the foot. (Jaussen 1948[1907]:327; see Whitehead 1988[1921]:119–121 for a remarkably similar account of madness-like possession in south India)

Although there is no clear psychopathology associated with demon possession, listlessness, depression, guilt feelings, fainting, and dissociation are frequently reported. Acute or chronic stress (or emotional or psychic "tension") are features habitually cited as precipitating and accompanying noninstitutionalized cases of possession. Institutionalized cases tend to have more noticeably psychotic pathologies, such as schizophrenic hallucination, epileptic confusion, mania, and senility. In one institutionalized Chinese sample of possessed patients, Yap (1960) reported mainly hysterics (48.5 percent), schizophrenics (24.3 percent), and depressives (12.2 percent).

In Trinidad, demon possession occurs predominantly among lower- and lower-middle-class blacks and East Indians associated with the Pentacostal Church (C. Ward and Beaubrun 1980). Case studies suggest a common pattern. The victims, whether men or women, have intense sexual conflicts (incestuous or illicit love affairs, unwanted abortions), domestic difficulties (unwanted or unhappy marriage, conflicts with in-laws or step-relatives), or both. Incubi enter the body at night, sometimes engaging in sexual intercourse. The conflicts and difficulties are long-standing, sometimes stretching out over many years. Victims usually report feelings of depression, lack of motivation, headaches, dissociation, and other types of physical malaise. Possessed persons come to the church for faith-healing and exorcism only after repeatedly visiting the doctor or trying other folk remedies with no relief. All the case subjects required repeated exorcisms to keep the demons out and the mind and body under control.

In south India, even relatively high-caste Hindu women go to a village holy man (*pūjārī*) to exorcise evil spirits when medical help is to no avail: "It is said to be a common belief among many Hindus that barrenness in females is sometimes the result of possession by evil spirits, some of whom have to be propitiated, while others are terrified into leaving their victims" (Whitehead 1988[1921]:119). According to C. Ward and Beaubrun (1980), possession exorcism affords positive advantages to the individual in such cases: direct escape for a conflict situation and dimunition of stress and guilt feelings by projecting blame onto the intruding spirit. The critical advantage of the Pentacostal Church or the village holy man over doctors and folk healers is community support. The group accepts the cause of a person's difficulties to lie beyond the individual's responsibility or control and also accepts the collective burden of comforting, caring for, and eventually curing the individual.

Other types of possession may involve benevolent rather than malevolent spirits. Here, too, there is a fine line beween madness and possession or ecstatic experience (see McDaniel 1989 on ecstatic experiences in Bengal). The precipitating factors (chiefly sexual or domestic problems) and accompanying relief (stress and anxiety reduction) are also often similar. For example, among the Edo of Benin (Nigeria), only women who are possessed by the spirit of Olokun (senior son of Osanobua, the creator god) become priestesses of the Olokun cult that manages the relations between the dry land and deep waters of the Edo cosmos. Following a proper diagnosis by a diviner, the women are initiated into the priesthood. During initiation, they come to realize that their previous difficulties in life were imposed on them by Olokun so that they could now truly understand, enjoy, and spread the opposite benefits of His kingdom. Unlike the repeated exorcisms and temporary relief associated with demon possession in Trinidad, stress relief among Edo priestesses appears to be permanent. This is because their status in society and life conditions change completely after initiation: "the psychological benefits of participation are not temporary outlets but a real redefinition of the self" (Ben-Amos 1994:119).

In both the Trinidad and Edo examples, depossession, relief of depression, and stress reduction occur in conjunction with social synchronization of rhythmic auditory, vestibular, and graphic movements: speaking in tongues, dancing, designing with chalk, and so forth. Studies by Susan Nolen-Hoeksema (1991) indicate that active responses to depression, such as directed activities (work, hobbies, etc.), are more likely to alleviate it than are ruminative responses. In cases of possession, religious intervention may actively redirect attention away from ruminative notions of helplessness and "being stuck."

Stress (associated with guilt and anxiety) appears to be especially manifest before religious conversions. Clark (1929) first reported that among those who had a sudden conversion, 55 percent suffered from guilt feelings compared with only 8.5 percent of his total sample. Roberts (1965) found that 52 percent of sudden converts and 41 percent of slow converts (in a sample of 40 subjects) expressed a sense of guilt before conversion. Spellman, Baskett, and Byrne (1971) administered the Taylor Manifest Anxiety Scale (MAS) to three groups in a Protestant town: those who had a sudden religious conversion, those who had a more gradual religious development, and those who were not religious at all. The nonreligious and gradual religious development groups did not differ from each other on manifest anxiety, but the sudden conversion group scored significantly higher on the MAS than the other two groups combined. There are substantial positive correlations between MAS and scales of guilt feelings (Lowe 1964) and substantial negative correlations between MAS and social desirability (Edwards 1957).

Deutsch (1975) observed that individuals with low self-esteem and a history of troubled relationships are more frequent religious converts. Recent studies by Kirkpatrick (1997, 1998) reveal that positive religious change is predicted by negative models of self and positive models of others. In one study of adult women over a four-year period, women who initially registered as either anxious or avoidant on measures of social attachment were significantly more likely than secure women to report having "found a new relationship with God" over the four-year study interval (Kirkpatrick 1997). In addition, women who were initially anxious were significantly more likely than either avoidant or secure women to report having had "a religious experience or conversion" during the intervening four years, with marginally greater likelihood of being "born again" or "speaking in tongues" (glossolalia).[12]

As in cases of possession, cult converts often seek professional help before conversion. For example, around 40 percent of persons surveyed who joined the Divine Light Mission and Unification Church (Galanter 1982) and Hare Krishna (Rochford, Purvis, and Eastman 1989) reported having sought counseling or medical assistance prior to conversion. Nearly half of the Hare Krishna sample (48 of 103) claimed that they were anxious about life before converting.

Stress and anxiety also seem to be factors in acute religious experience. Hay (1982) found that 50 out of 100 British adults who reported a religious mystical experience claimed to have been "distressed and ill at ease." In a sample of 192 Christians reporting a religious mystical experience, Spilka, Brown, and Cassidy (1992) found that subjects experienced a greater sense of union with God and felt more at ease with themselves. Several studies indicate that the anxiety and stress associated with a life crisis, dissatisfaction with standard religion, and social encouragement are all reliable predictors of glossolalia (Kildahl 1972; Richardson 1973; Maloney and Lovekin 1985). In brief, *linked feelings of guilt, anxiety, and social alienation are often conspicuous factors in religious possession, conversion, and mystical experience*.

In discussions of the physiological mechanisms underlying religious conversion generally, Sargant (1957, 1969) proposes that stress disrupts existing patterns of thought and behavior, which become dysfunctional, as in prolonged bereavement. This creates the opportunity for new or suppressed patterns to assert themselves. At least in Britain and the United States, the majority of religious conversions appear to occur during adolescence (puberty to adulthood), when emotional turbulence and doubts about the self and the future are particularly acute (Brandon 1960). Persons joining religious sects in the United States are generally unmarried adolescents (Richardson 1995). In our society, adolescence is when individuals are most likely to question (Allport, Gillespie, and Young 1948; Ozorak 1989), change (Spilka, Hood, and Gorsuch 1985), confirm, or abandon religion (Sloane and Potvin 1986). Levels of stress hormones among adolescents are significantly elevated compared to those of the more "settled" adult population (Persinger 1987:37–38).

Converts to religious cults in Japan (A. Miller 1992) and to Evangelical sects in Central America (Roberts 1968) also tend to be younger and socially unattached or marginal (e.g., recent immigrants to cities). In Britain and the United States, the highest measures of religious commitment and the most radical forms of "traditional" religious affiliation (Pentacostal, Baptist, Jehovah's Witnesses, Seventh-Day Adventists, etc.) are registered among the most marginal or underprivileged social groups, especially minorities and persons at the bottom of the socioeconomic totem pole (i.e., lowest SES; Gerard 1985; A. Walker 1985; Kosmin and Lachman 1993; Iannaccone 1994). By contrast, stress and anxiety levels seem to be reduced in elderly populations, which are more prone to intensify their social and religious affiliations than other age groups (T. Johnson 1995; McFadden 1996). In general, then, *the intense pursuit of religious identity in large-scale industrial societies is often sought by adolescents and socially marginal individuals whose stress levels are high and whose levels of self-esteem are low or unstable*.

Converts to religious sects, such as Hare Krishna and the Moonies, report reduced anxiety and heightened self-esteem (Galanter et al. 1979; J. Frank and Frank 1991). Nevertheless, there appears to be no reliable improvement in mental health (Weiss and Mendoza 1990), except in reducing substance abuse (Galanter 1982; Volinn 1985). In our society at least, such religious cults generally suffer high rates of defection and attrition (Bird and Reimer 1982; Wright 1988), which implies a limited ability to provide the psychological stability that its adherents often seek. Like sudden converts, apostates tend to have more distant and stressful relations with parents and society at large (Hunsberger and Brown 1984). *Like demon exorcism and sudden conversion, intense religious experiences among socially and psychologically maladjusted individuals usually provides only little or limited long-term relief.*[13]

Long-term reduction of stress and anxiety may be more prevalent among highly committed "mainstream" religious believers. In a survey of over 1,600 Midwestern adults, Poloma and Pendleton (1991) found that subjects who reported a religious experience during prayer were more likely to consider themselves happy and to express a sense of well-being. L. Brown (1994) also found prayer to be a stress-reducing means to deal with the existential anxiety that accompanies uncontrollable events (diagnosis of cancer, death of a loved one, combat fears, etc.). Summarizing the literature on the psychotherapeutic effects of religious commitment and prayer, Worthington et al. (1996) note consistently reliable correlations between indices of hope and feelings of subjective well-being in religious subjects. Prayer appears to be a common coping method of addressing distress, regardless of level of religious commitment. Many Catholics go to confession to alleviate stress, reduce guilt, and relieve anxiety. Prayer may also help to alleviate everyday stress—a factor that may partially account for the finding that over 60 percent of Americans and 40 percent of British adults surveyed report praying daily (Poloma and Gallup 1991).

In line with this speculation, Spellman, Baskett, and Byrne (1971) also found that regular churchgoers tended (marginally) to have the lowest levels of anxiety. More clearly, R. Williams and Cole (1968) showed that highly committed "mainstream" religious subjects manifested less general anxiety than the least religious subjects (as measured by galvanic skin response and by frequency of extreme scores on the Minnesota Multiphasic Personality Inventory). Contrary to expectations that closeness to death might lead to increased anxiety in elderly populations, their stress and anxiety levels are actually lower than those of other age cohorts. Elderly populations, it appears, are more prone to intensify their social and religious affiliations than other age groups (T. Johnson 1995; McFadden 1996). A tentative conclusion is that *the more traditionally and continuously religious the person, the less likely to suffer depression and anxiety in the long run.*

6.7. Routine Ritual: Rehearsal with Only the Promise of Resolution

Most often, religious rituals involve repeated, generally voluntary, and usually reversible states of emotional communion in the context of formulaic social ceremonies. Here, supernatural agents, through their surrogates and instruments, manifest themselves in people's affections. The ceremonies reoccur not so that religion becomes a conditioned reflex (Persinger 1987) or is well remembered (Whitehouse 2000). They repetitively occur to make highly improbable, and therefore socially unmistakable, displays of mutual commitment. Within the congregation's coordinated bodily rhythms (chanting, swaying, tracking, etc.)—often in conjunction with primate displays of submission (bowing, kneeling, prostrating, etc.)—individuals show and feel that they identify themselves with, and give over part of their being to, the intensely felt existential yearnings of others. This demonstration, in turn, conveys the *intention* or *promise* of self-sacrifice by and toward others (charity, care, defense, support, etc.), without any particular person or specific situation necessarily in mind.

It makes little difference that most participants of a Latin Mass, an American Jewish service, an Indonesian Moslem pilgrimage, or a Zimbabwean Pentacostal revival hardly understand a word of Latin, Hebrew, Arabic, or what is spoken in tongues, or that the incense and bells of a Greek Orthodox or Hindu ceremony signal nothing in particular, or that a Sufi or Bantu dance has no specified point to make. Indeed, specific content, referents, and objectives would just preempt the promissory potential of affective coordination and the "understanding" of future cooperation.

In a general sense, ritual displays that aim to ensure reciprocation through the repetitive and rhythmic synchronization of affective body states pervade the animal kingdom, especially species of social vertebrates. According to Lorenz:

> In their original form, such intention movements are quite undoubtedly *inconsequential by-products* of the instinctive motor patterns as far as survival of the species is concerned. At most, they may serve some function in the sense of self-stimulation. But in a great many vertebrates these incompletely performed motor patterns . . . have acquired a new, extremely important function in that they have been converted into a "means of communication." This highly interesting phylogenetic process [evident, for example, with] chichilid fish, lizards, and birds, probably originated through the development in socially living species of an "understanding" of the intention movements of conspecifics. (1996:252)

Tinbergen (1951) has described these communicative forms of incompletely performed intention movements as "ritualized social releasers." Social releasers exhibit sense-evident properties, "either of shape, or colour, or special movements, or sound, or scents," which readily elicit a well-timed and well-oriented cooperative response in a conspecific: for mating, parenting, fighting, defense, food gathering, and the like. Courtship, for example, can include sounds (chirping of locusts and crickets, calls of frogs and toads, bird songs), scent (butterflies and moths, dogs and pigs), visual display (ceremonial flights, stickleback or peacock "fanning"), manner of movement (fiddler crabs, pigeons), tactile display ("purring," "quivering"), or various multisensory combinations of sign stimuli.

To serve as a social identification mechanism, the display of releasers must involve an unmistakable and highly improbable sequence of sign stimuli: "Such displacement reactions, originally serving as an outlet of a surplus of motor impulses, may, when secondarily acquiring survival value in social releasers, become ritualized, that is, adaptively refashioned according to the needs of a social releaser: simplicity, conspicuousness, specificity" (Tinbergen 1951:191–192). Although each of the elements may not be sufficiently improbable and specific to prevent mimicking or use by other species, their concatenation is usually unlikely enough to be inimitable. Thus, for the male stickleback, "a mating partner must be red and must perform a zigzag dance; it must also lead her to the nest, show her the nest entrance and deliver the very special tactile stimuli which the male delivers by 'quivering'" (124–125). True, even inanimate red mail vans may catch a stickleback's attention ("fooling" a male stickleback into responding to it as a potential rival), but the whole sequence and setting is sufficiently discriminating to prevent fertilization by the wrong individuals.

Humans, too, have instinctual motor patterns that function as social releasers, for example, bared teeth and swaying of clenched fists to communicate aggression, or hugging, rocking, and cooing to communicate affection (Darwin 1965[1872]). Even with these most instinctual human behaviors, cultural manipulation and elaboration infuse them with indefinitely many greater degrees of freedom and arbitrariness for indefinitely many varied purposes. Unlike the "automatic-rhythmic stimulus production" characteristic of the "innate releasing mechanisms" of other animals (Lorenz 1996; Tinbergen 1951), religious ritual is characterized by largely voluntary-rhythmic stimulus production. Humans, it appears, are the only animals that spontaneously engage in creative, rhythmic bodily coordination to enhance possibilities for cooperation (e.g., when hammering with a stranger, swaying in a crowd).

Moreover, incomplete intention movements in other animals lead to accumulation of response-specific arousal energy that is usually released only when the wanted object or response is obtained, as in orgasm. In religious ritual, emotional release (abreaction) usually occurs without a specific object or behavioral response being targeted or obtained. The bliss of a ritually induced "God high" may strike some as like orgasm, but nothing so concrete is emitted or acquired. Rather, what is achieved is an intensely felt "personal experience" of intimacy and fellowship, whose unimpeachable source (the self) and unquestionable ardor (emotional passion) guarantee the "truth" of whatever specific thought contents and behaviors are allied in the course of time (Turner 1969; Rappaport 1999).[14]

A key feature of the creativity of human worship is that all religions use music in social ritual. Even the Taliban, who prohibited nearly all public displays of sensory stimulation, promoted a cappella religious chants. In a survey of persons who reported a religious experience (Greeley 1975), music emerges as the single most important elicitor of the experience (49 percent of cases), followed by prayer (48 percent) and attending group services (41 percent). Reading the Bible (31 percent) and being alone in church (30 percent) trail significantly behind. Psychological studies indicate that listeners reliably associate basic or primary emotions to musical structures, such as happiness, sadness, fear, and anger (Wedin 1972; Cupchik, Rickert, and Mendelson 1982; Panksepp 1995). Even 3-year-olds consistently associate musical scores and emotions (Cunningham and Sterling 1988; Trainor and Trehub 1992). Recent electrocortical measures of frontal brain activity suggest that fear, joy, happiness, and sadness are associated with distinct frontal EEG signatures. People exhibit greater relative left frontal activity to joyful and happy music and greater relative right frontal activity to fearful and sad music, with activity greater for fearful than sad reactions and for joyful than happy reactions (Schmidt and Trainor 2001).

Music invites interpersonal relationships, creating emotional bonds between people, through the "attunement" of somatic states—much as the rocking and cooing behavior of mother and infant attunes the parental bond (Stern 1985). This is especially apparent in "call-response" format, as in Yoruba dances and Hebrew services. Attunement involves more than mere "entrainment" or "getting under one's skin." Entrainment is simply the causal uptake of sensory movements (as when flashing lights entrain an epileptic fit). Attunement is further mediated by interpretation, that is, cognitive representations (Guck 2002); for example, in somatic attunement of empathy (see section 4.8). Interpretation is not fixed, but is variable across persons in the audience (including performers). The messages conveyed are indeterminate, as are the perceived loci of music (in the world and in the body, Walton 1994). Even when attached to literal texts, and affixed to definite movements of affect (surging, fleeting, fading, etc.), music "speaks" to people personally. It evokes idiosyncratic memories, inferences, and beliefs that, if successful, go way beyond the thin layers of common textual meanings.

Music, which involves patterned modulation of people's sense of time, arouses and manipulates affective states and cognitive representations in ways inaccessible to consciousness. Moreover, especially in religious contexts, music is experienced as authorless, like the sacred texts that often accompany it (see section 4.4). The pre-tonal religious music of small-scale societies usually has its mythic beginnings in the origins of the world, which invites audiences to share in a sense of timeless intimacy. In one view advanced by the Catholic Church, Gregorian chants were taught to men by birds sent from heaven; and even Bach, Mozart, and Beethoven were but *vehicles* of The Divine.

Most often, religious music is set to words, as in much prayer. Music structures and word structures are both generative in that they allow indefinitely many combinations and variations with finite and few means. Words infuse music with a sense of meaning and purpose; music imbues words with emotional salience and sentiment. Together, music and words inspire personal conviction in social commitment.

In sum, religious rituals involve sequential, socially interactive movement and gesture (chant, dance, murmur, etc.) and formulaic utterances (liturgies, canonical texts, etc.) that synchronize affective states among group members in displays of cooperative commitment. Unlike, say, avian mating calls and flight formations, human music and body dance (which are omnipresent in worship) can be arbitrarily and creatively elicited, transferred, combined, or interpolated to fit many different purposes and contexts (e.g., from use of love songs in mating displays to use of mating displays in sales jingles).

6.8. Summary: Ritual and Revelation; Extraordinary Displays of Ordinary Means

Religion arises when (1) hard-to-fake emotions (2) ally with thought content whose truth implications are logically and factually impossible to evaluate (3) but that together convincingly evoke commitment to cultural mores. Religious beliefs and experiences cannot be consistently validated by social consensus either through deductive or inductive inference. Validation occurs only by satisfying the very emotions that motivate religious beliefs and experiences.

Intense religious episodes—severe initiations, sudden conversions, mystical revelations—combine aspects of personal memory for stressful events (e.g, an unforgettably traumatic, life-orienting occurrence) and socially widespread cognitive schema (scripted coactivation of publicly accessible categories and connecting pathways) to ensure life-long effect. The culturally manipulated, or God-given, sentiment of religious experience affectively stirs and assuages the same existential anxieties that incite religious belief in the first place. Even more frequent, less emotionally intense rituals—daily prayer, weekly services, yearly festivals—affectively manipulate and rhythmically coordinate actors' minds and bodies into convergent expressions of public sentiment: a sort of N-person courtship.

Humans, it appears, are the only animals that spontaneously engage in creative, rhythmic bodily coordination to enhance possibilities for cooperation (e.g., singing and swaying as they work together). Rituals intensify these natural movements to emotionally validate, and sanctify, any number of different cultural sets of moral sentiments. These religious sentiments feel right and good, and the religious quasi propositions that express them become truly held. No human society has long survived without such seemingly arbitrary but sanctified sentiments.

7 Waves of Passion

The Neuropsychology of Religion

As with emotionally drawn-out religious initiations, neurobiological studies of stress disorders indicate that subjects become intensely absorbed by sensory displays. Unlike chronic stress sufferers, however, participants in even the most emotionally aversive initiations end their ordeal through positive affirmations of social acceptance. Previous neurobiological studies of religion have focused on tracking participants' neurophysiological responses during episodes of religious experience and recording individual patterns of trance, vision, revelation, and the like. This has favored comparison of religious experience with temporal lobe brain wave patterns during epileptic seizures and acute schizophrenic episodes. Cognitive structures of the human mind/brain in general, and cognitions of agency in particular, are usually represented in these studies in simple-minded terms (e.g., binary oppositions, holistic vs. analytical tensions, hierarchical organization) that have little input from, or pertinence to, recent findings of cognitive and developmental psychology. Perhaps more telling is recent work on the role of the prefrontal cortices in processing concepts of agency and self and in cognitive mediation of relevant emotions originating in (what was once called) the limbic system. Still, for those religious believers who never have an emotionally intense encounter with the Divine—including the overwhelming majority of persons in our society—the neurophysiological bases of faith remain a complete mystery.

7.1. Neurobiological Evidence: The Amygdala and Stress Modulation

The neuroanatomical loci of memory processing include cortical regions (e.g., prefrontal, anterior cingulate) and subcortical structures (e.g., hippocampus, amygdala). Experiments by neurobiologists Antonio Damasio (1994) and Joseph LeDoux (1996) indicate that the neural system underlying emotional memory critically involves the amygdala—a core feature of what is often termed the limbic system (MacLean 1990)—and structures with which it is connected. In this chapter, I sketch out some of the neurobiological factors that researchers have implicated in studies of the sort of religious rituals and mystical experiences described in the previous chapter.[1]

The amygdala, which receives inputs from memory and sensory brain structures, is a small almond-like formation tucked under the temporal lobe, next to the hippocampus. When the amygdala is removed, monkeys attempt to eat unusual things, like excrement and stones, and try to mate with members of other species. Lesioned monkeys and rats lose fear of objects that they had previously been conditioned to fear by electric shock, and they also lose fear of things that frighten normal monkeys and rats. Nevertheless, animals with the amygdala removed are not generally amnesic: they remember where food and other objects are located as well as do nonlesioned animals (D. Schacter 1997:212–213; Aggleton and Passingham 1991).

The amygdala does not seem to contribute directly to the details or accuracy of memory but to level of emotional arousal and sensory vividness: "It might even be possible to explain amygdala contributions to cognition [including memory] . . . in terms of the loss of the affective qualities of cognition" (LeDoux 1993:69). Damasio's (1994) research suggests that people with amygdala damage cannot assess how important or unimportant a situation or decision may be. Although they are often able to cognitively represent and analyze the schematic or propositional structure of a situation, they have great difficulty coming to any decision about it or even understanding that some decision may be necessary in a given situation. They appear to master cognitive processes of representation but not the emotional and sensory indices required to cope with it.

When the amygdala detects an emotionally arousing situation it triggers the autonomic nervous system. The autonomic nervous system, in turn, activates the adrenal gland, which releases adrenaline into the bloodstream. Adrenaline then appears to influence the ability to form an explicit memory of the situation (perhaps through the hippocampal system; LeDoux 1996:207).[2]

Results in experimental psychology support the presence of such an emotional system. Christianson and colleagues (1991) found that subjects presented with emotionally aversive scenes (of victims of traffic accidents, war, famine, etc.) for very short durations (50 ms) recognized those scenes better than neutral scenes from everyday life or emotionally positive scenes (nudes in a summer scene). Similarly, memories for emotional stimuli, like blood or an eye injury, were much the same at short exposures (180 ms) as at longer exposures. The evolutionary implication seems to be that it's crucial to survival to rapidly remember unpleasant emotional events as threats requiring fast, effective responses (fight, freeze, or flee). Severe initiations and other extreme religious rituals ride piggyback on this evolutionary disposition.

Perhaps the closest analogous case in the neuropsychological literature to what follows from once-in-a lifetime religious events is posttraumatic stress disorder (PTSD). Research into PTSD began with an almost exclusive focus on combat veterans but has come to include other sorts of trauma, such as rape, child abuse, natural disasters, and terrorism. The research now extends also to laboratory studies of animals and the development of more generalized animal models of traumatic stress (for a review, see Newport and Nemeroff 2000). The third edition of the *Diagnostic and Statistical Manual of Mental Disorders* (American Psychiatric Association 1980) describes PTSD in terms of three sets of readily apparent symptoms: reexperiencing the trauma (nightmares, intrusive memories, flashbacks), avoidance (amnesia of the event, refusal to talk or think about it), and hyperarousal (startle response, fitful sleep, poor concentration) (for an update see American Psychiatric Association 1994:424–429). Ethnographic descriptions of terrifying and prolonged initiation rites appear to resemble PTSD on a variety of these phenomenological criteria; however, there has been no comparable neurobiological study of religious and tribal initiations so that any comparison with PTSD can only be speculative and suggestive.

Perhaps most relevant for the present discussion is PTSD's effects on memory processing. PTSD sufferers often "relive" their traumatic experiences through flashbacks caused by sounds or sights that bear some (often remote) resemblance to aspects of the original event; for example, just about any loud sound or flying object may cause a PTSD combat veteran or war refugee to reexperience the original panic. These symptoms appear to be associated with alterations in levels of two catecholamines, dopamine and norepinephrine, which chemically mediate transmission of sympathetic nerve impulses. Stress-related hormones, such as adrenaline, stimulate release of these chemical messengers in reaction to emotional arousal.

In PET and other studies comparing Vietnam combat veterans with PTSD to combat veterans without PTSD and to noncombat controls, only the PTSD group showed heightened left amygdala activation in response to combat sounds (Liberzon et al. 1999). Vietnam veterans with PTSD who were exposed to combat sounds and pictures showed decreased medial prefrontal blood flow and alterations in anterior cingulate functioning when compared to combat veterans without PTSD (Bremner, Staib, et al. 1999). This suggests that subcortical connections between the amygdala and relevant areas of the prefrontal cortex may be disturbed. PET scans of PTSD subjects who are remembering personal traumas show exaggerated activity in the right amygdala as well as the visual cortex but decreased activity in Broca's region (a key cortical area for language production). Functional MRI studies of PTSD subjects also indicate heightened amygdala response to masked facial stimulation. These results and other neurobiological data suggest that traumatic recollections are accompanied by intense emotion and sensory display.

Medical studies intimate that *chronic, long-term stress suppresses immune function* and sustained ability to cope with injury, infection, and stressful situations (Khansari et al. 1990; Glaser et al. 1994). It appears, however, that *acute, short-term stress enhances immune response* directed toward injury or infirmity. Plausibly, this immune response to acute stress evolved to serve a protective role against stress-inducing agents (parasites, aggressors, etc.):

> Stress hormones may direct the body's "soldiers" (leukocytes), to exit their "barracks" (spleen and bone marrow), travel the "boulevards" (blood vessels), and take position at potential "battle stations" (skin, lining of gastrointestinal and urinary-genital tracts, and draining lymph nodes). . . .

> Thus, a hormonal alarm signal released by the brain on detecting a stressor may prepare the immune system for potential challenges (wounding or infection) that may arise from the actions of stress-inducing agents (e.g., a predator or attacker). In contrast, it is likely that chronic stress suppresses immune function by decreasing leukocyte redistribution. (Dhabhar and McEwen 1999:1059)

PTSD studies are pertinent to our understanding of the evolutionary dimensions of stressful religious initiations. Like participants in emotionally drawn-out religious initiations, PTSD subjects are intensely absorbed by sensory displays (visual, auditory, olfactory, gustatory, kinesthetic) associated with stressful events. Their recollections tend to be vivid and enduring but telescoped on central, autobiographically relevant details of the event structure: who (agents) did or practiced what (instruments and actions) on whom (patients). As with severe religious or secular initiations, persons suffering abuse are often threatened or cajoled into not talking about their experiences and may become incapable of rendering an explicit and thorough verbal account of what happened when.

Still, there are also important differences between PTSD and stressful initiations. PTSD subjects who permanently lose memory and undergo reduced immune response often suffer from chronic stress and lack of effective social support. By contrast, even the most severe and emotionally aversive religious initiations end in positive exhibitions of social acceptance. Arguably, such exhibitions are meant to assuage acute stress (as Freud might say) by channeling it into cultural accomplishment.[3]

7.2. Adrenaline-Activating Death Scenes Heighten Religiosity: An Experiment

Throughout I have claimed that emotionally eruptive existential anxieties motivate religious beliefs, and that this motivation has been sorely lacking in cognitive theories of religion. This section summarizes a recent experiment by Ara Norenzayan, Ian Hansen, and myself that links adrenaline-activating death scenes to increased belief in God's existence and the efficacy of supernatural intervention in human affairs. Results show that people cognitively commit themselves more to the supernatural under stressful interpretations of events involving other people than they do when events are emotionally uneventful. This is so even when those uneventful events specifically involve a religious component. Commitment theories of religion neglect special attention to the supernatural.

Our experiment builds on a study by Larry Cahill and colleagues (1994) in the laboratory of James McGaugh, entitled "Beta-Adrenergic Activation and Memory for Emotional Events." They showed college students a series of slides and a storyline about a boy riding a bike. Some subjects were exposed to an uneventful story: the boy rides his bike home, and he and his mother drive to the hospital to pick up his father (who is a doctor). For the other participants, the story begins and ends in much the same way, but the middle is very different: the boy is hit by a car and rushed to the hospital's emergency room, where a brain scan shows severe bleeding from the boy's brain and specialized surgeons struggle to reattach the boy's severed feet. After exposure to the stories, and before being tested for recall, half the subjects were given either a placebo pill or a drug (propranolol) that blocks the effects of adrenaline. The placebo and drug groups recalled the uneventful story equally well. Only the placebo group, however, remembered the emotional story more accurately than the uneventful one. (Similar effects are reported with patients suffering from amygdala damage, McGaugh et al. 1995.)

Our hypothesis was that stressful events associated with existential anxieties (e.g., death) not only deeply affect how people remember events but also their religious coloring of those events. We first controlled for religious background and measured for religious identification. Then we primed each of three groups of college students with a different story (see table 7.1): Cahill et al.'s uneventful story (neutral prime), Cahill et al.'s stressful story (death prime), and another uneventful story whose event-structure matched the other two stories but which included a prayer scene (religious prime). Afterward, each group of subjects read a reprint from a *New York Times* article (2 Oct. 2001) whose lead ran: "Researchers at

Table 7.1. Three stories with matching events used to prime feelings of religiosity: Neutral (uneventful), Death (stressful), Religious (prayer scene)

	Neutral	Death	Religious
1	A mother and her son are leaving home in the morning.	A mother and her son are leaving home in the morning.	A mother and her son are leaving home in the morning.
2	She is taking him to visit his father's workplace.	She is taking him to visit his father's workplace.	She is taking him to visit his father's workplace.
3	The father is a laboratory technician at Victory Memorial Hospital.	The father is a laboratory technician at Victory Memorial Hospital.	The father is a laboratory technician at Victory Memorial Hospital.
4	They check before crossing a busy road.	They check before crossing a busy road.	They check before crossing a busy road.
5	While walking along, the boy sees some wrecked cars in a junk yard, which he finds interesting.	While crossing the road, the boy is caught in a terrible accident, which critically injures him.	While walking along, the boy sees a well-dressed man stop by a homeless woman, falling on his knees before her, weeping.
6	At the hospital, the staff are preparing for a practice disaster drill, which the boy will watch.	At the hospital, the staff prepares the emergency room, to which the boy is rushed.	At the hospital, the boy's father shows him around his lab. The boy listens politely, but his thoughts are elsewhere.
7	An image from a brain scan machine used in the drill attracts the boy's interest.	An image from a brain scan machine used in a trauma situation shows severe bleeding in the boy's brain.	An image from a brain scan that he sees reminds him of something in the homeless woman's face.

Table 7.1. *(Continued)*

	Neutral	Death	Religious
8	All morning long, a surgical team practices the disaster drill procedures.	All morning long, a surgical team struggles to save the boy's life.	On his way around the hospital, the boy glances into the hospital's chapel, where he sees the well-dressed man sitting alone.
9	Make-up artists are able to create realistic-looking injuries on actors for the drill.	Specialized surgeons are able to re-attach the boy's severed feet, but can not stop his internal hemorrhaging.	With elbows on his knees, and his head in his hands, the man moves his lips silently. The boy wants to sit beside him, but his father leads him away.
10	After the drill, while the father watches the boy, the mother leaves to phone her other child's pre-school.	After the surgery, while the father stays by the dead boy, the mother leaves to phone her other child's pre-school.	After a brief tour of the hospital, while the father watches the boy, the mother leaves to phone her other child's pre-school.
11	Running a little late, she phones the pre-school to tell them she will soon pick up her child.	Barely able to talk, she phones the pre-school to tell them she will soon pick up her child.	Running a little late, she phones the pre-school to tell them she will soon pick up her child.
12	Heading to pick up her child, she hails a taxi at the number nine bus stop.	Heading to pick up her child, she hails a taxi at the number nine bus stop.	Heading to pick up her child, she hails a taxi at the number nine bus stop.

Columbia University, expressing surprise at their own findings, are reporting that women at an in vitro fertilization clinic in Korea had a higher pregnancy rate when, unknown to the patients, total strangers were asked to pray for their success." The article was given to students under the guise of a different story about "media portrayals of scientific studies." Finally, the students rated the strength of their belief in God and the power of supernatural intervention on a nine-point scale.

Results show that strength of belief in God's existence (fig. 7.1) *and in the efficacy of supernatural intervention* (fig. 7.2) *are reliably stronger after exposure to the death prime than either to the neutral or religious prime* (there were no significant differences between either uneventful story). This was the case regardless of students' religious background or prior degree of religious identification. In sum, *emotional stress associated with death-related scenes seems a stronger natural motivator for religiosity than mere exposure to emotionally unstressful religious scenes, such as praying.*

This provides some confirmation of the claim that emotionally eruptive existential anxieties motivate belief in the supernatural. We also plan to test the further claim that invocation of the supernatural not only cognitively validates these eruptive emotions, but is affectively validated by assuaging the very emotions that motivate belief in the supernatural (see chapter 6). With this in mind, it is worth noting that uncontrollable arousal mediated by adrenergic activation (as for sub-

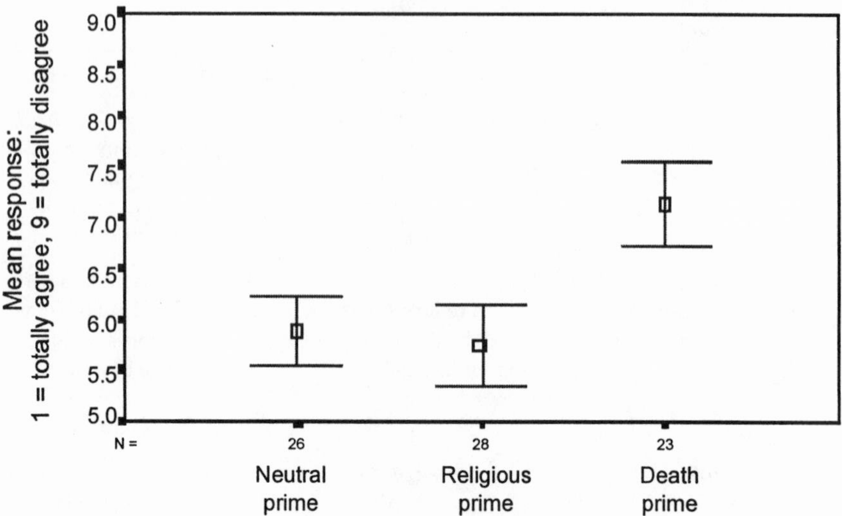

Figure 7.1. Strength of belief in God's existence after priming (neutral, religious or death) and then reading a newspaper article about effects of prayer on pregnancy (vertical bars represent margin of error at $p = .05$)

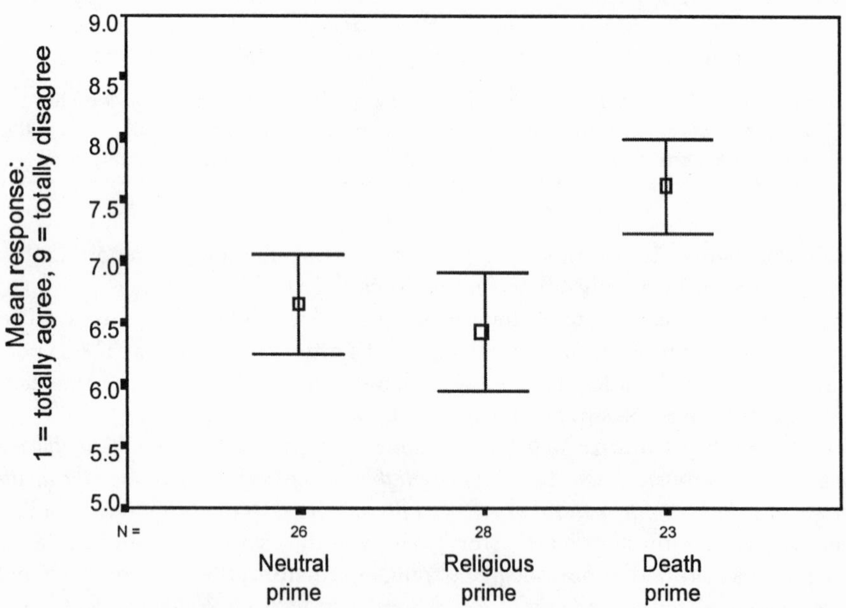

Figure 7.2. Strength of belief in supernatural power after priming (neutral, religious or death) and then reading a newspaper article about effects of prayer on pregnancy (vertical bars represent margin of error at $p = .05$)

jects exposed to death scenes) may lead to PTSD if there is no lessening of terror and arousal within hours; however, adrenergic blockers (propranolol, clondine, guanfacine, and possibly antidepressants) can "interrupt the neuronal imprinting that leads to long-term symptoms" (McReady 2002:9). A possibility arises, then, that heightened expressions of religiosity following exposure to death scenes that provoke existential anxieties could also serve this blocking function.

7.3. Neurotheology: Science and Moonshine

In their most intense manifestations, ritual ceremonies and liturgy rivet attention on specific and conspicuous sources of sensory stimulation, including stimulation emanating from one's own body: drums or clapping hands, dancing or nodding, incense or sweat secretion, incantation or deep breathing, the light through stained-glass scenes, or the making of signs and designs. Often, these actions and the associated stimuli induce altered states of consciousness, for example, through hyperventilation in whirling dance, deep-breathing meditation, or "going up to the mountain" (where the rarefied air leads to the effect). This focused sensory stimulation, in turn, undoubtedly arouses powerful emotional responses in the limbic system (hippocampus, amygdala, hypothalamus) much as naturally provoked surprise, fear, anger, and joy do (but in more controlled and sustained doses).

A possible scenario is that the overly stimulated amygdala goes into undirected hyperactivity. It is unable to process the emotional significance of individual stimuli, though perhaps producing a general sense of foreboding. Consistent with this scenario (but by no means proving it), EEG patterns of electrical activation during "mystical experiences" bear striking similarities to those recorded during bouts of temporal lobe epilepsy (Persinger 1983; Gloor et al. 1982; Geschwind 1983). The hypothalamus receives this confounding flood of information, relaying it to the autonomic nervous system. This provokes increased discharges in both the sympathetic (or egotropic) and parasympathetic (or trophotropic) branches of the autonomic nervous system.

The sympathetic branch is reponsible for priming the body for action, such as fight or flight. The parasympathetic branch carries signals that relax or quiet the body, such as for rest and sleep. Augmented sympathetic discharges increase: heart rate, blood pressure, sweat secretion, pupillary dilation, skeletal muscle tone, level of stress hormones (e.g., adrenaline), and cortical excitation. Augmented parasympathetic discharges lead to corresponding decreases in visceral and skeletal reactions. In normal states, increased activation in the activity of one branch usually leads to decreased activity in the other. In mystical states, both branches appear to be activated simultaneously, although one or the other is usually dominant.

In meditative states, such as Zen Buddhist or Hindu yoga, EEG patterns indicate a "trophotropic syndrome." Here, parasympathetic activity dominates, although continued sympathetic activity "seems in some way to be a correlate of the heightened perceptual sensitivity reported by such subjects" (Gellhorn and Kiely 1972:399). According to Gellhorn and Kiely, "The principal psychological distinction from the normal would appear to be the suspension of autonomous will or intentionality" (402). More frenzied mystical states, such as viscerally charged (rather than meditative) trance possession and Sufi whirling, may be characterized by an "ergotropic syndrome." Sympathetic activity dominates but continued parasympathetic activity may be associated with a concurrent sense of catharsis that is often compared to the aftereffects of sexual orgasm.[4]

The hippocampus, which modulates the expression of emotions elicited by hypothalamic stimulation and provides conceptual significance to the emotions through projections to the amygdala (LeDoux 1993), may also go into overdrive during rhythmically induced mystical experiences. As a result, the regular channels of neural transmission are thrown out of balance. Evidence from SPECT (single photon emission computed tomography) brain imaging is consistent with this possibility. Blood flow, and therefore traffic flow of signals between neurons, increases to the frontal lobes but decreases to the posterior superior parietal lobe (Newberg et al. 2001). PET imaging indicates that the frontal lobes, particularly the prefrontal cortices, are associated with the executive conceptual functions of will and self-control, as well as the self's temporal orientation (Wheeler, Stuss, and Tulving 1997). The top back portion of the parietal cortex, especially the left side, is associated with three-dimensional body imaging and spatial orientation (J. Lynch 1980). Possibly, the asymmetric flow of information toward the lower front of the brain and away from the upper back of the brain may have something to do with the most outstanding aspect of reported mystical experiences, namely, a vivid but diffusely conceived awareness of a boundless universe, centered on (joined to, merged with) a self that has no physical markers or constraints.

Of course, this is all rank speculation. At present, the only thing known is that some types of mystical states roughly tend to exhibit certain gross patterns of brain activation. But even this conclusion must be hedged because there are usually too few subjects and repeated trials in clinical and laboratory studies to guarantee statistical reliability. Moreover, "much the same probably holds for people (who have ecstatic experiences) at rock concerts" (D. Medin, personal communication, 2001). Still, scientists in the emerging field of neurotheology do not shy from even more sweeping claims about the neuropsychological bases and particularities of religion.[5]

The most completely developed neurotheological theory of brain and religion stems from the work of two colleagues at the University of Pennsylvania School of Medicine, Eugene d'Aquili and Andrew Newberg. The authors use their own brain-imaging (SPECT) studies of meditating Buddhists and Franciscan nuns at prayer to demonstrate that the experience of God, or "Absolute Unitary Being" (AUB), is hardwired into the human brain (d'Aquili and Newberg 1998, 1999; Newberg, d'Aquili, and Rause 2001). For example, in subjects who reported a feeling of boundless perspective and self-transcendence during meditation, the researchers found decreased blood flow in the brain's "object association areas," where perceptions between boundary and self are normally processed. They speculate that the ultimate mystical state of "hyperlucid unitary consciousness often experienced as God" (Nirvana, *unio mystica*, etc.) occurs when the sympathetic and parasympathetic systems are both discharging at maximal levels, with neither predominating (d'Aquili and Newberg 1998:200, 1999:26). They provide no empirical evidence whatever for this latter speculation.

The authors see religious experiences as the result of normal, healthy physiology, and not pathological or random events. With this I agree. They conclude that the experience of God, which is potentially within us all, is as "real" as the experience of ordinary objects and events (Newberg, d'Aquili, and Rause 2001). With this I have problems.

D'Aquili and Newberg (1998, 1999) leave open the issue of whether God is also a being that exists outside of our brain and body. They affirm that science cannot decide whether ordinary, baseline perception and conception or the mystical perception and conception of God is "more real." Just as quantum physics intimates that we may never know the ultimate reality of matter, so we may never know the ultimate reality of God. This is a specious argument. What evolutionary science *can* tell us is that without our ordinary, baseline reality our species would have had no natural means of emerging from the evolutionary process. If our ordinary perceptions and inferences were not at least approximately veridical with respect to everyday objects and events, then how—without constant divine intervention—could our ancestors have possibly avoided falling off cliffs or being eaten by wild animals at every turn?

Moreover, the natural and cognitive sciences get better and better at extending and dissecting our commonsense world. Ever more accurately and completely, they describe and predict many of its objects and relations. By contrast, science *can't* tell us whether or not God has an external existence because notions of God have no fixed logical or referential properties to even begin the processing of external identification, verification, or falsification. As far as science is concerned, "reason suggesteth nothing" about God but a heck of a lot about matter and mind.

D'Aquili and Newberg postulate exactly seven functionally localized "cognitive operators" that are "likely to be preprogammed into the brain." These operators "represent the way the mind functions on all input into the brain . . . sensory input, thoughts and emotions" (1999:51–57, 164–176):

1. The Holistic Operator (right parietal lobe) allows us to conceive the world as a whole and "to apprehend the unity of God and the oneness of the universe."
2. The Reductionist Operator (left parietal lobe) gives us our "scientific, logical, and mathematical approach . . . to the universe" but is also critical to understanding the totality of God and the universe in each of the parts.
3. The Causal Operator (left frontal lobe and left posterior superior parietal lobe) "permits reality to be viewed in terms of causal sequences."
4. The Abstractive Operator (inferior portion of the parietal lobe in the left hemisphere) forms general concepts from individual facts, including the concepts of "mathematics, government, justice, culture, and family."
5. The Binary Operator (inferior parietal lobe) permits us to extract meaning from the world "by ordering its abstract elements into dyads . . . (e.g., good versus evil)." It is crucial to "mythic structure": "Myths . . . develop the notion that the opposites we see are actually illusory, a notion that comprises part of the ideologies of Buddhism and Hinduism."

6. The Quantitative Operator (inferior parietal lobe close to areas underlying the Binary and Abstractive Operators) abstracts quantity from the perception of various elments.
7. The Emotional Value Operator (limbic system) assigns affective values to percepts and concepts.

These are much the same operators that d'Aquili (1978) proffered two decades before. They are allegedly responsible for religious experience.

Operators 1 and 2 are relics of Gestalt psychology and are so vague and general as to apply to virtually anything and everything. Consequently, they apply to nothing in any scientifically significant or surprising way. No set of empirical tests or experiments could confirm or disconfirm their operation. As the Maharishi Mahesh Yogi intoned: "The atom and the solar system, the macrocosm and the microcosm, the self and the universe, are all one and the same." Talk of preprogrammed operators in such cases is vacuous.

Operator 3 is a bit more specific and more plainly wrong. For the past couple of decades, researchers in developmental and cognitive psychology have begun describing functionally quite different causal mechanisms, including various types of mechanical and teleological causes (Sperber et al. 1995). For example, the type of mechanical causality (kinetics) employed by human neonates to interpret the movements of inanimate substances entails physical contact between causally related objects and spatiotemporal contiguity along any causal path. By contrast, the type of teleological causality (agency) that children apply to the interpretation of the causal interactions between animate objects, especially humans, assumes no physical contact between interacting objects or spatiotemporal contiguity. Agentive causality is more closely associated with the prefrontal cortices. Moreover, these different types of causality have distinct maturation schedules in the brain.

Operator 4 is a relic of behaviorist psychology. "Abstraction" per se logically implies an infinite regress and so is unrealizable in real time. First, to learn that something is an instantiation of a fact (e.g., this is a cat) requires that one has *already* generalized or "abstracted" across instances (i.e., one has to know what makes this a cat and not a chicken or a telephone). If twentieth-century philosophy of science has accomplished anything, it has at least employed like reasoning to abandon the once common idea that there are "observational facts" or "pretheoretical facts" (Nagel 1961).

Second, we know from experiments in cognitive and developmental psychology and anthropology that people do not first learn only specific facts before they abstract general ones (Rosch et al. 1976; Atran et al. 1997). For example, people first come to understand that something is *simultaneously* an *animal* of a certain *generic kind* (e.g., a cat); only later do they come to categorize it as also being a more specific (e.g., tabby) or general (e.g., mammal) sort of animal. The learning sequence may be very different for other domains. Thus, people everywhere are more prone to initially individuate persons than to individuate animals or plants or rocks. This makes good evolutionary sense. It usually matters whether your conflict or liaison is with this Jones or that Smith, but not which bear can eat you or which apple you can eat. It makes little evolutionary sense to have a domain-general operation of abstraction or generalization.

Concerning Operator 5, d'Aquili and Newberg reason that "lesions in the inferior parietal lobe . . . prevent patients from being able to name the opposite of any word prescribed to them. This area is thus the seat of . . . the binary operator" (1999:55). Cutting the neural pathways in the area that facilitate antonymy no more proves this area to be the "seat" of antonymy than cutting off air traffic over the mid Atlantic proves the mid Atlantic to be the seat of the air industry. In any event, antonymy is only one kind of binary contrast (e.g. "cat" isn't an antonym of "dog," "mouse," or "kitten" but can be opposed to them).

Operator 5 is derived from anthropologist Claude Lévi-Strauss's structural analysis of myths (Lévi-Strauss 1963a; cf. d'Aquili 1986). Lévi-Strauss's gift resides in an idiosyncratically marvelous ability to reveal startling, multidimensional contrasts in ethnographic details and to create from them a symphony-like exposition of autochthonous ideas and themes. Like poetry, his work is inimitable.[6] As with the notion of similarity, however, "binary opposition" is meaningless without some prior dimension in mind along which to array "opposites." Otherwise, anyone can oppose anything to everything else in infinitely many ways. Even along a single dimension (e.g., high versus low), without prior imposition of a structural grid, there remain indefinitely many possible binary oppositions (e.g., low-medium-high vs. low-medium-low, or medium-medium-high, or high-low-high). One could as readily posit a Tripartite Operator (high–in between–low, the Holy Trinity, Brahma-Vishnu-Shiva, the Sacred Triangle, etc.), which would be just as meaningless.

Operator 6 supposedly accounts for quantification. Recent work by Harvard psychologists Marc Hauser, Susan Carey, and Elizabeth Spelke with monkeys, apes, and children suggests that even the simplest quantitative operation involves at least two different brain mechanisms: one for simple counting (1, 2, 3, 4, many) and one for relative proportion (the interval from 1 to 3 is the same as from 2 to 4). There may be other components (Hauser 2000b). For example, Chomsky (1988) suggests that the notion of discrete infinity attaching to number is a by-product of the language faculty.

Quantity is not extracted from the perception of elements but is imposed by placing them in one-to-one correspondence with an abstract cardinal set (class of similar classes), such that the last correspondence counted is the number assigned (7 windows and 7 flocks of birds are both just 7). There is much anecdotal evidence in anthropology, and a recent unpublished study in psychology, indicating that some nonliterate peoples can't determine cardinality (past four) because they simply haven't had the cultural need to put the various components of quantification together. (Needless to say, all such societies have religion.) Apparently, such people perceive a difference between, say, 24 and 32 claps but not between 22, 23, 24, 25, or 26 claps (Susan Carey, personal communication 2000). Similarly, the application of number to space (extension), which characterizes Western science (rulers, coordinates, etc.), was until recently alien to the rest of the world (and to the world's religions). There is no evidence that these cultural breakthroughs involved rewiring of the inferior parietal lobe or that even the simpler components of number reside there.

Operator 7 is merely a catch-all for "affect." Cognitive theories of emotion, such as appraisal theory (Leventhal and Scherer 1987; Ellsworth 1991), suggest that the value structure of emotions is organized very differently from the relations among emotions in the limbic system. In an aversive situation, for example, anger and sadness may have nearly matching cognitive value structures (anger involves the perception of a responsible external agent, sadness doesn't), as may fear and hope (which differ only on valence; Keltner, Ellsworth, and Edwards 1993). Nevertheless, anger has more physiological and "limbic" manifestations in common with fear than anger has with sadness or fear has with hope.

In brief, apart from overgeneralizations based on poor and fragmentary empirical evidence, and confounding casuistry with scientific modesty, there is more serious trouble. Neurotheology takes almost no account of progress in cognitive and developmental psychology and cognitive anthropology over the past quarter century or so. In fact, if claims about cognitive operators were true, most recent advances in cognitive science would be moonshine.

7.4. A "God Module" in the Temporal Lobe? Not Likely

> The Shaman lives a life apart, practises or pretends to practise various austerities, wears mysterious and symbolical garments, and performs noisy incantations in which a sacred drum or an enchanted rattle takes a leading part. On occasion he should be able to foam at the mouth and go into a trance or fit, during which his soul is supposed to quit his body and wander away into space. By some these seizures have been ascribed to epilepsy.
>
> —W. Crooke, *The Native Races of Northern India* (1907)

In *The Neuropsychological Bases of God Beliefs*, Michael Persinger argues: "God experiences and religious rituals are evolutionary consequences of neural organization" (1987:137). The neural substrate of religious experience is available to everyone. Most people activate it some of the time, but some people do so relatively infrequently (many scientists) and others abuse it (religious fanatics). These are claims that can be shared with the neurotheologists. But Persinger considers these evolutionary consequences to be more accidents than adaptations. At this level of generality, I have no objections. The detail of Persinger's thesis is another matter.

More specifically, Persinger holds that "the God experience is an artifact of transient changes in the temporal lobe, and religious principles are maintained by the classic principles of conditioning" (1987:137). Using routine EEG measures, Persinger (1984) tracked a Transcendental Meditation teacher for 10 seconds during a peak experience and a member of a Pentacostal sect who experienced protracted intermittent episodes of glossolalia (speaking in tongues). Neither subject had any psychiatric history. EEG patterns exhibited transient, focal, epileptic-like charges in the temporal lobe. But even if *all* religious experiences involved characteristic electrical perturbations of the temporal lobe (and there is scant evidence for any such claim), without the frontal lobes, there would be no awareness of self or agency, much less a supernatural agency such as God (Passingham 1993; Damasio 1994; Corcoran, Mercer, and Frith 1995; Baron-Cohen 1995; Wheeler, Stuss, and Tulving 1997).

Like Freud and the attachment theorists, Persinger sees the adult's readiness to believe in God as a psychological compulsion to recover the lost parental security of childhood. This innate drive is conceptually generalized to God by stimulus-response conditioning through reward and punishment. Learning to generalize to God need involve little more than simple word association: "In this way, the properties of objects [e.g., parents] are transferred to words [e.g., 'God']": "The parents no longer have the properties of omnipotence and omnipresence. Through experience, the adult has learned that parents are discrete and mortal beings with limited space and little time. The childhood expectations have been generalized to God" (1987:66). Details of the God concept are determined by a person's culturally conditioned experiences. Thus, "Matrilineal societies . . . have female gods. In patrilineal societies, where the male line is most important, the god is portrayed with clear masculine features" (67). These and similar claims that religious beliefs are forged through conditioning and association are either vague or false.

Findings reported earlier suggest that preschoolers can represent different types of nonhuman agents and that these agents do not merely simulate what people are supposed to believe about persons (J. Barrett et al. 2001; Knight et al. 2001; see section 3.7). Interestingly, only God's relationship to truth and falsity is fixed early on in a way that does not change with development. The child, in fact, learns at least some specific aspects of the God concept *before* learning the proper scope and limits of a mother or parent concept. The God concept is neither generalized from the parent concept nor particularly associated with it by words or other means.

Although it is vaguely true that the deities of different societies take on culturally specific aspects of those societies (Durkheim 1995[1912]), there is often no simple mapping or straightforward projection of social structures onto God features. For example, the matrilineal Nair (Warrior Caste) of Kerala in south India have the same pantheon of 330 male and female deities as do patrilineal Hindus. Off the Arabian Sea's Kerala coast, the matrilineal Lakshadsweep Islanders have no God but Allah and worship Mohammed as His Prophet, just as the patrilineal Arabs do.

Some of the syncretic Moslem and Christian societies of Asia and Africa have high-ranking women deities and even important animal and plant deities. A recurrent myth in male-dominated patrilineal societies of Africa, such as the Gola of Liberia (d'Azevedo 1973), is that female deities originate what men desire to control (Horton 1963:94–95). For the patrilineal Tsembaga of New Guinea, the most important single spirit is Smoke Woman (Kun Kaze Ambra), who "acts as an intermediary between the living and all other categories of spirits." She is clearly a female deity in that "Smoke Woman might, out of jealousy, do mischief to any woman with whom a [male] novice of hers consorts" (Rappaport 1979:102–104).

Finally, how could one possibly learn by word association or conditioned generalization from Mom's or Dad's behavior that, perhaps, "God appealed to Johnny to like himself" is a perfectly fine God thought, but that "God appeared to Johnny to like himself" isn't? Mom or Dad can be vain, but God supposedly can't be (at least in our society). For that matter, how could one possibly learn the difference between "appear" and "appeal" as applying to God—or anything else—by conditioned association unless one already knew a lot about God (or, by infinite regress, whatever else "appear" and "appeal" are supposed to apply to)?

In fact, generalization from a few fragmentary examples to an indefinitely extended set of complexly related cases by conditioned association is *logically impossible*. This is simply because there are infinitely many ways to go at each step of the generalization regardless of how many "correct" inferences are rewarded and how many "incorrect" inferences are punished (Hume 1955[1758]; N. Goodman 1965; Chomsky 1971). This is true even for rats (Garcia, Ervin, and Koelling 1966). For example, if a rat gets sick a full day after eating something, how can the rat figure out by "context-dependent learning," "stimulus generalization," or "contiguity" (Persinger 1987:63–67) that it was the food that made it sick and not the innumerably many other things that came before getting sick (or even before eating the food)? Unless the rat already had a built-in preparedness for associating food to illness, it would soon be dead (Seligman 1971). This is not to say that acquiring a socially appropriate notion of God requires a "God module" in the brain. It implies only that whatever conceptual structures distinguish thoughts about God from thoughts about other things (including Mom and Dad) have to be available in the mind beforehand, for example, that God can't be vain or, more generally and universally, that gods are supernatural but that parents aren't.

7.5. Religion and Psychopathology: Epilepsy, Schizophrenia, Autism

In every society, the auditory and visual hallucinations that our medical establishment associates with certain forms of temporal lobe epilepsy and schizophrenia often take on a religious color. They become the "voices" and "visions" of personal revelation for the subjects themselves and, depending on the society, they may become the charge of local religion as well. In some societies, epileptics may be preferentially chosen as shamans (Crooke 1907:259–260; Eliade 1964) and persons prone to schizophrenia may find themselves better suited for a more cloistered religious life (Kelley 1958).

One prominent neurobiological focus of these extreme religious experiences—as well as nonpathological experiences involving glossolalia, trance, and meditative ecstatic visions—is the amygdala-hippocampus complex (Slater and Beard 1963; Dewhurst and Beard 1970; Bear 1979; Gloor et al. 1982; Geschwind 1983; Persinger 1984). Accounts of visual and auditory hallucinations among some of history's leading religious converts and mystics intimate possible temporal lobe epilepsy. A particularly controversial case concerns the dramatic conversion of the Apostle Paul. Paul was a vicious persecutor of Christians. One day, he collapsed on the road to Damascus and suddenly experienced auditory and visual hallucinations. As a result, he converted to Christianity and became perhaps the single most important figure in fostering its spread beyond a few marginal Jewish communities of the Roman Empire. Psychologist William James (1902) surmises that Paul's newfound voice of conscience may have been "a physiological nerve storm or discharging lesion like that of epilepsy," although lack of of evidence for subsequent mental deterioration argues against temporal lobe epilepsy (Woods 1913). Another famous case concerns a sixteenth-century saint, Theresa of Avila. She experienced vivid visions, intense headaches, and fainting spells, followed by "such peace, calm, and good fruits in the soul, and . . . a perception of the greatness of God" (St. Theresa 1930 [1577]:171). Biographers suggest that she may well have experienced epileptic seizures (Sackville-West 1943), similar perhaps to the fits suffered by the great nineteenth-century Russian writer and religious mystic, Fyodor Dostoevsky.

The absence of details precludes an accurate diagnosis in such cases. Yet, there is little doubt that extreme and even pathological religious experiences have been interpreted through the ages as unequivocal signs of divine enlightenment or possession in different times and places. In contemporary Europe and North America, however, such manifestations more often lead to confinement in a mental asylum (except in the movies). In studies of schizophrenia-like psychoses of epilepsy in British hospitals, A. W. Beard and colleagues found that 38 percent of patients had hallucinations and mystical delusions, although fewer than 9 percent had religious convictions prior to the onset of symptoms (Beard 1963; Slater and Beard 1963). Typical reports of religious experiences among temporal lobe epileptics include "greater awareness"; "seeing Christ coming down from the sky"; "seeing Heaven open"; "hears God speak"; "feels himself transfigured and even believes that he is God" (cf. Karagulla and Robertson 1955; Geschwind 1983).

A study of sudden religious conversion among six temporal lobe epileptics (three of whom also had epileptogenic areas in the frontal lobes) revealed the following: hearing "divine music and angelic voices"; "she heard a church bell ring in her right ear; and the voice said: 'Thy Father hath made thee whole, Go in peace!' "; having "a day-time visual hallucination in which he saw angels playing with their harps"; "he had a sudden dream-like . . . flash of light, and exclaimed 'I have seen the light' "; feeling "heavenly voices abusing him, felt rays were being shone on him to punish him (a sensation of burning)"; "terrified that [he] would not be able to carry out . . . the love of God . . . he . . . he also became paranoid, believing that he was being poisoned and refusing to take his tablets"; sensing "a holy smell"; believing "that he was able to pick up other people's thoughts"; "believed that he could understand other people's thoughts," and so on (Dewhurst and Beard 1970).

Sudden alterations of activity in the hippocampus and amygdala can affect auditory, vestibular, gustatory, tactile, and olfactory perceptions and lead to hallucinations involving voices or music, feelings of sway or physical suspension, the tastes of elixirs, burning or caressing, the fragrance of Heaven or the stench of Hell. For example, because the middle part of the amygdala receives fibers from the olfactory tract, direct stimulation of that part of the amygdala will flood co-occurring events with strong smells. In religious rituals, incense and fragrances stimulate the amygdala so that scent can be used to focus attention and interpretation on the surrounding events. In temporal lobe epilepsy, the sudden electrical spiking of the area infuses other aspects of the epileptic experience with an odorous aura.

The hippocampus processes verbal and vocal signals, helping to link the intentions behind those signals (originating in the prefrontal cortices) to appropriate states of arousal and emotivity (via the amygdala and hypothalamus). Religious rituals sequence and rhythmically pattern these signals (prayers, preaching, incantations, chants) to infuse them with sustained affect and to increase the motivation for any uses to which they may be put. In temporal lobe epileptics, the hippocampus may be spontaneously stimulated to produce or interpret verbal signals as eruptive "voices" of unknown source and uncertain intention, which may threaten in the acute phase of schizophrenic-like hallucination or soothe during remission (cf. Larkin 1979).

Hallucinations can involve different sensory modalities. Thus, the brain's auditory, vestibular, and visual channels are closely intertwined. The inner ear conveys both sounds and a sense of balance. In religious ritual, music or chanting can set the body to swaying, triggering pleasant feelings. Loud noises and irregular sound patterns can cause sudden, disorienting movements, triggering surprise and fear and temporarily throwing the body out of kilter (although people can become habituated to noise levels and idiosyncracies in sound patterns, so that what feels unpleasant to some feels pleasant to others). Loud music or sudden noises (as well as bright or flashing lights) can drive the epileptic into seizures marked by feelings of terror and paranoia.

Because of the innate adaptation of our moving body to the gravitational conditions on Earth, the coordination of the retina's frame with the inner ear's frame gives us a proper sense of movement only when we are upright from the ground. When the two frames are thrown out of whack (moving on a boat, whirling in a dance, suddenly rising after lying down), the body tells you that you're moving but the ground lets you know that you're not. Notions of "up," "down," "side," ceiling," "floor," and "wall" become confused. When ritually controlled, this disynchronization often induces an emotionally positive sense of floating, suspension, or slow motion in a fast-moving world. When uncontrolled, as in epileptic experiences, it can provoke a frightening, emotionally aversive sense of dislocation and bewilderment. It can also produce nausea (as in motion sickness) and perhaps a sense of being poisoned (nausea and vomiting are plausibly adaptations for the elimination of toxins from the body).

These and other findings concerning relations between religious experiences and temporal lobe epilepsy provide a main support for Persinger's (1987:113) claim that transient patterns of stimulation in the temporal lobe—especially around the amygdala-hippocampal complex—"create the God experience." As I indicated, the main problem with his hypothesis from a neuropsychological standpoint is that it takes little account of the importance of agency and relations with the prefrontal cortices. The key issue here is that of *functional connectivity*, that is, temporal correlations between spatially remote physical events. In particular, frontal temporal connectivity—and not just temporal activation as such—implies a distributed rather than localized neural substrate for many types of religious experience. For example, disinhibited functions in the temporal lobes (e.g., seizure foci) will generally elicit a compensatory response from inhibitory circuits in the frontal lobes. If Newberg, d'Aquili, and Rause (2001; Newberg et al. 2001) are right about systematic alterations in the activity of the parietal lobe's orientation association area, then issues of connectivity become correspondingly more complex. For the present, though, I want to concentrate on what I think are the least controversial, or at least the most empirically supported, arguments about frontal temporal connectivity in religious experience.

Brain imaging shows heightened electrical stimulation and increased blood flow to this area of the brain during bouts of epileptic seizure, schizophrenic hallucination, speaking in tongues, trance, and deep meditation and prayer. But whereas schizophrenia-like episodes of epilepsy and schizophrenic hallucinations appear to be associated with *decreased* activity in the frontal cortices (Stern and Silbersweig 1998), meditation and prayer seem to be associated with *increased* activity (Newberg, d'Aquili, and Rause 2001; Newberg et al. 2001). In pathological cases there is a corresponding, clinically apparent lack of awareness of reality, whereas in nonpathological cases there is a reported hyperawareness of reality.

Numerous studies of schizophrenia indicate that sufferers experience their hallucinations as objectively real and as directing their thoughts and behaviors. Auditory hallucinations are by far the most common, followed by visual hallucinations, and then by tactile and olfactory or gustatory hallucinations. Tactile, olfactory, and gustatory hallucinations are stongly correlated with one another. Global severity of the illness correlates best with visual hallucinations (Mueser, Bellack, and Brady 1990). Owing to frequency of occurrence, however, research on auditory hallucinations in schizophrenia is by far the most advanced.

In a study of 60 inpatients with schizophrenic or schizophrenic-like auditory hallucinations, Oulis and colleagues (1995) found high levels of conviction about the reality of the sensory stimuli, clarity of content, location of their source, and lack of volitional control. The voices associated with such pathological states indicate a dampening of subcortical interactions with the prefrontal cortices and an absence or submission of will (Damasio 1994). The louder and more intrusive the hallucinations and intensity of delusional beliefs, the more anxious and fearful patients become, whether diagnosed as schizophrenics (Hustig and Hafner 1990) or as temporal lobe epileptics (LaBar et al. 1995). A study of command hallucinations among 106 schizophrenic outpatients revealed the hallucinations to be often violent in content, leading to attempts to harm others (including innocent bystanders) or self (including two cases of command suicide; Zisook et al. 1995).

The hallucinations and delusions associated with pathological states indicate a disconnection between self-will and the (supernatural) will commanding the hallucinations. Schizophrenics (and schizophrenic-like temporal lobe epileptics) may say "I am God" or "I am God's slave" or both. According to Stern and Silbersweig, such "delusions of control (or passivity) could result when a self-generated movement [e.g., self-generated verbally mediated thought] is not associated with a sense of volition and/or is mistakenly believed to arise from another source, or both" (1998:239). These authors show that medial temporal activations (hippocampus) are prominent in hallucinating schizophrenics, but absent when control subjects listen to or imagine voices. Such temporal lobe activations occur in the setting of a relative lack of prefrontal activity and corresponding deficits in executive functions that assign volition and agency.

By contrast, in nonpathological cases, neuropsychologist Patrick Macnamara observes:

> [In] most accounts of mystical experience . . . the subject is invited to consent to the experience before it is given or "revealed" (see the account of the Anunciation to Mary in the New Testament as the paradigmatic example). The suspension of agency and will, if anything, is antithetical to mystical experiences (if not to hallucinatory experience). . . . If there is a central focus to religious belief I would place it in the effort to develop the right relationships to the deity/deities . . . and all this in service to development of greater self-awareness. . . . These, after all, are major functions of both orbitofrontal and dorsolateral frontal lobes. (personal communication, 2000)

Consistent with this idea, a literature review reveals that intense prayer encourages self-control and self-esteem in ways that reduce both acute and chronic stress and that appear to depend heavily on prefrontal activation (Worthington et al. 1996). Thus, Newberg, d'Aquili, and Rause (2001; Newberg et al. 2001) report EEG and SPECT data showing increased electrochemical activity in and blood flow to the inferior frontal and dorsolateral prefrontal cortical regions during intense meditation and prayer. These areas send inhibitory efferents directly on to a number of limbic and brainstem sites implicated in stress: amygdala, hippocampus, hypothalamus, and locus ceruleus (the nuclei that manufacture the stress hormone norepinephrine; Hugdahl 1996). There is often a marked delusional misidentification of faces, even familiar ones, which "may well be related to the misinterpretation of social interactions found in such subjects" (Phillips and David 1995).

More generally, experiments from cognitive neuropsychology indicate that such schizophrenic patients have a deficit in their ability to appreciate other people's mental states. Subjects fail in the performance of tasks involving social inferences, such as correctly assessing intentions from indirect speech (Corcoran, Mercer, and Frith 1995). This points to a *malfunctioning "theory of mind" and intentional agency*, which is patently not the case for most people who have deep or periodic episodes of religious experience (including many of our political leaders).[7]

Finally, schizophrenics with prefrontal deficits also seem unable to properly formulate or process counterfactual propositions that require imagining oneself in possible social worlds that are different from the actual one. For example, after a career failure or the death of a loved one, nonpsychotic persons often imagine "what might have been, if I had only done such and such." This is an ordinary behavior that seems to be lacking among some schizophrenics (Knight and Grabowecky 1995; Hooker, Roese, and Parks 2000). Although a common occurrence after the death of a loved one is "dream sleep" (vivid and realistic dreams concerning the deceased that burst into awareness), the grieving subject is usually aware of the difference between dream and reality. Understanding counterfactual situations may be important for dissociating imaginations of the supernatural (e.g., the transubstantiated body and blood of Christ) from factually mundane observation and existence (ordinary wine and wafers), that is, dissociating the quest for self-awareness from the awareness needed for survival.

Autism is another form of psychopathology that is increasingly associated with deficits in "theory of mind" and faulty appraisals of social intentions (Leslie and Frith 1987, 1988; Baron-Cohen 1995). The term "autism" was coined by Kanner in 1943; however, until the mid-1960s, when the first epidemiological survey of autism was conducted in England (Lotter 1966), autism was considered a precocious form of schizophrenia (Goldfarb 1964). As with certain forms of schizophrenia and temporal lobe epilepsy, autistics often show abnormalities in the limbic region and associated areas of the brain stem. Autistic children have trouble remembering and processing recent verbal-auditory material, which is consistent with autopsy reports and clinical analyses indicating abnormalities in the hippocampus (Bauman and Kemper 1985; DeLong 1992). Studies of lesioned monkeys with damage to the amygdala reveal autistic-like behavior associated with "hypoemotionality" (unnaturally fearless or tame, impairment in social interaction, aimless examination of objects; Klüver and Bucy 1939; Aggleton and Passingham 1981; Zola-Morgan et al. 1991; Bachevalier and Merjanian 1994).

Autistics also tend to manifest repetitive, rhythmic movements and "fixed memory" formulaic sequences akin to some forms of ritual behavior, but to no evident purpose. Catherine Johnson, a mother of two autistic children and coauthor of *Shadow Syndromes* (Ratey and Johnson 1998), nevertheless sees the use of these ritualistic movements as a stepping-stone for religious education: "A child with autism can 'get' the idea of God. . . . For one thing, the repetition and ritual of religion is perfect, . . . For another, I'm hoping that the visual power of the high church ceiling activates the 'God part' of his brain. . . . Neuroscientists have found there is a region of the brain that, when stimulated, causes people to experience the presence of God" (www.feat.org/search/news.asp, "Autism and God," 18 September 2000).

One apparent problem with autism, as with certain forms of schizophrenia described above, is an inability to imagine counterfactual situations. This can be particularly striking in children suffering from Asperger's syndrome, a high-functioning form of autism. They seem to be very literal-minded and to believe exactly what they are told, as the following excerpts from a Web forum on Asperger's syndrome suggest:

> We went overseas, and when the plane was over the clouds, he asked me: "So this is where God lives? I can't see him." (accesscom.com/~hcross/mindblind.htm)

> My daughter is fixated with angels. My son told her that when you die you go to heaven and become an angel. . . . (Excited at this pointed) ("Goody, Goody!") . . . I barged right in the room and told her not to listen to her brother [for fear she would try to kill herself right there and then]. (Listserv by St. John's University for Asperger syndrome)

To deal with such deficits in counterfactual thinking, St. Paul's Catholic Church in Alabama has instituted an intensive learning program for autistic children aimed at helping them to undertsand and take First Communion:

> "The church requires that children who receive Holy Communion be able to recognize the difference between ordinary bread and the Eucharist," said the Rev. Sam Sirianni, director of the office of worship for

> the Diocese of Trenton. The St. Paul's program was designed to teach the difference . . . but it also taught more basic things, like how to behave properly in church . . . learning how to behave in a crowded situation like a Mass was good for the children . . . people with autism often find crowds frightening, and the more situations they learn to deal with, the better. (Albert Raboteau, "Celebrating a Milestone," *Austism Society of Alabama: National and World News Forum* [Web site], 25 June 2000)

Unlike hallucinating schizophrenics or temporal lobe epileptics, however, autistics do not usually misrepresent their own voices and intentions as those of other agents (including supernatural agents) or misinterpret the intentions of others as those of demons or deities. Rather, severe autistics show little evidence of inferring *anybody's* intentions. This may be so despite retaining most other aspects of intelligence and intellect intact. Their world appears to be populated not by supernatural agents, or even natural agents like friends and enemies, but by mindless, zombie-like beings that have no autonomous will, desires, or thoughts.

In some religious contexts, the usually sad spectacle of an autistic child droning on and on in his or her own world is sometimes taken to be an indication of an intensely absorbing divine state of grace. For example, anthroposophy-theosophy, a Christian spiritual education and healing movement widespread in Europe, Australia, and the Americas, considers autistic children as well as those with Down syndrome (mongolism) to be angels who are "heaven blessed" (*Béni des cieux*; Geuter-Newitt, 1956:27). These "annointed" children are almost certainly better off than those more commonly isolated or committed by our society. More problematic, perhaps, are cultural diagnoses of autism as cases of spirit possession requiring exorcism, as in Moslem societies such as Saudi Arabia and Pakistan. Although the exorcism ceremony may offer social support, it also may inflict pain and harm. Having no awareness of the social support offered, or of an invitation to consent, the child is assailed from an unknown source to no apparent purpose. Arguably, this might initiate the child into an even deeper incomprehension of the fragmentary cognitive and emotional states that make up those social worlds that ordinary people find coherent.

Recent studies indicate that in largely secular societies, like our own, where there is a history of separation between Church and state, extreme mystical states are generally attributed to cerebral pathology. But in societies where institutional religions dominate, the contents of hallucinations, delusions, and possessed beliefs, as well as the diagnoses of their causes, are more generally taken to be religious in origin (Kent and Wahass 1996; Wahass and Kent 1997). Religious treatment may have positive or negative effects, depending on the community's beliefs about the supernatural origins of the illness, such as whether the person is blessed by God or possessed by Satan.

These differences in belief, which determine different moral judgments about the mutual responsibilities of individuals and societies, can lead to social or political conflict. For example, in an unprecedented ruling, Chicago immigration officials recently decided to grant political asylum to a 10-year-old autistic boy whose mother had claimed his disability and sporadically violent behavior is so misunderstood in Pakistan, their homeland, that he would be tortured and persecuted if he returned there. In her successful application to the Chicago Office of Asylum, she stated: "He was forced to undergo various degrading and dangerous mystical treatments consistent with the curse of 'Allah,' which is how the Islamic majority in Pakistan view his condition" (Deardoff 2001).[8]

In Moslem Pakistan and Saudi Arabia, the religious community is obliged to recognize the violent behavior of an autistic child as a social problem that requires the forceful intervention of the religious community. From the secular standpoint of U.S. immigration officials and their medical advisors, this leads the boy's homeland community to "violate" the individual's rights. By contrast, in some states of the United States (e.g., Texas) medical diagnoses of severe and violent autism imply no special secular or religious responsibility of the community toward an individual who breaks a law that he or she cannot understand. In such cases, the individual may be even more radically isolated from society in prison and prosecuted (Western Europeans would say "persecuted") unto death (execution).

Whatever the religious take, there is an increasing scientific consensus that autism owes at least in part to alterations in the normal functioning of the prefrontal cortices, especially the ventromedial region that is involved in the affective assessment of social interactions and intentions (cf. Damasio 1994). There are massive subcortical connections among the prefrontal cortices, the temporal lobes, and the limbic system. None of the religious pathologies that I have summarized—temporal lobe epilepsy, schizophrenia, autism—implies a localized neural substrate for extreme religious experiences in the temporal lobe (or anywhere else in the brain).

More significant, neither is there any evidence that less extreme, more "routine" religious experiences have some characteristic brain activation pattern. Many people never have a full-fledged mystical experience, yet are affectively committed religious believers. Although about 25 to 33 percent of American and British subjects polled report having had some kind of "religious experience" in their lives (Hay 1990; Spilka, Brown, and Cassidy 1992), only 2 to 3 percent claim to have had an intensely emotional "mystical experience," such as experiencing that all things in the world are one (Thomas and Cooper 1978; Hay and Heald 1987 cited in Beit-Hallahmi and Argyle 1997:79). We know next to nothing about the neurobiology of the vast majority of run-of-the-mill religious experiences and beliefs that sustain most people's faith.

7.6. Summary: Mystical Episodes Inspire New Religions, but Don't Make Religion

Stressful personal episodes become religious experiences by instantiating publicly relevant schemas. Within such cultural schemas, even the eccentric voices and visions of clinically diagnosed schizophrenics and epileptics can become publicly sanctioned revelations, as they are in some societies. The religious hallucinations and delusions of schizophrenics, the sensory enlightenments of temporal lobe epileptics (possibly the Apostle Paul, more likely Saint Theresa de Avila), and the mystical visions and voices of persons are at the extreme end of the "normal" distribution (Jacob, Jesus, Mohammed, Paliau, Maharishi Mahesh Yogi?).

In historically seminal moments, their unpredictable, "miraculous" revelations have undoubtedly inspired common belief in divine intention and grace. Malfunctioning or hyperactive theories of mind and intentional agency are cognitively and emotionally ripe for supernatural co-optation. Revivalist and starter cults are more likely than established religions to acknowledge the divine character of these more extreme mystical experiences. As Adam Smith noted, this is because such religious sects aim to radically reform or recreate religious obeisance "by carrying it to some degree of folly or extravagance" (1993[1776]:439). A startling episode of intense sensory arousal in a face-to-face encounter with the supernatural may prove unforgettable and emotive enough to permanently inculcate religious belief in a person, and perhaps to jump-start new belief in society.

For the most part, however, relatively few individuals have emotionally arousing mystical experiences, at least in our society, although the overwhelming majority of individuals consider themselves to be religious believers. Neither is there any evidence that more "routine" religious experiences have a characteristic temporal lobe signature or any other specified type of brain activity pattern. The neurophysiological bases that commit the bulk of humanity to the supernatural remain a complete mystery.

PART 4

Mindblind Theories

Culture is both superindividual and superorganic. . . . [T]here are certain properties of culture—such as transmissibility, high variability, cumulativeness, value standards, influence on individuals—which is difficult to explain, or to see much significance in, strictly in terms of organic personalities and individuals.

—A. L. Kroeber, *Anthropology: Culture Patterns and Processes* (1963[1923])

Culture is inherited habit. . . . All cultures seek to constrain the raw selfishness of human nature through the establishment of unwritten moral rules . . . to affirm an ethical code . . . by simple habituation.

—Francis Fukuyma, *Trust: The Social Virtues and the Creation of Prosperity* (1995)

Culture is something I put in the same category as unicorns.

—Noam Chomsky to Lawrence Hirschfeld, Royaumont Conference, Paris (October 1975)

8 Culture without Mind

Sociobiology and Group Selection

Sociobiological and group selection theories of human societies, which posit norms as the functional units of cultural selection, are improbable. There is no compelling psychological evidence for norms as packages of learned information, stored as discrete units, clustered into higher-order knowledge structures, encoded as specific memory traces in neural tissue, or expressed in clearly recognized and denumerable bundles of behavior. Those who propose norms as the units of culture make almost no effort to describe how norms are formed and represented in the minds that supposedly produce them or to causally spell out how they actually work in producing behaviors. Much of the purported evidence for norms as units of cultural selection is skimmed from the ethnographic digests of colonial anthropologists and other lone fieldworkers who have tried to expeditiously make sense of alien cultures as "social machines." These norms are convenient or commonsense summaries of socially relevant and recurrent ideas and behaviors.

Most widely accepted, sacred, or morally absolute norms are only signposts of behavioral tendencies. They are not shared rules. Like the Ten Commandments, they have little if any context-free content or directive. They are customarily summoned in particular situations, with reference to known and generally accepted examples (shared prototypes), so as to bring about successful communication or consensus in regard to new or unresolved contexts. Lacking reliable content or boundaries, they can't replicate with any degree of fidelity adequate for Darwinian selection. There is also no clear sense to the notion of "fitness consequences at the level of whole cultures," because cultures have no readily definable boundaries but do have enormously varied ways of enduring, expanding, mixing, assimilating, and transforming. A "garden experiment" in the Maya Lowlands helps to make the case and gives a new twist to religion's role in resolving "the Tragedy of the Commons."

8.1. Sociobiology, or Mystical Materialism

> In reference to any feature of a system we can ask how it contributes to the working of the system. That is what is meant by . . . its *social function*. When we succeed in discovering the function of a particular custom, i.e., the part it plays in the working system to which it belongs, we reach an understanding and explanation of it. . . . It is only when changes are seen as changes in organization of a functioning system that they can be understood.
>
> —A. R. Radcliffe-Brown, Introduction to *African Systems of Kinship and Marriage* (1950)

Traditional sociobiology attempts to account for cultural behaviors directly in terms of task-specific genetic preparedness for those behaviors. For example, according to anthropologist Marvin Harris (1974), the Aztec religious practice of large-scale human sacrifice stems from the fact that Mesoamerica has relatively few large mammals; hence, apart from the other humans they eat, people in the region have few substantial sources of protein. Indeed, declares biologist Edward O. Wilson, "some of the most baffling of religious practices in history might have an ancestry passing in a straight line back to the ancient carnivorous practices of humankind" (1978:98). Similarly, the cult of the sacred cow of India allegedly owes to the cow being more ecologically efficient as a sustained source of labor, dung, and milk than as a one-shot source of protein (Harris 1966; E. Wilson 1978).

But why, then, was there not large-scale human sacrifice in every chiefdom or civilization where game was scarce? And why did other Mesoamerican peoples religiously practice human sacrifice even into colonial times (Clendinnen 1990), although game was apparently abundant? For example, in the country of the Lowland Yukatek and Itza' Maya, known even from pre-Columbian times as "the Land of the Deer and the Wild Turkey" (Landa 1985[1566]): "The Indians of this land are very dexterous with bow and arrow, and so are great hunters, and they raise dogs, with which they hunt deer, peccaries, coatimundis . . . rabbits, armadillos, iguanas . . . wild turkey, pheasants and many others" (López de Cogolludo 1971[1656]:I:242; cf. Villagutierre Soto-Mayor 1701: bk.10, xi–xii; Atran 1993, 1999 for Itza' species lists).

And why is it that for other cultures, such as the Azande and the peoples they conquered, apparently routine cannibalism required no religious ritual: "The motive was simply a taste for human meat" (Evans-Pritchard 1960:256)? How could Moslem peoples of the Indian Subcontinent, who often spoke the same language and exploited the same habitat as Hindus, afford to eat cows? Even more significant, why did such elaborate and materially inefficient religious theater emerge within which human sacrifice and the sacred cow played only a part, and how could such exorbitant display endure for centuries if not millennia?

Sacrifice of humans, animals, plants, or artifacts often involves partial redistribution among the population of the items sacrificed, such as cows among the Sudanese Nuer (Evans-Pritchard 1940), pigs among the Maring of New Guinea

(Rappaport 1968), buffaloes, lambs, chickens, and rice among the Tamil of south India (Whitehead 1988[1921]). But such redistribution is by no means obligatory in all societies that practice sacrifice, such as among ancient Maya who destroyed their own cities and temples or the Ancient Hebrews who offered first grains. Noncannibalistic human sacrifice is a prime example. Thus, archaeologist Johann Reinhard (in Fagan 2000) has recently discovered evidence that the Inca of Peru sacrificed young girls and boys to mountain gods, bundled and mummified them in rich cloths, and buried them with fine textiles, clays pots containing meat, and dozens of gold, silver, and shell statues of humans and llamas. Noncannibalistic child sacrifice is reported throughout human history and from around the world: Ancient Greece and Rome (Pliny 1829 [ca. A.D. 70]), Phoenicia and Carthage (Burkert 1996), South American Inca (de la Vega Inca 1986[1609]), preconquest Pawnee and Iroquois (Lowie 1924), India until outlawed in 1835 (J. Wilson 1855; Whitehead 1988[1921]), Ancient Chinese Shang civilization, some forms of contemporary Afro-Brazilian voodoo (P. Stewart 2000), and so forth.

Numerous and varied other forms of expensive and materially unreciprocated offerings are culturally widespread. Examples include chopping off one's fingers for the slain among the Dani and other Papuan New Guinea tribes (R. Gardner and Heider 1968) as well as among the Crow and other Plains Indians (Lowie 1924); knocking out one's teeth during ritual initiation among aboriginal tribes of central Australia (B. Spencer and Gillen 1904); and periodic and painful blood letting from the tongue and penis by pre-Columbian Maya (Schele and Freidel 1990). There are also extravagant engineering and art works that serve no material function, such as the pyramids of Egypt, Mesoamerica, and Cambodia and the statues and tombs of ancestors everywhere. Only the dead use them.

The material benefits to a population of the redistributions that are often associated with sacrifice are rarely efficient in terms of the time and energy expended and generally do not offset the material costs (Firth 1963; see also section 5.1 above). Religious individuals nonetheless *perceive* these redistributed benefits as tantamount to return gifts bestowed by religious powers, that is, as a form of reciprocal altruism with supernatural agents and their priestly representatives. Perceived reciprocal altruism may result in a culturally stable strategy as long as defectors can be detected and excluded and as long as the actual material costs do not so outweigh the benefits that physical survival is compromised.

Even when a threat to physical survival is evident in some cultural strategy, people may steadfastly cling to it. In cases of collective martyrdom, such a strategy may extinguish itself by killing off the individuals holding it, as with the zealots of ancient Masada or contemporary Jonestown. In ways akin to sexual selection (Cronin 1991; G. Miller 2000), frequency-dependent cultural selection (follow the majority) or dominance-dependent cultural selection (follow those who are successful) can lead to chaotic and maladaptive outcomes (Laland Richerson, and Boyd 1996; Boyd and Richerson 1985). This often happens with social fashions and crazes (e.g., body building and steroid-induced impotence; body piercing and infection) and also in societies ruled and led to destruction by charismatic megalomaniacs (e.g., Hitler's Germany, Pol Pot's Cambodia). In some situations, an often successful but somewhat risky strategy may succumb to its inherent risk, for example, fundamentalist movements that thrive by fomenting internal purges and external wars but that, in the end, may generate more potent enemies than such movements are able to suppress (e.g., the Taliban).

Moreover, the apparently rational material aspects of religious practice and belief, such as associated distributions of food and labor, may create the very material conditions (ecological and institutional) that favor the continued cultural selection and survival of religious practice and belief. This cultural form of "ecological engineering" resembles biological niche construction (Laland, Olding-Smee, and Feldman 2000). Thus, the burrowing behavior of numerous mammal species (gophers, ground squirrels, marmots, moles, rabbits, rats, etc.) creates material conditions that favor the further selection of systems of burrow defense, maintenance, and regulation (R. Nowak 1991). Similarly, once a redistributive system is in place, there is further motivation for the material maintenance and ideational regulation of that system and for the whole religious edifice in which that system is embedded. With such an ecologically self-rationalizing strategy, the motivational conditions for success and survival are realized through religious practice. There is a looping effect whereby religious practice enhances its "cultural fitness" over time, even if it is materially inefficient initially or in its own right.

In sum, sociobiological accounts often invoke ordinary material causes (genetic adaptations for carnivorous behavior) to explain ordinary material effects (cannibalism). Nevertheless, they fail to provide a hint of how the putative distal causes (genetic) enter into known material relationships with more proximate causes (mental and public representations) to actually produce the forms of behavior to be explained (religious beliefs and practices causally connected within and between human minds and bodies). Sociobiological accounts of cultural behaviors readily complement so-called materialist accounts in anthropology, by waving away the superstructure or ideology of cultural forms as nonmaterial or epiphenomenal "by-products" of underlying material causes (ecological, economic, or genetic).

Materialism in anthropology, including versions of Marxism, consist largely of reasons that include no material causes known to the natural sciences (e.g., modes of production that generate ideologies). It relies instead on open-textured metaphors drawn from the natural sciences, such as "power" and "revolution" taken from physics or "reproduction" and "evolution" taken from biology. Usual sociobiological accounts of religion and other cultural forms differ from such materialism only by substituting this metaphorical and immaterial causality (the production of nonmaterial effects by material means) with silence as to the actual material antecedents and proximate causes of cultural practices and beliefs.

In his last work, political anthropologist Eric Wolf (1999) suggests that the massive ritual human sacrifice practiced by the Aztecs resulted from extreme political, economic, and demographic-ecological dislocation. The Aztecs experienced deep anxiety about the future that compelled them to adopt frenzied, cosmic ideologies. This somewhat resembled Nazi Germany's efforts to exterminate non-Aryan races or exaggerated forms of potlatching in which Northwest Coast Indians engaged in gift-giving competitions that spiralled out of control (after introduction of European luxury goods) into ruthless destruction of wealth and wealth-based status. To claim that the Aztecs practiced ritual sacrifice to offset protein deficiency may be no more justified than to claim that Nazis set up extermination camps to solve problems of overpopulation or labor shortages.

Shielding cognition from omnipresent eruptive and rationally unresolvable anxieties (e.g., catastrophe, loneliness, injustice, death) and sharing emotional and conceptual commitment to some resolution are as likely to be as much functional motivations for, or constraints on, religion as are ecologically variable conditions of nutrition or resource management. In the cultural evolution of religion, proactive displays of commitment may prevail over whatever functional, functionless, or dysfunctional ecological utility they might promote.

8.2. Are Norms Units of Cultural Evolution?

Sociobiological and genetic coevolution models of cultural evolution are normative models that assume that cultures are systems of widely shared rules or ideas that maintain heritable variation (Lumsden and Wilson 1981; Cavalli-Sforza and Feldman 1981; Boyd and Richerson 1985, 2001a, 2001b; Durham 1992; Laland and Olding-Smee 2001; Laland, Olding-Smee, and Feldman 2000). Trait models of group selection for human cultures are also normative models (D. Boehm 1996; Sober and Wilson 1998; Rappaport 1999; Boyd and Richerson 2001a, 2001b; D. Wilson in press). There are important differences between individual and group selection models, but not with respect to their basic characterization of the definable units of cultural selection as "norms" (Irons 1996a; Axelrod 1997).

In the following sections I discuss some of these differences. Nevertheless, my central argument will be that all such normative models of cultural organization and evolution are "mindblind" in the sense that they ignore the cognitive and computational architecture of the human mind/brain and so may seriously misconstrue the nature of human cultures. Meme theories, too, are essentially normative, mindblind accounts of cultural evolution (Dawkins 1976; Dennett 1995; A. Lynch 1996; Blackmore 1999; Aunger 2001); however, they have a somewhat original slant that merits separate attention (see chapter 9).

There are other presumptively evolutionary theories that have norms as a principal means for regulating human social behavior but that make no particular claims about the actual selection processes that might generate such norms. For example, there is the notion that moral rules are embodiments of passionate commitments that evolved under natural selection to offset the short-sightedness of immediate biological self-interest (R. Frank 1988; Nesse 1999; cf. Schelling 1960; Hirshleifer 1977). Emotionally uncontrollable, and thus sincere and convincing, displays of love ("in sickness as in health until death do us part"), tolerance ("turn the other cheek"), and vengeance at any price ("an eye for an eye" even if it costs the avenger the other eye) are some of the sentiments that function in the long run to forestall cheating, defection, and harmful actions by those to whom the displays are targeted. Religions everywhere seem to codify such social commitment strategies in normative dogmas and doctrines, such as the Ten Commandments, Calvin's "Principles," Islamic Hadiths and Fatwas, and the moral prescriptions inculcated during the emotionally intense initiation rites of certain Native American, African, Melanesian and Australian aboriginal groups.

Individual and group selection theorists simply go a bit further in proposing specific selection models for these and other moral sentiments and injunctions.

Whether immediate self-interest is overridden for the sake of long-term individual self-interest or for the sake of some group interest that requires an individual's unreciprocated sacrifice is one of the issues that distinguishes individual from group selectionists. For both individual and group selectionists, norms are supposed to play a role in cultural evolution that is lawfully analogous to the role genes play in biological evolution. Norms are culturally transmitted beliefs and values that specify which behaviors are good or bad, honorable or shameful, commendable or punishable. Just as genes are heritable units of biological information that are stored in body cells to instruct the organism how to behave and develop in different environmental settings, so norms are heritable units of cultural information stored in networks of neural tissue, or "minds," to instruct people how to develop and behave in different social (and socially relevant ecological) settings.

The cultural analogues of genetic evolution are not meant to be metaphors. They are hypothesized to be literal instantiations of general Darwinian laws that theoretically apply to any biological or nonbiological evolutionary process in any situation or possible world that is governed by nomological laws of cause and effect and thermodynamics. Such a Darwinian scenario occurs whenever information can proliferate and be edited by a process of selection, where the selection affects the information at a greater rate than competing processes, such as mutation (random alteration and spontaneous transformation) or drift (helter-skelter accumulation and chance isolation; G. Williams 1992). For example, computer viruses could maintain their effect in the face of antivirus programs by replicating themselves with a relatively high fidelity that is not quite perfect, allowing random variation in parts of their instructional code. If some of the replicating variants are better able than others to resist the antivirus programs and to produce more copies than others can, then these strains will evolve in Darwinian fashion.

Norms are supposedly "inherited" from one individual to another in the sense that they can be transmitted "vertically" from parent to offspring (e.g., rules for caste adherence, ritual circumcision, family occupation) or "horizontally" across peer cohorts and other groups of nonkin (ideas for new laws, fashions, protocols) or both vertically and horizontally (e.g., religious commandments, common law, ethnic bias). Normative rules in the mind are parts of a culture's analogue of the "genotype," whereas the normative behaviors that these rules generate under environmental prodding and influence are parts of the culture's "phenotype." Normative behaviors are "adaptive" when they promote cultural "fitness" by contributing to the survival and spread of the population that carries the norms of which those behaviors are the naturally selected phenotypic expressions. (In meme theories, it is the norms themselves that are selected, rather than the populations that carry the norms or memes.)

8.3. Emulation, Display, and Social Stabilization

To be selected in Darwinian fashion, the units of selection must survive with recognizable continuity and replicate with relatively high fidelity so that they resemble one another more than they do unrelated competitors. They must be longer-lasting and produce more copies or like variants than do other forms to contribute to differential fitness or reproductive success. Norms supposedly acquire relatively long life and high fidelity through a number of means, such as imprinting, classical and operant conditioning, formal and informal teaching, and imitation.

The focal process for most normative theories of cultural evolution is imitation without explicit instruction. Imitation is a fairly economic and efficient way to produce behaviors that best fit the circumstances compared to more costly efforts, such as creation through trial and error or "reinventing the wheel." Most commonly, groups of people can eventually change their habits and traditions to further ensure survival because, when in doubt, individuals tend to look out for, observe, and copy the apparently more successful behaviors of others.

In the hills of Bali, for example, the religious institution of water temples ritually functions to regulate and optimize rice cultivation under antagonistic ecological constraints (e.g., irrigation vs. pest control, upstream vs. downstream). The temples encourage farmers to systematically monitor immediately adjacent plots, to emulate the scheduling practices of more successful neighbors, and so coordinate local activities to maintain a relatively constant level of productivity. According to Lansing and Kremer (1993), the physical placement of water temples at key forks in the water distribution system, and associated communal rites, emerged to morally underwrite and facilitate the quest of individual farmers to balance competing cultivation schedules and shifting ecological contingencies. Indeed, computer simulations of the water flow problem (i.e., much water breeds many pests, little water yields few crops) that rely exclusively on ecological and demographic variables show precisely those forks where temples occur to be the best placements for water control gates. By imitating neighbors, farmers maximize yields in the long run.

Although functional success in ecological accommodation and material production is often important to the selection of norms, these are not the only selection factors. Social punishments and rewards are also critical to the spread and stabilization of norms. Punishments may have explicit public representation, for example, legal criteria for fines, imprisonment, and exile, or bodily torture, mutilation, and execution (e.g., severing the hands of thieves and stoning or decapitating adulterers). Punishments can also be implicit, as when potential job candidates in high-status business or politics are rejected because they fail to wear the appropriate uniform of coat and tie or pantsuit at an interview, or when would-be members of lower-status peer groups are mocked because they fail to sport the right brand of tennis shoes or orient their baseball caps in the appropriate direction. Rewards also can be explicit, as when successful executives acquire greater decision-making powers and monetary rewards. And rewards can be implicit, for example, when successful politicians acquire enhanced reputations, greater self-esteem, a wider range of potential mates, and greater access to sexual favors. ("Power," former U.S. Secretary of State Henry Kissinger is supposed to have said, "is the ultimate aphrodisiac.")

The norms that govern secondary displays of commitment to primary norms provide a social environment of rewards and punishments that leads to stabilization of primary norms. For example, a decree from the Taliban leader in Afghanistan, Mullah Mohammed Omar, emphasized complete subservience to Islamic law and custom by banning male citizens without beards from jobs or any other services ("Growing Beard Is the Tradition of Islam's Prophet Mohammed That Must Be Followed by Muslims," Reuters News Service, 6 November 2000). Similarly, the Taliban requires full head and body veils for women who venture out in public on pain of stoning. This encourages Afghanis to be good Taliban Muslims whatever their personal inclinations.[1]

Social anthropologist Richard Antoun (1968:687) suggests that the "modesty code" for Moslem Arab women forms part of a conceptually integrated, religiously absolute, and socially exclusive system of norms that functions to identify and control sociocultural boundaries. In this sociocultural system, "practical norms" (e.g., illicit sexual relations) can be realized only through "espousal of all the norms connected with a particular value" (e.g., seclusion, veiling). The normative value of secondary displays, such as veiling, is amplified and raised to parity with primary behaviors, such as illicit sex, so as to reinforce discouragement of those primary behaviors. Accordingly, "It was not unusual . . . that the affirmation of the [primary] norm was as complete as the punishment was harsh and the violation of the [display of] modesty flagrant" (ibid.)

The cultural evolution of secondary social displays somewhat parallels the biological evolution of animal signaling behavior. In social primates, fundamental action schema and derivative display schema are homologous structures that are related to the same ancestral problem context. They share much in the way of form but function very differently. For example, the baring of teeth in humans and other social primates communicates anger or aggression, whereas baring of fangs in other mammals is a motor priming for actual biting. Nevertheless, this particular form of signaling behavior, snarling, makes sense only as a derivative adaptation from the original adaptation of behavior for attack (Lorenz 1965a). In general, derivative behaviors carry lower costs than fundamental behaviors in terms of energy expenditure and risk. Seeing some person or animal with teeth bared makes one think twice about approaching and engaging.

Secondary normative displays that promote adherence to primary norms also tend to carry lower commitment costs than direct adherence to primary norms themselves. It is easier to pledge allegiance to the flag and signal that one is willing to sacrifice oneself for one's country than have to prove one's pledge. It is also easier for others to monitor displays for failure to signal one's commitment than to monitor actual commitments (e.g., in one's own house or in other situations where surveillance is difficult and unlikely).

Moreover, secondary displays tend to amplify the effects of primary behaviors over a population and thus to further the proliferation of the norms such behaviors represent (cf. Sober and Wilson 1998). Friendly people who display eagerness to help others are more likely to inspire confidence and trust in critical situations than are people who display social distance and meanness. A friendly person who seeks out others is also more likely to communicate and thus propagate a help ethic than a misanthrope is likely to transmit a selfish ethic.

There are, however, trade-offs: fixation on secondary displays allows for greater latitude in deception and defection in the performance of primary duties and obligations. But there are also countervailing means to augment the reliability of secondary displays: the accompanying of hard-to-fake emotions will often enable a jury to make the right decision, and efforts to punish those who fail to punish defectors work to spread and lessen the individual costs of policing both secondary displays and primary behaviors. As a whole (on average), individuals in the group benefit by performing and monitoring secondary displays of commitment at less individual cost (on average) than if there were only primary behaviors to attend to.

The joint operation of imitation, reward, and punishment can generate conformity to *any* norm, including norms that are clearly nonadaptive (Edgerton 1992). Conformity to social fashions often has no inherent social or ecological value, for example, body piercing, wearing silk ties, or eating soup by scooping with a spoon down and away from the mouth rather than up toward it. By contrast, the ritual sealing of group covenants is often decidely dysfunctional, at least for the individuals who risk infection, death, and loss of reproductive potential, for example, in removing the clitoris (female circumcision in the Sudan [Barclay 1964] and West Africa [d'Azevedo 1994]), cutting the penis to expose the uretha (subincision in aboriginal Central Australia [B. Spencer and Gillan 1904; Meggitt 1965]), or scarring the back of the skull (Candomblé Nagô initiation in Bahia, Brazil [Omari 1994]).

These biologically nonadaptive norms and normative behaviors seem to arise via a process of runaway "conformist transmission" (Boyd and Richerson 1985; Henrich and Boyd 1998): an organism's genes (or memory) compel it to go with the fashion because the very fact that the trait is preferred by the majority is often a good indication of the trait's (and trait bearer's) success in getting genes (or ideas) spread in the population (see Dugatkin and Alfieri 1991 on conformist transmission in guppies). But once the trait is preferred by the majority, it may evolve in ways that run contrary to its original function. When in doubt, the majority of the population will continue to imitate the fashion as signaling the most adequate behavior, although the pressures toward conformity through reward and punishment may have become so great as to foreclose the option of adopting behaviors more adequate to an environmental shift. Like reasoning may explain other types of conformist transmission, such as "follow the leader" (see Wilkinson 1992 on emulating the most successful hunters among vampire bats). In this way, a group might continue to follow its initially successful leaders into the abyss (e.g., the people of Hitler's Germany or Pol Pot's Cambodia) or emulate its successful fashion and sports stars by falling into the advertiser's clutches (e.g., Cindy Crawford's watch brand, Michael Jordan's shoe brand).

Group selection theorists acknowledge that within-group selection pressures driven by the rewards and punishments of conformist transmission can produce ecologically dysfunctional norms. In the long run, however, between-group competition and selection is expected to whittle away the irrational excesses of runaway conformism. The result should be an adaptive core of social norms among the surviving groups.

8.4. Functionalism Rules Group Selection

The theory most widely used and cited by group selectionists is functionalism (Boyd and Richerson 1985; Soltis, Boyd, and Richerson 1995; Boehm 1993, 1996;

Sober and Wilson 1998; D. Wilson 2002). This is a doctrine elaborated in anthropology and sociology during the first half of the twentieth century, with beginnings in the late nineteenth century. According to Robert Boyd (in press):[2] "Many social scientists are convinced that societies show evidence of design: societies are structured for the good of the whole. Functionalism, an old and still influential school in anthropology and sociology, holds that beliefs, behaviors and institutions exist because they promote the healthy functioning of social groups." For Boehm (1993, 1996), cultures are based on discrete lists of behaviors that are desirable or undesirable, functional or dysfunctional. Societies have an enumerable set of moral values (Kluckholn 1952) as their "worldview" or "ethos" (Kroeber 1948).

According to philosopher Elliot Sober and biologist David Sloan Wilson, "In most human social groups, cultural transmission is guided by a set of norms that identifies what counts as acceptable behavior" and that "function largely (although not entirely) to make human groups function as adaptive units." Norms are functioning parts of a "complex and sophisticated machine designed to forge groups into corporate units" (1998:150–176). Sober and Wilson cite numerous examples from a worldwide ethnographic survey, *The Human Relations Area Files*, first compiled by George Murdock (1949) over half a century ago.

For Murdock (1949), the HRAF was specifically constructed to help sociology and anthropology develop a true science of human society according to two overriding, interdependent theoretical principles: functionalism and behaviorism. On his view, the most important contribution of the social sciences in his time was "the discovery that a culture is adaptive or 'functional,' subserving the basic needs of its carriers and altering through time by a sort of mass trial-and-error process which is truly evolutionary, i.e., characterized by orderly adaptive changes" (xii). Murdock attributes the rise and general acceptance of functionalism to Bronislaw Malinowski. Malinowski (1961[1922]) argued that the anthropologist must strive to filter through individual variation and idiosyncracy in search of the normative causal structures of society: "As sociologists, we are not interested in what A or B may feel qua individuals, in the accidental course of their own personal experiences—we are interested only in what they feel and think *qua* members of a given community. Now, in this capacity, their mental states receive a certain stamp, become stereotyped by the institutions in which they live" (23).

For Murdock, the clearest theoretical presentation of functionalism in social anthropology could be found in the work of A. R. Radcliffe-Brown, who argued that the scientific anthropologist should restrict himself to "social structure," that is, "the arrangement of persons in institutionalized relationships" (1950:43). One discovers how discrete parts, or "organs," of the social structure function to form and stabilize the whole society, or "body," through comparative "analysis," that is, "a process of abstractive generalization . . . that can only be applied to something that is in itself a whole or a synthesis. By it we separate out, in reality or thought, the components of a complex whole and thereby discover the relation of these components to one another within the whole" (2). Murdock (1949:xiv–xv) surmises that this view of society leads rightly to A. L. Kroeber's (1963[1923]:61–62) conception of "the nature of culture" as a "superorganism."

Finally, Murdock argues that anthropology should not only seek to weed out, and so virtually ignore, individual variation in search of an ideal stereotype—

nowadays referred to as the "omniscient informant." It should also refuse to consider individual mental processes—nowadays called "cognition"— as unscientific fictions: "Of all the systematic approaches to the study of human behavior known to the author, [behaviorism] exceeds all others in scientific rigor and objectivity, and it is the only one against which he can level no serious criticism" (1949:xvi).

I have gone through this rather tedious process of citation to explain how Murdock set up the HRAF. First, societies, or "cultures," are postulated (and not discovered) to be discrete functional systems that operate as an integrated coordination of discrete functional parts. Second, these discrete parts, or institutions, allegedly function in complex unison on the basis of rules, which are putative causal laws (of an entirely metaphorical nature, e.g., social "forces"). Third, these institutionalized laws drive human bodies to act in certain stereotyped ways, that is, in accordance with behavioral norms. Fourth, human minds may store representations of normative behaviors in the brain, but they do little else. Human minds are assumedly passive vehicles that (in wholly mysterious ways) directly translate institutional norms into customary behaviors. Individual difference and variation results simply from a faulty translation process that owes to internal (e.g., emotional) or external (e.g., impinging ecological) perturbations.

Boyd and Richerson (in press) and Sober and Wilson (1998) surmise that a "random" survey of citations from 25 of 700 societies represented in the HRAF supports claims for the functionalism of norms and group selection. This is not surprising in light of the fact that the original entries were selected for the HRAF precisely on the basis of such claims. In brief, analyses based on the HRAF that purportedly demonstrate the functionalism of norms and group selection are basically circular, and therefore demonstrate nothing at all.

Sober and Wilson defend their reliance on the *HRAF* disingenuously: "[W]e have been told that many early ethnographies (which contribute disproportionately to the HRAF) overemphasize the importance of social norms in tribal societies. Further research on the same societies often reveals more flexible and individualistic aspects of behavior. . . . However, it is important to avoid the assumption that knowledge always advances and that modern ethnographers are invariably more enlightened than their predecessors" (1998:163). This is a startling argument as it stands, in that there is no attempt whatever to examine the theoretical objections to functionalism that have marked most advances in the field for the past half century. Even more striking, reputable biologists who seriously question whether there is anything at all to group selection in explaining the biology of colonies of nonhuman organisms, blithely accept Sober and Wilson's pronouncements on the functional role of social norms in the group selection of human cultures. These are characterized as the "most rewarding" (Maynard-Smith 1998) and "most valuable" (Reeve 2000) aspects of Sober and Wilson's work and as the primary (and perhaps only) novel contribution of goup selection theory to evolutionary theory (cf. G. Williams 1992).

It is as if anthropologists were to tell biologists to ignore the theories and discoveries of the past fifty years (e.g., DNA, neurotransmitters, cloning) in favor of those of a bygone era. Of course, it is entirely possible that there have been no interesting advances in anthropological understanding of human throught and behavior during the second half of the twentieth century; however, the argument would have to be made through analysis, not fiat. In fact, there has been notable progress that bears directly on functionalist claims.

8.5. Leapfrogging the Mind

In these group selection theories, functionalism, which is alive and well in biology, is confounded with functionalism in anthropology, which has been in decline for at least half a century. Functionalism in anthropology, where it is a dying metaphor, was initially derived from nineteenth-century biological functionalism, which has since developed into an insightful and instrumental research strategy. One immediate drawback to functionalism in the study of human societies is that it takes no account of intention and other critical aspects of human cognition. In biology, disregard of intention led to a breakthrough in understanding. In anthropology and psychology, it led to the dead end of behaviorism.

Ever since Chomsky's (1959) devastating attack on behaviorism, that doctrine has faded to near oblivion in cognitive science. Group selection theorists today make no mention of behaviorism. But neither do they mention any cognitive structures or causal processes of the human mind that might affect how information is structured to causally produce behaviors. There is no appeal to the different components of brain and computational architecture and of their very different causal roles in the production of behavior, much less of individual variation and differences in cognition.

Mental structures are simply "proximate mechanisms" to be ignored—at least at the initial stage of study—in trying to make scientific sense of culture. Although human cultures perhaps developed "to function as adaptive units via many proximate mechanisms" (Sober and Wilson 1998:182), it is possible to study cultures as "phenotypes" without describing the proximate computational machinery that generates them: "As long as the proximate mechanisms result in heritable variation, adaptations will evolve by natural selection. There is a sense in which the proximate mechanism doesn't matter. If we select for long wings in fruit flies and get long wings, who cares about the specific developmental pathway? . . . Similarly, if humans have evolved to coalesce into functionally organized groups, who cares how they think and feel?" (193).

There are, in fact, two sets of people who care about what others think and feel: most humans in their everyday lives and many cultural anthropologists and psychologists. Arguably, the first set regularly behaves as it does because its members regularly think and feel as they do. For the past forty years or so, the second set has made a science of trying to figure out these causal regularities, namely, cognitive science.

For example, we have seen that religion in general—and gods, ghosts, devils, and demons in particular—are culturally ubiquitous because they invariably meet or systematically manipulate modular input conditions of the human mind/brain. Children can initially communicate with their parents about such physically imperceptible agents on the basis of very poor and fragmentary data and little instruction. The same goes for communication about supernatural agents among peers or between anthropologists and their informants. Similarly, people require little or no instruction to acquire understanding of what the difference is between pretense and fact in any culture, where the middle or side is of any object or figure, how to form a question from a declarative in any language, and whether a person is happy or sad. Without such biologically poised competencies—the products of millions of years of biological and cognitive evolution—a child's acquisition of such a wide range of cultural knowledge in a few short years would be miraculous. This is also true for any adult's ability to network such a vast repository of detailed information in a mere lifetime, or for any anthropologist's ability to understand something of an alien culture in a season or two of fieldwork.

Norm theorists in general, and group selection theorists in particular, might acknowledge all of this but still claim it's not where the action is: "On this argument, humans can easily and naturally do the things we are really adapted to do like learn a language or understand the feelings of others. . . . If we had to do so [e.g., reinvent technology] could we be able to reinvent that stuff, just as Fang children invent the properties of their ghosts, or children can invent a grammar? Good questions, but we think the answer is almost certainly 'Are you nuts?'!" (Boyd and Richerson 2001a). For example, surviving alone in the Australian outback with little more than one's birthday suit is a common feat for a central Australian Aborigine, just as months alone in the rainforest is for a Lowland Maya Indian. Except for a few wilderness freaks, most Western "individualists" would expire in these circumstances in a matter of days. Obviously, a tourist caught in such a situation would be better off seeking instruction from a native than trying to elaborate on innate capacities.

It is also highly improbable that an ignorant person unschooled in reading, writing, or mathematics—like the ignorant Greek slave in Plato's *Meno*—would ever spontaneously come up with the Pythagorean theorem, although without some innate recognition of straight lines, object boundaries, proportion, and relative position even Socrates could never have gotten a geometry lesson started. Perhaps an untutored person does have all the necessary intellectual components; however, there is no guarantee that these would ever be sufficient. Similarly, although all working components of the internal combustion engine were known well before the automobile appeared (e.g., gears, pistons, spark plugs or flint locks, carburetors or liquid sprayers), the internal combustion engine represented a systemic level of complexity that could not be predicted from its previously known component systems (the example is John Holland's). This is so regardless of the "ecological" factors in play, such as the industrial demand for individual control of a horseless carriage.

Moreover, from a cognitive standpoint, some cultural aspects are genuinely arbitrary: different election or accounting principles, administrative boundaries and borders, driving on the left versus right side of the street, and so on. Once in place, they may have cascading effects throughout the network of mental and public representations that constitute a population's "culture," and their violation can wreak social havoc. People often have to expend considerable time and energy learning and navigating with such rules and regulations. From this perspective, notes economist Robert Frank, "society's norms are an important part of its capital, no less than its roads or factories" (1988:253, citing sociologist James Coleman).

Nonetheless, three questions arise: Do human societies consist essentially of collections of such normative rules and practices? Are norms the fundamental units of historical selection in cultural evolution? Do norms develop for the benefit of the group at the expense of the individual? To each question, I think the answer is no.

8.6. Nebulous Norms

There is no ready way of deciding what counts as a norm. There is no set of criteria for determining whether the chosen units or "chunks" of information actually cut up societies at their natural joints. Without definable operational units, little by way of cumulative scientific insight can be expected.

Norm selection accounts of cultural evolution are modeled primarily on molecular-genetic accounts of biological evolution. In biological evolution, the "definable units" of genetic selection may be fairly discrete traits, such as sex, or fairly continuous traits, such as height. Continuous traits, in turn, may be "blended," such as height and skin color. These evolve if there are high enough rates of mutation to maintain sufficient variation for selection to produce reliable differences in survival and production of organisms. Similarly, in cultural evolution, normative traits may be fairly discrete, such as literal representations of the Ten Commandments, or fairly continuous, such as ideological conviction. Continuous traits, in turn, may be blended, as with ideological conviction and socioeconomic status. Nevertheless, to be naturally selected, continuous and blended traits must survive transmission with reliably measurable frequency and fidelity to produce "selectable" differences in survival and productions of organisms (or ideas and behaviors).

The existence of particular combinations of blended traits at one time need not imply the further existence of those particular combinations at a later time. Consider color as an analogy. At one time red, yellow, and blue may be apparent, but the next round of combinations might produce green, orange, and brick. Still, one could appropriately talk of colors as heritable, blended traits. Similarly, past ideologies (e.g., communism, fascism, anarchism) may blend and evolve into new and different ideologies, although historians might well recognize a common heritage. From this standpoint, the cultural evolution of blended traits would be more akin to stellar evolution than to biological evolution. For, in stellar evolution, the state of things at a later time is predictable from the state of things at an earlier time, despite few if any features being fully shared at both times.

Even with all of these caveats, however, norms fail to qualify as causally operational units for selection. Individual minds seldom fully represent norms (at least as described by the anthropologist or political scientist) or consistently practice normative behavior. Norms typically involve collective representations and actions. But the actual, as opposed to ideal-typical, distributions of representations and behaviors that norms are supposed to summarize also lack coherent boundaries or cohesive structure.

For example, consider the following description of courtship "rules" among the Bontok of the northern Philippines: "The norm of youthful conduct could be stated thus. A boy cannot enter an *olag* [girl's house] in which there are immediate relatives such as his sister or step-sister. . . . Should he have a somewhat less close female relative, such as a first cousin, aunt, or niece, he may enter, but should 'hold back' instead of joining the fun. Such rules are the more effective in that boys and girls rarely have opportunities for close association outside the *olag*" (Keesing 1949:589; cf. Lawrence and Murdock 1949). Here, the supposed norm is that degree of kin relatedness determines the degree to which a Bontok boy refrains from partying in the girl's house. If he violates the norm, he is punished with disapproval that may (or may not) affect his future relationships. It is difficult to see what precise chunk of ideas or behaviors could possibly constitute a "unit of selection," in the sense of a trait that replicates, repeats, or persists with fairly high fidelity across individuals over time. Even the Arab "modesty code" described above, which is one of the most widely accepted normative descriptions in popular thought (in the Middle East and elsewhere) as well as in the anthropological and sociological literature, faces a similar objection.

Consider an abstract model of how social convergence could be fostered from normative displays that are essentially contentless. The model adopts an agent-based account of social influence grounded in the principle that communication is most effective between people who are already somewhat alike. In other words, the probability that a given cultural attribute will spread from one individual or group to another is a function of how many other attributes they have in common. Formal models of this sort demonstrate that similarity favors interaction, and interaction fosters even greater similarity without, however, generally leading to complete convergence. This is so for models that treat only one trait at a time (Boyd and Richerson 1985) or several traits simultaneously over time (Axelrod 1997).

Let's allow the model to be set up in accordance with some of the general views of norm theorists. Assume that each individual (or goup) is associated with a set of discrete cultural attributes represented by an N-tuple, where each attribute can have any number of different values (Arabic numerals). For example, one cultural attribute may be I = "political orientation" (0 = conservative, 1 = liberal, 3 = green, etc.) and another II = "social hair" (0 = skinhead, 1 = short military or business cut, 2 = long-hair expressions of social identity, and so forth; on "social hair," see Hallpike 1969). One individual (or group) can thus be described as a list of digits (e.g., [I]2, [II]1, etc.) and another individual as a different list (e.g., [I]1, [II]0, etc.).

Assume that every actor (individual or group) is randomly assigned a set of cultural attributes and each actor is associated with a particular site (e.g., a house in the village = a cell in a matrix) in a locale (e.g., the village = the matrix). The process of social influence can be represented in a series of repeated events, as follows: (a) activate a site at random and pick an adjacent site; (b) with probability equal to the number of values they share, let these two sites interact; (c) whenever two adjacent sites interact, select a random attribute on which the active site and its neighbor differ and change the neighboring site's value on this attribute to the active site's value on this attribute. In the lingo of "complexity theory," we can thus model cultural evolution as a random walk through a parameter space (Kauffman 1993).

Consider, as a simple example, only (male) individuals possessing two attributes (I = "political orientation" and II = "social hair"), each with two possible values (I: 0 = "conservative" or 1 = "liberal"; II: 0 = "short" or 1 = "long"). Thus, any given individual might be a short-haired conservative (00), a short-haired liberal (01), a long-haired conservative (10), or a long-haired liberal (11). Suppose there is a region, a street of houses, each with only one adjacent site (four houses in a row). Assume an initial random distibution of values among the four sites: 00, 01, 10, 11. Suppose the leftmost site is the one first activated (by a militant who is out to activate others). If a neighboring site already shares a value, then the neighbor will adopt the value of the activated site not initially shared. The following evolution should then occur: 00, 01, 10, 11 → 00, 00, 01, 11 → 00, 00, 00, 11, with no further change possible even if direction were reversed. Thus, most people on the block would wind up as short-haired conservatives, with a minority long-haired liberal, and no one else in between.

Suppose, however, that activation started with the rightmost site. Then the street culture could evolve differently: 00, 01, 10, 11 → 00, 00, 11, 11 → 00, 11, 11, 11, with no further change possible. The street would have a majority of long-haired liberals with a minority short-haired conservative. Different initial distributions of values would produce different results. For example, take the distribution 00, 01, 11, 00. If activated from the leftmost site, the street culture should evolve as follows: 00, 01, 11, 10 → 00, 00, 11, 11, and stop (deadlock). If activated from right to left, it might evolve differently: 00, 01, 10, 10 → 00, 00, 10, 10 → 00, 10, 10, 10 → 10, 10, 10, 10 (unanimity). Different patterns of activation also could yield different results for the same initial distributions (e.g., if first activated from the middle of the block), such as a plurality of long-haired conservatives (e.g., some Orthodox Jews, Moslems, and Hindus).

The point of this exercise is not to claim that such norm selection models are in any sense adequate accounts of cultural evolution. It is only to show that even if one accepts basic aspects of norm modeling, the norms modeled need not have the role in human thought and behavior that such accounts assume. In these examples, normative displays (e.g., haircut) have equal weight with primary ideas or behaviors (e.g., political orientation and activity, such as pro-life vs. pro-choice), as in the real-world Taliban case cited earlier. They equally drive cultural evolution. Still, they may have no propositional content or further direct behavioral implications in themselves, for example, the Hebrew "Here O Israel, the Lord Thy God, the Lord Is One"; the Catholic "Hail Mary Mother of God"; the Moslem "There Is No God but Allah and Mohammed Is His Prophet"; or Lowland Maya recitations of the *Chilam B'alam* (*Spokesman of the Jaguar*) and Highland Maya incantations of the Popul Vuh.

Such religious displays can serve to identify potentially kindred spirits (similar actors) and so spread other normative creeds and displays piggyback, as well as ideas and behaviors that have more concrete and direct functional value. Some displays may be so weighted, though, that they undermine basic tenets of influence models. For example, warring sides in the Balkans and Northern Ireland may be more similar to one another than to any other cultural groups, but difference in religious display may be so emotionally charged as to impede rather than promote convergence.

8.7. Group Selection in Biology: A Notational Variant of Inclusive Fitness

According to Sober and Wilson (1998:95), human societies are "superorganisms" in much the same way that bee hives are. Let's consider first the claims of group selection theory for biology in general, and then go on to explore some more specific claims for the value and role of norms in cultural evolution.

During the first part of the twentieth century, group selection was widely current in biology and anthropology. In biology, the earlier views of group selection culminated in Wynne-Edwards's (1962) claim that animals restrict their own reproduction so that the population will not outpace its food supply. He argued that selection must be operating on the whole population or species, even at the cost of individual fitness. In anthropology, similar arguments were offered to explain the readiness of individuals to sacrifice even their own lives for the good of their society (Service 1962; Fried 1967).

There was little attempt to describe any actual mechanisms for human group selection. Still, group selection seemed the only plausible alternative to pure self-interest and hedonism as the driving force of human affairs. It still does for many anthropologists today, some of whom continue to state the thesis rather than empirically attempt to show it (Kuper 1996; Rappaport 1999). To oppose biological theories of individual fitness and apparently similar theories of economic self-interest was also to reject the egocentric and ethnocentric biases of early twentieth-century theories of human and social evolution. For the most part, these theories were racist and elitist in their association with eugenics, fascism, and colonial capitalism.

In biology, opinion shifted decidely against group selection after publication of Hamilton's (1964) theory of altruism in terms of "inclusive fitness." The sacrifice of an organism for its relatives—a mother for her children, a brother for his siblings, an ant for its colony, a bee for its hive—lowers an organism's individual fitness (also called "classical" or "Darwinian" fitness) because it compromises the individual's ability to bear and raise offspring. Nevertheless, such kin altruism may also enhance the individual's inclusive fitness by allowing surviving relatives to pass on many of the individual's genes to future generations.

According to Hamilton's principle of kin selection, altruists should benefit the fitness of each of their fellow group members by a value b, at a cost to themselves c, depending on a member's degree of biological relatedness R; that is, $b > Rc$. When an individual's sacrifice benefits genetic relatives and thereby increases the total of its genes returned to the population's gene pool, then self-denial is more apparent than real. The individual organism is used as a propagating or facilitating vehicle, or "interactor" (Hull 1988), and then discarded by its selfish, immortality-seeking genes (Dawkins 1976).

The "new" group selection theory, also called "multilevel selection theory," dates from D. S. Wilson's (1975) "trait group" model. Populations divide into trait groups. Within trait groups, individuals vary in degree from pure selfishness to pure altruism. Whenever altruists are reliably able to associate with other altruists and to avoid associating with nonaltruists, then altruism can evolve in the population. There is no argument between inclusive fitness theorists and group selection theorists that (1) the initial structure of a population, and the distribution of traits within it, affect the way the structure of the population and the distribution of traits will evolve, and (2) altruistic behavior can evolve under certain initial conditions (Maynard-Smith 1998).

Multilevel selection models simply, though at times nontrivially, provide an alternative perspective on the same selective processes described by "gene's-eye" models (G. Williams 1992). Whenever sufficiently detailed for formalized treatment, group selection models can be mathematically represented in terms of inclusive fitness models, and vice versa. In other words, they are *notational equivalents*, much as the mathematical product G(i+j) is equivalent to iG + jG, where G may be called the group component, and i and j called individual components. It suffices to know that multiplication is distributive relative to addition.

Thus, let E(x) be ego's production of offspring and A(x) be an associate's production of offspring. According to Hamilton, selection will act on x to maximize the inclusive fitness quantity: *R*eE(x) + *R*aA(x), where *R*e is ego's relatedness to its own offspring and *R*a is ego's relatedness to its associate's offspring. Then, "kin altruism" occurs to the extent that ReE(x) decreases relative to *R*aA(x).

A group selection variant of this quantity is as follows: let E(x) be the fraction of the association's total offspring produced by ego, F(x), times the group's total production, G(x), and let A(x) be the associate's fraction of the group's product, 1−F(x), times the group's total, G(x), such that: *R*eE(x) + *R*aA(x) = *R*eF(x)G(x) + *R*a[1−F(x)]G(x) = G(x)[*R*a + (*R*e − *R*a) F(x)] = G(x) *R*eF(x) whenever *R*a = 0 (i.e., whenever the associate is a nonrelative). Then, "group altruism" occurs when behavior increases group production G(x) while decreasing the selfish component *R*eF(x), and a group-level advantage accrues to the degree that G(x) is maximized. The only difference between inclusive fitness theory and group selection theory is that the former takes kin altruism as the paradigm view of altruism and the latter takes group altruism as the paradigm view of altruism. And that's really all there is to it, at least in biology (see Reeve 2000).

8.8. Case Studies of Human Group Selection? Hardly

One purported example of human group selection is D. S. Wilson's (1998) reanalysis of the "tolerated-theft model" in hunter-gatherer societies. That model, best articulated by Blurton Jones (1984, 1987), maintains that hunters share game with members of their group because it would be more costly for them not to share for two reasons. First, starving scroungers are more apt to struggle for a share of meat than successful and satisfied hunters are willing to fight against sharing. Second, there are indirect social and economic perks to sharing that offset and surpass individual costs of sharing, such as "successful nice guy" reputations that lead to higher social status, access to a wider range of sexual partners, and ready assistance from others in times of need (cf. Hill and Kaplan 1993).

In Wilson's account, however, individuals who share may never be fully compensated for their outlay within their own group. Selection within the group would favor the scrounger, but selection between groups would favor the hunter.

Groups containing cooperators would outcompete groups consisting exclusively of selfish noncooperators within a larger metapopulation. The relative fitness of hunters will be greater in the metapopulation although lower within any group that contains both scroungers and hunters.

Thus, selection within groups seems insensitive to group welfare. In fact, inclusive fitness theory indicates that group welfare and individual fitness are intimately related: if the individual cost of cooperating within a group is less than the absolute benefit of being a group member, then individual cooperators who sacrifice self-interest can still profit more in the long run from the advantages of group membership than if they were miserly pariahs. If cooperators are aware of the social rewards of sharing or punishments for not sharing, then these incentives figure in an individual's overall calculations of "self-interest."

D. S. Wilson responds that social incentives are themselves group-selected norms that operate more for the benefit of the group as a whole than for the individuals who must follow them willy nilly: "[C]omparing human groups to beehives and single [super]organisms . . . appears more reasonable on the basis of social control mechanisms" (1998:93). If sharing is performed voluntarily in accordance with social incentives but at individual cost, then the person who shares is an altruist. A society with at least some true altruists will have an advantage in organic solidarity over rival societies because more can be achieved by pooling together than acting alone or divided.

Much seems to hinge on the notion of "voluntary" self-sacrifice. One problem is that rewards and punishments may be implicit and distant and their inclusion into any "voluntary" act of game sharing may not be readily apparent (Kaplan and Hill 1985; Hawkes, O'Connell, and Rogers 1997). R. Frank (1988) argues that the seemingly uncontrollable emotion that underscores some commitments, such as romantic love and religious passion, may actually be a naturally selected response to distant rewards. By making apparently irrational commitments here and now in the sacrifice of immediate self-interest (getting more mates, doing productive work) one involuntarily convinces oneself and thus others of sincerity. This, in turn, promotes long-term reciprocity and future aid when one is most likely to be in need.

Another problem concerns normative descriptions themselves, which may be a product of how anthropologists interview informants. As any fieldworker knows, interviews often place informants on their best behavior (Freeman 1983). This "leads them to present a normative account. Such accounts are often neat and tidy and can mesh with romanticized views about their ways of life, thus reinforcing them, as in the case of game-sharing rules and the collective appropriation of nature" (Peterson 1993:870). For example, although anthropologists stress that aboriginal hunter-gatherers themselves emphasize generosity, "observation and ethnographic evidence suggest that much giving and sharing is in response to direct verbal and/or nonverbal demands" (860). *If generosity is voluntary, then why does it have to be so often and energetically solicited against seemingly contrary stinginess?* In brief, apparent cases of voluntary self-sacrifice may prove on deeper analysis to be more subtle or nonconscious involuntary responses to individual needs.

Another example of the alleged importance of group-selected traits comes from a variation on the "garden experiment" in biology. When members of a species have different phenotypes in different environments, samples are taken from both environments and replanted in only one environment. If the differences still exist, they are probably genetic (two genotypes); if not, they are probably environmental (one genotype producing two phenotypes). Similarly, "the best evidence for the importance of culturally transmitted norms on behavior is data which show that groups of people who have different cultural histories behave differently in the same environment" (Boyd and Richerson in press).

Boyd and Richerson (in press) and Sober and Wilson (1998) cite Ray Kelly's (1985) analysis of the Nuer and Dinka of Sudan. Kelly's study is an insightful reevaluation of Evans-Pritchard's (1940) classic monograph *The Nuer*, which was organized according to the standard functionalist view of social structure current at the time. The colonial government of the Anglo-Egyptian Sudan had commissioned Evans-Pritchard to undertake a study of "the chief values of the Nuer" to provide "a true outline of their social structure" (Evans-Pritchard 1940:7,15).

Evans-Pritchard represented Nuer society as a segmented system of patrilineages that could become organized into a hierarchy of levels (single village, tribal segment, whole tribe) as a function of the scale of outside threats. The segmentary lineage system also enabled the Nuer to fuse their patrilineal segments into larger groups that were able to conquer smaller groups, such as the neighboring Dinka. R. Kelly (1985) argues that the value placed by the Nuer on a high bride price in terms of livestock, together with rules of patrilineal reckoning, provided a competitive advantage over the Dinka. The Dinka didn't have a segmentary lineage system reinforced by high bride price. They could coalesce only in small groups because they had fixed residences in the wet season and because they distributed goods and obligations bilaterally, among both patrilateral and matrilateral relatives.

Somewhat similar arguments concern the ability of Arab tribes to fission and fuse along segmentary patrilineal lines as ecological, economic, and political conditions warranted and, historically, to conquer their neighbors and embark on vast campaigns of conquest (Murphy and Kasdan 1959; Atran 1985a). The Arab case differs in that high bride price is preferentially waived in favor of patrilateral endogamy (preference for marriage with father's brother's daughter), with higher bride prices established as a function of the genealogical distance between marriage partners (reckoned patrilineally). As with the Nuer, the application of normative preferences in Arab kinship and marriage arguably allowed the various Arab tribes to constitute an effective social organization at the level of larger groups, and thus to outcompete rival tribes who did not have the normative machinery that promoted larger unification. (The same segmentary tendencies, however, would also permit social fission and extreme political division during internecine conflict.) Because rivals share the same ecology, mode of subsistence, and warfare technology, differential success likely owes to different normative systems of social organization, such as shallow genealogical reckoning and bilateral marriage ties versus extensive (patrilineal) genealogical reckoning and preferentially related forms of marriage and bride price.

These are useful and informative summaries of normative ideas and behaviors, although the actual mechanics of alliance formation and segmentation are decidedly more nuanced and complicated (Cuisenier 1975; Atran 1985b). Peters

(1960, 1967), in his detailed studies of lineage segmentation and feuding patterns among the Beduoin of Cyrenaica (Libya), points out that the so-called segmentary lineage system is much more rigidly "normative" in the anthropological literature than among the natives themselves. This is because colonial governments encouraged normative descriptions of tribal customs for administrative purposes of political control. When the natives failed to conform to these norms (e.g., in neatly segmenting and delimiting tribal territories) they were directly or indirectly made to do so by colonial authorities. The result was something of a self-fulfilling prophecy: colonial anthropologists and administrators helped to impose the normative behavior that they meant to describe.

In such cases, claims of group "fitness" based on differential selection of "heritable" norms are highly dubious. Not all the normative descriptions of social structure cited by group selectionists come from colonial accounts or the HRAF. But their summary and sometimes tendentious aspect is much the same. For example, Boehm's (1993:27) study of "egalitarian society" cites claims by French Marxist anthropologist Maurice Godelier (1986[1982]) for the Baruya of New Guinea, where "differences between individuals are only permitted . . . insofar as they work for the common good." This may be true, but we have basically only Godelier's say-so to go on.

8.9. Cultural Epidemiology: A Garden Experiment in the Maya Lowlands

There is little or no detail available in typically normative accounts of social structure anywhere (and none that I am aware of in the HRAF) that would allow evaluation of patterns of individual variation, agreement, and disagreement within and between groups. Without such detail, normative claims are difficult to verify or falsify. The overarching reason is simple: anthropologists are typically instructed to go out into the field alone for some months or, in exceptional cases, some few years and bring back a description of the society studied. The popular image of the anthropologist with a pith helmet and notebook is not very far off the mark, only now the pith helmet is a baseball cap or canvas fedora and the notebook is a PC. In this situation, there is little alternative to normative description (or the "narratives" of antipositivist postmodernists).

Detailed analyses of the relations among ecology, technology, social networks, and so forth require large interdisciplinary efforts, over many field seasons, at a cost that usually exceeds typical ethnographic fieldwork by one or several orders of magnitude. The pertinent academic and government funding institutions are not set up for this kind of project, and so the effort is rarely made. I have been fortunate to be a part of one such effort that involves the sort of critical "garden experiment" of the Nuer-Dinka type that group selectionists call for. In what follows, I report on studies that isolate the influence of certain sociocultural factors (social networks, cognitive models) from environmental management and maintenance.

Our research team assessed folkecological mental models and behaviors with respect to interactions among rainforest species among three linguistically distinct groups exploiting the same habitat in the Municipality of San José, in Guatemala's

Department of El Petén: native Lowland Maya (Itza'), immigrant Maya from the neighboring Highlands (Q'eqchi'), and immigrant Spanish-speaking Ladinos (mixed European and Amerindian descent; Atran et al. 1999). There were no reliable between-group differences in regard to sources and level of income, family and population size, or ability to recognize local species. Our studies employed multiple measures, including (1) biodiversity, biomass, and soil composition among different types of forest holdings for each informant; (2) mental models of plant-animal-human ecological relationships, and (3) statistical relationships between 1 and 2.

Only the area's last native Itza' Maya (who have few cooperative institutions) show systematic awareness of ecological complexity involving animals, plants, and people and practices clearly favoring forest regeneration. Spanish-speaking immigrants prove closer to native Maya in thought, action, and social networking than do immigrant Q'eqchi' Maya (who have highly cooperative institutions). For example, given the results from our sample plots, Q'eqchi' destroy more than five times as much forest, but Ladinos less than twice as much, as Itza' (Atran et al. 2002).

In this context, Itza' appear to behave "irrationally" insofar as their restraint subsidizes another group's profligacy: the more cooperators produce for free riders, the more the free-riding population is able to expand and lay waste (Axelrod and Hamilton 1981). But within the more localized municipal context, Itza' seem ecologically rational insofar as their behavior is "attracting" another group (the Ladinos) toward effective cooperation and sustainability. Factor-analytic assessments of mental models show that cognitive preferences strongly reflect, and reliably predict, behavior regularities (Atran et al. 1999).[3] Notice that these findings call into question an operating principle of agent-based normative models (Axelrod 1997), namely, that societies that don't share normative values (e.g., Itza' and Ladinos) are less likely to interact and converge than societies that do (e.g., Itza' and Q'eqchi').

Social network analysis bears out the close relationship in mental models and behaviors between Itza' and Ladinos. For each community we began with six men and six women not immediately related by kinship or marriage. Each informant was asked to name, in order of priority, the seven people outside of the household "most important for your life." Informants were asked in what ways the people named in this *social network* were important for their lives. Some days later each informant was asked to name, in order of priority, the seven people "to whom you would go if there were something that you do not understand and want to find out about the forest." Informants were asked about the kind of information they would seek in these *expert networks*.

After performing these tasks with our initial group of informants, we used a "snowball method" to extend these ego-centered networks to the wider context of patterned social communication in which they operate. Social interaction and expert networks were elicited from the first and last persons named in the social network. The three populations markedly differ in their social and expert network structures, with different consequences for the flow of information about the forest.

The Q'eqchi' show a dense, highly interconnected social network, with no dominant individual or subgroup. This redundant social structure favors communal and ceremonial institutions that organize accountability and that are manifestly richer among Q'eqchi' than among Itza' or Ladinos. Only Q'eqchi' practice agroforestry in corporate groups: neighbors and kin clear and burn each household's plot, kin groups seed together, and the community sanctions unwarranted access to family stands of copal trees (*Protium copal*), whose resin is ritually burned to ensure the harvest. This implies that institutional monitoring of access to resources, cooperating kin, commensal obligations, a vibrant indigenous language, and knowledge of the land (including recognition of important species) may not suffice to avoid ruin of common pool resources.

For the immigrant Q'eqchi', continued corporate and ceremonial ties to the sacred mountain valleys of the Q'eqchi' Highlands do not carry corresponding respect for Lowland ecology. A relatively closed corporate structure that channels information focused on internal needs and distant places may function to impede access to ecological information relevant to commons survival. The Q'eqchi' expert networks suggest that information pertinent to long-term survival of the forest comes from outside organizations with little long-term experience in Petén. What outside information there is seems unlikely to penetrate deeply into the Q'eqchi' community because it is not conveyed by socially relevant actors.

For the Itza', in no case could we discern a statistical relationship between knowledge agreement among any subgroup of informants and their social or expert network proximity. In line with this result, Itza' acknowledge consulting their experts on difficult problems about the forest, but mostly claim to acquire the knowledge elicited in our tasks by "walking alone" in the forest they call "the Maya House." For Itza', diffusely interconnected social and expert networks suggest multiple social pathways for individuals to gain, and for the community to assimilate and store, information about the forest. Cultural stories, values, and the like bias the interpretation of experience in different ways; for example, a bird or monkey eating fruit is observed as transparently harmful by Q'eqchi' and Ladinos but can be inferred by Itza' to be helpful. Although culturally channeled in this way, Itza' knowledge of specific plant-animal interactions appears to be acquired through individual experience and exploration.

Statistical analyses of response patterns show that Ladinos have a distributive network of folkecological beliefs that is clearly parasitic on the Itza' network. Whereas Itza' observe the forest for what is important, Ladinos also observe the Itza' for what is important.[4] Over time, socially well-connected male Ladinos converge toward the consensus of Itza' experts. For example, we found that judgments of hundreds of plant-animal interactions by the Ladino most highly rated as an expert by other Ladinos composed a *proper subset* of the pairwise judgments made by the Itza' who was most highly rated by the top Ladino himself and by the other Itza' (Atran et al. 2002). It is highly improbable that Ladinos who approximate Itza' response patterns actually observe and copy Itza' dealings with the hundreds of species relationships in question. Rather, individual Ladinos seem to project fragmentary observations of Itza' behavior to a richly textured cognitive model of folkecology *by inference*. Consider the following.

In line with evolutionary models of prosocial learning, let's assume that people, when in doubt or ignorance about some domain of activity vital to everyday life, will look to emulate those with knowledge (Boyd and Richerson 1985; Lansing and

Kremer 1993; Henrich and Boyd 1998). Also assume that they don't have direct access to the deep knowledge they wish to emulate, but only to surface signs or "markers" of that knowledge (much as people who wish to be like a famous academician, powerful politician, or celebrity adopt that person's outward trappings in the hope that these will help guide them to success). One reasonable strategy is to first look for knowledge from those to whom deference (respect) is shown by others (Henrich and Gil-White 2001). In many small-scale societies, knowledge bearers tend to be elders, political leaders, and economically well-off.

In the Itza' case, forest experts are expert in a variety of relevant domains (birds, mammals, trees, soils), elder males, and former political town leaders. Ladinos express doubt about their own forest knowledge and also express a desire to acquire knowledge from Itza'. Apparently, the most respected and socially well-connected Ladinos attend to those Itza' to whom other Itza' defer; these Ladinos, in turn, become subjects of emulation and sources of knowledge for other Ladinos. But how do Ladinos obtain relevant knowledge without initially knowing how it's relevant? Besides patterns of deference, which carry no knowledge content, precisely how and what do Ladinos learn?

The evidence indicates that neither Ladino experts nor the wider Itza' or Ladino populations are learning norms about the forest from Itza' experts or from imitating one another. Itza' express no content-specific normative or prototypical attitudes to the forest other than to "care for the forest as it cares for us." Even the notion of "reciprocity" that we invoke to describe Itza' patterns is only a gloss for statistically consensual patterns of thought and behavior, with considerable variation in content. Ladinos may be acquiring knowledge in part through different isolated examples that trigger preexisting inferential structures to generate convergent patterns, and in part through stories and other evocative conduits.

Thus, a Ladino may observe or hear about a specific exemplar of ecological knowledge from a respected Itza' (perhaps embedded in a tale), such as observing that Itza' elders look for fallen ramon fruits after spider monkeys have passed through trees. Itza' pick up the fruits that aren't chewed through and leave the rest, knowing also that half-chewed fruits are even more likely than unchewed fruits to generate new ramon stands. From such Itza' behavior, a Ladino observer may readily deduce that (1) ramon is desired and useful for people, and (2) spider monkeys can negatively affect ramon seeds. But Ladinos don't generally learn that (3) spider monkeys can also positively affect ramon seeds and so help both the forest and people in it. Although Ladino observers seem to lack the Itza' cultural bias of conceiving species relationships reciprocally, they still spontaneously induce much more from a single instance of experience than simply (1) and (2).

On this account, patterns of generalization may be directly predictable from the Ladino-Itza' correspondence of taxonomic and ecological groupings. For example, we should expect Ladinos to generalize their observations along much the same lines as Itza' do when Itza' and Ladino taxonomies coincide. In the above scenario, Ladinos should "automatically" infer that howler monkeys and kinkajous similarly affect ramon because Ladinos, like Itza', recognize both folk species as belonging to the same intermediate folk taxon as the spider monkey (see Lopez et al. 1997). Further correspondences are predictable from the similarity between the two groups' appreciation of ecological associations. For both groups, the ramon tree and the chicle tree have very similar ecological profiles. Accordingly, both groups should readily generalize relations from, say, spider monkeys and ramon trees to kinkajous and chicle trees. (Q'eqchi' are not looking to Itza' for ecologically relevant content and so cannot generalize.) An analysis of response patterns indicates that this is the case.

Another constraint on inductive inference is the interpretation of the base event itself. If a Ladino observer lacks a cultural propensity for conceiving of species relationships reciprocally, then he will neither learn that spider monkeys help ramon trees nor infer that kinkajous help chicle trees. In short, individual Ladinos project fragmentary observations of Itza' behavior to a richly textured cognitive model of folkecology by inference and evocation from background knowledge and story structures rather than through imitation or invocation of norms.

Social learning arguably involves inferential processes that are mobilized according to several factors: (1) domain-specific cognitive devices (e.g., taxonomy for biological kinds),[5] (2) prior cultural sensitivity to certain kinds of knowledge (e.g., species reciprocity in ecological relationships), (3) awareness of lack of knowledge and the motivation to acquire it (doubt), (4) selective attention (e.g., Ladino focus on the patterns of deference to and the behavior of Itza' elders, vs. Itza' deference and attention to the forest itself), and (5) preexisting values (weighted preferences) with respect to a given cognitive domain (e.g., overvaluing economic utility relative to other determiners of interest, like sacredness or role in the economy of nature; see section 8.10). Here the culturally specific learning landscape (3–5) further constrains the canalization process of our specieswide evolutionary landscape (1). Much as rain falling anywhere in a mountain valley tends to converge into the same natural river basin and be further channeled through the gates of a dam constructed there, so each person's knowledge converges toward the same cultural basin of thought and action.

This "learning landscape" shapes the way inferences are generalized from particular instances (experiences, observations, exemplars). It channels the information acquired toward convergence with a general body of knowledge (an emergent structural pattern that achieves a statistical consensus in a population). It produces convergence toward the emergent consensus even though specific inputs vary widely in richness and content (just as many different people, observing many different exemplars of *dog* under varying conditions of exposure to those exemplars, all still generate more or less the same general concept of *dog*).

Other learning factors may be involved in channeling and transmitting knowledge, including normative prototypes and narratives, but not in exclusive or straightforward ways. Thus, Ladino protoypes and stories of Itza' experts as forest wizards may share little actual content with the normative pronouncements and narratives of the Itza' themselves. Moreover, Itza' disavow teaching the Ladinos anything about the forest. How, then, might Ladinos eventually attain Itza'-like "spiritual" awareness? The line of reasoning that follows is frankly speculative and anecdotal, but one that should motivate further research.

Seeking to interview the two most cited Itza' experts, we found that both had gone on that particular day to the Ladino town of La Nueva. When they returned we asked them in separate interviews if they ever teach anything about the forest to the Ladinos; both denied doing so. Then, we asked why they had gone to La Nueva and what they did there. One said that he had gone because there were no lemons to be found in San José but he knew of some in La Nueva. He said that he had stayed so long in La Nueva after finding the lemons because he was trying to figure out with people there how it would be best to plant lemon trees. The other Itza' said that he had gone from our field station to visit his daughter, who is married to the son of the most cited Ladino expert. There he stayed telling stories of the screeching barn owl (*ajxooch'* = *Tyto alba*) whose call augurs the death of strangers; people familiar with it cannot die from it. The Ladinos listened to every detail with obvious fascination.

A final anecdote concerns the sounds of the forest. This sensibility is not one merely of perception but of affective value. For example, Itza' give the short-billed pigeon (*Columba nigrirostris*) the onomatopoeic name *ixku'uktz'u'uyeen*. Itza' decompose this low, mournful sound into meaningful constituents, interpreted as follows. Pigeon was frightened of Jaguar's coming. Squirrel saw this and told Pigeon to leave her young with Squirrel for protection. Pigeon came back to find that Squirrel had eaten her young and that's why, as long as there is forest, one will hear Pigeon lament that "Squirrel (*ku'uk*) tricked (*tz'u'uy* = entangle) me (*een*)." But when we ask identifications from Ladinos, we are sometimes told that this bird's name, Uaxactun-Uaxactun, signifies a lament for the ancient Maya spirits of Uaxactun and that's why "Itza" named it like that. Unlike Tikal, these Classical Maya ruins were given the name Uaxactun (*waxaktun* = "eight stone") early last century by an American archaeologist, Sylvanus Morley. Thus, it is hardly likely that an Itza' elder would ever describe the pigeon's sound as these Ladinos think the Itza' do. Such misinterpretation, then, seems to reflect a sense of what a native Maya should attend to in the forest.

By and large, Ladino knowledge is a subclass of Itza' knowledge that underrepresents the ecological complexity and spiritual integrity of Itza' knowledge. To be sure, the Ladinos use their own taxonomic and ecological knowledge of the forest to generalize their inferences from Itza' behavior, but they do not appear to have learned yet how "to walk alone in the forest," as Itza' do, nor to effectively map spiritual values onto ecological relationships. Nevertheless, from studies of other Ladino communities in Petén, it seems that some "Petenero" Ladino communities have learned to think and act much as Itza' do after three or four generations of the kind of contact described between our Itza' and Ladino samples (N. Schwartz 1990). This may well involve assimilating "spiritual values" of an Itza' kind.

8.10. The Spirit of the Commons

> Upixan-oo' kinukuch ch'ib'al kuxlajoo' taanil ti diyoos.
> (The spirits of our great lineage [ancestors] lived before God.)
> —Yun Domingo Chayax Suntecun,
> Itza' Maya elder (1993)

Anthropologists and sociologists target norms as functional building blocks of cultures and societies. Economists and political scientists see norms as institutional means to solving public goods problems, such as "the Tragedy of the Commons" (Hardin 1968; Fukuyama 1995). The general idea is that to solve problems of rational choice inherent in balancing individual with collective needs, individuals must be made to forsake a measure of self-interest and to sacrifice resources in accordance with institutional norms that function to maintain the public good(s).

The Tragedy of the Commons and other similar social dilemmas are variants of a basic problem in decision theory and game theory known as "the Prisoner's Dilemma." Consider a group of *n* persons who share a common territory of fixed size on which they hunt animals. Each hunter has one of two choices: he can cooperate with others by not overhunting the commons, or he can hunt in a way advantageous to him but that ultimately results in overuse and destruction of the common resource. The second option appears more rational in the short term. This is because the short-term advantage to one who overhunts (e.g., 1) always outweighs the short-term disadvantage to him when that disadvantage is equally distributed among the other hunters ($1/n$). If all cooperate, the commons is preserved. But if the rationale of self-interest pervades the camp, no one will be motivated to cooperate and all will defect.

Field and laboratory studies indicate that individual calculations of rational self-interest collectively lead to a breakdown of a society's common resource base unless institutional or other normative mechanisms are established to restrict access to cooperators (Berkes et al. 1989; Atran 1986). This is so even when people's "basic needs" are satisfied, no matter how small the group or how informed of the looming tragedy (White 1994; but see Ostrom 1998 on strangers cooperating, at least for low-cost items). Yet, evidence from our garden experiment neither indicates the primacy of norms in explaining cultural differences in regard to the Tragedy of the Commons, nor does it indicate that institutional mechanisms are exclusive or primary means for preserving common resources.

One puzzle that our findings present for rational theories of utility and decision making is this: How do people sustainably manage limited resources without apparent institutional or other obvious normative constraints to encourage and monitor cooperation? Theories of rational action predict that increases in the number of noncooperative players in the environment and their apparent disregard for the future should lead even native cooperators to abandon long-term interest for short-term gain, unless institutional restraints can compel individual action toward the common good. Yet, native Itza' Maya, who have few cooperative institutions, show awareness of ecological complexity and reciprocity among animals, plants, and people, whereas immigrant Q'eqchi' Maya, who have highly cooperative institutions, acknowledge few ecological dependencies. No doubt economic rationality and institutional constraints are important factors in determining and describing actions on common pool resources, but they may not suffice. There also appears to be an important cognitive dimension to behavioral research on how people learn to manage environmental resources.[6]

One tentative line of reasoning is that Itza', and perhaps other native peoples with a long history of ecological maintenance, might not treat resources as traditional decision and game theory suggests, that is, as objects of a payoff matrix (extensional items substitutable along some metric, such as one that assigns monetary value to every object). Instead, some people may treat resources, such as species, as intentional, relational entities that are subjectively defined, like friends or enemies (cf. Rappaport 1979; Posey 1983).

To explore this idea, we asked people from each of the three Petén groups to rank-order 21 plant species in terms of their importance according to (1) members of their own community, (2) and (3) members of each of the other two communities, (4) God, and (5) the forest spirits. Only Itza' see the forest spirits as actively protecting the forest: Itza' rankings from the point of view of the forest spirits are significantly related to Itza' models of human impact as well as ecological centrality. For example, multiple regressions show that Itza' consensus on spirits together with the overall Itza' consensus on combined use (wood + shelter + cash) account for most of the variance in human impact, with spirits and use equally weighted predictors.

The most reliable combination of predictors for what (Itza' believe) the spirits think about a species is its ecological centrality (measured by number of recognized relations of a given species with other species) and what (Itza' believe) God thinks about it. Ladinos and Q'eqchi' state belief in forest spirits, and Ladinos even provide normative and narrative accounts of spirit life similar to those of Itza'. Moreover, Ladino beliefs about God's preferences and Itza' preferences are nearly identical. Yet, among Q'eqchi' and Ladinos belief in spirits and God is not reliably linked to forestry practice.[7] Itza' rankings of God's preferences are related to the measure of combined use, but ecological centrality is not. Recall (section 3.7) that our other studies indicate that Lowland Maya consider forest spirits and God to be intentional beings that are superior to people in their ability to avoid deception (N. Knight et al. 2001).

To date, rational-decision and game-theoretic accounts involving human use of nonhuman resources have not considered the possibility of resources (e.g., species) and humans both as "players" in the same game. Prima facie, such consideration is not plausible, because species are assumed not to have motives, desires, beliefs, or strategies for cooperation or deception that would be sensitive, and systematically responsive, to corresponding aspects of human intention. Nevertheless, both in increasingly globally oriented ecological movements in the industrial world and in religious practices of small-scale societies there are public pronouncements of respect for species. Indeed, one claim for "animistic" and "anthropomorphic" interpretations of species in many small-scale societies is that the "intention gap" between humans and species is thus bridged (at least to human satisfaction) with outcomes mutually beneficial to the survival of species and of the human groups that live off of those species (cf. Ingold 1996; Bird-David 1999).

From a long-term cultural vantage spirit preferences may represent a summary history of sustained human-species interactions over many generations. When asked, Itza' men and women express the belief that they will be punished if they violate spirit preferences, although women are less clear about what such preferences are likely to be. Especially for men, the spirits are intermediaries or "spokesmen" for the forest species, although there is wide individual variation in response to what the spirits say about any given species. This has intriguing implications for ecological decision and game theory in that individual Itza' may be basing cognitive and behavioral strategies for sustaining the forest more by playing a game with spirits than by playing a game with other people (on the wider role of spirits in Itza' life and religion, see Atran 2001a).

Note that evolution itself provides mechanisms for interactive "games" that at least implicitly commensurate the incommensurable, for example, the interacting "strategies" of bacteria and their hosts. Human minds may further explicitly commensurate apparently incommensurable entities, such as people and plants, by semantically modeling their biological and mechanical interactions as an intentional game, mediated and refereed by supernatural agents. In this way, spiritual values may be ascribed to people's interactions with nature, which reduce or refine evolutionary pressures to deal exclusively with the environment on the basis of short-term self-interest. Protecting some interactions with nature as sacred and rendering some forms of exploitation and exchange taboo (Fiske and Tetlock 1997; Medin et al. 1999) may be a path that humans gravitate toward in their collective efforts to sustain life in culturally familiar, long-term ways.

In sum, our valuation studies suggest that cognition of supernatural agents may serve not only to guarantee trust and foster cooperation between nonkin, as standard commitment theories assume (R. Frank 1988; Irons 1996a,b), but also to foster human interaction with nonhuman resources in relations of "indirect reciprocity" (Alexander 1987). Society as a whole arguably benefits: Itza' agroforestry practice has endured conquest and competition for centuries, if not millennia (Atran 1993; Atran and Ucan Ek' 1999). But so, too, do the individuals who most sacrifice: they are respected, consulted, socially connected, and politically supported (the most cited Itza' experts also have been elected political leaders). Nevertheless, there is a clear absence of high-fidelity norms with heritable variation (consensus among Itza' on spirit preferences accounts for only 50 percent of the variance in response patterns). Consequently, there can be no selection of norms in any definite sense for either individual or group benefit.

8.11. Belief Systems as Group Evolutionary Strategies? Don't Believe It

> And thou shalt not glean thy vineyard, neither shalt thou gather every grape of thy vineyard; thou shalt leave them for the poor and the stranger. . . . Ye shall not steal, neither deal falsely, neither lie with one another. . . . Thou shalt not go up and down as a talebearer among thy people: neither shalt thou stand against the blood of thy neighbour. . . . Thou shalt not hate thy brother in thine heart: thou shalt not in any wise rebuke thy neighbour, and not suffer sin upon him. Thou shalt not avenge, nor bear any grudge against the children of thy people but thou shalt love thy neighbour as thyself.
>
> —Leviticus 19:10–18

> When thou comest nigh into a city to fight against it, then proclaim peace unto it. . . . [if] it make thee the answer of peace, and open up unto thee, then it shall be, that all the people that is found therein shall be tributaries unto thee, and they shall serve thee. And if they

> will make no peace with thee . . . thou shalt smite every male thereof. . . . But the women, and the little ones, and the cattle, and all that is in the city . . . shalt thou take unto thyself. . . . Thus shalt thou do unto all the cities which are very far from thee. . . . But of the cities of these people, which the Lord thy God doth give thee for an inheritance, though shalt save alive nothing that breatheth: But thou shalt utterly destroy them; namely, the Hittites, the Canaanites, and the Perizzites, the Hivites, and the Jebusites. . . . that they may not teach you not to do after all their abominations, which they have done unto their gods; so should ye sin against the Lord your God.
>
> —Deuteronomy 20:10–18

In *Darwin's Cathedral,* David Sloan Wilson (2002) more closely examines religion as a blueprint for the construction of a community superorganism by interpreting literature pertaining to a few select cases. In his account, Balinese water temples, Calvin's principles and practices, Judaic brotherhood, Early Christian altruism, and most other examples of religious doctrine and ritual are normative pronouncements and displays that serve to define in-group morality. In fact, the key evolutionary "design feature" of religion is the use of norms as "isolating mechanisms" (see also Gil-White 2001). For example, Jewish circumcision rites (*brit*), food taboos (*kashrut*), and other costly displays "force group members to demonstrate their commitment." The Ten Commandments and other religious rules "regulate the behavior of group members in minute detail." And the enforcing "penalties specified by Jewish law for violating these norms were sometimes so extreme that they put Calvinism to shame" (Wilson 2001 website draft of ch. 4, www.santafe.edu/files/workshops/bowles).

According to Wilson, inclusive fitness theories that ignore group selection utterly fail to explain the moral foundations of group life: "Within-group selection by itself creates a world without morality in which individuals merely use each other to maximize their relative fitness" (Ch. 4). By normatively defining in-group morality, religions almost automatically cast out groups—that is, potential competitors—as not moral. If the out-group is a known and near competitor, it is often explicitly condemned as immoral. If the out-group is relatively unknown and far off, it is implicitly amoral. For example, the Old Testament God of the Israelites required His chosen people to love one another as themselves, to subjugate far-off cities obedient to unknown deities, and to annihilate all groups worshipping false gods in the lands where Israelites sought to dwell (Leviticus 19:10–18; Deuteronomy 20:10–18).

As among Jews over the past two millennia or so, a self-reinforcing interactional bias fostered in-group convergence and cooperation. At the same time, this cognitive bias reduced the risk, energy, and time involved in discriminating and interacting with out-groups that would more likely contain potential enemies. By sanctifying and steadfastedly implementing an "Us versus Them" strategy, Jews survived over time as a group but also continually generated hostility from other groups. Moreover, by practicing fairly strict and close endogamy (e.g., first-cousin marriage) and selective breeding (e.g., based on religious reputation and scholarly intelligence), Jews evolved a particularly effective group-enhancement strategy:

"Human groups whose members are both genetically related and unified by a moral system should be very cooperative indeed. . . . The many mechanisms employed by religions to encourage brotherhood within groups could build upon a foundation of real brotherhood in the case of Judaism" (Wilson 2001: ch. 4). From this "group evolutionary perspective," major Western anti-Semitic movements are fundamentally collectivist responses to real conflicts of interests with Jews, no matter how many self-deceptions and false beliefs may also be involved on both sides (see also MacDonald 1998a,b). This exemplifies the darker side of our groupish nature.

For Wilson, who follows Durkheim (1995[1912]) in certain respects, religion's normative system is a "functional algorithm" with two essential components. On the one hand, there are direct prescriptions of "secular utility," which ensure basic human activities required for the survival and reproduction of the group. On the other hand, there is a "metaphysical side," which provides the overarching moral authority for the system to work in a practical sense. What distinguishes the metaphysical side is not the supernatural but "the sacred." By rendering some ideas and actions sacred, and thereby making them obligatory for the collective, religion serves to confer a fitness advantage on the group vis-à-vis other groups.

Especially in the early stages of a religion, when the group seeks to gain a foothold in a hostile environment, individuals may be called on for great sacrifice. Thus, Christ's crucifixion and the many early examples of martyred saints explicitly mark extreme altruism as a defining distinction between early Christianity and its nearest rivals, Jewish monotheism and Roman pantheism. Moreover, the early Christians were able to expand their membership beyond the Jewish community and into the heart of gentile Rome through several converging group-evolutionary strategies. One strategy consisted of fine-tuning the biologically evolved relationship between pleasure and procreation by rigidly controlling sex for maximum propagation of group membership. Another strategy involved universalizing the notion of sacrifice for one's fellow man and actually practicing what one preached, for example, risking contagion by caring for gentile strangers during epidemics (see also Stark 1997). This latter strategy shows a potentially brighter side of religion and group formation by illustrating how groups may expand their moral circles to wider and less exclusive coverage of other humans.

I have no argument with claims that Balinese water temples, Calvinist doctrine, Jewish liturgy, and Early Christian practice represent examples of group survival and enhancement strategies that have proven effective in particular ecological and historical contexts. What I doubt is that these are evolutionary strategies that have anything to do with group selection. People form and sacrifice for their own groups because, on the average and in the long-run, it is to individual advantage.

Group selection arguments require the additional demonstration that average individual fitness within the group decreases so that the overall fitness of the group increases relative to the overall fitness of other, competing groups. There is nothing approaching such a demonstration in Wilson's account. To be sure, the empirical arguments that Wilson presents, which are based largely on his reading of secondary literature, allow the possibility of group selection, as well as any number of non-group-selection arguments. There aren't sufficient data on individual variation in any of these case studies to decide the case one way or another.

The one case where data have actually been amassed in direct support of group selection concerns the Jews. Again, there are too few data on individual variation to evaluate the competing claims of group selection and accounts that don't invoke group selection. Nevertheless, the data and claims made from them are sufficiently spelled out for us to assess the plausibility of the group selection argument in this case. Much of Wilson's analysis of this case derives from Kevin MacDonald's (1994, 1998a, 1998b) recent books on Judaism as a group evolutionary strategy. Wilson is much more cautious than MacDonald in extrapolating from behavioral data to actual intentions, but he accepts MacDonald's central thesis, [8] namely, that Judaism is a naturally selected, biological, and intellectual program for group-level adaptation.

According to MacDonald, the data show that for the past two millennia or so Judaism has consisted of a set of ideological structures and behaviors that have resulted in the following features: (1) segregation of the Jewish gene pool from surrounding gentile societies, (2) resource and reproductive competition with gentile host societies, (3) high levels of within-group cooperation and altruism among Jews, and (4) eugenic efforts directed at producing high intelligence, high-investment parenting, and commitment to group rather than individual goals. The sad but supposedly true implication from all of this is that: "From an evolutionary perspective, in the absence of actual genetic assimilation one is left to conclude that this Jewish sense of moral and religious idealism, which results in genetic segregation, is in fact a mask for a self-interested evolutionary strategy aimed at promoting the interests of a kinship group that maintains its genetic integrity during a diaspora" (MacDonald 1994:64).

Jewish cultural and genetic separatism, combined with resource competition and other conflicts of interest, tend to result in division and hatred within the larger society. From this viewpoint, anti-Semitism is a "defensive" response of the larger society from which Jews isolate themselves in order to better dominate it. In recent times, the prime example of defensive anti-Semitism is Nazism, which gave blunt meaning to the old adage "The best defense is a good offense." Indeed, Nazism was a striking "mirror image" of the Jewish eugenics program enunciated in the first five books of the Old Testament (cited at the beginning of this section). This is allegedly evident in Nazism's active promotion of an Aryan race of supermen whose members were entirely subordinate to the state, in its plan to enslave other potentially competitive "races," and in its ruthless annihilation of the all-too-familiar and competitive Jews in its heartland (MacDonald 1998a).

Finally, Jewish group evolutionary strategies, like those of its competitor groups and even those of other animal species, depend crucially on deception and self-deception (MacDonald 1998b). In the Jewish case, a key (self?) deception is to deny that proactive Judaism is a direct cause of anti-Semitism.[9] Jewish "self-perceptions are systematically distorted as they relate to the role of Jewish behavior in causing anti-Semitism, as is evident in Jewish historiography written by Jews." A recurring form of this self-serving deception is to denounce as antihumanist those who bring to light this embarrassingly obvious truth. Victims of such denunciations include David Irving, the British historian who denies that Jews were ever gassed to death at Auschwitz, and MacDonald himself, who felt morally obliged to testify in defense of Irving's libel case against Jewish "slander" that labeled denial of the Holocaust "a lie." Here is part of that testimony:[10]

> The effectiveness of Jewish strategizing has been facilitated by several key features of Judaism as group evolutionary strategy—particularly that the IQ of Ashkenazi Jews is at least one standard deviation above the Caucasian mean. In all historical eras, Jews as a group have been highly organized, highly intelligent, and politically astute, and they have been able to command a high level of financial, political, and intellectual resources in pursuing their group goals. . . . Jewish organizations commissioned writings in opposition to "scientific anti-Semitism," as exemplified by academically respectable publications that portrayed Jews in negative terms. . . . Jewish organizations have used their power to make the discussion of Jewish interests off limits. (Statement of Kevin MacDonald, 31 January 2000, posted on David Irving's Web site, *www.fpp.co.uk*)

Like most other human groups, Jews compete more with others than among themselves. Unlike most other human groups, Jews have developed a highly sophisticated and pernicious two-faced moral system. One face pretends to be humanist and universalist and is intended for show mainly to non-Jews. The other is deeply racist and isolationist and is designed to maintain moral integrity among Jews alone. When others discover this "truth," "reactive" anti-Semitism naturally breaks out. But one doesn't necessarily need to be an anti-Semite to discover the truth about Judaism. MacDonald claims that he makes no "moral judgment" about Judaism, but only reaches "scientific" conclusions. Unfortunately, the Jewish cabal does not distinguish between classical anti-Semitic reactions and valid scientific inferences to many of the same classical anti-Semitic conclusions (the one novel argument from "science" being the MacDonald-Wilson notion of group selection).

By and large, MacDonald's contemporary data come from the United States. Here, the mostly Ashkenazi population of Jews, uprooted from their orginal Eastern European homes, have diligently sought to establish, or reestablish, a sense of community, in part by forging relations of real and fictive kinship. In France, though, neither the older European Ashkenazi population nor the more recently arrived North African Sephardis seem quite as taken with notions of biological community.

More critical to MacDonald's argument is the claim that Jews maintain "genetic integrity." Studies in epidemiology and population genetics merely indicate that, with respect to certain genetically linked traits, some groups of Jews scattered throughout the world have more in common with one another than with groups that have been coresident with these Jews for generations. It tells us nothing about any "Jewish gene pool." For example, Jews of mostly Eastern European origin (Ashkenazi Jews) are more likely to carry certain recessive disorders (e.g., Tay-Sachs disease) than are other Jews (e.g., Sephardic Jews) or non-Jews. The genetic bases of such traits have been established through sophisticated techniques of tissue culture, enzyme analysis, and DNA proofing. There is, however, no overall Jewish DNA signature.

There is nothing of comparable sophistication or demonstration concerning the heritability of IQ. For one thing, nobody has the slightest idea which genes, singly or in combination, might affect IQ. For another, there is no reason to believe, and much reason not to believe, that the measure of a so-called Intelligence Quotient in any way reflects some basic cognitive capacity or "natural kind" of the human mind. The domain-general measure of IQ is not motivated by any recent discovery of cognitive or developmental psychology. It thoroughly confounds domain-specific abilities, which are the only cognitive abilities for which an evolutionary account seems plausible in terms of natural selection for task-specific competencies. Nowhere in the animal or plant kingdoms does there ever appear to have been natural selection for a task-general adaptation. An overall measure of intelligence or mental competence is akin to an overall measure for "the body," taking no special account of the various and specific bodily organs and functions, such as hearts, lungs, stomach, circulation, respiration, and digestion. A doctor or biologist presented with a single measure for "Body Quotient" wouldn't be able to make much of it.[11]

If Jewish intellectual superiority is based, in part, on a genetically inherited tendency for IQ scores that are higher than those of the general population, then why don't Sephardic Jews of Southern European and Middle Eastern origin meet the bill? And why do Ashkenazi Jews exceed the general population by a standard deviation only with respect to verbal tasks but not mathematical tasks, if indeed Ashkenazis owe their survival to a calculating ability to dominate the economy of their host countries?

One can imagine all sorts of just-so stories to deal with these contingencies. The Sephardic Jews encountered *less* hostility among Moslems than Ashkenazis did among Christians, and so could gain more (wealth, political dominance, etc.) with less (intelligence, social exclusivity, etc.). A variant of this argument forms part of the Spanish Inquisition's judgment of the Jews as allies of the Moors who had to be expelled from Christendom. Or, Sephardis were attacked *more* often and intensely in Moslem societies than the Ashkenazis were in Christian societies, so that the Sephardis were unable to fully implement their eugenics program. This is MacDonald's explanation, which depends on the rather extravagant assumption that Moslems were more fanatical in their suppression and discrimination of Jews than were Christians. As for Ashkenazi superiority in verbal skills but not necessarily in mathematical skills, it's obvious (isn't it?) that verbal reasoning is the more critical for deception and self-deception, the key "evolutionary group strategy" for deflecting gentile attention and discrimination.

By incorporating a looping notion of self-serving deception, *any* belief or behavior can be interpreted as implying something and its contrary: antiracism is really racism, anti-Semitism can be cryptohumanism or even crypto-phylo-Semitism, and so forth. Admittedly, deception and self-deception are integral aspects of human beings' naturally selected endowment, but their actual functioning needs to be demonstrated through specific chains of cause and effect. This necessarily involves an analysis of psychological states. Intent cannot just be inferred from the behavioral setting, especially when the setting is mostly reconstructed from rather selective and fragmentary historical data. Neither can argument by similarity and analogy be any more than weakly suggestive. There are indefinitely many relations of similarity and analogy that can be established between any pair of items. To intimate that aspects of Hitler's *Mein Kampf* "mirror image" aspects of what God told the People of Israel in Leviticus and Deuteronomy may be as far from a true causal account as almost *anything* we might imagine.

Finally, claiming anti-Semitism to be chiefly a defensive strategy against Jewish deception fails entirely to explain why members of violent anti-Semitic organizations (at least in the United States) seem to be generally young, unattached males who often have a dysfunctional history of social (broken families, few steady jobs) and psychological (fearful anxieties, high alcoholism rates) problems (Ezekiel 1995). In fact, MacDonald's thesis rests on three spurious assumptions akin to the "Holy Trinity" of racist belief: (1) race is biologically real (there are underlying genetic essences that distinguish all or some human groups), (2) competition for power and dominance is the main driving force behind human relationships (rather than just one among many), and (3) nothing is what it seems (deception and conspiracy is everywhere other than among one's own kind).

From almost any evolutionary perspective, it is embarrassingly obvious that Jews, and most or all other religious groups, cooperate among themselves to better compete against other groups. Most or all social groups of *any* human or other animal kind do so. But understanding evolution doesn't even remotely entail accepting MacDonald's strong conspiracy theory of Judaism, namely, as a truly coherent, albeit somewhat self-deceiving, biological strategy for group enhancement through intellectual domination of gentiles. Accepting an evolutionary basis for thought and behavior also doesn't lead to Wilson's weaker thesis of Jewry and other religious or ideological groups as "adaptive superorganisms," each with an internal, normative morality—a morality that no member owns but that all members must pay for so that the group may profit as a whole.

As in much sociobiology, there is no attempt to comprehend the subjective psychological content of religious beliefs and their causal effects on behavior. The mental causes of behavior are of little consequence in the actual analysis of behavior. Only the supposed "fitness consequences" of the "culture," or the "whole social system," merit scrutiny. Discussion of the human mind is restricted to metapsychological categories such as altruism, deception, and emotion, which tell us nothing about how people actually think and put their thoughts into action.

Even if we accepted the historically far-fetched MacDonald-Wilson analysis of Judaism as a coherent group-level belief system, what in the world does it mean for it, on any other group-level belief system, to have fitness consequences at the level of a whole culture or social system? As Dan Sperber noted in email comments on Wilson's earlier work to the Human Evolution and Behavior Society (31 March 1996):

> Only a few social systems have "offsprings" of a sort through fission and colonization of new territories. Surely, having offsprings of this kind, though conceivable [as] a sign of fitness, is not a necessary condition for it. Is then fitness a matter of the size of the population belonging to the social system? Of variations in this size (e.g., expansion)? Of the duration of

the social system? Of some weighted combination of size and duration? If a social system both expands and changes rapidly, as has been the case with most imperial systems, success seems to be at the expense of heritability. What, then, exhibits fitness?

8.12. Summary: Norms and Group-Level Traits Are Notional, Not Natural, Kinds

There is no clear sense to the notion of "fitness consequences at the level of whole cultures or societies." This is because cultures and societies have no readily definable external boundaries and because, internally, they have no systemically identifiable structural functions. They do have enormously varied ways of enduring, expanding, mixing, assimilating, and transforming. But exactly where in all of this is *the* culture? *It* is nowhere and in no way precise enough to pin down *its* fitness consequences.

Normative morality is largely a convenient fiction—not because it masks what it really is but because it represents too many underdetermined possibilities, and therefore represents nothing in particular. Social scientists, political leaders, and ordinary people in ordinary groups use these normative conveniences to identify their audience and track its flow of information. These normative conveniences do not contain much information at all. They only signal where relevant information may be found. They are signs that point to many similar, different, and even contrary meanings and referents. They are not the sorts of replicating units of information, or even reliably blending clusters of information, that can be objects of Darwinian selection.

In everyday life, the routine prejudice of confounding the signal with the flux of information, the sign with its open-ended meanings and multiple referents is of little consequence. Ordinary principles of communicative relevance amply serve to disambiguate meaning and reference in context (Sperber and Wilson 1986). Allowing this commonsense prejudice to persist in science is a different matter, because it leads to context-general theories that are founded on shifting sand.

Anthropologists normatively describe the societies they study for the same reasons that people everywhere normatively represent their own societies to one another: to facilitate communication and promote consensus in thought or action. But the commonsense use of norms should not be confused with the scientific analysis of their causal import. There is a similar point to the following observation. In our society, most of us think that we understand enough of what others mean by "germ," "unhappiness," or "consciousness" to make sense of what is being talked about. But this does not entail that such terms will have a causally coherent extension. On the contrary, it is doubtful they refer to any scientifically recognizable "natural kind" of lawfully regular material object, physiological state, or neural network.

Norms are not shared rules and human societies and cultures are not clustered and aggregated sets of rules that functionally determine some definitely bounded "social system" or "cultural worldview." At best, norms are public representations that help to orient causal analyses of cultural phenomena—for the person in the street as well as for the social scientist—by stereotyping those public exhibitions and performances whose recurring tokens are especially relevant to social communication and coordination. But any scientific analysis needs to treat real material tokens rather than ideal types. In like manner, evolutionary and molecular biologists must deal with actual organisms and gene pools rather than species as categorical kinds. Group-selected social traits and cultures as functional systems of traits are notional, not natural, kinds. They are not units of Darwinian selection.

For the most part, social norms and cultural traits are commonsense notions. They are synthetic digests of information partially and intermittently shared among the causally linked population of human minds that constitutes a "culture." At best, these stereotypical constructs are public displays, like statutes in law books, the Apostles' Creed, or signs at roadsides or on public buildings. When displayed in their appropriate ecological context, they assist in causally linking up diverse private (mental) and public (manifest) representations within and between individual minds by channeling relations among these representations in time and space. They operate to ensure enough similarity of content between diverse representations to establish communication between individual minds and make coordinated action possible.

This is, in part, how the distributed networks of representations that we commonly call cultures and religions are created. Norms are nodes with ever shifting significance and control in these information networks. They are activated by ecological and historical contingencies, and they operate only within structural parameters fixed by the cognitive and computational architecture of the human mind/brain.

9 The Trouble with Memes

Inference versus Imitation in Cultural Creation

Memes are hypothetical cultural units, an idea or practice, passed on by imitation. Although nonbiological, they undergo Darwinian selection like genes. Cultures and religions are supposedly coalitions of memes seeking to maximize their own fitness, regardless of fitness costs for their human hosts. Cognitive study of multimodular human minds undermines memetics: unlike in genetic replication, high-fidelity transmission of cultural information is the exception, not the rule. Constant, rapid "mutation" of information during communication generates endlessly varied creations that nevertheless adhere to modular input conditions. The sort of cultural information most susceptible to modular processing is that most readily acquired by children, most easily transmitted across individuals, most apt to survive within a culture, most likely to recur in different cultures, and most disposed to cultural variation and elaboration. The supernatural and other aspects of religious beliefs and practices are prime examples.

9.1. Memes Are Nonbiological but Strictly Darwinian

The concept of *meme*, introduced by Richard Dawkins in 1976 in *The Selfish Gene*, is now defined in the Oxford English Dictionary as "an element of culture that may be considered to be passed on by non-genetic means, esp. imitation."[1] Candidate memes include a word, a sentence, a thought, a belief, a melody, a scientific theory, an equation, a philosophical puzzle, a religious ritual, a political ideology, an agricultural practice, a fashion, a dance, a poem, a recipe for a meal, table manners, court etiquette, and plans for cars, computers, and cell phones. Derived from the Greek root *mimeme*, with allusions to memory and mime (and the French word *même*, or "same"), a meme is supposed to replicate from mind to mind in ways analogous to the ways a gene replicates from body to body.

Memes undergo natural selection in a Darwinian sense. The process of natural selection requires only that elements of selection be units of hereditary information that control the matter that encodes the information and for which there is a bias to selection over time that greatly exceeds the rate of endogenous change: "Information can proliferate and be edited by natural selection only if the selection affects the information at a greater rate than competing processes such as mutation and drift" (G. Williams 1992:12). The matter that encodes the information selected can be DNA or RNA, as with genes and proteins; electrochemical neural networks or written languages, as with memes; or nonbiological electric circuits, as with computer viruses.

The units of selection must have fecundity. They or their carriers must "be fruitful and multiply"; otherwise, there is little morphological or behavioral variation among units from which to select because of lack of abundance of different elements. The heritable variants must be copied with high fidelity so that they resemble one another more than they do unrelated forms. Only then can they be repeatedly chosen as favorable or eliminated as unfavorable by selection. The replicating variants must be relatively long-lived. They must survive at least long enough to produce more copies than do other forms to contribute to differential fitness or reproductive success. Finally, the elements of selection must be in competition for survival over scarce resources that sustain them in a given environment (e.g., cell, body soma, ecological niche, mind, computer memory) or else there would be no pressure for selection.

A general theory of the evolution of replicators under natural selection requires *fecundity* and *variation*, *heredity* and *high fidelity*, *longevity* and *fitness*, and *competition for survival-enhancing resources*. Whenever all such interrelated factors are present, in whatever possible nomological world where laws of cause and effect and thermodynamics hold, different lineages of self-replicating forms should evolve from one or a few original forms. As new forms evolve, so must the environments to which the forms are constantly added and adapted. The cultural evolution of ideas (memes), including changes wrought by ideas on the cognitive and social environments that ideas adapt to, seems to fit the bill.

Although the relation of memes to genes is one of analogy, the relation is no more intended as a metaphor than was the Rutherford-Bohr analogy of the atom to the solar system at the beginning of the past century. The meme-gene analogy itself is meant to function as a research program that will hopefully lead to a science of "memetics," much as the atom–solar system analogy was briefly viewed by some scientists as a research program to help unify physical processes at the microscopic (e.g., electromagnetism) and macroscopic (e.g., gravity) levels. The initial stage of memetics, then, is to specify whether and how the analogy between meme and gene holds up under testable scrutiny. If the analogy can be informatively sustained, it must be able to reliably predict significant and surprising scientific discoveries about specific causal structures. If the analogy cannot be informatively sustained, as with the atom–solar system analogy, then it must be eventually discarded as a scientific endeavor. In this latter eventuality, the analogy might still be maintained as a pedagogic device, which could introduce novices into a field that has developed, in part, by failed efforts to make the analogy informative.

I lean to the latter eventuality. Nevertheless, I recognize the likelihood that such an original and enticing idea as the meme will endure with significantly altered content or as an expedient trope that orients attention, like the etiological notion of germ. In any event, if the meme concept is eventually to work for science, I think that it cannot be as a replicator that copies information to the mind. It might work as an elicitor that draws out inferences and information from the mind.

9.2. What Is Unique about Memes?

Other Darwinian approaches, such as coevolution models of genes and cultural traits or social norms, offer similar perspectives on cultural life (Cavalli-Sforza and Feldman 1981; Boyd and Richerson 1985; Durham 1991; Sober and Wilson 1998). But Dawkins's proposal has an original response to the key evolutionary question Cui bono? Who benefits? (Dennett 1995). The answer: not brains, individuals, or societies but memes themselves. Just as genes or viruses seek serial immortality by successively using, then discarding the individual organisms that host them, so memes seek to perpetuate themselves by nesting and nurturing in mind after mind. In the mind, a meme associates itself with other memes in a package, or "memeplex" (Blackmore 1999). Together, memes in a memeplex act to restructure the mind's computational architecture.

Restructuring includes instructions that cause the mind to transmit the memeplex to other minds. Take the evangelist's dictum "Spread, but dare not alter, the Word of God." The underlying message, but not its surface form, appears replicated in a review of the Bible that was originally posted at Amazon.com and then reprinted in newspapers: "Nonbelievers need to read this in any form. I don't want to spoil the end, but let's just say YOU NEED TO READ THIS BOOK AS SOON AS POSSIBLE" (*International Herald Tribune*, 18 July 2000, p. 22). Colonization by a memeplex also further renders the mind susceptible to invasion and transformation by a memeplex, like increasing devotion to dependence on religion or science or addiction to dialogue on the Internet.

Like genes, memes can pass supposedly "vertically" from parent to child, for example, in the religious practice of circumcision. Memes can also copy themselves "horizontally" from person to person—between peers or from leaders to followers—as with the concept of meme itself. In our hominid past, when sustainable transmission was largely vertical and horizontal transmission was restricted to a few cultural artifacts, the fitness of memes depended almost exclusively on the fitness of the population that hosted them. With language, the computational possibilities of horizontal transmission exploded.

Once the newer, faster-paced memetic evolution took off, it was no longer subservient to the older, slow-moving pace of genetic evolution, or necessarily bound to it at all. Memes could even afford to kill off their hosts if given the time and the medium to broadcast themselves to new victims before the hosts' demise, as with well-publicized cases of religious or political martyrdom. With Internet and globalization of information transmission, the evolutionary rate of memetic change appears to be once again on the verge of exponential takeoff, with unforeseeable evolutionary consequences. Now there is even less pressure on memes to guarantee the physical survival of brains as more and more memetic activity shifts from biospace to cyberspace.

In fact, as David Hull points out (personal communication, 2000), the memetic distinction between vertical and horizontal transmission makes little sense in the case of ideas. In gene-based biological evolution, vertical is defined as the way genes go. Genes usually go the way organisms go: a mother passes on half her genes to her children. In horizontal transmission, a virus might pick up a gene and transfer it to a non-family member. From a genetic perspective, the difference between a parent teaching something to his or her children and anyone else teaching them is irrelevant; the process by which memes move is the same in both cases. Moreover, information "explosions" are not restricted to ideas. For example, millions of T cells are manufactured every day in the thymus gland, 97 percent of which are reabsorbed before they ever leave the thymus gland. Of those that do, 99.99 percent never meet an antigen they recognize. Biological selective processes often require massive waste (e.g., sperm) for remarkably little creation and innovation. Finally, at least some processes of genetic evolution are as fast as or faster than any memetic change: the immune system was designed to cope with rapid change of viruses and bacteria, and no conceptual change in a population, not even cell phones, has ever surpassed the speed of some viral infections. Rapid, horizontal spread is thus not unique to memes.

9.3. Brain and Mind Building

For psychologist Susan Blackmore (1999), the human brain, language, and the self evolved because they primarily gave advantage to memes, not genes. The brain grew large in order to function as a better and better copying machine for memes. The brain evolved as a genetic fax built for and run by memes. Similarly, language was selected for meme transmission. Language evolved as a genetic telephone line built for memes to call one another. The self, too, was created by and for the replication of memes. The "I," with its illusion of free will, is in reality a meme stronghold for defense against displacement by masses of fearless competitors invading from the surrounding social environment.

There is a novel account of altruism and friendliness. Nice guys who are available and helpful to others have more chances to influence others; they are "meme fountains." People who keep to themselves are "meme sinks" that other memes and their supporting folk would do better to avoid. Meme fountains spread "altruism memes" and other good memes (e.g., tolerance) and bad memes (e.g., faith) that ride piggyback on the altruism meme. Bad memes that hitch onto the altruism meme are said to use "the altruism trick" to insinuate their way into unsuspecting minds. Bad religion memes co-opt the altruism meme and insinuate themselves into minds to form an infectious memeplex of comemes (Dawkins 1993; A. Lynch 1996; Dennett 1997).[2]

Blackmore's account, like nearly all other stories of the evolution of the big brain and language, provides neither empirical evidence nor substantive proposals for how one might go about gathering and testing evidence. No insight is provided into any specific brain structure or neural organization, for example, concerning the structure of the late-evolving prefrontal cortices and their relationship to language comprehension and production centers in the temporal and parietal lobes of the dominant hemisphere. Neither is there a hint about specific semantic or syntactic structures, such as *wh*-movement, case assignment, and anaphora. The operative analogy, of course, is that minds are built for memes as bodies are built for genes. As masterful work by Hamilton (1964), G. Williams (1966), and Dawkins (1976) demonstrates, grudging acceptance of the gene's-eye view of body building in biology, which is still hotly debated, required considerable detailed biological groundwork. The meme's-eye view of mind building requires no detailed knowledge or evidence concerning the computational architecture of the human brain/mind and provides no specifiable structural constraints on allowable cultural forms.

9.4. Good and Bad Memes

For Dawkins, as for Blackmore and philosopher Daniel Dennett (1995), there are bad memes and good memes. Bad memes and memeplexes include Nazi ideology, deconstructionism, hard-to-forget advertising jingles, alien abduction crazes, new-age medicine and witchcraft, astrology and divination, palmistry and fortune telling, second-rate scientific articles, creationism, and religious faith. Good memes and memeplexes include democracy and tolerance of free speech, a Mozart or Beethoven symphony, modern medicine, evolutionary theory, and first-rate science. The distinction between good and bad memes really has no theoretical import. The distinction serves to illustrate how different kinds of memes spread and interact, although the way the distinction is set up counts as a moral tale that is aggressively atheist and embarrassingly intellectualist.

Bad memes can sometimes be spread along with the good memes they happen to be linked to. For example, in the political and social climate of post-Weimar Germany, people were more likely than today to adopt Wagner's pernicious anti-Semitism as adding reason and force to his music. Similarly, people then were more likely than people now to adopt evolutionary theory for its link to racism, and vice versa. Once linked, special effort may be needed to unhinge good memes from bad. Israeli society is bitterly divided over whether the Israeli Philharmonic should include Wagner in its repertoire ("Israel Court Allows Wagner Concert," Associated Press, 24 October 2000). A similar decoupling problem shows in the way many in cultural anthropology lump theories of human evolution and evolutionary psychology with eugenics, racism, and elitism.

From the meme's-eye view, the only bad memes are ones that lead to their own extinction. These may include good memes from a humanist standpoint, such as the time-consuming practice of elders telling moral tales and wondrous stories to youngsters, a practice being rapidly erased in small-scale societies around the globe as television expediently offers unwary minds facile sitcoms, game shows, and endless movies that tease the emotionally inexhaustible theme of "lethal sex." Like the fast-food industry that gainfully manipulates and amplifies human beings' innate yearning for fat, salt, and sugar—a yearning adapted for an ancestral time when availability of these food items was naturally scarce—so the entertainment industry channels and exploits innate dreads and desires in marketable and often mischievous ways.

9.5. Mindblind Memetics

In *The Extended Phenotype,* Dawkins appeared to backtrack from forceful advocacy of a memetic science of mind and culture: "its main value lies not so much in helping us understand human culture as in sharpening our perception of genetic natural selection. . . . I do not know enough about the existing literature on human culture to make an authoritative contribution to it" (1982:112). By then, two major objections had arisen. First, there was no ready way of deciding what counts as a meme. There was no set of criteria for determining whether the chosen units or "chunks" of information actually cut up culture at its natural joints. Even if memes could be operationally isolated, they still might not constitute a theoretical expedient. Without definable or at least agreed upon operational units, little by way of cumulative scientific argument could advance.

For genes, there is a rather straightforward operational definition: those DNA-encoded units of information that dependably survive reproductive division, that is, meiosis (although crossover can occur anywhere along a strand of DNA, whether at the divisions of functionally defined genes or within them). "Definable units" may be fairly discrete (e.g., sex) or continuous (e.g., skin color) traits. Whether discontinuous and digital or continuous and analog, selectable traits must in themselves be cohesive in definite and coherent proportions, and not because someone wishes or decides to attach numbers to "operational units" that have no fixed content or boundaries.[3]

The second objection poses a more serious challenge to the possibility of memetics. Unlike genes, ideas rarely copy with anything close to absolute fidelity. In the overwhelming majority of cases, an idea undergoes some sort of modification during communication (Atran 1996; Sperber 1996). For example, arbitrarily select any news item and see how the different news media present it. The real mystery is how any group of people manages an effective degree of common understanding given that transformation of ideas during transmission is the rule rather than the exception. If transformation (mutation or drift) affects the information at a greater rate than high-fidelity replication, then a favorable or unfavorable selection bias cannot develop for the replicated (hereditary) information. In such cases, Darwinian selection becomes impossible. Moreover, unlike genetic lines, descendent ideas cross and merge so quickly and thoroughly that there can be no identification of "species" or "lineages" of memes, only variably defined "influences," for example, the influence of black African and classical European rhythms on American blues and the further looping of these three strains of music on rock and roll. Although eminent biologists and philosophers of biology have continued to view culturally persistent or widespread ideas as true replicators (G. Williams 1992; Hull 1988), these objections greatly threaten to undermine the nascent memetics movement.

In a recent essay, Dawkins (1999:xvi) gives Dennett (1995) and Blackmore (1999) much of the credit for his renewed faith in "the possibility that the meme might one day be developed into a proper hypothesis of the human mind"—a possibility that now appears at hand. According to Dennett (1995:356), what *Romeo and Juliet* and *West Side Story* memetically share is not text and "syntactic structure" (phenotype), but the underlying story and "semantic structure" (genotype). In this case, there are historical records indicating that the authors of *West Side Story* got the thematic idea from *Romeo and Juliet*, and so one can claim them to be instances of the same underlying meme or descendent memes in the same memetic lineage. Of course, in the absence of historical records it may be impossible to distinguish independently evolved analogies from genealogically related homologies: "consider the fact that two widely separated cultures both used boats; this is no evidence at all of a shared cultural heritage," unless the boats of both cultures shared some arbitrary design, such as blue hexagons on their bows (357).

One potentially serious obstacle to this account is anthropologist Dan Sperber's (1985a) insight that the key to understanding how ideas become cultural representations lies not with their formal (semantic) structure but with their *causal* relationship to multimodular minds. Dennett (1995:379) is well aware of recent advances in cognitive and developmental psychology with respect to domain-specific, modular structures. He allows that prior mental structures facilitate the nesting of memes in the brain (much as certain trees or building structures may facilitate specific kinds of bird nesting) and that memes sometimes "enhance and shape preexisting structures, rather than generating entirely new structures." Nevertheless, Dennett dismisses the role of the biologically evolved mind with a hand wave: "The peculiarities of human psychology (and human digestion, for that matter . . .) are important *eventually*, but they don't stand in the way of a scientific analysis of the phenomena. . . . You can finesse your ignorance of the gory mechanical details of how the information got from A to B, at least temporarily, and just concentrate on the fact that it *did* get there" (358–359).

This seems a reasonable strategy only if the mind, or at least higher-order cognition, is in effect a huge parallel machine, or "central processor," which gets reprogrammed by memes via language and culture. In such a mind, whatever cognitive modules there may be function primarily at lower levels of perceptual processing (cf. Fodor 1983). At higher levels modular processes have little presence, except perhaps as coves for memes to harbor in and work over the mind. Dawkins (1976) also acknowledges that the mind has prior cognitive structure, but he considers those who concentrate on the role of evolved cognitive faculties in generating and selecting cultural ideas as "begging just as many questions as I am." Coming from an evolutionary biologist, this is a curious position. To explain how genes function and adapt, Dawkins describes rich adaptive landscapes: conglomerations of fitness-relevant environmental factors from conspecifics to predators to sunlight. For memes, he merely alludes to the cognitive architecture of the mind as part of the adaptive landscape under which memes evolve and then dismisses concern with the adaptive landscape as "question begging."

I suspect that Dawkins and colleagues tend to disregard or underplay the role of evolved cognitive architecture in constituting culture for many of the same reasons that motivate Stephen Gould (1980) and colleagues to take a similar stance: as an answer to vulgar sociobiology (i.e., identifiable classes of genes directly cause identifiable classes of cultural behavior). The central message of memetics is that human beings can still be purely Darwinian creatures and yet possess a significant measure of independence from their selfish genes and from the blind processes of natural selection that ruthlessly govern biological evolution. But sociobiology is not the only Darwinian alternative to memetics.

The multimodular mind, too, allows for obvious human creativity and much free play in thought. Unlike memetic hand waving, it does so by attempting to actually specify the cognitive tools available and the recurrent rules of their use in building cultures. Imagine if you were to build a city: Would you have more creative possibilities with some simple or general-purpose tools, or with a richly endowed tool kit that could be used to build further complex building tools (e.g., cranes; Tooby and Cosmides 1992; Pinker 1997)? Imagine also a game plan with few or no rules and instructions to keep it that way: How could increased skills and ever more refined strategies take hold and evolve? They might, if time was unlimited and randomly produced patterns could stabilize and surreptitiously pass for new rules. In general, though, the more specific and multiple the rules, as with chess versus checkers, the greater the possibilities for increased skill, choice, and complexity in play.

9.6. The Multimodular Mind: Evidence for an Alternative

The recent evolutionary approach to cognitive and cultural phenomena focuses on what functional arguments from sociobiology and so-called materialist anthropology generally ignore, namely, the mental mechanisms that cause behavior. Research into these mental mechanisms owes to a convergence of several late twentieth-century theoretical developments in cognitive and developmental psychology, psycholinguistics, evolutionary biology, and cognitive and cultural anthropology: (1) computational thinking (the mind is a computer; Marr 1982), (2) domain specificity (the mind is a multimodular computer; Hirschfeld and Gelman 1994), (3) nativism (different mental modules are innate; Fodor 1983), (4) adaptationism (modules were functionally designed under natural selection to solve vital problems in ancestral environments; Barkow, Cosmides, and Tooby 1992), and (5) cultural epidemiology (beliefs and practices spread, develop, and survive under cultural selection to the extent that they are susceptible to modular processing; Sperber 1996). Each modular faculty, or "mental organ," is presumably governed by a specific set of (genetically prescribed) core principles that interpret and generalize the behavior and properties of entities in the world belonging to (falling under) the faculty's domain (Chomsky 2000).

The evolutionary argument for a naturally selected cognitive disposition involves converging evidence from a number of venues: functional design (analogy), ethology (homology), universality, precocity of acquisition, independence from perceptual experience (poverty of stimulus), selective pathology (cerebral impairment), resistance to inhibition (hyperactivity), and cultural transmission. None of these criteria may be necessary, but the presence of all or some is compelling, if not conclusive. Examples to which these criteria may be successfully applied include folkmechanics, folkbiology, and folkpsychology.

As an illustration, consider these evidential criteria for modularity in folkbiology:[4]

1. *Functional design*: All organisms must function to procure energy to survive, and they also must procure (genetic) information for recombination and reproduction (Eldredge 1986). The first requirement is primarily satisfied by other species and an indiscriminate use of any individual of the other species (e.g., energywise, it does not generally matter which chicken or apple you eat). The second requirement is usually satisfied only by genetic information unique to individual conspecifics (e.g., genetically, it matters who is chosen as a mate and who is considered kin). On the one hand, humans recognize other humans by individuating them with the aid of species-specific triggering algorithms that "automatically" coordinate perceptual cues (e.g., facial recognition schemata, gaze) with conceptual assumptions (e.g., intentions). On the other hand, people do not spontaneously individuate members of other species in this way, but as examplars of the (generic) species that identifies them as belonging to only one essential kind.

   Natural selection basically accounts only for the appearance of complexly well-structured biological traits that are designed to perform important functional tasks of adaptive benefit to organisms. In general, naturally selected adaptations are structures functionally "perfected for any given habit" (Darwin 1883[1872]:140), having "very much the appearance of design by an intelligent designer . . . on which the wellbeing and very existence of the organism depends" (Wallace 1901[1889]:138). Plausibly, the universal appreciation of generic species as the causal foundation for the taxonomic arrangement of biodiversity, is one such functional evolutionary adaptation. But a good story is not enough.
2. *Ethology*: One hallmark of adaptation is a phylogenetic history that extends beyond the species in which the adaptation is perfected; for example, ducklings crouching in the presence of hawks, but not other kinds of birds, suggests dedicated mechanisms for something like species recognition. Some nonhuman species can clearly distinguish several different animal or plant species (Cerella 1979; Lorenz 1966; Herrnstein 1984). Chimpanzees may even have rudimentary hierarchical groupings of biological groups within groups (D. Brown and Boysen 2000). Nevertheless, only humans appear to have taxonomies that readily allow assimilation of indefinitely many new species, and that reliably guide indefinitely many inferences about the distribution of biologically related properties in the face of uncertainty. As an evolved cognitive adaptation applicable to any number of species from any number of habitats, it may well have facilitated humans spreading over the globe. But this is still just a tale.

3. *Universality*: Ever since the pioneering work of Berlin and colleagues, evidence from ethnobiology and experimental psychology has accumulated that all societies have similar folkbiological structures (Berlin 1992; Berlin, Breedlove, and Raven 1973; Atran 1990a, 1999). These striking cross-cultural similarities suggest that a small number of organizing principles universally define folkbiological systems. Basic aspects of folkbiological structure (taxonomic ranking, primacy of generic species) seem to vary little across cultures as a function of theories or belief systems. This is fact.
4. *Ease of acquisition*: Acquisition studies indicate a precocious emergence of essentialist folkbiological principles in early childhood that are not applied to other domains (Gelman and Wellman 1991; Keil 1994; Hatano and Inagaki 1999; Atran et al. 2001).
5. *Independence from perceptual experience*: Experiments on inferential processing show that humans do not make biological inductions primarily on the basis of perceptual experience or any general similarity-based metric, but on the basis of imperceptible causal expectations of a peculiar, essentialist nature (Atran et al, 1997; Coley, Medin, and Atran 1997).
6. *Pathology*: Cerebral impairments (Williams syndrome, brain lesions caused by certain types of herpes virus, etc.) suggest selective retention or loss of folkbiological taxonomies or of particular taxonomic ranks. Neuropsychological studies have reported a pathological performance in recognition at the life-form and generic-species levels (e.g., recognizing an item as an animal but not as a bird or robin) and dissociation at the life-form level (e.g., not recognizing items as trees). Existing studies, however, do not say anything about the generic-species rank as the preferred level of representation for reasoning, perhaps because of methodology (linked to averaging over items and failure to include sets of generic species; Warrington and Shallice 1984; Sartori and Job 1988; Job and Surian 1998; Caramazza 2002).
7. *Inhibition and hyperactivity*: One characteristic of an evolved cognitive disposition is evident difficulty in inhibiting its operation (Hauser 2000a). Consider beliefs in biological essences. Such beliefs greatly help people explore the world by prodding them to look for regularities and to seek explanations of variation in terms of underlying patterns. This strategy may help bring order to ordinary circumstances, including those relevant to human survival. But in other circumstances, such as wanting to know what is correct or true for the cosmos at large, such intuitively ingrained concepts and beliefs may hinder more than help. For example, the essentialist bias to understand variation in terms of deviance is undoubtedly a hindrance to evolutionary thinking. In some everyday matters, the tendency to essentialize or explain variation in terms of deviation from some essential ideal or norm (e.g., people as mental or biological "deviants") can be an effortlessly "natural" but wrong way to think.

Because intuitive notions come to us so naturally they may be difficult to unlearn and transcend. Even students and philosophers of biology often find it difficult to abandon commonsense notions of species as classes, essences, or natural kinds in favor of the concept of species as a logical individual: a genealogical branch whose endpoints are somewhat arbitrarily defined in the phyletic tree and whose status does not differ in principle from that of other smaller (variety) and larger (genus) branches. Similarly, racism—the projection of biological essences onto social groups—seems to be a cognitively facile and culturally universal tendency (Hirschfeld 1996). Although science teaches that race is biologically incoherent, racial or ethnic essentialism is as notoriously difficult to suppress as it is easy to incite (Gil-White 2001).

8. *Cultural transmission*: Human cultures favor a rapid selection and stable distribution of those ideas that (1) readily help to solve relevant and recurrent environmental problems, (2) are easily memorized and processed by the human brain, and (3) facilitate the retention and understanding of ideas that are more variable (e.g., religion) or difficult to learn (e.g., science) but contingently useful or important. Folkbiological taxonomy readily aids humans everywhere in orienting themselves and surviving in the natural world. Its content tends to be stable within cultures (high interinformant agreement, substantial historical continuity) and its structure isomorphic across cultures (Berlin, Breedlove, and Raven, 1973; López et al. 1997). Folkbiological taxonomy also serves as a principled basis for transmission and acquisition of more variable and extended forms of cultural knowledge, such as certain forms of scientific and religious belief—for example, systematics and totemism (Atran 1990a, 1998).

Within our species' evolutionary landscape of medium-size objects and actors that are snapshots in a single lifespan of geological time, biologically poised mental structures channel cognitive development but do not determine it. Cultural life, including science, can selectively target and modify parts of this landscape but cannot simply ignore it or completely replace it. For example, modern systematics emerged from folkbiology's cultural domain.

Consider three corresponding ways in which ordinary folk and biologists think of plants and animals as special (Atran 1998). First, people in all cultures classify plants and animals into species-like groups that biologists generally recognize as populations of interbreeding individuals adapted to an ecological niche. Second, there is a commonsense assumption that each generic species has an underlying causal nature, or essence, that maintains the organism's integrity even as it causes the organism to grow, change form, and reproduce. For example, a tadpole and a frog are in a crucial sense the same animal although they look and behave very differently and live in different places. Evolutionary biologists reject the notion of essence as some sort of metaphysical reality. Nevertheless, biologists have traditionally

> interpreted this conservation of identity under change as due to organisms having separate genotypes and phenotypes.
>
> Third, in addition to the spontaneous division of local flora and fauna into essence-based species, such groups have "from the remotest period in . . . history . . . been classed in groups under groups. This classification [of generic species into higher- and lower-order groups] is not arbitrary like the grouping of stars in constellations" (Darwin 1859:431). Such taxonomies not only organize and summarize biological information, they also provide a powerful inductive framework for making systematic inferences about the likely distribution of organic and ecological properties among organisms. In scientific taxonomy, this strategy receives its strongest expression in "the fundamental principle of systematic induction" (Warburton 1967).
>
> Folkbiological species and groups of folkspecies are inherently well-structured, attention-arresting, memorable, and readily transmissible across minds. As a result, they readily provide effective pegs on which to attach knowledge and behavior of less intrinsically well-determined social groups. In this way totemic groups can also become memorable, attention-arresting, and transmissible across minds. These are the conditions for any meme (elicitor) to become culturally viable. A main feature of totemism that makes it "good to think" is that it enhances both memorability and capacity to grab attention by pointedly violating the general behavior of biological species (Lévi-Strauss 1962, 1963b). Members of a totem, unlike species members, don't interbreed, but only mate with members of other totems to create a system of social exchange. Notice that this violation of core knowledge is far from arbitrary. It is such a pointed violation of human intuitive ontology that it readily mobilizes most of the assumptions people ordinarily make about biology in order to help build societies around the world.
>
> Similarly, supernatural agents, which are banished from science but enthroned in religion, lie within folkpsychology's cultural domain. In other words, supernatural agent concepts are created from cultural manipulations of modular cognitive schema for recognition and interpretation of agents, such as people and animals. By conscientiously violating innate, modularity-induced ontological commitments (e.g., endowing spirits with movement and feelings but no body) processing can never be brought to factual closure and indeterminately many interpretations can be generated for indefinitely many newly arising situations.

In brief, these enduring aspects of human cultures need not be, and often are not, fixed in terms of perceptual or conceptual content. Unlike genetic transmission and replication, high-fidelity transmission of cultural information is the exception rather than the rule. Constant and rapid "mutation" of information during cultural transmission results in endlessly varied proliferation of information that nevertheless continues to meet modular input conditions. The sort of cultural information that is most susceptible to modular processing is the sort of information most readily acquired by children, most easily transmitted from individual to individual, most apt to survive within a culture over time, most likely to recur independently in different cultures and at different times, and most disposed to variation and elaboration.

In genetic evolution, there is only "weak selection" in the sense that there are no strong determinants of directional change. As a result, the cumulative effects of small mutations (on the order of one in a million) can lead to stable directional change. By contrast, in cultural evolution, there is very "strong selection" in the sense that modularized expectations powerfully constrain transmitted information into certain channels and not others. As a result, despite frequent "error," "noise," and "mutation" in socially transmitted information, the messages tend to be steered (snapped back or launched forward) into cognitively stable paths. Cognitive modules, not memes themselves, enable the cultural canalization and survival of beliefs and practices.

9.7. No Replication without Imitation, Therefore No Replication

We are increasingly witness to a rapid and global spread of anonymous electronic messages that many of us would prefer to do without yet cannot seem to avoid. This adds much to the sentiment that these messages are authorless, active, aggressive, and alive. I believe this sentiment is an illusion. Ideas don't reproduce or replicate in minds. They don't nest in and colonize minds, and they don't generally spread from mind to mind by imitation. It is minds that produce and generate ideas. Minds structure certain communicable aspects of the ideas produced, and these communicable aspects generally trigger or elicit ideas in other minds through *inference and evocation, not imitation*.

Consider: when millions of Chinese in a rally hold up Mao's *Little Red Book* and recite the statement "Let a thousand flowers bloom," you can bet most do not have the same flowers in mind, or any flowers at all, or even a medium-fidelity version of what others have in mind. What the crowd has in common is a context, for example, a rally against "Western influence." The shared context mobilizes background knowledge in people's minds, for example, that Western ideas, practices, preferences, and so on have heretofore dominated in China. This background knowledge is then used to infer the statement's "real" or "true" underlying message: that autochthonous ideas, practice, preferences should be adopted. This presumptively true message may be interpreted in widely varying ways by different people: that a single-party political system is better than a multiparty system, that acupuncture and herbal medicine should be exclusively or also used in the local hospital, that peasants should determine the priorities of scientific research, that violins should be banned, or that every village should have a politically correct dance company.

To test this speculation, I presented the expression "Let a thousand flowers bloom" to East Asian and American students at the University of Michigan. Students were asked to write down the meaning of the expression on a piece of paper. The responses of one group of East Asian students were as follows: "Many good things will happen"; "Let all in your group be able to express their inner thoughts"; "May there be much crop growth and productivity"; "Make the world a beautiful place, use your talents to help others"; "Allow the flowers to bloom"; "Help your environment, don't pollute"; "Allow life to try to reproduce"; "Let things go on their own and see how things turn out"; "Let us enjoy the beauty and serenity of meadows"; "Grow and flourish"; "Let things be in peace and good things will happen"; "Prosperity, health and happiness." American responses were, if anything, even more wide-ranging.

True, this is a rather extreme example of successful low-fidelity communication via inference instead of imitation. But it is by no means uncommon. Communication involving religious beliefs is often of this sort. For example, in another set of classroom experiments, I asked students to write down on a piece of paper the meanings of three of the Ten Commandments: (1) Thou shall not bow down before false idols; (2) Remember the sabbath; (3) Honor thy father and thy mother. Despite the students' own expectations of consensus, little was apparent. One class of 10 students interpreted 1 as "Only worship the Christian God"; "Don't follow anyone else's rules but God's"; "Only believe in what is good or you go to Hell"; "Be careful not to pay too much attention to wealth and material things"; "Be true to yourself and don't compromise your ideals just to satisfy short-term goals"; "Believe in the system your parents inflicted on you"; "Why not believe in celebrities?"; "Don't follow bad examples"; "You should not worship objects, persons or gods outside your religion"; "It means that person who is false—a person who does not show cooperation should not be someone I follow." These responses, in turn, were presented to another class, and students were again asked to give the meaning of the expressions read. Not one produced a recognizable version of the first Commandment. Interpretations of the other Commandments showed similar variation.

One student project (by Amol Amladi) aimed to show that at least members of the same church have some normative notion of the Ten Commandments, that is, some minimal stability of content that could serve for memetic selection. Twenty-three members of a Bible class at a local Pentecostal church participated in the study, including the church pastor. They were given identical pieces of paper and pens and asked to define seven expressions: the three Commandments listed above as well as "Thou shalt not kill," "The Golden Rule," "Lamb of God," and "Why did Jesus die?" Only the last two elicited consensus (such that the meaning expressed elicited something close to the original on a different occasion). I suspect that similar results would obtain for almost any congregation, despite widespread claims that the Ten Commandments and the Golden Rule are among the most constant norms of contemporary America (R. Frank 1988), with meanings little changed since biblical times (Schlesinger 1999).

By contrast, instances of successful high-fidelity transmission strictly or mainly by imitation are often frequent but minimally informative. Examples include formal salutations (handshakes, wolf whistles, "Dear X . . . Sincerely Y," etc.), standing in line or marching in formation, public applause, driving on the right side of the street rather than the left or vice versa, setting a table, copying addresses and telephone numbers, mimicking another person's mannerisms, humming a tune you heard somewhere and would rather forget, dancing the Twist or the Macarena, reciting a prayer in Latin or Hebrew without understanding a word, ear piercing. Other examples include emulation learning of minimal but sometimes important skills: lighting a fire, artificial respiration, putting babies in baby carriages, cutting paper with a scissors, opening cans with a can opener, the Heimlich maneuver (a recently acquired technique that helps to offset our evolutionary susceptibility to choke on food). Only occasionally does imitated behavior carry information that explicitly includes instructions for replicating that information, as with chain letters, computer viruses, or messages such as "Please forward," "Tell a friend," "Do someone else this favor." But the rarity of information with active instructions for its own propagation is not a significant objection to the meme perspective. It is enough that the cognitive environment *reacts* to memes in reliably productive ways.

Nevertheless, most high-fidelity communication is overwhelmingly inferred rather than imitated. Consider the simple proposition expressed by the statement "Cats chase birds." When you read the statement you do not have the proposition replicate in your mind. This is so even if the context in which the statement is expressed is as poor as can be (e.g., receiving only this statement in a letter with no indication of who sent it or why). Decoding the expression's syntactic structure is not the end of an ordinary communication process but only the beginning. Once syntactically decoded, semantic elements of the proposition are recovered in ways that "automatically" activate a rich set of conceptual structures. These structures are partly innate and partly enhanced through personal experience and previous testimony from others.

For example, because of the universal character of folkbiological taxonomy, you infer that members of a familiar biological species likely have it in their nature to prey upon a wide variety of known and unknown biological species, although this underlying biological disposition may not actually be realized for various reasons (some cats are too sick to chase birds, others may be trained to not chase birds, some large raptors are probably too big for cats to handle, etc.). You further infer that all of these species whose members a cat might chase, if circumstances were right, belong to a taxonomic level superordinate to the level of the species, on a par with the category *fish* or even the category *tree*. Innumerable further inferences could be easily generated from just this entry into your folkbiological taxonomy if the context of the utterance or statement warranted it. In addition to automatic taxonomic inferencing, various aspects of learned encyclopedic knowledge might be mobilized about cat and bird behaviors, predator-prey relationships, and so on. Episodic memories associated with personal recollection could also be stimulated, as when a particular cat chased a certain bird on a given occasion, or when a cat chased a mouse (maybe you've never seen a cat chase a bird). Further inference and interpretation can vary from person to person, depending on differences in extent of encyclopedic knowledge and content of personal memory (for fuller discussion, see Atran 1998).

Unless the context warrants further interpretation and inference, though, most people's inferential processing of a statement is remarkably rapid and economical (Sperber and Wilson 1986; Gigerenzer and Todd 1999). It *stops* just as soon as *enough sense* is made of a statement to be *relevant* (by providing important new knowledge or rejecting of old knowledge). In the present example, this "stopping rule" can apply only after activation of taxonomic knowledge that is shared among minds in the population by virtue of their innate, modular structure.[5]

9.8. Commandments Don't Command and Religion Doesn't Reproduce

Unlike genes, normative ideas like memes rarely copy with anything close to absolute fidelity. The real mystery is how any group of people manages an effective degree of common understanding given that transformation of ideas during transmission is the rule rather than the exception. If transformation (mutation or drift) affects the information at a greater rate than high-fidelity replication, then a favorable or unfavorable selection bias cannot develop for the replicated (hereditary) information. In such cases, selection is not possible.

Moreover, unlike genetic lines, descendent ideas cross and merge so quickly and thoroughly that there can be no identification of "species" or "lineages" of norms, only variably defined "influences." For example, the influence of conservative versus liberal ideas on political, economic, and social behavior may be figuratively stereotyped as that of a "Strict Father" versus a "Nurturing Mother" (Lakoff 1996). Such quasi-metaphorical notions only vaguely summarize open-textured clusters of ideas and behavioral tendencies because that is all there is to them. There are no reliable context-free predictions and no fixed set of associated propositions or contents. For example, no general responses ensue from such seemingly fundamental questions as Should the U.S. Constitution be changed? or Ought government aid industries in difficulty? or If your baby cries at night, do you pick her up?

In the overwhelming majority of religious prescriptions, the meaningful content of a normative idea undergoes modification during horizontal (contemporaneous) and vertical (historical) transmission. For example, the Golden Rule—Do unto others as you would have them do unto you—can mean very different things to different people even within the same local congregation, and can mean different things to the same person at different times. Sometimes, the Golden Rule may suggest noninterference in one another's affairs; at other times, it may be invoked as a call for mutual assistance.

Consider the debate over religion in schools that has recently been agitating U.S. politics. According to then Republican presidential candidate George W. Bush, a "standard version" of the Ten Commandments should be posted in schools and public places (Reuters News Service, 24 June 1999). This echoes a congressionally approved measure whose aim, argues House Republican Representative Henry Hyde, is to "slow the flood of toxic waste in our kids' minds" (Associated Press, 17 June 1999). For Alabama Republican Robert Aderholt: "The recent shootings of Littleton, Colorado, provide an unfortunate picture of terror infested in our school today, children killing children in the halls of our schools, children who do not understand the basic principles of humankind" (Reuters News Service, 17 June 1999). Representative Bob Barr of Georgia suggested during the House debate on the measure that the school shootings would never have happened if the Ten Commandments had been posted in each public classroom. For the

Republican candidate for chief justice of the Alabama Supreme Court: "There is an absolute truth . . . in the Bible . . . upon which this nation was founded and is the basis of the laws of our nation" (Associated Press, 20 October, 2000). In displaying the Commandments in the courtroom, we may thus begin to reverse the process by which the United States has become a "moral slum" by banishing God from public view. This, despite the fact that Jews, Catholics, and Protestants do not necessarily agree on a "standard version."

Another argument for posting the biblical laws was to remind people that the Democratic President flagrantly violated one or more Commandments in his affair with White House intern Monica Lewinsky. Commentaries on the House debate cited two recent books in defense of the measure: former Secretary of Education William Bennett's *The Death of Outrage* (1998) and television personality Dr. Laura Schlesinger's *The Ten Commandments* (1999). Bennett argued that the country was at serious risk of losing its moral bearings without passionate and uncompromising commitment to basic Judeo-Christian principles that condemned President Clinton's behavior.

In her book, Schlesinger claims that the solution to the moral dilemma is really very simple. The sacred Commandments provide clear guidelines in a day-to-day context, enabling us to "elevate our lives above mere frantic, animal existence" in "making healthy, loving and correct choices": "The Ten Commandments are the first direct communication between a people. . . . Each . . . asserts a principle . . . a moral focal point for real-life issues relating to God, family, sex, work, charity, property, speech, and thought. These principles . . . are as relevant today as they were in Biblical times" (1999). For example, the Commandment "Thou shalt not recognize the gods of others" actually means "Attaining money, power, stimulation, professional success, and accumulating possessions, while legitimate pursuits, are not the ultimate purpose of life." "Thou shalt not steal" signifies that "Respecting the property and reputation of others provides mutual safety, peace and propsperity." "Honor thy Father and thy Mother" is for "reinforcing the concepts of treating others responsibly in spite of sentiment or situation." "Remember the Sabbath" is designed to give people time for "refocusing on family, obligations to others, prayer, kindness, justice, and decency." "Thou shall not commit adultery," underscores "the family stability necessary for individual growth and health, community peace, and societal welfare." Thou shalt not kill" tells us that "Not only can a life be physically taken, but demoralization and humiliation can kill our souls." And so on.

The supposed relevance of each Commandment does indeed have a contemporary ring that is flexibly (or vaguely) attuned to everyday life in postindustrial America: beware of overcommitment to money and too much competitive striving for professional success (job stress, the legal pitfalls of insider trading); respect people's property and reputation (vandalism, cutthroat politics and reporting); be responsible and civil (in fierce competition); be kind and decent (help the elderly and infirm, reject child abuse); don't undermine individual growth and health with promiscuous sex (AIDS); don't deaden your own spirit by killing others (school shootings, gang wars, see what happened in Kosovo). There is, however, an admittedly large degree of freedom for individuals to interpret what each Commandment means at any given moment in life, as well as wide latitude for political and social debate. For example, some people, including the hierarchy of U.S. Catholic Bishops, consider the death penalty to violate the Commandment not to kill (Associated Press, 15 November 2000); others, including a majority of the U.S. Congress, consider it an appropriate punishment for violating that same Commandment.

In fact, there is little evidence to support claims for historical continuity in the meaning and relevance of the Ten Commandments. Example-based interpretations in the Old Testament are clearly more pertinent to a bygone era of semi-nomadic pastoralism based on patrilineal social organization. For example, "Thou shalt not bow down to other gods" (Exodus 20:5) is explicitly used to support war and conquest or annihilation of groups competing with the Israelites for control of Canaan: "for I the Lord thy God am a jealous God, visiting the iniquity of the fathers upon the children unto the third and fourth generation" (i.e., in accord with traditions of kin-based patrilineal feuding still found among Middle Eastern pastoralists; Atran 1985a). Thus, "He that sacrificeth to any god, save unto the Lord only, he shall be utterly destroyed" (Exodus 5:20): "So let thine enemies perish, O Lord: but let them that love him be as the sun when he goeth forth in his might" (Judges 5:31). The Spanish Conquistadores, too, violently implemented the "same" Commandment in a different social context. Fray Bernardino de Sahagun reports:

> This is what the Spaniards did to the Mexican Indians because they provoked them by being faithless in honoring their idols. . . . [T]he Spaniards entered with their weapons and ranged themselves all along the inner walls of the courtyard. The Indians thought that they were just admiring the style of their dancing and playing and singing, and so continued their celebration and songs. At this moment, the first Spaniards to start fighting suddenly attacked those who were playing the music for the singers and dancers. They chopped off their hands and their heads so that they fell down dead. Then all the other Spaniards began to cut off heads, arms, legs and to disembowel the Indians. . . . Now that nearly all were fallen and dead, the Spaniards went searching for those who had climbed up the temple and those who had hidden among the dead, killing all they found alive. (1989[1585]: 20:76–77)

According to Bishop Bartolomé de Las Casas (1552), the Mexicans were hanged and burned at the stake in groups of thirteen to honor Christ and his twelve apostles. This is a far cry from mere caution against becoming too attached to money or things.

Disobedience to parents in ancient Israel had little to do with accommodating the needs of others. It was more a prototype of unpardonable refusal to submit to absolute authority: "And he that curseth his father, or his mother, shall surely be put to death" (Exodus 21:17); "A son honoureth his father, and a servant his master" (Malachi 1:6).[6] The Commandment against fornication and adultery was focused on ensuring the patrilineal purity on which rested social and political legitimacy: "If . . . the tokens of virginity not be found for the damsel: Then they shall bring out the damsel to the door of her father's house, and the men of her city shall stone her with stones that she die: because she has wrought folly in Israel, to play whore in her father's house. If a man be found lying with a woman married to an husband, they shall both of them die" (Deuteronomy 22:20–22).

Keeping the sabbath holy did not serve as a simple nudge to timely reflection on family and social obligations. Rather, it was a costly display of devotion and submission whose neglect meant execution: "Six days shall work be done, but on the seventh day there shall be to you an holy day, a sabbath day of rest to the Lord: whosoever doeth work therein shall be put to death. Ye shall kindle no fire throughout your habitations on the sabbath day" (Exodus 35:2–3). Murder, too, was adjudged by pastoral customs of kin-based blood revenge, blood money, exile, and so on. The Old Testament sabbath also functioned to manage long-term fallowing and grazing schedules: "And six years thou shalt sow thy land, and shalt gather in the fruits thereof. But the seventh *year* thou shalt let it rest and lie still; that the poor of thy people may eat: and what they leave the beasts of the field shall eat. In like manner thou shalt deal with thy vineyard, *and* with thy olive yard" (Exodus 23:10–11). Prohibitions against theft likewise reflected the times and circumstances: "If a man shall steal an ox, or a sheep, and kill it, or sell it; he shall restore five oxen for an ox, and four sheep for a sheep. . . . If the theft be certainly found in his hand alive, whether it be ox, or ass, or sheep; he shall restore double" (*Exodus* 22:1–4).

There is little, if any, historically fixed content in interpretation of Old Testament Commandments even within Judaism. Following the Babylonian conquest of Judea (586 B.C.) and exile to more urbanized Persian-ruled lands, relevance to pastoral life lessened and interpretations focused on maintaining group identity in the diaspora. Observance of the sabbath, a markedly public aspect of communal life, equaled or surpassed in importance all of the other Ten Commandments combined. Numerous exegetical volumes were incorporated during the next millennium as "interpretations" (*amoraim*) on the Commandments (in the Talmud). Their aim was to guide normative practices and they acquired the weight of rabbinical law in religious courts and communal services.

The following millennium produced many further interpretive commentaries, including Rashi's (eleventh-century) dialectical *responsa* form of question-and-answer (*tosafot*) and Maimonides' (twelfth-century) books of *Review* (*Mishne Torah*), *Precepts* (*Sefer ha-mitzvot*), *Laws* (*Hilkhot Yerushalmi*), and *Guide* (*Dalālat al-harīn*). Even at the time of their inception, these commentaries were hotly debated (e.g., in 1233, Rabbi Solomon of Montpellier had the Church burn Maimonides's *Guide* in an auto-da-fé). Today, Reform Judaism favors individual leeway and use of *responsa*. Orthodox Judaism prefers more direct and authoritative forms of consultation. For example, Orthodox U.S. Senator Joseph Leiberman indicated that he would not engage in "ordinary" political activity on Saturdays so as "to stop, take stock, have a day of mental and physical rest" (Reuters News Service, 4 November 2000). Nevertheless, he would consult with rabbis if elected vice president to determine when an "emergency" warrants acting on the sabbath for the sake of the nation. A casual glance at television evangelists shows still greater divergence and idiosyncracy in the interpretation of God's "laws."

In the case of religion, the future deeds to be performed in accordance with the appropriate covenants need not be specified in detail, or even at all. All that is required is the convincingly expressed commitment to perform appropriately when some as yet unarticulated need arises. For example, if someone promises to do "God's bidding," then that person, or others, may interpret any number of as yet undetermined actions as satisfying the promise. Of course, embedded within religious liturgies there are also promises that refer to more or less determinate situations that can be observed or discovered to conform to the promise made in rather straightforward and ordinary ways (e.g., I promise to obey the Commandment "Thou shalt not steal"). More often, however, religious prescriptions and commandments do not constitute social norms or memes in the sense of shared rules or injunctions that determine behavior. Instead, they stipulate only a bare, skeletal frame for collectively channeling thought and action. Their expression performatively signals and establishes a cognitive and emotional commitment to seek convergence, but does not specify *what* people should be converging to. Faith in God (or other supernatural agents) is a promissory belief that He (or they) will take care of *that*.

In brief, although the Ten Commandments are commanding, in the sense of drawing attention or priority, they do not command definite behaviors. A similar moral tale could be told of other normative ideas, such as Calvin's 20 or so "Principles" or the Articles of the U.S. Constitution. They are invoked according to the circumstances, with passing notices to already known cases, so as to foster communication and consensus in regard to new or unresolved cases. Their importance lies in the causal links they establish between minds and not in their information content as such.

9.9. Imitation versus Inference

Coevolution theories examine cultural traits from the standpoint of a number of different learning processes: observational experience, imprinting, classical and operant conditioning, formal and informal teaching, and imitation. For memeticists, imitation is often all that is necessary (and sufficient) for replication of information. Only because of imitation can replicated information subsequently undergo natural selection. Imitation occurs when an individual copies a new skill or behavior by observing the behavior of someone else. This allows an individual to benefit directly from the efforts of others without having to pay the original cost of seeking out and testing the behavior. What is copied is not the rote sequence of motor movements but structure-dependent behaviors. This involves simultaneous awareness of distal as well as proximate causal relationships between behavioral elements and anticipation of behavioral consequences that transcend the actual learning context.

Clear examples of imitation among other animals are scarce (Heyes and Galef 1996). In some instances of social learning, one individual may reproduce the novel behavior of another individual without copying it. This is one interpretation of the celebrated case of sweet potato washing by Japanese macaques (Kawai 1965). After a young female found that she could wash sand off her sweet potatoes, others in the group eventually adopted the practice, beginning with relatives and close associates of the discoverer. Arguably, however, the initiator's actions simply drew the attention of others to a context consisting of sweet potatoes, sand,

and water. The other macaques would recognize the context and begin to manipulate its elements. Eventually, after two years on average, some of the other macaques would stumble on the same discovery, in effect "reinventing the wheel" (Heyes and Galef 1996).

The case for imitation is stronger among chimpanzees and bonobos (Boesch 1991). For example, some groups of wild chimpanzees (at Bossou and Kibale) crack nuts, using selected sticks as "hammers" and other objects as "anvils" on which to break the hard casing. Mothers monitor and routinely intervene in attempts by their young to crack nuts. On occasion they take the youngster's club and slowly rotate it (for up to a minute) until the right striking position is attained, and then back away as the youngster practices. Even with apes, however, emulation is rare enough so that there are too few novel behaviors and too few behavioral differences for cumulative combinations of new behaviors to evolve (Tomasello 1994).

On the memeticist view there is no true imitation without replication and no true replication without imitation. The key point about imitation is not that it triggers or elicits or produces or reproduces information. Rather, it both *causes replication* as well as *provides the information to be replicated*. The process of imitation causes replication by including, as part of the information it provides, instructions for copying the information. This entails that the information carried by a replicator will always contain instructions for copying the instructions. The building plan incorporates the builder.

For Dawkins (1999:xi–xii), who follows Blackmore in this regard, considerations associated with copying-the-instructions (replicating the genotype), rather than copying-the-product (reproducing the phenotype), "greatly reduce, and probably remove altogether, the objection that memes are copied with insufficient fidelity to be compared with genes." To illustrate the point, Dawkins offers a thought experiment that compares two games involving representation of a Chinese junk. In the first game, a child is shown a picture of a Chinese junk and asked to draw it. A second child is then shown the drawing but not the original picture and is asked to make her own drawing of it. A third child is asked to make a drawing from the second drawing, and so on down the line. By the time several unskilled drawings are completed, the last drawing in the series will probably differ so much from the first that it would be unrecognizable as a Chinese junk. There is too much "mutation and drift" to sustain the design.

In the second game, the first child is taught by (wordless) demonstration to make a model of a Chinese junk with origami, the art of paper folding. The first child then demonstrates to a second child how to make an origami junk. As the skill passes down the line, it's a good bet that an independent judge will recognize later productions as more or less faithful versions of the original model. If, in the first game, the child also learned by demonstration to draw the junk, later productions might be as recognizable as in the second game. And if, in the second game, the child were given no demonstration of the art of paper folding but simply shown a finished product, then later productions would likely be as unrecognizable as in the first game.

A critical difference between the two games is that only the second has a demonstration that allows the observer to induce the instructions, for example,

"Take a square sheet of paper and fold all four corners exactly into the middle." Although actual productions rarely involve perfect squares or folding to the exact middle, such surface (phenotypic) imperfections tend to cancel out in the long run because the underlying (genotypic) code is "self-normalizing": "what passes down the line is the ideal essence of junk, of which each actual junk is an imperfect approximation." Plato would be grinning. "For me," opines Dawkins, "the quasi-genetic inheritance of language, and of religious and traditional customs, teaches the same lesson" (1999).

Either I have misunderstood the memetic program or there is an insurmountable inductive barrier of the kind Hume and Nelson Goodman described—a logical barrier akin to the physical barrier that disallows mass from exceeding the speed of light and arriving at a destination before it starts out. How in the world is a person ever going to induce a unique rule from any given display of behavior? Rules of grammar, principles of origami, and techniques of drawing are always underdetermined by the behaviors they produce. Any such behavior can be logically associated with indefinitely many alternative interpretations (rules, principles, instructions, techniques, etc.). The only way a person understands one of indefinitely many fragmentary instances of experience as an example of a general rule is by being able to project that instance to an indefinitely large set of complexly related instances (e.g., there are infinitely many imperfect squares or middle lines that satisfactorily instantiate the concepts "square" and "middle" in the origami instruction; Sperber 2001a). But to do *that*, either you must already have the rule in mind or you must be able to *infer* the rule from other premises available in your mind.

Notice that for language, you obviously need a very rich prior inferential structure, including much built-in information content, to be able to infer the same rule from strikingly different behaviors or different rules from remarkably similar behaviors. For example, (1) "John kissed Mary" has nearly the same underlying syntactic structure as (2) "The dog bit the cat." Both are transitive sentences with practically identical phrase structure. By contrast, (3) "John appeared to Peter to do the job" has a very different underlying syntactic structure from (4) "John appealed to Peter to do the job." Sentence 3 involves a recursive structure of two embedded sentences with subject-control (John appeared to Peter → John does the job), whereas sentence 4 involves a recursive structure of two embedded sentences with object-control (John appealed to Peter → Peter does the job). What "self-normalizing" instruction could possibly be read off these "phenotypic" surface forms that would justify including 1 and 2 under the same "genotypic" rule but 3 and 4 under different types? The language learner's task is not to imitate and induce; it is to use the surface form of sentences to test the applicability of preexisting and observationally "invisible" syntactic structures, such as transitive phrase structure and subject-controlled versus object-controlled embeddings (Chomsky 1986).

Like considerations apply to "traditional customs." In the United States, the same experimentally controlled physical or verbal behavior can lead to radically different interpretations and responses depending on whether the person grew up in the South or the North (Nisbett and Cohen 1996). For example, Southerners tend to justify violent responses to a perceived insult, whereas Northerners are more likely to let it pass. Identical observations may produce very different interpretations depending on the observer's cultural background, and quite different observations can lead to similar interpretations in one culture but not another (for a review, see Nisbett et al. 2001). For example, when shown an animated cartoon of a school of fish swimming in unison and a lone fish swimming on the outside, Americans interpret the outlier as a leader who is more intelligent and daring than the others, whereas Chinese interpret the outlier as an outcast, lacking in promise and ignorant of responsibility. Americans tend to interpret mass murders as caused by the inherent mental instability of the murderer; Chinese tend to interpret the same events as caused by situational and social factors such as the prior rejection of the murderer by colleagues at work (M. Morris, Nisbett, and Peng 1995). Given triads of items (man/woman/child, chair/table/bowl), Americans tend to isolate the nonfunctional, categorical dyad (man + woman = adult, chair + table = furniture); Chinese tend to factor out the functional, thematic dyad (mother + child = nurturing, table + bowl = meal; Chiu 1972).

Don't such robust and systematic cultural differences actually reinforce the memeticist's claim instead of refuting it? Dennett (1995:365) suggests that the structure of Chinese or Korean minds is "dramatically different" from that of American or French minds because of differences in prior meme activity. Yet, the experiments cited, and others (Norenzayan 1999), also show that Americans and East Asians have little trouble making sense of one another's preferences. The preferences of one cultural group are also latent alternatives in the other cultural group and can be readily elicited. Notice, for example, that members of neither cultural group interpret the animated fish cartoon simply as changing patterns of illumination, as a lifeless screen, as a moving cluster and point, as a temporal sequence of clusters and points, as a school of fish and a singular object, as a clustered object and a single fish, or any of the infinitely many other logically possible interpretations of the scene observed. This implies operation of richly textured, built-in computational structures that severely constrain the space of logically possible interpretations of experience to a much narrower range of spontaneously accessible, or "natural," interpretations.

To drive the point home, consider a set of three somewhat informal experiments, which I gave to students in two different classes at the University of Michigan (one cotaught with Richard Nisbett). In the first experiment, I flashed a piece of paper for 10 seconds and asked the students to copy what was written on it: "Through the air underground as they fly marry bachelors." None of the students got it perfect, but most captured a few chunks, like "through the air" and "as they fly," and there was also a case of "merry bachelors." Then I showed the following to the students in another class: "Bachelors the through marry fly they underground as." Most got as far as "Bachelors" and then muddled the rest. To the students in the other class I showed "Bachelors marry underground as they fly through the air." Although the last string of words is as meaningless as the other two, all of the students copied it correctly. The reason students got this string right is not because they induced some self-normalizing instruction, but because they were readily able to process it syntactically.

Humans everywhere automatically seek to process word strings as meaningful sentences. To be meaningful a sentence must, first of all, be a sentence, that is, a morphosyntactic structure that fits a set of grammatical rules. The first two strings fail to meet this preestablished cognitive threshold. The first string, however, contains syntactic fragments that, if passed on serially as in the origami experiment, might bias students down the line to alter syntactic structure and lexical combinations in ways that ultimately stabilize into a grammatically correct and meaningful pattern. Such a pattern, if it arises, would not likely be predictable from the original. Chances are more remote that the second string would stabilize because the lack of initial structure allows too much leeway for mutation in every copying episode.

Only the third string is readily inferred to be grammatically well-structured. This stable structure would be initially more resistant to change in a serial transmission than a less well-structured string. Possibly, it would succumb to selective pressures to be *both* grammatically well-formed *and* meaningful, so that it would eventually transform into a meaningful expression as well as a grammatical one. Perhaps the string would stabilize down the line as a statement about "merry bachelors" or a proposition about bachelors who like airplanes rather than subways. Selective pressures leading to both grammatical well-formedness and meaningfulness owe to the mind's modular landscape: in this case, the innate language faculty (Pinker 1994) in conjunction with universal pragmatic constraints on semantic relevance (Sperber and Wilson 1986).

In a second experiment I asked students in two classes to copy a row of nine circles flashed on a piece of paper for 10 seconds. Going from left to right, the last circle in line was smallest; the first circle was the next smallest; the second, third, and fourth circles where all medium size; the fifth circle was largest; and the other circles were all a shade smaller than the fifth. In one class, few students copied the correct number of circles, and no students correctly reproduced their relative sizes, except for the last circle. In the other class, I prefaced the copying instruction with the statement "These are the planets." Nearly all students got the number and relative sizes of the circles right. What happened in the second case was that the students brought to bear a rich repository of background knowledge that enabled them to infer the number and relative size of the objects observed and to at least partially verify what they inferred from what they observed. They did not copy what was presented to them, but used what was visually and verbally presented as inferential stepping-stones toward a more complete representation.

The third experiment is a variation on a thought task that Dan Sperber suggested to me (cf. Sperber 2001a). In one class, I asked students to copy a drawing of a square outlined by eight broken lines, two on each side. All students more or less faithfully reproduced the square, although the overall size of the figure and the lengths of broken lines varied from person to person. Some of the representations were more rectangular than square, and some representations connected all of the broken lines. In the other class, I asked students to copy a drawing that preserved significant features of the square, such as the number and length of broken lines, four right angles, and contiguity among the four right angles (separated only by the length of the gap between the original broken lines). Few students could reproduce the original figure, although most figures produced contained only right angles and one student produced a swastika (with no underlying intent, I'm sure). Logically speaking, there was no difference in the quantity and complexity of information presented to the two classes for copying. Students in the first class, however, all spontaneously inferred that the object of the task was to copy a *square* or *rectangle*.

The information pertinent to being a square or a rectangle was not wholly or even mostly carried in the drawing itself, and the drawing together with the copying instruction did not produce a replication of the drawing. Rather, the drawing triggered a chain of inferences in each person's mind that resulted in the production of a representation that selectively shared particularly significant aspects of the original drawing. The selection of significant shared elements came entirely from the cognitive architecture of the mind—in particular, computational structures that determine the well-formedness of geometric shapes—and not from the broken figure itself. Indeed, the broken lines and angles *could* have been interpreted in indefinitely many other ways. Possible interpretations include a rotated diamond, a digital L together with an inverted L, a digital C and a digital I, a digital D, eight separate lines, one figure consisting of one right angle and three lines conjoined with another figure consisting of two right angles and five lines, a window, the outline for cutting a hole in a piece of paper, pairs of birds flying off in opposite directions, and so forth ad infinitum.

If one objects that many of these logically possible interpretations violate expectations of symmetry or require additional cognitive effort beyond considerations of geometric form, such objections prove the point: broken lines don't make a square. To make a square requires inferences from broken lines to preexisting computational structures. This specific piece of human cognitive architecture selectively reduces the set of all possible relations between stimuli to only those that fit prior determinations of what counts as geometric well-formedness.

Another factor that militates against memes as cognitive replicators transmitted via imitation concerns the role of the emotions in cognitive preference. Religious ideas, for example, are loaded with emotional valence. In fact, without passionate commitment to religious ideas and practice, they would be indistinguishable from Mickey Mouse cartoons or a high school football game and parade. Emotional behaviors do not imitate well or at all (Ekman 1992). True, actors can learn to control some outward manifestations of emotional signaling, such as crying, but even the best actor cannot, by imitation, fall in love, become honest or hateful, be truly vengeful or remorseful, fair or faithful (R. Frank 1988). And crying itself isn't imitated, but elicited.

Emotional preference may also depend on congruence with, or violation of, modular structures. Good geometric forms are "pleasing," deities and demons that violate ontological assumptions (e.g., sentient but bodiless, able to pass through solid objects) are surprising and attention-arresting and hence memorable, and so on (Atran and Sperber 1991; Boyer 1994). Iambic pentameter and couplets that rhyme are culturally specific; but though culturally specific, their pleasingness has to do with innate preference in humans for rhythmic structures.

Memeticists might grant all this and argue that, somehow, memes insinuate themselves into minds to activate the emotions that sustain them, much as a virus can insinuate itself into cells to stimulate certain cell processes that facilitate viral spread and transmission. Nevertheless, relations between emotions and cognitions may also depend on universal structures that cannot be learned simply by imitation or association. Thus, experimental studies of emotion indicate that people cognitively appraise situations in terms of elements such as pleasantness, certainty, anticipated effort, control, legitimacy, and perceived obstacle (Ellsworth 1991).

Distinct emotions tend to be associated with different combinations of appraisals. A perceived obstacle (barrier to a goal) thought to be caused by an external agent is associated with anger; a perceived obstacle that is a person's own responsibility is associated with guilt; a perceived obstacle that has no apparent source is associated with sadness, and a perceived obstacle characterized by uncertainty is associated with fear and anxiety (Keltner, Ellsworth, and Edwards 1993). Like the idea of "good form," the concept of "perceived obstacle" comes from the mind itself and is not implanted by memes.

9.10. Summary: Cognitive Constraints on Culture

Cultures and religions are causally distributed assemblages of mental representations and resultant behaviors. Representations that are stable over time within a culture, like those that recur across cultures, do so because they are readily produced, remembered, and communicated. The most memorable and transmissible ideas are those most congenial to people's evolved, modular habits of mind. These habits of mind evolved to capture recurrent features of hominid environments relevant to species survival. Once emitted in a cultural environment, such core-compatible ideas will spread "contagiously" through a population of minds (Sperber 1985a). They will be little affected by subsequent changes in a culture's history or institutional ecology. They are learned without formal or informal teaching and, once learned, cannot be easily or wholly unlearned. They remain inordinately stable within a culture and are by and large structurally isomorphic across cultures. An example is the categorization and reasoning schema in folkbiological taxonomy.

"Prosthetic devices," such as Bibles and bombs, and natural or constructed ecological features, such as colleges and churches, further constrain and extend the distributions of thoughts and actions that our cognitive endowment favors. By further channeling and sequencing thoughts and actions, these aspects of institutional ecology allow harder-to-learn representations and behaviors to develop and survive, like the science of biology or totemic religion.

One positive message that memetics brings is that evolutionary psychology might profit from a source barely tapped: the study of cultural transmission. Some bodies of knowledge have a stability of their own, only marginally affected by social change (e.g., intuitive mechanics, basic color classification, folkbiological taxonomies); others depend for their transmission, and so for their existence, on specific institutions (e.g., totemism, creationism, evolutionary biology). This suggests that culture is not an integrated whole, relying for its transmission on undifferentiated cognitive abilities. But the message is also one of "charity" about mutual understanding of cultures (Davidson 1984): anthropology is possible because underlying the variety of cultures are diverse but universal commonalities. This message also applies to the diversity and comprehensibility of the various sciences and religions (Atran 1990a, 1998).

Would-be memeplexes, like beliefs in natural causes and supernatural agents, are universally constrained by specific structures of the multimodular human mind. The computational architecture of the human brain strongly and specifically determines reception, modification, and tendency to send any meme on its way again to elicit similar responses from other minds. Even harder-to-learn cultural ideas—such as science, theology, or politics—are subject to modular constraints, at least in their initial stages and conception. Indeed, it is only by pointedly attempting to transcend, violate, or enrich modular expectations about folkmechanics, folkbiology, folkpsychology, and other universal, species-specific cognitive domains that more varied and elaborate cultural ideas acquire life.[7]

10 Conclusion

Why Religion Seems Here to Stay

On a long railroad journey through what was then Indian territory, the author, sitting next to a traveling salesman of "undertaker's hardware" . . . casually mentioned the still impressively strong church-mindedness. Thereupon the salesman remarked, "Sir, for my part everybody may believe or not believe as he pleases; but if I saw a farmer or a businessman not belonging to any church at all, I wouldn't trust him with fifty cents. Why pay me, if he doesn't believe in anything?"

—Max Weber, "The Protestant Sects and the Spirit of Capitalism," in *From Max Weber: Essays in Sociology* (1946)

Civilization requires civility. . . . That, in turn, requires belief in the deeper proposition that, underneath everything, there is truth. . . . because at the end of the day everything finally makes sense and is headed somewhere decent and good. That proposition enables civilized people to trust in argument with one another, in the confidence that truth will win out. Its absence compels barbarians to rely on clubs. . . . The minority of Americans who do not believe in the God described in the Declaration [of Independence] is very small indeed. Polls suggest perhaps 8 percent.

—Michael Novak, *International Herald Tribune* (5 September 2000)

> America is a nation guided by faith. Someone called us a nation with the soul of a church. Ninety-five percent of Americans say they believe in God, and I'm one of them.
>
> —President George W. Bush, addressing students at Tsinghua University, China, 21 February 2002, *The New York Times* (22 February 2002)

10.1. Religions are costly, hard-to-fake commitments to counterintuitive worlds

This book began with a rough-and-ready characterization of religion as a community's costly and hard-to-fake commitment to a counterintuitive world of supernatural causes and beings. The criterion of costly commitment appears to rule out purely cognitive theories of religion as sufficient. Such theories are motiveless. In principle, they can't distinguish cartoon fantasy from religious belief. The criterion of belief in the supernatural rules out commitment theories of religion as sufficient. Such theories are mindblind, in that they ignore the cognitive structure of the mind and its causal role. In principle, such theories can't distinguish strong secular ideologies from religious belief.

All human societies pay a price for religion's material, emotional, and cognitive commitments to unintuitive, factually impossible worlds. From an evolutionary standpoint, it's odd that natural selection wouldn't have forestalled the emergence of such an expensive ensemble of brain and body behaviors. Evolutionary arguments for religion often try to offset its clear functional disadvantages with greater functional benefits. There are many different and contrary explanations for why religion exists in terms of beneficial functions served. These include functions of social (bolstering group solidarity, group competition), economic (sustaining public goods, surplus production), political (mass opiate, rebellion's stimulant), intellectual (explain mysteries, encourage credulity), and emotional (terrorizing, allaying anxiety) utility. Many of these functions have obtained in one cultural context or another, yet all also have been true of cultural phenomena besides religion.

Such explanations of religion are not wrong; however, none predicts the cognitive peculiarities of religion that this book attempts to account for. These include the predominance of agent concepts in religion; the cultural universality of supernatural agent concepts; why some supernatural agent concepts are more easily conceived, remembered, and transmitted than others; how it's possible to validate the truth about supernatural agent concepts when they can't be factually confirmed or logically scrutinized; and how it's possible to block people from simply denying and defecting from religion's moral authority or to prevent them from merely feigning acceptance through deception.

10.2. Religions aren't adaptations but do conform to an evolutionary landscape

To begin with, we found that religions are not adaptations and they have no evolutionary functions as such. There is no such entity as "religion" and not much sense in asking how "it" evolved. Unlike the case for language, for religion there is no integrated set of cognitive principles that could represent a task-specific evolutionary design.

Evolutionary adaptations are functional biological designs naturally selected to solve important and recurrent problems in ancestral environments, such as teeth for masticating food. Evolutionary by-products are necessary concomitants of adaptations that were not initially selected to have any direct utility, such as the whiteness of teeth (owing to much calcium and little bacteria). Nevertheless, by-products can acquire or co-opt functions for which they were not originally designed, such as white teeth as a sign of health for attracting mates.

Religious belief and practice involve a variety of cognitive and affective systems, some with separate evolutionary histories and some with no evolutionary history to speak of. Of those with an evolutionary history, some parts plausibly have an adaptive story and others are more likely by-products. Both adaptations and by-products, in turn, have been culturally co-opted, or "exapted," in religion to new functions absent from ancestral environments and which may have little, if any, systematic relationship to genetic fitness, such as spiritual fulfillment, artistic creation, mass scarification, and human sacrifice.

This book's chosen metaphor for thinking about the evolutionary history and underpinnings of religion in particular, and culture in general, is a mountain-valley landscape formed by different mountain ridges. This landscape is shaped by natural selection. It is ancestrally defined by specific sets of affective, social, and cognitive features (different mountain ridges). Each mountain ridge in this landscape has a distinct contour, with various peaks whose heights reflect evolutionary time.

One such evolutionary ridge encompasses panhuman emotional faculties, or "affect programs." Some of these affect programs, such as surprise and fear, date at least to the emergence of reptiles. Others, such as grief and guilt, may be unique to humans. Another ridge includes social-interaction schema. Some of these may go far back in evolutionary time, such as schema involved in detecting predators and seeking protectors or that govern direct tit-for-tat reciprocity (you scratch my back and I'll scratch yours). Other social-interaction schema appear to be unique to humans, such as committing to nonkin. Still another ridge encompasses panhuman mental faculties, or cognitive "modules," such as folkmechanics, folkbiology, and folkpsychology. Folkmechanics is the oldest part of this evolutionary ridge, perhaps stretching back in part to amphibian brains. Folkpsychology is the newest, with foreshadowing among the great apes. Only humans, however, seem able to formulate the abstract notion of CONTROLLING FORCE that applies to agents, and without which religion is inconceivable. Only humans, it appears, can conceive of multiple models of other minds and worlds, including those of the supernatural.

Human experience that lies anywhere along this evolutionary landscape converges on more or less the same life paths, just as rain that falls anywhere in a mountain-valley landscape drains into a limited set of lakes or rivers. As humans randomly interact and "walk" through this evolutionary landscape, they naturally tend to converge toward certain forms of cultural life, or *cultural paths*. All cultural paths include religious paths as well. The *domain of religion* is the set of *all possible religious paths*. Cultures and religions do not exist apart from the individual minds that constitute them and the environments that constrain them, any more than a physical path exists apart from the organisms that tread and groove it and the surrounding ecology that restricts its location and course.

All religions follow the same structural contours. They all invoke supernatural agents to deal with emotionally eruptive existential anxieties, such as loneliness, calamity, and death. They all have malevolent and predatory deities as well as more benevolent and protective ones. They all systematically, but minimally, violate modularized expectations about folkmechanics, folkbiology, and folkpsychology.

In brief, there are multiple elements in the naturally selected landscape that channel socially interacting cognitions and emotions into the production of religions. These include evolved constraints on emotional feelings and displays, on modularized conceptual and mnemonic processing, and on social commitments and attentiveness to information about cooperators, protectors, predators, and prey. These various landscape features are mutually constraining. For example, emotional reactions to different sorts of social actors involve modularized processes of agent detection. The evolutionary canalization of emotions, cognitions, and social commitments into a natural basin of possibilities, from which interacting individuals select their cultural paths, favors the emergence of religion for the life of our species.

10.3. Supernatural agents arise by cultural manipulation of stimuli in the natural domain of folkpsychology, which evolved trip-wired to detect animate agents

One ridge explored in this evolutionary landscape includes the conceptual modules that shape religious beliefs, with the focus on the summit of folkpsychology (attribution of intentions, beliefs, and desires to other minds). A critical derivative is the concept of supernatural agent common to all religions. The concept of supernatural agent is culturally derived from innate cognitive schema—"mental modules"—for the recognition and interpretation of agents, such as people and animals. In particular, such concepts are triggered by an agent-detection module. This is a sort of innate releasing mechanism, whose proper (naturally selected) domain encompasses animate objects but whose actual domain (of stimuli that mimic the proper domain) extends to moving dots on computer screens, voices in the wind, faces in the clouds, and smoke from a burning building. By "culturally derived," I mean that numbers of people acting together causally manipulate the agent-detection module's actual domain in historically contingent ways, much as makeup and masks involve culturally collective, contingent, causal manipulation of innate, modular sensibilities to secondary sexual characteristics and human facial cues.

Souls and spirits, which derive much of their inductive force from analogy to the dissociated thoughts of dreams and the disembodied movements of shadows, are near-universal candidates for religious elaboration. This is because souls, spirits, dreams, and shadows have many psychologically co-occurring thematic associations (e.g., immateriality and unworldliness, night and death). They also systematically manipulate innate, modularized expectations about folkmechanics, folkbiology, and folkpsychology.

All supernatural agent concepts trigger our naturally selected agency-detection system, which is trip-wired to respond to fragmentary information, inciting perception of figures lurking in the shadows and emotions of dread or awe. Mistaking a nonagent for an agent would do little harm, but failing to detect an agent, especially a human or animal predator, could well prove fatal; it's better to be safe than sorry. The evolutionary imperative to rapidly detect and react to rapacious agents encourages the emergence of malevolent deities in every culture, just as the countervailing evolutionary imperative to attach to caregivers favors the apparition of benevolent deities. This is one way that the conceptual ridge of our evolutionary landscape connects to the ridge of social interaction schema, in particular with the evolutionary design for avoiding and tracking predators and prey.

10.4. Metarepresentation allows moral deception but also enables one to imagine supernatural worlds that finesse modular expectations so as to parry the problem

A key evolutionary design feature of a fully developed human agency module (i.e., folkpsychology) is the capacity to represent alternative worlds and states of mind, to model different models of things. This metamodeling or metarepresentational ability has varied and wide-ranging consequences for human survival. It allows people to conceive of alternative worlds and to entertain, recognize, and evaluate the differences between true and false beliefs. Given the ever-present menace of enemies within and without, concealment, deception, and the ability to both generate and recognize false beliefs in others would favor survival. But because human representations of agency and intention include representations of false belief and deception, human society is forever under the threat of moral defection.

Supernatural causes and beings are always metarepresented as more or less vague ideas about other ideas, like a metaphor that metarepresents the Earth as a mother but not quite, or an angel as a winged youth but not quite. The supernatural can never be simply represented as a proposition about a state of affairs in the world whose truth, falsity, or probability can be factually or logically evaluated. No statement or thought about the supernatural can ever be empirically disconfirmed or logically disproven.

One significant distinction between fantasy and religion is knowledge of its source. People know or assume that public fictions (novels, movies, cartoons, etc.) were created by specific people who had particular intentions for doing so. Religious believers, however, assume that the utterances or texts connected with religious doctrines are authorless, timeless, and true. Consequently, they don't apply ordinary relevance criteria to religious communications to figure out the speaker's true intentions or check on whether God is lying or lacking information. Timelessness implies that cues from the surrounding environment, background knowledge, and memory are all irrelevant. So God's message can apply to any context and to each context in indefinitely many and different ways.

By now it should be patent that supernatural agency is the principal conceptual go-between and main watershed in our evolutionary landscape. Secular ideologies are at a competitive disadvantage in the struggle for cultural survival as moral orders. If some truer ideology is likely to be available somewhere down the line, then, reasoning by backward induction, there is no more justified reason to accept the current ideology than convenience—either one's own or worse, someone else's. To ensure moral authority transcends convenient self-interest, everyone concerned—whether King or beggar—must truly believe that the gods are ever vigilant, even when one knows that no other person could possibly know what is going on. This is another way that the conceptual ridge of our evolutionary landscape connects with the ridge of social interaction, in particular with the evolutionary imperative to cooperate in order to compete.

Supernatural agents seem to vary as much as anything possibly could in human imagination, from talking mountains to jealous but bodiless spirits. Still, the range of supernatural agency is strikingly limited on two counts: the ways such agents actually astonish us obeys a fairly rigid ordering of cognitive categories, and what is left over after we are astonished is remarkably ordinary and mundane.

All cultures have supernatural beliefs that are attention-arresting because they are deeply counterintuitive; that is, they violate innate, modular expectations about basic ontological categories, such as LIVING KINDS (ANIMATE [PERSON, ANIMAL], PLANT) and STUFF (ARTIFACT, SUBSTANCE [OBJECT, MASS]). Nevertheless, religious beliefs remain integrally bound to factual, commonsense beliefs and inferences. For example, bodiless spirits still have indefinitely many sorts of mundane emotions, beliefs, desires, and needs.

A few fragmentary narrative descriptions or episodes are enough to mobilize an enormously rich network of implicit background beliefs. It follows that religious concepts need little in the way of overt cultural representation or instruction to be learned and transmitted. Our memory experiments also indicate that belief sets composed of a mixture of a few counterintuitive beliefs plus mostly intuitive beliefs are recalled with greater fidelity over time than belief sets that are entirely intuitive, with entirely counterintuitive belief sets least remembered of all.

Religious beliefs in the supernatural, then, are always *quasi-propositional* beliefs. Quasi-propositional beliefs may have the superficial subject-predicate structure of ordinary logical or factual propositions, but they can never have any fixed meaning because they are counterintuitive. Their cognitive role is to mobilize a more or less fluid and open-textured network of ordinary commonsense beliefs to build logically and factually impossible worlds that are nevertheless readily conceivable and memorable. Thus, the same metacognitive abilities that make possible lying and deception, and that perpetually endanger any moral order, also provide the hope and promise of eternal and open-ended solutions via representations of counterintuitive worlds.

10.5. Emotionally motivated self-sacrifice to the supernatural stabilizes in-group moral order, inspiring competition with out-groups, so creating new religious forms

All religions require their members to sacrifice immediate self-interest in displays of moral commitment to a community way of life whose rightness and truth is God-given. Because commitment is useless if not successfully communicated, displays of commitment are as necessary as the behavioral commitments they are meant to signify. In general, a promissory display to commit is less costly to individuals than the act of actually carrying out the commitment, and the cumulative benefits to people in society are greater.

Displays of commitment are convincing only if people *are* sincerely committed to live up to their promises no matter what the cost—including sacrificing one's own life if need be. Sincere commitments must be emotionally expressed and passionately held, like uncompromising vengeance or true love. Such apparently irrational commitments insinuate more far-sighted cooperative interests into the overriding preoccupation with short-sighted self-interest, thus optimizing evolutionary strategies for survival in the statistical long run and on average. In this way, both the conceptual and social-interaction ridges of our evolutionary landscape connect with the ridge of emotions.

Sanctified displays and sacred vows of passionate commitment are promissory notes to others to deal with future needs arising from existential anxieties, where there is no predictable outcome, rational solution or prospect of reward. This gives people faith in one another's uncalculating good will. That's the good news.

The bad news is that just as a marriage commitment to one person precludes similar commitment to another, so a religious commitment to one society or moral order usually precludes commitment to another. It is not that all religions explicitly insist on mutually exclusive commitments, though many do. Rather, every religion professes absolute and nonnegotiable commitments that set the limits of tolerance. This adversarial process leads to unending development of new religious and cultural forms, for example, the world order ensuing from the Crusades or after September 11, 2001.

Evolutionarily, at least some basic emotions preceded conceptual reasoning: surprise, fear, anger, disgust, joy, sadness. These may have further evolved to incite reason to make inferences about situations relevant to survival decisions. This was plausibly an important selection factor for the emergence of reason itself. Existential anxieties are by-products of evolved emotions, such as fear and the will to stay alive, and of evolved cognitive capacities, such as episodic memory and the ability to track the self and others over time. For example, people cannot avoid overwhelming inductive evidence predicting their own death and that of persons to whom they are emotionally tied, such as relatives, friends, and leaders. The emotions compel such inductions and make them salient and terrifying. This is "the Tragedy of Cognition." Consistent with this line of reasoning, experiments show that getting people to think about death increases both their feelings of religiosity and group commitment. This is another byway in the evolutionary landscape linking the conceptual, social, and emotional ridges.

10.6. Existential anxieties (e.g., death) motivate religious belief and practice, so only emotional assuaging of such anxieties—never reason alone—validates religion

To better understand the affective ties that religiously bind multiple human minds and bodies, we examined the psychology and neurobiology of religious performance and experience. The focus was on communal rituals, such as initiation rites and exorcisms, and mystical states, such as divine visions and revelations. As with emotionally drawn-out religious initiations, neurobiological studies of stress disorders indicate that subjects become intensely absorbed by sensory displays. Recollections of stressful events tend to telescope on central, autobiographically relevant details of the event structure: who (agents) did or practiced what (instruments and actions) on whom (patients). Unlike chronic stress sufferers, though, participants in even the most emotionally aversive initiations end their ordeal through positive affirmations of social acceptance. Severe initiations, sudden conversions, mystical revelations, and other intense religious episodes combine aspects of personal memory for stressful events (e.g., traumatic, life-changing experiences) and social scripts (coactivation of public categories and connecting pathways) to ensure life-long effect.

Because religious beliefs are counterintuitive their truth cannot be validated by logical inference or empirical observation. Validation occurs only by satisfying or assuaging the very emotions that motivate such beliefs. Communal rituals rhythmically coordinate emotional validation of, and commitment to, moral truths in worlds governed by supernatural agents. Humans, it appears, are the only animals that spontaneously engage in creative, rhythmic bodily coordination to enhance possibilities for cooperation. Rituals involve sequential, socially interactive movement and gesture and formulaic utterances that synchronize affective states among group members in displays of cooperative commitment.

10.7. Neurobiological comparisons of mystical states (e.g., trance) to pathological states (schizophrenia, epilepsy) underplay agency and prefrontal cortical activity

Previous neurobiological studies of religion have focused on tracking neurophysiological responses during episodes of intense religious experience and recording individual patterns of trance, vision, revelation, and the like. This has favored comparison of religious experience with temporal lobe brain wave patterns during epileptic seizures and acute schizophrenic episodes. Most of these studies have little input from, or pertinence to, recent findings of cognitive and developmental psychology.

In so-called neurotheology, for example, cognitive structures of the human mind/brain in general, and cognitions of agency in particular, are usually represented in simple-minded terms: binary oppositions, holistic versus analytical tensions, hierarchical organization, and so forth. Without an adequate understanding and description of the cognitive structures involved in religious experience, the relevance of neuroimaging and other neurophysiological measures remains obscure. Also neglected in most neurobiological accounts of religion is the role of the prefrontal cortices in processing concepts of agency and self and in cognitive mediation of relevant emotions originating in (what was once called) the limbic system. Moreover, for those religious believers who never have an emotionally intense encounter with the Divine—including the overwhelming majority of persons in our society—the neurophysiological bases of faith remain a complete mystery.

Stressful personal episodes become religious experiences by instantiating publicly relevant schemas. Within such cultural schemas, even the eccentric voices and visions of clinically diagnosed schizophrenics and epileptics can become publicly sanctioned revelations, as they are in some societies. In historically seminal moments, which are often times of intense social conflict, such "miraculous" revelations can inspire new belief. Revivalist and starter cults that seek radical religious reform are more likely than established religions to acknowledge the divine character of these more extreme mystical experiences. For the most part, though, relatively few individuals have emotionally arousing mystical experiences, at least in our society. Yet the overwhelming majority of individuals consider themselves to be religious believers. Mystical episodes may inspirit religions—especially new religions—but don't make religion.

Public acts of aggressive "martyrdom," such as suicide bombings, are generally alien to our own society but are usually neither senseless nor crazy. Unlike, say, command suicide, which is a psychotic condition associated with schizophrenia and auditory hallucinations that nobody else can hear, religiously motivated self-sacrifice is neither psychopathic nor sociopathic. Even the most violent cases of martyrdom don't appear to be proximately motivated by sudden bouts of stress or anxiety or correlated with social marginality (at least regarding their own social circles). On the contrary, would-be martyrs often have long periods of indoctrination, careful training, patient dedication, and a relatively stable and positively reinforcing social milieu (see also section 5.6).

The religious path of martyrdom is a cultural path that is deeply grooved, psychologically and socially. It is usually accompanied by a profound sense of injustice whose reversal requires violent death in this life to realize the promise of peace and justice in afterlife. In and along this path, personal and religious identities may have completely fused—often in the social camaraderie of adolescence, when unsettled identities become stabilized—and institutionally detonated in a way that propels those willing to bear the costs of ultimate vengeance to the end of the garden path, in paradise.

10.8. Sociobiology (unknown genes direct religious behaviors) and group selection theory (religious cultures are superorganisms) ignore minds as causes of religion

The overall implication from various empirical case studies and experiments analyzed in this book is that cultural formation and transmission do not consist primarily in shared rules or norms (defined as functional units of cultural selection). Rather, they proceed through the linking and communication of complex patterns of causally connected mental models, values, and behaviors across individual minds and bodies. Much of the purported evidence for norms as units of cultural selection is skimmed from the ethnographic digests of colonial anthropologists and other lone fieldworkers who have tried to expeditiously make sense of alien cultures as "social machines." In much sociobiology, for instance, almost no effort is made to describe how cultural norms are formed and represented in the minds that supposedly produce them, or to causally spell out how they actually work in producing behaviors. It is simply assumed that, in some as yet wholly mysterious ways, specific combinations of unidentified genes are responsible.

Group selection theories also assume that norms are the defining units of religions, the operational units of natural selection and cultural evolution, and the primary "isolating mechanisms" of human societies. The motivating idea of group selection theory applied to humans is that cultures are superorganisms in much the same way that bee hives are. People sacrifice individual fitness to form groups that can outcompete other groups. The key concept is that of "fitness consequences at the level of whole societies." Yet, there is no clear sense to this concept. Because societies constantly transform and merge, they have no stable external physical boundaries or internal structural functions. Societies do not endure, expand or reproduce in any definite, or fitness-definable, sense.

By focusing on the causal pathways that determine how groupwide distributions of cognitions in general, and spiritual values in particular, affect environmental management and group survival, I offered an alternative picture of the causal processes whereby cultures are formed and transformed. Borrowing the set-up of a garden experiment in biology, I provided a detailed example of the ways that a culturally specific learning landscape further constrains the canalization process of our specieswide evolutionary landscape.

We found that three groups living off the same rainforest habitat manifest strikingly distinct behaviors, cognitions, and social relations relative to the forest. Only the area's last native Itza' Maya (who have few cooperative institutions) reveal systematic awareness of ecological complexity involving animals, plants, and people and practices clearly favoring forest regeneration.

We sought to operationalize the role of "noneconomic" entities and values, such as supernatural being, in environmental cognition and behavior. Projective valuation techniques enabled us to measure people's own preferences against others' preferences, including members of other groups, forest spirits, and God. For the Itza', and likely for at least some other small-scale societies with long-standing attachments to their native habitat, nonhuman forest species may come to have intentions and act as negotiating partners through spirits.

For the Itza', species seem to be relationally defined entities, like enemies or friends. As such, they cannot simply be treated as freely interchangeable objects, like items in a shopping mall. This aspect of religion suggests limitations to standard economic and decision theories in accounting for the ways people deal with one another and their resource environment. It also suggests a nonobvious role for religion in helping human societies to resolve "the Tragedy of the Commons" and other ecologically pertinent forms of "the Prisoner's Dilemma." Supernatural agents not only may serve to guarantee trust and foster cooperation among nonkin, as standard theories of social commitment assume. This intentional and affective sense of supernatural agency may also act to allow humans to engage nonhuman resources in relations of indirect or mediated reciprocity so as to better monitor and accommodate to nature's requirements for continuing her human support.[1]

This is, in part, how the distributed networks of representations that we commonly call "cultures" are created. Norms are nodes with ever shifting significance and control in these information networks. Lacking reliable content or boundaries and the requisite fidelity in transmission, norms are not the sorts of replicating units of information, or even reliably blending clusters of information, that can be objects of Darwinian selection. Norms are notional, not natural, kinds.

10.9. Religious notions don't replicate as memes imitated in host minds but recreate across minds through inferences and evocations driven by modular constraints

A quarter-century ago, biologist Richard Dawkins introduced the notion of a meme as a hypothetical cultural unit passed on by imitation, for example, a religious commandment or ritual. Memes provide a novel take on the evolutionary query, Who benefits? Fitness accrues not to brains, individuals, or societies but to memes themselves. Just as genes strive for eternity by successively using individual organisms as disposable vehicles to perpetuate themselves, so memes survive the individual minds that serially host and spread memetic messages. Memes cohere into reproducing bundles or "memeplexes," such as religious liturgies, that restructure the mind's computational architecture, thus making minds safe harbors for like messages and fortresses against messages of competing memeplexes. Cultures and religions are coalitions of memes seeking to maximize their own fitness, regardless of fitness costs for their expendable hosts.

Meme theory has increased in notoriety as we have become increasingly bombarded by anonymous electronic messages that seem authorless, active, aggressive, and alive. But seeming is not being. Ideas do not invade, nest in, colonize, and replicate in minds, and they don't generally spread from mind to mind by imitation. It is minds that create ideas. Minds structure certain communicable aspects of the ideas produced, and these communicable aspects generally trigger or elicit ideas in other minds primarily through *inference and evocation, not imitation and replication*.

Constant, rapid "mutation" of information during communication generates endlessly varied creations that nevertheless adhere to modular input conditions. Beliefs and practices that are stable over time within a culture, like those that recur across cultures, do so because they are readily produced, remembered, and communicated. The most memorable and transmissible beliefs and practices are those most congenial to people's evolved, modular habits of mind. These habits of mind evolved to capture recurrent features of hominid environments relevant to species survival.

The sort of cultural information most susceptible to modular processing is that most readily acquired by children, most easily transmitted across individuals, most apt to survive within a culture, most likely to recur in different cultures, and most disposed to cultural variation and elaboration. Natural or constructed ecological features, such as colleges and churches, further constrain and extend the distributions of thoughts and actions that humans evolved to produce, so that harder-to-learn representations and behaviors can emerge and endure, like various sciences and religions.

10.10. Secular Science and Religion: Coexistence or a Zero-Sum Game?

> "Science cannot tell us what we *ought* to do, only what we *can* do."
>
> —Jean-Paul Sartre, *Being and Nothingness* (1993[1943])

> Sophisticated theologians who do not literally believe in the Virgin Birth, the Six Day Creation, the Miracles, the Transubstantiation or the Easter Resurrection are nevertheless fond of dreaming up what these events might actually *mean*. It is as if the double helix model of DNA were one day to be disproved and scientists, instead of accepting that they had simply got it wrong, sought desperately for a symbolic meaning so deep as to transcend factual refutation. "Of course," one can hear them saying, "we don't literally believe *factually* in the double helix any more."
>
> —Richard Dawkins, *Unweaving the Rainbow* (1998)

> People have known for years that you can have the Earth circle around the sun and still believe in God.
>
> —U.S. Vice President Al Gore to White House reporters, *Drudge Report*, Internet news service (28 May 1999)

Despite the rise of secular ideologies and science, and corresponding predictions of religion's inevitable demise, new religious movements (NRMs) continue to arise at a furious pace—perhaps at the rate of two or three per day (Lester 2002). In Africa, for example, the Winner's Church, a Pentacostal church that celebrates new-found market wealth and success, is only a dozen years old. It already has more than 50,000 members in 32 branches on the continent (Onishi 2002). During the same period, the Falun Gong and Al Qaida have also emerged on a continental, if not world, scale.

There are hundreds of distinct forms of Christianity, Islam, Hinduism, and Buddhism, dozens of which include millions of people. The world's religious panorama is a kaleidoscope of forms that continuously develop, split, merge, transform, decay, and reemerge in a relentless process of competitive agitation. Behind this constant movement, however, the evolutionary contours of the religious panorama remain fairly stable and predictable through all historical, cultural, and scientific change.

Roughly, science is the attempt to associate the flux of our perceptible experiences into a logically thorough structure of thought, in which each event is uniquely and convincingly correlated with that structure in ways that are collectively identifiable and clearly replicable. Science aims to reveal how verifiable facts are systematically coordinated with, and conditioned by, one another. Religion, by contrast, is less interested in how the world is than in how it ought to be, whatever the cost to consistency and actuality. It is not concerned with the rational foundation of material existence but with the moral worth of human values and goals that neither necessitate nor lend themselves to logical justification or empirical confirmation. From this perspective, a conflict between secular science and religion is not inevitable (cf. Einstein 1950). That there has been conflict, however, is undeniable.

The secularization of Europe effectively began with the Peace of Westphalia in 1648, which wound down the horrendously long and violent religious conflict known as the Thirty Years War. Advent of the Enlightenment in the next century fired anticlerical revolutions in France and throughout the European continent and inspired the economic triumphs of science-driven technology and warfare. Ever since, philosophers, economists, political theorists, moralists, and scientists have predicted the inevitable demise of religion. Edward Gibbon (1845[1776–1788]), in his great work *Decline and Fall of the Roman Empire*, set the tone of a new antireligious intellectual tradition with a twofold claim:

- Religion (e.g., Christianity) basically corrodes civilization (e.g., secular Roman law and military discipline).
- Religions (e.g., theistic empires) fetter the sort of competition in the economic, political, and intellectual spheres that leads to creation and progress in civilization (e.g., as with the competing Greek city states, or the enlightened rivalry among European nation-states).

Empirical philosophers Bertrand Russell (1948) and Karl Popper (1950) championed this sentiment. Biologist Jared Diamond's (1997) Pulitzer prize-winning short history of the world also echoes this message, as does biologist Richard Dawkins's (1998) call to substitute the "poetry" of scientific reason for religion.

According to philosopher Kai Nielsen, "In Western societies, during the 19th and early 20th centuries, belief versus unbelief or theism versus atheism was a hotly debated issue, but today atheism among intellectuals is as common as blackberries in North Carolina" (1996:595). This is a good thing because "We should not be like children who tell ourselves fairy tales, even consoling fairy tales." A positive view of science and economy has often spawned a negative view of religion as apparently irrational on two counts: as logically incoherent and economically impractical. Yet, despite increasingly secular globalization and scientific advance—and arguably because of them—religious renewal is on the rise the world over. Gibbon did not foresee the nineteenth-century rise of the Mormons, Ahmadis and Bahai, much less the twentieth-century emergence of the Moonies, Al Qaida and Falun Gong.

There are now nearly 2 billion self-proclaimed Christians (about one-third of humanity), 25 percent of whom are Pentacostals or charismatics (people who stay in mainstream Protestant and Catholic churches that have adopted Pentacostal practices like healings, speaking in tongues, casting out demons, and laying hands upon the sick; Goodstein 2000:24). Polls indicate that 88 percent of Americans and 61 percent of Europeans believe in the soul (Gallup and Newport 1991; Humphrey 1995). Fundamentalism among Islam's 1.3 billion people has progressed apace and has also made significant inroads into Judaism's two largest national communities (Israel and the United States).

The United States, the world's most economically powerful and scientifically advanced society, is also one of the world's most professedly religious societies.

Evangelical Christians and fundamentalists include about 25 percent of Americans (Talbot 2000:36) and together with charismatics constitute about 40 percent of the American population. About the same number believe that God speaks to them directly (H. Bloom 1999:120–123). Among Americans, 90 percent pray for God's intervention in life and 90 percent believe God cares for them (H. Bloom 1999); 69 percent believe in angels and 50 percent believe in ghosts, the devil, and the literal interpretation of Genesis (polls cited in Pinker 1997; Dennett 1995).

Although 83 percent of Americans surveyed support the teaching of creationism, 79 percent agree that a person can believe in evolution and still believe that God created humans and guided their development (Glanz 2000: A1, A10). Most people seem to believe that the mechanistic laws of physics and biology proximally constitute the natural stage of human existence, but that the first or ultimate cause of existence, as well as the final say at any given moment in development, is God's will (Evans 2001). In other words, most people in our society accept and use both science and religion without conceiving of them in a zero-sum conflict. Genesis and the Big Bang theory can perfectly well coexist in a human mind. According to several polls, about 40 percent of scientists believe in God (Blakesee 1999).

A few poll numbers hold particular interest: 94 to 96 percent of Americans profess belief in God (E. Wilson 1978:177; H. Bloom 1999), but 98 percent would not vote for an atheist for President (Elliot 1985:784). Such sentiments seem to change little over the years. Thus, a century ago, while visiting the United States, Max Weber (1946:46) observed that even the most hard-headed capitalist would make it his business to advertise his faith in order to display his trustworthiness to others. More recently, U.S. President George Bush appears to have surmised that the end of the cold war was truly at hand when Russian President Vladimir Putin confided that he was deeply worried that he had lost a cross that his mother had given him in a burning building. A worker found the cross, and Putin reportedly said to Bush: "It was as if something meant for me to have the cross." Bush replied: "Mr. Putin, President Putin, that's what it's all about—that's *the* story of the cross." And that's when the U.S. President knew that the Russian President could be trusted: "[Putin] basically seemed he was saying there was a higher power" (cited in Noonan 2001).

One interpretation of this sentiment is that true religious belief is almost always reckoned as sincere social commitment, whereas beliefs about everyday empirical facts, science, or economics are generally not. Of course, professions of religious belief are not guarantees of actual faith or honesty, much less of good or moral action. Nevertheless, people apparently infer that explicit professions of faith carry the implicit message that trusworthiness matters—in the unblinking and forever watchful eyes of God—and commitments will be met even at great cost and even when there is no hope of reward. Science and secular ideology are poor competitors in this regard.

One conceptual difference between science and religion is the way they process (meta)representations. Science, like religion, uses metarepresentation in cosmology building, for example, in analogies where some initially more familiar domain (e.g., the solar system, computers, genetic transmission) is used to model some initially less familiar system (e.g., the atom, mind/brain, ideational transmission). In fact, science and religion may use the same analogies; however, there is a difference in these uses.

For example, the Rutherford-Bohr analogy of the atom with the solar system was an acceptable conceptual frame for research in physics from about 1912 to 1925. Its empirical disconfirmation remains a valuable pedagogic guide to understanding more likely theories. Followers of the Maharishi Mahesh Yogi, too, put out yearly advertisements in the *International Herald Tribune* claiming that the microcosm and macrocosm, the atom and the solar system, and gravity and electromagnetism combine into a unified religious-scientific "field theory." But the Maharishi's disciples, unlike those of Einstein and Bohr, seek an eternal "truth" that harmonizes smaller bodies (especially human bodies) with larger nature (especially the surrounding ecology). This truth is sustained by faith in the authority of those charged with continually reinterpreting it and fitting it to new circumstances.

Science aims to reduce the analogy to a factual description, where the terms of the analogy are finally specified, with no loose ends remaining and nothing left in the dark: atoms are scientifically like solar systems if and only if both can be ultimately derived from the same set of natural laws. Whereas science seeks to kill the metaphor, religion strives to keep it poetic and endlessly open to further evocation. In the case of religion, these metarepresentational ideas are never fully assimilated with factual and commonsensical beliefs. They are always held metarepresentationally: they are displayed, discussed, interpreted, and reinterpreted as doctrines, dogmas, sacred texts, or "norms" that further illustrate beliefs and behaviors rather than describe beliefs and behaviors. The fact that religious beliefs do not lend themselves to any kind of clear and final comprehension allows their learning, teaching, exegesis, and circumstantial application to go on forever.

A second, more deeply affecting difference between science and religion is that humans are only incidental elements of the scientific universe, whereas they are central to religion. A science that neglected to make reference to humans would, as Bertrand Russell (1948) commented, "suffer at most a trivial imperfection." Religion without humans would be senseless. A closely related difference is the enthronement of agency in the religion versus its banishment as a causal force from science. The result is that religion fares poorly against science in knowledge of impersonal affairs, whereas science cannot compete well morally with religion in human affairs. Militant creationist attempts to place Genesis on a theoretical par with Darwin appear more ludicrous than lucid, whereas attempts by scientists and philosophers of science to replace religion with science generally prove more embarrassing than effective.

A third difference that seems crucial to social life is that religons are morally absolute, however conceptually flexible and open-textured, whereas science endlessly pursues ever changing truth by strict and rigid means. Religion establishes truth to provide moral and social stability. Science sacrifices surety to discover truth's illusions. Religion abhors the competition for truth. Science can't live without it.

The constant danger of replacement by other possible moral worlds does not primarily concern the everyday physical world of substances and species, locomotion and lakes, hawks and handsaws. There are more or less independent commonsense grounds for discovery and validation of knowledge about natural kinds and relations in the everyday physical world. This occurs through routine processes of perceptual verification that are conceptually allied to inference programs (sometimes rigidly via mental modules). These verification and inferential processes do not (and often cannot) appreciably change the nature of the entity or relation scrutinized. (I'm obviously not talking about the phenomena of quantum physics.) No such grounds exist for independent discovery and evaluation of the truth about socially constituted relationships and human kinds, such as reciprocity and responsibility, honor and humility, good and evil, or who should be pauper and who should be prince.

Supernatural agents contribute to maintaining the cooperative trust of actors and the trustworthiness of communication by sanctifying the actual order of mutual understandings and social relations as the only morally and cosmically possible one. Moreover, the causal scope of supernatural agents subsumes both the physical and social elements of the environment under a sanctified moral order. Whatever certainty, coherence, or verifiability is attached to physical understanding becomes solid inductive evidence for corresponding certainty, coherence, and verifiability with respect to the social and cosmic order governed by supernatural agents.

Thus, a fourth difference between science and religion is that factual knowledge as such is *not* a principal aim of religious devotion but plays only a supporting role. Only in the past decade has the Catholic Church reluctantly come to acknowledge the factual plausibility of the ideas of Copernicus, Galileo, and Darwin (Geitner 1999). The earlier rejection of their theories stemmed from the challenges posed to a cosmic order unifying the moral and material worlds. Separating out the core of the material world would be like draining the pond where a water lily grows. A long lag time was necessary to refurbish and remake the moral and material connections in such a way that would permit faith in a unified cosmology to survive.

Religion survives science as it does secular ideology not because it is prior to, or more primitive than, science or secular reasoning, but because of what it affectively and collectively secures for people. Consider: the norms that serve as prototypes of shared knowledge and understanding, and that reinforce the stability of the distributed network of cognitions and behaviors that constitute cultural identity, are always vulnerable. They are susceptible to rejection by individuals within the society and ultimate replacement by other norms emanating from within or without. In times of stress, internal defection and outside competition are often conjoined: people are most apt to defect to external competitors when internal cooperation is most needed. This, according to the fourteenth-century Arab historian and philosopher Ibn Khaldûn (1958: II,iii:41), is a regular and perhaps unavoidable aspect of the history of human societies.

If people learn that all apparent commitment is self-interested convenience or, worse, manipulation for the self-interest of others, then their commitment is debased and withers. In times of vulnerability and stress, social deception and defection in the pursuit of self-preservation are more likely to occur. As a result, whole societies are more liable to disintegrate when people need their protection most. Everyone becomes poorer off and on their own. Religion passionately rouses hearts and minds to break out of this viciously rational cycle of self-interest and to adopt group interests that may benefit individuals in the long run. Even from a primarily economic standpoint, religion provides a backdrop of trust and "social capital" (Coleman 1988) that reduces "transaction costs" associated with the legal costs of holding self-interest in check (lawyers, litigation, enforcement, monitoring, etc.).[2] More generally, religion underpins the "organic solidarity" (Durkheim 1933[1893]) that makes social life more than simply a contract among calculating individuals. It creates the arational conditions for devotion and sacrifice that enable people and societies to endure against even terrible odds.

In breaking one vicious cycle, however, religions almost invariably set in motion another. The more strongly individuals hold to group interests, the more they risk excluding or fighting the interests of other groups. The absolute moral value that religions attach to in-group interests practically guarantees that the ensuing conflict and competition between groups will be costly and interminable and only resolved in specific cases by banishment, annihilation, or assimilation of outgroups and their ideas. Principles of evolution do not discourage, and may in fact encourage, this sort of creatively destructive spiral.

Within this spiral, the "secular" democracies of North America and Europe have arguably lessened the compulsion of religious exclusion. They have done this not so much by dampening religious passion (more true anyway of Europe than the United States), as by channeling religious conviction into more or less *voluntary* association and action. As Weber (1958:23) noted, Western capitalism itself is a "civic economy" rooted in a Protestant religious ethic of volitional membership in a moral community. In the United States, it was neither the family nor the state that was traditionally the primary locus and focus of capitalist production, but town and city as corporate communities (Fukuyama 1995). Here, religious and civic commitment was, at least legally, if not always practically, by elective choice and not by obligation. The faithful exercise of choice, in turn, became a prime measure of moral commitment to customers, creditors, employers, and employees who were also neighbors, friends, helpers, and defenders. This, too, was the ideal of "One Nation Under God" in the "pusuit of happiness," which was framed by "founding fathers" who well understood the importance of religion for the common trust, despite wide variation in strength and kind of belief.

Purely ideological commitments to moral principles also lack interactive aspects of personal agency—and the emotional intimacy that goes with it—as well as the promise to allay the eruptive and uncontrollable existential anxieties for which there appears to be no rational expectation of resolution, such as vulnerability (to injustice, pain, dominance), loneliness (abandonment, unrequited love), and calamity (disease, death). In such matters, science also has little reassuring to propose, other than that everyone is in the same boat. At best, this is cold comfort.

All of this isn't to say that *the* function of religion is to neutralize moral relativity and establish social order anymore than *the* function of religion is to promise resolution of all outstanding existential anxieties, or to give meaning to an otherwise arbitrary existence, or to explain the unobservable origins of things, and so forth. Religion has no evolutionary function per se. It is rather that moral sentiments and existential anxieties constitute—by virtue of evolution—ineluctable elements of the human condition, and that the cognitive invention, cultural selection, and historical survival of religious beliefs owes, in part, to success in accommodating these elements.

There are also other factors in this success, involving naturally selected elements of human cognition, such as the inherent susceptibility of religious beliefs to modularized conceptual and mnemonic processing. Although certain structural aspects of religious belief and practice are recurrently identifiable across cultures, generations, and minds, the actual contents of religious beliefs and practices vary widely from one culture, generation, or mind to another. With such substantial variation, any stability in particular contents over time or space cries out for explanation, for example, the sentient but bodiless supernatural agents that crop up across cultures and history. Such explanation cannot be reduced to one or a few timeless causes (e.g., class domination) or categories (e.g., mythic archetypes). A big part of any such explanation is that the indefinitely many unpredictable historical and ecologically contingent factors that affect religious beliefs and practices are constrained by naturally selected elements of human cognition to converge toward a restricted set of cultural paths.

In this book, I have sketched a particular evolutionary landscape in which all human experience occurs. This landscape's naturally selected structures of cognition, emotion, and social relations canalize the thoughts and actions of interacting individuals into cultural paths that tend to be also religious paths, which accounts for religion's enduring cross-cultural success. Religion is not an evolutionary adaptation, but it does more or less describe a natural space of possibilities—a set of paths—in the basin of this landscape. Supernatural agency is a main watershed in this evolutionary landscape.

This book harbors no claim about whether or not supernatural agency in particular, and religion in general, has overall fitness benefits. Its arguments suggest only that no other mode of thought and behavior deals routinely and comprehensively with the moral and existential dilemmas that panhuman emotions and cognitions force on human awareness and social life, such as death and deception. As long as people share hope beyond reason, religion will persevere. For better or worse, religious belief in the supernatural seems here to stay. With it comes trust in deities good and bad, songs of fellowship and drums of war, promises to allay our worst fears and achieve our most fervent hopes, and heartfelt communion in costly homage to the absurd. This loss and gain persist as the abiding measure of humanity. No other seems able to compete for very long. And so spirituality looms as humankind's provisional evolutionary destiny.

NOTES

Chapter 1

1. As I was preparing the final version of this manuscript, Pascal Boyer published his *Religion Explained* (New York: Basic Books, 2001), which takes up some similar cognitive issues in original ways. Both of us were first introduced to such issues in the theory of religion by Dan Sperber.

2. Dialectical materialism postulates, as a historical "axiom," a "natural law" of "unconditional" progress in revealing nature's "absolute truth." This includes "absolutely objective knowledge" of communism's ultimate historical triumph (Lenin 1972[1908]:153). Market fundamentalism assumes absolute faith in the wisdom and moral value of an unfettered marketplace, where capitalism's "invisible hand" is thought to inexorably drive society to produce the greatest good for the greatest number—a mathematical and physical impossibility if resources remain limited while population grows (Hardin 1968).

Chapter 2

1. Hare et al. (2000; Hare, Call, and Tomasello 2001) showed that subordinate chimps would take only whichever food item was visually occluded from a dominant chimp. In one experiment, the dominant chimp, who originally saw where a banana was placed, was made to exit the scene. The experimenters then occluded the banana before reintroducing the dominant onto the scene. The subordinate still would not take the banana. But when a *different* dominant chimp was introduced onto the scene after the banana was occluded, the subordinate would take it. The implication is that the chimps can mentally represent one another's intentional focus, at least when that

focus is on a perceptual event (cf. Suddendorf and Whiten 2001). But these intriguing findings have so far failed attempts at replication in different laboratories (Povinelli 2001).

2. Domain-specific accounts of cognitive ontogenesis bear little relation to Piaget's (1970) well-known but largely specious account of the "organic" transformation from the child's sensorimotor intelligence and object recognition to ego-centered preoperational intelligence and linguistic concepts, to final metamorphosis into context-free science and logic via the causally opaque process of "reflective abstraction."

3. Neanderthal gravesites in Europe and the Middle East were clearly intentional. The cadaver was usually placed in a sleeping or fetal position. Some remains have been found with fauna placed in the hands or on the body, along with red ocher. Sometimes a Neanderthal couple and several children were buried together, suggesting that families remained united after death. For example, at Shanidar Cave in Iraq, remains were carefully placed in the fetal position on a bedding of woven woody horsetail, a local plant. Pollen samples reveal several different species of flowers: cornflowers, groundsel, grape hyacinths, yarrow, St. Barnaby's thistle, woody horsetail, and mallow. According to paleoanthropologist Ralph Solecki, several have medicinal qualities that "range from relief from toothache and inflammation to uses as poultices and for spasm" (1971:249).

Seven individual Neanderthal graves were found at La Ferrassie, in southwest France: a man, a woman, two children, and three infants. The man, about 45 years old, had been buried lying on his back, slightly inclined toward the left, with flexed legs. Three flat stones were placed with the body, one by the skull and the others on the arms. The grave also contained incised large bones, bone splinters, and flint flakes. Near the male grave was the skeleton of a woman age 25 to 30, buried in a way suggesting that she had been tied up before burial (Shackley 1980:87). A child skeleton, of about 4 years of age, "was headless; the skull was buried a short distance away, covered with a large stone marked with a series of artificial, cuplike depressions" (Trinkaus and Shipman 1993:255). Nearby pits and trenches contained animal bones.

At Le Moustier, also in southern France, a man's remains had been sprinkled with red ocher: "His head rested on a pillow of flints, and burned wild cattle bones were scattered about, as if in offering" (Shreeve 1995:53). At Teshik-Tash in Uzbekistan, a child of about 9 years of age was buried with mountain goat horns arranged vertically, in pairs, forming a circle around the body, with the pointed ends driven in the ground.

At Drachenlock, in Switzerland, "a number of bear skulls were found stacked in a stone chest" (Kennedy 1975:92). In Regourdou, southern France, a rectangular pit contained the remains (mostly skulls) of at least 20 bears, covered by a stone slab weighing nearly a ton. Nearby lay remains of a Neanderthal in another stone pit, along with a bear humerus, a scraper, a core and some flakes (Chase and Dibble 1987).

In sum, the collective evidence suggests that Neanderthals ritually interred their dead. Still, some paleoanthropolgists question whether Neanderthals ceremoniously dealt with death: "Neanderthals buried their dead only to discourage scavengers and eliminate odor" (Rudavski 1991:44). Flower pollen could have been carried to the grave by the wind or the feet of mourners (Johanson and Edgar 1996:100). Underground streams could have led to accumulation of bear bones in cave niches and to groups of fallen roof blocks; this would produce the illusion of an intentionally made storage pit (Chase and Dibble 1987). There is also the possibility that the conventional aspects of Neanderthal burials may have lacked symbolic charge owing to deficient prefrontal cortical development (a sharper flexion of the cranial base in modern humans tucked the face under the frontal lobes to allow prefrontal development, Balter 2002:1221).

4. I have serious doubts (Atran 2001e) about Leda Cosmides's (1989) interpretation of the Wason selection task (see also Gigerenzer and Hug 1992; Fiddick, Cosmides, and Tooby 2000). But these doubts suggest only that the Wason task is not the appropriate one for testing her very plausible hypothesis, namely, that maintaining a variety of concrete forms of social cooperation among nonkin leads to selection pressures for abstract computational algorithms to detect cheaters on implicit or explicit social contracts.

5. Depression seems to be particularly contagious during economic recessions in the wealthier countries of the industrialized world. For example, "Cases of clinically identified depression have surged in recent years [in Japan, whose economy has been mired in stagnation for a decade], doubling from more than 200,000 in 1994 to about 430,000 in 1998, the latest year for which figures are available" (M. Nakomoto, *Financial Times*, 9–10 June 2001, p. 4). In the United States, plans are being instituted for a national "network of comprehensive depression centers" (Imperio 2002:10).

Chapter 3

1. For the Lacandon, the term for dream, *wayak'*, also implies magic and the supernatural. Among Yukatekan-speaking Mayan groups (Yukatek, Itza', Mopan, Lacandon), the root *waay* refers to sorcery and also appears to be the root of *way-äl*, "metamorphose" (e.g., caterpillar to butterfly, ice or hailstones to water): "It may also be the root of wy-s-ik, 'create.' This gives us linguistic support for the close association between religion, dreams and magic" (Bruce 1975:14). The Lacandon Onen is a vestigial totemic notion that persists today only in regard to the interpretation of dreams. Among pre-Columbian Yukatekan groups, the concept *waay* denoted the animal spirit-companions of gods, ancestors, kings, and queens (equivalent to the idea of *nawal* among Nahuatl-speaking Mexican groups, such as Toltecs and Aztecs). A person's spirit-companion was that person's "heart" or "essence" (*ch'ulul;* cf. Freidel, Schele, and Parker 1993).

2. The possible, though not obligatory, interpretation of dreams through reversal allows almost limitless ways to fathom events in terms of something and its contrary:

> CAESAR: Calphurnia here, my wife, stays me at home: She dreamt to-night she saw my statua, which like a fountain with a hundred spouts, Did run pure blood; And many hasty Romans Came smiling, And did bathe their hands in it. . . .
>
> DECIUS BRUTUS: The dream is all amiss interpreted; It was a vision fair and fortunate: Your statue spouting blood in many pipes, In which so many smiling Romans bath'd, Signifies that from you great Rome shall suck Reviving blood. (Shakespeare, *Julius Caesar*, Act II, scene 2)

3. For example, the spirits of the Kayans of Borneo fall into three principal classes (House & McDougall 1912:II, 28–32):

1. Anthropomorphic spirits that dwell in remote and vaguely conceived regions, and that intervene very powerfully in human affairs: "Towards these the attitude of the Kayans is one of supplication and awe, gratitude and hope. . . . These spirits must be admitted to be gods in a very full sense."

2. Spirits of living and deceased persons and of other anthropomorphically conceived spirits: "Such are those embodied in the omen animals and in the domestic pig, fowl, dog, in the crocodile, and possibly the tiger-cat and a few other animals." These are less powerful than spirits of the first class.
3. The third class is more heterogeneous and comprises all the spirits that seem always at hand. Some are good, but many are malevolent. The latter include spirits attached to the heads hung in houses: "The dominant emotion in the presence of these is fear; and the attitude is that of avoidance and propitiation."

There is little here, save for the spirits of the heads hung in houses, that is not also present in popular Christianity, Islam, Hinduism, and so forth.

4. For Fodor (2000), the primary criterion for modularity is "encapsulation," that is, exclusive access to a proprietary input. Encapsulation is supposedly true only of perceptual modules, such as language or facial recognition. In ordinary circumstances, internal principles of grammar, phonetic rules, and lexical structures provide a database for rapidly processing linguistic input with practically no regard for, or influence from, other cognitive systems. Similarly, folkbiological taxonomy arguably provides a database for nearly "automatic" recognition of plant and animal exemplars in terms of the (folk)species to which they uniquely belong.

Of course, almost by definition *any* conceptual *system* has *some* functional *autonomy* and is therefore "encapsulated." Virtually any game (e.g., chess) or routine activity (e.g., car driving) relies on a restricted database that gives it privileged access to a certain range of input. This would seem to trivialize the notion of modularity and rob it of any descriptive or explanatory force. Indeed, according to Fodor (2000:23), the best case that can be made for the computational theory of mind (i.e., the view that all conceptual processes are Turing-like computations over syntacticlike representational structures) is in terms of conceptual modularity; however, because conceptual modularity "is pretty clearly mistaken," then, very likely, so is the claim that the computational theory of mind has much to tell us about how the mind configures the world. For Sperber (2001b), Fodor's pessimism is unwarranted because it ignores the fact that privileged access to an input set *depends on the competition for mental resources*. Evolutionary task demands generally favor certain naturally selected modular structures for processing certain types of naturally occurring and statistically relevant input (*ceteris paribus*). In sum, an explanatory account of modularity in terms of evolutionary and developmental considerations of modularity is preferable to a purely descriptive account in terms of "encapsulation," "mandatoriness," and the like.

5. The Csibra et al. (1999) experiment establishes necessary, but not necessarily sufficient, conditions for understanding the abstract causal notion of CONTROLLING FORCE. It's an open question whether apes would perform successfully; an experiment by Uller and Nichols (2000) purporting to show chimps pass the test has since been retracted (Uller and Nichols 2001). Experiments by Povinelli (2000) and colleagues indicate that chimps understand causal relations between perceptible events (cf. Premack and Woodruff 1978) and generalize from observed statistical regularities and causal asymmetries (e.g., knife cuts apple but not vice versa) to similar causal events (scissors cuts paper but not vice versa). But they don't seem capable of abstracting unobservable causal notions, such as FORCE and WEIGHT, from observable events. For example, in one study chimps and young children were both fairly adept at trying to figure out how a block with one flat end and one beveled end could be made to stand (seeing that the block would fall if set down on the beveled end, they soon felt for the

beveled end before setting down the block on its flat end). In another study, a hidden weight was placed in a block resembling an inverted "L." When the weight was set in the vertical part of the block, the block would stand; when the weight was set in the horizontal part of the block, it would tip over. The children soon figured out that by paying attention to differences attributable to an unobservable concept of CENTER OF GRAVITY, they could make the block stand. The chimps never did.

6. Epicurus and Lucretius tried to argue that people shouldn't fear death—nor, therefore, invoke gods for help—because death is simply nonexistence: if people aren't worried by the fact that they didn't exist for some indeterminate time in the past, then there is no reason they should be worried about not existing for some indeterminate time in the future. But death is quite different from nonexistence. There is a lot more anxiety about losing what you have, especially your own life or that of someone dear, than of never having something (Kahneman and Tversky 1979).

7. We tested 28 college students ($n = 14$ in the experimental group, $n = 14$ in the control group). The experimental group was more likely to feel religious, $t(1, 26) = 2.03$, $p = .05$, and to believe in God, $t(1, 26) = 2.33$, $p < .05$.

8. The Cubeo Indians of southeastern Colombia dread the deep forest (*maqáno*), wherein lurk the "*abuhuwa,* canabilistic monsters living in the forest" (I. Goldman 1940:244). Qechua of northern Ecuador warn people to be watchful after sunset because of the "*auqui,* night-wandering spirits, particularly harmful to infants . . . exposed towards evening to the gaze of ghost children who may look like animals" (Parsons 1940: 220). For the Kuranko of Sierre Leone, Africa, "Such persons are known as *yelalafentiginu* ('change thing masters') and regarded with awe because . . . [they shapeshift] in the form of predatory or dangerous animals" (Jackson 1990:59). The long-haired *ixtab'ay* of the Lowland Maya forests—part woman, part animal, part plant—tempt their victims with songs and cakes, bringing them to perdition much as the water sirens of Homer's *Odyssey* enticed ancient Greek mariners. In the paintings of the Ajanta caves, executed when Buddhism dominated north India, "the female, or Rākshasi, is represented as a gobline in the shape of a handsome woman, red, fair, or dark, with flowing hair, killing men and feeding on their flesh and blood" (Crooke 1907:238). In the folk Buddhism of Chinese villages, "certain animals . . . appear in human form" to seduce or otherwise outfox men, "especially . . . foxes (transformed into women)" (Wieger 1927:667).

9. North American students report God as being more similar sometimes to father and sometimes to mother (Vergote and Tamayo 1980) and sometimes similar to both father and mother (Birky and Ball 1987). Findings vary according to religion (Catholics vs. Protestants; Rees 1967 in Beit-Hallahmi and Argyle 1997), sex and age of respondent (Deconchy 1968), and education level (Tamayo and Dugas 1977). Non-Christian Japanese kindergartners identify God more with teachers than with parents (Saski and Nagasaki 1989).

10. The sacrifices are often gruesome, including mutilation and beheading of animals (buffalo, pig, lamb, goat, chicken). The officiating holy man (*pūjārī*) sometimes leaps at the animal's neck, bites through its jugular vein, and then parades the streets with the animal's entrails around his neck and its liver in his mouth (Whitehead 1988[1921]: 140–143). Persons who deviate or interfere with the ceremony may be killed by irate villagers. In her pre-Brahmanistic manifestation as Ammavaru (before the invading Indo-European Aryans subjugated Dravidian south India), the village goddess also seems to have required human sacrifice (*narayāga*; J. Wilson 1855; Thurston 1907; Crooke 1907).

11. Kāli was also chief goddess of the "Thugs" (*sthagati* = "he covers, conceals"), a religious fraternity of professional killers who roamed in gangs throughout northern

India from the mid-fourteenth to mid-nineteenth centuries. In many ways, the Thugs resembled the Moslem "Assassins" (*hashāshīn* = *Cannabis* smokers) of Crusader times. According to Marco Polo, the Assassins, who belonged to the schismatic sect of Nizārī Ismā'īlites, would drug themselves into a religious fervor to get a foretaste of eternal bliss before setting out to kill or conquer. In the early twelfth century, the Assassins extended their base of operations from Persia to Syria, where conquests by the Seljuk Turks had led to anarchy, rebellion, and banditry among local Shī'ite minorities. From the fortress of Masyāf in the An-Nusayrīyah mountains, Rashīd ad-Dīin as-Sinān and his successors, known as Shaykh al-djebel ("Mountain Leader," which the Crusaders rendered as "The Old Man of the Mountain"), instituted a reign of terror. The Assassins and Thugs did not refrain from attacking Europeans, but their primary prey were less radical or rival coreligionists. There are obvious historical parallels with contemporary Islamic radicals in methods though not much in aims. Current aims are more revolutionary and thoroughly modern: to violently uproot the Judeo-Christian foundations of Western bourgeois capitalism and replace its corrupting influence on world civilization with an Islamic universalism that rules all human social, political, and economic life: "The Caliphate is the only and best solution to the predicaments and problems from which Muslims suffer today . . . It will remedy economic underdevelopment which was bequeathed upon us as a political dependence on an atheist East and infidel West" (cited in Rohde and Chivers 2002: A18).

Chapter 4

1. I thank Brian Malley for highlighting to me the importance of the relationship between religious texts and conditions of relevance.

2. A proposition is the smallest string of meaningful ideas about which one can reasonably assert truth (or likelihood) or falsity (or unlikelihood; B. Russell 1919). It is usally represented in terms of an abstract, language-like formulation that is not tied to any specific sensory modality (Fodor 1975). A proposition is *about* a state of affairs in the world and, if truthful, something like an accurate picture of things (Wittgenstein 1961[1921]).

3. J. Barrett and Nyhof list as common items "a being that can see or hear things that are not too far away"; "a species that will die if it doesn't get enough nourishment or if it is severely damaged"; "an object that is easy to see under normal lighting conditions" (2001:79). Indeed, such items fall so far below ordinary expectations that items communicated should carry some new or salient information that Barrett and Nyhof report: "common items were remembered so poorly relative to other items. . . . In some instances of retelling these items, participants tried to make the common property sound exciting or unusual" (82–83). In other words, some subjects apparently tried to meet minimum conditions of relevance (Sperber and Wilson 1986). For the most part, however, common items failed these minimum standards for successful communication.

4. A paired-samples t-test revealed superiority of intuitive (INT) over minimally counterintuitive beliefs (MCI): $M = 1.28$ vs. $M = 1.09$ respectively, $t(79) = 4.01$, $p < .001$.

5. As one might expect, there was a massive overall memory degradation, from immediate recall (INT $M = 1.30$ and MCI $M = 1.09$) to delayed recall after a week (INT $M = .55$ and MCI $M = .45$). Nevertheless, the superiority of INT beliefs relative to MCI beliefs persisted (excluding the "All INT" condition again): $t(67) = 2.97$, $p < .005$.

6. There was a linear decrease of recall as a function of ontological status for immediate recall, $F(4, 124) = 6.75$, $p < .001$, and for delayed recall, $F(4, 104) = 9.51$, $p < .001$. Recall was highest for intuitive items, lowest for maximally counterintuitive ones. The data correspond to a linear pattern for both immediate and delayed recall: $p < .001$.

7. Four intuitive bizarre (BIZ) items were remembered as minimally counterintuitive (5.6 percent), and five BIZ items were remembered as intuitive (INT) (7 percent).

8. The highest degradation was observed in the Mostly MCI condition and the All INT condition, conforming to an inverse quadratic function: $F(3, 89) = 4.49$, $p < .05$. Memory degraded least in the Mostly INT condition, and increased as the proportion of MCI beliefs increased, resulting in a linear trend: $F(2, 65) = 3.53$, $p = .06$.

Chapter 5

1. Essentially the same Islamic sacrificial ceremony accompanied each victory of the Northern Alliance over the Taliban in Afghanistan (November 2001).

2. For humans, who presumably are able to compute relative costs and benefits associated with future events (e.g., obtaining an inheritance), Hamilton's (1964) rule does *not* imply that a person should always be more altruistic to a more closely related individual than to a less closely related individual. Actual choice and behavior is contingent on the environmental context, that is, on the perceived availability of relative costs and benefits. If the benefits are high enough (e.g., inheriting a fortune), it pays to be altruistic to a less closely related individual (e.g., a friend who will kill your relative to enable you to get the fortune). Behavioral ecologist Robin Dunbar (2001) has accumulated historical evidence that supports the point.

3. The concept of "fictive kin" fails to capture the absolute reckoning, or essentializing, of human groups. Human groups are essentialized more as fictive species than as fictive kin, in the sense that people attribute to them an underlying causal nature or hidden essence ("genotype") that is assumed to be responsible for producing the apparent features of the group ("phenotype"). There is a debate as to whether the attribution of underlying causal essences to human groups owes to an innate "essentialist mode of construal" that applies indiscriminately to biological species, human groups, and perhaps natural kind substances (Sperber 1994; Hirschfeld 1996; Gelman and Hirschfeld 1999), or whether essentialization of human groups derives from manipulation of innate parameters evolved specifically for processing biological species (Atran 1990a, 1998, 2001c; Boyer 1994; Gil-White 2001). All sides in the debate agree that people everywhere essentialize human groups into causal kinds, albeit using organizing criteria that are more culturally variable than in the case of biological kinds.

4. According to anthropologist Anthony Wallace: "War is the sanctioned use of lethal weapons by members of one society against members of another. It is carried out by trained persons working in teams that are directed by a separate policy-making group and supported in various ways by the non-combatant population. . . . There are few, if any, societies that have not engaged in at least one war in their known history" (1968:173).

5. In a survey of over 400 new religious cults in the United States, Stark and Bainbridge (1985) found that membership in most cults was declining, and rising in only 6 percent.

6. Historically, new religions emerge by borrowing, merging, and transforming beliefs and practices of earlier and surrounding religions. For example, the Greeks and Romans offered wine to accompany the animal sacrifices given as food for the gods, much as wine was served to accompany food at the ordinary person's dinner table. For the Hebrews, too: "And the fourth part of an hin of wine for a drink offering shalt thou prepare with the burnt offering, or sacrifice, for one lamb" (Numbers 15:5). But the Hebrews also directly identified wine as "the blood of the grape" and poured it at the base of the altar where the sacrificial blood of animals also collected (Robertson Smith 1972[1891]:230). In the Eucharist, the early Christians merged these symbolic notions of wine. In communion with Christ, the worshipper drinks the wine and takes the wafer as the blood and flesh of the sacrificial "lamb" (i.e., Christ).

7. According to Kathleen Gough (1978, 1981), the Parayar were already complete outcastes by the third or fourth century A.D., during the period of the first Chola Kingdom. Nevertheless, there is some evidence that Parayar priests (Valluvan) were still performing temple functions under the Pallava kings as late as the ninth century: "Sri [an honorific title] Valluvan Pūvanan, the Uvachan [temple administrator], will employ daily six men and do the temple service" (ninth-century Vattellutu inscription, cited in Stuart 1891: 3:267–268; cf. Manickam 1993:103).

8. In our society, older age is reliably associated with heightened religious identification (T. Johnson 1995; McFadden 1996) and also with more intimate and succoring social networks (Carstensen, Isaacowitz, and Charles 1999), which helps to offset the stronger individualism of the young.

9. Conflicting emotions may activate simultaneously, such as fear and hope, grief and relief, disgust and joy. Different sequences of emotions can arise from the same situation depending on the order in which structural conditions are sampled and processed. For example, initial surprise at the unexpected can turn to fear if the situation is anticipated to be dangerous, or joy if it is greeted as serendipitous (Ellsworth 1991). Fear, in turn, may lead to anger if the danger is considered intentionally caused, or sadness if the danger "just happens."

10. R. Frank's (1988) theory expands on earlier discussions of the adaptive value of social commitment strategies, particularly those of economist Jack Hirshleifer (1977, 1978) and political strategist Thomas Schelling (1960). Schelling, for instance, pointed out that a sincere but apparently irrational commitment to mutually assured destruction (MAD) could actually diminish the likelihood of nuclear confrontation.

11. For a number of years I lived in a Levantine Druze village. Druze are highly endogamous non-Moslem Arabs (Atran 1985a). Druze men and women would frequently tell stories of how kinsmen tracked down wayward kinswomen and offending men to Egypt and the United States. Only once in my years with the Druze was there an honor killing (a brother knifed a sister for marrying against her father's wishes and went to prison). Despite the rarity of such events, women who know full well that they risk unrelenting pursuit and eventual killing by close kinsmen, whatever the legal safeguards, do not often risk disobeying community protocol.

12. Nothing in this account of religion warrants appeal to group selection (contra Sober and Wilson 1998; Rappaport 1999). Statistically reliable, long-term individual benefits suffice.

13. Consider this recent New York City trial of alleged police homicide:

> From the start . . . the prosecution tried to show that the vestibule where Mr. Diallo died was well lighted, which should have allowed the officers not to mistake his wallet for a gun, and the officers should have realized their mistake and stopped firing. Ultimately, their approach apparently failed to reg-

> ister with the jury. . . . Instead, the jury quickly focused on what the defense had long said would determine the verdict: the dramatic testimony by the officers on what they said happened that night. When the officers took the stand, defense lawyers were able to humanize the men, especially Sean Carroll, one of the two officers who fired 16 shots each, who broke down in tears on the stand. ("The Diallo Verdict: The Jury Speaks and the City Reacts," *New York Times*, 26 February 2000, A13)

Convincing displays of emotion often carry more weight than reason and fact in judging a person's intentions.

14. In many societies, institutionally sanctioned mating is often separated from romance. For example, marriage preferences and prohibitions in most sub-Saharan societies appear to "have as their social function to preserve, maintain, or continue existing kinship structures as a system of institutional relations" (Radcliffe Brown 1950:62). Still, "romantic love played a larger part in traditional African family systems than is generally conceded" (W. Goode 1970:174). Romantic love appears to be culturally universal, and marriages by mutual consent based on love "are reported from everywhere but the implications of such love matches vary enormously" (Lowie 1920:24; Westermarck 1922).

Chapter 6

1. The first Crusade was driven in part by a radical new theological doctrine but also by divine promise of relief from unrelenting misery, limitless booty, and forgiveness for any imaginable cruelty toward non-Christians. The Roman Catholic will to dominate Europe and the Middle East began at the Abbaye de Cluny in Paris (then the building encompassing the largest indoor space in the world, like the Pentagon today). From there, in 1073, future Pope Gregory VII started preaching a doctrine of Conquest for Christ that forbade Christians to kill other Christians who agreed with Gregory, but forgave killing all others, especially Saracens. The Crusades officially began in 1095 under Pope Urban, Gregory's successor and kindred spirit. The initial wave, led by Peter the Hermit, was composed of tens of thousands of Western European peasants and vagabonds who had just barely survived a horrendous decade of famine, drought, and plague (Cohn 1962). Urban promptly announced that as long as those who killed and pillaged did not turn back until they either died or reached Jerusalem, God would fulfill all of their material needs and remit all of their sins in this world and the next. The first to be looted and massacred were the Jews of Germany (in Worms, Meinz, Cologne, etc.), a practice that would be repeated intermittently in other times of social crisis and economic hardship, and under somewhat similar religious and mystical doctrines, well into the twentieth century.

After ferrying the Crusaders across the Bosphorus Straits, Byzantine Christians reported their horror at witnessing the Crusading knights and peasants skewering and roasting children on spits, as the invaders advanced from Nysea in Anatolia (where many of the victims were actually Cappadocian Christians living under Turkish rule) to Marj Uyun in the Lebanon. When the soldiers finally took Jerusalem in 1099, they celebrated their victory by burning alive all the Jews they could find, massacring Moslem women and children, and destroying most mosques and every synagogue in the Holy City. For two hundred years, claims James Reston, the Crusades unleashed "a frenzy of hate and violence unprecedented before the technological age and the scourge of Hitler" (2001).

The Crusades left a deep impression on both Western and Moslem politics and historical sentiment. Indeed, notes Reston, "in July 1920 when the French general Henri Gourard took charge of Damascus, he strode to Saladin's tomb next to the Grand Mosque and exclaimed, to the everlasting disgust of modern Arabs, 'Saladin [the Kurdish Sultan who united the Moslems of Syria and Egypt and retook Jerusalem in 1187], we have returned. My presence here consecrates the victory of the Cross over the Crescent'" (2001). Whatever basic differences there may be in the current predicaments of Palestine, Iraq, and Afghanistan, masses of Moslems perceive a similar pattern and feel an old wound. Thus, in a recent taped interview, radical Islamist Osama bin Laden declared the killing of Americans and Jews to be a sacred duty: "We will see Saladin carrying his sword, with the blood of unbelievers dripping from it" (cited in Burns, 2001).

2. The emergence of doctrinal religion coincides with Jared Diamond's (1997) idea of "true religion" as coincidental with the rise of kleptocracies in Sumer and elsewhere.

3. Whitehouse acknowledges his debt to anthropologist Ruth Benedict (1935: 56–57), who had earlier distinguished more sensually driven "Dionysian" rites from more intellectually driven "Apollonian" practices. She characterizes Dionysian rites as extreme psychological states (revelation, illumination, hallucination, trance, etc.) and Apollonian practices as being more normalized and dogmatic. Benedict's distinction stems from philosopher Friedrich Nietzsche's (1956[1872]) description of "the birth of tragedy" in ancient Greece. Nietzsche distinguishes two tendencies: the Apollonian, which has dominated Western society since Aristotle's time, and the pre-Hellenistic Dionysian, which is characterized by a longing to surpass all norms in the manner of the drunken and cacophonous orgies of Dionysian festivals. Nietzsche's distinction, in turn, is a development of Aristotle's analysis of tragedy in *The Poetics*: "Tragedy first arose without deliberate intent, as did comedy also. The former originated with the leaders of the dithyramb [a choral performance in honor of Dionysus], the latter with the leader of phallic songs which even today remain customary in many cities" (1958b:9). Aristotle stresses that tragedy emerged as an organized play that aimed to harness emotions so as to convey an appropriate social message. In a proper play, each incident, or "episode" (*épeisódion*) of the story must be scripted into a relevant slot and must not become an isolated or "episodic" (*épeisodiōdēz*) incident that only distracts from the plot: "The episodic are the worst of all plots and actions; and by episodic I mean one in which episodes have no probable or inevitable connection" (20).

4. Fundamental religious beliefs only *look like* propositions insofar as they may take a subject-predicate form (e.g., "God is incorporeal"). Ever since Aristotle's *Categories* (1963), from the vantage of deductive logic it makes no sense to try to verify or falisfy utterances about the supernatural because they are "category violations." Examples include utterances about four-footed water, an emotional but bodiless deity, and a building or sentence that came down with AIDS (Ayer 1950; Sommers 1963; Keil 1979). Such an utterance allows contradictory inferences (e.g., emotions do and don't involve the activation of bodily states; AIDS is caused by a virus and AIDS is not biological), and therefore permits any inference to follow and so precludes no inference in principle (Quine 1960). If one doesn't wish to hold logic to a "positivist" characterization of category violations as "senseless," then also from the vantage of "fuzzy" and nonquantificational logics the allowable inferences are too "open-textured" or semantically underdetermined to reliably generate intuitions of truth, falsity, verisimilitude, likelihood, probability, warrantedness, or justifiability.

5. In their recent book, *Bringing Ritual to Mind* (2002), philosopher Robert McCauley and religious studies expert E. Thomas Lawson adopt key facets of White-

house's analysis of the relationship among ritual, memory, and emotion. But in bringing lessons to bear from their previous study of the cognitive structure of ritual action (Lawson and McCauley 1990), the authors wish to make performance frequency a dependent, rather than independent, variable, by deriving differences in frequency from differences in form. On this account, all religious rituals have a formal action structure that typically involves (1) an *agent*, acting on (2) somebody or something (a *patient*), (3) usually by means of an *instrument*, (4) to effect a certain state of affairs through supernatural causation. Except for intervention of the supernatural, there is no difference between the action structures of religious rituals and those of mundane, nonreligious ceremonies and events. Frequency and low arousal occur when the most immediate connection between some element of the current ritual and the supernatural agent is through the ritual's instruments or patient rather than through its agent, no matter how central the ritual is to the religion. For example, although the Eucharist is central to Catholicism it is frequently repeated with a fairly low level of sensory pageantry: "the agents [e.g., the priests] are more distant (ritually) from the religious system's [supernatural] agents than are either the instruments they use (e.g., holy water) or the patients (e.g., the body and blood of Christ). . . . [M]ore rituals intervene between the agent in the current ritual and the gods than intervene between the gods and either the instruments or the patient of that ritual" (McCauley and Lawson 2002: ch. 4). By contrast, in rituals where the connection with a supernatural agent first arises with the performing agent, there will be higher levels of sensory pageantry. For example, in a Catholic wedding it is (1) the priest performing the wedding, who (2) has been ordained by the Church, which (3) is the direct link to Christ. Although the supernatural agent (Christ) first appears at level 3 in the marriage ritual, it does so via an agent (the priest). True, a priest also presides over the Eucharist; however, Christ initially enters the ritual as patient (the wine and wafer that are consumed as His blood and body) at level 1. The pageantry aims indelibly to impress on the ritual's participants "not only that they have undergone fundamental changes but also that the [supernatural] agents, who are ultimately responsible for those changes, are *vitally* important to them and . . . their community." These emotionally grounded convictions, in turn, *motivate* the participants *to remember and transmit* this information to others. The heightened sensory pageantry that signals these superpermanent effects is designed to convince participants in a *single exposure*. The participants, as patients, need directly experience these effects only once.

McCauley and Lawson's account is enlightening in two ways. First, it emphasizes an *affective motivation* for ritual as the spur for emotional memory, rather than merely as an adjunct to or consequence of memory constraints. Second, it stresses the *priority of supernatural agents* in ritual over magical or mechanical instruments or actions. This has experimental support. J. Barrett and Lawson (2001) presented students in a Protestant college with several variations on a hypothetical ritual, such as (1) "A *priest* sprinkles *sacred* water on a pregnant woman and her baby is born healthy"; (2) "A *priest* sprinkles ordinary water . . ."; (3) "A layperson sprinkles *sacred* water . . ."; (4) "An ordinary cloud sprinkles *sacred* water . . ."; and so forth. They asked the students to rate on a 7-point scale how likely each of the alternatives was "to find favor with the gods and cause a baby to be born healthy?" Italics indicate a link with the supernatural, or "S-marker." (Students saw no italics and the order of presentation was randomized.) Subjects judged that rituals with the most S-markers are the most effective (1 > 2); S-markers in the agent position are more effective than S-markers in the instrument position (2 > 3); and agents are more effective than nonagents (3 > 4).

All in all, differences between Whitehouse's and McCauley and Lawson's interpretations of the relationship between performance frequency and sensory pageantry are minor and based largely on differing intuitions about the same cases. There are really no clear cases for trying to choose between the two models because there are no reliable methods for evaluating cases. There are no measures of ritual "frequency" (is a motorway blessing a type of its own, or a token of a miscellaneous class of mundane blessings?) or of degree of "participation" versus "witnessing" (does a daughter's or friend's wedding count like one's own?). Neither are there reliable criteria for determining "levels of embedding" (at what level of a priest's ordaining does one place the anointing of the Pope, who appoints the bishop, who authorizes the ordaining?) or whether or where in a given ritual a supernatural power first imbues an agent, instrument, or patient (in a baptism does the Holy Spirit first make contact with the priest or the holy water?).

6. A frame also contains default assumptions concerning slot values. If a text or memory fails to mention or recall some piece of information, the default value is assumed. For example, suppose Mary is described or remembers herself as a little girl looking at a bear eating the popcorn that fell from her bag. We, like Mary, can reliably assume that she was accompanied by an adult (and wasn't alone); the accompanying adult paid for the popcorn (and did not steal it); the bear was behind a protective barrier of some sort (so that Mary was relatively safe); and so forth. Slots contain restrictions on what kind of information they may contain: an animal-in-a-cage slot cannot be filled in with the accompanying adult, and a popcorn-seller slot cannot be filled by a bear.

7. Consider fear of flying, whose onset is often caused by a single, surprising, and threatening event, such as a sudden drop in altitude on an otherwise routine flight or violent shaking that leads one to expect a crash. Those who continue to fly after such an experience often continue to be fearful, especially of anything resembling the initial event (e.g., turbulence). Yet, people conscientiously use their cognitive system for calculating probabilities and likely outcomes (e.g., the probability of crashing is very small, even with turbulence), which allows them to "rationally" overcome or control the fear. In the long run, however, an emotionally undiminished "irrational" avoidance of such a low-probability, high-risk event could be a lifesaver (people who don't fly *never* die in plane crashes; thoughts from a discussion with Douglas Medin and Peter Railton 2001).

8. These results still leave open the possibility that high levels of initial arousal and accurate recall may obtain for persons with firsthand participation in momentous events. To test this, Neisser et al. (1996) studied people's memories about the Loma Prieta earthquake that shook the California Bay area in 1989. Reported levels of emotional arousal did not correlate with accuracy of recall. Most Californians did not consider themselves to be in danger at the time of the quake, presumably because earthquakes in California are not uncommon. They learned about this particular earthquake's relative importance only after the fact, presumably through news reports and discussions detailing the extent of damage in the region, such as the collapse of the Bay Bridge (which scored 5.28 on a 7-point arousal scale). Here, again, narrative consolidation seems to account better for flashbulb memory effects than does emotional arousal.

9. Hamond and Fivush (1991) found that children's recall contained more than twice as many propositions for Florida's Hurricane Andrew as an extended family visit to Florida's Disneyworld. Parker and colleagues (1998) found a curvilinear relation between stress and recall. Based on mothers' ratings of the storm's severity (in terms of physical damage to their home), children who experienced severe consequences from the storm recalled less than children who experienced only moderate consequences. Minor but stressful medical emergencies, such as voiding cystourethro-

gram or treating a facial laceration, are recalled accurately and consistently over a six-week period by children age 3 to 7 (Ornstein 1995). Children who *talked about* the procedure with the attending physician, however, had the better memory for it—again suggesting the importance of narrative consolidation in maintaining singular memories. Moreover, children's memories were positively correlated with "warmth," including mother's supportive presence and talk with the child about the experience (G. Goodman et al. 1994). But children who scored high on behavioral ratings of stress (e.g., nightmares) recalled less accurately than children who had lower ratings.

10. Only children who were younger than age 3 years at the time could not verbally recall their experience, even after they had developed language (a finding consistent with the literature on "infantile amnesia" for *any* memory of events before age 3; Terr 1990; cf. Meltzoff 1995b; Perner and Ruffman 1995). Even with the youngest children, though, an unarticulated "emotional memory" of a traumatic event might conceivably persist into adulthood as a panic disorder or phobia (e.g., an "irrational" fear of buses).

11. Establishing solidarity among initiation cohorts is often a crucial aspect of small-scale group morality and cohesion, such as mutual commitment in warfare. A student project by Andrew Baron based on interviews with World War II and Vietnam combat veterans suggests that the physical ordeal of a shared initiation in battle motivates small-group solidarity and sacrifice. As with hazings at college fraternities, severe initiations may help to create cohesive social units within otherwise large-scale and diffuse social organizations, such as modern armies and universities.

12. Ullman (1982) found converts to have more negative perceptions of parents than did persons with a continuous religious identity. Also, more fathers tended to be absent among the converts. Beit-Hallahmi and Nevo (1987) compared 59 male converts to Orthodox Judaism with matched controls and found converts to identify less with parents and to score lower on measures of self-esteem. Orphans or persons without parents seem to be more likely to join religious cults, such as the Moonies and Hare Krishna (Galanter et al. 1979, Poling and Kenney 1986).

13. Among a sample of manic depressive patients, 52 percent had religious experiences versus 20 percent for controls, but such experiences did not ameliorate their chronic condition (Gallenmore, Wilson, and Rhoads 1969). A study of religious beliefs and practices among 52 psychiatric inpatients in Minnesota revealed the rate of belief in the major tenets of faith (God, the devil, and an afterlife) to be uniformly high; however, patients with depressive and anxiety disorders tended to score lower than those with other diagnoses on a wide variety of indices of religious commitment (Kroll and Sheehan 1989). Those who come to religious sects and claim to be healed of their physical handicaps also report overall improvement in well-being. Follow-up studies indicate that their actual physical condition does not improve (Pattison, Lapins, and Doerr 1973; Glik 1986). Nevertheless, psychological support from the healing group may allow its members to ignore or deny lack of improvement and so perhaps live more easily with their misfortune. A survey of Christian healing groups suggests that, at the very least, group participation enhances the self-esteem and sense of well-being of those seeking help (McGuire 1983).

14. Grooming and greeting behaviors of higher primates, including some monkeys and most apes, is intermediate between involuntary animal rituals and voluntary human rituals. Like human rituals, they convey promissory potential for cooperation and commitment (Watanabee and Smuts 1999). But manipulation of signal stimuli appears to be pretty much limited to use of instinctual gestures, whereas in humans they can become fairly arbitrary (expressing submission by a salute or courtship by a display of etchings).

Chapter 7

1. In 1878, the French neurologist Paul Broca noted that on the medial surface of the mammalian brain, just underneath the cortex, there is an area of gray matter that he called the "limbic lobe" (from the Latin *limbus*, implying circle, surrounding) because it rings the brain stem. Years later, Paul MacLean (1952) argued that the "limbic system" developed with the emergence of primitive mammals. Also called the paleopallium or "old mammalian" brain, the limbic system supposedly commands behaviors crucial to the survival of all mammals, such as those involved in a mammal's ability to care for its own or to fight, flee, or freeze in the face of a predator. In particular, it modulates specific affective functions that allow a mammal to distinguish the agreeable from the disagreeable.

Basic emotions are primate functions originating in the limbic system. Some of these, like surprise and fear, seem to have neuronal links that go back even further into the archipallium, or primitive "reptilian" brain that comprises the structures of the brain stem (LeDoux 1996). Other, socially attuned emotions, such as guilt and empathy, are more tied to the neopallium, or "new mammalian" brain, which includes both hemispheres of the neocortex. The peculiarly human manifestations of these feelings, which may be subject to considerable cultural manipulation (Griffiths 1997), appear to be mediated by the most recently evolved prefrontal cortices (Damasio 1994).

MacLean argued that the hippocampus was the limbic system's principal emotion modulator, but more recent research grants that role to the neighboring amygdala. In fact, the hippocampus appears to modulate consciousness and declarative memory more than it does emotion (Zola-Morgan et al. 1991). Conscious awareness and verbal memory are hardly "primitive" or "old mammalian" functions. Moreover, although there are important structural connections between the amygdala and hippocampal formation, there are also important connections between these two formations and the brain stem and neocortex. This suggests that there may be no structural integrity to the limbic system as such (cf. LeDoux 1993, 1996:98–102).

2. Adrenaline and other stress-related hormones seem to affect the relationship between emotion and memory regardless of whether a person has been traumatized. Many communities use adrenaline-inducing sensory stimuli or drugs to trigger religious experiences of various kinds. The same drug can often stimulate contrary emotions, thoughts, and behaviors depending on personal history and the social context in which it is taken. Schachter (1967) found that the same adrenaline-enhancing drug could produce feelings of ecstasy or aggression, depending on the ambient environment.

3. Unlike the case of nontraumatized persons, PTSD sufferers tend to show *decreased* accuracy of detailed and verbal recall for emotional memories. Decreased activity in Broca's area and alterations in prefrontal cortical activity among PTSD subjects appear to be associated with deficits in verbal memory for traumatic events. PTSD subjects suffering from child abuse, sexual abuse, or combat fatigue show evidence of a significant correlation between decreased right-sided activation or atrophy of the hippocampal formation and deficient verbal recall (Bremner et al. 1995; Bremner Narayan et al. 1999; Bremner, Staib et al. 1999). The hippocampus appears to play an important role in our ability to explicitly remember ongoing or recent incidents in our lives (Marr 1971). It seems to bind together diverse episodes of a specific event (Damasio 1989).

Stress-induced impairments of "explicit memory" (Schacter 1987) or "declarative memory" (Squire 1992), whose contents can be consciously brought to mind and described, are experimentally associated with loss of neurons and a decrease in the branching of dendrites in the hippocampus (McEwen and Sapolsky 1995). This may owe to the fact that high levels of glucocorticoids released during stress increase the vulnerability of neurons to toxic levels of amino acids. Glucocorticoids modulate synaptic plasticity over hours and also produce long-term changes in dendritic structure. Evidence from animal studies also indicates that severe stress results in atrophy of hippocampal neurons and long-term memory impairment owing to glucocorticoid influence on cognitive function (Magariños et al. 1996; de Quervain, Roozendaal, and McGaugh 1998). Studies of Gulf War syndrome further suggest that synaptic concentrations of the excitatory neurotransmitter acetylcholine suffer long-lasting decrease with PTSD (Saplosky 1998). Even mild stress, or "burnout," seems to provoke short-term verbal memory loss, as with persons "stressed out" before an exam or job interview.

4. Konrad Lorenz describes an arousal syndrome in vertebrate predators similar in ways to the "ergotropic syndrome." After prolonged effort and heightened arousal associated with chasing prey, an avian or mammalian carnivore experiences an acute "sensual pleasure" after catching it through the rapid, rhythmic movement of "shaking to death." This is followed by a particular form of emotional release:

> A striking predator finds itself in an exceptional state of maximal arousal. . . . Immediately after striking its prey, the bird shows the same degree of abreaction as a human being . . . directly after orgasm. Far from greedily beginning to devour, the raptor—even if it is very hungry—will first sit still for several minutes on its prey . . . and then embark on the slow, laborious process of plucking its prey, as though half-asleep. Even when the raptor finally begins to eat it, it does so in a "dispassionate," mechanical nature, as though not quite conscious. (1996: 267–268)

5. James Ashbrook (1984) first coined the word "neurotheology" as an attempt to integrate neuropsychology with theology, although the project was first elaborated by psychiatrist Eugene d'Aquili and anthropologist Charles Laughlin nearly a decade before (d'Aquli and Laughlin 1975). The principal outlet for neurotheology is *Zygon: The Journal of Religion and Science*. The journal has attracted prestigious academicians and scientists, including anthropologist Victor Turner (1983) and neurophysiologist and Nobel laureate Roger Sperry (1991, 1992). Neurotheology, with its promise to show how religion plays out in the brain, has recently become popular with the mass media (e.g., "Religion and the Brain," *Newsweek*, 7 May 2001:50–58).

6. In 1974 I interviewed Lévi-Strauss (intending to invite him to a debate I was organizing between Noam Chomsky and Jean Piaget), transcribing my notes shortly afterwards. I asked him why he believed binary operators to be one of the fundamental structures of the human mind. He shrugged and sighed, and then replied, "When I started there was still no science of mind. [Ferdinand] Saussure [the French linguist who elaborated the method of contrasting minimal pairs], [Karl] Marx [who employed the dialectical method of analysis for resolving historical contradictions], [Marcel] Mauss [the French sociologist who, in *The Gift*, saw reciprocity as the foundation of human society], and music were my guides. Since then things have changed. Psychology now has something to say."

7. Gordon Claridge (1985) proposed the term "shizotypy" to describe a personality predisposition to schizophrenia (much as high cholesterol predisposes a person to heart attacks). Claridge's (1997) basic idea is that the features of psychotic disorders such as schizophrenia actually lie on a continuum with, and form part of, normal behavior and experience. Jackson (1991, cited in Beit-Hallahmi and Argyle 1997:92) found the schizotypy scale to correlate modestly but reliably with religious

experience (accounting for one-fourth of the variance). There is no evidence, however, that nonschizophrenic "schizotypes" exhibit any of the prefrontal deficits often associated with schizophrenia.

8. A study of 75 schizophrenic patients in Britain and Saudi Arabia found no difference along dimensions of loudness, frequency, clarity, and perceived validity of auditory hallucinations in the two populations. Nevertheless, "much of the content of the hallucinations of the Saudi Arabian patients was religious and superstitious in nature [e.g., black magic], whereas instructional themes and running commentary was common in British patients" (Kent and Wahass 1996). Similarly, responses from 281 patients attending their general practitioners indicated that "those living in Saudi Arabia were most likely to believe that hallucinations were caused by Satan or due to magic, while the UK sample were more likely to cite schizophrenia or brain damage. While the Saudi sample believed that religious assistance would be most effective, the UK sample supported medication and psychological therapies" Wahass and Kent surmise, however, that the Saudi patients may in fact be *more* socially isolated than their British counterparts insofar as the community perceives them to be possessed by Satan.

Chapter 8

1. As the Quran makes clear, face and body covers for women signal and encourage chaste behavior. Adherence to the norm of chastity, in turn, ensures the impeccable patrilineal pedigree on which Arab (and many other Moslem) social polities are based: "Tell the believing women . . . to draw their veils over their bosoms [24:31] . . . to draw their cloaks close around them [33:59]. As for women past childbearing, who have no hope of marriage, it is no sin for them if they discard their (outer) clothing. . . . But to refrain is better for them [24:60]." The Quran, like nearly all other religious and civil traditions, advances the norm-reinforcing principle of the carrot and the stick: "Whosoever doeth right . . . We shall quicken with good life, and We shall pay them a recompense in proportion to the best of what they do [16:97]. Whoso doeth an ill deed . . . will be repaid the like thereof [40:40]."

2. Although I am critical of Boyd and colleagues' past use of norms and group selection as key components of cultural selection and evolution, more recent work modeling intra- and intercultural variation in the distribution and transmission of cultural practices is a valuable contribution to our understanding of cultural epidemiology and evolution (cf. response to F. Gil-White in Atran et al. 2002). In this work, norms are not necessarily discrete, widely shared, or rule-like. Instead, they reflect more complex statistical distributions of cognitions, behaviors, and ecological contexts (Henrich and Boyd 2002). There is no comparable sophistication in D. S. Wilson's (or Sober's) views of culture, however much I respect some of their work in biology.

3. When, as happened for each group, there is a cultural consensus in the formal sense (i.e., a single-factor solution in a principal components analysis), we are justified in aggregating individual responses into a "cultural model" (Romney, Weller, and Batchelder 1986). In some cases, the consensual model may show an emergent coherence and systematicity over and above the simple accretion of its individual components (like an eddy that emerges from a water flow) and be used to predict further response patterns in the population with statistical reliability (e.g., López et al. 1997). This statistical technique not only justifies the aggregation of individual responses into a "cultural model," but also allows the possibility of combining the consensual cultural

models of different populations into a "metacultural" model of the sort that group selection arguments require (e.g., to show how average within-group patterns compare to between-group patterns). Culture-consensus modeling allows exploration of possible pathways of learning and information exchange between cultural groups. This, in turn, can illuminate more general processes of cultural formation, transformation, and evolution. Notice that unlike normative accounts of relations among culture, cognition, and behavior, the models thus generated are not synthetic interpretations of people's thoughts and behaviors but emergent cultural patterns derived statistically from measurements of individual cognitions and behaviors.

4. More generally, the highest competence scores among the Ladinos in the combined Itza'-Ladino model of plant-animal relations belong to those Ladinos who most cite Itza' as their experts. Furthermore, these Ladino experts are also the most socially well-connected members of the Ladino community and the persons most cited as experts by the rest of the Ladino community. Putting these findings together not only suggests that Ladinos are learning from Itza' but also that the social and expert network structure strongly facilitates this learning between the Ladino and Itza' communities as well as within the Ladino community.

5. People in every society readily generate richly structured folkbiological taxonomies from fragmentary samples of plant and animal kinds owing to an evolved, task-specific ("modular") system for folkbiological induction (Atran 1998). To illustrate: using standard taxonomic sorting experiments, we elicited highly consensual mammal taxonomies. The aggregated Ladino taxonomy correlated equally with Itza' and Q'eqchi' taxonomies (r = .85), indicating very similar stuctures and content (Atran et al. 2002).

6. This bears on the seemingly intractable problem of "upscaling" lessons of local commons to increasingly mobile and multicultural societies: even in a relatively open-access environment (with uncontrolled immigration), if there is ready access to relevant information, then ecologically sound behaviors may be learned by relative newcomers who have no cognitive or cultural predisposition favoring commons survival. (But having the time to learn poses a daunting problem: rates of cultural and environmental degradation in neotropical areas are awesome by any standard, owing to global economic and political processes that function similarly across such areas.)

7. We also asked 17 representatives of several nongovernmental organizations (NGOs) at a workshop on the Maya Biosphere Reserve (December 1999) to rank the same trees as did Itza', Ladinos, and Q'eqchi' (in terms of importance to forest life). For the NGOs, there was marginal consensus. The most valued species for NGO representatives are, in rank order: mahogany, tropical cedar, allspice, and chicle. These are the most important trees for the extractive economy and export market. NGO preferences partially predict the consensus on preferences expressed by Ladinos and Itza'; however, the worst predictor of NGO rankings is Itza' rankings of spirit preferences and Itza' ratings of ecological centrality.

8. See Wilson's comments on MacDonald as "developing a general theory of human social groups, of which Judaism is an example" and whose "major themes . . . are well worth defending" (www.csuib.edu/~kmacd/wilson_comment2.html).

9. Other forms of deception are allegedly evident in twentieth-century intellectual movements in the United States that were spearheaded by Jews, particularly in New York City. One example is Boasian anthropology, the dominant school of American cultural anthropology for much of the past century (MacDonald 1998b). Under the tutelage of Franz Boas, a German Jewish refugee and professor at Columbia University in New York, a generation of American cultural anthropologists actively

sought to debunk the eugenics movement and racialist thinking hitherto predominant in anthropology and psychology (as well as politics and law). MacDonald suggests that by denying the reality of biological determinism and attacking the wider eugenics movement, the Jews' own eugenics program could better thrive unhindered by gentile criticism or competition. Not that Boas or his students were consciously aware that they were actually promoting the Jews' group evolutionary strategy. On the contrary, they were probably self-deceivingly unaware, which makes the deception all the more convincing and effective. Thus, Boas's student Margaret Mead, although an Anglo-Saxon Protestant, may have unwittingly served Jewish interests in her endeavor to show that the emotional troubles of adolescence were not as biologically preordained as supposed, or that "primitive races" were every bit as sophisticated in categorization and reasoning ability as Westerners. Proof of her (self)deception is an apparently willful blindness to readily available counterevidence of the sort presented in Derek Freeman's (1983) exposé *Margaret Mead and Samoa: The Making and Unmaking of an Anthropological Myth*.

As in many of MacDonald's arguments, there is substantial fact and truth: New York City had a large proportion of Jewish intellectuals; Boaz was a Jew, and he and many other Jewish intellectuals opposed the eugenics movement; Mead did ignore some readily available evidence countering her claims that Samoan adolescence was relatively untroubled; and so forth. But the inference to all of this instantiating a Jewish "group evolutionary strategy" is no more commendable than that of any similarly specious conspiracy theory.

10. Unlike Irving, MacDonald doesn't deny the Holocaust, but he agrees with Irving that attempts to prevent historical comparison with other real or alleged cases of genocide often serve political interests. In part, I agree and have written at length on this and related issues (Atran 1987c, 1987d, 1989b, 1990b), also addressing public audiences on these matters in the United States, France, England, Israel, and Palestine. Unlike Irving and MacDonald, however, I've never had an inkling of a Jewish conspiracy to silence such thoughts (although people have argued that I've been wrong).

11. IQ is a general measure of socially acceptable categorization and reasoning skills. IQ tests were designed in behaviorism's heyday, when there was little interest in cognitive structure. The scoring system was tooled to generate a normal distribution of scores with a mean of 100 and a standard deviation of 15. In other societies, a normal distribution of some general measure of social intelligence might look very different, in that some "normal" members of our society could well produce a score that is a standard deviation from "normal" members of another society on that society's test. For example, in forced-choice tasks East Asian students (China, Korea, Japan) tend to favor field-dependent perception over object-salient perception, thematic reasoning over taxonomic reasoning, and exemplar-based categorization over rule-based categorization (Nisbett et al. 2001). American students generally prefer the opposite. On tests that measure these various categorization and reasoning skills, East Asians average higher on their preferences and Americans average higher on theirs. There is nothing particularly revealing about these different distributions other than that they reflect some underlying sociocultural differences.

There is a long history of acrimonious debate over which, if any, aspects of IQ are heritable. The most compelling studies concern twins raised apart and adoptions. Twin studies rarely have large sample populations. Moreover, they often involve twins separated at birth because a parent dies or cannot afford to support both, and one is given over to be raised by relatives, friends, or neighbors (Lewontin 1995:100–102). This disallows ruling out the effects of social environment and upbringing in producing convergence among the twins. The chief problem with adoption studies is that the mere fact of adoption reliably increases IQ, regardless of any correlation between the IQs of the children and those of their biological parents.

Chapter 9

1. David Hull informs me that Richard Semon (1921[1904]) coined the term "mneme" in 1904 for an entity that functions much like the meme: "In the evolution of language, 'meme' and 'mneme' are homoplasies [analogies], not homologies."

2. Boyd and Richerson (1985:11) allow that successful cultural traits, such as social norms, do not always enhance the chances of an individual who follows the norms to maximize transmission of his or her genes to the next generation. But it is the group as a whole that benefits, not the idea of altruism per se that benefits. Memes break links to biology, making their own way in the world.

3. A possible response is that the basic unit of cultural information more properly analogous to the gene is the word/morpheme, that is, the smallest unit of consistent sound-meaning correspondence (or its semantic referent). A memeplex, then, is a complex "wordplex," such as a proposition. Rather than replicate, word-plexes "recombine" into more intricate forms of inference and predication. I fail to see how this maneuver gains anything. Take the command "Eat cake!" The actual intent and inferred meaning of the command, and the informational content that is transmitted over time, may have very little to do with the command's explicit propositional content (e.g., when uttered to a starving person begging for bread).

4. Paul Griffiths (2001) argues that because the items on any such symptomatic list don't necessarily co-occur in any given case and can't unequivocally demonstrate innateness, notions of innateness are inherently confused and should be discarded. The same could be said against modularity. But the list represents only a family of evidentiary heuristics, and does not pretend to be a causal analysis of innateness or modularity.

5. Economy is not always good. Gigerenzer and Todd (1999) argue that "fast and frugal" cognitive heuristics "make us smart." But they may often be as likely to make us stupid. Racial stereotypes are culturally widespread and cognitively economical but biologically incoherent and often socially dysfunctional. Perhaps intellectual innovation is difficult because of economy.

6. Notice that there is no need for a religious commandment to "Honor thy children," any more than "Thou shalt eat and reproduce," inasmuch as people's minds are likely evolutionarily wired for such actions anyway.

7. Arguably, my claim that there are no "species" or "lineages" of memes is belied by multivariate analysis of linguistic and cultural traits (cf. Romney and Moore 2001). One issue is whether there are scientifically identifiable "traits" or "norms" at all, or whether such "cultural units" are simply commonsense summaries of complex and variable behaviors (see chapter 7).

Chapter 10

1. This doesn't entail that pantheism is conceptually better for the environment than monotheism. There are monotheistic "deep ecology" movements that are quite environment-friendly. They see God as protector of, and perhaps mediator between, the respective interests of all living and some nonliving kinds. But there may be a

problem of scale: it is difficult to monitor all the world's kinds to get right their relative interests.

2. For example, the Islamic practice of *hawala,* based on personal trust among believers, allows relatively paperless and cost-free money transfers almost anywhere in the world, whether in large or small amounts or to friends or strangers.

REFERENCES

Abelson, R. 1981. Psychological status of the script concept. *American Psychologist* 36:715–729.

Aggleton, J. and R. Passingham. 1981. Syndrome produced by lesions of the amygdala in monkeys (*Macaca mulatta*). *Journal of Comparative and Physiological Psychology* 95:961–977.

Ahn, W.-K., C. Kalish, S. Gelman, D. Medin, C. Luhmann, S. Atran, J. Coley, and P. Shafto. 2001. Why essences are essential in the psychology of concepts. *Cognition* 82:59–69.

Aiello, L., and P. Wheeler. 1995. The expensive-tissue hypothesis. *Current Anthropology* 36:199–221.

Alexander, R. 1981. Evolution, culture, and human behavior. In R. Alexander (ed.), *Natural selection and social behavior*. New York: Chiron Press.

———. 1987. *The biology of moral systems*. New York: Aldine de Gruyter.

———. 1989. Evolution of the human psyche. In C. Stringer (ed.), *The human revolution*. Edinburgh: University of Edinburgh Press.

Alexander, R., and K. Noonan. 1979. Concealment of ovulation, parental care and human social evolution. In N. Chagnon and W. Irons (eds.), *Evolutionary biology and human social organization*. North Scituate, MA: Duxbury.

al-Issa, I. 1995. The illusion of reality or the reality of illusion: Hallucinations and culture. *British Journal of Psychiatry* 166:368–373.

Allport, G. 1956. *The nature of prejudice*. Cambridge, MA: Harvard University Press.

Allport, G., J. Gillespie, and J. Young. 1948. The religion of the post-war college student. *Journal of Psychology* 25:3–33.

Alston, J., and B. Aguirre. 1979. Congregational size and the decline of sectarian commitment: The case of Jehovah's Witnesses in South and North America. *Sociological Analysis* 40:63–70.

Alston, W. 1967. Religion. In P. Edwards (ed.), *The encyclopedia of philosophy*, vol. 7. London: Collier Macmillan.

al-Thakeb, F., and J. Scott. 1982. Islamic fundamentalism. *International Review of Modern Sociology* 12:175–195.

Antoun, R. 1968. On the modesty of women in Arab Muslim villages. *American Anthropologist* 70:671–697.

American Psychiatric Association. 1980. *Diagnostic and statistical manual of mental disorder*, 3rd ed. (DSM-III). Washington, DC.

American Psychiatric Association. 1994. *Diagnostic and statistical manual of mental disorder*, 4th ed. (DSM-IV). Washington, DC.

Aquinas, Saint Thomas, 1955 (1265–1273). *Somme théologique [Summa theologiae]*, 6 vols., trans. A.-M. Rouget. Paris: Desclée.

Archaeological Survey of India, 1992. *Chola temples*. New Delhi: Director General, Archaeological Survey of India.

Arias, A. 1990. Changing Indian identity: Guatemala's violent transition to modernity. In C. Smith (ed.), *Guatemalan Indians and the state: 1540–1988*. Austin: University of Texas Press.

Aristotle. 1958a. *The politics of Aristotle*. London: Oxford University Press.

———. 1958b. *Aristotle on poetry and style*, trans. G. Grube. New York: Bobbs-Merrill.

———. 1963. *Aristotle's categories and de interpretatione*, trans. J. L. Ackrill. Oxford: Clarendon.

Armstrong, K. 2000. *The battle for God*. New York: Knopf.

Aronson, E., and J. Mills. 1959. The effect of severity of initiation on liking for a group. *Journal of Abnormal and Social Psychology* 59:177–181.

Ashbrook, J. 1984. Neurotheology. *Zygon* 19:331–350.

Astington, J., and A. Gopnik. 1991. Theoretical explanations of children's understanding of the mind. *British Journal of Developmental Psychology* 9:7–31.

Astington, J., P. Harris, and D. Olson. 1989. *Developing theories of mind*. New York: Cambridge University Press.

Atran, S. 1980. Commentary. In M. Piatelli-Palmarini (ed.), *Language and learning: The debate between Jean Piaget and Noam Chomsky*. Cambridge, MA: Harvard University Press.

———. 1982. Constraints on a theory of hominid tool-making behavior. *L'Homme* 22:35–68.

———. 1985a. Managing Arab kinship and marriage. *Social Science Information* 24:659–696.

———. 1985b. Démembrement social et remembrement agraire dans un village palestinien. *L'Homme* 25:111–135.

———. 1986. *Hamula* [patriclan] organisation and *masha'a* [commons] tenure in Palestine. *Man* 21 :271–295.

———. 1987a. Ordinary constraints on the semantics of living kinds. *Mind and Language* 2:27–63.

———. 1987b. Origins of the species and genus concepts. *Journal of the History of Biology* 20:195–280.

———. 1987c. Construction de l'identité palestinienne. In *Vers des sociétés pluriculturelles*. Actes du Colloque International de l'AFA, Paris, 9–11 January 1986. Paris: Editions de l'Orstom.

———. 1987d. Le question foncière en Palestine. *Annales Economies Sociétés Civilisations*, no. 6:1361–1389.

———. 1989a. Basic conceptual domains. *Mind and Language* 4:7–16.

———. 1989b. The surrogate colonization of Palestine. *American Ethnologist* 16:719–744.

———. 1990a. *Cognitive foundations of natural history*. Cambridge, UK: Cambridge University Press.

———. 1990b. Stones against the iron fist, terror within the nation: Alternating structures of violence in the Israeli-Palestinian conflict. *Politics and Society* 18:481–526.
———. 1991. L'ethnoscience aujourd'hui. *Social Science Information* 30:595–662.
———. 1993. Itza Maya tropical agro-forestry. *Current Anthropology* 34:633–700.
———. 1996. Modes of thinking about living kinds: Science, symbolism and common sense. In D. Olson and N. Torrance (eds.), *Modes of thought: Explorations in culture and cognition*. New York: Cambridge University Press.
———. 1998. Folkbiology and the anthropology of science: Cognitive universals and cultural particulars. *Behavioral and Brain Sciences* 21:547–609.
———. 1999. Itzaj Maya folk-biological taxonomy. In D. Medin and S. Atran (eds.), *Folk biology*. Cambridge, MA: MIT Press.
———. 2001a. The vanishing landscape of the Petén Maya Lowlands: People, plants, animals, places, words and spirits. In L. Maffi (ed.), *On biocultural diversity: Linking language, knowledge, and the environment*. Washington, DC: Smithsonian Institution Press.
———. 2001b. The case for modularity: Sin or salvation? *Evolution and Cognition* 7:46–55.
———. 2001c. Are ethnic groups of the essence for humankind? *Current Anthropology* 42:537–538.
———. 2001d. The trouble with memes: Inference versus imitation in cultural creation. *Human Nature* 12:351–381.
———. 2001e. A cheater-detection module? Dubious interpretations of the Wason Selection Task. *Evolution and Cognition* 7:187–193.
———. 2002. Cognitive modularity in biological reasoning. In P. Carruthers, S. Stich, and M. Siegal (eds.), *Cognitive foundations of science*. New York: Oxford University Press.
Atran, S., P. Estin, J. Coley, and D. Medin. 1997. Generic species and basic levels: Essence and appearance in folk biology. *Journal of Ethnobiology* 17:22–45.
Atran, S., and X. Lois. 2001. Anti-anti-Cartesianism. *Current Anthropology* 42:498–500.
Atran, S., X. Lois, and E. Ucan Ek'. (In press). *Plants of the Petén Itza' Maya*. Ann Arbor: memoirs of the University of Michigan Museums, vol. 37.
Atran, S., D. Medin, E. Lynch, V. Vapnarsky, E. Ucan Ek', J. Coley, C. Timura, and M. Baran. 2002. Folkecology, cultural epidemiology, and the spirit of the commons: A garden experiment in the Maya Lowlands, 1991–2001. *Current Anthropology* 43:421–450.
Atran, S., D. Medin, E. Lynch, V. Vapnarsky, E. Ucan Ek', and P. Sousa. 2001. Folkbiology doesn't come from folkpsychology: Evidence from Yukatek Maya in cross-cultural perspective. *Journal of Cognition and Culture* 1:3–42.
Atran, S., D. Medin, N. Ross, E. Lynch, J. Coley, E. Ucan Ek', and V. Vapnarsky. 1999. Folkecology and commons management in the Maya Lowlands. *Proceedings of the National Academy of Sciences U.S.A.* 96:7598–7603.
Atran, S., and D. Sperber. 1991. Learning without teaching: Its place in culture. In L. Tolchinsky-Landsmann (ed.), *Culture, schooling and psychological development*. Norwood, NJ: Ablex.
Atran, S., and E. Ucan Ek'. 1999. Classification of useful plants among northern Petén Maya. In C. White (ed.), *Reconstructing ancient Maya diet*. Salt Lake City: University of Utah Press.
Au, T., and L. Romo. 1999. Mechanical causality in children's "folkbiology." In D. Medin and S. Atran (eds.), *Folkbiology*. Cambridge, MA: MIT Press.
Augustine, Saint. 2000(413–426). *The city of God*. New York: Modern Library.
Aunger, R., ed. 2001. *Darwinizing culture: The status of memetics as a science*. New York: Oxford University Press.
Austin, J. 1962. *How to do things with words*. Oxford: Oxford University Press.
Avis, J., and P. Harris. 1991. Belief-desire reasoning among Baka children. *Child Development* 62:460–467.

Axelrod, R. 1984. *The evolution of cooperation*. New York: Basic Books.

———. 1997. *The complexity of cooperation*. Princeton: Princeton University Press.

Axelrod, R., and W. Hamilton. 1981. The evolution of cooperation. *Science* 211:1390–1396.

Ayer, A. J. 1950. *Language, truth, and logic*. 2d ed. New York: Dover.

Bachevalier, J., and P. Merjanian. 1994. The contribution of medial temporal lobe structures in infantile autism: A neurobehavioral study in primates. In L. Bauman and T. Kemper (eds.), *The neurobiology of autism*. Baltimore: Johns Hopkins University Press.

Baer, H., and M. Singer, 1993. *African-American religion in the twentieth century*. Knoxville: University of Tennessee Press.

Bailenson, J., M. Shum, S. Atran, D. Medin, and J. Coley. (2002) A bird's eye view: Biological categorization and reasoning within and across cultures. *Cognition* 84:1–53.

Baillargeon, R. 1987. Object permanence in 3.5 and 4.5-month-old infants. *Developmental Psychology* 23:655–664.

Baker, A. 2001. *The gladiator: The secret history of Rome's warrior slaves*. New York: St. Martin's.

Baker, M. 1996. *The polysynthesis parameter*. New York: Oxford University Press.

Balch, W., D. Myers, and C. Papotto. 1999. Dimensions of mood in mood-dependent memory. *Journal of Experimental Psychology: Learning, Memory, and Cognition* 25:70–83.

Balter, M. 2002. What made humans modern? *Science* 295:1219–1225.

Baran, M. 2000. Agency, animacy and intentionality. Paper presented at Evolutionary Epistemology seminar, Culture and Cognition Program, University of Michigan, April.

Barber, B. 2002. Adolescents as activists and victims: Lessons from Gaza and Bosnia. Paper presented to the seminar series, "The Psychology of Extremism," Institute for Social Research, The University of Michigan, Ann Arbor, March 25.

Barber, E., and A. Peters. 1992. Ontogeny and phylogeny: What child language and archaeology have to say to each other. In J. Hawkins and M. Gell-Mann (eds.), *Studies in the science of complexity. Proceedings of the Santa Fe Institute*, 11. Redwood City, CA: Addison Wesley.

Barclay, H. 1964. *Buurri al Lamaab: A suburban village in the Sudan*. Ithaca, NY: Cornell University Press.

Barkow, J., L. Cosmides, and J. Tooby, eds. 1992. *The adapted mind*. New York: Oxford University Press.

Barkun, M. 1974. *Disaster and the millennium*. New Haven: Yale University Press.

Baron, J., and M. Spranca, 1997. Protected values. *Organizational Behavior and Human Decision Processes* 70: 1–16.

Baron-Cohen, S. 1995. *Mindblindness: An essay on autism and theory of mind*. Cambridge, MA: MIT Press.

Barrett, J. 2000. Exploring the natural foundations of religion. *Trends in Cognitive Science*. 4:29–34.

Barrett, J. 1998. Cognitive constraints on Hindu concepts of the divine. *Journal for Scientific Study of Religion* 37:608–619.

Barrett, J., and F. Keil. 1996. Conceptualizing a non-natural entity: Anthropomorphism in God concepts. *Cognitive Psychology* 31:219–247.

Barrett, J., and E. T. Lawson. 2001. Ritual intuitions: Cognitive contributions to judgments of well-formedness. *Journal of Cognition and Culture* 1:183–201.

Barrett, J., and R. Newman. 1999. Knowing what God knows: Understanding the importance of background knowledge for interpreting static and visual displays. Poster presented at the Cognitive Development Society meeting, Chapel Hill, NC, October.

Barrett, J., and M. Nyhof. 2001. Spreading nonnatural concepts. *Journal of Cognition and Culture* 1:69–100.

Barrett, J., R. Richert, and A. Driesenga. 2001. God's beliefs versus mother's: The development of nonhuman agent concepts. *Child Development* 72:50–65.

Barrett, L., R. Dunbar, and J. Lycett, 2001. *Human evolutionary psychology*. Basingstoke, UK: Macmillan.

Barth, F. 1953. *Principles of social organization in southern Kurdistan*. Oslo: Universitetets Etnografiske Museum, Bulletin 7.

———. 1975. *Ritual and knowledge among the Baktaman of New Guinea*. New Haven: Yale University Press.

Bartlett, F. 1932. *Remembering*. Cambridge, UK: Cambridge University Press.

Bartsch, K., and H. Wellman. 1995. *Children talk about the mind*. New York: Oxford University Press.

Bar-Yosef, O., and S. Kuhn. 1999. The big deal about blades: Laminar technologies and human evolution. *American Anthropologist* 101:322–338.

Bates, E., L. Benigni, I. Bretherton, L. Camaioni, and V. Voletera. 1979. *The emergence of symbols*. New York: Academic Press.

Bateson, G. 1958. *Naven*. Stanford: Stanford University Press.

Batson, C. 1975. Rational processing or rationalization: The effect of disconfirming information on a stated religious belief. *Journal of Personality and Social Psychology* 32:176–184.

Bauman, M., and T. Kemper. 1985. Histoanatomic observations of the brain in early infantile autism. *Neurology* 35:866–874.

Bear, D. 1979. Temporal lobe epilepsy. *Cortex* 15:357–384.

Beard, A. 1963. The schizophrenia-like psychoses of epilepsy, 2: Physical aspects. *British Journal of Psychiatry* 109:113–129.

Beit-Hallahmi, B. 1992. *Despair and deliverance: Private salvation in contemporary Israel*. Albany: State University of New York Press.

Beit-Hallahmi, B., and M. Argyle. 1997. *The psychology of religious behavior, belief, and experience*. London: Routledge.

Beit-Hallahmi, B., and B. Nevo. 1987. "Born-again" Jews in Israel. *International Journal of Psychology* 22:75–81.

Ben-Amos, P. G. 1994. The promise of greatness: Women and power in an Edo spirit possession cult. In T. Blakely, W. van Beek, and D. Thomson (eds.), *Religion in Africa*. Portsmouth, NH: Heinemann.

Benedict, R. 1935. *Patterns of culture*. London: Routledge & Kegan Paul.

Bennett, J. 2002. Arab press glorifies bomber as heroine. *The New York Times*, February 11.

Bennett, W. 1998. *The death of outrage: Bill Clinton and the assault on American ideals*. New York: Simon & Schuster.

Bering, J., and D. Bjorklund. 2002. Simulation constraints on the development of death representation: Are there natural foundations of afterlife beliefs? Paper presented to the International Conference, "Minds and Gods: the Cognitive Study of Religion," The University of Michigan and The John Templeton Foundation, Ann Arbor, March.

Berkes, F., D. Feeny, B. McCay, and J. Acheson. 1989. The benefit of the commons. *Nature* 340:91–93.

Berlin, B. 1992. *Ethnobiological classification*. Princeton: Princeton University Press.

Berlin, B., D. Breedlove, and P. Raven. 1973. General principles of classification and nomenclature in folk biology. *American Anthropologist* 74:214–242.

Biklen, D. 1990. Communication unbound: Autism and praxis. *Harvard Educational Review* 60:291–314.

Bird, F., and B. Reimer. 1982. Participation rates in new religious and parareligious movements. *Journal for the Scientific Study of Religion* 21:1–14.

Bird-David, N. 1999. "Animism" revisited. *Current Anthropology* (supplement) 40:S67–S92.

Birky, I., and D. Ball. 1987. Parental trait influence on God as an object representation. *Journal of Psychology* 122:133–137.

Blackmore, S. 1999. *The meme machine*. Oxford: Oxford University Press.

Blakely, T., W. van Beek, and D. Thomson, eds. 1994. *Religion in Africa*. Portsmouth, NH: Heinemann.

Blakeslee, S. 1999. Pro-Darwinian center helps school fight creationism. *International Herald Tribune* (New York Times Service), 31 August.

Bliss, E., E. Larson, and S. Nakashima. 1983. Auditory hallucinations and schizophrenia. *Journal of Nervous and Mental Disease* 171:30–33.

Bloom, H. 1992. *The American religion*. New York: Simon and Schuster.

———. 1999. Billy Graham. *Time*, 14 June.

Bloom, P., and C. Veres. 1999. The perceived intentionality of groups. *Cognition* 71: B1–B9.

Blurton Jones, N. 1984. A selfish origin for human food sharing. *Ethology and Sociobiology* 5:1–3.

———. 1987. Tolerated theft. *Social Science Information* 26:31–54.

Bock, W. 1973. Philosophical foundations of classical evolutionary taxonomy. *Systematic Zoology* 22:275–392.

Boehm, C. 1993. Egalitarian society and reverse dominance hierarchy. *Current Anthropology* 34:227–254.

———. 1996. Emergency decisions, cultural selection mechanics and group selection. *Current Anthropology* 37:763–793.

———. 1997. The impact of the human egalitarian syndrome on Darwinian selection mechanics. *American Naturalist* 150:100–121.

Boesch, C. 1991. Teaching in wild chimpanzees. *Animal Behaviour* 41:530–532.

Boetius, J., and E. Harding. 1985. A re-examination of Johannes Schmidt's Atlantic eel investigations. *Dana* 4:129–162.

Boster, J. 1986. Exchange of varieties and information between Aguaruna manioc cultivators. *American Anthropologist* 88:428–436.

Bower, G. 1967. A descriptive theory of memory. In D. Kimble (ed.), *Organization of recall*. New York: The New York Academy of Sciences.

Bower, G., and J. Mayer. 1989. In search of mood-dependent retrieval. *Journal of Social Behavior and Personality* 4:133–168.

Bowlby, J. 1969. *Attachment and loss, vol. 1. Attachment*. New York: Basic Books.

Boyd, R. In press. Population structure, equilibrium selection and the evolution of norms. In U. Pagano (ed.), *Evolution*. New York: Cambridge University Press.

Boyd, R., and J. Henrich. 2001. On modelling cognition and culture. Paper presented to Innateness and Structure of the Mind Workshop, University of Sheffield, November.

Boyd, R., and P. Richerson. In press. Solving the puzzle of human cooperation. In S. Levinson (ed.), *Evolution and culture*. Cambridge, MA: MIT Press.

Boyd, R., and P. Richerson. 1985. *Culture and evolutionary process*. Chicago: University of Chicago Press.

———. 1989. The evolution of indirect reciprocity. *Social Networks* 11:213–236.

———. 1990. Group selection among alternatively stable strategies. *Journal of Theoretical Biology* 145:331–342.

———. 1991. Punishment allows the evolution of cooperation (or anything else) in sizable groups. *Ethology and Sociobiology* 13:171–196.

———. 1995. Why does culture increase human adaptability? *Ethology and Sociobiology* 16:125–143.

———. 2001a. Memes: Universal acid or a better mouse trap. In Robert Aunger (ed.), *Darwinizing culture: The status of memetics as a science*. New York: Oxford University Press.

———. 2001b. Norms and bounded rationality. In G. Gigerenzer and R. Selten (eds.), *The adaptive toolbox*. Cambridge, MA: MIT Press.

Boyer, P. 1994. *The naturalness of religious ideas*. Berkeley: University of California Press.

———. 1996. What makes anthropomorphism natural: Intuitive ontology and cultural representations. *Journal of the Royal Anthropological Institute* (NS) 2:83–97.

———. 1997. Cognitive tracks of cultural inheritance. *American Anthropologist* 100:876–889.

———. 2000. Functional origins of religious concepts. *Journal of the Royal Anthropological Institute* (NS) 6:195–214.

Boyer, P., and C. Ramble. (2001). Cognitive templates for religious concepts: Cross-cultural evidence for recall of counter-intuitive representations. *Cognitive Science* 25:535–564.

Boysen, S., V. Kuhlmeier, P. Halliday, and Y. Halliday. 1999. Tool use in captive gorillas. In S. Parker, R. Mitchell, and H. Miles (eds.), *The mentalities of gorillas and orangutans*. Cambridge, UK: Cambridge University Press.

Brams, S. 1980. *Biblical games: A strategic analysis of stories in the Old Testament*. Cambridge, MA: MIT Press.

Brandon, E. 1960. *The battle for the soul: Aspects of religious conversion*. London: Hodder and Stoughton.

Bransford, J., and J. Johnson. 1973. Consideration of some problems in comprehension. In W. Chase (ed.), *Visual information processing*. New York: Academic Press.

Bremner, J. D., M. Narayan, L. Staib, S. Southwick, T. McGlashan, and D. Charney. 1999. Neural correlates of memories of childhood sexual abuse in women with and without posttraumatic stress disorder. *American Journal of Psychiatry* 156:1787–1795.

Bremner, J. D., P. Randall, E. Vermetten, L. Staib, R. Bronen, S. Capelli, C. Mazure, G. McCarthy, S. Charney, and R. Innis. 1995. MRI-based measurement of hippocampal volume in combat-related posttraumatic stress disorder. *American Journal of Psychiatry* 152:973–981.

Bremner, J. D., L. Staib, D. Kaloupek, S. Southwick, R. Soufer, and S. Charney, 1999. Neural correlates of exposure to traumatic pictures and sound in Vietnam combat veterans with and without posttraumatic stress disorder. *Biological Psychiatry* 45:806–816.

Bricker, V. 1981. *The Indian Christ, the Indian king: The historical substrate of Maya myth and ritual*. Austin: University of Texas Press.

Bromley, D., ed. 1992. *Making the commons work*. San Francisco: Institute for Contemporary Studies Press.

Brown, D. 1991. *Human universals*. New York: McGraw-Hill.

Brown, D., and S. Boysen. 2000. Spontaneous discrimination of natural stimuli by chimpanzees (*Pan troglodytes*). *Journal of Comparative Psychology* 114:392–400.

Brown, L. 1962. A study of religious belief. *British Journal of Psychology* 53:259–272.

———. 1994. *The human side of prayer*. Birmingham, AL: Religious Education Press.

Brown, R., and J. Kulik. 1977. Flashbulb memories. *Cognition* 5:73–99.

Brown, R., and J. Kulick, 1982. Flashbulb memory. In U. Neiser (ed.), *Memory observed: Remembering in natural contexts*. San Francisco: W. H. Freeman.

Bruce, R. 1975. *Lacandon dream symbolism*. Mexico City: Ediciones Euroamericanas.

Bruner, J. 1990. *Acts of meaning*. Cambridge, MA: Harvard University Press.

Burkert, W. 1996. *Creation of the sacred*. Cambridge, MA: Harvard University Press.

Burland, C. 1973. *Eskimo art*. London: Hamlyn.

Burns, J. 2001. America the vulnerable meets a ruthless enemy. *The New York Times*, September 12.

Buss, D. 1995. *The evolution of desire*. New York: Basic Books.

Buss, D., T. Shackelford, A. Bleske, and J. Wakefield. 1998. Adaptations, exaptation, and spandrels. *American Psychologist* 53:533–548.

Byron, G. (Lord). 1998(1812). *The works of Lord Byron*. Ware, Hertsfordshire: Wordsworth Poetry Library.

Cahill, L., B. Prins, M. Weber, and J. McGaugh. 1994. Beta-adrenergic activation and memory for emotional events. *Nature* 371:702–704.

Cain, D. 1974. The role of the olfactory bulb in limbic mechanisms. *Psychological Bulletin* 18:654–671.

Calvin, J. 1956 (1559). *On God and political duty*. 2d ed. New York: Bobbs-Merrill.

Campbell, D. 1979. Comments on the sociobiology of ethics and moralizing. *Behavioral Science* 24:37–45.

Campbell, J. 1975. *The mythic image*. Princeton: Princeton University Press.

Caramazza, A. (2002). The organization of conceptual knowledge: The view from neuropsychology. Paper presented at the British Academy, London, June.

Carey, S. 1995. On the origin of causal understanding. In D. Sperber, D. Premack, and A. Premack (eds.), *Causal cognition*. Oxford: Clarendon Press.

Carneiro, E. 1940. The structure of African cults in Bahia. *Journal of American Folk-Lore* 53:271–278.

Carstensen, L., D. Isaacowitz, and S. Charles. 1999. Taking time seriously. *American Psychologist* 54:165–181.

Cavalli-Sforza, L. 1991. Genes, peoples, languages. *Scientific American* 265:104–110.

Cavalli-Sforza, L., and M. Feldman. 1981. *Cultural transmission and evolution*. Princeton: Princeton University Press.

Cerella, J. 1979. Visual classes and natural categories in the pigeon. *Journal of Experimental Psychology: Human Perception and Performance* 5:68–77.

Chase, P. and H. Dibble. 1987. Middle Paleolithic symbolism. *Journal of Anthropological Archaeology* 6:263–296.

Cheney, D., R. Seyfarth, and B. Smuts. 1986. Social relationships and social cognition in nonhuman primates. *Science* 234:1361–1366.

Cheng, P., K. Holyoak, R. Nisbett, and L. Oliver. 1986. Pragmatic versus syntactic approaches to training deductive reasoning. *Cognitive Psychology* 18:293–328.

Chiu, L.-H. 1972. A cross-cultural comparison of cognitive styles in Chinese and American children. *International Journal of Psychology* 7:235–242.

Chomsky, N. 1959. A review of B. F. Skinner's *Verbal behavior. Language* 35:26–58.

———. 1971. *Problems of knowledge and freedom*. New York: Vintage Books.

———. 1986. *Knowledge of language*. New York: Praeger.

———. 1988. *Language and problems of knowledge: The Managua lectures*. Cambridge, MA: MIT Press.

———. 2000. Minimalist inquiries: The framework. In R. Martin, D. Michaels, and J. Uriagereka (eds.), *Step by step*. Cambridge, MA: MIT Press.

Christianson, S.-Å. 1989. Flashbulb memories: Special, but not so special. *Memory & Cognition* 17:435–443.

———. 1992. Emotional stress and eyewitness memory: A critical review. *Psychological Bulletin* 112:284–309.

Christianson, S.-Å., E. Loftus, H. Hoffman, and G. Loftus. 1991. Eye fixations and memory for emotional events. *Journal of Experimental Psychology: Learning, Memory, and Cognition* 17:693–701.

Claridge, G. 1985. *Origins of mental illness*. Oxford: Blackwell.

———. 1997. *Schizotypy: Implications for illness and health*. New York: Oxford University Press.

Clark, E. 1929. *The psychology of religious awakening*. New York: Macmillan.

Clements, W., and J. Perner. 1994. Implicit understanding of belief. *Cognitive Development* 9:377–395.

Clendinnen, I. 1990. *Ambivalent conquests*. New York: Cambridge University Press.
Cochrane, G. 1970. *Big men and cargo cults*. Oxford: Clarendon Press.
Cohn, N. 1962. Medieval millenarism. In S. Thrupp (ed.), *Millenial dreams in action*. The Hague: Mouton.
Coleman, J. 1988. Social capital in the creation of human capital. *American Journal of Sociology* (supplement) 94:S95–S120.
Coley, J. 1995. Emerging differentiation of folkbiology and folkpsychology. *Child Development* 66:1856–1874.
Coley, J., D. Medin, and S. Atran. 1997. Does rank have its privilege? Inductive inferences in folkbiological taxonomies. *Cognition* 63:73–112.
Conrie, B. 1976. *Aspect*. New York: Cambridge University Press.
Corcoran, R., G. Mercer, and C. Frith. 1995. Schizophrenia, symptomatology and social inference: Investigating "theory of mind" in people with schizophrenia. *Schizophrenia Research* 17:5–13.
Cosmides, L. 1989. The logic of social exchange: Has natural selection shaped how humans reason? Studies with Wason Selection Task. *Cognition* 31:187–276.
Cosmides, L., and J. Tooby. 1992. Cognitive adaptations for social exchange. In J. Barkow, L. Cosmides, and J. Tooby (eds.), *The adapted mind: Evolutionary psychology and the generation of culture*. New York: Oxford University Press.
Cranston, R. 1988. *The miracle of Lourdes*. New York: Image Books.
Crapanzano, V. 1985. *Waiting: The whites of South Africa*. New York: Random House.
Cresswell, R. 1976. Lineage endogamy among Maronite mountaineers. In J. Peristiany (ed.), *Mediterranean family structures*. Cambridge, UK: Cambridge University Press.
Cronin, H. 1992. *The ant and the peacock*. New York: Cambridge University Press.
Crooke, W. 1907. *The native races of northern India*. London: Archibald Constable.
Cruickshank, B. 1966 (1853). *Eighteen years on the Gold Coast of Africa*, 2 vols. London: Cass.
Csibra, G., G. Gergely, S. Bíró, O. Koós, and M. Brockbank. 1999. Goal attribution without agency cues: The perception of "pure reason" in infancy. *Cognition* 72:237–267.
Cuisenier, J. 1975. *Economie et parenté*. Paris: Mouton.
Culbert, T. P., and D. Rice, eds. 1990. *Precolumbian population history in the Maya Lowlands* Albuquerque: University of New Mexico Press.
Cunningham, J., and R. Sterling. 1988. Developmental changes in the understanding of affective meaning in music. *Motivation and Emotion* 12:399–412.
Cupchick, C., M. Rickert, and J. Mendelson. 1982. Similarity and preference judgments of musical stimuli. *Scandinavian Journal of Psychology* 23:273–282.
Curtiss, S. 1902 (1892). *Primitive Semitic religion to-day*. Chicago: Fleming H. Revell Co.
Damasio, A. 1989. The brain binds entities and events by multiregional activation from convergence zones. *Neural Computation* 1:123–132.
———. 1994. *Descartes' error*. New York: Avon Books.
Daniels, D. 1983. The evolution of concealed ovulation and self-deception. *Ethology and Sociobiology* 4:69–87.
d'Aquili, E. 1978. The neurobiological bases of myth and concepts of deity. *Zygon* 13:257–275.
———. 1986. Myth, ritual, and the archetypal hypothesis. *Zygon* 21:141–160.
d'Aquili, E., and C. Laughlin. 1975. The biopsychological determinants of religious ritual behavior. *Zygon* 10:33–58.
d'Aquili, E., and A. Newberg. 1998. The neuropsychological basis of religions, or why God won't go away. *Zygon* 33:187–201.
———. 1999. *The mystical mind*. Minneapolis: Fortress Press.
Darnton, R. 1984. *The great cat massacre and other episodes in French cultural history*. New York: Basic Books.

Darwin, C. 1859. *On the origin of species by means of natural selection*. London: Murray.
———. 1883 (1872). *On the origin of species by means of natural selection*. 6th ed. New York: Appleton.
———. 1965 (1872). *The expression of the emotions in man and animals*. Chicago: University of Chicago Press.
Davidson, D. 1984. On the very idea of a conceptual scheme. In *Inquiries into truth and interpretation*. Oxford: Clarendon Press.
Davis, P. 1990. Repression and the inaccessibility of emotional memories. In J. Singer (ed.), *Repression and dissociation*. Chicago: University of Chicago Press.
Dawkins, R. 1976. *The selfish gene*. New York: Oxford University Press.
———. 1982. *The extended phenotype*. Oxford: Oxford University Press.
———. 1986. *The blind watchmaker*. London: Penguin.
———. 1993. Viruses of the mind. In B. Dahlbohm (ed.), *Dennett and his critics: Demystifying mind*. Oxford: Blackwell.
———. 1996. *Climbing mount improbabale*. New York: Norton.
———. 1998. *Unweaving the rainbow*. Boston: Houghton Mifflin.
———. 1999. Foreword to *The meme machine*, by S. Blackmore. Oxford: Oxford University Press.
d'Azevedo, W. 1973. Mask makers and myth in western Liberia. In A. Forge (ed.), *Primitive art and society*. London: Oxford University Press.
———. 1994. Gola womanhood and the limits of masculine omnipotence. In T. Blakely, W. van Beek, and D. Thomson (eds.), *Religion in Africa*. Porstmouth, NH: Heinemann.
Deardoff, J. 2001. Mom wins asylum for son with autism. *Chicago Tribune* February 21.
Deconchy, J. P. 1968. God and parental figures. In A. Godin (ed.), *From cry to word*. Brussels: Mumen Vitae.
de la Vega Inca, Garcilaso. 1986 (1609). *Commentarios reales*, 3 vols. Lima, Peru: La Confianza.
DeLong, G. 1992. Autism, amnesia, hippocampus, and learning. *Neuroscience and Behavioral Reviews* 16:63–70.
Dennett, D. 1978. Response to Premack and Woodruff: Does the chimpanzee have a theory of mind? *Behavioral and Brain Sciences* 4:568–570.
———. 1987. *The intentional stance*. Cambridge, MA: MIT Press.
———. 1995. *Darwin's dangerous idea*. New York: Simon and Schuster.
———. 1997. Appraising grace: What evolutionary good is God? *The Sciences* 37:39–44.
de Quervain, D., B. Roozendaal, and J. McGaugh. 1998. Stress and glucocorticoids impair long-term retrieval of spatial memory. *Nature* 394:787–790.
Descartes, R. 1681. *Les principes de la philosophie*. 4th ed. Paris: Theodore Gerard.
Deutsch, A. 1975. Observations on a sidewalk ashram. *Archives of General Psychiatry* 32:166–175.
Devasahayam, N. 1990. The museum approach to Tamil Nadu tribes. In *The Tamil Nadu Tribes. Bulletin of the Madras Government Museum* 16(3)(NS). Madras: Director of Stationery and Printing, Government of Tamil Nadu.
de Waal, F. 1982. *Chimpanzee politics*. London: Jonathan Cape.
———. 1986. Deception in the natural communication of chimpanzees. In R. Mitchell and N. Thompson (eds.), *Deception*. Albany: State University of New York Press.
Dewhurst, K., and A. Beard. 1970. Sudden religious conversions in temporal lobe epilepsy. *British Journal of Psychiatry* 117: S497–S507.
Dhabar, F., and B. McEwen. 1999. Enhancing versus suppressive effects of stress hormones on skin immune function. *Proceedings of the National Academy of Sciences U.S.A.* 96:1059–1064.
Diamond, J. 1997. *Guns, germs, and steel*. New York: Norton.

Díaz del Castillo, B. 1989 (1632). *Historia verdadera de la conquista de la Nueva España*. 8th ed. Madrid: Espasa-Calpe.

Dostoyevsky, F. n.d. (1880). *The brothers Karamazov*. New York: Modern Library.

Douglas, M. 1966. *Purity and danger*. London: Routledge & Kegan Paul.

———. 1973. *Natural symbols*. New York: Vintage Books.

Douyon, E. 1966. L'examen au Rorschach des voudouisants Haitiens. In R. Prince (ed.), *Trans and possession states*. Montreal: R. M. Bucke Memorial Society.

Dugatkin, L., and M. Alfieri. 1991. Guppies and the tit for tat strategy. *Behavioral Ecology and Sociobiology* 28:243–246.

Dunbar, R. 1996. *Grooming, gossip and the evolution of language*. London: Faber & Faber.

———. 2001. Mental modules versus phenotypic plasticity. Paper presented at the Evolution and Mind Workshop, Institute of Advanced Studies, University of Western Australia, August.

Dunn, J. 1988. *The beginnings of social understanding*. Cambridge, MA: Harvard University Press.

Dunn, J., J. Brown, C. Slomkowski, C. Tesla, and L. Youngblade. 1991. Young children's understandings of other people's feelings and beliefs. *Child Development* 62:1352–1366.

Dunn, J., and N. Dale. 1984. I a daddy: 2-year-olds' collaboration in joint pretend play with sibling and with mother. In I. Bretherton (ed.), *Symbolic play*. New York: Academic Press.

Durham, W. 1992. *Coevolution: Genes, culture and human diversity*. Stanford: Stanford University Press.

Durkheim, E. 1933 (1893). *The division of labor in society*. New York: Macmillan.

———. 1995 (1912). *The elementary forms of religious life*. New York: Free Press.

Echevarría, J.-U. 1963. *Fiesta de la Tirana de Tarapaca*. Valparaiso, Chile: Ediciones Universitaria de Valparaiso.

Eckberg, D., and T. Blocker. 1989. Varieties of religious involvement and environmental concerns. *Journal for the Scientific Study of Religion* 28:509–517.

Edgerton, R. 1992. *Sick societies*. New York: Free Press.

Edmonson, M. 1982. *The ancient future of the Itza: The book of the Chilam Balam of Tizimin*. Austin: University of Texas Press.

Edwards, A. 1957. *The social desirability variable in personality assessment and research*. New York: Dryden Press.

Eich, E. 1995. Searching for mood-dependent memory. *Psychological Science* 6:67–75.

Einstein, A. 1950. *Out of my later years*. New York: Philosophical Library.

Eisenberg, N., and J. Strayer. 1987. *Empathy and development*. New York: Cambridge University Press.

Ekman, P. 1992. An argument for basic emotions. *Cognition and Emotion* 6:169–200.

Eldredge, N. 1986. Information, economics, and evolution. *Annual Review of Ecology and Systematics* 17:351–369.

Eliade, M. 1964. *Myth and reality* London: Allen & Unwin.

Ellickson, R. 1994. *Order without law*. Cambridge, MA: Harvard University Press.

Elliot, E. 1985. Religion, identity and expression in American culture. *Social Science Information* 24:779–797.

Ellsworth, P. 1991. Some implications of cognitive appraisal theories of emotion. In K. Strongman (ed.), *International review of studies of emotion*, vol. 1. New York: Wiley.

Erikson, E. 1963. *Childhood and society*. 2d ed. New York: Norton.

Ettlinger, G., and W. Wilson. 1990. Cross-modal performance. *Behavioral Brain Research* 40:169–192.

Evans, M. 2001. Cognitive and contextual factors in the emergence of diverse belief systems: Creation versus evolution. *Cognitive Psychology* 42:217–266.

Evans-Pritchard, E. 1937. *Witchcraft, oracles and magic among the Azande*. Oxford: Clarendon Press.

———. 1940. *The Nuer*. Oxford: Oxford University Press.

———. 1960. Zande cannibalism. *Journal of the Royal Anthropological Institute* 90:238–258.

———. 1965. *Theories of primitive religion*. Oxford: Clarendon Press.

Ezekiel, R. 1995. *The racist mind: Portraits of American neo-nazis and Klansmen*. New York: Viking Penguin.

Fagan, B. 2000. Archaeology. In *2000 Britannica book of the year*. Chicago: Encyclopaedia Britannica.

Feinman, S., and M. Lewis. 1983. Social referencing at 10 months. *Child Development* 54:878–887.

Festinger, L., H. Riecken, and S. Schachter. 1956. *When prophecy fails*. Minneapolis: University of Minnesota Press.

Feuerbach, L. 1972(1843). *The fiery book: Selected writings of Ludwig Feuerbach*. Garden City, NY: Anchor Books.

Fiddick, L., L. Cosmides, and J. Tooby. 2000. No interpretation without representation. *Cognition* 75:1–79.

Firth, R. 1963. Offering and sacrifice. *Journal of the Royal Anthropological Institute* 93:12–24.

Fisher, H. 1995. *Anatomy of love*. Fawcett Books.

Fisher, R. 1958. *The genetical theory of natural selection*. 2d ed. New York: Dover.

Fiske, A., and P. Tetlock. 1997. Taboo trade-offs. *Political Psychology* 18:255–297.

Fivush, R., J. Gray, and F. Fromhoff. 1987. Two-year-olds talk about the past. *Cognitive Development* 2:393–410.

Flavell, J. 1986. The development of children's knowledge about the appearance-reality distinction. *American Psychologist* 41:418–425.

Flavell, J. H., X.-D. Zhang, H. Zou, Q. Dong, and S. Qui. 1983. A comparison of the appearance-reality distinction in the People's Republic of China and the United States. *Cognitive Psychology* 15:459–466.

Fodor, J. 1975. *The language of thought*. New York: Thomas Crowell.

———. 1983. *Modularity of mind*. Cambridge, MA: MIT Press.

———. 1987. *Psychosemantics*. Cambridge, MA: MIT Press.

———. 1998. The trouble with psychological Darwinism. *London Review of Books*, 15 January.

———. 2000. *The mind doesn't work that way: The scope and limits of computational psychology*. Cambridge, MA: MIT Press.

Fortes, M. 1959. *Oedipus and Job in West Africa*. Cambridge, UK: Cambridge University Press.

Foster, R., and J. Keating. 1992. Measuring androcentrism in the Western God-concept. *Journal for the Scientific Study of Religion* 31:366–375.

Fox, E., A. Sitompul, and C. Van Schaik. 1999. Intelligent tool use in wild Sumatran orangutans. In S. Parker, R. Mitchell and H. Miles (eds.), *The mentalities of gorillas and orangutans*. Cambridge, UK: Cambridge University Press.

Fox, R. 1967. *Kinship and marriage*. Cambridge: Cambridge University Press.

Frank, A. 1993(1947). *The diary of a young girl*, trans. B. Mooyaart. Upper Saddle River, NJ: Prentice Hall.

Frank, J. D. and B. Frank. 1991. *Persuasion and healing*. Baltimore: Johns Hopkins University Press.

Frank, R. 1988. *Passions within reason*. New York: Norton.

Freed, S., and R. Freed. 1964. Spirit possession as an illness in a North American village. *Ethnology* 3:152–197.

Freeman, D. 1983. *Margaret Mead and Samoa*. Cambridge, MA: Harvard University Press.

Freidel, D., L. Schele, and J. Parker. 1993. *Maya cosmos*. New York: Morrow.

Freud, S. 1955(1913). *Totem and taboo*. In J. Strachey (ed.), *The standard edition of the complete psychological works of Sigmund Freud*, vol. 13. London: Hogarth Press.

———. 1955(1921). *Group psychology and the analysis of the ego*. In J. Strachey (ed.), *The standard edition of the complete psychological works of Sigmund Freud*, vol. 18. London: Hogarth Press.

———. 1957a(1915). Thoughts for the time on war and death. In J. Strachey (ed.), *The standard edition of the complete psychological works of Sigmund Freud*, vol. 14. London: Hogarth Press.

———. 1957b(1915). Repression. In J. Strachey (ed.), *The standard edition of the complete psychological works of Sigmund Freud*, vol. 14. London: Hogarth Press.

Fried, M. 1967. *The evolution of political society*. New York: Random House.

Fukuyama, F. 1995. *Trust*. New York: Free Press.

Galanter, M. 1982. Charismatic religious sects and psychiatry. *American Journal of Psychiatry* 139:1248–1253.

Galanter, M., R. Rabkin, F. Rabkin, and A. Deutsch. 1979. The "Moonies." *American Journal of Psychiatry* 136:165–169.

Gallenmore, J., W. Wilson, and J. Rhoads. 1969. The religious life of patients with affective disorders. *Diseases of the Nervous System* 30:483–487.

Gallup, G., and F. Newport. 1991. Belief in paranormal phenomena among adult Americans. *Skeptical Inquirer* 15:137–146.

Galvin, J., and A. Ludwig. 1961. A case of witchcraft. *Journal of Nervous and Mental Disease* 133:161–168.

Garcia, J., F. Ervin, and R. Koelling. 1966. Learning with prolonged display of reinforcement. *Psychonomic Science* 4:123–124.

Gardner, B., and R. Gardner. 1971. Two-way communication with an infant chimpanzee. In A. Schrier and F. Stollnitz (eds.), *Behavior of non-human primates*, vol. 4. New York: Academic Press.

Gardner, R., and K. Heider. 1968. *Gardens of war: Life and death in the New Guinea Stone Age*. New York: Random House.

Garnham, W., and J. Perner. 2001. Actions do speal louder than words—but only implicitly: Young children's understanding of false beliefs in action. *British Journal of Developmental Psychology* 19:413–432.

Geertz, C. 1966. Religion as a cultural system. In M. Banton (ed.), *Anthropological approaches to the study of religion*. London: Tavisock.

———. 1975. Common sense as a cultural system. *Antioch Review* 33:5–26.

Geitner, P. 1999. Pope praises Copernicus. Associated Press Wire, 7 June.

Gellhorn, E., and W. Kiely. 1972. Mystical states of consciousness. *Journal of Nervous and Mental Disease* 154:399–405.

Gelman, S., and L. Hirschfeld. 1999. How biological is essentialism? In D. Medin and S. Atran (eds.), *Folkbiology*. Cambridge, MA: MIT Press.

Gelman, S., and H. Wellman. 1991. Insides and essences. *Cognition* 38:213–244.

Gerard, D. 1985. Religious attitudes and values. In M. Abrams, D. Gerard, and N. Timms (eds.), *Values and social change in Britain*. London: Macmillan.

Gerard, H., and G. Mathewson. 1966. The effects of severity of initiation on liking for a group: A replication. *Journal of Experimental Social Psychology* 2:278–287.

Gergely, G., Z. Nádasdy, G. Csibra, and S. Bíró. 1995. Taking the intentional stance at 12 months of age. *Cognition* 56:165–193.

Gerrard, N. 1968. The serpent-handling religions of West Virginia. *Trans-Action* 5: 22–28.

———. 1970. Churches of the stationary poor in southern Appalachia. In J. Photiadis and H. Schwarzweller (eds.), *Change in rural Appalachia*. Philadelphia: University of Pennsylvania Press.

Geschwind, N. 1983. Interictal behavioral changes in epilepsy. *Epilepsia* (supplement 1)24: S23–S30.

Geuter-Newitt, I. 1956. *Pour les parents d'un enfant mongoloïde*. St. Preux, Switzerland: Editions Association Institut de Pédagogie Curative.

Gibbon, E. 1845(1776–1788). *Decline and fall of the Roman empire*, 6 vols. New York: International Book Co.

Gigerenzer, G. 1997. The modularity of social intelligence. In A. Whiten and R. Byrne (eds.), *Machiavellian intelligence II*. Cambridge, UK: Cambridge University Press.

Gigerenzer, G., and K. Hug. 1992. Reasoning about social contracts. *Cognition* 43:127–171.

Gigerenzer, G., and P. Todd. 1999. *Simple heuristics that make us smart*. New York: Oxford University Press.

Gil-White, F. 2001. Are ethnic groups biological "species" to the brain? *Current Anthropology* 42:515–554.

Glanz, J. 2000. Survey finds support is strong for teaching 2 origin theories. *New York Times*, 11 March.

Glaser, R., D. Peral, J. Kiecolt-Glaser, and W. Malarkey. 1994. Chronic stress modulates the immune response to a pneumococcal pneumonia vaccine. *Psychoneuroendocrinology* 19:765–772.

Glik, D. 1986. Psychosocial wellness among spiritual healing participants. *Social Science and Medicine* 22:579–586.

Gloor, P., A. Olivier, F. Quesney, F. Andermann, and S. Horowitz. 1982. The role of the limbic system in experiential phenomena of temporal lobe epilepsy. *Annals of Neurology* 12:129–144.

Godelier, M. 1986 (1982.) *The making of great men: Male dominance and power among the Baruya of New Guinea*. Cambridge, UK: Cambridge University Press.

Goldfarb, W. 1964. An investigation of childhood schizophrenia. *Archives of General Psychiatry* 11:620–634.

Goldman, A. 1989. Interpretation psychologized. *Mind and Language* 4:161–185.

Goldman, I. 1940. Cosmological beliefs of the Cubeo Indians. *Journal of American Folk-Lore* 53:242–247.

Goldsmith, T. 1990. Optimization, constraint, and history in the evolution of eyes. *Quarterly Review of Biology* 65:281–322.

Gómez-Pompa, A., J. Flores, and V. Sosa. 1987. The *pet kot*: A man-made tropical forest of the Maya. *Interciencia* 12:10–15.

Goodall, J. 1986. *The chimpanzees of Gombe*. Cambridge, MA: Harvard University Press.

Goode, E. 2000. What provokes a rapist to rape? *New York Times*, 15 January.

Goode, W. 1970. *World revolution and family patterns*. New York: Free Press.

Goodenough, W. 1990. Evolution of human capacity for beliefs. *American Anthropologist* 92:597–612.

Goodman, G., J. Quas, J. Batterman-Fauce, M. Riddlesberger, and J. Kuhn. 1994. Predictors of accurate and inaccurate memories of traumatic events experienced in childhood. *Consciousness and Cognition* 3:269–294.

Goodman, N. 1965. *Fact, fiction and forecast*. Indianapolis: Bobbs-Merrill.

Goodstein, L. 2000. A direct line to God in an impersonal era. *New York Times*, 1 January.

Gopnik, A., and H. Wellman. 1992. Why the child's theory of mind really *is* a theory. *Mind and Language* 7:145–171.

Gordon, R. 1996. "Radical" simulationism. In P. Carruthers and P. Smith (eds.), *Theories of theories of mind*. Cambridge, UK: Cambridge University Press.

Gough, K. 1973. Harijans in Thanjivur. In K. Gough and H. Sharma (eds.), *Imperialism and revolution in South Asia*. New York: Monthly Review Press.

———. 1978. *Dravidian kinship and modes of production*. New Dehli: Indian Council of Social Science Research.

———. 1981. *Rural society in southeast India*. Cambridge, UK: Cambridge University Press.

Gould, S. 1980. *The panda's thumb*. New York: Norton.

———. 1991. Exaptation: A crucial tool for evolutionary psychology. *Journal of Social Issues* 47:43–46.

———. 1997. The exaptive excellence of spandrels as a term and prototype. *Proceedings of the National Academy of Sciences U.S.A.* 94:10750–10755.

Gould, S., and E. Vrba, 1982. Exaptation: A missing term in the science of form. *Paleobiology* 8:4–15.

Gould, S., And R. Lewontin. 1979. The Spandrels of San Marco and the Panglossian Paradigm: A Critique of the Adaptionist Program. *Proceedings of the Royal Society of London* B 205:581–598.

Granberg, D., and K. Campbell. 1973. Certain aspects of religiosity and orientations toward the Vietnam War among Missouri undergraduates. *Sociological Analysis* 34:40–49.

Greeley, A. 1975. *The sociology of the paranormal*. London: Sage.

———. 1991. Religion and attitudes towards AIDS policy. *Sociology and Social Research* 75:126–132.

———. 1993. Religion and attitudes toward the environment. *Journal for the Scientific Study of Religion* 32:19–28.

Greenberg, J., T. Pyszczynski, S. Solomon, A. Rosenblatt, M. Veeder, S. Kirkland, and D. Lyon. 1990. Evidence for terror management theory II: The effects of mortality salience on reactions to those who threaten or bolster the cultural worldview. *Journal of Personality and Social Psychology* 58:308–318.

Greenberg, U. 1937. *The book of denunciation and belief*. Jerusalem: Sadar.

Griffiths, P. 1997. *What emotions really are*. Chicago: University of Chicago Press.

———. 2001. What is innateness? *The Monist* (special issue, ed. K Sterelny).

Grünberg, J., and V. Ramos. 1998. *Base de datos sobre población, tierras y medio ambiente en la Reserva del la Biosfera Maya, Petén, Guatemala*. Guatemala City: CARE/CONAP.

Guck, M. 2002. Music as a (dis-)embodiment of human behavior, as an invitation to (human) relationship. Paper presented to the University of Michigan "Culture and Cognition Program," March 8.

Guglielmino, C., C. Viganotti, B. Hewlett, and L. Cavalli-Sforza. 1995. Cultural variation in Africa. *Proceedings of the National Academy of Sciences U.S.A.* 92:7585–7589.

Guthrie, S. 1993. *Faces in the clouds: A new theory of religion*. New York: Oxford University Press.

Hallpike, C. 1969. Social hair. *Man* 4:256–264.

———. 1976. Is there a primitive mentality? *Man* 11:253–270.

Hamilton, W. 1964. The genetical evolution of social behavior. *Journal of Theoretical Biology* 7:1–52.

Hamilton, W., and G. Orians. 1965. Evolution of brood parasitism in altricial birds. *Condor* 67:361–382.

Hamond, N., and R. Fivush. 1991. Memories of Mickey Mouse. *Cognitive Development* 6:433–448.

Hardin, G. 1968. The tragedy of the commons. *Science* 162:1243–1248.

Hare, B., J. Call, B. Agenta, and M. Tomasello. 2000. Chimpanzees know what conspecifics do and do not see. *Animal Behaviour* 59:771–785.

Hare, B., J. Call, and M. Tomasello. 2001. Do chimpanzees know what conspecifics know? *Animal Behaviour* 61:139–151.

Harmon-Jones, E., and J. Mills, eds. (1999) *Cognitive dissonance*. Washington, DC: American Psychological Association.
Harris, M. 1966. The cultural ecology of India's sacred cattle. *Current Anthropology* 7:51–65.
———. 1974. *Cows, pigs, wars, and witches*. New York: Random House..
———. 1975. *Culture, people, nature*. 2nd ed. New York: Thomas Crowell.
Harris, P. 1992. From simulation to folk psychology. *Mind and Language* 7:12–144.
———. 1994. Understanding pretence. In C. Lewis and P. Mitchell (eds.), *Children's early understanding of mind*. Hove, UK: Erlbaum.
Hatano, G., and K. Inagaki. 1999. A developmental perspective on informal biology. In D. Medin and S. Atran (eds.), *Folkbiology*. Cambridge, MA: MIT Press.
Hauser, M. 2000a. *What animals really think*. New York: Henry Holt & Company.
———. 2000b. What do animals think about numbers? *American Scientist* 88:144–151.
Havemeyer, L. 1929. *Ethnography*. Boston: Ginn and Company.
Hawkes, K. 1993. Why hunter-gatherers work. *Current Anthropology* 34:341–361.
Hawkes, K., J. O'Connell, and L. Rogers. 1997. The behavioral ecology of modern hunter-gatherers, and human evolution. *Trends in Ecology and Evolution* 12:29–31.
Hay, D. 1982. *Exploring inner space*. Harmondsworth, UK: Penguin.
———. 1990. *Religious experience today*. London: Mowbray.
Hayes, K., and C. Hayes. 1951. The intellectual development of a home-raised chimpanzee. *Proceedings of the American Philosophical Society* 95:105–109.
Hediger, H. 1955. *Studies in the psychology and behavior of animals in zoos and circuses*. London: Buttersworth.
Heider, F., and S. Simmel. 1944. An experimental study of apparent behavior. *American Journal of Psychology* 57:243–259.
Henderson, J., and M. Oakes. 1990. *The wisdom of the serpent*. Princeton: Princeton University Press.
Henrich, J., and R. Boyd. 1998. The evolution of conformist transmission and the emergence of between-group differences. *Evolution and Human Behavior* 19:215–241.
———. 2002. Culture and Cognition: Why cultural evolution does not require replication of representations. *Journal of Culture and Cognition* 2.
Henrich, J., and F. J. Gil-White. 2001. The evolution of prestige. *Evolution and Human Behavior* 22:165–196.
Hermann, B., and S. Whitman. 1984. Behavioral and personality correlates of epilepsy. *Psychological Bulletin* 95:451–497.
Herrnstein, R. 1984. Objects, categories, and discriminative stimuli. In H. Roitblat (ed.), *Animal cognition*. Hillsdale, NJ: Erlbaum.
Hesse, M. 1961. *Forces and fields*. London: Nelson & Sons.
Heuer, F., and D. Resiberg. 1992. Emotion, arousal, and memory for detail. In S.-Å. Christianson (ed.), *Handbook of emotion and memory*. Hillsdale, NJ: Erlbaum.
Heyes, C. 1993. Anecdotes, training, trapping, and triangulation: Do animals attribute mental states? *Animal Behaviour* 46:177–188.
———. 1998. Theory of mind in nonhuman primates. *Behavioral and Brain Sciences* 21:101–148.
Heyes, C., and B. Galef, eds. 1996. *Social learning in animals*. New York: Academic Press.
Hijuelos, O. 1995. *Mr. Ives' Christmas*. New York: HarperCollins.
Hill, K. 1999. Evolution of the human life course. Paper presented to the Evolution and Human Adaptation Program, Institute for Social Research, University of Michigan, Ann Arbor, 9 February.
Hill, K., and H. Kaplan. 1993. On why male foragers hunt and share food. *Current Anthropology* 34:701–706.

Hillard, A. 2000. *For the time being*. New York: Knopf.
Hirschfeld, L. 1996. *Race in the making*. Cambridge, MA: MIT Press.
Hirschfeld, L., and S. Gelman, eds. 1994. *Mapping the mind: Domain-specificity in cognition and culture*. New York: Cambridge University Press.
Hirshleifer, J. 1977. Economics from a biological viewpoint. *Journal of Law and Economics* 20:1–52.
Hobbes, T. 1901 (1651). *Leviathan*. New York: Dutton.
Holland, J. 1995. *Hidden Order*. New York: Addison-Wesley.
Holloway, R. 1969. Culture: A human domain. *Current Anthropology* 10:395–412.
Holloway, R. 1983. Human paleontological evidence relevant to language behavior. *Human Neurobiology* 2:105–114.
Holyoak, K., K. Koh, and R. Nisbett. 1989. A theory of conditioning. *Psychological Review* 96:315–340.
Hood, R., and R. Morris. 1981. Sensory isolation and the differential report of visual imagery in intrinsic and extrinsic subjects. *Journal for the Scientific Study of Religion* 20:261–273.
Hooker, C., N. Roese, and S. Parks. 2000. Impoverished counterfactual thinking is associated with schizophrenia. *Psychiatry* 63:336–338.
Hornick, R., N. Risenhoover, and M. Gunnar. 1987. The effects of maternal, positive, neutral, and negative affective communications on infant responses to new toys. *Child Development* 58:937–944.
Horowitz, M. 1979. Psychological response to serious life events. In V. Hamilton and D. Warburton (eds.), *Human stress and cognition*. New York: Wiley.
Horton, R. 1963. The Kalabiri Erkine society. *Africa* 33:94–114.
———. 1967. African thought and Western science. *Africa* 37:50–71, 159–187.
———. 1973. Lévy-Bruhl, Durkheim and the scientific revolution. In R. Horton and R. Finnegan (eds.), *Modes of thought: Essays in thinking in Western and non-Western societies*. London: Faber & Faber.
Houlihan, P. 1996. *The animal world of the pharaohs*. London: Thames & Hudson.
House, C., and W. McDougall. 1912. *The pagan tribes of Borneo*. London: Macmillan.
Howell, F. C. 1965. *Early man*. New York: Time-Life Books.
Hubel, D. 1988. *Eye, brain, and vision*. New York: Scientific American.
Hugdahl, K. 1996. Cognitive influences on human autonomic nervous function. *Current Opinion in Neurobiology* 6:252–258.
Hull, D. 1988. *Science as a process*. Chicago: University of Chicago Press.
Hume, D. 1955 (1758). *An inquiry concerning human understanding*. New York: Bobbs-Merrill.
———. 1956 (1757). *The natural history of religion*. Stanford: Stanford University Press.
———. 1978 (1739). *A treatise of human nature*. New York: Oxford University Press.
Humphrey, N. 1995. *Soul searching: Human nature and supernatural belief*. London: Chatto & Windus.
Hunsberger, B. 1996. Religious fundamentalism, right-wing authoritarianisms, and hostility towards homosexuals in non-Christian groups. *International Journal for the Psychology of Religion* 6:39–49.
Hunsberger, B., and L. Brown. 1984. Religious socialization, apostasy, and the impact of family background. *Journal for the Scientific Study of Religion* 23:239–251.
Hustig, H., and R. Hafner. 1990. Persistent auditory hallucinations and their relationship to delusions and mood. *Journal of Nervous and Mental Disease* 178:264–267.
Huston, N. 1998. *L'empreinte de l'ange*. Paris: ACTES SUD.
Iannaccone, L. 1994. Why churches are strong. *American Journal of Sociology* 99:1180–1211.

Ibn Khaldûn 1958. *The Muqaddimah*. 3 vols. London: Routledge & Kegan Paul (originally composed in 14th century).

Imperio, W. 2002. First depression center. *Clinical Psychiatry News*, February.

Inagaki, K., and G. Hatano. 1987. Young children's spontaneous personification as analogy. *Child Development* 58:1013–1020.

———. 1993. Young children's understanding of the mind-body distinction. *Child Development* 64:1534–1549.

Ingold, T. 1996. The optimal forager and economic man. In P. Descola and G. Pálsson (eds.), *Nature and society*. London: Routledge.

Irons, W. 1996a. Morality, religion, and human nature. In W. M. Richardson and W. Wildman (eds.), Religion and science. New York: Routledge.

———. 1996b. In our own self image: The evolution of morality, deception, and religion. *Skeptic* 4:50–61.

Izard, C. 1977. *The face of emotion*. New York: Appleton-Century-Crofts.

Jackendoff, R. 1990. What would a theory of the evolution of language have to look like? *Behavioral and Brain Sciences* 13:737–738.

Jackson, M. 1990. The man who could turn into an elephant: Shape-shifting among the Kuranko of Sierre Leone. In M. Jackson and I. Karp (eds.), *Personhood and agency: The experience of self and other in African cultures*. Washington, DC: Smithsonian Institution Press.

Jacobs, M. 1934. *Northwest Sahaptin texts*. New York: Columbia University Press.

James, W. 1902. *The varieties of religious experience*. London: Longmans.

Jaussen, A. 1948 (1907). *Coutumes des Arabs au pays de Moab*. Paris: Adrien-Maisonneuve.

Jenkins, J., and J. Astington. 1996. Cognitive factors and family structure associated with theory of mind development in young children. *Developmental Psychology* 32:70–78.

Jerison, H. 1976. The paleoneurology of language. In S. Harnad, H. Steklis, and J. Lancaster (eds.), *Origins and evolution of language and speech. Annals of the New York Academy of Sciences* 280:370–382.

Jeyifous, S. 1985. Atimodemo: Semantic conceptual development among the Yoruba. Ph.D. diss., Cornell University.

Job, R., and L. Surian. 1998. A neurocognitive mechanism for folk biology? *Behavioral and Brain Sciences* 21:577–578.

Johanson, D., and B. Edgar. 1996. *From Lucy to language*. New York: Simon and Schuster.

Johnson, S., A. Booth and K. O'Hearn. 2001. Inferring the goals of a non-human agent. *Cognitive Development* 16:637–656.

Johnson, S., V. Slaughter and S. Carey. 1998. Whose gaze will infants follow? The elicitation of gaze in 12-month-olds. *Developmental Science* 1:233–238.

Johnson, T. 1995. The significance of religion for aging well. *American Behavioral Scientist* 39:186–208.

Jones, G. 1998. *The conquest of the last Maya kingdom*. Stanford: Stanford University Press.

Josephus Ben Mathias. 1981. *The Jewish war* (67–73 A.D.) New York: Dorset Press (originally written in 1st century A.D.).

Kahneman, D., and A. Tversky. 1979. Prospect theory: An analysis of decision under risk. *Econometrica* 47:263–291.

Kaldor, P. 1994. *Winds of change*. Hoebush West, Australia: Anzea.

Kanner, L. 1943. Autistic disturbances of affective contact. *The Nervous Child* 2:217–250.

Kant, E. 1951 (1790). *Critique of judgement*. New York: Hafner Press.

Kanter, R. 1972. *Commitment and community*. Cambridge, MA: Harvard University Press.

Kaplan, H., and K. Hill. 1985. Food sharing among Ache foragers. *Current Anthropology* 26:223–246.

Karagulla, S., and E. Robertson. 1955. Physical phenomena in temporal lobe epilepsy and the psychoses. *British Medical Journal* 1:748–752.

Kauffman, S. 1993. *The origins of order*. New York: Oxford University Press.
Kawai, M. 1965. Newly acquired precultural behavior of the natural troop of Japanese monkeys on Koshima islet. *Primates* 6:1–30.
Kawaruma, S. 1959. The process of sub-culture propagation among Japanese macaques. *Primates* 2:43–60.
Keegan, J. 1993. *A history of warfare*. New York: Knopf.
Keesing, F. 1949. Some notes on Bontok social organization, northern Philippines. *American Anthropologist* 51: 578–601.
Keil, F. 1979. *Semantic and conceptual development*. Cambridge, MA: Harvard University Press.
———. 1994. The birth and nurturance of concepts by domains. In L. Hirschfeld and S. Gelman (eds.), *Mapping the mind*. New York: Cambridge University Press.
Keller, J. and F. Lehman. 1993. Computational complexity in the modelling of cosmological ideas. In P. Boyer (ed.), *Cognitive aspects of religious symbolism*. Cambridge, UK: Cambridge University Press.
Kelley, M. 1958. The incidence of hospitalized mental illness among religious sisters in the United States. *American Journal of Psychiatry* 115:72–75.
Kelly, M., and F. Keil. 1985. The more things change . . . : Metamorphoses and conceptual structure. *Cogntitive Science* 9:403–416.
Kelly, R. 1985. *The Nuer conquest*. Ann Arbor: University of Michigan Press.
Keltner, D., P. Ellsworth, and K. Edwards. 1993. Beyond simple pessimism: Effects of sadness and anger on social perception. *Journal of Personality and Social Psychology* 64:740–752.
Kennedy, K. 1975. *Neanderthal man*. Minneapolis: Burgess.
Kent, G. and S. Wahass. 1996. The content and characteristics of auditory hallucinations in Saudi Arabia and the UK. *Acta Psychiatrica Scandinavica* 94:433–437.
Khansari, D., A. Murgo, and R. Faith. 1990. Effects of stress on the immune system. *Immunology Today* 11:170–175.
Kierkegaard, S. 1955. *Fear and trembling* and *The sickness unto death*. New York: Doubleday (*Fear and trembling* originally published in 1843).
Kildahl, J. 1972. *The psychology of speaking in tongues*. New York: Harper and Row.
Killany, R., and M. Moss. 1994. Memory function and autism. In L. Bauman and T. Kemper (eds.), *The neurobiology of autism*. Baltimore: Johns Hopkins University Press.
Kilson, M. 1972. Ambivalence and power: Mediums in Ga traditional religion. *Journal of Religion in Africa* 4:171–177.
Kingsley, M. 1899. *West African studies*. London: Macmillan.
Kintsch, W., and E. Greene. 1978. The role of culture-specific schemata in the comprehension and recall of stories. *Discourse Processes* 1:1–13.
Kirkpatrick, L. 1997. A longitudinal study of changes in religious belief and behavior as a function of individual differences in adult attachment style. *Journal for the Scientific Study of Religion* 36:207–217.
———. 1998. God as a substitute attachment figure. *Personality and Social Psychology Bulletin* 24:961–973.
Kluckholn, C. 1952. Values and value-orientations in the theory of action. In T. Parsons and E. Shils (eds.), *Toward a general theory of action*. Cambridge, MA: Harvard University Press.
Kluckholn, C., and D. Leighton. 1974 (1946). *The Navaho*. Cambridge, MA: Harvard University Press.
Klüver, H., and P. Bucy. 1939. Preliminary analysis of function of the temporal lobe in monkeys. *Archives of Neurology* 42:979–1000.
Knight, N., J. Barrett, S. Atran, and E. Ucan Ek'. (2001). Understanding the mind of God: Evidence from Yukatek Maya children. Paper presented at the annual meeting of the Society for the Scientific Study of Religion, Columbus, OH, October.

Knight, R., and M. Grabowecky. 1995. Escape from linear time: Prefrontal cortex and conscious experience. In M. Gazzaniga (ed.), *The cognitive neurosciences*. Cambridge, MA: MIT Press.

Koenigsberger, H. 1966. The Reformation and social revolution. In J. Hurstfield (ed.), *The Reformation crisis*. New York: Harper & Row.

Köhler, W. 1927 (1917). *The mentality of apes*. Trans. E. Winter. London: Routledge & Kegan Paul.

Kosmin, B., and S. Lachman. 1993. *One nation under God*. New York: Harmony Books.

Kramer, S. 1963. *The Sumerians*. Chicago: University of Chicago Press.

Krebs, J., and R. Dawkins. 1984. Animal signals: Mind-reading and manipulation. In J. Krebs and N. Davies (eds.), *Behavioral ecology*, 2d ed. Sunderland, MA: Sinauer Associates.

Kroeber, A. L. 1963 (1923). *Anthropology: Culture patterns and processes*. New York: Harcourt, Brace and World.

Kroll, J., and W. Sheehan. 1989. Religious beliefs and practices among 52 psychiatric inpatients in Minnesota. *American Journal of Psychiatry* 146:67–72.

Kuhl, P., and J. Miller. 1975. Speech perception by the chinchilla. *Science* 190:69–72.

Kummer, H., G. Anzenberger, and C. Hemelrijk. 1996. Hiding and perspective taking in long-tailed macaques (*Macaca fascicularis*). *Journal of Comparative Psychology* 110:97–102.

Kundera, M. 1991. *Immortality*. New York: Grove Weidenfeld.

Kuper, A. 1996. *The chosen primate*. Cambridge, MA: Harvard University Press.

LaBar, K., J. LeDoux, D. Spencer, and E. Phelps. 1995. Impaired fear conditioning following unilateral temporal lobectomy in humans. *Journal of Neuroscience* 15:6846–6855.

Lack, D. 1968. *Ecological adaptations for breeding in birds*. London: Methuen.

Laitman, J. 1983. The evolution of the hominid upper respiratory system and implications for the origins of speech. In E. de Grolier (ed.), *Models of scientific thought, vol. 1, Glossogenetics*. Paris: Harwood Academic.

Lakoff, G. 1996. *Moral politics*. Chicago: University of Chicago Press.

Laland, K., and J. Olding-Smee. 2001. The evolution of memes. In Robert Aunger (ed.), *Darwinizing culture: The status of memetics as a science*. New York: Oxford University Press.

Laland, K., J. Olding-Smee, and M. Feldman. 2000. Niche construction, biological evolution and cultural change. *Behavioral and Brain Sciences* 23:131–146.

Laland, K., P. Richerson, and R. Boyd. 1996. Developing a theory of animal social learning. In C. Heyes and B. Galef (eds.), *Social learning in animals*. San Diego: Academic Press.

Landa, Diego de. 1985 (1566). *Relación de la cosas de Yucatán*. Ed. M. Rivera Dorado. Crónicas de America, no. 7. Madrid: Historia 16.

Lansing, S., and J. Kremer. 1993. Emergent properties of Balinese water temple networks: Coadaptation on a rugged fitness landscape. *American Anthropologist* 95:97–114.

Larkin, A. 1979. The form and content of schizophrenic hallucination. *American Journal of Psychiatry* 136:940–943.

Las Casas, Fray Bartolomé de 1552. *Breuissima relacion de la destruycion de las Indias*. Sevilla: Sebastian Trugillo.

Latour, B. 1987. *Science in action*. Cambridge, MA: Harvard University Press.

Lawrence, W., and G. Murdock. 1949. Murgin social organization. *American Anthropologist* 51:58–67.

Lawson, E. T. 1993. Cognitive categories, cultural forms and ritual structures. In P. Boyer (ed.), *Cognitive aspects of religious symbolism*. Cambridge, UK: Cambridge University Press.

Lawson, E. T., and R. McCauley. 1990. *Rethinking religion*. Cambridge, UK: Cambridge University Press.

Leach, E. 1976. *Culture and communication*. Cambridge, UK: Cambridge University Press.

Leakey, R., and R. Lewin. 1977. *Origins*. New York: Dutton.

LeBar, K., J. LeDoux, D. Spencer, and E. Phelps. 1995. Impaired fear conditioning following unilateral temporal lobectomy in humans. *Neuroscience* 15:6846–6855.

LeDoux, J. 1993. Emotional memory systems in the brain. *Behavioural Brain Research* 58:69–79.

———. 1994. Emotion, memory and the brain. *Scientific American* 270:32–39.

———. 1996. *The emotional brain*. New York: Simon and Schuster.

Leeming, D., and M. Leeming. 1994. *A dictionary of creation myths*. New York: Oxford University Press.

Legertsee, M. 1994. Patterns of 4-month-old infant responses to hidden, silent, and sounding people and objects. *Early Development and Parenting* 3:71–80.

Leiberman, P., E. Crelib, and D. Klatt. 1972. Phonetic ability and related anatomy of the newborn and adult human, Neanderthal man, and the chimpanzee. *American Anthropologist* 74:287–307.

Leiris, M. 1958. *La possession et ses aspects theatreaux chez les Ethiopiens de Gender*. Paris: Plon.

Lemert, C. 1974. Cultural multiplexity and religious polytheism. *Social Compass* 21:241–253.

Lenin, V. 1972 (1908). *Materialism and empirio-criticism*. Peking: Foreign Language Press.

Leroi-Gourhan, A. 1964. *Le geste et la parole: Technique et langage*. Paris: Albin Michel.

Leslie, A. 1982. The perception of causality in infants. *Perception* 11:173–186.

———. 1987. Pretense and representation. *Psychological Review* 94:412–426.

———. 1991. The theory of mind impairment in autism. In A. Whiten (ed.), *Natural theories of mind*. Oxford: Blackwell.

———. 1994. ToMM, ToBy, and agency. In L. Hirschfeld and S. Gelman (eds.), *Mapping the mind*. New York: Cambridge University Press.

Leslie, A., and U. Frith. 1987. Metarepresentation and autism: How not to lose one's marbles. *Cognition* 27:291–294.

———. 1988. Autistic children's understanding of seeing, knowing, and believing. *British Journal of Developmental Psychology* 6:315–324.

Leslie, A., and L. Thaiss. 1992. Domain specificity in conceptual development: Neuropsychological evidence from autism. *Cognition* 43:225–251.

Lester, T. 2002. Supernatural selection. *Atlantic Monthly*, February 8.

Lettvin, J., H. Maturana, W. Pitts, and W. McCulloch. 1961. Two remarks on the visual system of the frog. In W. Rosenblith (ed.), *Sensory communication*. Cambridge, MA: MIT Press.

Leventhal, H., and K. Scherer. 1987. The relationship of emotion to cognition. *Cognition and Emotion* 1:3–28.

Lévi-Strauss, C. 1962. *Totemism*. Boston: Beacon Press.

———. 1963a. *Structural anthropology*. New York: Anchor Books.

———. 1963b. The bear and the barber. *Journal of the Royal Anthropological Institute* 93:1–11.

———. 1966 (1962). *The savage mind*. Chicago: University of Chicago Press.

———. 1969 (1964). *The raw and the cooked* (*Mythologiques*, vol. 1) New York: Harper.

———. 1971. *L'homme nu*. (*Mythologiques*, vol. 4) Paris: Plon.

Lévy-Bruhl, L. 1966 (1923). *Primitive mentality*. Boston: Beacon Press.

Lewis, I. 1971. *Ecstatic religion*. Harmondsworth, UK: Penguin.

Lewontin, R. 1970. The units of selection. *Annual Review of Ecology and Systematics* 1:1–18.

———. 1995. *Human diversity*. New York: Scientific American Library.

Liberzon, I., S. Taylor, R. Amdur, T. Jung, K. Chamberlain, S. Minoshima, R. Koeppa, and L. Fig. 1999. Brain activation in PTSD in response to trauma-related stimuli. *Biological Psychiatry* 45:817–826.

Lieberman, P. 1984. *The biology and evolution of language*. Cambridge, MA: Harvard University Press.

Lilliard, A. 1998. Ethnopsychologies: Cultural variations in theory of mind. *Psychological Bulletin* 123:3–32.

Lipkind, W. 1940. Carajá cosmography. *Journal of American Folk-Lore* 53:248–251.

Lois, X. 1998. Gender markers as "rigid determiners" of the Itzaj Maya world. *International Journal of American Linguistics* 64:224–282.

López, A., S. Atran, J. Coley, D. Medin, and E. Smith. 1997. The tree of life: Universals of folk-biological taxonomies and inductions. *Cognitive Psychology* 32:251–295.

López Austin, A. 1989. *Cuerpo humano e ideología: Las concepciones de los antiguos nahuas*, vol. 1. Mexico City: UNAM.

López de Cogolludo, Fray Diego. 1971 (1656). *Los tres siglos de la dominación española en Yucatán*, 2 vols. Graz, Austria: Akademische Druck.

Lorenz, K. 1965a. Preface to *The expression of the emotions in man and animals*, by Charles Darwin. Chicago: University of Chicago Press.

———. 1965b. *Evolution and the modification of behavior*. Chicago: University of Chicago Press.

———. 1966. The role of gestalt perception in animal and human behavior. In L. White (ed.), *Aspects of form*. Bloomington: Indiana University Press.

———. 1996. *The natural science of the human species: An introduction to comparative research. The "Russian manuscript" (1944–1948)*. Cambridge, MA: MIT Press.

Lotter, V. 1966. Epidemiology of autistic conditions in young children, 1: Prevalence. *Social Psychology* 1:124–137.

Lowe, C. 1964. The equivalence of guilt and anxiety as pathological constructs. *Journal of Consulting Psychology* 28:553–554.

Lowie, R. 1920. *Primitive society*. New York: Horace Liveright.

———. 1924. *Primitive religion*. New York: Boni and Liveright.

Ludwig, A. 1965. Witchcraft today. *Diseases of the Nervous System* 26:288–291.

Lumsden, C., and E. Wilson. 1981. *Genes, mind and culture*. Cambridge, MA: Harvard University Press.

Lynch, A. 1996. *Thought contagion*. New York: Basic Books.

Lynch, J. 1980. The functional organization of posterior parietal association cortex. *Behavioral and Brain Sciences* 3:485–499.

Macauley, D., L. Ryan, and E. Eich. 1993. Mood dependence in implicit and explicit memory. In P. Graff and M. Masson (eds.), *Implicit memory*. Hillsdale, NJ: Erlbaum.

MacDonald, K. 1994. *A people that shall dwell alone*. Westport, CT: Praeger.

———. 1998a. *Separation and its discontents: Toward an evolutionary theory of anti-Semitism*. Westport, CT: Praeger.

———. 1998b. *The culture critique: An evolutionary analysis of Jewish involvement in twentieth-century intellectual and political movements*. Westport, CT: Praeger.

MacLean, P. 1952. Some psychiatric implications of physiological studies on frontotemporal portion of limbic system (visceral brain). *Electroencephalography and Clinical Neurophysiology* 4:407–418.

———. 1990. *The triurne brain*. New York: Plenum Press.

Mack, J. 1994. *Abduction: Human encounters with aliens*. London: Simon and Schuster.

Magariños, A. M., B. McEwen, G. Flügge, and E. Fuchs. 1996. Chronic psychosocial stress causes apical dendritic atrophy of hippocampal CA3 pyramidal neurons in subordinate tree shrews. *Journal of Neuroscience* 16:3534–3540.

Malinowski, B. 1961 (1922). *Argonauts of the western Pacific*. New York: Dutton.

Malley, B. 1995. Explaining order in religious systems. *Method & Theory in the Study of Religion* 7:5–22.

Maloney, H., and A. Lovekin. 1985. *Glossolalia*. New York: Oxford University Press.

Mandler, J. 1992. How to build a baby: II, Conceptual primitives. *Psychological Review* 99:587–604.

Manickam, S. 1993. *Slavery in the Tamil country*. Madras, India: Christian Literature Society.

Marks, I. 1987. *Fears, phobias, and rituals*. New York: Oxford University Press.

Markus, H., and S. Kitayama. 1991. Culture and the self. *Psychological Review* 98:224–253.

Marr, D. 1971. Simple memory. *Philosophical Transactions of the Royal Society of London*, series B. 262:23–81.

———. 1982. *Vision*. New York: W.H. Freeman.

Marshack, A. 1976. Some implications of the Paleolithic symbolic evidence for the origin of language. In S. Harnad, H. Steklis, and J. Lancaster (eds.), *Origins and evolution of language and speech*. *Annals of the New York Academy of Sciences* 280:289–311.

Martin-Baro, L. 1990. Religion as an instrument of psychological warfare. *Journal of Social Issues* 46: 93–107.

Marx, K. 1972 (1842). Religion and authority. In F. Bender (ed.), *Karl Marx: The essential writings*. New York: Harper.

Masur, E. 1983. Gestural development, dual-directional signaling, and the transition to words. *Journal of Psycholinguistic Research* 12:93–109.

Matasuzawa, T. 1996. Chimpanzee intelligence in nature and in captivity. In W. McGrew, L. Marchand, and T. Nishida (eds.), *Great apes*. New York: Cambridge University Press.

Mauss, M. 1990 (1925). *The gift: The form and reason for exchange in archaic societies*. Trans. W. Halls. New York: Norton.

Maynard-Smith, J. 1998. The origin of altruism. *Nature* 393:639–640.

McArthur, A., and J. Clark. 1988. Body temperature of homeotherms and conservation of water and energy. *Journal of Thermal Biology* 13:9–13.

McCauley, R., and E. T. Lawson. 2002. *Bringing ritual to mind*. New York: Cambridge University Press.

McClelland, D. 1975. *Power: The inner experience*. New York: Irvington.

McDaniel, J. 1989. *The madness of saints: Ecstatic religion in Bengal*. Chicago: University of Chicago Press.

McEwen, B., and R. Sapolsky. 1995. Stress and cognitive function. *Current Opinion in Neurobiology* 5:205–216.

McFadden, S. 1996. Religion, spirituality, and aging. In J. Birren and K.W. Shaie (eds.), *Handbook of the psychology of aging*, 4th ed. New York: Academic Press.

McGaugh, J., L. Cahill, M. Parent, M. Mesches, K. Coleman-Mesches, and J. Salinas. 1995. Involvement of the amygdala in the regulation of memory storage. In J. McGaugh, F. Bermudez-Rattoni and R. Prado-Alcala (eds.), *Plasticity in the central nervous system*. Hillsdale, NJ: Erlbaum.

McGuire, M. 1983. Words of power: Personal empowerment and healing. *Culture, Medicine and Psychiatry* 7:221–240.

McReady, N. 2002. Adrenergic blockers shortly after trauma can block PTSD. *Clinical Psychiatry News*, February.

Mead, M. 1932. An investigation of the thought of primitive children with special reference to animism. *Journal of the Royal Anthropological Institute* 62:173–190.

———. 1956. *New lives for old: Cultural transformations—Manus, 1928–1953*. New York: Mentor Books.

Medin, D., and A. Ortony. 1989. Psychological essentialism. In S. Vosniadou and A. Ortony (eds.), *Similarity and analogical reasoning*. New York: Cambridge University Press.

Medin, D., B. Ross, and E. Markman. eds. 2001. *Cognitive psychology*, 3d ed. New York: Wiley.

Medin, D., H. Schwartz, S. Blok, and L. Birnbaum. 1999. The semantic side of decision making. *Psychonomic Bulletin & Review* 6:562–569.

Meggitt, M. 1965. *The desert people: A study of the Walbiri of central Australia*. Chicago: University of Chicago Press.

Meltzoff, A. 1995a. Understanding the intention of others: Re-enactment of intended acts by 18-month-old children. *Developmental Psychology* 31:838–850.

———. 1995b. What infant memory tells us about infantile amnesia. *Journal of Experimental Child Psychology* 59:497–515.

Merari, A. 2002. The psychology of suicide terrorists. Paper presented to the seminar series, "The Psychology of Extremism," Institute for Social Research, The University of Michigan, Ann Arbor, February 11.

Miller, A. 1992. Predicting nonconventional religious affiliation in Tokyo. *Social Forces* 71:397–410.

Miller, G. 2000. *The mating mind*. New York: Doubleday.

Mills, J. 1993. The appeal of tragedy. *Basic and Applied Social Psychology* 14:255–271.

Mills, J. and P. Mintz. 1972. Effect of unexplained arousal on affiliation. *Journal of Personality and Social Psychology* 24:11–13.

Mineka, S., M. Davidson, M. Cook, and R. Keir. 1984. Observational conditioning of snake fear in rhesus monkeys. *Journal of Abnormal Psychology* 93:355–372.

Mitchell, P. and H. Lacohée. 1991. Children's early understanding of false belief. *Cognition* 39:107–127.

Mitchell, S., L. Daston, N. Sesardic, P. Sloep, and G. Gigerenzer. 1997. In the service of pluralism and interdisciplinarity. In P. Weingart, P. Richerson, S. Mitchell, and S. Maasen (eds.), *Human nature: Between biology and the social sciences*. Hillsdale, NJ: Erlbaum.

Mol, H. 1970. Religion and sex in Australia. *Australian Journal of Sociology* 59:454–465.

Montgomery, D. 1996. The role of action-initiation in young children's causal explanation of action. *Cognitive Development* 11:467–489.

Morris, M., D. Nisbett, and K. Peng, 1995. Causal understanding across domains and cultures. In D. Sperber, D. Premack, and A. Premack (eds.), *Causal cognition*. Oxford: Oxford University Press.

Morris, R., and D. Morris. 1965. *Men and snakes*. London: Hutchinson.

Moser, S. 1976. Inferential reasoning in episodic memory. *Journal of Verbal Learning and Verbal Behavior* 15:193–212.

Mueser, K., A. Bellack, and E. Brady. 1990. Hallucinations in schizophrenia. *Acta Psychiatrica Scandinavica* 82:26–29.

Munkur, B. 1983. *The cult of the serpent*. Albany: State University of New York Press.

Murdock, G. 1949. *Social structure*. New York: Macmillan.

Murphy, R. and L. Kasdan. 1959. The structure of parallel cousin marriage. *American Anthropologist* 61:17–29.

Musil, A. 1908. *Arabia Petraea*. Vienna: Ethnologischer Reisebericht.

Nagel, N. 1961. *The structure of science*. New York: Harcourt, Brace & World.

Nansen, F. 1893. *Eskimo life*. Trans. W. Archer. London: Longmans, Green.

National Geographic Society. 1995. *The new chimpanzee*. Television documentary.

Neisser, U., and N. Harsch. 1992. Phantom flashbulbs. In E. Winograd and U. Neisser (eds.), *Affect and accuracy in recall*. Cambridge, UK: Cambridge University Press.

Neisser, U., E. Winograd, E. Bergman, C. Schreiber, S. Plamer, and M. Weldon. 1996. Remembering the earthquake: Direct experience versus hearing the news. *Memory* 4:337–357.

Nesse, R. 1989. Evolutionary explanations of emotions. *Human Nature* 1:261–289.
———. 1999. The evolution of commitment and the origins of religion. *Science and Spirit* 10:32–33, 46.
———, ed. 2002. *Evolution and the capacity for commitment*. New York: Russell Sage Foundation.
Newberg, A., A. Alavi, M. Baime, M. Pourdehand, J. Santanna, and E. d'Aguili. 2001. The measurement of cerebral blood flow during the complex cognitive task of meditation. *Psychiatry Research: Neuroimaging* 106:113–122.
Newberg, A., E. d'Aquili, and V. Rause. 2001. *Why God won't go away*. New York: Ballantine.
Newport, D. J. and C. Nemeroff. 2000. Neurobiology of posttraumatic stress disorder. *Current Opinion in Neurobiology* 10:211–218.
Nielsen, K. 1996. *Naturalism without foundations*. Amherst, NY: Prometheus Books.
Nietzsche, F. 1956 (1872). *The birth of tragedy* and *The genealogy of morals*. New York: Anchor.
Nisbett, R., and D. Cohen. 1996. *Culture of honor*. Boulder, CO: Westview Press.
Nisbett, R., K. Peng, I. Choi, and A. Norenzayan. 2001. Culture and systems of thought: Holistic vs. analytic cognition. *Psychological Review* 108:291–310.
Nolen-Hoeksema, S. 1991. Responses to depression and their effects on the duration of depressive episodes. *Journal of Abnormal Pychology* 100:569–582.
Noonan, P. 2001. *When character was king: A story of Ronald Reagan*. New York: Viking.
Norenzayan, A. 1999. *Rule-based and experience-based thinking*. Ph.D. diss., University of Michigan, Ann Arbor.
Norenzayan, A., and S. Atran. 2002. Cognitive and emotional processes in the cultural transmission of natural and nonnatural beliefs. In M. Schaller and C. Crandall (eds.), *The psychological foundations of culture*. Hillsdale, NJ: Erlbaum.
North, D., and R. Thomas. 1977. The first economic revolution. *Economic History Review* 30:229–241.
Novak, M. 1999. How Christianity created capitalism. *Wall Street Journal*, 27 December.
———. 2000. Politics in the language of the Torah. *International Herald Tribune*, September 5.
Nowak, M. and K. Sigmund. 1998. Evolution of indirect reciprocity by image scoring. *Nature* 395:573–577.
Nowak, R. 1991. *Walker's mammals of the world*, 5th ed. Baltimore: Johns Hopkins University Press.
Obeyesekere, G. 1984. *The cult of the goddess Pattini*. Chicago: University of Chicago Press.
Omari, M. 1994. Candomblé: A socio-political examination of African religion and art in Brazil. In T. Blakely, W. van Beek, and D. Thomson (eds.), *Religion in Africa*. Portsmouth, NH: Heinemann.
Onishi, N. 2002. Africans fill churches that celebrate wealth. *New York Times*, March 13.
Oppenheim, L. 1964. *Ancient Mesopotamia*. Chicago: University of Chicago Press.
Ornstein, P. 1995. Children's long-term retention of salient personal experiences. *Journal of Traumatic Stress* 8:581–606.
Ostrom, E. 1998. A behavioral approach to the rational choice theory of collective action. *American Political Science Review* 92:289–316.
Ostrom, E., R. Gardner, and J. Walker. 1994. *Rules, games, and common-pool resources*. Ann Arbor: University of Michigan Press.
Otterbein, K. 1999. A history of research on warfare in anthropology. *American Anthropologist* 101:794–805.
Oulis, P., V. Mavreas, J. Mamounas, and C. Stefanis. 1995. Clinical characteristics of auditory hallucinations. *Acta Psychiatrica Scandinavica* 92:97–102.

Ozorak, E. 1989. Social and cognitive influences on the development of religious beliefs and commitment in adolescence. *Journal for the Scientific Study of Religion* 28:448–463.

Paine, R. 1967. What is gossip about? *Man* 2:278–285.

Paley, W. 1836. *Natural theology*, vol. 1. London: Charles Knight.

Panksepp, J. 1995. The emotional source of "chills" induced by music. *Music Perception* 13:171–207.

Parker, J., L. Bahrick, B. Lundy, R. Fivush, and M. Levitt. 1998. Effects of stress on children's memory for a natural disaster. In *Eyewitness memory: Proceedings of the first annual conference of the Society for Applied Research on Memory and Cognition*. Mahwah, NJ: Erlbaum.

Parsons, E. C. 1940. Cosmography of Indians of Imbabura Province, Ecuador. *Journal of American Folk-Lore* 53:219–224.

Passingham, R. 1993. *The frontal lobes and voluntary action*. Oxford: Oxford University Press.

Patterson, F., and F. Linden. 1981. *The education of Koko*. New York: Holt, Rinehart and Winston.

Pattison, E., N. Lapins, and H. Doerr. 1973. A study of personality and function. *Journal of Nervous and Mental Disease* 157:397–409.

Pehrson, R. 1966. *The social organization of the Marri Baluch*. Chicago: University of Chicago Press.

Peng, K., and R. Nisbett. 1998. Cross-cultural similarities and differences in the understanding of physical causality. In M. Shield (ed.), *Proceedings of the seventh interdisciplinary conference on science and culture*. Frankfort: Kentucky State University Press.

Pennell, T. L. 1909. *Among the wild tribes of the Afghan frontier*. London: George Bell & Sons.

Peristiany, J., ed. 1976. *Mediterranean family structures*. Cambridge, UK: Cambridge University Press.

Perner, J., U. Frith, A. Leslie, and S. Leekman. 1989. Exploration of the autistic child's theory of mind. *Child Development* 60:789–700.

Perner, J., and T. Ruffman. 1995. Episodic memory and autonoetic consciousness. *Journal of Experimental Child Psychology* 59:516–548.

Perrin, J.-P. 2001. Oints et parfumés avant le "martyre." *Libération* (Paris daily), August 12.

Persinger, M. 1983. Religious and mystical experiences as artifacts of temporal lobe function. *Perceptual and Motor Skills* 57:1255–1262.

———. 1984. Striking EEG profiles from single episodes of glossolalia and transcendental meditation. *Perceptual and Motor Skills* 58:127–133.

———. 1987. *Neurophysiological bases of God beliefs*. New York: Praeger.

———. 1997. "I would kill in God's name:" Role of sex, weekly church attendance, report of a religious experience, and limbic lability. *Perceptual and Motor Skills* 71:817–818.

Peters, E. 1960. The proliferation of segments in the lineage of the Bedouin in Cyrenaica. *Journal of the Royal Anthropological Institute* 90:29–53.

———. 1967. Some structural aspects of the feud among the camel herding Bedouin of Cyrenaica. *Africa* 37:261–282.

Peterson, N. 1993. Demand sharing. *American Anthropologist* 95:860–874.

Pfeiffer, J. 1982. *The creative explosion*. New York: Harper & Row.

Phillips, M., and A. David. 1995. Facial processing in schizophrenia and delusional misidentification. *Schizophrenia Research* 17:109–114.

Piaget, J. 1967. *The child's conception of the world*. Totowa, NY: Littlefield and Adams.

———. 1969. *The psychology of the child*. New York: Basic Books.

———. 1970. *Genetic epistemology*. New York: Columbia University Press.

Pinker, S. 1994. *The language instinct*. New York: Morrow.

———. 1997. *How the mind works*. New York: Norton.

———. 1998. The evolutionary psychology of religion: Does the brain have a "God module"? Paper presented at conference, Religious belief: A human universal, MIT Dept. of Brain Sciences and the McDonnell-Pew Center for Cognitive Neuroscience, Cambridge, MA.

Pinker, S, and P. Bloom. 1990. Natural language and natural selection. *Behavioral and Brain Sciences* 13:707–727.

Plato. 1958. *Meno, Phaedo*. Trans. B. Jowett. In I. Edwin (ed.), *The works of Plato*, 3d ed. New York: Modern Library.

Pliny [Pline]. 1829 (ca. A.D. 70). *Historie naturelle de Pline* [*Historiarum mundi*], 20 vols. Paris: Panckoucke.

Plotkin, H. 1997. *Evolution in mind*. Cambridge, MA: Harvard University Press.

Plutchik, R. 1980. *Emotion: A psychoevolutionary synthesis*. New York: Harper & Row.

Podhoretz, N. 1999. Science hasn't killed God. *Wall Street Journal*, 30 December.

Poling, T., and J. Kenney. 1986. *The Hare Krishna character type*. Lewiston, NY: Edwin Mellen.

Poloma, M., and G. Gallup. 1991. *The varieties of prayer*. Philadelphia: Trinity Press International.

Poloma, M., and B. Pendleton. 1991. *Religiosity and well-being: Exploring neglected dimensions of quality of life research*. Lewiston, NY: Edwin Mellon.

Popper, K. 1950. *The open society and its enemies*. Princeton: Princeton University Press.

———. 1963. *Conjectures and refutations*. New York: Harper & Row.

Posey, D. 1983. Indigenous ecological knowledge and development of the Amazon. In E. Moran (ed.), *The dilemma of Amazonian development*. Boulder, CO: Westview Press.

Potter, G. 1966. Zwingli and Calvin. In J. Hurstfield (ed.), *The Reformation crisis*. New York: Harper & Row.

Povinelli, D. 2000. *Folk physics for apes*. New York: Oxford University Press.

———. 2001. Chimpanzee theory of mind and folk physics. Paper presented to the "Innateness and Structure of the Mind" Workshop, University of Sheffield, November.

Povinelli, D., and T. Eddy. 1996. What young chimpanzees know about seeing. *Monographs of the Society for Research in Child Development* 61(3).

Povinelli, D., K. Nelson, and S. Boysen. 1992. Comprehension of social role reversal by chimpanzees: Evidence for empathy? *Animal Behaviour* 43:633–640.

Povinelli, D., K. Parks, and M. Novak. 1992. Role reversal by rhesus monkeys, but no evidence of empathy. *Animal Behaviour* 44:269–281.

Powell, B., L. Steelman, and C. Peek. 1982. Fundamentalism and sexism. *Social Forces* 60:1154–1158.

Prem Nath, C. S. 1996. *Hinduism*. New Delhi: Crest Publishing House.

Premack, D. 1990. The infant's theory of self-propelled objects. *Cognition* 36:1–16.

Premack, D., and A. Premack. 1995. Origins of social competence. In M. Gazzaniga (ed.), *The cognitive neurosciences*. Cambridge, MA: MIT Press.

Premack, D., and G. Woodruff. 1978. Does the chimpanzee have a theory of mind? *Behavioral and Brain Sciences* 1:515–526.

Pressel, E. 1974. Umbanda trance and possession in São Paulo, Brazil. In F. Goodman, J. Henney, and E. Pressel (eds.), *Trance healing and hallucination*. London: Wiley.

Price, B. 2000. The biology of culture. *Anthropology News* 41:24.

Prosser, C. 1973. *Comparative animal physiology*, 3d ed. Philadelphia: Saunders.

Putney, S., and R. Middleton. 1961. Rebellion, conformity, and parental religious ideologies. *Sociometry* 24:125–135.

Pynoos, R., and K. Nader. 1989. Children's memory and proximity to violence. *Journal of the American Academy of Child and Adolescent Psychiatry* 28:236–241.

Pyszczynski, T., R. Wicklund, S. Floresku, H. Koch, G. Gauch, S. Solomon, and J. Greenberg. 1996. Whistling in the dark: Exaggerated consensus estimates in response to incidental reminders of mortality. *Psychological Science* 7:332–336.

Quine, W. 1960. *Word and object*. Cambridge, MA: Harvard University Press.

Radcliffe-Brown, A. R. 1950. Introduction to A. R. Radcliffe-Brown and D. Forde (eds.), *African systems of kinship and marriage*. London: Oxford University Press.

Rappaport, R. 1968. *Pigs for the ancestors*. New Haven: Yale University Press.

———. 1979. *Ecology, meaning, and religion*. Berkeley: Atlantic Books.

———. 1999. *Ritual and religion in the making of humanity*. Cambridge, UK: Cambridge University Press.

Ratey, J., and C. Johnson. 1998. *Shadow syndromes*. New York: Bantam Doubleday.

Rauch, S., P. Whalen, L. Shin, S. McInerney, M. Maklin, N. Lasko, S. Orr, and R. Pitman. 2000. Exaggerated amygdala response to masked facial stimuli in posttraumatic stress disorder: A functional MRI study. *Biological Psychiatry* 47:769–776.

Reddy, V. 1991. Playing with others' expectations: Teasing and mucking about in the first year. In A. Whiten (ed.), *Natural theories of mind*. New York: Blackwell.

Redfield, R., and A. Villa Rojas. 1934. *Chan Kom: A Maya village*. Chicago: University of Chicago Press.

Reed, N. 1964. *The caste war of Yucatan*. Stanford: Stanford University Press.

Reeve, H. 2000. Review of "Unto others." *Evolution and Human Behavior* 21:65–72.

Reina, R. 1966. *The law of the saints: A Pokoman pueblo and its community culture*. Indianapolis: Bobbs-Merrill.

Repacholi, B., and A. Gopnik. 1997. Early reasoning of desires: Evidence from 14- to 18-month-olds. *Developmental Psychology* 33:12–21.

Reston, J. 2001. *Warriors of God: Richard the Lionheart and Saladin in the third crusade*. New York: Doubleday.

Rhode, D., and A. Chivers. 2002. Qaeda's grocery lists and manuals of killing. *New York Times*, March 17.

Richardson, J. 1973. Psychological interpretations of glossolalia. *Journal for the Scientific Study of Religion* 12:199–207.

———. 1995. Clinical and personality assessment of participants in new religions. *International Journal for the Psychology of Religion* 5:145–170.

Richerson, P., and R. Boyd. 1998. The evolution of human ultra-sociality. In I. Eibl-Eibisfeldt and F. Salter (eds.), *Indoctrinability, ideology, and warfare: Evolutionary perspective*. New York: Berghahn Books.

Roberts, B. 1968. Protestant groups and coping with urban life in Guatemala. *American Journal of Sociology* 6:753–767.

Roberts, F. 1965. Some psychological factors in religious conversion. *British Journal of Social and Clinical Psychology* 4:185–187.

Robertson Smith, W. 1894. *Lectures on the religion of the Semites*, London: A. & C. Black.

———. 1972 (1891). *The religion of the Semites*. New York: Schocken.

Rochford, E., S. Purvis, and N. Eastman. 1989. New religions, mental health, and social control. *Research in the Social Scientific Study of Religion* 1:57–82.

Rogers, E. 1995. *Diffusion of innovations*, 4th ed. New York: Free Press.

Rokeach, M. 1960. *The open and closed mind*. New York: Basic Books.

Romney, A. K., and C. Moore. 2001. Systemic culture patterns as basic units of culture transmission and evolution. *Cross-Cultural Research* 35:154–178.

Romney, A. K., S. Weller, and W. Batchelder. 1986. Culture as consensus: A theory of culture and informant accuracy. *American Anthropologist* 88:313–338.

Rosch, E., C. Mervis, W. Grey, D. Johnson, and P. Boyes-Braem. 1976. Basic objects in natural categories. *Cognitive Psychology* 8:382–439.

Ross, N. In press. Cognitive aspects of intergenerational change: Mental models, cultural change and environmental behavior among the Lacandon Maya in southern Mexico. *Human Organization*.

Roszak, T. 1970. *The making of counter-culture*. London: Faber.

Rudavsky, S. 1991. The secret life of the Neanderthal. *Omni* 14:42–44, 55–56.

Ruffman, T., J. Perner, M. Naito, L. Parkin, and W. Clements. 1998. Older (but not younger) siblings facilitate false belief understanding. *Developmental Psychology* 34:161–174.

Rumbaugh, D., S. Savage-Rumbaugh, and R. Sevcik. 1994. Biobehavioral roots of language. In R. Wrangham, W. McGrew, F. de Waal, and P. Heltne (eds.), *Chimpanzee cultures*. Cambridge, MA: Harvard University Press.

Ruppell, Von G. 1986. A "lie" as a directed message of artic foxes (*Alopex lagopus* L.). In R. Mitchell and N. Thompson (eds.), *Deception*. Albany: State University of New York Press.

Russell, B. 1919. *Introduction to mathematical philosophy*. London: George Allen and Unwin.

———. 1940. *An inquiry into meaning and truth*. London: George Allen and Unwin.

———. 1948. *Human knowledge: Its scope and limits*. New York: Simon and Schuster.

———. 1950. An outline of intellectual rubbish. In *Unpopular essays*. New York: Simon and Schuster.

Russell, E. 1971. Christianity and militarism. *Peace Research Reviews* 4:1–77.

Sackville-West, V. 1943. *The eagle and the dove*. London: Michael Joseph.

Sader, S. 1999. Deforestation trends in northern Guatemala: A view from space. In *13 ways of looking at a tropical forest: Guatemala's Biosphere Reserve*. Washington, DC: Conservation International.

Safer, M., S.-Å. Christianson, M. Autry, and K. Österlund. 1998. Tunnel memory for traumatic events. *Applied Cognitive Psychology* 12:99–117.

Sahagun, Fray Bernardino de. 1989. *Conquest of New Spain, 1585 revision*. Salt Lake City: University of Utah Press.

Sahlins, M. 1976. *The use and abuse of biology: An anthropological critique of sociobiology*. Ann Arbor: University of Michigan Press.

Sapolsky, R. 1998. Molecular neurobiology: The stress of Gulf War syndrome. *Nature* 393:308–309.

Sargant, W. 1957. *Battle for the mind*. London: Heinemann.

———. 1969. The physiology of faith. *British Journal of Psychiatry*. 115:505–518.

Sartori, G., and R. Job. 1988. The oyster with four legs: A neuro-psychological study on the interaction of semantic and visual information. *Cognitive Neuropsychology* 5:105–132.

Saski, H., and H. Nagasaki. 1989. The mental distance: Its difference in educational circumstances. *Journal of Human Development* 25:1–10.

Savage-Rumbaugh, S., S. Shanker, and T. Taylor. 1998. *Ape, language and the human mind*. New York: Oxford University Press.

Scaife, J., and J. Bruner. 1978. The capacity for joint visual attention in the infant. *Nature* 253:265–266.

Schachter, J. 1967. The interaction of cognitive and physiological determinants of emotional states. *Advances in Experimental Social Psychology* 1:49–80.

Schacter, D. 1987. Implicit memory. *Journal of Experimental Psychology: Learning, Memory, and Cognition* 13:501–508.

———. 1997. *Searching for memory*. New York: HarperCollins.

Schank, R., and R. Abelson. 1977. *Scripts, plans, goals and understanding*. Hillsdale, NJ: Erlbaum.

Schele, L., and D. Freidel. 1990. *A forest of kings: The untold story of the ancient Maya*. New York: Morrow.

Schelling, T. 1960. *The strategy of conflict*. Cambridge, MA: Harvard University Press.

Schlesinger, L. 1999. *The Ten Commandments: The significance of God's laws in everyday life*. New York: HarperCollins.

Schmidt, L., and L. Trainor. 2001. Frontal brain electrical activity (EEG) distinguishes *valence* and *intensity* of musical emotions. *Cognition and Emotion* 15:487–500.

Schwartz, N. 1990. *Forest society*. Philadelphia: University of Pennsylvania Press.

Schwartz, T. 1962. The Paliau movement in the Admiralty Islands, 1946–1954. *Anthropological Papers of the American Museum of Natural History* 49:210–421.

Searle, J. 1969. *Speech acts*. Cambridge, UK: Cambridge University Press.

Sedikides, C., and J. Skowronski, J. 1997. The symbolic self in evolutionary context. *Personality and Social Psychology Review* 1:80–102.

Seidenberg, M. 1986. Evidence from the great apes concerning the biological bases of language. In W. Demopoulos and A. Marras (eds.), *Language learning and concept acquisition*. Norwood, NJ: Ablex.

Seligman, S. 1971. Phobias and preparedness. *Behavioral Therapy* 2:307–320.

Semon, R. 1921. *The Mneme*, trans. L. Simon London: *Allen & Unwin* (originally published in 1904 as *Die Mneme als erhaltendes Prinzip in Wechsel des organischen Geschehens*, Leipzig: W. Engelmann).

Service, E. 1962. *Primitive social organization*. New York: Random House.

Sethi, S., and M. Seligman. 1993. Optimism and fundamentalism. *Psychological Science* 4:256–259.

Shackley, M. 1980. *Neanderthal man*. Hamden, CT: Archon Books.

Shanker, S. 2001. What a child knows when she knows what a name is: The non-Cartesian view of language acquisition. *Current Anthropology* 42:481–513.

Sheils, D. 1980. The great ancestors are watching: A cross-cultural study of superior ancestral religion. *Sociological Analysis* 41:247–257.

Shin, L., M. Kosslyn, R. McNally, N. Alpert, W. Thompson, S. Rauch, M. Macklin, and R. Pitman. 1997. Visual imagery and perception in posttraumatic stress disorder. *Archives of General Psychiatry* 54:233–241.

Shreeve, J. 1994. Phenomena, comment and notes. *Smithsonian* 25: 17– 20.

———. 1995. *The Neanderthal enigma*. New York: William Morrow.

Simpson, J. 1984. High gods and the means of subsistence. *Sociological Analysis* 45:213–222.

Slater, E., and A. Beard, 1963. The schizophrenia-like psychoses of epilepsy. I, V. *British Journal of Psychiatry* 109:95–112, 143–150.

Sloane, D., and R. Potvin. 1986. Religion and delinquency. *Social Forces* 1:87–105.

Smidt, C., and J. Penning. 1982. Religious commitment, political conservatisms, and political and social tolerance in the United States. *Sociological Analysis* 43:231–246.

Smith, A. 1993 (1776). *An inquiry into the nature and causes of the wealth of nations*. Oxford: Oxford University Press.

Smith, J. M. 1998. The origin of altruism. *Nature* 393:639–640.

Smith, P. 1979. Naissances et destins: Les enfants de fer et les enfants de beure. *Cahiers d'Etudes Africaines* 19:330–351.

Smuts, B., and J. Watanabee. 1990. Socialized relationships and ritualized greetings in adult male baboons (*Papio cynocephalus anubis*). *International Journal of Primatology* 11:147–172.

Sobel, D. 2000. *Galileo's daughter*. New York: Penguin.

Sober, E., and D. S. Wilson. 1998. *Unto others: The evolution and psychology of unselfish behavior*. Cambridge, MA: Harvard University Press.

Solecki, R. 1971. *Shanidar: The first flower people*. New York: Knopf.

Soltis, J., R. Boyd, and P. Richerson. 1995. Can group functional behaviors evolve by cultural group selection? An empirical test. *Current Anthropology* 36:473–494.

Sommers, F. 1963. Types and ontology. *Philosophical Review* 72:327–363.

Soros, G. 2000. *Open society: The crisis of capitalism revisited*. New York: Public Affairs.

Spanos, N., P. Cross, K. Dickson, and S. DuBreuil. 1993. Close encounters: An examination of UFO experiences. *Journal of Abnormal Psychology* 102:624–632.

Spelke, E. 1990. Principles of object perception. *Cognitive Science* 14:29–56.

Spelke, E., A. Phillips, and A. Woodward. 1995. Infants' knowledge of object motion and human action. In D. Sperber, D. Premack, and A. Premack (eds.), *Causal cognition*. Oxford: Clarendon Press.

Spellman, C., G. Baskett, and D. Byrne. 1971. Manifest anxiety as a contributing factor in religious conversion. *Journal of Consulting and Clinical Psychology* 36:245–247.

Spencer, B. and F. Gillen. 1904. *The northern tribes of central Australia*. London: Macmillan.

Spencer, H. 1873–1881. *Descriptive sociology, or groups of sociological facts*, 8 vols. New York: D. Appleton.

Sperber, D. 1975. *Rethinking symbolism*. Cambridge, UK: Cambridge University Press.

———. 1985a. Anthropology and psychology: Towards an epidemiology of representations. *Man* 20:73–89.

———. 1985b. *On anthropological knowledge*. Cambridge, UK: Cambridge University Press.

———. 1994. The modularity of thought and the epidemiology of representations. In L. Hirschfeld and S. Gelman (eds.), *Mapping the mind*. New York: Cambridge University Press.

———. 1996. *Explaining culture*. Oxford: Blackwell.

———. 1998. Are folk taxonomies "memes"? *Behavioral and Brain Sciences* 21:589–590.

———. 2001a. An objection to the memetic approach to culture. In Robert Aunger (ed.), *Darwinizing culture*. New York: Oxford University Press.

———. 2001b. In defence of massive modularity. Paper presented to the Innateness and Structure of the Mind workshop, University of Sheffield, November.

Sperber, D., F. Cara, and V. Girotto. 1995. Relevance theory explains the selection task. *Cognition* 57:31–95.

Sperber, D., D. Premack, and A., Premack, eds. 1995. *Causal cognition*. Oxford: Oxford University Press.

Sperber, D. and D. Wilson. 1986. *Relevance*. Oxford: Blackwell.

Sperry, R. 1991. Search for beliefs to live by consistent with science. *Zygon* 26:237–258.

———. 1992. Paradigms of belief, theory and metatheory. *Zygon* 27:245–259.

Spilka, B., G. Brown, and S. Cassidy. 1992. The structure of religious mystical experience. *International Journal for the Psychology of Religion* 2:241–257.

Spilka, B., R. Hood, and R. Gorsuch. 1985. *The psychology of religion*. Englewood Cliffs, NJ: Prentice-Hall.

Spiro, M., and R. D'Andrade. 1958. A cross-cultural study of some supernatural beliefs. *American Anthropologist* 60:456–466.

Squire, L. 1992. Memory and the hippocampus: A synthesis from findings with rats, monkeys, and humans. *Psychological Review* 99:195–231.

Stark, R. 1997. *The rise of Christianity*. New York: HarperCollins.

Stark, R., and W. Bainbridge. 1980. Networks of faith. *American Journal of Sociology* 85:1376–1395.

———. 1985. *The future of religion*. Berkeley: University of California Press.

Stark, R., and R. Finke. 2000. *Acts of faith*. Berkeley: University of California Press.

Stark, R., and C. Glock. 1968. *American piety*. Berkeley: University of California Press.

Stern, D. 1985. *The interpersonal world of the infant*. New York: Basic Books.

Stern, E., and D. Silbersweig. 1998. Neural mechanisms underlying hallucinations in schizophrenia: The role of abnormal fronto-temporal interactions. In M. Lenzenweger and R. Dworkin (eds.), *Origins and development of schizophrenia*. Washington, DC: American Psychological Association.

Stevens, J., H. Vernon, F. Erwin, P. Pacheco, and K. Suemastu. 1969. Deep temporal lobe stimulation in man. *Archives of Neurology* 21:157–169.

Stewart, P. 2000. Brazil vodoo priests arrested for child sacrifice. Reuters News Wire, 25 August.

Stewart, S. 1980. *Grammatica Kekchi*. Guatemala City, Guatemala: Editorial Academica Centro Americana.

Stoll, D. 1994. Jesus is Lord of Guatemala: Evangelical reform in a death-squad state. In M. Marty and R. Abbleby (eds.), *Accounting for fundamentalisms*. Chicago: University of Chicago Press.

Stuart, H. 1891. *Census report: Madras, 1891*. Madras, India: Government Press.

Subbotsky, E. 2000. Metaphysical foundations of science and child development. Paper presented to the international conference, The Cognitive Basis of Science, Hang Seng Center for Cognitive Science, University of Sheffield, 29 June.

Suddendorf, T. 1999. The rise of the metamind. In M. Corballis and S. Lea (eds.), *The descent of mind*. New York: Oxford University Press.

Suddendorf, T., and M. Corballis. 1997. Mental time travel and the evolution of the human mind. *Genetic, Social, and General Psychology Monographs* 123:133–167.

Suddendorf, T., and A. Whiten. 2001. Mental evolution and development: Evidence for secondary representation in children, great apes, and other animals. *Psychological Bulletin* 127:629–650.

Swanson, G. 1967. *Religion and regime*. Ann Arbor: University of Michigan Press.

Tager-Flusberg, H. 1993. What language reveals about the understanding of minds in children with autism. In S. Baron-Cohen, H. Tager-Flusberg, and D. Cohen (eds.), *Understanding other minds*. Oxford: Oxford University Press.

Talbot, M. 2000. A mighty fortress. *New York Times Magazine*, February 27.

Tamayo, A., and A. Dugas. 1977. Conceptual representation of mother, father and God according to sex and field of study. *Journal of Psychology* 97:74–84.

Tambiah, S. 1973. Form and meaning of magical acts. In R. Horton and R. Finnegan (eds.), *Modes of thought: Essays in thinking in Western and non-Western societies*. London: Faber and Faber.

———. 1981. *A performative approach to ritual*. London: British Academy.

Taylor, G. 1959. *Sex in history* London: Thames and Hudson.

Terkel, J. 1996. Cultural transmission of feeding behavior in the black rat (*Rattus rattus*), In C. Heyes and B. Galef (eds.), *Social learning in animals*. San Diego: Academic Press.

Terr, L. 1983. Chowchilla revisited: The effects of psychic trauma four years after a school-bus kidnapping. *American Journal of Psychiatry* 140:1543–1550.

———. 1990. *Too scared to cry: Psychic trauma in childhood*. New York: Harper and Row.

Terrace, H. 1979. *Nim: A chimpanzee who learned sign language*. New York: Knopf.

Theresa of Avila, Saint. 1930 (1577). *Interior castle*. London: Thomas Baker.

Thomas, L., and R. Cooper. 1978. Measurement and incidence of mystical experience. *Journal for the Scientific Study of Religion* 17:433–437.

Thornhill, R. 1997. The concept of evolved adaptation. In *Characterizing human psychological adaptations* Ciba Foundation Symposium. Chichester, UK: Wiley.

Thornton, R. 1986. *We shall live again: The 1870 and 1890 Ghost Dance movements as demographic revitalization*. Cambridge, UK: Cambridge University Press.

Thrupp, S., ed. 1962. *Millennial dreams in action*. The Hague: Mouton.

Thurston, E. 1907. *Ethnographic notes in southern India*. Madras, India: Government Press.

Tinbergen, N. 1951. *The study of instinct*. London: Oxford University Press.

Tomasello, M. 1994. The question of chimpanzee culture. In R. Wrangham, W. McGrew, F. de Waal, and P. Heltne (eds.), *Chimpanzee cultures*. Cambridge, MA: Harvard University Press.

Tomasello, M., and J. Call. 1997. *Primate cognition*. New York: Oxford University Press.

Tomasello, M., R. Strosberg, and N. Akhtar. 1996. Eighteen-month-old children learn words in non-ostensive contexts. *Journal of Child Language* 23:157–176.

Tomkins, S. 1962. *Affect, imagery, consciousness*. New York: Springer.

Tooby, J., and L. Cosmides. 1990a. The past explains the present: Emotional adaptations and the structure of ancestral environments. *Ethological Sociobiology* 11:375–424.

———. 1990b. Towards an adaptationist psycholinguistics. *Behavioral and Brain Sciences* 13:760–762.

———. 1992. The psychological foundations of culture. In J. Barkow, L. Cosmides and J. Tooby (eds.), *The adapted mind*. New York: Oxford University Press.

Tozzer, A. 1957. *Chichen Itza and its cenote of sacrifice*. Memoirs of the Peabody Museum 11–12. Cambridge, MA: Peabody Museum.

Trainor, L., and S. Trehub. 1992. The development of referential meaning in music. *Music Perception* 9:455–470.

Trinkaus, E., and P. Shipman. 1993. *The Neandertals*. New York: Knopf.

Trivers, R. 1971. The evolution of reciprocal altruism. *Quarterly Review of Biology* 46:35–57.

Tulving, E. 1972. Episodic and semantic memory. In E. Tulving and W. Donaldson (eds.), *Organization of memory*. New York: Academic Press.

———. 1976. Rôle de la mémoire sémantique dans le stockage et la récuperation de l'information épisodique. *Bulletin de Psychologie* (special issue):19–25.

———. 1983. *Elements of episodic memory*. New York: Oxford University Press.

Tulving, E., and M. Watkins. 1975. Structure of memory traces. *Psychological Review* 82:261–275.

Turnbull, C. 1962. *The forest people: A study of the pygmies of the Congo*. New York: Simon and Schuster.

Turner, V. 1969. *The ritual process*. New York: Aldine.

———. 1983. Body, brain, and culture. *Zygon* 18:221–245.

Tuzin, D. 1982. Ritual violence among the Ilahita Arapesh. In G. Herdt (ed.), *Rituals of manhood: Male initiation in Papua New Guinea*. Berkeley: University of California Press.

Tygart, C. 1971. Religiosity and university student anti–Vietnam War attitudes. *Sociological Analysis* 32:120–129.

Tylor, E. 1930 (1881). *Anthropology*, 2 vols. London: Watts & Co.

———. 1958 (1871). *Primitive culture*, 2 vols. New York: Harper.

Uller, C., and S. Nichols. 2000. Goal attribution in chimpanzees. *Cognition* 76:B27–B34.

———. 2001. Retraction of "Goal attribution in chimpanzees." *Cognition* 80(3):iii.

Ullman, C. 1982. Cognitive and emotional antecedents of religious conversion. *Journal of Personality and Social Psychology* 43:183–192.

Van Lawick-Goodall, J. 1971. *In the shadow of man*. London: Collins.

Van Valen, L. 1975. Group selection, sex, and fossils. *Evolution* 29:87–94.

Vatsyayana. 1984 [ca. 100–500]. *The Kama Sutra*. Trans. R. Burton and F. Arbuthnot. New York: Diadem Books.

Vendler, Z. 1967. Verbs and times. In *Linguistic philosophy*. Ithaca, NY: Cornell University Press.

Vergote, A. 1969. *The religious man*. Dublin: Gill & Macmillan.

Vergote, A., and A. Tamayo. 1980. *The parental figures and the representation of God*. The Hague: Mouton.

Villagutierre Soto-Mayor, Juan de. 1701. *Historia de la Conquista de la Provincia de el Itza*. Madrid: Lucas Antonio de Bedmar y Narvaez.

Volinn, E. 1985. Eastern meditation groups: Why join? *Sociological Analysis* 46:147–156.

Waddington, C. 1959. Canalisation of development and the inheritance of acquired characteristics. *Nature* 183:1654–1655.

Wagner, A. 1978. Expectancies and the priming of STM. In S. Hulse, H. Fowler, and W. Honig (eds.), *Cognitive processes in animal behavior*. Hillsdale, NJ: Erlbaum.

Wahass, S., and G. Kent. 1997. A comparison of public attitudes in Britain and Saudi Arabia towards auditory hallucinations. *International Journal of Social Psychiatry* 43:175–183.

Walden, T., and A. Baxter. 1989. The effect of context and age on social referencing. *Child Development* 60:1511–1518.

Walker, A. 1985. From revival to restoration: The emergence of Britain's new classical Pentecostalism. *Social Compass* 32:261–271.

Walker, S. 1972. *Ceremonial spirit possession in Africa and Afro-America*. Leiden, Netherlands: Brill.

———. 1992. Supernatural beliefs, natural kinds and conceptual structure. *Memory and Cognition* 20:655–662.

Wallace, A. R. 1901 (1889). *Darwinism*. New York: Macmillan.

Wallace, A. 1968. Psychological preparations for war. In M. Fried, M. Harris and R. Murphy (eds.), *War*. New York: Natural History Press.

Wallin, P. 1957. Religiosity, sexual gratification, and marital satisfaction. *American Sociological Review* 22:300–305.

Walton, K. 1994. Listening with imagination: Is music representational? *The Journal of Aesthetics and Art Criticism* 52:49–61.

Warburton, F. 1967. The purposes of classification. *Systematic Zoology* 16:241–245.

Ward, C., and M. Beaubrun. 1980. The psychodynamics of demon possession. *Journal for the Scientific Study of Religion* 19:201–207.

Ward, K. 1998. *Religion and human nature*. Oxford: Clarendon Press.

Warner, R. 1977. Witchcraft and soul loss. *Hospital and Community Psychiatry* 28:686–690.

Warren, A., and J. Smartwood. 1992. Developmental issues in flashbulb memory research. In E. Winograd and U. Neisser (eds.), *Affect and accuracy in recall*. New York: Cambridge University Press.

Warrington, E., and T. Shallice. 1984. Category specific impairments. *Brain* 107:829–854.

Watanabee, J., and B. Smuts. 1999. Explaining ritual without explaining it away. *American Anthropologist* 101:98–112.

Weber, M. 1946. The Protestant sects and the spirit of capitalism. In *From Max Weber: Essays in sociology*. Trans. and ed. C. Wright Mills and H. Gerth. New York: Oxford University Press.

———. 1958. *The Protestant ethic and the spirit of capitalism*. Trans. T. Parsons. New York: Charles Scribner's Sons.

Wedin, L. 1972. A multidimensional study of perceptual-emotional qualities in music. Scandinavian Journal of Psychology 13 :241–257.

Weiss, A., and R. Mendoza. 1990. Effects of acculturation into the Hare Krishna movement on mental health and personality. *Journal for the Scientific Study of Religion* 29:173–184.

Welch, K. 1981. An interpersonal influence model of traditional religious commitment. *Sociological Quarterly* 22:81–92.

Wellman, H. 1990. *The child's theory of mind*. Cambridge, MA: MIT Press.

Werner, E. T. C. 1961 (1932). *A dictionary of Chinese mythology*. New York: Julian Press.

West-Eberhard, M. 1980. Horned beetles. *Scientific American* 242:166–181.

Westermack, E. 1922. *The history of human marriage*, 3 vols., 5th ed. New York: Allerton Book Company.

Wheeler, M., D. Stuss, and E. Tulving. 1997. Toward a theory of episodic memory: The frontal lobes and autonoietic consciousness. *Psychological Bulletin* 121:331–354.

White, S. 1994. Testing an economic approach to resource dilemmas. *Organizational Behavior and Human Decision Processes* 58:428–456.

Whitehead, H. 1988 (1921). *The village gods of South India*. Madras, India: Asia Education Services.

Whitehouse, H. 1992. Memorable religions. *Man* 27:777–797.

———. 1995. *Inside the cult: Religious innovation and transmission in Papua New Guinea*. Oxford: Oxford University Press.

———. 1996. Rites of terror: Emotion, metaphor and memory in Melanesian cults. *Journal of the Royal Anthropological Institute* (NS) 2:703–715.

———. 2000. *Arguments and icons*. Oxford: Oxford University Press.

Whiting, J., C. Kluckholn, and A. Anthony, 1958. The functions of male initiation ceremonies at puberty. In E. Maccoby, T. Newcomb, and E. Hartley (eds.), *Readings in social psychology*, 3d ed. New York: Holt, Rhinehart & Winston.

Wieger, L. 1927. *Histoire des croyances religieuses et des opinions philosophiques en Chine depuis l'origine, jusqu'à nos jours*, 3d ed. Sienhsien, China: Hien-hien.

Wilkinson, G. 1984. Reciprocal food sharing in the vampire bat. *Nature* 308:181–184.

———. 1992. Information transfer at evening bat colonies. *Animal Behaviour* 44:501–518.

Williams, G. 1966. *Adaptation and natural selection*. Princeton: Princeton University Press.

———. 1992. *Natural selection*. New York: Oxford University Press.

———. 2000. The adaptation concept. Lecture delivered to the ISR Evolution and Human Adaptation Program, Adaptation, Maladaptation and Natural Selection, University of Michigan, Ann Arbor, 25 January.

Williams, R., and S. Cole, 1968. Religiosity, generalized anxiety, and apprehension concerning death. *Journal of Social Psychology* 75:111–117.

Wilson, B. 1973. *Magic and the millennium*. New York: Harper & Row.

Wilson, D. S. 1975. A general theory of group selection. *Proceedings of the National Academy of Sciences* 72:143–146.

———. 1998. Hunting, sharing, and multilevel selection. *Current Anthropology* 39:73–97.

———. 2002. *Darwin's cathedral: Evolution, religion, and the nature of society*. Chicago: University of Chicago Press.

Wilson, D. S., and L. Dugatkin, 1997. Group selection and assortative interactions. *American Naturalist* 149:336–351.

Wilson, D. S., and E. Sober. 1994. Reintroducing group selection to the human behavioral sciences. *Behavioral and Brain Sciences* 17:585–654.

Wilson, E. O. 1978. *On human nature*. Cambridge, MA: Harvard University Press.

Wilson, J. 1855. *History of the suppression of infanticide in western India under the government of Bombay*. Bombay: Smith, Taylor and Co.

Wimmer, H., and J. Perner. 1983. Beliefs about beliefs: Representation and constrain function of wrong beliefs in children's understanding of deception. *Cognition* 13:103–128.

Wisniewski, E., and D. Medin. 1994. On the interaction of theory and data in concept learning. *Cognitive Science* 18:221–281.

Wittgenstein, L. 1958. *Philosophical investigations*. London: Basil Blackwell & Mott.

———. 1961 (1921). *Tractatus logico-philosophicus*. London: Routledge and Kegan Paul.

Wolf, E. 1999. *Envisioning power: Ideologies of dominance and crisis*. Berkeley: University of California Press.

Woods, M. 1913. *Was the Apostle Paul an epileptic?* New York: Cosmopolitan Press.

Woodward, A. 1998. Infants selectively encode the goal object of an actor's reach. Cognition 69:1–34.

Worsely, P. 1968. *The trumpet shall sound*. New York: Schocken.

Worthington, E., T. Kurusu, M. McCullough, and S. Sandage. 1996. Empirical research on religion and psychotherapeutic processes of outcomes. *Psychological Bulletin* 19:448–487.

Wright, S. 1988. Leaving new religions. In D. Bromley (ed.), *Falling from the faith*. Newbury Park, CA: Sage.

Wynne, C. 2001. *Animal cognition*. Basingstoke, UK: Macmillan.

Wynn, T. 1979. The intelligence of Later Acheulean hominids. *Man* 14:371–391.

Wynne-Edwards, V. 1962. *Animal dispersion in relation to social behavior*. New York: Hafner.

Yap, P. 1960 The possession syndrome. *Journal of Mental Science* 106:114–137.

Young, R. 1992. Religious orientation, race and support for the death penalty. *Journal for the Scientific Study of Religion* 31:76–87.

Youngblade, L., and J. Dunn. 1995. Individual differences in young children's pretend play with mother and sibling. *Child Development* 66:1472–1492.

Zahavi, A. 1977. The testing of a bond. *Animal Behaviour* 25:246–247.

Zajonc, R. 1984. On the primacy of affect. *American Psychologist* 39:117–123.

Zisook, S., D. Byrd, J. Kuck, and D. Jeste. 1995. Command hallucinations in outpatients with schizophrenia. *Journal of Clinical Psychiatry* 56:462–465.

Zola-Morgan, S., L. Squaire, P. Alvarez-Royo, and R. Cower. 1991. Independence of memory functions and emotional behavior. *Hippocampus* 1:207–220.

INDEX